Foundations of Financial Planning: An Overview

Financial Advisor Series

Walt J. Woerheide, Editor

Sales Skills Techniques

Techniques for Exploring Personal Markets

Techniques for Meeting Client Needs

Techniques for Prospecting: Prospect or Perish

Product Essentials

Essentials of Annuities

Essentials of Business Insurance

Essentials of Disability Income Insurance

Essentials of Life Insurance Products

Essentials of Long-Term Care Insurance

Essentials of Multiline Insurance Products*

Planning Foundations

Foundations of Estate Planning

Foundations of Financial Planning: An Overview

Foundations of Financial Planning: The Process

Foundations of Investment Planning

Foundations of Retirement Planning

* Course under development

Financial Advisor Series: Planning Foundations

Foundations of Financial Planning: An Overview

Second Edition

C. Bruce Worsham, Editor

The American College Press/*Bryn Mawr, Pennsylvania*

This publication is designed to provide accurate and authoritative information about the subject covered. While every precaution has been taken in the preparation of this material, the editor, the authors, and The American College® assume no liability for damages resulting from the use of the information contained in this publication. The American College is not engaged in rendering legal, accounting, or other professional advice. If legal or other expert advice is required, the services of an appropriate professional should be sought.

*© 2009 The American College Press
270 S. Bryn Mawr Avenue
Bryn Mawr, PA 19010
(888) AMERCOL (263-7265)
www.theamericancollege.edu
All rights reserved*

*Library of Congress Control Number 2008940914
ISBN 1-932819-75-4*

Printed in the United States of America

*Knowledge is the key to professionalism.
The road to knowledge begins with the turn of the page*

Contents

	Preface	xi
	The American College	xiii
	Acknowledgments	xv
	About the Authors	xvii
	Special Notes to Advisors	xix
	About the Financial Advisor Series	xxi
	Overview of the Book	xxiii
1.	**The Financial Planning Process**	**1.1**

    Emergence of a New Profession   1.2
    What Is Financial Planning   1.3
    How Is Financial Planning Conducted?   1.16
    Financial Planning Areas of Specialization   1.19
    Content of a Comprehensive Financial Plan   1.20
    Trends Creating Opportunities for Financial Planning Advisors   1.27
    Consumer Needs for Financial Planning   1.30
    The Final Word   1.34
    Chapter Summary   1.35
    Chapter Review   1.39

2. Insurance Planning and Risk Management   **2.1**

    Importance of Protection Objectives   2.2
    Risk   2.2
    Types of Pure Risks   2.5
    Planning for Pure Risks: Insurance and Other Techniques   2.6
    A Survey of Personal Insurance Coverages   2.28
    The Final Word   2.59
    Chapter Summary   2.60
    Chapter Review   2.62

3. Employee Benefits Planning — 3.1

Scope and Significance of Employee Benefits	3.2
Importance of Benefit Planning	3.6
Eligibility for Benefits	3.9
Types of Employee Benefits	3.11
Cafeteria Plans	3.52
The Final Word	3.56
Chapter Summary	3.56
Chapter Review	3.58

4. Investment Planning — 4.1

The Meaning of Investment	4.3
Service to the Client	4.7
Categories of Investment Assets	4.11
Sources of Investment Risk	4.21
Special Portfolio Considerations	4.25
Investment Returns	4.31
Investment Principles, Strategies, and Techniques	4.35
Investment Markets and Regulation	4.41
The Final Word	4.45
Chapter Summary	4.46
Chapter Review	4.48

5. Income Tax Planning — 5.1

The Purpose of Income Tax Planning	5.3
The Principle of Gross Income	5.3
Exclusions from Gross Income	5.5
Deductions	5.5
Personal and Dependency Exemptions	5.11
Tax Rates and Brackets	5.11
Tax Credits	5.14
The Alternative Tax Credits Minimum Tax (AMT)	5.14
Tax Periods and Accounting Methods	5.15
Three Important Issues	5.16
Basic Income-Tax-Planning Concepts	5.19
Taxable Entities	5.30
The Final Word	5.30
Chapter Summary	5.31
Chapter Review	5.34

6. Retirement Planning — 6.1

- Starting Retirement Planning When Young — 6.2
- The Role of the Retirement Advisor — 6.4
- The Art of Financial Planning for Retirement — 6.11
- Developing a Retirement Plan — 6.16
- Potential Sources of Retirement Income — 6.25
- Overcoming Inadequate Retirement Resources — 6.48
- The Final Word — 6.51
- Chapter Summary — 6.51
- Chapter Review — 6.54

7. Estate Planning — 7.1

- The Goals of Estate Planning — 7.2
- Starting the Process — 7.3
- Types of Property Interest — 7.5
- Estate Planning Documents — 7.9
- Transfers at Death — 7.16
- Taxes Imposed on Transfers of Wealth — 7.19
- Preserving the Client's Wealth — 7.31
- The Final Word — 7.45
- Chapter Summary — 7.45
- Chapter Review — 7.48

8. Social Security, Medicare, and Medicare Supplements — 8.1

- Social Security and Medicare — 8.2
- Coverage to Supplement Medicare — 8.31
- The Final Word — 8.36
- Chapter Summary — 8.36
- Chapter Review — 8.39

Appendix A–Topic List for CFP® Certification Examinations — A.1

Appendix B–Risk Identification Questionnaire — B.1

Glossary — Glossary.1

Answers to Review Questions and Self-Test Questions — Answers.1

Index — Index.1

Preface

The mission of this book is to introduce you to the financial planning profession. Financial planning is a rapidly evolving, multidisciplinary profession. The book describes the financial planning process and all of the major planning areas that define the profession. As the book's title suggests, this material represents a beginning. Each chapter addresses a topic that is covered in much greater detail in other books. Nonetheless, the material in this book will provide you with an overview of the financial planning process and the major planning components that make up a comprehensive plan.

While much of the text material will be new to you, some will, no doubt, refresh knowledge you acquired in the past. In either case, all of the text material is both valuable and necessary if you aspire to be a successful financial advisor. The benefits you gain from studying the text material will be directly proportional to the effort you expend. So read each chapter carefully and answer both the essay and multiple-choice review questions for the chapter (preferably before looking in the back of the book for the answers); to do less would be to deprive yourself of a unique opportunity to become familiar with the financial planning process and all that it entails.

The book includes numerous features designed to focus your study of financial planning. Among the features found in each chapter of the book are

- learning objectives and a chapter outline
- a chapter summary
- key terms and concepts
- review questions (essay format)
- self-test questions (multiple-choice format)

Features located in the back of the book are

- a glossary
- appendixes
- an answers-to-questions section
- an index

Finally, all of the contributing authors as well as those individuals noted on the acknowledgments page made this a better book, and I am grateful. However, in spite of the help of all these fine folks, some errors have undoubtedly been successful in eluding my eyes. For these I am solely responsible. At the same time, however, I accept full credit for giving those of you who find these errors the exhilarating intellectual experience produced by such discovery

C. Bruce Worsham

The American College

The American College® is an independent, nonprofit, accredited institution founded in 1927 that offers professional certification and graduate-degree distance education to men and women seeking career growth in financial services.

The Center for Financial Advisor Education at The American College offers both the LUTCF and the Financial Services Specialist (FSS) professional designations to introduce students in a classroom environment to the technical side of financial services, while at the same time providing them with the requisite sales training skills.

The Solomon S. Huebner School® of The American College administers the Chartered Life Underwriter (CLU)®; the Chartered Financial Consultant (ChFC)®; the Chartered Advisor for Senior Living (CASL)®; the Registered Health Underwriter (RHU)®; the Registered Employee Benefits Consultant (REBC)®; and the Chartered Leadership Fellow® (CLF)® professional designation programs. In addition, the Huebner School also administers The College's CFP Board–registered education program for those individuals interested in pursuing CFP® certification, the CFP® Certification Curriculum.

The Richard D. Irwin Graduate School® of The American College offers the master of science in financial services (MSFS) degree, the Graduate Financial Planning Track (another CFP Board-registered education program), and several graduate-level certificates that concentrate on specific subject areas. It also offers the Chartered Advisor in Philanthropy (CAP)® and the master of science in management (MSM), a one-year program with an emphasis in leadership. The National Association of Estate Planners & Councils has named The College as the provider of the education required to earn its prestigious AEP designation.

The American College is accredited by:

> The Middle States Commission on Higher Education
> 3624 Market Street
> Philadelphia, PA 19104
> 215.662.5606

The Middle States Commission on Higher Education is a regional accrediting agency recognized by the U.S. Secretary of Education and the Commission on Recognition of Postsecondary Accreditation. Middle States accreditation is an expression of confidence in an institution's mission and goals, performance, and resources. It attests that in the judgment of the Commission on Higher Education, based on the results of an internal institutional self-study and an evaluation by a team of outside

---

Certified Financial Planner Board of Standards, Inc., owns the certification marks CFP®, CERTIFIED FINANCIAL PLANNER™, and CFP (with flame logo)®, which it awards to individuals who successfully complete initial and ongoing certification requirements.

peer observers assigned by the Commission, an institution is guided by well-defined and appropriate goals; that it has established conditions and procedures under which its goals can be realized; that it is accomplishing them substantially; that it is so organized, staffed, and supported that it can be expected to continue to do so; and that it meets the standards of the Middle States Association. The American College has been accredited since 1978.

The American College does not discriminate on the basis of race, religion, sex, handicap, or national and ethnic origin in its admissions policies, educational programs and activities, or employment policies.

The American College is located at 270 S. Bryn Mawr Avenue, Bryn Mawr, PA 19010. The toll-free number of the Office of Student Services is (888) AMERCOL (263-7265), the fax number is (610) 526-1465, and theamericancollege.edu is the home page address.

Acknowledgments

Publication of this edition of the book required the collaborative efforts of the authors as well as many other individuals. I am especially grateful to Evelyn M. Rice and Patricia A. Perillo for production assistance. I would also like to thank the following individuals for their past work in authoring and/or editing materials used in this book:

- David M. Cordell, a former faculty member of The American College, for his contributions to chapter 1.
- The late Robert M. Crowe, a former faculty member of The American College, for his contributions to chapter 1.
- Charles E. Hughes, a former faculty member of The American College, for his contributions to chapter 2.
- The late William J. Ruckstuhl, a former faculty member of The American College, for his contributions to chapter 4.
- Lynn Hayes, the former Director of the Editorial/Production Services at The American College, for editing the 1st edition of the book.

I also wish to thank Walt J. Woerheide, Vice President and Dean of the Faculty at The American College and Editor of the Financial Advisor Series, for his encouragement and support in the development of this book

Finally, many other members of the faculty and staff of The American College contributed in countless ways, and I offer my appreciation to all of them.

C. Bruce Worsham
Associate Professor of Taxation & Insusrance
The American College

About the Authors

C. Bruce Worsham, CLU, is an associate professor of taxation and insurance at The American College. He has been with The College since 1969, and his current responsibilities include the development of course materials for The College's LUTCF and FSS programs.

Mr. Worsham earned his BS from The University of California at Berkeley and an MA from the University of Pennsylvania. He received his JD from Widener University School of Law and an LLM in taxation from Villanova University School of Law.

Burton T. Beam, Jr., CLU, CPCU, ChFC, CASL, is an associate professor of insurance at The American College, where he is responsible for developing courses on group benefits and health insurance.

Mr. Beam obtained his BA and MBA from the University of Oregon and his MA from the University of Pennsylvania. He is a member of the National Association of Health Underwriters, the CPCU Society, and the Society of Financial Service Professionals.

Robert W. Cooper, is the Employers Mutual Distinguished Professor of Insurance at Drake University. He has published widely in the fields of insurance and business ethics and has received several grants and awards.

Dr. Cooper earned his BS from the University of Connecticut and his MA and PhD from the University of Pennsylvania.

Constance J. Fontaine, CLU, ChFC, is an associate professor of taxation and holder of the Larry R. Pike Chair in Insurance and Investments at The American College. Her primary responsibility is course development in the estate and gift tax planning areas.

Ms. Fontaine received her BS from Arcadia University; her JD from Widener University School of Law; and her LLM in taxation from Villanova University School of Law.

James F. Ivers III, ChFC, is a professor of taxation and associate dean at The American College. He has professional experience in the areas of estate, gift, and income taxation as well as business and personal financial planning.

Mr. Ivers received his BA from Villanova University and his JD and LLM in taxation from Boston University School of Law. He is a member of the bar in Pennsylvania and Florida.

Theodore T. Kurlowicz, CLU, ChFC, AEP, is a professor of taxation and holder of the Charles E. Drimal Estate Planning Professorship at The American College. His responsibilities at the College include preparation of text materials and courses in estate planning, planning for business owners and professionals, and charitable giving.

Mr. Kurlowicz received his BS from the University of Connecticut, his MA from the University of Pennsylvania, his JD from Widener University School of Law, and his LLM in taxation from Villanova University School of Law. He is a member of the Pennsylvania and American Bar Associations.

David A. Littell, CFP, is the Joseph E. Boettner Chair in Financial Gerontology and a professor of taxation at The American College. He is responsible for course and textbook development in the pension and retirement planning area.

Mr. Littell holds a BA from Northwestern University and a JD from Boston University School of Law.

Kenn B. Tacchino, is a professor of taxation at Widener University and director of the New York Life Center for Retirement Income at The American College. He is also editor of the *Journal of Financial Service Professionals*.

Mr. Tacchino received his BA from Muhlenberg College, his JD from Western New England Law School, and his LLM from Widener University School of Law. He is a member of the American Bar Association and National Council on Aging.

Walt J. Woerheide, CFP, is a vice president and dean of academics at The American College; he holds the rank of professor of investments.

Dr. Woerheide earned his BA from Brown University and his MBA and PhD from Washington University. He is a member of the Academy of Financial Services.

Special Notes to Advisors

Text Materials Disclaimer

This publication is designed to provide accurate and authoritative information about the subject covered. While every precaution has been taken in the preparation of this material to ensure that it is both accurate and up to date, it is still possible that some errors eluded detection. Moreover, some material may become inaccurate and/or outdated either because it is time sensitive or because new legislation will make it so. Still other material may be viewed as inaccurate because your company's products and procedures are different from those described in the book. Therefore, the editor, the authors, and The American College assume no liability for damages resulting from the use of the information contained in this book. The American College is not engaged in rendering legal, accounting, or other professional advice. If legal or other expert advice is required, the services of an appropriate professional should be sought.

Caution Regarding Use of Illustrations

Any illustrations, fact finders, sales ideas, techniques, and/or approaches contained in this book are not to be used with the public unless you have obtained approval from your company. Your company's general support of The American College's programs for training and educational purposes does not constitute blanket approval of any illustrations, fact finders, sales ideas, techniques, and/or approaches presented in this book unless so communicated in writing by your company.

Use of the Terms "Financial Advisor" or "Advisor"

Use of the term "financial advisor" as it appears in this book is intended as the generic reference to professional members of our reading audience. It is used interchangeably with the term "advisor" so as to avoid unnecessary redundancy. "Financial advisor" takes the place of the following terms:

Account Executive	Financial Planning	Producer
Agent	Professional	Property & Casualty Agent
Associate	Financial Services	Registered Investment
Broker (stock or	Professional	Advisor
insurance)	Health Underwriter	Registered Representative
Employee Benefit	Insurance Professional	Retirement Planner
Specialist	Life Insurance Agent	Senior Advisor
Estate Planner	Life Underwriter	Tax Advisor
Financial Consultant	Planner	
Financial Planner	Practitioner	

Answers to the Questions in the Book

The answers to all essay and multiple-choice questions in this book are based on the text materials as written.

About the Financial Advisor Series

The mission of The American College is to raise the level of professionalism of its students and, by extension, the financial services industry as a whole. As an educational product of The College, the Financial Advisor Series shares in this mission. Because knowledge is the key to professionalism, a thorough and comprehensive reading of each book in the series will help the practitioner-advisor to better service his or her clients—a task made all the more difficult because the typical client is becoming more financially sophisticated every day and demands that his or her financial advisor be knowledgeable about the latest products and planning methodologies. By providing practitioner-advisors in the financial services industry with up-to-date, authoritative information about various marketing and sales techniques, product knowledge, and planning considerations, the books of the Financial Advisor Series will enable many practitioner-advisors to continue their studies so as to develop and maintain a high level of professional competence.

The books that make up the Financial Advisor Series are spread across three separate subseries, each with a special focus. The first subseries, *Sales Skills Techniques,* focuses on enhancing the practitioner-advisor's marketing and sales skills but also covers some product knowledge and planning considerations. The second subseries, *Product Essentials,* focuses on product knowledge but also delves into marketing and sales skills, as well as planning considerations, in many of its books. The third subseries, *Planning Foundations,* focuses on various planning considerations and processes that form the foundation for a successful career as a financial services professional. When appropriate, many of the books in this third subseries also touch upon product knowledge and sales and marketing skills. Current and forthcoming titles are listed earlier in this book.

Overview of the Book

Foundations of Financial Planning: An Overview is designed to be an overview of the major planning components that make up a comprehensive financial plan. Although each of these components is covered in more depth in other American College publications, this is the one College text where all these components are brought together to show what needs to be covered in a truly comprehensive financial plan.

Chapter 1 begins the discussion by explaining that financial planning is a six-step process that can involve a single-purpose, multiple-purpose, or comprehensive approach, with the focus being on the later. The content of a comprehensive financial plan should include a discussion of each of the major planning areas. Which phase of the financial life cycle that the client is currently in strongly influences the priority given to the goals for each of the planning areas. Financial planning is a process that should be ongoing throughout the client's financial life.

Chapters 2 through 7 introduce the major planning components that make up comprehensive financial planning. Chapter 2 discusses insurance planning, including the risk management process and insurance coverages. Chapter 3 examines employee benefits planning, since many of the financial needs of a client and his or her family may be met—or at least partially met—with benefits provided by and/or through an employer. Chapter 4 is an introduction to investment planning. It describes basic risk/return concepts, financial risk tolerance, asset allocation models, categories of investments, and several portfolio considerations. In chapter 5, basic concepts of income taxation are presented with an emphasis on tax planning. In chapter 6, retirement planning concepts are addressed, including retirement income needs and the types of retirement plans available. Chapter 7 covers estate planning, the final major planning area. The chapter 7 discussion focuses on preserving the client's wealth for his or her family.

Although the Social Security and Medicare programs could have been covered in earlier chapters as subparts of one of the major planning areas, they are dealt with separately in chapter 8 because of their importance as the foundation upon which the client's comprehensive financial plan should be built. The last part of chapter 8 is devoted to explaining the various types of coverages designed to supplement Medicare.

Foundations of Financial Planning: An Overview

1

The Financial Planning Process

Robert W. Cooper
C. Bruce Worsham

Learning Objectives

An understanding of the material in this chapter should enable you to

1-1. Explain the six steps in the financial planning process.

1-2. Describe three different approaches to financial planning, and identify several areas of specialization in which advisors concentrate their activities.

1-3. Identify the subjects that should be included in a comprehensive financial plan.

1-4. Describe what is meant by a person's financial life cycle, and explain how it relates to life-cycle financial planning.

1-5. Describe how a comprehensive financial plan can be organized around the steps in the financial planning process, and explain how a plan can be organized in three stages over a period of time.

1-6. Explain the trends that are creating opportunities in the financial planning marketplace.

1-7. Identify the principal financial goals/concerns of most consumers, and describe three major obstacles that prevent them from achieving these goals.

Chapter Outline

EMERGENCE OF A NEW PROFESSION 1.2
WHAT IS FINANCIAL PLANNING? 1.3
    Financial Planning Is a Six-Step Process 1.3
    Steps in the Financial Planning Process 1.5
HOW IS FINANCIAL PLANNING CONDUCTED? 1.16
    Single-Purpose Approach 1.17
    Multiple-Purpose Approach 1.18
    Comprehensive Approach 1.18

FINANCIAL PLANNING AREAS OF SPECIALIZATION 1.19
CONTENT OF A COMPREHENSIVE FINANCIAL PLAN 1.20
    Life-Cycle Financial Planning 1.22
    Format of a Comprehensive Financial Plan 1.24
TRENDS CREATING OPPORTUNITIES FOR FINANCIAL PLANNING ADVISORS 1.27
CONSUMER NEEDS FOR FINANCIAL PLANNING 1.30
    Obstacles Confronting Consumers 1.34
    Role of Financial Planning Advisors 1.34
THE FINAL WORD 1.34
CHAPTER SUMMARY 1.35
CHAPTER REVIEW 1.39

This chapter begins by looking at the emerging new profession of financial planning and then explains that financial planning is a six-step process for helping clients achieve their financial goals. Next, the chapter describes three approaches for conducting financial planning and identifies the key areas of specialization in which financial advisors concentrate their activities. The chapter then summarizes the recommended content of a comprehensive financial plan, introduces the concepts of financial life cycle and life-cycle financial planning, and reviews two approaches for organizing a comprehensive plan. Finally, the chapter discusses a number of trends that are creating opportunities for financial advisors to serve clients, looks at the main financial concerns of American consumers that drive them to seek professional financial planning help, and identifies some of the obstacles that advisors must help clients overcome if financial goals are to be achieved.

EMERGENCE OF A NEW PROFESSION

Although providing financial planning advice and services to clients is a relatively new and still-emerging field of professional endeavor, very affluent individuals have had access to such help for many years. Moreover, some financial advisors, such as accountants and life insurance agents, argue that they have been practicing financial planning all their professional lives. Perhaps they are correct. However, it is generally recognized that financial planning services that cover a spectrum of client concerns have become available to most Americans in the middle- and upper-middle-income brackets only in the past 35 to 40 years.

Financial advisors claiming to be practicing financial planning first appeared in numbers in the late 1960s, a period of rising inflation and interest rates. The financial planning movement grew rapidly during the 1970s as the general trend of prices continued upward. By the late 1970s and into the early 1980s, inflation and interest rates were virtually out of control. Confronted with very high income tax rates along with these inflation and interest rates, American consumers clamored for help. The growth of the financial planning movement was explosive. Often, however, what advisors labeled as financial planning consisted mostly of selling "get rich quick" products and elaborate income tax dodges, usually accompanied by an abundance of "hype." A few advisors, sometimes with near-messianic zeal, preached the message of comprehensive financial planning as the financial salvation of the American household.

By the mid-1980s, much of the turbulence in economic conditions began to settle down. In addition, when income tax reform eliminated the most extreme types of tax shelters from the marketplace, many so-called financial planning advisors disappeared from the scene. Many advocates of the comprehensive approach to financial planning came to realize that this type of financial planning is practical for only a small, affluent clientele, especially when provided solely on a fee-for-service basis. Also, with the oldest members of the "baby boom" generation entering their 40s, retirement planning became an increasingly important component of financial planning practices.

In the 1990s, the financial planning profession gained some stability and maturity. Now it is possible to describe more realistically what financial planning is and what client needs it can fulfill.

WHAT IS FINANCIAL PLANNING?

financial planning

One factor that has hampered the development of *financial planning* as a discipline and as a profession is the fact that there has been very little agreement among advisors as to what exactly financial planning is. Indeed, it sometimes seems that there are as many definitions of financial planning as there are people who believe they are engaged in financial planning. This ongoing debate among financial advisors[1] is not merely an exercise in semantics; it becomes intensely practical when questions are raised about such issues as who shall regulate those advisors engaged in financial planning, who shall set standards for the financial planning profession, what sort of education should these advisors have, or which advisors may hold themselves out to the public as practicing financial planning.

Financial Planning Is a Six-Step Process

Despite the ongoing controversy among advisors, financial planning can be defined conceptually as a process that accomplishes both of the following:

- ascertaining the client's financial goals
- providing a plan for achieving the client's goals

financial planning process

Whether used by financial advisors or self-planning individuals, the *financial planning process* is divided into the following six steps:

(1) Establish and define the advisor-client relationship.
(2) Determine goals and gather data.
(3) Analyze and evaluate the data.
(4) Develop and present a plan.
(5) Implement the plan.
(6) Monitor the plan.

Advisors who use this process in their practices find it both flexible and accommodating because it can be applied to the full range of a client's problems and/or goals using a comprehensive approach or it can be applied to a smaller subset of those problems and/or goals using a multiple-purpose approach. In fact, it can even be applied to a single client problem or goal using a single-purpose approach. (These three approaches to financial planning are discussed later in this chapter.) It is not, however, the range of client problems and/or goals addressed that determine whether an advisor is engaged in financial planning. Rather, it is the advisor's use of the process to address the client's problems and/or goals that is the determining factor.

Advisors who primarily sell traditional financial products (such as insurance policies, stocks and bonds, and mutual funds) generally view the financial planning process as a selling/planning process that has eight steps—the six steps similar to those in the financial planning process preceded by two additional steps: (1) identify the prospect, and (2) approach the prospect. The eight steps of the selling/planning process are

(1) Identify the prospect.
(2) Approach the prospect.
(3) Meet the prospect.
(4) Gather information and establish goals.
(5) Analyze the information.
(6) Develop and present the plan.
(7) Implement the plan.
(8) Service the plan.

Thus, the six-step financial planning process is an integral part of the eight-step selling/planning process. (see table 1-1 for a comparison of the eight-step selling/planning process with the six-step financial planning process.)

Although not all financial advisors sell traditional financial products, the financial plans they develop are themselves considered financial products that must be marketed and sold. Except for the few advisors who have prospects calling them for appointments, even fee-only advisors have to market and sell their financial planning expertise in developing plans. In other words, the eight-step selling/planning process reflects what the majority of financial advisors face: the necessity to market and prospect. In spite of this fact, however, the discussion of financial planning in this book will be based on the six-step process because the subject of prospecting, while extremely important to financial advisors, is beyond the scope of this book.

TABLE 1-1
Comparing the Eight-Step Selling/Planning Process With the Six-Step Financial Planning Process

Step	Selling/Planning Process	Financial Planning Process	Step
1	Identify the Prospect		
2	Approach the Prospect		
3	Meet the Prospect	Establish and Define the Advisor-Client Relationship	1
4	Gather Information and Establish Goals	Determine Goals and Gather Data	2
5	Analyze the Information	Analyze and Evaluate the Data	3
6	Develop and Present the Plan	Develop and Present a Plan	4
7	Implement the Plan	Implement the Plan	5
8	Service the Plan	Monitor the Plan	6

Steps in the Financial Planning Process

The following pages present a brief discussion of the six steps in the financial planning process.

Step 1: Establish and Define the Advisor-Client Relationship

The first step in the financial planning process is to establish and define the advisor-client relationship. This normally begins at the first client meeting, although it can start prior to this meeting through telephone interactions and/or disclosure documents sent to the client. In any event, the first client meeting is essential for establishing the framework for a successful advisor-client relationship. This meeting is where the advisor begins building trust with the client, ensuring client satisfaction, and creating a relationship with the client that it is hoped will span the client's entire financial life.

Establishing the advisor-client relationship when the client is a couple is a more complex challenge because the advisor needs to build trust and rapport with both parties. Covering the goals of both parties in one financial plan requires the advisor to be aware of the goals that both have in common and how their needs may differ.

In any kind of planned and purposeful communication setting, the first element that needs attention is structuring. Structuring serves to determine both the format and the subject matter of the interaction that is to follow. The financial advisor's task in structuring is to make the purpose of the initial meeting and those that follow clear to the client at the outset. This would include the inevitable introductions, an explanation of the financial planning process, a discussion of forms that are used (for example, a fact-finder form and a disclosure form) and the amount of time that will be required to complete them, a discussion of the confidential nature of the relationship, and some prediction of what kinds of outcomes the client might reasonably expect. This structuring need not be lengthy and cumbersome; in fact, it is far better to structure communication in a clear, straightforward, and succinct fashion.

More specifically, structuring for the financial planning process requires the advisor to explain how he or she works and the types of products and/or services that he or she is able to provide. It requires the advisor to explain the financial planning process and how that process is used to develop financial plans for clients. It may even require the advisor to give examples of how some of his or her products and/or services can be utilized to help clients meet their financial goals and objectives.

At the first meeting, the financial advisor also needs to disclose his or her background, philosophy, and method of compensation, whether that be fee-only, commission, or a combination of the two. If the advisor does not live up to the client's expectations during the first meeting, there will be no second or follow-up meeting. The first meeting with the client sets the stage for future meetings and the eventual implementation of a financial plan.

Step 2: Determine Goals and Gather Data

Once having established and defined the advisor-client relationship, the advisor is ready to move on to step 2 of the financial planning process. Time permitting, this step can begin during the first meeting with the client and may even be completed during this session if the client's goals are few in number and relatively straightforward, and the data is easy to gather. This however, is rarely the situation.

While it is true that few people begin a vacation without a specific destination in mind, it is also true that millions of people make significant financial decisions without a specific financial destination in mind. Determining a specific financial destination, that is goal setting, is critical to creating a successful financial plan. However, before the advisor can develop a financial plan to help the client achieve his or her financial goals, the client, along with the help of the advisor, must determine exactly what those goals are.

A financial plan can never be right for the client if the client does not know what his or her goals are and when he or she wants to achieve them. Even if the client wants to have zero involvement in implementing plan strategies and turn it all over to the advisor, the advisor cannot possibly make the right decisions for the client if the advisor does not know what the client is trying to achieve. And how can the advisor possibly know what the client is trying to achieve if the client does not know?

Clients typically express concern about a whole host of financial topics. A few clients may actually enumerate specific, prioritized goals, but most clients are likely to present a vague list of worries that suggest anxiety and frustration rather than direction. The advisor's responsibility is to first help the client transform these feelings into goals and then to integrate the goals into a workable financial plan.

Very few clients invest simply to make money. The money represents goals that clients want to achieve. Money is just the means to an end. This is why it is so important for clients to define what their goals are. Every client has a different value system, and what is important to one client may not be important to another. Determining what a client is trying to achieve also makes it much easier to actually save and invest, because the advisor can formulate clear-cut strategies that, if followed, will make the client's goals achievable.

Advisors should question clients to learn what they are trying to accomplish. Usually the response is couched in general terms, such as, "Well, we want to have a comfortable standard of living when we retire." At first glance this seems to be a reasonable goal, but a closer evaluation reveals that it is far too vague. When do they want to retire? What is meant by "comfortable"? Do they want to consider inflation? Do they want to retire on "interest only" or draw down their accumulated portfolio over their expected lives?

Skillful questioning may reveal a more precise goal, such as, "We want to retire in 20 years with an after-tax income of $60,000 per year in current dollars, and we want the income to continue as long as we live without depleting the principal." Helping the client set goals that are SMART[2] (that is, goals that are Specific, Measurable, Achievable, Relevant, and have a Target date) is one of the most valuable services the financial advisor can provide.

Goal setting is the process of deciding which needs and wants to pursue, based on the client's values. Each client's goals will differ depending on the number and ages of children, the standard of living desired, attitudes toward risk, the number of wage earners in the client's family, obligations toward dependents, the ability and desire to forgo current consumption to achieve future goals, and prospects for increased earnings in future years, among other things. By helping the client set goals that are SMART, the client will have a clear vision of them and thus be more motivated to work toward achieving them.

While setting goals, many clients discover that they have multiple goals all competing for a prominent place in their financial plans. Should they save for their children's college educations or pay off their mortgage early? Should they max out their retirement savings or pay off their high-interest credit cards? When there are so many financial goals all competing against each other, it seems impossible to focus on just one or two goals. As with goal setting, advisors also play an important role by helping clients prioritize their goals.

financial planning pyramid

One approach to setting and prioritizing goals is to place them into relevant categories. These categories typically include income protection and security goals, accumulation goals, and goals dealing with the management of retirement and estate assets. Categorizing goals in this fashion also serves to help prioritize them. Goals placed in the income protection and security category collectively receive the highest priority rating and are designated as Level 1 goals. Goals placed in the accumulation category collectively receive the second highest priority rating and are designated as Level 2 goals. Goals dealing with the management of retirement and estate assets collectively receive the lowest priority rating and are designated as Level 3 goals. To help in understanding how these levels fit together in a comprehensive financial plan, one needs to look at the *financial planning pyramid* in figure 1-1.

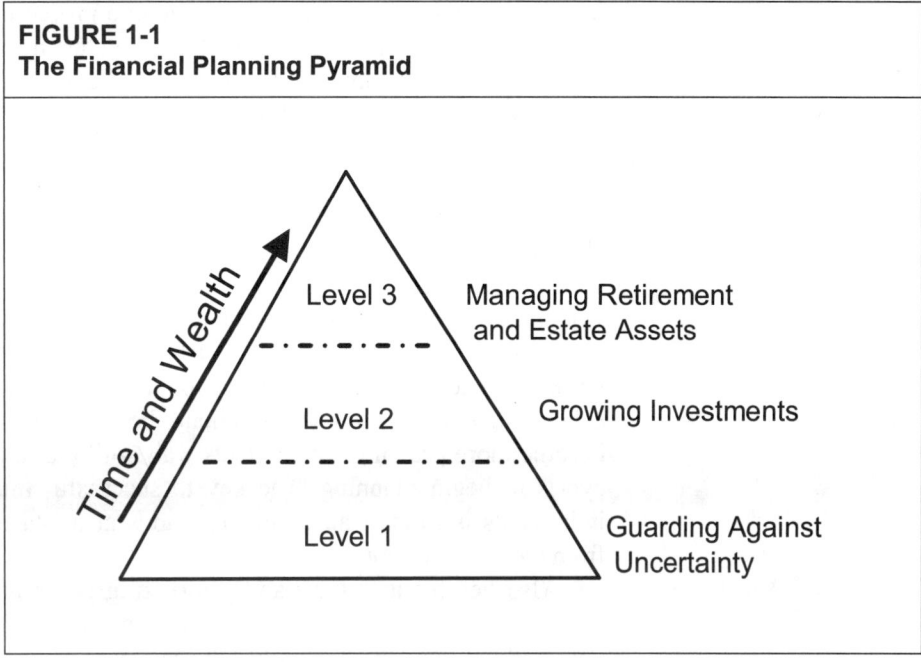

FIGURE 1-1
The Financial Planning Pyramid

The pyramid illustrates how developing a comprehensive financial plan begins with a sound foundation and proceeds in an orderly fashion. The financial goals represented by Level 1, the foundation of the pyramid and collectively the highest priority goals, have as their objective protecting the client against life's financial uncertainties. Level 2, the middle part of the pyramid, is the wealth accumulation component of the financial plan. As the client moves up the pyramid (that is, as the client's financial well-being improves), the focus of the plan shifts from income protection and security goals to wealth accumulation goals. This typically involves growing money through various types of investments. Level 3, the top part of the pyramid, becomes important once the client has achieved most of his or her accumulation goals. This last component of the financial plan addresses both the management of retirement assets and the preservation and distribution of the estate. This part of the financial plan typically is carried out by an estate plan and other advanced planning strategies, including trusts and an updated will.

Even though goals can be collectively prioritized by placing them into relevant categories or pyramid levels, they still need to be individually prioritized within their respective categories or pyramid levels. However, it may be possible to work on achieving several goals at the same time, in which case more than one goal can receive the same priority rating.

Moreover, all goals in the Level 1 income protection and security category do not have to be fully completed before starting on the top-priority goals in the Level 2 accumulation category. Likewise, all Level 2 accumulation goals do not have to be fully completed before moving on to the top-priority Level 3 goals that deal with the management of retirement and estate assets.

Collectively prioritizing goals in the manner described works best if the client is at the beginning of his or her financial life cycle and has previously not done any financial planning. It is more difficult to begin planning for clients who are in the middle of their financial life cycles because they have less time to accumulate funds needed for achieving goals, whether they be income protection and security goals or accumulation goals. Goals that would have had a fairly low priority for young clients because of their distant time horizons become more pressing when clients wait until the middle of their financial life cycles to begin planning. The key to successful financial planning for most individuals is to start accumulating funds at an early age in order to benefit from the magic of compounding.

Also helpful in setting and prioritizing goals is to separate them within their respective categories into short-term, intermediate-term, and long-term goals. Short-term goals should take no more than about 3 years to achieve. Intermediate-term goals should be achievable within 3 to 10 years. Long-term goals typically take more than 10 years to achieve.

Before the financial advisor begins the information-gathering process, he or she should discuss a couple of concerns with the client. First, the client should be made aware that he or she will have to invest time, perhaps a significant amount of time, in the information-gathering stage of financial planning. Even though part of the financial advisor's responsibility is to avoid consuming the client's time unnecessarily, this commitment of the client's time is essential. The magnitude of the needed time commitment will depend on the scope and complexity of the client's goals and circumstances, but the proper development of even a narrowly focused and fairly uncomplicated plan requires information that only the client can furnish.

Second, the client should be made aware that he or she probably will have to provide the advisor with some information that is highly confidential, perhaps even sensitive or painful, for the client to reveal. Again, the scope and complexity of the client's goals will influence this matter. The creation of even straightforward plans, however, may require clients to disclose such things as their income and spending patterns, their attitudes toward other family members or their opinions as to the extent of their own financial responsibilities to others.

After the advisor has helped the client set goals and discussed the information-gathering process, the advisor is ready to gather information about the client that is relevant to achieving the goals. The more complex the client's situation and the more varied the number of goals, the greater the information-gathering task. In fact, assembling complete, accurate, up-to-date, well-organized, and relevant information about the client is the single most important task in financial planning. Without such information, the advisor cannot possibly begin to develop a financial plan tailored exclusively for the client's situation.

Two broad types of information will need to be gathered: objective and subjective. A few examples of objective (factual) information that might be needed from the client include

- personal and family information
- an inventory of assets including securities holdings
- an inventory of liabilities
- the current estate plan and/or will
- a list of annual income and expenditures
- a summary of present insurance coverages
- the current financial plan

financial risk tolerance

Of at least equal importance is the subjective information about the client. In addition to the client's financial goals, this may include information about the client's hopes, fears, values, preferences, attitudes, and nonfinancial goals. There is, however, one piece of subjective information about the client worthy of special attention and that is his or her *financial risk tolerance*.

With the help of a risk tolerance questionnaire like The American College's Survey of Financial Risk Tolerance,[3] the advisor must determine the client's attitude toward financial risk before developing a plan and making recommendations. The Survey of Financial Risk Tolerance provides the type of information that can help the advisor suggest financial strategies and investment alternatives that are truly appropriate for the client. The information also helps the advisor avoid (or at least defend) unsuitability lawsuits from a dissatisfied client. Financial risk tolerance is discussed again in chapter 4 in conjunction with investment planning.

fact finder form

A prerequisite for the effective gathering of client information is a systematic approach to the task. Although there are many possible ways to systematize the gathering of information, one way that has proven helpful is using a structured *fact-finder form*[4]. Some fact finders are only a few pages long and ask for basic information, while others are thick booklets that seek very detailed data on each asset and amount. Most fact finders are designed for specific financial planning software to simplify data entry. For many client situations, a formal fact finder elicits considerably more information than needed. The sections that should be completed depend on the particular areas of concern to be addressed in each client's financial plan.

Obviously, information gathering is far more than asking the client a series of questions during an interview in order to fill out a fact-finder form. Certainly that is required, but usually information gathering also requires examination and analysis of documents—such as wills, tax returns, employee benefit plan coverage, and insurance policies—supplied by the client or the client's other financial advisors. It also requires counseling, advising, and listening during face-to-face meetings with the client (and spouse). These skills are especially important because the advisor needs to help the client (and spouse) identify and articulate clearly what he or she really wants to accomplish and what risks he or she is willing to take in order to do so. Moreover, no matter how the information is gathered, it must, as previously stated, be accurate, complete, up-to-date, relevant to the client's goals, and well organized. Otherwise, financial plans based on the information will be deficient—perhaps erroneous, inappropriate, and inconsistent with the client's other goals, or even dangerous to the client's financial well-being.

Before leaving the step 2 discussion, two things need to be clarified. First, while many advisors focus their efforts on setting goals before gathering information, many advisors reverse this order and gather information first. The choice of whether to focus first on setting goals or gathering information is really up to each individual advisor and/or the specifics of the particular engagement. In fact, setting goals and gathering information are both frequently done simultaneously by advisors because setting goals is more meaningful when done with at least some knowledge of the client's current financial situation. Second, a client in the very beginning of his or her financial life cycle may not have much in the way of financial information for the advisor to gather. For example, he or she probably has not yet made any investments in stocks, bonds, and/or mutual funds. Nevertheless, the advisor still needs to gather all available financial information from the client in order to develop a suitable financial plan for the client.

Step 3: Analyze and Evaluate the Data

Once the client's goals have been determined and data has been gathered, organized, and checked for accuracy, consistency, and completeness, the financial advisor's next task is to analyze and evaluate the client's present financial status. The objective here is to determine where the client is now in relationship to the client's goals that were established in step 2.

This analysis may reveal certain strengths in the client's present position relative to those goals. For example, the client may be living well within his or her means, and thus resources are available with which to meet some wealth accumulation goals within a reasonable time period. Maybe the client has a liberal set of health insurance coverages through his or her employer, thereby adequately covering the risks associated with serious disability. Perhaps the client's will has been reviewed recently by his or her attorney and brought up-to-date to reflect the client's desired estate plan.

More than likely, however, the financial advisor's analysis of the client's present financial position will disclose a number of weaknesses or conditions that are hindering achievement of the client's goals. For example, the client may be paying unnecessarily high federal income taxes or using debt unwisely. The client's portfolio of investments may be inconsistent with his or her financial risk tolerance. Maybe the client's business interest is not being used efficiently to achieve his or her personal insurance protection goals, or important loss-causing possibilities have been overlooked, such as the client's exposure to huge lawsuits arising out of the possible negligent use of an automobile by someone other than the client.

One conclusion from the advisor's analysis may be that the client cannot attain the goals established in step 2. For example, the client's resources and investment returns may preclude reaching a specified retirement income goal. In this case, the advisor helps the client to lower the goal or shows what changes the client must make to achieve the goal. Postponing retirement, saving more money, seeking higher returns, and deciding to deplete principal during retirement are four ways to help achieve the goal. Presented with alternatives, the client can restate the original goal by either lowering it or revising restrictive criteria to make it achievable.

Step 4: Develop and Present a Plan

financial plan

After the information about the client has been analyzed and, if necessary, the goals to be achieved have been refined, the advisor's next job is to devise a realistic *financial plan* for bringing the client from his or her present financial position to the attainment of those goals. Since no two clients are alike, a well-drawn financial plan must be tailored to the individual, with all the advisor's recommended strategies designed for each particular client's needs, abilities, and goals. The plan must be the client's plan, not the advisor's plan.

It is unlikely that any individual advisor can maintain an up-to-date familiarity with all the strategies that might be appropriate for his or her clients. Based on his or her education and professional specialization, the advisor is likely to rely on a limited number of "tried and true" strategies for treating the most frequently encountered planning problems. When additional expertise is needed, the advisor should always consult with a specialist in the field in question to help him or her design the client's overall plan.

Also there is usually more than one way for a client's financial goals to be achieved. When this is the case, the advisor should present alternative strategies for the client to consider and should explain the advantages and disadvantages of each strategy. Strategies that will help achieve multiple goals should be highlighted.

The financial plan that is developed should be specific. It should detail who is to do what, when, and with what resources.

Implicit in plan development is the importance of obtaining client approval. It follows that the plan must not only be reasonable, it must also be acceptable to the client. Usually interaction between advisor and client continues during plan development, providing constant feedback to increase the likelihood that the client will approve the plan.

Normally, the report describing the plan should be in writing. Since the objective of the financial planning report is to communicate, its format should be such that the client can easily understand and evaluate what is being proposed. Some financial advisors take pride in the length of their reports, although lengthy reports are often made up primarily of standardized or "boilerplate" passages. In general, the simpler the report, the easier it will be for the client to understand and adopt. Careful use of graphs, diagrams, and other visual aids in the report can also help in this regard.

After the plan has been presented and reviewed with the client, the moment of truth arrives. At this time the advisor must ask the client to approve the plan (or some variation thereof). As part of this request, the advisor must ask the client to allocate money for the plan's implementation. While there are those who frown at the mere mention of selling in connection with financial planning, the truth is that financial planning does involve selling. Even financial advisors who are compensated entirely on a fee-for-service basis must sell the client on the need to work with the advisor to develop and implement a plan.

Step 5: Implement the Plan

The mere giving of financial advice, no matter how solid the foundation on which it is based, does not constitute financial planning. A financial plan is useful to the client only if it is put into action. Therefore, part of the advisor's responsibility is to see that plan implementation is carried out properly according to the schedule agreed upon with the client.

Financial plans that are of limited scope and limited complexity may be implemented for the client entirely by the advisor. For other plans, however, additional specialized professional expertise will be needed. For example, such legal instruments as wills and trust documents may have to be drawn up, insurance policies may have to be purchased, or investment securities may have to be acquired. Part of the advisor's responsibility is to motivate and assist the client in completing each of the steps necessary for full plan implementation.

Step 6: Monitor the Plan

The relationship between the financial advisor and the client should be an ongoing one that hopefully will span the client's entire financial life. Therefore, the sixth and final step in the financial planning process is to monitor the client's plan. Normally the advisor meets with the client at least once each year to review the plan, or more frequently if changing circumstances warrant it. The first part of this review process should involve measuring the performance of the implementation vehicles. Second, updates should be obtained concerning changes in the client's personal and financial situation. Third, changes that have occurred in the economic, tax, or financial environment should be reviewed with the client.

If this periodic review of the plan indicates satisfactory performance in light of the client's current goals and circumstances, no action needs to be taken. However, if performance is not acceptable or if there is a significant change in the client's personal or financial circumstances or goals or in the economic, tax, or financial environment, the advisor and client should revise the plan to fit the new situation. This revision process should follow the same six steps used to develop the original plan, though the time and effort needed will probably be less than in the original process.

Summary

The financial planning process described above is depicted schematically in figure 1-2. The blocks on the left represent the six steps in the process, while the blocks on the right indicate the main substantive activities that should occur in each step.

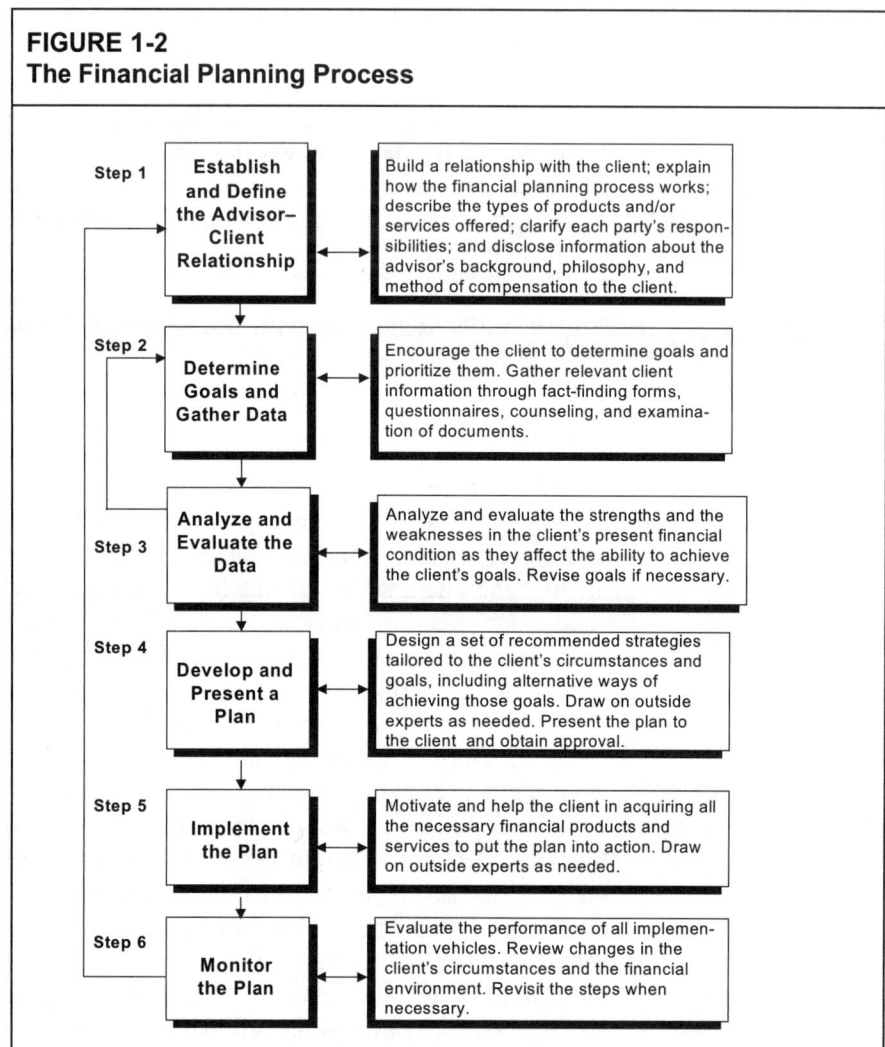

FIGURE 1-2
The Financial Planning Process

HOW IS FINANCIAL PLANNING CONDUCTED?

The ongoing debate over what financial planning is and, thus, who is engaged in financial planning has often centered on the breadth of services provided to clients. Some have contended that the financial advisor who focuses on solving a single type of financial problem with a single financial product or service is engaged in financial planning. Others have argued that true financial planning involves consideration of all of the client's financial goals and all the products and services available to achieve those goals. What if the advisor's focus is somewhere in between these two extremes?

Once financial planning is recognized as being a process, the traditional debate is relatively easy to resolve. Regardless of the breadth of services provided, an advisor is engaged in financial planning if he or she uses the six-step financial planning process in working with a client to develop a plan for achieving that client's financial goals. Thus, as previously noted, true financial planning can involve a single-purpose, multiple-purpose, or comprehensive approach to meeting a client's financial goals as long as the six-step financial planning process is utilized in doing so.

Single-Purpose Approach

Some advisors take the position that the simple selling of a single financial product or service to a client in order to solve a single financial problem constitutes financial planning. Clearly, these advisors would be incorrect if the financial planning process was not used to determine whether the problem their product solves is, in fact, the specific client's financial problem and if so, whether it is the most appropriate product or service for solving that client's problem. In this case, the advisor would be involved in product sales, not financial planning.

single-purpose approach

However, if an advisor sells a client a product to implement the recommendation of a plan developed according to the financial planning process and approved by the client, the service provided by the advisor constitutes financial planning. According to this specialist or *single-purpose approach,* all the following individuals would be engaged in financial planning as long as they use the financial planning process in working with their clients:

- a stockbroker who advises a customer to buy shares of common stock of a particular company
- a salesperson who sells to a client shares in a real estate limited partnership
- a preparer of income tax returns who suggests that a client establish an IRA
- a banker who opens a trust account for the benefit of a customer's handicapped child
- a life insurance agent who sells key person life insurance to the owner of a small business
- a personal finance counselor who shows a client how to set up and live within a budget

Multiple-Purpose Approach

Client financial needs and financial products and services are often seen as falling into one of the major planning areas: insurance planning and risk management, employee benefits planning, investment planning, income tax planning, retirement planning, and estate planning. Rather than taking a single-purpose approach of just solving a single financial problem with a single financial product or service, many financial advisors take a *multiple-purpose approach* by dealing with at least a large part of one of these planning areas, and perhaps some aspects of a second planning area. According to the multiple-purpose approach, the following individuals would be engaged in financial planning as long as they use the financial planning process in working with their clients:

- a multiline insurance agent who sells all lines of life, health, property, and liability insurance
- a tax attorney who assists clients with their income, estate, and gift tax planning
- an investment adviser who is registered as such with the Securities and Exchange Commission
- a life insurance agent who also sells a family of mutual funds to meet both the protection and wealth accumulation needs of clients

Comprehensive Approach

Still other advisors take a *comprehensive approach* to providing financial planning services. Comprehensive financial planning considers all aspects of a client's financial position, which includes the client's financial goals and objectives, and utilizes several integrated and coordinated planning strategies for fulfilling those goals and objectives. The two key characteristics of comprehensive financial planning are

- that it encompasses all the personal and financial situations of clients to the extent that these can be uncovered, clarified, and addressed through information gathering and counseling
- that it integrates into its methodology all the techniques and expertise utilized in more narrowly focused approaches to solving client financial problems

Because of the wide range of expertise required to engage in comprehensive financial planning, effective performance commonly requires a team of specialists. The tasks of the advisor managing the team are to coordinate the efforts of the team and to contribute expertise in his or her own field of specialization.

In its purest form, comprehensive financial planning is a service provided by the managing advisor on a fee-only basis. No part of the managing advisor's compensation comes from the sale of financial products, thus helping to ensure complete objectivity in all aspects of the plan. Some team specialists also are compensated through fees, while others might receive commissions from the sale of products, while still others might receive both fees and commissions. In its less pure but often more practical form, comprehensive financial planning provides the managing advisor with compensation consisting of some combination of fees for service and commissions from the sale of some of the financial products. Again, other members of the team might receive fees, commissions, or both.

Furthermore, in its purest form, comprehensive financial planning is performed for a client all at once. A single planning engagement by the managing advisor and his or her team of specialists creates the one plan that addresses all the clients concerns and utilizes all the needed financial strategies. This plan is then updated with the client periodically and modified as appropriate. In its less pure form, comprehensive financial planning is performed incrementally during the course of several engagements with the client. For example, the advisor in one year might prepare a plan to treat some of the client's tax and estate concerns as well as his or her insurance planning problems. In another year, the advisor might focus on the client's retirement concerns and investment planning problems and then dovetail the strategies for dealing with them with the previously developed tax, estate, and insurance strategies. In a third engagement, the advisor might address the remaining issues in the tax, estate, insurance, retirement, and investment planning areas and coordinate all the recommended strategies and previously developed plans. Again, each incremental part, as well as the overall plan, is reviewed periodically and revised as appropriate.

FINANCIAL PLANNING AREAS OF SPECIALIZATION

Regardless of the breadth of the approach to financial planning—single-purpose, multiple-purpose, or comprehensive—employed by a particular advisor in working with clients, financial advisors tend to have areas of specialization in which they concentrate their activities. A survey conducted by the CFP Board of Standards[5] in 1999 identified the following areas of specialization which, in turn, give an indication of the types of services provided by advisors to clients.

- investment planning/advice—90 percent (of those surveyed)
- pension/retirement planning—87 percent

- comprehensive planning—73 percent
- estate planning—73 percent
- portfolio management—67 percent
- income tax planning—60 percent
- insurance planning—59 percent
- education planning—55 percent
- elder/long-term care planning—46 percent
- closely-held business planning—37 percent
- financial planning employee education—31 percent
- income tax preparation—25 percent
- divorce planning—19 percent

CONTENT OF A COMPREHENSIVE FINANCIAL PLAN

As indicated in the previous section, many financial advisors see comprehensive financial planning as being one of their areas of specialization. In practice, however, it is the least frequently encountered type of financial planning engagement for most advisors for several reasons. First, not many clients are willing to invest as much of their own time in the undertaking as comprehensive financial planning requires. Second, usually only affluent clients are willing and able to pay for all the time of the advisor and his or her staff that is needed in developing a comprehensive financial plan. Third, not many clients can easily deal with the totality of their financial goals, capabilities, and difficulties all at one time. Instead, most clients prefer to concentrate on only one or a few related goals and/or problems at a time. (As has been mentioned, however, even clients who prefer to concentrate on only one or a few related goals and/or problems at any one time can still have a comprehensive financial plan developed and implemented for them, although development and implementation will take place in incremental stages over a period of time.)

When the advisor prepares a comprehensive financial plan for a client, whether entirely in one engagement or incrementally over a period of time, what should the plan contain? Clearly, comprehensive financial planning is such an ambitious and complex undertaking that it must cover numerous subjects. At a minimum, these subjects should include the major planning areas identified by the Certified Financial Planner Board of Standards in its Topic List for CFP Certification Examinations (reproduced in appendix A). These areas are

- general principles of financial planning (for example, personal financial statements, client attitudes and behavioral characteristics, and so forth)

- insurance planning and risk management
- employee benefits planning
- investment planning
- income tax planning
- retirement planning
- estate planning

A comprehensive financial plan should address all of these major planning areas as they relate to the client. If the financial advisor does not have the expertise to personally address each of the major planning areas in the development of the plan, he or she should form a team of specialists and serve as its manager. The advisor's role would then be to coordinate the efforts of the team and to contribute expertise in his or her own field of specialization. If, for some reason, one of the major planning areas does not apply to the client, the plan should spell out this fact. This will indicate that an important planning area was not overlooked in the development of the plan but was investigated and found not to apply to the client at this time.

FOCUS ON ETHICS
Beginning a Dialogue on Ethics

Every chapter contains an ethics dialogue box similar to this one. Ethics is a topic that should be implicit in any discussion of financial planning and the role of the financial advisor. This first box addresses a question that many advisors have asked: "Is the highly ethical advisor financially rewarded for being ethical." The answer is that he or she may be, but there is no guarantee. There are certainly some illustrations of the shady advisor reaping significant financial gains. Disciplined ethical conduct, by itself, does not guarantee financial success.

Perhaps the question should be addressed from a different perspective. Do clients want to do business with someone who really understands financial planning but who has questionable morals? Do clients want to do business with someone whose integrity is unassailable but whose financial planning skills are marginal? The answer to both questions is no.

The skilled financial advisor who is client centered and ethically well disciplined clearly has the attributes that clients desire and deserve. Again, ethical practice provides no guarantees of financial success. It is clear, however, that clients want to do business with financial advisors who have earned their trust and are technically competent.

In addition to the major planning areas that pertain to almost every client, there are a number of more specialized areas that are relevant to many, but not all, clients. These specialized areas are, for the most part, subsets of, and typically involve several of, the major planning areas. However, because all of these specialized areas are unique, they merit separate treatment. They should be made part of a client's comprehensive financial plan only if he or she is affected by them. Typically, a single-purpose or multiple-purpose financial plan that is focused on the particular planning need deals with these specialized areas.

The most important of these specialized areas in terms of the number of people it affects is educational funding. Most clients understand the need to save for college and are aware that college costs have risen at a faster pace than the *Consumer Price Index (CPI)*. Still, the vast majority of families accumulate far too little money for college by the matriculation date. They usually have to cut back on living expenses, borrow money, tap into retirement assets, or seek additional employment to meet the funding need. Often, they lower their sights and target a school that is less expensive than the one best suited to their children's needs. Consequently, planning to meet the costs of higher education has become a necessity for most parents.

Consumer Price Index (CPI)

The other specialized areas worthy of mention are those that can be categorized as financial planning for special circumstances. These areas typically include planning for

- divorce
- terminal illness
- nontraditional families
- job change and job loss, including severance packages
- dependents with special needs

As previously mentioned, all of these specialized planning areas are subsets of one or more of the major planning areas. For example, divorce planning could affect every single one of the major planning areas but, nevertheless, should not be part of a comprehensive financial plan unless the client is contemplating divorce. Even then, divorce planning would be better handled under a single-purpose or multiple-purpose financial plan because of its unique aspects and shorter planning horizon than the major planning areas.

Life-Cycle Financial Planning

financial life cycle

There are five distinct phases in an individual's *financial life cycle*. Starting at a relatively young age (that is, age 25 or younger), a career-minded person typically will pass through four phases en route to phase 5 and his or her retirement. These five phases and their corresponding age ranges are

1. early career (age 25 or younger to age 35)
2. career development (age 35 to age 50)
3. peak accumulation (age 50 to ages 58–62)
4. preretirement (3 to 6 years prior to planned retirement)
5. retirement (ages 62–66 and older)

Together, these five phases span a person's entire financial life. Although some people will not experience all of the phases or will spend more or less time in any one phase, the vast majority of career-minded people will go through all five phases.

As previously discussed, the first step in creating a comprehensive financial plan is for the advisor to establish and define the advisor-client relationship. Once the ground rules for the financial planning engagement have been set, the advisor's next task is to lead the client through the goal-setting process. Goal setting requires clients to recognize that there are several phases in their financial life; for young clients, the early career phase is the beginning of that life. The goals that young clients who are in this phase typically set reflect this fact. For example, a client who is in the early career phase often is newly married and has young children, and the client and/or his or her spouse are establishing employment patterns. This client should first be concerned about protecting his or her family from a potential financial disaster due to death or disability as well as building a cash reserve or emergency fund to meet unexpected contingencies. After addressing these income protection and security goals, the client can begin accumulating funds for a home purchase and saving for the children's college educations. In addition, accumulating funds for retirement should begin in earnest while the client is still young. However, other than having a simple will drafted, the client's goals that deal with the management of retirement and estate assets generally will not have a very high priority in the first few years of the early career phase, but they still need to be considered if the financial plan is to be a truly comprehensive one.

Once the client has a comprehensive financial plan, it is incumbent on the advisor to monitor the plan. As the client moves into the career development phase of his or her financial life cycle, some goals may need revision. This phase is often a time of career enhancement, upward mobility, and rapid growth in income. The phase usually includes additional accumulation and then expenditure of funds for the children's college educations. Moreover, the advisor should recommend coordinating the employee benefits of the client and his or her spouse and integrating them with insurance and investment planning goals.

As the client moves into the peak accumulation phase, the ever-vigilant advisor should be monitoring the plan for any needed changes. In this phase, the client is usually moving toward maximum earnings and has the greatest opportunity for wealth accumulation. The phase may include accumulating funds to increase net worth, but it is usually a continuation of accumulating funds to meet retirement goals.

The preretirement phase often involves winding down both the career and income potential, restructuring investment assets to reduce risk and enhance income, and a further emphasis on tax planning and evaluating retirement plan distribution options relative to income needs and tax consequences. Throughout this phase, the financial advisor should be actively involved in keeping his or her client's financial plan on target to meet all the client's goals.

The final phase in the client's financial life cycle is retirement. If the advisor has kept the client's financial plan fine-tuned, then this phase should be a time of enjoyment with a comfortable retirement income and sufficient assets to preserve purchasing power. While all of the major planning areas should have been receiving attention throughout the client's financial life cycle, now is the time for the advisor to make certain that his or her client's estate plan is in order.

life cycle financial planning

The advisor who monitors a client's financial plan throughout the client's financial life cycle is practicing *life-cycle financial planning*. A comprehensive financial plan that is developed for a relatively young client needs to be reviewed and revised periodically as the client ages and passes through the phases of the financial life cycle. Many of the client's financial goals will need adjusting as life's circumstances change; having the right goals is critical to creating a successful financial plan. As previously discussed, the advisor's role in setting goals is to help the client establish SMART goals (that is, goals that are Specific, Measurable, Achievable, Relevant, and have a Target date) and to set a positive tone for the entire financial planning process. The entire process encompasses not only the development of the client's first financial plan but also any future revisions and/or modifications to that plan.

The content of a comprehensive financial plan should, as already mentioned, include a discussion of each of the major planning areas. Which phase of the financial life cycle that the client is currently in strongly influences the priority given to the goals for each of the planning areas. Financial planning is a process that should be ongoing throughout the client's financial life. That is why financial planning over the client's financial life is called life-cycle financial planning.

Format of a Comprehensive Financial Plan

A financial plan, whether comprehensive or not, is essentially a report to the client regarding the advisor's findings and recommendations. This report results from the application of the financial planning process to the client's present situation in an effort to assist the client in meeting his or her financial goals. Although there are as many different formats for a comprehensive financial plan as there are financial advisors, it is easy to agree that every comprehensive financial plan should include certain types of information. For example, every comprehensive plan should cover all of the major planning areas. Every plan should be based on SMART goals set by the client. And every plan should be structured around strategies for achieving the client's goals. In addition, in the process of formulating strategies, assumptions have to be made and should be spelled out in the plan documents. Typical assumptions include the interest rate, the rate of inflation, and the client's financial risk tolerance, to name but a few. Finally, every plan is developed around information gathered during a fact-finding process. Much of this information, such as financial statements, should also be included in the plan.

Recognizing that there are many possible variations for organizing all of this information into a cohesive plan, one possible approach is to structure the plan to parallel the steps in the financial planning process. A single planning engagement with the advisor, generally with a team of specialists, utilizes several planning strategies and creates the one plan that addresses all the client's financial concerns.

A comprehensive financial plan organized to follow the financial planning process should start (paralleling step 1, establishing and defining the advisor-client relationship) by specifying the responsibilities of each party for implementing the plan and carrying it through to completion. Along with specifying responsibilities, the plan also needs to clarify how the advisor is to be compensated for his or her work in developing, implementing, and monitoring the plan. Covering these all-important ground rules at the beginning of the plan helps not only to define the advisor-client relationship but to set the tone for that relationship as well.

Next (paralleling step 2, determining goals and gathering data), the comprehensive financial plan should specify the client's stated goals, indicating the priority of each one and the time frame for achieving it. Each goal, as previously indicated, should be stated as SMART as possible and placed into relevant categories, such as income protection and security goals, accumulation goals, and goals dealing with the management of retirement and estate assets. Keep in mind that the best solution for a specific goal may involve a combination of the major planning areas; whatever approach is adopted for categorizing the goals, the plan should be designed to avoid confusing the client.

In addition to specifying the client's goals, the plan should also describe the client's present situation based on both the personal and financial data gathered from the client. In terms of the personal situation, this should include not only basic information about the client and his or her family, such as names, addresses, phone numbers, dates of birth, Social Security numbers, and so on, but also other relevant personal information that helps define the client's present situation and consequently will affect the financial plan. This other relevant information could include such topics as a child's serious health problem, a feeling of personal obligation to support aging parents, a desire to treat adopted or stepchildren differently from natural children, previous marriages and alimony or child-support obligations, and gifts or inheritances pending or anticipated.

Besides defining the client's present personal situation, the plan should include a description of the client's present financial situation. This is most commonly done by including a copy of the client's financial position statement on the plan date, listing his or her assets and liabilities and showing net worth; a cash-flow statement that identifies all the client's income and expenses and indicates his or her net cash flow for the latest period; and a copy of the client's most recent federal income tax return and an analysis thereof. The information presented should also include pro forma statements, that is, projections of future financial position relevant to understanding the client's current position. The client's current investment portfolio should also be presented with an indication of, among other things, its liquidity, diversification, and risk characteristics.

Next, for each goal, at least three critical areas of information should be presented:

- (paralleling step 3, analyzing and evaluating the data) the problem(s) identified by the advisor that the client would encounter in attempting to accomplish the goal
- (paralleling step 4, developing and presenting a plan) the recommended financial and tax services, products, and strategies for overcoming the identified problem(s) (including any underlying assumptions the advisor made in formulating the recommendation) so that the client can achieve the goal
- (paralleling step 5, implementing the plan) recommendations for implementing the proposed solution for achieving the goal

A second possible approach for structuring a comprehensive financial plan is to build the plan from the ground up in three stages. This type of plan typically requires several meetings with the client over a period of years. At the first stage or level of plan development, the advisor should concentrate his or her efforts on protecting the client against unexpected occurrences that could cause financial hardship. At the second stage or level, the advisor should focus on the client's wealth accumulation objectives. At the third and final stage or level, the advisor should address retirement and estate concerns. To help in understanding how these stages or levels fit together in a comprehensive plan, one needs to review the financial planning pyramid shown in figure 1-1. The pyramid illustrates how to develop a comprehensive financial plan in three stages or levels over a period of time.

Regardless of the format a financial advisor adopts to organize a comprehensive financial plan, the important point to remember is that the plan should be communicated to the client in the form of a written report. The format of this financial planning report should make it easy for the client to understand and evaluate what is being proposed. In general, the simpler the report, the easier it will be for the client to understand and adopt. Careful organization, as well as the use of graphs, diagrams, and other visual aids, can help in this regard.

TRENDS CREATING OPPORTUNITIES FOR FINANCIAL PLANNING ADVISORS

A number of trends having important implications for advisors engaged in financial planning have emerged in the United States in recent years. They all point to enormous opportunities for these advisors to render valuable service to clients.

One of the most important trends is that the population is growing older. The median age of Americans has risen more than 7 years in the past 3 decades, meaning that a larger proportion of the population has moved into the period of highest earnings. Also, as people get older, they tend to devote a smaller share of their income to current consumption and a larger share to savings and investments.

baby boom generation

One of the causes of the rising median age of Americans is that the members of the *baby boom generation* are no longer babies. The children born from 1946 to 1964 now range in age from their early 40s to their early 60s and constitute about 30 percent of the U.S. population. Another cause of the rising median age is that Americans are living longer. Approximately 12.4 percent of them are now age 65 or over as compared to 9.2 percent in 1960, and this percentage will continue to rise. Government statistics indicate that the average life expectancy for 65-year-old males is now over 16 years and for 65-year-old females is now over 19 years.

The aging of the American population means that more consumers need retirement planning assistance during both their remaining years of active work and their retirement years. An increasing proportion of the population also needs assistance in planning for the cost of their children's college educations.

A second important trend in the financial planning marketplace is that dual-income families are increasingly common. This trend results from an increasing percentage of women entering (and reentering) the labor force, even during the years when they have young children. Dual-income families typically have higher total incomes, pay higher income and Social Security taxes, and have less time to manage their finances. The opportunities for financial planning advisors to assist people in this situation are obvious.

A third broad trend is the increasing volatility of financial conditions in the American economy. Three indicators of this volatility confronting and confusing American households in the past 45 years are the changes that have occurred in inflation rates, in the level of interest rates, and in common stock prices. For example, during the first half of the 1960s, annual increases in the CPI averaged about 1.3 percent; the *prime interest rate* charged by banks on short-term business loans averaged about 4.68 percent, and the *Standard & Poor's 500 Index* of common stock prices averaged about 72. Consider the dynamic patterns of these indicators since then, as shown in table 1-2.

prime interest rate

Standard & Poor's 500 Index

Inflation and interest rates rose steadily in the late 1960s, and they were undoubtedly a motivating factor behind the growth in the number of advisors engaged in financial planning. Inflation and interest rates then cooled but bounced up again sharply in the mid-1970s. After a 3-year respite, they rose very sharply in the late 1970s and into the 1980s. Throughout this entire period, stock prices rose only modestly.

Inflation rates slowed again during the mid-1980s, as did the prime interest rate. Meanwhile the stock market rose dramatically but erratically. As the 1980s came to a close, inflation and interest rates were creeping up again and average common stock prices were gyrating sharply from day to day. Then in the early 1990s, inflation started cooling again, stock prices rose dramatically, and interest rates plummeted.

The mid-1990s saw continued moderation of inflation, yet interest rates crept upward while the stock market set record highs. Inflation in 1998 dropped to 1.6 percent, its lowest level in over 3 decades, and then rose again to 3.4 percent in 2000. From 1997 to 1999 the stock market soared to unprecedented highs, but also displayed unsettling volatility.

In 2000, the stock market turned downward and continued to drop in 2001 and 2002. From a high near 1500 in the middle of 2000, the S & P 500 fell below 900 by the end of 2002, quite close to where it was in the middle of 1997 near the beginning of the bull market. Inflation declined after 2000 to a low of 1.6 percent in 2002. Meanwhile, in response to actions of the Federal Reserve, interest rates dropped to their lowest levels in decades, declining from 9.50 percent during December 2000 to 4.00 percent in July 2003.

TABLE 1-2
Consumer Price Index Changes (Urban Consumers), the Prime Rate, and the Standard & Poor's 500 Stock Index: 1965–2007

Year	Percentage Change in CPI	Average Prime Rate %	Average S & P 500 Index
1965	1.6	4.54	88.47
1966	2.9	5.63	84.46
1967	3.1	5.63	92.18
1968	4.2	6.31	98.54
1969	5.5	7.96	97.58
1970	5.7	7.91	83.45
1971	4.4	5.73	98.21
1972	3.2	5.25	109.82
1973	6.2	8.03	106.51
1974	11.0	10.81	81.48
1975	9.1	7.86	87.13
1976	5.8	6.84	102.79
1977	6.5	6.83	97.48
1978	7.6	9.06	95.46
1979	11.3	12.67	103.33
1980	13.5	15.26	119.58
1981	10.3	18.87	127.84
1982	6.2	14.85	120.28
1983	3.2	10.79	160.72
1984	4.3	12.04	160.32
1985	3.6	9.93	188.97
1986	1.9	8.33	238.92
1987	3.6	8.21	285.99
1988	4.1	9.32	267.72
1989	4.8	10.87	326.31
1990	5.4	10.01	332.68
1991	4.2	8.46	381.53
1992	3.0	6.25	417.12
1993	3.0	6.00	453.45
1994	2.6	7.15	460.66
1995	2.8	8.83	546.88
1996	3.0	8.27	674.85
1997	2.3	8.44	875.86
1998	1.6	8.35	1,087.86
1999	2.2	8.00	1,330.60
2000	3.4	9.23	1,419.73
2001	2.8	6.91	1,186.00
2002	1.6	4.67	989.38
2003	2.3	4.12	967.93
2004	2.7	4.34	1,132.60
2005	3.4	6.19	1,207.75
2006	3.2	7.96	1,318.31
2007	2.8	8.05	1,478.10

Percentage change in CPI calculated from data provided by the U.S. Department of Labor, Bureau of Labor Statistics and available at: www.bis.gov/cpi/home.htm. The source for Average Prime Rate is: "H.15 Selected Interest Rates: Historical Data" (updated weekly), the Federal Reserve Board available at: www.federalreserve.gov/releases/h15/data.htm. Average S&P 500 Index is based on monthly data provided by The Financial Forecast Center™ and available at: www.forecasts.org, except for 2006 and 2007 data, which is available at: www.econstats.com/eqty/eqem_mi_1.htm.

In addition to the volatility of inflation rates, interest rates, and stock market prices, another destabilizing factor faced by American consumers has been important U.S. income tax law changes that affect all aspects of financial planning. Still another element of instability in the financial environment has been the failure rate among financial institutions, including some very large ones. In the 1980s and early 1990s failure rates among savings and loan associations, banks, and insurance companies were higher than they had been in many years. In mid 2008, several financial institutions found themselves on shaky ground because of the mortgage crisis.

With the possible exception of the bull markets of the late 1990s and mid 2000s where many investors felt they could "do it themselves" without either professional advice or paying much attention to risk,[6] volatile economic conditions generally create greater demand for financial planning services. They also emphasize the need for financial advisors to continuously monitor their clients' financial circumstances and to adjust the plans as circumstances dictate. These volatile financial conditions make it doubly important that advisors thoroughly understand and abide by their clients' risk tolerances. With the two most recent declines in the stock market that began in 2000, and again in late 2007, along with their impact on the value of invested assets, investors are again recognizing the value of financial planning services and the need to consider risk as well as return in attempting to achieve their financial goals.

A fourth major trend in the financial planning market is the technological revolution that has occurred in the financial services industry. This revolution has made possible the creation of many new financial products and has made it easier to tailor these products to individual client needs. Also the technology has made possible improved analysis of the performance of these products by advisors with the skills to do so.

CONSUMER NEEDS FOR FINANCIAL PLANNING

A basic and inescapable principle of economics is the law of scarcity. In every society, human wants are unlimited whereas the resources available to fill those wants are limited. The available resources must be somehow rationed among the wants. This rationing problem creates the need for financial planning even in affluent societies, such as the United States, and even among the most affluent members of such societies. To put it colloquially, there is just never enough money to go around.

What are the main financial concerns of American consumers? Are they able to handle those concerns on their own or do they need professional help? In short, do U.S. consumers have a significant need and effective demand for professional financial planning services in the early years of the new millennium?

A national consumer survey conducted by the CFP Board of Standards in 2004 identified the following top-10 reasons people begin financial planning:[7]

- building a retirement fund (82 percent of those surveyed)
- home purchase/renovation (41 percent)
- building an "emergency fund" (40 percent)
- managing/reducing current debt (34 percent)
- vacation/travel (34 percent)
- building a college fund (32 percent)
- accumulating capital (31 percent)
- providing insurance protection (29 percent)
- sheltering income from taxes (26 percent)
- generating current income (25 percent)

In reporting the results of its 2004 Consumer Survey, the CFP Board of Standards also broke the findings down according to three key groups of respondents—"up and coming," "mid-life," and "retirement cusp." Table 1-3 shows the financial planning focus of each of the groups and highlights the relative importance of retirement planning to all three consumer groups.

The 2008 Retirement Confidence Survey conducted by the Employee Benefits Research Institute[8] also indicated that there is a strong need for professional help in planning effectively for one's retirement. The survey results showed

- Retirement worries growing—Americans' confidence in their ability to afford a comfortable retirement dropped to its lowest level in 7 years, reflecting worries about health costs, the economy, and home values. Decreases in confidence occurred across all age groups and income levels but were particularly acute among younger workers and those with lower incomes.
- Overall retirement confidence drops sharply—The percentage of workers very confident about having enough money for a comfortable retirement decreased sharply, down from 27 percent in 2007 to 18 percent in 2008.
- Health care costs have become a big issue for retirees—Among retirees who left the work force earlier than planned, 54 percent indicated they did so because of health problems or disability. 44 percent of retirees say they have spent more than expected on health care expenses, while 54 percent of retirees say they are now more concerned about their financial future than they were right after they retired, a 14 percentage-point increase from 2007.

TABLE 1-3 Financial Planning Needs		
Consumer Group	Who Are They?	Financial Planning Focus
Up and Coming	Ages: 20-39 28% have a written financial plan 52% completed plan within the last 3 years Most tolerant of risk More likely to use the Internet for financial purposes Most likely to have financial software	Prepare for retirement Manage/reduce debt Build an emergency fund Build a college fund Save for a home purchase/renovation
Mid-Life	Ages: 40-54 39% have a written financial plan 56% completed plan at least 4 years ago More likely to use a financial professional to develop a plan Highest amount of household income Have low to moderate risk tolerance	Prepare for retirement (strongest focus of all three consumer groups) Build an emergency fund Vacation/travel Finance college education Manage/reduce current debt Shelter income from taxes
Retirement Cusp	Ages: 55-69 47% have a written financial plan 62% completed plan at least 5 years ago Higher net worth and lower risk tolerance Most likely to have a financial professional as a primary advisor	Prepare for retirement Vacation/travel Accumulate capital Generate income Shelter income from taxes Provide for future medical needs Build an emergency fund
Source: 2004 Consumer Survey, Certified Financial Planner Board of Standards, Denver, CO.		

- Workers may be waking up to the lack of health insurance in retirement—The survey found that 34 percent of workers expect to have access to employer-paid health insurance in retirement, down 8 percentage points from the 2007 results. Although 41 percent of retirees say they currently have access to health insurance through a former employer, many employers are eliminating health care coverage for future retirees.
- Retirement planning is up, but still not high—47 percent of workers say they and/or their spouse have tried to calculate how much money

they will need for a comfortable retirement, up from the 42 percent measured in 2004–2006. The survey found that 44 percent who actually calculated a retirement income goal changed their retirement planning, and of those 59 percent of them started saving or investing more.

- Most savings levels are modest—While 72 percent of workers say they have saved for retirement, 49 percent report total savings and investments (not including the value of their primary residence or any defined benefit plans) of less than $50,000. Amazingly, 22 percent of workers and 28 percent of retirees say they have no savings at all.

Baby boomers are now in midlife with many on the verge of retirement. A research report written for the American Association of Retired Persons (AARP) Public Policy Institute in January 2008,[9] found that at least half of baby boomers are on track to a comfortable retirement, although substantial numbers of them are not. The gap between the haves and the have-nots is likely to be greater than in previous generations and could create a class of seniors more heavily dependent on government and support from younger generations. In addition, the report pointed out that many boomers—even those on the verge of retiring—are clueless about how much income they will need in retirement. Moreover, boomers who are single, divorced, or widowed when they begin retirement as well as those who did not graduate from high school are the ones most likely to outlive their financial resources.

Another study of baby boomers conducted by The Allstate Corporation in 2001 suggests that many baby boomers are likely to encounter a retirement that is quite different in financial terms from the past.[10] Among other things, the survey revealed that during retirement, more than one in three baby boomers will be financially responsible for parents or children, 7 percent will be financially responsible for both parents and children, one in five will pay college tuition for one or more children, and more than 70 percent will continue to work. The survey also suggests that baby boomers appear to be poorly prepared for this financially burdensome retirement with survey respondents having saved an average of only 12 percent of the total they will need to meet even basic living expenses in retirement and having far underestimated the predicted increase in the cost of living over the next 20 years.

sandwiched generation

The baby boom generation has also become known as the *sandwiched generation* because many of its members are already faced with helping finance their children's college educations and aiding their aging parents at the same time that they themselves should be saving for their own retirements. Retirement, college funding, and long-term care are important to everyone, but especially to sandwiched boomers.

Obstacles Confronting Consumers

The results of the surveys discussed above and similar studies make it clear that many American households still have not gained control of their financial destinies. Certainly, there are many reasons why they have not developed financial plans that will enable them to do so. Three of the most important obstacles they face are the following:

- the natural human tendency to procrastinate—Among the reasons for putting off the task of establishing a financial plan may be a lack of time due to a hectic lifestyle, the seeming enormity of the task of getting one's finances under control, and the belief that there is still plenty of time to prepare for achieving financial goals.
- the very common tendency for Americans to live up to or beyond their current income—The pressure in households to overspend for current consumption is enormous, and many families have no funds left with which to implement plans for the achievement of future goals.
- the lack of financial knowledge among consumers—Although in recent years there has undoubtedly been some growth in the financial sophistication of Americans, there is still widespread ignorance about how to formulate financial objectives and how to identify and properly evaluate all the strategies that might be used to achieve them.

Role of Financial Planning Advisors

A basic inference that can be drawn from the results of consumer surveys is that Americans need help in managing their personal finances to achieve their financial goals. Moreover, many Americans seem to realize that they would benefit from professional help, and with better education, most others would reach the same conclusion. A major part of the challenge facing advisors who are doing financial planning is to help clients overcome obstacles by educating them and motivating them to gain control of their own finances.

THE FINAL WORD

The major planning areas that follow the General Principles of Financial Planning are discussed in chapters 2 through 7. The order, as well as the corresponding chapter in which these planning areas are discussed, is as follows:

- chapter 2: Insurance Planning and Risk Management
- chapter 3: Employee Benefits Planning
- chapter 4: Investment Planning
- chapter 5: Income Tax Planning
- chapter 6: Retirement Planning
- chapter 7: Estate Planning

These areas are viewed as the major planning areas that fall under the financial planning umbrella. Even though each one of these planning areas is a specialty unto itself, together they make up the totality of what is known as comprehensive financial planning. The order in which these planning areas are covered in this book is identical to the order that they appear on the Topic List for CFP® Certification Examinations (reproduced in appendix A).

Chapter 8 is devoted exclusively to Social Security, Medicare, and Medicare supplements. Even though the government and quasi-government programs stemming from these three areas could just as easily be discussed under insurance planning, employee benefits planning, and retirement planning, they are dealt with separately in this book because of their importance in providing a minimum floor of protection. They are viewed by advisors as the foundation upon which comprehensive financial planning builds.

CHAPTER SUMMARY

Although providing financial planning advice and services to clients is a relatively new and still-emerging field of professional endeavor, very affluent individuals have had access to such help for many years. However, comprehensive financial planning is now available to most Americans in the middle-and upper-middle income brackets. Moreover, as a profession, financial planning gained some stability and maturity in the 1990s, and consequently, it is now possible to describe more realistically what financial planning is and what client needs it can fulfill.

Conceptually, financial planning can be defined as a process that accomplishes both (1) ascertaining the client's financial goals, and (2) providing a plan for achieving those goals. The process is divided into six steps: (1) establish and define the advisor-client relationship, (2) determine goals and gather data, (3) analyze and evaluate the data, (4) develop and present a plan, (5) implement the plan, and (6) monitor the plan.

Advisors who use the six-step process in their practices find it both flexible and accommodating because it can be applied to the full range of a client's problems and/or goals or it can be applied to a subset of those problems and/or goals. In fact, it can even be applied to a single client problem or goal. It is not, however, the range of client problems and/or goals addressed that determine whether an advisor is engaged in financial planning. Rather, it is the advisor's use of the six-step process to address the client's problems and/or goals that is the determining factor.

As already stated, the first step in the financial planning process is to establish and define the advisor-client relationship. This normally starts at the first client meeting where advisors begin building trust with their clients by explaining to them how they work and the types of products and/or services they provide. They also must explain the financial planning process and how that process is used to develop financial plans. In addition, they need to disclose their background, philosophy, and method of compensation, whether that be fee-only, commission, or a fee and commission. Lastly, advisors must clarify not only what their responsibilities for the relationship are but also what is expected from their clients.

Once having completed step 1 of the process, the advisor is ready to determine goals and gather data in step 2. Goal setting is critical to creating a successful financial plan. The advisor's responsibility is to help the client set SMART financial goals, prioritize them, and then integrate them into a workable financial plan. One approach to setting and prioritizing goals is to place them into relevant categories or pyramid levels that can help in understanding how goals fit together in a comprehensive financial plan.

After the advisor has helped the client set goals, the advisor is ready to gather information about the client. Assembling complete, accurate, up-to-date, well organized, and relevant information about the client is the single most important task in financial planning. Without such information, the advisor cannot possibly begin to develop a financial plan tailored exclusively for the client's situation. A prerequisite for the effective gathering of client information is a systematic approach to the task. In financial planning, this usually requires using a structured fact-finder form.

Once the client's goals have been determined and data gathered, the advisor moves on to step 3 where he or she is required to analyze and evaluate the data in order to determine the client's present financial status. The objective here is to determine where the client is now in relationship to the client's goals that were established in step 2. If the advisor's analysis reveals that the client cannot possibly attain one or more of the goals, the advisor helps the client determine the changes that need to be made to achieve the goals.

After information about the client has been analyzed and, if necessary, the goals refined, step 4 requires the advisor to develop and present a plan for achieving the client's goals. Since no two clients are alike, a well-drawn financial plan must be tailored to the individual, with all the advisor's recommended strategies designed for each particular client's needs, abilities, and goals. The plan must be the client's plan, not the advisor's plan.

The report describing the financial plan should be presented to the client in writing. Since the objective of the report is to communicate, its format should be such that the client can easily understand and evaluate what is being proposed. Moreover, implicit in plan development is the importance of obtaining client approval. It follows that the plan presented to the client must not only be reasonable, it must also be acceptable to and approved by the client.

Step 5 is to implement the plan. A financial plan is useful to the client only if it is put into action. Therefore, the advisor must see that plan implementation is carried out.

Step 6, the final step of the financial planning process, is to monitor the plan. If the review of the plan indicates satisfactory performance, no action needs to be taken. However, if performance is unacceptable, the plan will need to be revised.

The single-purpose approach to financial planning is when the financial planning process is applied to a single client problem or goal. When more than one problem and/or goal is dealt with, the advisor is practicing the multiple-purpose approach to financial planning; and when the full range of a client's problems and/or goals is dealt with, the advisor is pursuing the comprehensive approach to financial planning.

When a financial advisor prepares a comprehensive financial plan for a client, whether entirely in one engagement or incrementally over a period of time, the plan should address all the major planning areas identified by the Certified Financial Planner Board of Standards. Besides covering the general principles of financial planning, the plan should address (1) insurance planning and risk management, (2) employee benefits planning, (3) investment planning, (4) income tax planning, (5) retirement planning, and (6) estate planning.

There are five distinct phases in an individual's financial life cycle. These five phases and their corresponding age ranges are (1) early career (age 25 or younger to age 35), (2) career development (age 35 to age 50), (3) peak accumulation (age 50 to ages 58–62), (4) preretirement (3 to 6 years prior to planned retirement), and (5) retirement (ages 62–66 and older). Together, these five phases span a person's entire financial life.

Although there are as many different formats for a comprehensive financial plan as there are financial advisors, one possible approach is to structure the plan to parallel the steps in the financial planning process. This type of plan typically is developed for the client in a single planning engagement. A second possible approach for structuring a comprehensive plan is to build the plan from the ground up in three stages. This type of plan typically requires several meetings with the client over a period of years and is best exemplified by the levels of the financial planning pyramid.

A number of trends having important implications for advisors engaged in financial planning have emerged in the United States in recent years. These trends are (1) the population is growing older, (2) dual-income families are increasingly common, (3) the increasing volatility of financial conditions, and (4) the technological revolution in the financial services industry.

A basic and inescapable principle of economies is the law of scarcity. In every society, human wants are unlimited whereas the resources available to fill those wants are unlimited. The available resources must be somehow rationed among the wants. This rationing problem creates the need for financial planning even in affluent societies, such as the United States, and even among the most affluent members of such societies. To put it colloquially, there is just never enough money to go around. American consumers have many financial concerns. Consequently, consumers have a significant need and effective demand for professional financial planning services.

Obstacles thwarting consumers from embracing financial planning include (1) the natural human tendency to procrastinate, (2) the very common tendency for Americans to live up to or beyond their current income, and (3) the lack of financial knowledge among consumers. A major part of the challenge facing advisors is to help clients overcome these obstacles.

The previously noted major planning areas fall under the financial planning umbrella. Even though each one of these planning areas is a specialty unto itself, together they make up the totality of what is known as comprehensive financial planning.

CHAPTER REVIEW

Key Terms and Concepts are explained in the Glossary. Answers to the Review Questions and Self-Test Questions are found in the back of the book in the Answers to Questions section.

Key Terms and Concepts

financial planning
financial planning process
financial planning pyramid
financial risk tolerance
fact-finder form
financial plan
single-purpose approach
multiple-purpose approach

comprehensive approach
Consumer Price Index (CPI)
financial life cycle
life-cycle financial planning
baby boom generation
prime interest rate
Standard & Poor's 500 Index
sandwiched generation

Review Questions

1-1. Identify the six steps in the financial planning process and briefly indicate the kinds of activities involved in each step.

1-2. Describe each of the following approaches to financial planning:
   a. single-purpose approach
   b. multiple-purpose approach
   c. comprehensive approach

1-3. At a minimum, what subjects should be included in a comprehensive financial plan?

1-4. Explain what is meant by life-cycle financial planning.

1-5. Explain the significance of the financial planning pyramid to the development of a comprehensive financial plan.

1-6. Describe the opportunities for financial planning advisors resulting from each of the following trends:
   a. rising median age
   b. increasing number of dual-income families
   c. volatility of financial conditions
   d. increasing use of sophisticated technology by the financial services industry

1-7. What are the top-10 reasons why people begin financial planning?

1-8. Describe three important obstacles preventing households from gaining control of their own financial destinies.

Self-Test Questions

Instructions: Read chapter 1 first, then answer the following questions to test your knowledge. There are 10 questions. For questions 1 through 4, match the statement with the step in the 6-step financial planning process to which it relates; for questions 5 through 10, circle the correct answer. When finished with the test, check your answers with the answer key in the back of the book.

Match each statement below with the step in the 6-step financial planning process to which it relates.

1-1. This step is where the advisor does fact-finding.   __B__

1-2. This step is where the advisor reviews changes in the client's circumstances and the financial environment.   __F__

1-3. This step is where the advisor identifies the strengths and weaknesses in the client's present financial condition.   __C__

1-4. This step is where the advisor motivates and helps the client acquire all the necessary financial products and services.   __E__

    (A) Establish and define the advisor-client relationship.
    (B) Determine goals and gather data.
    (C) Analyze and evaluate the data.
    (D) Develop and present a plan.
    (E) Implement the plan.
    (F) Monitor the plan.

1-5. According to a 2004 consumer survey conducted by the CFP Board of Standards, the top reason why people begin financial planning is to

    (A) accumulate capital
    (B) purchase or renovate a home
    (C) build a retirement fund
    (D) generate current income

1-6. Which of the following financial advisors using the financial planning process would be considered to be practicing multiple-purpose financial planning?

(A) A multiline insurance agent who sells life, health, property, and liability insurance to a client
(B) A personal finance counselor who shows a client how to set up and live within a budget
(C) A stockbroker who advises a customer to buy shares of common stock in the "XYZ" Company
(D) A banker who opens a trust account for the benefit of a customer's handicapped child

1-7. Trends creating opportunities for advisors engaged in financial planning include which of the following?

   I. Longevity among Americans is increasing.
   II. The financial environment is becoming more stable.

(A) I only
(B) II only
(C) Both I and II
(D) Neither I nor II

1-8. Which of the following statements correctly describe(s) a characteristic of comprehensive financial planning in its purest form?

   I. The managing advisor's compensation is usually a combination of fees and commissions.
   II. The plan is created by the managing advisor and his or her team of specialists in a single planning engagement.

(A) I only
(B) II only
(C) Both I and II
(D) Neither I nor II

1-9. Financial advisor activities considered to be part of step 4 (develop and present a plan) in the financial planning process include all the following EXCEPT

(A) obtaining the client's approval of the plan
(B) presenting alternative plan strategies to the client
(C) writing a report for the client that describes the plan
(D) reviewing the plan to see that it is performing satisfactorily

1-10. The results of the 2008 Retirement Confidence Survey conducted by the Employee Benefits Research Institute showed all the following EXCEPT that

(A) health care costs have become a big issue for retirees
(B) retirement planning is up but still not high
(C) overall retirement confidence increased significantly
(D) retirement savings levels for most workers are modest

NOTES

1. Shelley A. Lee, "What is Financial Planning, Anyway," *Journal of Financial Planning*, December 2001, pp. 36-46.
2. See www.extension.org/pages/SMART_Financial_Goal_Setting.
3. *Survey of Financial Risk Tolerance*, The American College, Bryn Mawr, PA 1992. The Survey of Financial Risk Tolerance is also published as appendix B in both *The Foundations of Financial Planning: The Process,* Bryn Mawr, PA: The American College Press, 2005, and the *Foundations of Investment Planning*, Bryn Mawr, PA: The American College Press, 2008.
4. For an example of a structured fact-finder form, see Richard A. Dulisse, Kirk S. Okumura, Glenn E. Stevick, and C. Bruce Worsham, *Foundations of Financial Planning: The Process*. Bryn Mawr, PA: The American College Press, 2005, appendix A: Personal Financial Planning Fact Finder, or C. Bruce Worsham, *Foundations of Investment Planning.* Bryn Mawr, PA: The American College 2008, appendix A: Comprehensive Financial Planning Fact Finder.
5. First Annual CFP Practitioner Survey: Executive Summary of Findings, Certified Financial Planner Board of Standards, Denver, CO, Summer 1999, p. 7. The telephone survey of 661 CFP practitioners was conducted by Market Facts, Inc.
6. Nancy Opiela, "The State of Financial Planning: A Grassroots Perspective," *Journal of Financial Planning*, December 2002, pp. 8-16.
7. *2004 Consumer Survey,* Certified Financial Planner Board of Standards, Denver, CO. This was a survey of 1,122 upper-quartile households of all ages (income ranged from $60,000+ to $100,000 depending on the householders' ages).
8. *The 2008 Retirement Confidence Survey*, Employee Benefit Research Institute, Washington, DC, January 2008. A telephone survey was conducted of 1,322 individuals (1,057 workers and 265 retirees) age 25 or older in the United States.
9. Sophie Korczyk, In Brief: Who is Ready for Retirement, How Ready, and How Can We Know? Research Report written for the American Association of Retired People (AARP) Public Policy Institute, January, 2008. This report examines the financial challenges baby boomers face in retirement.

10. *Retirement Reality Check*, The Allstate Corporation, Northbrook, IL, December 2001. Harris Interactive polled 1,004 people born between 1946 and 1961, with household incomes ranging from $35,000 to $100,000. The results of this survey can be found online at http://seniorjournal.com/NEWS/Retirement/12-05-1Sandwished.htm.

2

Insurance Planning and Risk Management

Robert W. Cooper

Learning Objectives

An understanding of the material in this chapter should enable you to

2-1. Define risk and explain its two categories: pure risk and speculative risk.

2-2. Describe the various types of pure risks faced by individuals and families.

2-3. Explain how the financial planning process can be used to deal with the possibility of financial loss associated with pure risks.

2-4. Describe the various types of insurance coverages available for meeting personal risks.

2-5. Describe the various types of insurance coverages available for meeting property and liability risks.

Chapter Outline

    IMPORTANCE OF PROTECTION OBJECTIVES 2.2
    RISK 2.2
    TYPES OF PURE RISKS 2.5
    PLANNING FOR PURE RISKS: INSURANCE AND OTHER
        TECHNIQUES 2.6
        Establish and Define the Advisor-Client Relationship 2.6
        Determine Goals and Gather Data 2.8
        Analyze and Evaluate the Data 2.11
        Develop and Present a Plan 2.18
        Implement the Plan 2.27
        Monitor the Plan 2.28
    A SURVEY OF PERSONAL INSURANCE COVERAGES 2.28
        Meeting Personal Risks 2.28

Meeting Property and Liability Risks 2.49
THE FINAL WORD 2.59
CHAPTER SUMMARY 2.60
CHAPTER REVIEW 2.62

This chapter begins with a brief discussion of the importance of protection objectives. It then reviews the meaning of risk for insurance and financial planning purposes, which requires distinguishing between pure risk and speculative risk. Next, the chapter identifies types of pure risks and provides an in-depth look at planning for pure risks using insurance and other techniques. Finally, the chapter surveys the various insurance coverages available for dealing with the pure risks faced by individuals and families.

IMPORTANCE OF PROTECTION OBJECTIVES

Financial planning represents an integrated approach to the development and implementation of plans for the achievement of individual or family financial objectives. Although financial objectives may differ in terms of individual circumstances, goals, attitudes, and needs, all integrated plans should include an analysis and recommendations that satisfy the client's protection objectives.

While planning for the accumulation of wealth may be more exciting, the protection of that accumulated wealth cannot be overlooked. Most people work to acquire assets (wealth) such as homes, automobiles, savings, and investments, but the pleasure associated with this wealth is sometimes interrupted by the chilling thought that some event over which there is little or no control could cause assets to be damaged or destroyed. To find some method of protecting assets, or preserving the wealth represented by those assets, against the possibility of loss is a challenge nearly all people face. Efforts by individuals and families to meet this challenge are aimed at dealing with the problem of risk.

RISK

risk

Because risk is the basic problem with which insurance deals, it is important to understand what risk is if it is to be dealt with efficiently through the use of insurance and/or other risk handling techniques. For insurance and financial planning purposes, the term *risk* means the possibility of financial loss. In applying this definition of risk, it is important to recognize that there are two ways a financial loss can occur. The most common notion of a loss involves a reduction in the value of something that an individual already possesses—for example, the value of a family's home can be reduced by a fire, the value of one's income-earning ability can be reduced by death or disability, or the value of an investor's bond portfolio can be reduced by an increase in interest rates. However, in addition to a reduction in the value of something that an individual already possesses, a loss can arise from a reduction in the value of something that an individual does not already possess but, rather, expects to receive in the future—for example, earning only a 5 percent return on an investment that the investor expected would yield 10 percent, or receiving a smaller inheritance than one had expected because the deceased's financial advisor had done a poor job of minimizing taxes and estate settlement costs in providing the deceased with estate planning advice. Recognizing that a loss can arise from a reduction in either the value of something an individual already possesses or in the value of something an individual expects to receive in the future, risk can be said to involve the possibility of a financial loss. Defined in this way, risk can be divided into two categories:

pure risk
speculative risk

- *pure risk*—involves only the possibility of financial loss
- *speculative risk*—involves not only the possibility of financial loss, but also the possibility of financial gain

Both pure and speculative risks involve the possibility of financial loss. However, with pure risk the possibility of gain is essentially absent, and all that remains is the alternative of loss or no loss (no change).

The difference between pure and speculative risk can be illustrated by the situation of a client who owns a home. The possibility of damage or destruction to the home due to fire is a pure risk. What are the possible outcomes? Either a fire occurs and causes damage that results in a loss, or no fire occurs and there is no change or loss. In contrast, the risk that the home could appreciate or depreciate in market value is a speculative risk. In this case, the client may realize either a gain or a loss from the sale of the home. With few exceptions, insurance is a technique for dealing with pure, rather than speculative, risk.

Two additional points are important in fully understanding what risk is:

- Risk and uncertainty are not the same.
- Risk is not the probability of loss.

Although risk can give rise to uncertainty, risk is not uncertainty. Unlike uncertainty, which is a state of mind characterized by doubt, risk exists as a state of the world. As a result of this difference, the following may occur:

- A client can be uncertain in a situation in which no risk exists.
- Risk can exist in a situation where a client lacks knowledge of the risk and, thus, is not uncertain.
- Two clients facing the same risk can experience different degrees of uncertainty.

peril

Recognizing this difference between risk and uncertainty enables financial advisors to prepare their clients to view and deal with risk in an objective manner. Although effective handling of a client's risk from a particular cause of loss (a *peril*) can reduce the client's uncertainty about incurring a financial loss due to the occurrence of that peril, mere reduction of uncertainty does not reduce the risk—the possibility of a financial loss—that exists as a state of the world. This can be illustrated by considering the situation of a client who is a 25 year old single mother with two young dependent children. Transferring the risk associated with the client's death to an insurance company by purchasing life insurance would reduce the client's uncertainty about her dependent children suffering a severe financial loss upon her death. However, suppose instead the client merely reasoned that since she was young and not likely to die in the near future there was really no sense in buying life insurance at that time. While the client may have succeeded in reducing her own uncertainty, her low level of uncertainty had no effect on the risk—possibility of financial loss—faced by her children. If she is one of the relatively few females aged 25 who die in the next year, her dependent children will lose all the financial support that her income would have provided.

A second point that is important in understanding risk is that while risk may be measurable in terms of probabilities, it need not be measurable to exist. That is the reason risk is defined as the possibility, not the probability, of financial loss. In order for risk to be measurable in terms of probabilities, there must be a considerable number of similar exposures to which the probability can be applied in estimating the outcome. An insurance company that insures many similar houses in an area (many similar exposures) can use probabilities to measure its risk of loss—that is, the chance that the ratio of houses that burn to houses insured in the next year will exceed the ratio of houses expected to burn during that year. However, even knowing the probability that a house of a particular type in an area will burn within the next year does not help a client measure the risk he or she faces. With only one house (one exposure), the client will either have a loss or no loss. In this case, risk—the possibility of financial loss—exists; the client just cannot measure the risk he or she faces with probabilities because there is only a single exposure to loss.

TYPES OF PURE RISKS

personal risks
property risks
liability risks

As mentioned earlier, insurance is a technique for dealing primarily with pure risks—risks involving a chance of loss or no loss. Pure risks can be categorized as *personal risks, property risks*, and *liability risks*. These three types of pure risks can be described briefly as follows:

1. personal risks—involve the possibility of
   a. loss of income earning ability because of
      (1) premature death,
      (2) disability,
      (3) unemployment, or
      (4) retirement
   b. extra expenses associated with accidental injuries, periods of sickness, or the inability to perform safely some of the activities of daily living (ADLs) (that is, bathing, dressing, using the toilet, eating, transferring from bed to chair, and maintaining continence)
2. property risks—involve the possibility of
   a. direct losses associated with the need to replace or repair damaged or missing property
   b. indirect (consequential) losses, such as additional living expenses that are caused by a direct loss
3. liability risks—involve the possibility of
   a. loss from damaging or destroying the property of others
   b. loss from causing physical or personal injuries to others

Examples of personal risks include the possibility of a loss of income to family members upon a client's premature death, disability or retirement. In addition, the possibility of incurring increased expenses associated with medical and long-term care is a type of personal risk.

Clients are exposed to property risks through the ownership of real and personal property. Real property typically consists of the client's dwelling, and personal property includes such items as household goods, clothing, and automobiles. Direct losses to one's real or personal property can be the result of many perils (causes of loss) including, among others, fire, windstorm, theft, flood, earthquake, and automobile collisions. Indirect losses are associated with the loss of use of property following the occurrence of a direct loss. In addition to the indirect loss referred to as additional living expenses, other types of consequential losses include debris removal costs, rental income losses, and demolition losses. Of these, additional living expenses and debris removal are the more important indirect losses for most individuals and families.

The ownership, maintenance, or use of an automobile is the best known source of liability risk. However, individuals should be aware of the fact that potential losses also arise out of the ownership, maintenance, or use of real property and out of personal activities. It should also be noted that workers' compensation statutes can give rise to an exposure in certain states when a client has household employees.

PLANNING FOR PURE RISKS: INSURANCE AND OTHER TECHNIQUES

risk management

needs analysis

How is the financial advisor to approach his or her clients' pure-risk situations? The process used for dealing with pure risks has traditionally been called by different names depending upon the type of risk situation faced. When dealing with pure risks involving possible damage or destruction of property or legal liability, financial advisors have tended to use a process called *risk management*. On the other hand, when dealing with pure risks involving the loss of income earning ability due to death, disability, or old age, they have tended to use a process called *needs analysis*. However, as shown in table 2-1, the risk management and needs analysis processes not only contain steps similar to each other, but also contain steps similar to those of the financial planning process (as described in chapter 1). This should not really be surprising, since all three processes are essentially different statements of the same professional approach for helping to identify and solve a client's financial problem(s).[1] Given the similarity of the steps in the risk management, needs analysis, and financial planning processes, the financial planning process will be used in discussing the steps involved in helping individuals and families deal with the possibility of financial loss associated with pure risks.

Establish and Define the Advisor-Client Relationship

As described in chapter 1, the first step in the financial planning process is to establish and define the advisor-client relationship. For the advisor, this generally involves building trust with the client, ensuring client satisfaction, and creating a relationship with the client that will hopefully span the client's entire life. In order to do this, the advisor needs to explain how he or she works and the types of products and/or services he or she is able to provide. The advisor should also provide examples of how his or her products and/or services can help the client handle the pure risks he or she faces.

TABLE 2-1
Processes for Dealing with Pure Risks

Step	Risk Management	Needs Analysis	Financial Planning
1	Determination of objectives	Identify the client's needs in the event of death, disability, and/or retirement*	Establish and define the advisor-client relationship
2	Risk identification	Collect information on the client's current financial situation	Determine goals and gather data
3	Risk analysis	Determine the types and amounts of resources required to meet the client's needs Determine the types and amounts of resources currently available to meet the client's needs Subtract the resources currently available from the resources required to meet the client's needs to determine the gaps to be filled by additional resources	Analyze and evaluate the data
4	Consider alternative risk treatment devices and select the device(s) believed to be the best for treating the risk(s)	Develop a plan for filling the resource gaps with proceeds from additional insurance coverage(s) or resources from other relevant risk treatment devices	Develop and present a plan
5	Implement the decision	Buy additional life and/or disability income insurance; increase saving for retirement*	Implement the plan
6	Monitor	Monitor periodically for changes in the client's needs and/or external factors (inflation rate, rate of return that can be earned on investments, and so on)	Monitor the plan

* While loss of income earning ability due to retirement is a type of pure risk and some life insurance and annuity products can be used as savings vehicles for dealing with this risk, retirement planning for a client primarily involves investment and tax considerations rather than planning for insurance product acquisitions.

Determine Goals and Gather Data

Once the advisor-client relationship is established and defined, the advisor is ready to move on to step 2 of the financial planning process. The first part of step 2, determining the client's goals for handling pure risks, involves at least the following three activities:

- identifying the client's concerns related to various pure risks
- determining what the client's goals are in dealing with these concerns related to pure risks
- helping the client prioritize any competing goals

The client's concerns regarding various pure risks can be identified in a number of ways. For example, when discussing the client's general financial concerns or the specific concerns that directly caused the client to seek financial planning assistance, the advisor can listen for references to potential losses or other financial problems related to various types of pure risks. Alternatively, the advisor might present the client with an outline of the various types of pure risks and ask the client to indicate his or her degree of concern with each type and his or her reasons for concern. In addition to helping the advisor identify the client's key concerns related to pure risks, the latter approach may also help identify certain pure risks with which the client should be concerned, despite his or her apparent lack of concern at the beginning of the financial planning engagement. The advisor can then look for evidence of the need for greater concern about these pure risks during the process of gathering and then analyzing data.

Once the client's concerns about dealing with various pure risks have been identified, the financial advisor should query the client to learn what goals he or she has with respect to dealing with each of these concerns. For example, what is the client's goal with respect to the risk of loss due to his or her death? Perhaps it is to ensure that each of the children are fed, clothed, and sheltered until they reach a certain age when they presumably will no longer be dependent. This goal may also include ensuring that there will be adequate resources for each child to attend college at the state university and/or for the spouse to return to school to update his or her job skills. In discussing the client's goal for dealing with each pure risk he or she faces, the financial advisor, through skillful questioning, should help the client be as specific as possible in quantifying the goals.

Finally, where goals for dealing with various pure risks are competing, the financial advisor should help the client rank these goals. For example, for a family with young children and limited resources, protecting the dependent children against the financial consequences of a working parent dying until they graduate from high school might be more important to the client than funding the children's college educations, which in turn may have a higher priority than having only a $100 deductible for property damage covered by the family's auto and homeowners policies. Likewise, with a little education from the financial advisor, carrying adequate insurance to protect against liability risks is likely to be viewed as more important than maintaining low deductibles on insurance for property risks and personal health risks.

Once the client's goals for dealing with various types of pure risks have been established, the advisor needs to move on to the second part of step 2 and gather information from the client in order to identify the specific pure risks to which he or she is exposed. At a minimum, the advisor needs to gather the following types of objective and subjective information from the client:

- an inventory of assets and liabilities
- a description of the present arrangement for the distribution of the client's (and spouses) assets at death
- a list of annual income and expenditures
- a summary of present insurance coverages
- the client's preferences regarding such things as
  - the amount of income the family should have during various periods (e.g., when dependent children are still at home versus after they have left home) following the client's death,
  - the amount of income the family will need during various periods following a long-term disability suffered by the client,
  - the colleges the client would like the children to attend following his or her death or disability,
  - who should be responsible for managing the income and assets provided to the family and its members following the client's death, and
  - the role of the spouse (working versus staying home to raise young children) following the client's death or disability.

Once the advisor gathers this information from the client or while he or she is still in the process of gathering it, the advisor can use a checklist of property and activities to help identify the pure risks specifically faced by the client. One example of such a checklist is the Risk Identification Questionnaire (reproduced in appendix B). Using a checklist like this provides the advisor with a systematic approach to discovering a particular client's loss exposures.

> **FOCUS ON ETHICS**
> **When Responsibility Exceeds Knowledge**
>
> When financial advisors address a client's financial security, they often emphasize future income production and protection. The goal is to produce a level of wealth that will generate a sufficient stream of income that will prepare the client for retirement or will ensure a chosen lifestyle should there be an interruption in income production.
>
> Commission-based financial advisors are rarely licensed to sell property and liability insurance and frequently overlook the threat posed by property destruction or major liability claims. An underinsured home destroyed by fire or natural disaster can destroy the best financial plan. The same can happen if the client is underinsured and loses a major liability suit resulting from an accident, professional negligence, or other reason.
>
> The financial advisor must sensitize the client to these needs as well. Insurance can minimize the client's property and liability losses. Protecting the client's assets is an essential part of financial planning. Just because the advisor is less knowledgeable in these areas does not reduce the need or the responsibility.

To illustrate how risk identification might be done, assume that the information gathered from the client, Burt Beamer, indicates the following: Burt Beamer, aged 45, has a wife, aged 43, a son, aged 18, and a daughter, aged 16. Burt is a manager for a local firm and currently earns $78,000 annually. The Beamers purchased a home 5 years ago for $225,000. Last year they purchased a small cabin in the mountains for $45,000. They plan to use this cabin as much as possible during the summer months and occasionally on weekends during the balance of the year. They are also thinking about renting the cabin out periodically during the summer season. The Beamers own two automobiles, a 3-year-old station wagon and a one-year-old foreign compact.

Although this is a simplified example, a partial listing of the risks that the Beamer family faces is shown in table 2-2. In actual practice the advisor should seek additional information from the Beamer family to complete the list of their exposures to pure risk. The advisor would want to include other assets or property that might be owned or used by the Beamers. He or she would also be concerned with expanding the liability exposure to include any possible business pursuits and the use of nonowned autos. In this illustration, personal risks are limited to the premature death of Burt. In practice this area would be expanded to include premature death of Burt's spouse, risks associated with the loss of earning power because of periods of disability, the incurring of additional expenses for medical and long-term care, and the need for income at retirement. Even the needs under the premature death category might be expanded beyond those shown in this illustration.

TABLE 2-2
Risk Identification (Type of Risk)

Property risks
    Direct losses
        Dwelling
        Cabin
        Furniture, clothing, etc. (dwelling)
        Furniture, clothing, etc. (cabin)
        Automobiles
    Indirect losses
        Additional living expenses
        Debris removal

Liability risks
    Owned premises (dwelling, cabin)
    Owned automobiles
    Personal activities

Personal risks
    Premature death (of Burt)
        Education fund
        Mortgage redemption fund
        Lifetime income for spouse

The risk-identification process may appear to be a relatively simple task. Some financial advisors and clients may feel that it is a waste of time to formalize the risk-identification process. They need only be reminded that forgetting or neglecting an existing risk could have disastrous financial consequences.

In addition to risk identification, the information gathered provides the advisor with a basis for identifying potential problems the client's current situation may present for the achievement of the client's goals. For example, the types and amounts of some of the client's present insurance coverages may be either not appropriate or not efficient for meeting the client's goals. In analyzing the client's exposures to pure risk in the next step of the financial planning process, review of the present insurance coverages may reveal, among other things, that the client's liability insurance limits are too low, the type of life insurance coverage currently held is too costly to enable the client to purchase an adequate amount of insurance to protect his or her dependents, or a greater amount of risk can be retained by raising the deductibles in the client's property insurance policies.

Analyze and Evaluate the Data

Once the client's goals have been determined and information about the client has been gathered, organized, and checked for accuracy, consistency, and completeness, the advisor's next task in step 3 of the financial planning process is to analyze and evaluate the client's present financial condition with respect to the pure risks he or she faces. The objective here is to determine the weaknesses or conditions in the client's current financial situation that are hindering achievement of the client's goals established in step two of the financial planning process. In the case of pure risks, data analysis requires at least two important activities:

- measurement of the potential losses associated with the identified pure risks
- evaluation of these risks from the standpoint of their potential financial impact on the client

Risk Measurement

Theoretically, risk measurement should include information on both the frequency (probability of occurrence) and severity of loss. As mentioned earlier, in order for risk to be measurable in terms of probabilities, there must be a considerable number of similar exposures to which the probability can be applied in estimating the outcome. However, in most cases, the pure risk situations faced by a particular individual or family involve only one or a few exposures to loss. Therefore, probabilities of loss do not help measure the pure risks faced by such clients. As a result, the major emphasis in risk measurement must be on the severity of the loss. When dealing with pure risks faced by individuals and families, it is safest to assume total loss and identify this as the maximum possible loss.

Property Risks. The easiest asset to measure for loss purposes is cash; each one dollar bill is worth one dollar (except, of course, when it is numismatic property or when problems of foreign exchange enter the picture). For property other than cash, however, risk measurement problems begin to emerge. Three key terms of the measurement process that need to be understood are (1) actual cash value, (2) replacement cost, and (3) depreciation.

actual cash value

Actual cash value is an insurance term used in many property insurance contracts. These contracts often limit the insurer's liability for damaged property to its actual cash value at the time of loss. Actual cash value has generally been defined as replacement cost less a reduction resulting from depreciation and obsolescence. This is normally expressed simply as

$$\text{Actual cash value} = \text{Replacement cost} - \text{Depreciation}$$

Actual cash value is sometimes a difficult measurement to understand, primarily because of the confusion that arises from the interpretations of

replacement cost depreciation

replacement cost and *depreciation*. Although useful life is frequently used as a guideline in measuring depreciation, depreciation as a factor in measuring actual cash value differs from depreciation in an accounting sense. Depreciation is a function of the age of the asset, its use, its condition at the time of loss, and any other factor causing deterioration. In addition, anything that causes the property to become obsolete in any fashion is also included in the depreciation determination for purposes of calculating actual cash value.

Replacement cost is that cost necessary to replace or repair the damaged asset. For personal property this is replacement with a comparable asset at the current price. In the calculation of actual cash value, replacement cost would be reduced for the comparable age of the damaged property. For example, assume that an auto that had been purchased new 3 years ago for $11,995 was completely destroyed in an accident. The same auto purchased today would cost $15,000, which would be its replacement cost. The actual cash value is an amount sufficient to replace the destroyed auto with one of like age and condition. Note, however, that depreciation is deducted from the current price, not the original price. It is immaterial that the damaged auto cost $11,995 new 3 years ago. The actual cash value is $15,000 (replacement cost) less an allowance for depreciation.

When replacement cost is used for real property, such as a dwelling, it is normally interpreted to mean the cost to rebuild the same type dwelling on the same site for the same type of occupancy and with materials of like kind and quality. If the replacement cost for the dwelling is determined to be $160,000 and depreciation is $17,200, the measurement of the actual cash value will be

$$\begin{aligned} \text{Actual cash value} &= \text{Replacement cost} - \text{Depreciation} \\ &= \$160,000 - \$17,200 \\ &= \$142,800 \end{aligned}$$

Replacement cost has become the more practical measure of the maximum possible loss associated with a client's real property in pure-risk situations, especially when insurance is determined to be the technique most appropriate to treat the particular risk. Sometimes there is a temptation to use market value as the measurement of loss for real property. While this is the value that is most familiar to consumers and owners of real estate, market value is closely linked to supply and demand conditions and includes the value of land which is not likely to be lost, destroyed, or severely damaged as a result of the occurrence of a property risk. Thus, caution should be exercised in using market value as the measurement of maximum possible loss for pure-risk situations. Remember that pure risk is the possibility of loss or no loss; the concern is for the damage or destruction of property, not its transfer of ownership.

For insurance purposes, the measurement of loss for personal property such as furniture, clothing, and automobiles has traditionally been the item's actual cash value. Actually, however, the maximum possible loss is the replacement cost of the particular item. For an extra premium, most insurance companies will provide replacement cost coverage on personal property other than automobiles. For this reason, and for the purpose of showing the value differences, the maximum possible loss for personal property (and for real property as well) is measured on both a replacement cost and actual-cash-value basis. An example of this is shown in table 2-3.

TABLE 2-3
Risk Identification and Measurement

Type of Risk	Maximum Possible Loss	
	Actual Cash Value	Replacement Cost
Property risks		
Direct losses		
Dwelling	$160,000	$200,000
Cabin	30,000	42,000
Furniture, clothing, etc. (dwelling)	60,000	90,000
Furniture, clothing, etc. (cabin)	4,000	7,500
Automobiles	19,000	28,000
Indirect losses		
Additional living expenses		9,600
Debris removal		3,500
Liability risks		
Owned premises (dwelling, cabin)		unlimited
Owned automobiles		unlimited
Personal activities		unlimited
Personal risks		
Premature death (of Burt)		
Cash for cleanup fund		50,000
Education fund		78,000
Mortgage redemption fund		137,000
Lifetime income for spouse		1,100,000

Finally, for measurement purposes some loss exposures listed under the property risk category are not costs of replacing property but are indirect expenses incurred because of damage to property. The best example of this for most individuals is the category of additional living expenses. These are the costs over and above normal living expenses that would be necessary to provide living accommodations, food, and transportation if a dwelling could not be occupied due to damage or destruction. An estimate of these expenses should be made as the measurement of this loss exposure.

Liability Risks. No perfect method has been developed for measuring the maximum possible dollar loss that individuals can suffer from the liability exposure. A client can enter into certain contractual arrangements that will limit the extent of liability, but in most cases the liability loss will depend upon the severity of the future accident and the amount the court awards to the injured parties (or the amount of the out-of-court settlement agreement). Because a liability loss could range anywhere from a few dollars to $1 million or more, it is appropriate to recognize some uncertainty about the measurement of the liability loss and to identify this amount as "unlimited."

human-life-value method

Personal Risks. There are several ways of measuring the loss associated with personal risks. For example, the *human-life-value method* of measuring loss due to premature death is based on a calculation of the present value of a given dollar amount annually over a given number of years at some assumed interest rate. A major shortcoming of this approach is that it does not take into account the types or amounts of the dependent's needs following the client's death or the types or amounts of resources that will be available to meet those needs.

Another method of determining the loss associated with premature death is known as needs analysis. This commonly used approach (and the method used in this chapter for analyzing data related to key personal income risks) involves (1) identifying and attaching a dollar amount to the specific financial needs of the survivors, (2) identifying and attaching a dollar amount to the resources currently available to meet those needs, and (3) determining the gaps between the survivors' needs and the resources available to meet them. These gaps must be filled with additional financial resources if the survivors' needs are to be fully met. The needs analysis approach can also be used in measuring the loss that would be experienced by the client and his or her dependents as a result of serious disability. When needs analysis is applied to disability income planning, the financial needs of the disabled client as well as the needs of the dependent family members are substituted for the needs of the survivors in the premature death application.

In planning for the client's premature death, information gathered from the client in step 2 of the financial planning process is analyzed by the advisor to identify and measure the survivors' financial needs and the resources currently available to meet those needs. Generally, in the event of a client's death, the survivors' needs will include both lump-sum cash needs and income needs. For the Beamer family, the lump-sum cash needs are identified in table 2-3 as a cleanup fund, education fund, and mortgage redemption fund. The income need was identified as a lifetime income for the surviving spouse. To determine the amount of additional resources needed to meet the survivors' lump-sum and income needs, the amounts of currently available resources are subtracted from the needs. For example, any proceeds of existing life insurance policies on Burt's life and the after-tax balance of Burt's 401(k) plan would be available to reduce the amount needed to provide for the lump-sum cash needs at Burt's death. Similarly, any wages and employee retirement benefits expected to be earned by Burt's spouse as well Social Security benefits she would be entitled to at retirement are generally considered in determining the additional resources required to meet the spouse's income needs.

In table 2-3, the dollar amount shown for the cleanup fund is an estimate of the amount needed in addition to currently available resources for last illness expenses, funeral costs, outstanding debts, probate expenses, federal and state estate and inheritance taxes, and so forth. The dollar amount for the education fund is the present value of the projected future costs of educating the two Beamer children reduced by any resources currently available to help meet those costs. Planning for future education expenses has become a common part of the financial planning process, and the dollar amount needed for this item would most likely be provided in some other part of the total financial planning process. If not, some time should be spent in developing an estimate of these costs. The amount for the mortgage is typically the current unpaid balance shown in the amortization schedule less any resources currently available to help pay off the mortgage in the event of Burt's death.

The measurement of the amount needed to fund the lifetime income for the surviving spouse requires calculations beyond the scope of this chapter. In the advisor's discussions with the client it was determined that, in the event of his premature death, Burt wanted his widow to have the equivalent purchasing power of $4,000 per month throughout her lifetime. To calculate the value of the principal sum needed presently to satisfy this objective, it is necessary to make assumptions regarding future rates of inflation and future rates of interest earnings. For this case, these assumptions were 4.5 percent and 6.5 percent, respectively. It was also assumed that upon reaching the full retirement age for Social Security benefits (currently age 67 for Mrs. Beamer because her year of birth is after 1959) Mrs. Beamer would qualify for an inflation adjusted survivor benefit equal to 100 percent of Burt's PIA (currently about $1,000). Based on these assumptions and a projection of Mrs. Beamer's longevity of life, the current principal sum needed is calculated to be $1,100,000. This is the amount entered in table 2-3 as the maximum possible loss associated with the spouse's income need. Because Mrs. Beamer might live beyond the age indicated by the projection of the longevity of her life, an alternative approach that would truly guarantee her a lifetime income would be to determine the current principal sum needed to meet her income need until age 70 and then also determine the current capital sum needed to purchase her a life annuity of an appropriate amount if she is still living at age 70.

At this point, the risk identification and measurement activities should have been completed for all the pure risks to which the client is exposed. Table 2-3 illustrates the maximum possible loss values that were determined for the partial list of risks facing the Beamer family.

Risk Evaluation

Once all the pure risks have been identified and an appropriate value has been determined as the measure of the maximum possible loss for each, the second activity in analyzing the information gathered from the client is to evaluate these risks from the standpoint of their potential financial impact upon the client. The financial advisor can assist in this process by having the client assess the seriousness of each potential loss on his or her financial status and by ranking the various risks according to their severity. One method of showing this that will be useful later in selecting the most cost-effective technique(s) for handling each of the client's pure risk situations is to categorize losses as high severity or low severity. What is high or low severity must be interpreted in terms of the client's financial ability to absorb a risk situation's maximum possible loss. The risks listed for the Beamer family in table 2-3 are evaluated using this method in the Risk Impact Chart (table 2-4). In addition to the low severity property losses indicated in table 2-4, consideration should also be given to other low severity losses commonly experienced by individuals and families such as the first few hundred dollars of medical expenses each year, the income lost during the first few weeks of disability, and the expenses incurred during the first few weeks of long-term care.

One additional comment should be made about the evaluation of pure risks. It is a mistake to view these risks as isolated individual events; for example, the fire that causes damage to the dwelling should not be considered as a loss isolated from the concurrent loss due to fire damage of the furniture contained in that dwelling. All the losses that may result from a single event should be combined into one unit to obtain a true measure of the maximum possible loss. Therefore, the fire damage to the dwelling and furniture should be considered as one loss and the combined total should be utilized to determine the total financial impact on the individual or family.

> **TABLE 2-4**
> **Risk Impact Chart**
>
> High Severity
>   Liability losses
>   Owned premises (dwelling, cabin)
>   Owned automobiles
>   Personal activities
>
>   Property losses in excess of $500 per occurrence
>   Dwelling including debris removal and additional living expenses
>   Cabin
>   Furniture, clothing, etc. (from dwelling) including debris removal and additional living expenses
>   Furniture, clothing, etc. (from cabin)
>   Automobile (foreign compact)
>   Automobile (station wagon)
>
>   Personal losses
>   Cash for cleanup fund
>   Education fund
>   Mortgage redemption fund
>   Lifetime income for spouse
>
> Low Severity
>   Property losses of $500 or less

Develop and Present a Plan

After information about the client has been analyzed and, if necessary, the objectives to be achieved have been refined, the advisor's next job is to devise a realistic plan for bringing the client from his or her present financial position to the attainment of those objectives. In planning to deal with pure risks faced by the client, this step in the financial planning process involves consideration of the various alternative techniques for handling pure risks and identifying the most cost-effective technique(s) for dealing with each of the client's pure risk exposures. A plan containing the techniques identified by the advisor as being most appropriate are then shared with the client for approval.

Alternative Risk Treatment Devices

loss control

The techniques typically available to individuals and families for handling pure risks are grouped in two categories: loss control and loss financing. *Loss control* (sometimes referred to as risk control) is concerned with reducing the probability that events resulting in financial loss will occur and minimizing the magnitude of those losses that do occur. Since some

loss financing

risk avoidance
loss prevention
loss reduction
retention
insurance

losses will occur regardless of any loss control activities undertaken, *loss financing* is concerned with how to fund these losses.

Both loss control and loss financing include several alternative techniques for handling pure risks. Loss control techniques typically available to individuals and families include *risk avoidance, loss prevention* and *loss reduction*. The two loss financing techniques most commonly used for handling pure risks faced by individuals and families are *retention* and *insurance*.

Risk Avoidance. The objective of risk avoidance is the elimination of the activity or condition that gives rise to the particular risk so that the possibility of a loss becomes nonexistent. For example, since certain types of animals are known to be vicious or to become vicious at times, liability risk avoidance would be practiced by never owning such an animal or by selling or destroying such an animal if currently owned.

While this method is potentially the most powerful risk-treatment action, in many ways it is a very difficult treatment technique for an individual or family to practice. For example, if an individual is concerned about the liability loss exposure that arises from the ownership or use of an automobile, the application of risk avoidance would call for the complete elimination of the ownership and use of automobiles. In today's society this could be an extremely difficult objective to accomplish. Because it is neither possible nor practical to avoid all risks, it is therefore necessary to consider techniques that will forestall, minimize, or finance the losses.

Loss Prevention. Loss prevention attempts to reduce the frequency of loss associated with inescapable risks by preventing the occurrence of loss. Loss-prevention actions tend to be directed at hazards or conditions that increase the likelihood of a loss occurring. For example, if a cleint drives an auto, he or she can reduce the chance of being killed in a drunk-driving accident by no longer drinking before driving or by allowing someone who has not been drinking to drive him or her home after he or she has been drinking. While these loss prevention measures reduce the likelihood of loss, they do not totally eliminate the risk associated with drunk driving. The client still faces the inescapable risk that he or she may be killed by another motorist who has been drinking.

While many loss prevention activities involve things that should not be done, loss prevention activities can also be positive in nature. For example, the construction of a fence around the swimming pool in the client's backyard is an action designed to make it more difficult for individuals to gain access to the pool and, therefore, reduces the likelihood of a liability loss due to someone's use of the swimming pool without the client's knowledge.

While the goal of loss prevention activities is to eliminate the occurrence of the event, not all loss exposures can be totally prevented. Therefore, some effort should also be made to minimize the magnitude of the losses that do occur.

Loss Reduction. Loss reduction is a technique directed at reducing the severity of losses that do occur. It can be used before, during, or after a loss has occurred and is designed to minimize the magnitude of the loss and its financial impact on a family or individual.

Two examples of loss reduction actions directed at the possibility of fire are maintaining fire extinguishers in the home to extinguish flames before they spread and cause extensive damage to the property and installing smoke detectors to alert inhabitants that there is a fire so that they may extinguish the fire or call the fire department. Note, however, that these tools serve no loss-reduction purpose unless they are properly serviced and all household members are instructed in their use. Also, although it is discussed here as a loss-reduction action, installing smoke detectors also serves as a loss-prevention action because individuals should be instructed to vacate the property when the alarm sounds, thereby reducing the likelihood of death or injury due to fire.

Retention. Many individuals purchase insurance for pure risks and fail to consider other loss-financing techniques. Yet it is obvious that everyone retains some risks, either consciously or unconsciously. In many cases, voluntary risk retention can be a useful tool for handling pure risks. However, involuntary or unintentional risk retention due to failure to identify exposures can be a serious problem.

Risk retention is the process of financing or paying one's own losses. In cases where retention is consciously practiced, an individual may set aside funds earmarked for a particular risk. When the loss occurs, these funds are available to pay for the amount lost. However, this formal method of employing retention is rarely practiced—most retention is practiced informally by covering losses with funds in a savings account, by borrowing, or by paying for the loss on an out-of-pocket basis.

Retention is a cost-effective approach for handling pure risk when the maximum possible loss is too small to cause financial hardship—few people would insure the loss that would result from theft of a single inexpensive item of personal property. Such risk is appropriately retained through the use of deductibles in property insurance policies. In contrast, retaining risk where the probability of loss is small may not necessarily be a cost-effective choice. Retaining risks where the probability of loss is small but the potential amount of loss is severe is a dangerous practice for individuals since the application of probability is not appropriate for the single exposure unit of the individual. As mentioned earlier, while a young parent with dependent children might decide not to purchase life insurance because of the small probability of death at a young age, retention of the risk for this reason could have very serious consequences.

Retention is frequently practiced even when insurance is purchased for a particular risk. As mentioned above, a deductible may apply to losses covered by the insurance policy purchased, in which case the insured is retaining the first dollar amount of the loss. Similarly, the exposure to loss by causes excluded under an insurance contract is retained by the policyowner. These loss exposures may have to be retained by the policyowner simply because there is no alternative. Retention is also practiced when insurance policies exclude the loss to certain types of property or property at certain locations. Other provisions or exclusions in insurance policies may also preclude coverage for particular types of loss. Explaining the need for this sort of retention to purchasers of insurance is an important service provided by the financial advisor.

Insurance. Insurance is a risk-financing technique that involves the transfer of the financial burden of risk from one party called the insured to another party called the insurer for a price (premium). In addition, insurance involves pooling together a large number of similar risks by the insurer in an effort to make losses more predictable and thus, reduce risk. A technique for handling pure risk must have both of these features—risk transfer and pooling of similar risks—in order to be insurance.

The first part of the definition of insurance—risk transfer—describes how insureds view insurance whereas the second part—pooling of similar risks—is how insurers see it. From the viewpoint of an individual insured, insurance is a means for eliminating a pure risk they face by transferring it to an insurance company. The insurance company, in turn, accepts similar risks from a large number of insureds and by pooling them together, is able to reduce the risk it faces.

law of large numbers

To understand this last statement, it is necessary to review the insurance process. As insurers accept insureds, they pool those with similar loss exposures, and the combination of many similar exposure units permits the operation of the *law of large numbers*. From a statistical standpoint, as the number of exposure units increases, the deviation of actual from the expected experience diminishes. As the potential margin of error decreases, so also does the risk of loss faced by the insurer due to inaccurate predictions of the chance (frequency) and amount (severity) of loss. The application of the law of large numbers allows for greater predictability of probable losses and results in a reduction of risk for the insurer. This increased knowledge of probable loss frequency and severity also means that the insurer can determine a more suitable charge (premium) for accepting the transfer of risk from the insured.

The law of large numbers actually has a dual application in insurance. At the time an insurer determines the premium rate for insurance it will sell in the future, it does not know the actual frequency and severity of loss for those it will insure. As a result, the insurer must use data for similar loss exposures it insured in the past in order to estimate the frequency and severity of loss it expects to actually experience in the future when the premium rate is charged. Those estimates of frequency and severity from past data are used as a measure of expected future loss in determining the premium rate. If the insurer assumes that conditions affecting loss in the future will be the same as conditions affecting loss in the past, the insurer can, for example, first use the expected frequency of loss computed from past data to estimate the true underlying probability of loss and then, use the estimate of the true underlying probability of loss to estimate the actual frequency of loss in the future. Because two estimates are being made, there is a dual application of the law of large numbers:

- The larger the sample of past data used in calculating the expected frequency of loss, the more accurate will be the estimate of the true underlying probability of loss.
- The larger the number of exposure units insured in the future, the more accurate the estimate of the true underlying probability of loss will be of the actual frequency of loss in the future.

Because the law of large numbers is a statistical law, there are several assumptions that must be met in order for the pooling of a large number of similar exposure units to reduce the insurer's risk to a desired level. Stated in insurance-related terms these assumptions include

1. the ability to accurately determine when an insured loss has occurred and to accurately measure the amount of that loss
2. an equal probability of loss for each exposure unit that is pooled by the insurer (called homogeneous exposure units)
3. the existence of a sufficiently large number of exposure units to enable risk to be reduced to the desired level
4. a loss to one exposure unit does not affect the occurrence or nonoccurrence of a loss to another exposure unit (called independence)
5. to permit the dual application of the law of large numbers in insurance, conditions affecting loss in the future are the same as conditions affecting loss in the past

In some types of risk situations, violation of one or more of these assumptions may essentially eliminate the risk reducing effect of the law of large numbers and make the risk uninsurable, at least by privately-owned insurers. For example, violation of the assumption of independence by the risk of loss due to unemployment requires that unemployment insurance be provided by the government rather than by private insurers. However, in most insurable pure risk situations, violation of one or more of the assumptions merely reduces the effectiveness of the law of large numbers in reducing risk. For example, although life insurance violates assumptions 2 (not all individuals in a given rate class have the same probability of dying) and 5 (life expectancy is increasing—this actually works to the advantage of insurers in the case of life insurance), the line's strength in meeting the other three assumptions results in a high degree of risk reduction through the law of large numbers. In contrast, with violations of assumptions 1 (fraudulent claims), 3 (relatively few loss exposures in each rate class) and 5 (increasing frequency and severity of lawsuits), automobile liability insurance has considerably less accuracy of loss prediction than life insurance.

Regardless of how effectively the law of large numbers works in reducing risk for an insurer, all insurers continue to face some degree of risk that the actual frequency and/or severity of loss for insured exposures will exceed the expected frequency and/or severity computed from past experience and included in the premium rates. If this happens, an insurer may not collect enough premium to cover actual losses and expenses, and as a result, may suffer an underwriting loss. To handle the risk that continues to exist after the operation of the law of large numbers, insurers rely on three other techniques:

portfolio effect
- *portfolio effect*—reducing risk by writing different lines of insurance whose financial results vary inversely over time (the same risk reduction technique used by individuals who diversify their investment portfolios to reduce risk)

reinsurance
- *reinsurance*—an insurance company transferring part of its risk to other insurance companies (insurance for insurance companies)

financial capacity
- *financial capacity*—insurance companies hold at least minimum amounts of required surplus (net worth) to, among other things, absorb underwriting losses that are not covered by investment gains

Selecting Techniques for Handling a Client's Pure Risks

As shown in table 2-5, a commonly used approach for identifying the most appropriate risk treatment device(s) for handling the pure risk(s) faced by a client is based on two key risk characteristics—the potential frequency (probability) of loss and the potential severity (amount) of loss. The severity of loss for each pure risk situation faced by the client—maximum possible loss—was measured and evaluated in terms of seriousness in step 3 of the financial planning process. Thus, application of the financial planning process provides information for identifying high severity and low severity risk situations. As mentioned earlier, what is high or low severity must be interpreted in terms of the client's financial ability to absorb a risk situation's maximum possible loss.

TABLE 2-5
Risk Characteristics As Determinants of the Appropriate Risk Treatment Device(s)

	High Frequency	Low Frequency

High Severity	<ul><li>Voluntary retention is not realistic</li><li>Insurance/transfer is too costly</li><li>Loss control to reduce frequency through loss prevention will be productive only if either
	  – frequency is reduced sufficiently to make insurance/transfer economical, or
	  – severity is also reduced to a manageable level through loss reduction</li><li>Avoidance should be used if it is not possible either to reduce severity to a manageable level (through loss reduction), or to make insurance/transfer economical</li><li>Involuntary retention may be unavoidable if it is not possible to avoid, reduce or transfer the risk</li></ul>
		<ul><li>Voluntary retention is not realistic</li><li>Insurance/transfer and possibly also loss control through loss reduction
		  – Insurance/transfer will shift catastrophic loss at relatively low cost
		  – Loss control through loss reduction may reduce severity and thus, further reduce the cost of risk transfer</li><li>Loss control through loss reduction to reduce severity to a manageable level</li><li>Avoidance should be used if it is not possible either to reduce severity to a manageable level, or to transfer the risk</li><li>Involuntary retention may be unavoidable if it is not possible to avoid, reduce, or transfer the risk</li></ul>

Low Severity	<ul><li>Retention and loss control through loss prevention
	  – Retention is appropriate since high frequency implies that transfer will be costly
	  – Loss control through loss prevention is appropriate since a reduction of frequency will reduce the aggregate amount of losses to be borne under retention</li></ul>
		<ul><li>Retention is most appropriate since losses seldom occur and when they do, they are small</li></ul>

For reasons discussed earlier, no attempt is made to measure frequencies (probabilities) of loss in analyzing each of the pure risk situations faced by clients who are individuals or families. Thus, in using the risk characteristics approach for selecting techniques for dealing with the pure risks faced by a particular client, the advisor must categorize each of the client's pure risk situations as being high frequency or low frequency based on discussion with the client concerning the extent to which the client sees each risk situation as being likely to occur in his or her own situation.

Several key points about the use of insurance in handling the pure risks faced by a client are indicated in table 2-5. First, insurance is used most efficiently in dealing with risk situations involving low frequency, high severity losses. In this case, the consequences of a severe loss are transferred to the insurer for a premium that is economical due to the risk situation's low frequency. Some examples of low frequency, high severity risk situations where insurance is an especially cost-effective risk treatment device include

- the financial loss that young dependent children would experience upon the death of a young working parent
- the financial loss that an individual would experience as a result of a large liability judgment when a friend is accidentally injured at the individual's home
- the financial loss that would be experienced if a young working person were to become severely disabled and unable to work for the rest of his or her life
- the financial loss that would result from medical bills in the case of an extremely serious, long-term illness
- the financial loss that would result from the cost of long-term care services for a chronically ill individual
- the financial loss that would result from the total destruction of a family's home due to a fire

Second, even as loss frequency becomes higher and insurance premium rates increase significantly, insurance may still be the most effective technique for dealing with risk situations where loss severity is high. For example, although premium rates tend to be quite high for young male drivers or adult drivers with several accidents, auto liability insurance would still be the most appropriate technique for handling the risk of legal liability in a situation where the individual has no alternative form of transportation available for getting to work. Similarly, while life insurance rates increase considerably with age, life insurance would still be the most appropriate technique for handling the risk that would be encountered by young dependent children in the event of their 50 year old father's death, unless either the parents had already accumulated an adequate sum of money to meet that financial need or the mother's earnings at work would meet the family's needs following her husband's death. In cases such as these, eliminating the devastating impact of a very high severity loss through the purchase of insurance outweighs the high cost of the insurance coverage.

Third, insurance is not an efficient way for dealing with low severity risk situations, regardless of the frequency involved. Retention is clearly the most appropriate technique for dealing with low frequency, low severity risk situations, because losses seldom occur and when they do they are small. Even when the frequency of a low severity risk situation is high, retention is a more efficient technique than insurance because the high frequency makes insurance costly. For example, the probability of an individual visiting the doctor once a year is probably very close to one. If the doctor charges $75 for a single visit, buying insurance to cover the first visit would cost approximately $75 (1 x $75) plus a loading to cover the insurer's expenses, profit, and contingencies. Retaining the risk would cost only $75 when the individual goes to the doctor the first time. It is for this reason that retention through the use of deductibles is cost-effective in dealing with high frequency, small losses even when insurance is purchased to handle severe losses from the same cause. By removing the high frequency, low severity portion of a potential loss from coverage, a deductible leaves the low frequency, high severity portion of the potential loss to be covered by insurance, precisely the pure risk situation where insurance is most cost-effective.

Finally, in low frequency, high severity pure risk situations where insurance is an appropriate risk handling device, also employing loss reduction techniques may help to make insurance even more economical by reducing loss severity. For example, insurance companies give a discount in the premium for homeowners insurance for proper installation of an alarm system.

A Plan Using the Selected Techniques

Once the appropriate techniques have been identified, the advisor must formulate a plan for using the techniques to treat the pure risks faced by the client. Where insurance is to be used, he or she should be concerned with matching particular insurance policies to the various risks identified and measured earlier in the financial planning process. In addition, the advisor should identify specific opportunities to use risk retention and/or risk reduction to make the use of insurance as economical as possible. Finally, a plan to use insurance as a technique for treating risks cannot be formulated in isolation from insurance or other financial resources the client may already have. For example, it is highly probable that the client already has purchased a homeowners policy, an auto policy and life insurance, and has accumulated some personal savings. The client's employer probably provides employee benefits for health care financing, life insurance, income replacement for periods of disability and retirement, and Social Security will provide income during retirement and may provide income following the client's death or disability. The client's spouse may be employed and earning not only a salary, but also retirement benefits. Failure to consider these existing financial resources will result in a misleading picture of the types and amounts of insurance needed by the client.

Table 2-6 provides a sample of insurance policies for the Beamer family, taking into account opportunities for risk retention and consideration of resources the family already has available. The policy listing is broken down into the categories of essential, desirable, and useful insurance contracts to indicate the priority in the utilization of the client's premium dollars.

TABLE 2-6
Insurance Planning for the Beamer Family

Essential
1. Personal auto policy—$300,000 liability
2. Homeowners form 3—$180,000 dwelling (more than enough to satisfy the 80 percent replacement provision) with $500 deductible and $300,000 liability
3. Personal umbrella liability—$2 million
4. Dwelling form on cabin—$40,000 on cabin with $300,000 optional liability coverage
5. Life insurance policy on Burt—$50,000 for clean-up fund
6. Life insurance on Burt—$1,100,000 to provide lifetime income to surviving spouse

Desirable
1. Dwelling form for personal property (cabin)—$4,000 with theft endorsement
2. Personal auto policy—ACV for physical damage to the one-year-old compact auto; $500 deductible
3. Mortgage redemption policy—$137,000

Useful
1. Personal auto policy—ACV for physical damage to the 3-year-old station wagon; $500 deductible
2. Life insurance on Burt—$78,000 for education fund

Implement the Plan

Once the plan has been presented to and approved by the client, it must be implemented. The financial advisor's responsibility at this point is to motivate and assist the client in obtaining the insurance coverages necessary for plan implementation. If the financial advisor is a licensed insurance agent, he or she can help the client purchase the needed insurance policies. Otherwise, the advisor will need to work with a licensed agent in securing the necessary coverages. In either case, the advisor should ensure that the insurance companies recommended are financially stable and provide quality service, and that the premium costs for the coverages proposed are competitive.

Monitor the Plan

The advisor should meet with the client at least once each year to determine whether the plan is still satisfactory in light of the client's current objectives and circumstances. With changes in the client's personal or financial situation, the client may now be faced with some new pure risk situations and no longer faced with others. Also, the relative importance of certain pure risks may have shifted over time. Changes in the economic, tax, or financial environment may have affected the types and/or amounts of insurance protection needed. As a result of these changes, the advisor and client may need to revise the existing insurance plan by following the same six-step financial planning process used to develop the original plan.

A SURVEY OF PERSONAL INSURANCE COVERAGES

As mentioned earlier, insurance is often an appropriate technique for handling all or a portion of the losses associated with pure risks. The remainder of the chapter provides a brief summary of the various insurance coverages available for dealing with the pure risks typically faced by individuals and families.

Meeting Personal Risks

Personal risks are those pure risks that involve the loss of income earning ability due to premature death, disability, unemployment, and retirement. Personal risks also include the possibility of incurring extra expenses as a result of medical care for accidental injuries or sickness and long-term care for chronic illness. Since the occurrence of losses arising from unemployment lacks independence and thus, is potentially catastrophic in nature, private insurers are unable to insure the loss of income due to unemployment. Instead, only social insurance provided by the government can handle this pure risk situation. However, coverages for loss of income earning ability due to premature death, disability and retirement as well as for extra expenses incurred due to medical care are available from both private and social insurance programs. At present, long-term care coverage is available only from private insurers. The discussion that follows concentrates on products for handling personal risks that are available from private insurers.

Life Insurance

While many types of life insurance policies have cash surrender values that can be used alone or with other sources of savings and investment for meeting certain of the client's accumulation objectives, the feature that distinguishes life insurance from all other financial products is its unique ability to create an immediate large sum of money in the event of a client's premature death. Unlike decisions regarding the timing or extent of retirement over which a client may have some control or those related to disability which is not necessarily total or permanent, death is total, permanent, and nearly always unpredictable. As shown earlier, even when currently available resources (such as those from the client's existing savings, existing life insurance policies, and Social Security) are taken into account in step 3 of the financial planning process, there is often a very large amount of additional resources still needed to meet the various lump-sum cash and income needs of the surviving dependent members of a client's family in the event of his or her premature death. If a client were to die shortly after implementing his or her financial plan, life insurance is the only product in the plan that could immediately generate the large amount of additional resources required to meet the needs of the surviving dependent family members. It is for this reason that protection of a client's dependents in the event of his or her death is the most important personal use of life insurance and why it should be the key consideration in selecting the most cost-effective life insurance products for dealing with the risk of premature death.

Virtually all life insurance products that are widely marketed today are variations of the following three types of life insurance:

term life insurance
whole life insurance
universal life insurance

- *term life insurance*
- *whole life insurance*
- *universal life insurance*

Term Life Insurance. Term life policies provide insurance coverage for a limited period of time (the policy period), and thus, are generally well suited to situations where there is a temporary need for protection. The policy period in term life insurance policies is expressed as a number of years (such as 1, 5, or 20), or until a certain age of the insured (such as to age 60 or age 65). If the insured dies during the policy period, the specified amount (normally the face amount of the policy) will be paid to the designated recipient (beneficiary). Thus, with a $500,000 5-year term insurance policy, the beneficiary is paid $500,000 if the insured dies during the 5-year policy period. However, if the insured survives until the end of the policy period, no benefit is paid by the insurance company. A term policy not containing a renewability provision would expire at the end of the policy period and

renewability provision

satisfactory proof of insurability would be required to purchase a new policy if continued protection is needed. To prevent the loss of insurance due to bad health or failure to meet other underwriting requirements, clients should be encouraged to include a *renewability provision* in term insurance policies, especially those with policy periods of 10 years or less. If this provision is included, the policy can be renewed while protection is still needed without having to provide evidence of insurability to the insurer at the end of each policy period. While most insurers do not permit renewals to carry coverage beyond a certain age (generally 65 or 70), some companies now offer term insurance policies that are renewable to age 100.

The death benefit, or face amount, of a term life policy normally remains constant throughout the policy period. However, term life is also written on a decreasing death-benefit basis or, with some companies, on an increasing basis. A decreasing term policy may be appropriate for meeting all or at least a major portion of a client's needs that decline over time, such as the principal sum necessary to provide income to a dependent child over a shorter and shorter dependency period or the amount needed to liquidate a mortgage following the client's death. Increasing term life insurance may be used to "refund" the premiums paid on a whole life policy at the time of the insured's death or to have a policy's death benefit keep abreast of some index, such as the cost of living.

Because term life insurance provides protection for only a limited period of time, initial premium rates per $1,000 of coverage are lower for term policies than for whole life products issued at the same age. Moreover, initial premium rates per $1,000 for term policies issued at the same age are higher, the longer the policy period. For this reason, one-year term insurance permits a client to initially purchase the greatest amount of life insurance for a given outlay. Because the amount of insurance protection needed is generally greatest for a family with young dependent children but the funds available to pay premiums are often quite limited, one-year or perhaps 5-year term insurance with a renewability provision may provide a way for a client to afford a sufficient amount of life insurance to adequately protect a surviving spouse and dependent children and thus, meet the family's protection objective in the event of premature death. The client should be made aware that if the term coverage is to be renewed, the premium rate will increase to reflect the higher mortality rates in each successive policy period. Although these premium increases may be nominal at the younger ages, they increase rapidly at older ages.

In addition to the uses of term life insurance already mentioned, it should be recognized that term insurance can be the basis for one's future permanent insurance program. For example, when a client such as a young doctor or a new small business owner needs a large amount of life insurance but can afford only relatively small premiums at the present time, purchasing term insurance may be the only way to provide adequate protection for his or her

conversion provision

dependents. However, if permanent insurance will be needed in the future, consideration should be given to the inclusion of a *conversion provision* in the term policy at the time it is issued. This feature permits an insured to exchange the term policy for a whole life policy or another cash-value insurance contract without evidence of insurability.

Whole Life Insurance. All whole life policies promise to pay the face amount to the beneficiary upon the death of the insured, regardless of when death occurs. In order to price a whole life policy it is necessary to assume that all insureds die by a given age, normally age 100 (age 120 if the policy is based on the 2001 CSO Mortality Table). The few insureds who are still alive at age 100 are assumed to have died and are entitled to the face amount of their policy. Thus, unlike term insurance policies with their rather limited policy periods, whole life policies have long policy periods which end at age 100 (figure 2-1). Moreover, unlike term insurance policies where payment of a death benefit is an uncertainty because all insureds do not die during the policy period, payment of a death benefit is a certainty for each whole life policy (assuming premiums are paid and other policy provisions are complied with) because all insureds die (or are assumed to have died) during the policy period. Due to their longer policy period and the certainty of a death benefit payment, initial premiums for whole life policies are higher than for term insurance policies issued at the same age for the same face amount. However, with their life-long policy periods and lower premiums in the later years of life than term policies issued at the same age for the same face amount, whole life policies are often well suited for situations where there is a permanent need for protection, such as providing funds for estate liquidity, meeting a client's obligation under a business buy-sell agreement, or providing a client's spouse with a lifetime income following the client's death.

Due to the certainty of a death benefit payment, premium rates for whole life policies must be set high enough so that (taking into account interest) they can not only cover a policy's share of the death claims and expenses, but also build a fund called the reserve that will grow over the policy period. The reserve must equal the face amount of the whole life policy at age 100 (figure 2-1) so that the insureds who either die or survive during the last year of the policy period can each be paid the face amount of their policy. When the amount of the reserve in a given policy year is subtracted from the policy's face amount, the difference is the part of the policy's death benefit that is funded by loss sharing among policyowners in that year. Since a whole life policy's reserve increases over the policy period, the part of the death benefit paid by loss sharing declines (figure 2-1). As a result, whole life policies are often referred to as being composed of an increasing savings element (the reserve) and a decreasing protection element paid for by loss sharing among policyowners.

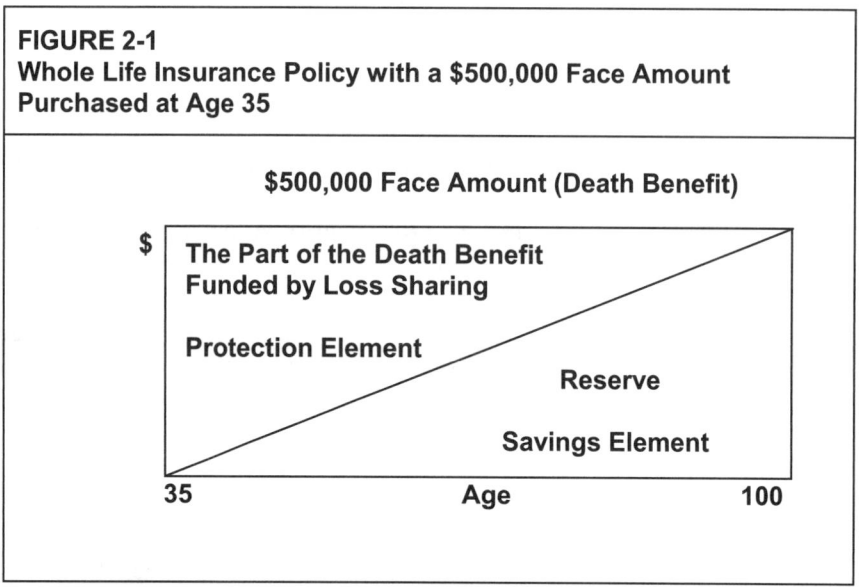

Policyowners can access part of the reserve called the cash value in several ways:

loan provision
- Under the policy's *loan provision,* part of the cash value can be borrowed either to provide the policyowner with cash or to be used to automatically pay premiums. In either case, the amount borrowed is charged interest at either the fixed or variable rate stated in the policy. If any part of the loan plus interest is outstanding at the time of the insured's death or at the time the policy is surrendered, the amount of the outstanding loan plus interest will be deducted from the policy's face amount or cash value, respectively.

nonforfeiture options
- Under the policy's *nonforfeiture options,* when a whole life policy is terminated, the policyowner has a choice of surrendering the policy for its cash value or exchanging the policy's cash value for either a reduced amount of paid-up insurance of the same type as the original policy or paid-up term insurance for the full face amount of the original policy.

While all whole life policies promise to pay the face amount to the beneficiary when the insured dies, these policies can differ from one another in the following ways:

- the length of the period over which premiums must be paid (the premium-paying period)
- whether they are participating or nonparticipating policies

- how and where the funds in the policy reserve (and thus, the cash value) are invested

Ordinary life policies are whole life policies where premiums are paid until the insured dies. In this case, the last annual premium might be paid at age 99. In contrast, limited-payment whole life policies require premiums to be paid only for a specified number of years or until the insured reaches a specified age at which time the policy is fully paid up. The policyowner is guaranteed that no additional premiums will be due once the policy is paid up. The shorter the premium-paying period for a whole life policy, the higher the premium rate. Thus, ordinary life policies have lower premiums than limited-payment whole life policies issued at the same age for the same face amount. However, due to their higher premiums, limited-payment whole life policies have a more rapid buildup of cash values than an ordinary life policy.

participating (par) policies

Participating (par) policies provide for, but do not guarantee, the payment of dividends to the policyowner. The dividends reflect the insurance company's past experience with respect to mortality, interest, and expenses. Favorable experience—lower mortality, lower expenses, and higher interest than expected—tends to increase the dividend scale, whereas unfavorable experience tends to have the opposite effect.

nonparticipating (nonpar) policies

current assumption whole life

In contrast to par policies, *nonparticipating (nonpar) policies* do not pay policyowner dividends. Today nearly all nonpar whole life policies, often called *current assumption whole life* policies, share the company's actual or anticipated experience by either changing the policy's premium or cash value. Favorable experience tends to lead to lower premiums or higher cash values, whereas unfavorable experience tends to have the opposite effects.

variable life insurance

Traditionally, the reserves (and thus, cash values) of whole life policies have been invested in the general assets of the insurance company where their allocation among various types of assets has been managed by the insurer. As a result, these traditional whole life policies contain a guaranteed interest rate which is the lowest interest rate with which policy funds can be credited. In contrast, some whole life policies, called *variable life insurance*, now permit the policyowner to allocate the funds generated by the policy among a variety of separate accounts each reflecting a different investment objective (similar to a family of mutual funds). Variable life policies shift the investment risk to the policyowner and provide no minimum guaranteed rate of return or guaranteed cash value. The rate of return credited to policy funds and thus, the amount of the cash value depend upon the investment success of the policyowner.

The performance of the separate account portfolio selected by the policyowner also affects the death benefit of a variable life insurance policy. In contrast to a traditional whole life policy whose death benefit is a stated face amount equal to the amount of insurance purchased, the face amount of a variable life policy can vary up and down above a minimum death benefit equal to the amount of insurance purchased depending upon investment performance.

The shorter the premium-paying period for whole life insurance, the smaller the death benefit (face amount) that can be purchased for a given amount of premium. Therefore, in planning for the use of whole life insurance it is necessary to clearly identify the client's objectives. Since whole life is most appropriate for permanent needs, the trade-off between a high amount of protection and a rapidly accumulating cash value should be considered carefully.

Universal Life Insurance. First sold in its current form in 1979, a universal life insurance (UL) policy is a flexible-premium, adjustable death benefit life insurance contract that enables the policyowner to see how premiums are allocated to the protection and cash value elements of the policy.

Universal life policies require at least a minimum level of premium payments during the first year of coverage. After the first year, the premium on this type of policy is truly flexible. Policyowners may pay whatever amounts at whatever times they wish, or even skip premium payments, as long as the cash value is large enough to cover required policy charges.

In addition to flexibility with regard to premium payments, universal life policyowners may also request a change in the face amount of the policy. Decreases in the policy death benefit can be made by policyowner request at any time. However, evidence of insurability may be required if an increase in the death benefit is requested.

Each year the policyowner of a universal life policy receives a report illustrating the flow of funds during the year. This report shows the amount in the cash value account at the beginning of the period which is increased by any premiums paid, reduced by mortality charges and expenses (if any), and increased by the interest earnings credited to the account. This type of detailed information is not generated for traditional whole life policyowners.

Universal life policies offer two death-benefit designs, usually labeled as options A and B. Option A provides a constant or level death benefit, like that of traditional whole life policies. However, at older ages the death benefit begins to increase because of the technical need to satisfy the Internal Revenue Code definition of life insurance. Option B provides a death benefit that at any time is equal to the sum of the original face amount of the policy and the accumulating cash value. The death benefit continues to increase as long as the cash value increases.

In addition to providing access to the policy's cash value through loans or full surrender of the contract, universal life insurance introduced a withdrawal (or partial surrender) feature which permits the policyowner to make partial withdrawals from the policy's cash value without incurring any indebtedness. Because the policy's cash value is reduced by the amount of the withdrawal, future interest earnings are also reduced. The policy death benefit is also reduced by the amount of the withdrawal so as not to invite *adverse selection* against the insurance company.

adverse selection

The cash value of a universal life policy is invested in the general assets of the insurance company where the investment allocation is managed by the insurer. To provide the policyowner with the ability to direct the investment of the cash value, variable universal life (VUL) insurance was developed by modifying the universal life policy. A *variable universal life* policy is identical to a universal life policy except that the cash value is invested by the policyowner in a variety of separate accounts rather than in the general assets of the insurance company. As with variable life insurance, variable universal life policies shift the investment risk to the policyowner and provide no minimum guaranteed rate of return. The rate of return credited to the policy's cash value depends upon the performance of the separate account(s) in which the policyowner invested the funds.

variable universal life

Some argue that the universal life or variable universal life policy is the only policy a person will need over an entire lifetime. They base the argument on the flexibility in premium payments and death benefits, which allows adjustments to be made to fit the client's needs at any time in the life cycle. Given their flexibility in meeting a client's changing needs, the features and potential uses of universal life and variable universal life policies should be understood by all financial advisors.

Annuities

Two important general challenges facing many clients in planning to deal with the pure risk associated with retirement are accumulating sufficient financial resources to meet their retirement objectives and distributing those resources in a manner consistent with those objectives. Annuities can be helpful in meeting both challenges.

Financial resources to meet retirement objectives can come from a number of sources, including Social Security retirement benefits, employer-sponsored retirement plans, private saving and investment for retirement, cash value life insurance owned by the client, and deferred annuities purchased by the client. For clients who wish to liquidate the financial resources accumulated for retirement without the risk of outliving their income, life annuities—both deferred and immediate—should be considered. Life annuities (and similar life income settlement options available for distributing the cash value of a life insurance policy for retirement) are the only financial products that can guarantee a client a lifetime income.

life annuities

The vast majority of the annuities sold by life insurance companies today are *life annuities* that provide for the systematic liquidation of a principal sum over the lifetime of the annuitant (the recipient of the payments). Life

immediate annuity

deferred annuities

annuities can be purchased either by a single premium or on an installment basis. An *immediate annuity* must be purchased with a single premium because it begins to pay periodic benefits at the end of the first payment period (such as one month) following the purchase date. The single premium used to purchase an immediate annuity can be financial resources accumulated by the client for retirement from any source other than the annuity itself. In contrast, *deferred annuities* that begin to pay periodic benefits at some specified future time can be purchased with either a single premium or on an installment premium basis. Prior to the date when the periodic payments begin (the accumulation period), the premiums paid for a deferred annuity are invested either in the general assets of the insurance company or in separate accounts where the allocation of funds for investment purposes is managed by the contract owner. Thus, while both immediate and deferred life annuities provide for the liquidation of financial resources over the lifetime of the annuitant, a deferred life annuity also provides a tool for accumulating financial resources before retirement.

Annuities can be purchased to provide periodic payments of a guaranteed fixed amount or a variable amount. When the variable annuity is elected, the periodic payment depends on the performance of the underlying investment portfolio, typically common stocks. As deferred annuities, variable annuities may be variable (invested in separate accounts) in both the accumulation and the payout periods or may be variable in the accumulation period and provide a guaranteed fixed amount during the payout period.

At a minimum, life annuities guarantee a lifetime income for the annuitant. Under a pure life annuity, payments cease upon the death of the annuitant, with no further obligations placed on the insurance company. Most annuity purchasers dislike this contingency basis and prefer arrangements that will also guarantee payments to the annuitant's survivors on some basis in the event the annuitant dies shortly after payments begin. This can be accomplished through the election of guaranteed payments for a certain period of time or through the selection of a cash or installment refund arrangement. However, regardless of any guarantees of payments to the annuitant's survivors, the annuitant of a life annuity would continue to receive payments for life if he or she lived beyond the period required to payout the minimum guaranteed payments. An alternative to a single life annuity with payments based on the life of one annuitant, the joint-and-survivor annuity bases payments on the lives of two or more annuitants, such as a husband and wife.

Annuities can be purchased on either a qualified or a nonqualified basis. In terms of annuity considerations received by life insurers in 2006, qualified and nonqualified annuities are both major components of the life annuity market, representing 56 percent and 44 percent of that market, respectively.[2] Because qualified annuities are generally purchased by employers for use in employee benefit plans, knowledge of annuities is important in understanding the funding of some forms of pension plans and the distribution options commonly available to participants in many qualified retirement plans. However, the financial advisor should also recognize that retirement purposes can be served through the purchase of individual life insurance policies with cash values. At some time in the future, the accumulated savings in a whole life or universal life policy can either be distributed using the life income settlement options (similar to life annuities) contained in the policy or be exchanged, typically at net cost, for an annuity to provide income to a client for the purpose of supplementing Social Security and other sources of retirement income.

Individual Health Insurance

As mentioned earlier, three pure risks associated with the loss of health include

- extra expenses incurred for medical care due to accident or sickness
- loss of income earning ability due to accident or sickness
- extra expenses incurred for long-term care due to the inability to perform safely some of the activities of daily living (ADLs)

medical expense insurance
disability income insurance
long-term care insurance

The types of health insurance available to help deal with these personal risks are *medical expense insurance*, *disability income insurance*, and *long-term care insurance*, respectively. Although each of these types of health insurance is available on either an individual basis (policies sold to individuals) or a group basis (policies sold most commonly to employers), the coverage in this chapter focuses on individual medical expense, disability income, and long-term care insurance. Group health insurance coverages are discussed in the next chapter on employee benefits.

Medical Expense Insurance. Because the bulk of medical expense insurance in the U.S. is provided on a group basis by employers, the types and providers of medical expense insurance are discussed in chapter 3. The popularity of the group, as opposed to the individual, approach to providing medical expense insurance coverage stems from both the opportunity for cost savings due to lower costs associated with the group mechanism as well as the favorable tax treatment of employer contributions made for payment of premiums. Unlike individual medical expense insurance premiums which are paid with after-tax dollars, employer contributions for medical expense insurance premiums are deductible by the employer and are not taxed to the employee. This last factor alone enables employer-provided medical expense coverage to be either less costly than comparable individual coverage or more comprehensive than individual coverage costing the same amount.

health savings account (HSA)

high-deductible health plan (HDHP)

An alternative to coverage under a traditional medical expense policy is the establishment of a *health savings account (HSA)*.[3] An HSA is a tax favored savings account that is used to pay for medical expenses not reimbursed by insurance. To establish an HSA, the individual must be covered by a *high-deductible health plan (HDHP)*. For purposes of HSA participation, an HDHP is defined as having the following deductibles and annual out-of-pocket limits for covered services in 2008 (as indexed):

- For self-only coverage, the deductible must be at least $1,100, and annual out-of-pocket expenses cannot exceed $5,600.
- For family coverage, the deductible must be at least $2,200, and annual out-of-pocket expenses cannot exceed $11,200.

Out-of-pocket expenses include the deductible amount, copayments, and any required percentage participation. They do not include the premium for coverage or any payments for services not covered by the HDHP.

The maximum annual contribution that an individual can make to an HSA in 2008 is $2,900 (as indexed) for self-only coverage and $5,800 (as indexed) for family coverage. Individuals aged 55 or older are also permitted an additional annual catch-up contribution of up to $900 in 2008 and up to $1,000 in 2009. Contributions are deductible for federal income tax purposes as above-the-line deductions (which are explained in chapter 5) even if the individual does not itemize deductions. Unused amounts in an HSA accumulate on a tax-free basis and carry over to subsequent years without limit. The size of an HSA balance carried over from prior years has no effect on a current year's contribution.

As an alternative to coverage under a group medical expense plan, many persons with HDHPs have coverage under an employer-provided plan, and employers may make contributions to the HSAs of employees. Employer-provided plans are briefly discussed in chapter 3.

Disability Income Insurance. One of the more frequently overlooked personal risk exposures is the loss of wages or earnings during periods of disability. Most people seem to be aware of the medical care costs associated with accident or illness and of the total discontinuation of earnings because of premature death, but tend to overlook the seriousness of the possible loss of income because of disability. At most ages the likelihood of a serious, long-term disability is considerably greater than the probability of death. Moreover, the severity of loss in terms of income needs is often greater in the case of serious, long-term disability than in the case of premature death, because the disabled income earner must be provided for in addition to the other dependent family members.

The financial advisor should begin the planning process for meeting the client's need for income replacement due to serious disability by examining the client's employee benefits package. In some disability income-replacement situations, the combination of Social Security disability benefits and employer-provided salary continuation or disability income benefits may provide most or all of the replacement income needed. However, individual disability income insurance is often needed in the following situations:

- self-employed individuals and high-income professionals in fields such as medicine or law who have no (or choose to have no) employer-provided disability income protection
- employees of companies, especially small private firms, that do not offer long-term disability income insurance as an employee benefit
- executives and middle-income earners who wish to supplement employer-provided disability income benefits in order to protect more of their earnings than are protected by their employer's plan
- businesses and their owners who require a source of funds to finance a buy-sell agreement or to provide protection against a loss of income and/or extra expenses incurred in the event of an owner's or key employee's disability

partial disability
residual disability

As discussed earlier, insurance is used most efficiently in handling pure risk situations involving the possibility of low frequency, high severity losses. Thus, while coverage is available to protect against *partial disability* and *residual disability*, disability income insurance is most efficiently used in dealing with the possibility of a client experiencing a long term, total disability. In this case, the consequences of a severe loss are transferred to the insurer for a premium that is economical due to the low frequency. Also, as mentioned earlier, retention is generally the most efficient way for dealing with low severity losses. Through the use of an appropriate *elimination (waiting) period*, retention can be achieved for low severity disability income losses when insurance is being used to handle the low frequency, high severity losses. In helping a client to use insurance efficiently in dealing with the risk of a serious, long term disability, the financial advisor should focus primarily on five key features of individual disability income insurance—the definition of *total disability*, the elimination period, the benefit period, the benefit amount, and the terms of renewability.

elimination (waiting) period

total disability

Definition of Total Disability. Definitions of disability in disability income policies are based on the ability of the insured to perform certain occupational tasks. One definition, typically called the any-occupation definition, states that insureds are considered to be totally disabled when they cannot perform the major duties of any gainful occupation for which they are reasonably suited by education, training, or experience.

A somewhat less restrictive definition is usually referred to as the own-occupation definition. With a pure own-occupation definition, insureds are deemed to be totally disabled when they cannot perform the major duties of their regular occupations. For purposes of this definition, the regular occupation is the one engaged in when the disability begins. Because this definition would allow an insured to work in some other capacity and still be entitled to benefits, many insurers now use a modified own-occupation definition which also provides that benefits either will not be paid or will be reduced if the insured chooses to work in any other occupation. In virtually all definitions of disability, insurers add a provision stipulating that the disabled person must be under the care and attendance of a physician.

Due to adverse claims experience, most companies no longer issue contracts of long benefit duration that have pure own-occupation definitions of disability for the contract duration. Instead, either a modified own-occupation definition or a dual definition of total disability is typically used in long-term disability income policies. With a dual definition, an own-occupation definition applies during the first few years of the benefit period, after which it is replaced by an any-occupation definition. Typically, the insured is given a choice between two options ranging from 2 to 5 years regarding the length of time the own-occupation definition of disability will remain in force.

Elimination Period. The elimination period is the number of days that must elapse between the start of disability and the start of benefit payments. It is sometimes called the waiting period or simply the deductible stated in time rather than dollars. The intent of this provision is to avoid coverage of the short-term illness or injury that temporarily disables an insured and for which retention is a more economical solution than insurance.

Elimination periods are generally available for periods ranging from 30 days to one year. The length of time recommended to a client should depend on the availability of other funds to support a risk retention program. For example, if a client's employer provides a salary continuation plan that will compensate the employee in full for 6 months, there is little need to add an individual disability income insurance policy that will pay benefits at the end of 30 days. However, if a short-term disability would cause financial hardship, a 30-day elimination period might be very appropriate. As with any deductible, the longer the elimination period selected, the lower the premium.

Benefit Period. The benefit period is the length of time during which income benefits will be paid after the elimination period is satisfied. Although a few companies still offer lifetime benefits, benefit periods typically range anywhere from 2 years in duration to until the insured reaches age 65 or 70. Historical data indicate that most disabilities are of short duration, but the likelihood of full productive recovery diminishes as the length of the disability increases. This means that long-term disabilities will be more devastating and that insurance is usually the best tool for dealing with this contingency. Therefore, the recommended benefit period should be of long duration. Of course, the longer the benefit period, the higher the premium, but a long elimination period might offset part of this higher cost.

Benefit Amount. Individual disability income policies specify the amount of monthly benefits payable for total disabilities continuing after the elimination period has been satisfied. At the time of policy issuance, the stated benefit amount should be in line with the client's income and provide fairly complete protection. However, over time, the stated amount is likely to become inadequate as the client's income increases because of both inflation and job promotions. Disability income policies are available with provisions to counteract such erosion in benefit levels. Prior to disability, disability income benefits can be kept in step with increased income in three ways—by purchasing new policies periodically (requires evidence of insurability), by purchasing a rider that guarantees the right to purchase additional coverage at specified future intervals up to some specified maximum age (such as 45, 50 or 55), or by purchasing a rider that automatically increases the benefit amount periodically. A cost-of-living (COLA) rider can be used to increase benefits once disability has commenced.

Insurance companies limit the amount of disability income coverage they will write so that the total benefit from all sources does not exceed a given percentage of the insured's earned income—about 65 percent for individuals in higher income brackets. One reason for this limitation is the fact that individually purchased disability income benefits are not taxable income to the recipient. Another reason is the potential disincentive for a disabled person to return to work if benefit payments are too high relative to predisability income.

Another limiting factor in purchasing disability income insurance is the maximum dollar benefit that companies are willing to write. This creates problems for higher income clients since they are unable to purchase an adequate level of benefit amount. The maximum benefit available tends to be in the $15,000 to $20,000 per month range for the more favorable risk classifications. The higher the benefit amount, the higher the premium.

Terms of Renewability. State laws specify that individually purchased disability income policies (and medical expense policies) must indicate the basis upon which the insured can continue the contract, a very important consideration to the insured.

noncancelable
guaranteed renewable

Most disability income policies sold to individuals are issued on either a *noncancelable* or *guaranteed renewable* basis. Under a guaranteed renewable contract, the insurer reserves the right to change premium rates for all insureds of the same class but cannot cancel or refuse to renew the policy.

Under a noncancelable policy, the insurer can neither change premium rates nor cancel the policy. A noncancelable policy costs more than a comparable guaranteed renewable one.

Other Available Coverages. Once the most catastrophic potential loss—a long-term, total disability loss—has been adequately covered, there are a number of supplemental benefits that might also be considered by the client in protecting against loss of income due to disability. Among others, these include

- residual-disability benefit—subject to a minimum percentage reduction in income, such as 20 percent, this benefit provides a reduced monthly benefit that reflects the percentage reduction in the insured's earnings when the insured returns to work at less than the amount of his or her income prior to disability
- partial-disability benefit—provides a stated percentage (usually 50 percent) of the total disability income benefit if the insured returns to work, but is unable either to perform a stated number of the duties of the insured's occupation or to be present at work for more than one-half the time normally spent performing the regular duties of that occupation
- Social Security supplement—because insurance companies usually take into account the level of Social Security disability benefits that might be payable in determining the amount of disability income insurance coverage the insured can purchase, this rider provides a supplemental monthly benefit when the insured meets the definition of total disability in the insurance policy but does not qualify for Social Security disability benefits

Following repeated underwriting losses and resulting market contraction and consolidation from the mid-1980s to 1998, the noncancelable disability income insurance business has experienced rising profits since 1999, resulting from the more restricted contractual features discussed above, higher pricing, tighter underwriting practices and more proactive claims management. With this improved environment, more insurers are entering the market and more products are becoming available for consideration by financial advisors in planning to meet the disability income risks faced by their clients. For example, one of these recently developed disability income products is the disability-to-long-term care conversion policy which is initially a disability income insurance policy that can be converted to long-term care coverage without evidence of insurability at the time of conversion and at lower cost than purchasing a new stand-alone long-term care policy later in life.

Long-Term Care Insurance. Another personal risk faced by individuals and families is the possibility of incurring extra expenses for long-term care due to the inability to perform safely some of the activities of daily living (ADLs). As Americans live longer, both the frequency and the severity of loss associated with this personal risk increase. Longer life spans today and in the future increase the chance that a client will experience a need for some long-term care services to assist with the ADLs. For example, while only one percent of persons between ages 65 and 74 reside in nursing homes, the percentage increases to 6 percent between the ages of 75 and 84 and to approximately 25 percent at age 85 and over. Also, because of the continuing increases in the costs of nursing home care and home health care, increasing life spans result in clients experiencing the costs of long-term care services at higher and higher levels. For example, already high annual nursing home costs of $30,000 to $60,000 or more and monthly part-time home health care costs of $2,500 or more are increasing faster than inflation because of the growing demand for nursing home beds and a shortage of skilled medical personnel. By 2030, the annual cost of nursing home care is expected to approximate $200,000 with comparable increases in home care charges. Also, while most nursing home stays are for less than two years, 25 percent last more than 3 years and 10 percent last more than 5 years.

As mentioned earlier, insurance is an efficient mechanism for handling pure risks involving the possibility of low frequency, high severity losses and retention is efficient for handling low severity losses. Since possible long-term care losses can be very severe, this risk should not be totally retained unless a client is willing to face the possibility of all, or a major portion of, his or her lifetime retirement savings and other assets being eaten up by long-term care expenses. In addition to the possibility of forcing the client and his or her dependents into poverty, this approach may also leave the client unable to meet the financial objective of leaving assets to heirs.

For most clients, the severity of the potential loss associated with long-term care expenses suggests that it be transferred by the purchase of long-term care insurance, especially if purchased at a younger age when the frequency of loss is relatively low. Retention can be used to efficiently handle low severity losses by choosing an appropriate elimination period.

A relatively new form of insurance coverage that was virtually nonexistent prior to the early 1980s, long-term care insurance has evolved to being an important form of insurance product carried by about 6.5 million persons. Currently, most long-term care insurance is sold on an individual, as opposed to a group, basis. Significant variations (and therefore differences in cost) exist among the individual long-term care policies sold by the approximately 100 companies that now offer this type of coverage.

Issue Age. While significant differences exist among insurance companies with respect to the age at which they will issue policies, a healthy client between the ages of 40 and 79 should be able to buy long-term care insurance from most companies. Most companies sell policies to persons as young as 18 and have an upper age in the range of 84 to 89 beyond which coverage is not issued.

Types of Care Covered. There are many types of care for which benefits may be provided under a long-term care policy. By broad categories, these can be categorized as nursing home care, assisted-living care, hospice care, Alzheimer's facilities, home health care, care coordination, and alternative sources of care. A long-term care policy may provide benefits for one, several, or all of these types of care.

Much of the variation among long-term care policies is related to the types of care for which benefits are provided. These benefit variations fall into three broad categories: facility-only policies, home health care only policies, and comprehensive policies. While policies providing benefits only if the insured is in a nursing home still exist, the term facility-only policy is now more commonly used to describe broader policies that provide benefits not only for nursing home care but also for care in other settings such as assisted-living facilities and hospices. A home health care only policy is designed to provide benefits for care outside an institutional setting.

Most long-term care policies written today can be described as comprehensive policies. A comprehensive long-term care insurance policy, sometimes referred to as an integrated policy, combines benefits for facility care and home health care into a single contract. However, variations exist within this type of policy with respect to what is covered as part of the standard policy and what is an optional benefit that the applicant may select. For example, some policies cover almost all care settings as part of their standard benefits; other policies provide facility-only coverage as a standard benefit with home health care covered as an option for an additional premium.

Benefit Amounts. When purchasing long-term care insurance, the applicant selects the level of benefit he or she desires up to the maximum level the insurance company will provide. Benefits are often sold in increments of $10 per day up to frequently found limits of $200 or $250 or, in a few cases, as much as $400 or $500 per day. Most insurance companies will not offer a daily benefit below $40 or $50. Some policies base benefits on a monthly (rather than daily) amount that can vary from $1,000 to $6,000 or more.

The same level of benefits is usually provided for all levels of institutional care. Most comprehensive policies that provide home health care benefits once limited the daily benefit to one-half the amount payable for institutional stays. However, many insurers now allow applicants to select home health care limits that are as high as 75 percent to 100 percent of the benefit for institutional care; a few insurers even offer limits as high as 125 percent or 150 percent. If a policy provides home health care benefits only, the daily amount of that benefit is what the applicant selects.

Policies pay benefits in one of two basic ways—reimbursement or per diem. The majority of newer policies pay benefits on a *reimbursement basis*. These contracts reimburse the insured for actual expenses up to the specified policy limit. Some policies provide benefits on a *per diem basis* once care is actually being received. This means that benefits are paid regardless of the actual cost of care.

reimbursement basis

per diem basis

Elimination Period. The applicant is required to select a period of time that must pass after long-term care commences but before benefit payments begin. The majority of long-term care insurers refer to this period as an elimination period. However, some insurers call it a waiting period or a deductible period. Most insurers allow an applicant to select from three to five optional elimination periods. For example, one insurer allows the choice of 20, 60, 100, or 180 days. Choices may be as low as zero days or as high as 365 days.

In a comprehensive policy, there is normally a single elimination period that can be met by any combination of days during which the insured is in a long-term care facility or receiving home health care services.

Maximum Duration of Benefits. Most insurers require the applicant to select the maximum period for which benefits are paid (often referred to as the benefit period), and they make several options available. For example, one insurer offers durations of 2, 3, and 5 years as well as lifetime benefits. This period begins from the time benefit payments start after satisfaction of the elimination period. The benefit period does not necessarily apply to each separate period for which long-term care services are received. Rather, it is a period that applies to the aggregate time benefits are paid under the policy.

In most cases, a single benefit period applies to long-term care no matter where it is received. A few policies, however, have separate benefit periods for facility care and home health care. There are also a few policies, usually of the per diem type, that specify the maximum benefits as a stated dollar amount such as $100,000.

There are actually two ways that the benefit period is applied in the payment of benefits. Under one approach, benefit payments are made for exactly the benefit period chosen. If the applicant selects a benefit period of 4 years and collects benefits for 4 years, the benefit payments cease. The other approach, most commonly but not exclusively used with reimbursement policies, uses a *pool of money*. Under this concept, there is an amount of money that can be used to make benefit payments as long as the pool of money lasts. The applicant does not select the amount in the pool of money; it is determined by multiplying the daily benefit by the benefit period

pool of money

selected. For example, if the daily benefit for institutional care is $200 and the benefit period is 1,460 days (or 4 years), then the pool of money is $292,000 ($200 x 1,460). Daily benefit payments from the pool of money cannot exceed the daily policy benefits for each type of care (in this case, $200 per day for institutional care).

Inflation Protection. Most states require that a long-term care policy offers some type of automatic inflation protection. The applicant is given the choice to select this option, decline the option, or possibly select an alternative option. The cost of an automatic-increase option is built into the initial premium, and no additional premium is levied at the time of an annual increase. The automatic option found in almost all policies is a 5 percent benefit increase that is compounded annually over the life of the policy. Under such a provision, the amount of a policy's benefits increases by 5 percent each year over the amount of benefits available in the prior year. A common alternative that many insurers make available is based on simple interest, with each annual automatic increase being 5 percent of the original benefit amount. Another alternative offered by some insurers is to allow the policyowner to increase benefits without evidence of insurability on a pay-as-you-go basis at specified intervals, such as every one, 2, or 3 years.

It is important to note that increases in benefits are often inadequate to offset actual inflation in the annual cost of long-term care, which has been in the double digits over the last decade.

Qualification for Favorable Tax Treatment. Long-term care policies that meet the prescribed standards of the Health Insurance Portability and Accountability Act (HIPAA) are treated as accident and health insurance for federal income tax purposes and are referred to as *tax-qualified contracts*. While most companies that write individual long-term care policies now issue only tax-qualified contracts, some companies issue both qualified contracts and *nonqualified contracts*, and a few companies issue only nonqualified contracts.

tax-qualified contracts

nonqualified contracts

Eligibility for Benefits. Almost all tax-qualified contracts use the same two criteria for determining benefit eligibility, with the insured being required to meet only one of the two. The first criterion is that the insured is expected to be unable, without substantial assistance from another person, to perform two of the six ADLs (eating, bathing, dressing, transferring from bed to chair, using the toilet, and maintaining continence) that are acceptable under HIPAA for a period of at least 90 days due to loss of functional capacity. The second criterion is that substantial supervision is required to protect the individual from threats to health and safety because of severe cognitive impairment.

Nonqualified contracts, on the other hand, have more liberal eligibility requirements. Many of these contracts use the same criteria that are in tax-qualified contracts, except there is no time period that applies to the inability to perform the ADLs. A small number of nonqualified contracts require only the inability to perform one ADL and/or use more than the six ADLs allowed by HIPAA. Finally, some nonqualified contracts make benefits available if a third criterion—medical necessity—is satisfied. This generally means that a physician has certified that long-term care is needed, even if neither of the other two criteria is satisfied.

Renewability. Long-term care policies currently being sold are guaranteed renewable, which means that an individual's coverage cannot be canceled except for nonpayment of premiums. While premiums cannot be raised on the basis of a particular applicant's claim, they can (and often are) raised by class.

Nonforfeiture Options. Most companies give an applicant for long-term care insurance the right to elect a nonforfeiture benefit, and some states require that such a benefit be offered. With a nonforfeiture benefit, the policyowner will receive some value for a policy if the policy lapses because the required premium is not paid in the future.

The most common type of nonforfeiture option is a shortened benefit period. With this option, coverage is continued as a paid-up policy, but the length of the benefit period (or the amount of the benefit if stated as a maximum dollar amount) is reduced. Some nonqualified policies offer a return-of-premium option, under which a portion of the premium is returned if a policy lapses after a specified number of years.

Premiums. The vast majority of long-term care policies have premiums that are payable for life and determined by the age of the insured at the time of issue. A few insurers, however, offer other modes of payment. Lifetime coverage can sometimes be purchased with a single premium. Some insurers offer policies that have premium payment periods of 10 or 20 years or to age 65, after which time the premium is paid up. These policies are particularly attractive to applicants who do not want continuing premium payments after retirement.

Most long-term care policies have a provision that waives premiums if the insured has been receiving benefits under the policy for a specified period of time, often 60 or 90 days.

Numerous factors affect the premium that a policyowner will pay for a long-term care policy. Among these factors are the following:

- age: While age plays a significant role in the cost of long-term care insurance, coverage can be obtained at a reasonable cost if it is purchased at a young age.
- types of benefits: Most policies cover care in a long-term care facility. However, many policies also cover home health care and other benefits provided to persons who are still able to reside in their own homes. This broader coverage increases premiums by 60 to 70 percent.
- duration of benefits: The longer the maximum benefit period, the higher the premium. The longer the elimination period, the lower the premium. With many insurers, a policy with an unlimited benefit period and no elimination period will have a premium about double that of a policy with a 2-year benefit period and a 90-day elimination period.
- inflation protection: All other factors being equal, the addition of a 5 percent compound annual increase in benefits can raise premiums by 50 to 100 percent.
- nonforfeiture benefits: The inclusion of a nonforfeiture benefit can increase a premium by anywhere from 20 to 50 percent or more, depending on the type of nonforfeiture benefit and other policy features.
- spousal coverage: Most insurance companies offer a discount of 10 percent to 15 percent if both spouses purchase long-term care policies from the company.
- nonsmoker discount: A few insurers offer a discount, such as 10 percent, if the insured is a nonsmoker.

Even if the provisions of several policies are virtually identical, premiums will vary among companies. For example, the premiums for three similar policies from three different companies are shown in table 2-7. Each policy has a daily benefit of $120 per day, a zero-day elimination period, a lifetime benefit period, and coverage for home health care.

TABLE 2-7
Comparison of Long-Term Care Premiums for Similar Policies

Age	Company A	Company B	Company C
40	$ 391	$ 549	$ 590
50	641	714	832
60	1,104	1,126	1,331
70	2,550	3,157	2,736
75	4,540	5,491	4,763

Meeting Property and Liability Risks

Individuals and families face a number of pure risks involving possible property and liability losses. As mentioned earlier, property risks involve direct and indirect losses arising from the need to replace or repair damaged or missing property. Liability risks involve the possibility of loss as a result of physical or personal injuries to others, or damage to or destruction of others' property.

Low severity property losses can be handled most efficiently through retention. However, given their potentially severe impact on a client's assets, large property losses and liability losses require transfer through the purchase of insurance. While some clients require specialized forms of insurance such as yacht policies, flood insurance, and professional liability insurance, the majority of the property and liability risks faced by clients and their dependents can be handled with the following types of insurance, using deductibles where appropriate to retain small property losses:

- homeowners insurance
- personal automobile insurance
- umbrella liability insurance

Homeowners Insurance

homeowners insurance

Homeowners insurance policies are package policies designed to provide protection for the following types of losses in one contract:

- with some exceptions including automobiles, the direct and indirect property losses typically faced by individuals and families
- with some exceptions including automobiles and business or professional activities, the bodily injury and property damage liability losses and defense costs typically faced by individuals and families
- without regard to whether or not legal liability exists, medical expenses incurred by a person other than a resident of the insured household when injured at an insured location or injured because of the insured's activities away from the insured location

To accomplish this, homeowners policies are divided into two parts—Section I which provides property coverage and Section II which provides liability and medical expense coverage.

The basis for the discussion of homeowners insurance policies in this chapter is the program introduced and made available by the Insurance Services Office (ISO). The ISO format has been adopted by many insurance companies throughout the country. There are, however, insurance companies that use their own policy forms, and regional or state variations that modify the basic forms.

In most states, there are six standard homeowners forms available:

- Homeowners 2—Broad Form
- Homeowners 3—Special Form
- Homeowners 4—Contents Broad Form
- Homeowners 5—Comprehensive Form
- Homeowners 6—Unit-Owners Form
- Homeowners 8—Modified Coverage Form

In making reference to these forms, it is common to call them Form 2, Form 3, and so on, or HO-2, HO-3, HO-4, HO-5, HO-6, and HO-8. The latter terminology is used in this chapter.

As shown in table 2-8, Section II in each of the homeowners forms is identical in providing both liability and medical expense insurance. However, Section I providing property insurance differs among the forms, depending upon the types of property for which they are used and the perils (causes of loss) they are designed to cover.

Four homeowners forms are available for clients who own their dwelling—HO-2, HO-3, HO-5 and HO-8 (used for certain types of older property). As shown in table 2-8, each of these forms provides four property coverages in Section I—Coverage A for the dwelling, Coverage B for other structures separated from the dwelling, Coverage C for personal property (contents), and Coverage D for loss of use (indirect loss). H0-4 for those who live in a rented dwelling or apartment and HO-6 for condominium unit-owners and members of cooperatives provide Coverage C for personal property (contents), and Coverage D for loss of use (indirect loss). In addition, Coverage A of HO-6 provides insurance protection for several items of property including fixtures and alterations made by the unit-owner.

named-perils approach

open-perils approach

The forms also differ as to the causes of loss—that is, the perils—for which coverage is provided. There are two general approaches for insuring property—named perils and open perils. With the *named-perils approach,* the policy lists the specific perils for which coverage is provided. Under the *open-perils approach,* losses caused by any peril are paid by the insurer unless the cause of loss is specifically excluded. Homeowners property insurance coverage is written using both approaches—the basic form provides coverage for losses caused by 10 named perils, the broad form extends the list of named perils to 16, and the special form provides coverage on an open-perils basis. Table 2-8 indicates where the basic, broad, and special forms are used to define the covered causes of losses in the homeowners program.

TABLE 2-8
Homeowners Forms

For Use By	Persons Who Own Their Home				Renters	Condo Owners
Forms	HO-2	HO-3	HO-5	HO-8	HO-4	HO-6
Section I – Property Coverages						
	Coverage A Dwelling	**Coverage A** Dwelling	**Coverage A** Dwelling	**Coverage A** Dwelling		**Coverage A** Unit-owner's Additions Flat $1,000
	Coverage B Other Structures	**Coverage B** Other Structures	**Coverage B** Other Structures	**Coverage B** Other Structures		
	Coverage C Personal Property	**Coverage C** Personal Property	**Coverage C** Personal Property	**Coverage C** Personal Property	**Coverage C** Personal Property	**Coverage C** Personal Property
	Coverage D Loss of Use	**Coverage D** Loss of Use	**Coverage D** Loss of Use	**Coverage D** Loss of Use	**Coverage D** Loss of Use	**Coverage D** Loss of Use
Perils Covered in Section I	Broad Form (16 named perils)	Coverages A & B Special Form (open perils) Coverage C Broad Form (16 named perils)	Special Form (open perils)	Basic Form (10 named perils)	Broad Form (16 named perils)	Broad Form (16 named perils)
Section II – Liability & Medical Payments Coverages						
	Coverage E Personal Liability	**Coverage E** Personal Liability	**Coverage E** Personal Liability	**Coverage E** Personal Liability	**Coverage E** Personal Liability	**Coverage E** Personal Liability
	Coverage F Medical Payments to Others	**Coverage F** Medical Payments to Others	**Coverage F** Medical Payments to Others	**Coverage F** Medical Payments to Others	**Coverage F** Medical Payments to Others	**Coverage F** Medical Payments to Others

Coverage A Dwelling. Dwelling coverage requires the selection of a limit or dollar amount of insurance coverage. For HO-2, HO-3, HO-5 and HO-8, this is the only part of Section I for which the insured must choose a limit of coverage. The limits for all other property covered by these homeowners forms are either a fixed-dollar amount or a fixed percentage of the limit on the dwelling. However, some of these limits can be changed by the insured.

A recommendation of the proper limit of coverage that the client should purchase on the dwelling should be made with care. With the exception of HO-8 where dwelling losses are settled on a functional replacement cost basis (e.g., plastered walls are replaced with plasterboard), if a loss should occur to the dwelling and at the time of loss the amount of insurance carried is equal to 80 percent or more of the full replacement cost of the dwelling, the loss will be settled on a full replacement-cost basis. If the current replacement cost of the dwelling is $200,000, a minimum limit of coverage on the dwelling of $160,000 and a maximum limit of $200,000 should be recommended. In most cases it would be appropriate to recommend the selection of a limit closer to the top of the range, particularly if the client would need to replace the entire dwelling following a total loss.

replacement-cost requirement

Protection against inflation can be provided in two ways. To help the insured satisfy the 80 percent *replacement-cost requirement* at the time of loss and reduce the chance of underinsurance due to increasing construction costs, the inflation guard endorsement periodically and automatically increases the limit of coverage on the dwelling by a specified percentage of the policy's original Coverage A limit. The guaranteed replacement cost coverage offered by some insurance companies guarantees the full cost of replacing the damaged dwelling even if that cost exceeds the Coverage A limit.

Coverage B Other Structures. Coverage B provides insurance on other structures located on the premises that are not attached to the dwelling. These include detached garages or tool-sheds and such things as fences, driveways, and retaining walls. Unless increased by the insured, the amount of coverage is 10 percent of the limit on the dwelling. Losses to these other structures are settled on a replacement-cost basis.

Coverage C Personal Property. Personal property includes the items normally contained in a dwelling, such as furniture, appliances, and clothing, and property stored in a garage, other structure, or outdoors. Unless increased, the limit of coverage on personal property for HO-2, HO-3, HO-5 and HO-8 is 50 percent of the dwelling limit. For HO-4 and HO-6, the insured selects the amount of coverage on personal property.

Personal property coverage is provided worldwide. When an insured has personal property normally situated at a secondary residence, coverage on such property is limited to either 10 percent of the Coverage C limit or $1,000, whichever is greater.

internal limits

Personal property is subject to *internal limits* of coverage on various items. Some examples of these internal limits include

- $200 on money, bank notes, bullion, coins, medals, scrip, and stored value and smart cards
- $1,500 on watercraft, including their trailers, furnishings, equipment, and motors
- $1,500 for loss by theft of jewelry, watches, furs, and precious and semiprecious stones
- $2,500 on property on the residence premises used primarily for business purposes

When the financial advisor identifies situations where client asset values exceed these limits, it is appropriate to suggest alternative ways of treating the exposure. Several alternatives are available depending upon the item(s) of property involved. Some of the internal limits in the client's homeowners policy can be increased for an additional premium. Certain types of valuable property such as furs, jewelry, fine arts, and antiques can be scheduled with a higher limit on an open-perils basis using the homeowners scheduled personal property endorsement. In some cases such as large or powerful watercraft, a separate policy may be the most effective means of providing not only adequate property insurance, but also essential liability insurance coverage.

Personal property is covered on an actual-cash-value basis. Sometimes it is desirable to place this coverage on a replacement-cost basis, which can be done by endorsement for an additional premium. Because the replacement cost of personal property will be greater than its actual cash value, it makes sense to increase Coverage C when loss settlement will be based on replacement cost.

Coverage D Loss of Use. Coverage D provides insurance protection for certain indirect losses. The primary loss-of-use coverage is for additional living expenses—those increased costs necessary to maintain normal living standards when the insured's dwelling is uninhabitable because of damage caused by a covered cause of loss. The automatic limit for this coverage is a percent of the coverage applicable to the dwelling for HO-2 (30 percent), HO-3 (30 percent), HO-5 (30 percent), and HO-8 (10 percent), and a percent of the coverage applicable to personal property for HO-4 (30 percent) and HO-6 (50 percent). Payment is limited to the period required to repair or replace the damage or if the insured permanently relocates, to the period required to resettle the household.

If a part of the residence premises is rented or held for rental to others, loss-of-use coverage is extended to the fair rental value of the rented portion. In effect, this coverage provides a continuation of the rent payment, less a deduction for expenses that do not continue. Coverage for additional living expenses or fair rental value is also provided if action by a civil authority prohibits the insured from using the residence premises because of direct damage to a neighboring premises that was caused by a covered peril in the insured's policy.

Coverage E Personal Liability. Personal liability insurance provides protection for activities and conditions at the premises where the named insured (the person named on the policy's declarations page) maintains a covered residence and for personal activities of the named insured and members of the his or her family anywhere in the world. All homeowners forms contain the same liability coverage.

Coverage E is similar to other liability insurance policies. Protection is provided for legal liability involving bodily injury or property damage, but not for personal injury. The latter includes such injuries as libel, slander, violation of privacy, malicious prosecution, and wrongful entry. These may be added by endorsement or covered under the umbrella liability policies discussed later in this chapter. The standard liability limit is $100,000 per occurrence, but may be increased for a relatively small additional charge. Given the potential severity of legal liability losses, clients should be advised to increase the Coverage E limit to the amount required as an underlying limit by an umbrella liability policy (commonly $300,000 for a homeowners policy).

Also, as with other liability policies, the insurer promises to defend the insured at the company's expense even if the suit is groundless, false, or fraudulent. The insurer may investigate and settle any claim that it feels is appropriate. The costs associated with investigating and defending a claim against an insured are paid in addition to the limit of liability.

Exclusions play an important role in liability insurance coverage, because the insurer is essentially promising to pay any claim involving bodily injury or property damage for which an insured is legally liable unless the particular situation is specifically excluded by the policy. Some of the exclusions found in homeowners policies should be expected, such as war and nuclear exposure. Others should be anticipated because the exposure can be covered with a different policy as in the case of motor vehicle, large and powerful watercraft, aircraft, workers' compensation, and business and professional service exposures. Liability arising out of the transmission of a communicable disease, sexual molestation or abuse, and the use, sale, manufacture, delivery, transfer, or possession of a controlled substance by an insured is also excluded. Finally, losses that are intentionally caused are not covered, nor is bodily injury to an insured.

Coverage F Medical Payments to Others. Coverage F provides medical benefits to persons, other than residents of the insured household, who suffer bodily injury at an insured location or who are injured because of an insured's activities away from the insured location. The basic limit for Coverage F is $1,000 per person. This amount is available for all necessary medical expenses incurred within 3 years of the date of the accident. Benefits under this coverage will be paid whether or not the insured is legally liable. While a client must carry an amount of coverage equal to the $1,000 basic limit, carrying higher limits would generally be an inefficient use of premium dollars, since an insured is protected by Coverage E if the injury was due to his or her negligence, and if not, the injured person should have his or her own medical expense insurance to cover such injuries.

Personal Auto Insurance

While there are several forms that are currently used to provide personal automobile insurance to individuals and families, ISO's Personal Auto Policy (PAP) is by far the most widely sold and, thus, will serve as the basis for discussion in this section. Because this policy is a very complicated contract, only the highlights can be covered here.

The PAP is a package policy that provides coverage for the three types of potential losses that may arise out of the ownership or operation of an automobile—legal liability, medical expenses, and damage to or loss of the auto. To accomplish this, the PAP offers the following four coverages:

 Part A, Liability Coverage
 Part B, Medical Payments Coverage
 Part C, Uninsured Motorists Coverage
 Part D, Coverage for Damage to Your Auto

Unlike homeowners insurance where the insured is required to carry at least a minimum amount of insurance for each of the coverages included in the particular policy form being used, the PAP, for the most part, provides the insured with a choice as to which of the coverages he or she desires and the amount of insurance for each coverage chosen.

Part A Liability Coverage. In addition to defending an insured at its own expense, the insurance company agrees to pay damages for bodily injury or property damage any insured becomes legally responsible for because of an auto accident. Part A of the PAP contains either

single limit of liability

- a *single limit of liability,* such as $300,000, which is the maximum amount that will be paid for all damages for bodily injury and property damage resulting from any one accident, or

split limit of liability

- a *split limit of liability,* such as $100,000/$300,000/$50,000, which is the maximum that will be paid for bodily injury to each person in an accident, for all bodily injury in an accident, and for all property damage in an accident.

Because the minimum limits available for auto liability insurance reflect the financial responsibility laws of the various states, they tend be quite low, such as $50,000 or $25,000/$50,000/$10,000. Given the potential severity of legal liability losses, clients should be advised to increase the Part A limit to the amount required as an underlying limit by an umbrella liability policy (such as, $500,000 or $500,000/ $500,000/ $50,000 for an auto policy).

The PAP identifies the named insured (the person named on the declarations page), the spouse, and any other family member as insureds for the liability exposure arising from the ownership, maintenance, or use of any auto. This means that unless a situation is specifically excluded by the policy (for example, legal liability for property damage to a rented auto), an insured is protected for legal liability whether or not the auto being operated is owned by the named insured. A family member in this case is anyone who is related to the named insured by blood, marriage, or adoption and who resides in the named insured's household. Other persons are also covered by the named insured's PAP for liability arising out of the use of the insured's covered auto.

A covered auto is any vehicle shown in the declarations of the policy. It also includes any trailer the named insured owns. If the insured purchases an additional vehicle during the policy period, it will be covered automatically as long as the insurance company is notified of this addition within 14 days. If the new vehicle is a replacement auto, the insurance company will provide coverage (other than coverage for Part D—Damage to Your Auto) until the end of the policy period without any notice being given. Finally, for all coverages other than Part D, a covered auto includes any auto or trailer not owned by the named insured while being used as a temporary substitute for another covered auto that is out of normal use because of breakdown, repair, servicing, loss, or destruction.

Clearly, the insuring agreement for the liability coverage portion of the PAP is broadly stated to provide coverage for a wide mix of individuals and autos. As might be expected, there are several exclusions applicable to this broad coverage. However, despite the number and complexity of the exclusions, the PAP continues to provide insureds with very broad auto liability insurance coverage.

Part B Medical Payments Coverage. Under the medical payments coverage of the PAP, the insurer will pay reasonable expenses incurred for necessary medical and funeral services because of bodily injury caused by an accident and sustained by an insured. Subject to certain exclusions, benefits are payable to the named insured and family members if injured while occupying any motor vehicle designed for public roads or if struck by a motor vehicle. This coverage differs from medical payments coverage under the homeowners policy where the named insured and members of the household are not covered, and coverage applies only to other persons injured on the premises or because of an insured's activities. In the PAP, medical expenses of other persons are also covered, but only while they are occupying a covered auto. Where no-fault benefits are required, medical payments coverage is normally replaced by the no-fault coverage.

Part C Uninsured Motorists Coverage. Uninsured motorists coverage is a rather unique addition to the PAP. It basically provides that if an insured sustains bodily injury (some states also include property damage) in an auto accident where the other driver was operating an uninsured motor vehicle, the insured may recover from his or her own insurance company those sums he or she is legally entitled to recover from the owner or operator of the uninsured motor vehicle.

An uninsured motor vehicle includes a motor vehicle to which no bodily injury liability insurance applies at the time of the accident, a motor vehicle for which the bodily injury liability insurance limit is less than the minimum limit required by the financial responsibility law of the state where the insured's covered auto is principally garaged, a hit-and-run vehicle, and a motor vehicle to which bodily injury liability insurance applies at the time of the accident, but the insurance company denies coverage or becomes insolvent.

The limit of liability for uninsured motorists coverage is typically the required limit of the financial responsibility law in the insured's state. However, the policy can be endorsed to add underinsured motorists coverage which increases this limit. The underinsured benefit provides payment when the at-fault driver or owner has liability insurance, but its limits are less than the limits purchased for the underinsured motorists coverage.

Part D Coverage for Damage to Your Auto. The physical damage coverage of the PAP is referred to as Part D—Damage to Your Auto. The two primary coverages in this part of the policy are *collision* and *other than collision*. The latter has historically been called "comprehensive" and is still referred to in this way by many in the insurance business. Collision is defined as the upset of the covered auto or its impact with an object or another vehicle. Other than collision is every other cause of loss except collision and those causes specifically excluded by the policy. The insured

collision
other than collision

has a choice of purchasing both the collision and the other-than-collision coverages, one of the coverages and not the other, or neither coverage.

The limit of liability for physical damage claims is the lesser of the actual cash value of the stolen or damaged property and the amount necessary to repair or replace the property. In addition, the damage amount is subject to a deductible that, within limits, can be selected by the named insured. A single deductible may apply to all losses or different deductibles may apply to collision losses and other-than-collision losses. An increase in the amount of the deductible can often result in a substantial premium savings.

Although this part of the PAP is called Coverage for Damage to Your Auto, coverage is also extended to nonowned autos. Nonowned autos include, among others, any private passenger auto, pickup, or van that is not owned by the named insured or a family member but is being driven by one of them. Nonowned autos also include vehicles that are rented on a temporary basis, such as when an insured is on a trip or a covered auto is out of service. In any event, coverage for nonowned autos is the broadest coverage applicable to any covered auto under the policy.

No-Fault Benefits. Approximately half the states have adopted some form of no-fault automobile insurance plan. Under a pure no-fault plan, legal liability arising out of automobile accidents would be abolished, and anyone suffering a bodily injury loss in an automobile accident would collect from his or her own insurance company. None of the plans now in existence have gone to this extreme. Rather, the right to sue another party either has not been altered or has been modified to eliminate suits for which losses are below a certain dollar limit (called a threshold) or below some verbalized statement regarding the severity of the injury. No-fault benefits typically include some combination of medical expenses, lost wages, replacement of services, survivors' benefits, and funeral expenses.

In those states with no-fault laws, individuals either must be offered the coverage or are required to carry insurance to compensate themselves, their families, and possibly passengers in their autos for their own bodily injuries. This is accomplished by adding the required endorsement to the PAP.

Umbrella Liability Insurance

The homeowners and automobile insurance policies are the basic coverages for most individuals and families. With the continual increase in the severity of legal liability judgments and settlements, there is an increasing need, particularly among the affluent, for liability limits greater than those provided by these two basic policies. One policy that is becoming increasingly popular for this purpose is the personal umbrella liability policy, also called excess liability or personal catastrophe liability insurance.

While there is no standardized personal umbrella liability insurance policy, a few generalizations can be made. These policies provide excess liability limits over underlying liability coverage limits and, in most cases, broader coverage than the underlying policies. Umbrella liability policies typically provide a liability limit of $1 million or more per occurrence, often up to a maximum of $5 or $10 million. The insured is required to carry certain underlying liability policies and limits—for example, a homeowners policy with a liability limit of $300,000 and an automobile liability policy with a single limit of $500,000. Other coverages may also be required if the exposures exist.

With respect to the underlying coverages, the umbrella liability policy provides excess coverage. For example, if an individual has an automobile liability policy with a single limit of $500,000 and an umbrella liability policy with a limit of $2,000,000, the first $500,000 of any claim arising out of an automobile accident would be payable under the automobile policy, and the balance (up to the policy limit) would be payable under the umbrella policy. Therefore, the insured would have total coverage amounting to $2,500,000.

The umbrella policy also covers situations not covered by underlying insurance policies, such as personal injury in the form of libel, slander, and invasion of privacy; or auto liability outside the United States and Canada. When the umbrella policy does provide coverage in these cases, it drops down to provide primary coverage over the insured's retained limit. A retained limit is like a deductible that must be paid by the insured. This can be as low as $250, but is typically in the $500 to $1,000 range.

Umbrella liability policies do contain some exclusions. Some typical ones are intentional acts, amounts payable under workers' compensation laws, business pursuits, and damage to the insured's own property. Professional liability may also be excluded, but insurance companies are now offering this coverage if the insured carries an underlying professional-liability policy.

The umbrella liability policy enables an individual to have protection against very severe bodily injury, personal liability, and property damage liability losses. Moreover, due to the relatively low frequency of such losses, the coverage is available at a very reasonable cost. The financial advisor should consider recommending this coverage to all clients.

THE FINAL WORD

Just as in planning for other areas of client needs, the financial planning process provides an organized approach for developing plans that help clients deal effectively with the various types of pure risks they face. While clearly not the most appropriate technique for handling all the pure risks faced by individuals and families, insurance is an efficient technique for dealing with those pure risk situations that involve the possibility of low frequency, high severity losses. When coupled with retention through the use of deductibles and elimination periods, insurance becomes an even more cost-effective technique for financing potentially severe losses that have a relatively small chance of occurring, but which could have a catastrophic impact on a client's overall financial plan if they do occur.

While this chapter has provided a survey of insurance coverages that are available to meet certain pure risks most commonly faced by individuals and families, the financial advisor must recognize two important points. First, the coverages discussed in this chapter are much more complex than the limited space allotted to each may suggest. A more in-depth knowledge of these coverages (or the assistance of an advisor who specializes in insurance) is essential if a financial advisor is to use even these basic coverages properly in working with clients. Second, since each client situation presents different problems to solve, additional study or help from an insurance advisor will also be needed in planning to effectively deal with the various rather unique pure risk exposures faced by different clients.

CHAPTER SUMMARY

While planning for the accumulation of wealth may be exciting, the protection of accumulated wealth should not be overlooked. Finding a method of protecting wealth against the possibility of loss is a challenge nearly all people face. Efforts by individuals and families to meet this challenge are aimed at dealing with the problem of risk.

Risk is the basic problem with which insurance deals, and it is important to understand what risk is in order to manage it efficiently through the use of insurance and/or other risk handling techniques. For insurance and financial planning purposes, the term risk refers to the possibility of financial loss. When defined in this way, risk can be divided into pure risk and speculative risk. The difference between these two categories of risk is that pure risk involves only the possibility of financial loss, while speculative risk involves not only the possibility of financial loss, but also the possibility of financial gain. With few exceptions, insurance is a technique for dealing with pure risk, not speculative risk.

Two additional points are important for fully understanding risk. First, risk and uncertainty are not the same. Second, risk is not the probability of loss. Although risk can give rise to uncertainty, risk is not uncertainty. Unlike uncertainty, which is a state of mind characterized by doubt, risk exists as a state of the world. Also, while risk may be measurable in terms of probability, it need not be measurable to exist. That is why risk is defined as the possibility, not the probability, of financial loss.

As previously mentioned, insurance is a technique for dealing primarily with pure risks, which can be categorized as personal risks, property risks, and liability risks. Given the similarity of the steps involved in the risk management, needs analysis, and financial planning processes, the financial planning process can be used to help individuals and families plan for the possibility of financial loss associated with pure risk.

The techniques typically available to individuals and families for handling pure risks are grouped into loss control techniques and loss financing techniques. Loss control techniques typically include risk avoidance, loss prevention, and loss reduction, while the two most commonly used loss financing techniques are retention and insurance. Once the appropriate techniques have been identified, the advisor needs to formulate a plan for using these techniques. Where insurance is to be used, the advisor must match particular insurance policies to the various pure risks that face individuals and families.

Pure risks categorized as personal risks include the loss of income earning ability due to unemployment, premature death, retirement, and disability. Personal risks also include the possibility of incurring extra expenses as a result of medical care for accidental injuries or sickness and long-term care for chronic illness. Private insurance can be used to cover all of these personal risks except for the risk of unemployment, which generally must be covered by social insurance.

With respect to the personal risk of premature death, life insurance is the only financial product that can immediately generate a sum of money large enough to protect an individual's dependents in the event of his or her premature death. Virtually all life insurance products marketed today are variations of (1) term insurance, (2) whole life insurance, and (3) universal life insurance.

With respect to the personal risk of retirement, two important general challenges facing many individuals are accumulating sufficient financial resources to meet their retirement objectives and distributing those resources in a manner consistent with those objectives. Annuities can be helpful in meeting both challenges.

Personal risks associated with the loss of health are (1) extra expenses incurred for medical care due to accident or sickness, (2) loss of income earning ability due to accident or sickness, and (3) extra expenses incurred for long-term care due to the inability to safely perform some of the activities of daily living (ADLs). The types of health insurance available to help deal with these risks are medical expense insurance, disability income insurance, and long-term care insurance, respectively. As an alternative to traditional medical expense insurance, an individual can establish a tax-favored health savings account (HSA) in conjunction with coverage under a high-deductible health plan (HDHP).

Individuals and families face a number of pure risks categorized as property risks and liability risks. Property risks involve direct and indirect losses arising from the need to replace or repair damaged or missing property. Liability risks, on the other hand, involve the possibility of loss as a result of physical or personal injuries to others, or damage to or destruction of others' property.

Property losses that are of low severity can be handled most efficiently through retention. However, large property losses and liability losses require transfer through the purchase of insurance, given their potentially severe impact on an individual's assets. While some individuals require specialized forms of insurance, such as yacht policies, flood insurance, and professional liability insurance, the majority of property and liability risks faced by individuals and families can be handled with (1) homeowners insurance, (2) personal automobile insurance, and (3) umbrella liability insurance. Where appropriate, deductibles can be used to retain small property losses.

CHAPTER REVIEW

Key Terms and Concepts are explained in the Glossary. Answers to the Review Questions and Self-Test Questions are found in the back of the book in the Answers to Questions section.

Key Terms and Concepts

- risk
- pure risk
- speculative risk
- peril
- personal risks
- property risks
- liability risks
- risk management
- needs analysis
- actual cash value
- replacement cost
- depreciation
- human-life-value method
- loss control
- loss financing
- risk avoidance
- loss prevention
- loss reduction
- retention
- insurance
- law of large numbers
- portfolio effect
- reinsurance
- financial capacity
- term life insurance
- whole life insurance
- universal life insurance
- renewability provision
- conversion provision
- loan provision
- nonforfeiture options
- participating (par) policies
- nonparticipating (nonpar) policies
- current assumption whole life
- variable life insurance
- adverse selection
- variable universal life
- life annuities
- immediate annuity
- deferred annuities

medical expense insurance
disability income insurance
long-term care insurance
health savings account (HSA)
high-deductible health plan (HDHP)
partial disability
residual disability
elimination (waiting) period
total disability
noncancelable
guaranteed renewable
reimbursement basis
per diem basis

pool of money
tax-qualified contracts
nonqualified contracts
homeowners insurance
named-perils approach
open-perils approach
replacement-cost requirement
internal limits
single limit of liability
split limit of liability
collision
other than collision

Review Questions

2-1. What does the term risk mean for insurance and financial planning purposes?

2-2. Identify the two categories of risk, and explain the meaning of each.

2-3. Identify the three types of pure risk, and briefly describe each type.

2-4. Explain the relationship of the financial planning process to the process called risk management and the process called needs analysis.

2-5. Distinguish between actual cash value and replacement cost as measures of loss associated with property risks.

2-6. What is the most appropriate measure of the loss associated with liability risks? Explain.

2-7. Describe two methods of measuring the financial loss associated with premature death.

2-8. Identify the two categories of techniques for handling pure risks, and briefly explain each one.

2-9. Briefly explain the operation of the law of large numbers.

2-10. Distinguish participating whole life policies from nonparticipating whole life policies.

2-11. Distinguish traditional whole life policies from variable whole life policies.

2-12. Describe the various ways in which disability may be defined in a disability income insurance policy.

2-13. What choices are typically available to a client who is considering the purchase of a long-term care insurance policy with respect to
    a. how the daily benefit amount is paid

b. how the benefit period is applied in the payment of benefits
c. the options for protecting against inflation

2-14. Summarize the coverage that is provided by homeowners forms HO-2 and HO-3 for damage to
a. the dwelling
b. other structures
c. personal property

2-15. Describe the coverage provided in a homeowners policy for loss of use of damaged property.

2-16. Describe the coverages provided by homeowners policies for
a. personal liability
b. medical benefits

2-17. Compare the medical payments coverage provided by the Personal Auto Policy (PAP) with that provided by a homeowners policy.

2-18. Compare the coverage provided in the Personal Auto Policy (PAP) for uninsured motorists with that provided by the endorsement for underinsured motorists.

2-19. Explain how a typical umbrella liability insurance policy works in conjunction with underlying coverages.

2-20. Why might umbrella liability insurance be needed by a client who has a homeowners policy with a high limit under the liability section of the policy?

Self-Test Questions

Instructions: Read chapter 2 first, then answer the following questions to test your knowledge. There are 10 questions; circle the correct answer, then check your answers with the answer key in the back of the book.

2-1. Insurance is used most efficiently in dealing with risk situations involving losses that are both

(A) low frequency and low severity
(B) low frequency and high severity
(C) high frequency and low severity
(D) high frequency and high severity

2-2. A variable universal life (VUL) policy differs from a universal life (UL) policy in which of the following ways?

(A) A VUL policy provides for a flexible premium after the first year.
(B) A VUL policy permits partial withdrawals from its cash value.
(C) A VUL policy permits the policyowner to decrease the death benefit at any time.
(D) A VUL policy allows the policyowner to direct the investment of the cash value.

2-3. If the daily benefit for institutional care in a long-term care insurance policy is $250 and the benefit period is 1,095 days (or 3 years), the policy's pool of money would be

(A) $91,250
(B) $182,500
(C) $273,750
(D) $821,250

2-4. For insurance and financial planning purposes, risk is defined to mean the

(A) possibility of financial loss
(B) uncertainty of financial loss
(C) probability of financial loss
(D) cause of financial loss

2-5. Umbrella liability policies typically exclude which of the following types of losses?

 I. Damage to the insured's own property
 II. Personal injury in the form of libel and slander

(A) I only
(B) II only
(C) Both I and II
(D) Neither I nor II

2-6. Which of the following statements concerning Coverage B (other structures) of homeowners insurance policies is (are) correct?

  I. Coverage B is found in all homeowners forms.
  II. All losses to other structures are settled on an actual cash value basis.

  (A) I only
  (B) II only
  (C) Both I and II
  (D) Neither I nor II

2-7. Which of the following statements concerning Part B (medical payments coverage) of the Personal Auto Policy (PAP) is (are) correct?

  I. Medical expenses of the named insured and/or family members are covered if they are struck by a motor vehicle.
  II. Medical expenses of persons other than the named insured and family members are covered if they are injured while in a covered auto.

  (A) I only
  (B) II only
  (C) Both I and II
  (D) Neither I nor II

2-8. Loss control techniques typically available to individuals and families include all the following EXCEPT

  (A) loss prevention
  (B) retention
  (C) risk avoidance
  (D) loss reduction

2-9. To handle the risk that continues to exist after the operation of the law of large numbers, insurers rely on all the following techniques EXCEPT

  (A) writing different lines of insurance
  (B) reinsuring part of their business
  (C) approving more claim payments
  (D) holding minimum amounts of surplus

2-10. The first part of step 2 in the financial planning process involves all the following activities EXCEPT

(A) identifying the client's concerns related to various pure risks
(B) measuring the potential losses associated with identified pure risks
(C) determining the client's goals in dealing with his or her pure risk concerns
(D) helping the client prioritize his or her competing goals

NOTES

1. The financial planning process essentially combines steps 1 and 2 of the risk management and needs analysis processes into step 2 and adds a new step 1—establish and define the advisor-client relationship. Realistically, however, to utilize either the risk management or needs analysis process, an advisor-client relationship would first have to be established. Therefore, even though not formally recognized as the first step in either of these processes, establishing an advisor-client relationship is, in reality, the first step in both the risk management and needs analysis processes.
2. *2007 Annuity Fact Book,* The Association for Insured Retirement Solutions, Reston, VA 20190.
3. For a comprehensive treatment of health savings accounts (HSAs), see Thomas P. O'Hare and Burton T. Beam, Individual Heath Insurance Planning: Medical, Disability Income, and Long-Term Care, (Bryn Mawr, PA: The American College Press, 2008), chapter 9.

3

Employee Benefits Planning

Burton T. Beam, Jr.

Learning Objectives

An understanding of the material in this chapter should enable you to

3-1. Describe the meaning of employee benefits, and explain why they have grown in significance.

3-2. Explain the importance of benefit planning.

3-3. Describe the eligibility requirements for employee benefits.

3-4. Describe the various types of employee benefits that can be categorized as traditional group insurance benefits, voluntary insurance benefits, and miscellaneous fringe benefits.

3-5. Explain the nature of cafeteria plans and how they can be used in financial planning.

Chapter Outline

    SCOPE AND SIGNIFICANCE OF EMPLOYEE BENEFITS 3.2
        Meaning of Employee Benefits 3.2
        Significance of Employee Benefits 3.3
        Growth of Employee Benefits 3.4
    IMPORTANCE OF BENEFIT PLANNING 3.6
        Benefit-Planning for the Employer 3.6
        Advisor Awareness of Employee Benefits 3.8
    ELIGIBILITY FOR BENEFITS 3.9
        Covered Classifications 3.10
        Full-Time Employment 3.10
        Probationary Periods 3.10
        Insurability 3.10
        Premium Contributions 3.11
        Termination of Coverage 3.11
    TYPES OF EMPLOYEE BENEFITS 3.11
        Medical Expense Insurance 3.12

Life Insurance 3.26
Disability Income Insurance 3.34
Dental Insurance 3.38
Vision Insurance 3.40
Voluntary Insurance Benefits 3.41
Miscellaneous Fringe Benefits 3.46
CAFETERIA PLANS 3.52
Nature 3.52
Types 3.53
THE FINAL WORD 3.56
CHAPTER SUMMARY 3.56
CHAPTER REVIEW 3.58

This chapter begins with a discussion of the meaning of employee benefits, their advantages, and the ways they can be used. The discussion then turns to a description of the eligibility requirements for the major types of employee benefits. Next, the chapter examines the various types of employee benefits that can be categorized as traditional group insurance benefits, voluntary insurance benefits, and miscellaneous fringe benefits. Finally, it concludes with a look at cafeteria plans, which can give employees a greater ability to customize their benefit packages.

SCOPE AND SIGNIFICANCE OF EMPLOYEE BENEFITS

Many of the financial needs of individuals and their families are met—or at least partially met—with benefits that are provided and/or available to them because of their employment. Employee benefits include a wide variety of benefits and services. They represent a major portion—and growing percentage—of total employee compensation. Financial advisors need to understand these benefits so they can incorporate them into the financial plans they are developing for their clients.

Meaning of Employee Benefits

There is not always agreement about what constitute employee benefits. No matter what definition is used, however, the magnitude of these benefits is significant.

The narrowest definition of employee benefits includes only employer-provided benefits for situations involving death, accident, sickness, retirement, or unemployment. On the other hand, the broadest definition of

employee benefits

employee benefits includes all benefits and services, other than wages for time worked, that employees receive in whole or in part from their employers. This chapter uses a broad definition and defines employee benefits as including the following five categories:

- legally required payments for government programs. These include employer contributions to such programs as Social Security, Medicare, unemployment compensation insurance, workers' compensation insurance, and temporary disability insurance.
- payments for private insurance and retirement plans. These include the cost of establishing such plans, as well as contributions in the form of insurance premiums or payments through alternative funding arrangements. Benefits are provided under these plans to cover loss exposures from personal risks, such as old age, death, disability, long-term care expenses, medical expenses, dental expenses, and legal expenses. In addition, a small number of employers have plans that cover some of the property and liability risks that employees are exposed to in their ordinary lives.
- payments for time not worked. These include family leave, vacations, holidays, jury duty, maternity leave, and National Guard duty.
- extra cash payments, other than wages and bonuses based on performance, to employees. Benefits in this category include educational assistance, moving expenses, suggestion awards, and Christmas bonuses.
- cost of services to employees, such as day care, adoption assistance, financial planning programs, subsidized meals, employee discounts, wellness programs, retirement counseling, and free parking

The first category of employee benefits is usually referred to as social insurance, and the last four categories are commonly called group benefits. This book covers many of the benefits from each of the categories, but not all of them are covered in this chapter. Retirement plans from the second category are covered in chapter 6, while social insurance programs from the first category are covered in chapter 8.

Significance of Employee Benefits

In a 2007 study of 453 companies, the U.S. Chamber of Commerce found that the average payment by employers for employee benefits was equal to 42.7 percent of payroll.[1] Of this figure, 9.5 percent of payroll went for the employer's share of legally required social insurance payments, 10.4 percent for payments to private retirement and savings plans, and 12.1

percent for medically related benefits. The remaining 10.7 percent was for all other types of benefits, with paid vacations being the single most costly item in this category. The study showed substantial variations among companies, with 15 percent of employers having benefit costs less than 24 percent of payroll and another 15 percent having benefit costs in excess of 50 percent. Also, larger companies offered a greater number of employee benefits to their employees than did smaller companies. Moreover, large variations were shown by industry. Within specific industries, the larger the company, the higher the costs of employee benefits as a percentage of payroll.

In addition to employer costs, employee payroll deductions for benefits amounted to 16.9 percent of payroll. Broken down into components, this amounted to 7.5 percent for Social Security and Medicare taxes, 5.6 percent for contributions to retirement and saving plans, and 3.8 percent for medically related benefits, including life insurance premiums.

The Chamber of Commerce study also showed that employees received an average of $21,527 in employer-paid benefits. However, there was a significant range, with the employees of 10 percent of companies at the high end of the range receiving more than $29,841 and the employees of 10 percent of companies at the low end of the range receiving $6,172 or less.

Growth of Employee Benefits

It is obvious from the previous section of this chapter that employee benefits comprise a significant portion of overall employee compensation. This has not always been the case, and this growth over the last 80 years stems from several factors that include industrialization, the influence of organized labor, wage controls, cost advantages, inflation, and legislation.

Industrialization

During the nineteenth and early 20th centuries, the United States made the transition from an agrarian economy to one characterized by increasing industrialization and urbanization. The economic consequences of death, sickness, accidents, and old age became more significant as individuals began to depend more on monetary wages than on self-reliance and family ties to meet their basic needs. As a result, some employers began to provide retirement, death, and medical benefits to their employees. While benevolence may have influenced the decision to provide such benefits, the principal reason was probably the employers' realization that it was in their own best interest to do so. Not only did such benefits improve morale and productivity, they also reduced employee turnover and the expenses associated with it.

While some of the earlier benefits were paid directly by employers, the development of group insurance and pension contracts enabled these benefits to be funded by systematic payments to another party, usually an insurance company. However, many employers still self-fund some of their benefit plans. For example, short-term sick pay benefits are commonly paid directly by many employers, and large employers often self-fund their medical expense plans. As employee benefits became more common, employers were faced with adopting new or better plans to remain competitive in attracting and keeping employees. This competition in employee benefits continues to exist.

Industrialization also led to more government benefits, such as Social Security, Medicare, unemployment insurance, and workers' compensation insurance.

Organized Labor

Labor unions have the right to legally negotiate for employee benefits for their members. Labor unions have also affected benefits for nonunion employees, because some employers provide generous benefit plans in an effort to discourage their employees from unionizing. In addition, employers with both union and nonunion employees often provide the same benefits for the nonunion employees as those stipulated in the union contracts.

Wage Controls

Employee benefit plans grew substantially during World War II and the Korean War. Although wages were frozen, no restrictions were imposed on employee benefits, thus making them an important factor in attracting and retaining employees in labor markets with little unemployment. Although unemployment increased after these conflicts ended, employee benefits were not cut back.

Cost Advantages

Because of the economies associated with group underwriting and administration, benefits can usually be obtained at a lower cost through group insurance than through separate policies purchased by individual employees. Similar savings can be realized by directly providing employees with certain services, such as financial planning, day-care centers, and subsidized meals. The Internal Revenue Code also provides favorable tax treatment to employer contributions for certain types of employee benefits. The employer may deduct most benefit contributions as usual business expenses, and employees often have no taxable income as a result of employer contributions in their behalf. In addition, employees may receive tax-free benefits from certain types of benefit plans, even if provided by employer contributions. The extent of the favorable tax treatment applicable to various employee benefits is discussed later in this chapter. Nevertheless, it should be noted here that the types of employee benefits with the most favorable tax treatment also tend to be the most prevalent.

Inflation

Inflation also affects employee benefits. When benefit levels are related to employees' wages, the level and cost of these benefits increase as wages increase; when benefit levels are stated as fixed amounts, inflation results in employee pressure for increases. For most employers, the cost of employee benefits has been increasing at a rate faster than wages, primarily because of the skyrocketing increase in the cost of providing medical expense benefits.

Legislation

Many states and the federal government have legislation that affects employee benefits. At the state level, benefit laws are often in the form of mandates regarding the provisions that must be included in group insurance contracts. Similar federal laws on the other hand typically apply to plans of any employer (with the possible exception of small employers), whether the plans are insured or not. These mandates include coverage for such conditions as maternity, mental illness, alcoholism, and drug abuse.

There are also benefit mandates—such as family leave—that apply to benefits that are traditionally uninsured.

IMPORTANCE OF BENEFIT PLANNING

The significant growth in employee benefits has called for increasingly complex decisions. Whether these decisions are by employers providing benefits, unions negotiating for benefits, or employees selecting benefit options, the need for proper benefit planning is crucial.

Before proceeding with a discussion of the types of benefits available to employees, it is important to look both at the benefit-planning process for employers and the reasons why financial advisors need to be aware of the benefits provided to and used by employees.

Benefit-Planning for the Employer

Employee benefit planning from the employer's perspective is a dynamic process that must continually be reviewed and modified if an overall benefit plan is to meet the needs of employees in a changing environment. Whether the planning is done by a benefits consulting firm or the employer's own benefits department, certain steps need to be followed. Using the six-step financial planning process introduced in chapter 1, the first step is to establish and define the advisor-client relationship. When the planning is to be done by a benefits consulting firm, the employer must select a consultant that it believes is capable of doing the job. When the employer's own benefits department does the planning, the rest of the employer's management team has to have confidence in the benefits department. If that confidence is lacking, a consulting firm will be brought in to assist the benefits department.

The second step of the planning process is divided into two components. The first component of this step is to determine the employer's goals for establishing a benefit plan or, as is more likely the case, modifying the present plan. Is the benefit package in line with the competition? Or should it be viewed as a leader, better enabling the firm to attract employees? An important part of this component is to prioritize the goals once they have been determined.

After the employer's goals are determined, the second component of this step is to gather data. This data must be accurate, complete, up-to-date, relevant to the employer's goals, and well organized.

The third step in the financial planning process is to analyze and evaluate the employer's present benefit plan, if there is one. The objective is to determine where the employer is now in relationship to the goals established in step two. The analysis will help to determine the kind of benefits to include in a new plan.

After the employer's present plan has been analyzed and evaluated, the fourth step in the process is also divided into two components. The first component of this step is to develop a new benefit plan for the employees. This may require a comparison of the present plan's costs to those for a new plan. If the costs for the new plan are excessive, the employer's goals may need to be revised. A major determinant of a benefit plan's cost is the method of funding. Should it be insured, funded from current revenues, or funded by some combination of the two approaches? Employers are increasingly using alternatives to traditional funding arrangements in an effort to reduce costs. Once a new plan is developed, the second component of this step is to present the plan to employees. However, if the new plan is presented poorly, it will be difficult for the employer's goals to be realized effectively. A good presentation is more than merely describing benefits; it also involves letting employees know the value of the benefits.

The fifth step in the financial planning process is to implement the plan. This may be as simple as adding an additional vacation day or as complex as taking competitive proposals for a pension plan from insurance companies, bank trust departments, or other providers of services.

The sixth and final step in the financial planning process requires employers to monitor the plan's performance and make any necessary changes. As new benefits or funding arrangements appear on the scene, should they be considered? Has the character of the work force changed so that a different benefit package would better meet the needs of employees?

Advisor Awareness of Employee Benefits

Employee benefits form the basis of almost all financial plans developed by advisors for their clients. Moreover, many employees are able to purchase additional life insurance and/or retirement benefits from their employer-sponsored plans. In addition, some executive level employees are able to negotiate their own compensation packages, including employee benefits.

The Basis of a Financial Plan

As previously indicated, part of the second step in the financial planning process is the gathering of data. This includes gathering information about employee benefits that are provided to employees. These benefits form the basis on which any sound financial plan is developed. For example, if an employee's goal is to have a retirement income of $70,000, it is important to know the extent to which this goal is already being met by Social Security and the employee's employer-provided retirement plan. As another example, an employee who should have $500,000 in life insurance may have a substantial portion of this need met by Social Security survivor benefits and employer-provided group life insurance.

The Purchase of Additional Insurance and Retirement Benefits

buy-up plan

voluntary benefit plans

The financial advisor needs to be aware of employee benefits that can be purchased through an employer-sponsored plan. For example, an employee may be provided with employer-paid group life insurance equal to one and one-half times salary. In addition, the employee may be able to purchase up to an additional two times salary with his or her own funds. This arrangement, called a *buy-up plan*, is common for life insurance and sometimes found with other types of group insurance.

Many employers are also the source for *voluntary benefit plans*. Under this type of arrangement, the employer does not share in the cost of the benefit, but merely makes it available to an employee who pays the entire cost of coverage if he or she elects the benefit. Long-term care insurance, dental insurance, and disability income benefits are often offered under voluntary plans.

In the case of both buy-up plans and voluntary benefit plans, the cost of coverage may be less expensive than comparable coverage in the individual marketplace. But this is not always the case, and individual insurance outside the employment relationship may be a more cost-effective purchase. Note, however, that the election of coverage through an employer-sponsored plan is usually accompanied by the ease of payroll deduction—a popular feature to employees. In addition, benefits can sometimes be purchased with before-tax dollars through a cafeteria plan or some other arrangement.

Finally, many retirement plans allow employees to make additional contributions to employer-provided retirement plans—often on a before-tax basis.

A Source for Negotiating a Compensation Package

Some employees are in a position where they can negotiate their own compensation packages, including employee benefits. These negotiations often result in the employer providing benefits to executives that are not made available to the same degree for all employees. These benefits may take the form of supplemental retirement income, additional life insurance coverage, enhanced medical expense coverage, and the like. The executives may also be provided with benefits that are not otherwise available to any employees, such as company cars, club membership, and long-term care insurance.

Executive benefits can often be provided to employees without the employees having any currently taxable income. However, as explained later in this chapter, nondiscrimination rules apply to certain types of benefits, and benefits may result in taxable income to specific categories of employees if the benefits are provided on a discriminatory basis.

While the previous discussion refers to executives as employees, it should be noted that these executives are often the majority stockholders or partners of their own businesses. As long as their overall compensation remains reasonable to the Internal Revenue Service, they can often design benefits plans that greatly benefit their own interests.

ELIGIBILITY FOR BENEFITS

Employee benefit plans are very precise in their definition of what constitutes an eligible person for coverage purposes. In general, an employee must be in a covered classification and work full-time. In addition, any requirements concerning probationary periods, insurability, premium contributions, and termination must be satisfied.

Covered Classifications

All employee benefit plans specify that an employee must fall into one of the classifications contained in the benefit schedule. While these classifications may be broad enough to include all employees of the organization, they may also be so limited as to exclude many employees from coverage. In some cases, these excluded employees may have coverage through union plans or under other employee benefit plans provided by the employer; in other cases, they may have no coverage because the employer wishes to limit benefits to certain groups of employees. For the most part, employers have significant flexibility to decide which groups of employees get which benefits. As mentioned later, however, some types of benefits are subject to nondiscrimination rules.

Full-Time Employment

Most types of employee benefits limit eligibility to full-time employees. Some benefits, however, may be provided to part-time employees. When this is done, the benefits may be smaller than those provided to full-time employees.

Probationary Periods

Employee benefit plans may contain a probationary period that must be satisfied before an employee is eligible for coverage. Such probationary periods are usually either 1 or 3 months and rarely exceed 6 months. An employee is eligible for the benefit on either the first day after the probationary period or on the first day of the month following the end of the probationary period. Different employee benefits often have different probationary periods.

Insurability

While most employee benefits are issued without individual evidence of insurability, in some instances underwriting practices require evidence of insurability. This commonly occurs when an employee fails to elect coverage under a contributory plan and later wants coverage or when an employee is eligible for a large amount of coverage. Evidence of insurability is also frequently required in voluntary benefit plans.

Premium Contributions

If an employee benefit plan is contributory, an employee is not eligible for coverage until the employer is given the proper authorization for payroll deductions.

Termination of Coverage

Employee benefit plans specify when coverage for an employee (or dependent) terminates. The coverage for any insured person terminates automatically (subject to any provisions for a continuation or conversion of coverage) when

- the employee terminates employment, including retirement
- the employee ceases to be eligible (for example, if the employee no longer satisfies the full-time work requirement or no longer falls into a covered classification)
- the policyowner or insurance company terminates a group insurance contract
- any required contribution by the employee has not been made (generally because the employee has notified the policyowner to cease the required payroll deduction)

However, most group insurance contracts provide that the employer may elect to continue coverage on employees during temporary interruptions of active full-time employment arising from leaves of absence, layoffs, or inability to work because of illness or injury. The employer must continue paying the premium, and the coverage may be continued only for a relatively short period of time, such as 3 months.

Employee benefit plans—particularly those providing health and life insurance coverage—make some provision for the continuation of coverage on employees whose active employment terminates due to disability.

TYPES OF EMPLOYEE BENEFITS

The types of employee benefits that are discussed in this chapter fall into three basic categories. The first is traditional group insurance plans for which the employer typically pays a major portion of the cost of an employee's coverage. These include medical expense insurance, 90 percent of which is obtained by Americans under age 65 through the workplace. For this reason there was little discussion of this topic in chapter 2. For the most part, the medical expense coverage available to persons outside the workplace is similar to employer-provided coverage. However, the deductibles and copayments are often higher, and there may be somewhat more restrictive exclusions.

There is also a discussion of other types of traditional group insurance coverage—life insurance, disability income insurance, dental insurance, and vision insurance.

The second category of employee benefits is voluntary benefit plans. And finally, there is a discussion of selected miscellaneous fringe benefits that take the form of payments for time not worked, payments to employees, and payments to cover the cost of specific services to employees.

The discussion of these benefits will focus on their nature and any resulting taxation to employees. As will be seen, taxation is not necessarily consistent from benefit to benefit and may or may not be affected by nondiscrimination rules that apply to many types of plans. It should be noted that while the tax treatment of benefits varies for an employee, the cost of providing benefits is almost always tax deductible to an employer as long as the overall compensation of the employee is reasonable.

Medical Expense Insurance

Medical expense insurance is arguably the most important employee benefit to most employees. It is also the single most expensive benefit for employers to provide. It is important for a financial advisor to understand a client's coverage in order to determine whether it is adequate. If not, supplemental coverages can sometimes be obtained. In addition, most employees have an option of two or more types of plans from which they can select. The advisor needs to understand the differences among these plans in order to properly advise clients. It is also important for the advisor to understand the alternatives that are available when a client's employment and/or insurance coverage terminates.

Types of Plans

major medical plans

Until the 1980s, most employees and their families were provided coverage under traditional *major medical plans*. These plans provide protection against catastrophic medical expenses, subject to some exclusions and limitations. Employees, however, must often assume part of their medical expenses because of deductibles and percentage participation (sometimes called coinsurance).

Example: Mary is covered under a major medical plan that has an annual deductible of $200 and a provision that requires her to assume 20 percent of her medical

> expenses in excess of the deductible. If she incurs annual medical bills of $2,200, she will have out-of-pocket costs of $600 (the deductible amount and 20 percent of her remaining $2,000 of charges). Thus, Mary will be reimbursed for only $1,600 of her medical expenses.

Although the example shows a deductible and percentage participation provision that applies to all expenses, some major medical contracts waive this cost sharing for certain types of medical expense. There is also often a maximum out-of-pocket amount (usually in the range of $1,000 to $3,000) that the insured is responsible for in any given year.

Traditional major medical plans, often referred to as indemnity contracts, require insureds to file claims for reimbursement and limit the reimbursement to reasonable and customary charges. The portion of any charge that exceeds this limit is not paid by the insurer, and the medical provider can (and usually) does bill the insured for this amount. Each insurer determines which is reasonable and customary, based on the range of fees normally charged for a given procedure by medical practitioners of similar training and experience within a geographic region.

One of the main attractions of traditional major medical plans is that the insured has complete freedom to use the physician or hospital of his or her own choice.

Historically, traditional major medical plans did little to control medical costs, monitor quality of care, or encourage preventive care. As a result, the 1970s saw the first large scale attempts to promote managed health care. Today, it is estimated that more than 90 percent of employees with medical expense insurance are covered under managed care plans. Two reasons account for this growth, but both are related to the fact that managed care plans are less expensive than traditional major medical plans. First, many employers offer only managed health care plans to their employees. And, second, employees who elect traditional major medical coverage when it is available are typically required to pay a larger share of the premium cost.

Despite reports of backlash over managed care, surveys indicate that a large majority of Americans are satisfied with their own managed care plans. In many cases, this backlash is aimed at the health care system in general. In other cases, criticism is aimed primarily at the tight controls over health care that are imposed by health maintenance organizations. However, many employees are covered by other types of managed care plans.

managed care plan

While variations exist, it is generally acknowledged that a true *managed care plan* should have five basic characteristics:

- controlled access to providers. It is difficult to control costs if participants have unrestricted access to physicians and hospitals. Managed care plans attempt to encourage or force participants to use predetermined providers. Because a major portion of medical expenses results from referrals to specialists, managed care plans tend to use primary care physicians as gatekeepers to determine the necessity and appropriateness of specialty care. By limiting the number of providers, managed care plans are better able to control costs by negotiating provider fees.
- comprehensive case management. Successful plans perform utilization review at all levels. This involves reviewing a case to determine the type of treatment necessary, monitoring ongoing care, and reviewing the appropriateness and success of treatment after it has been given.
- preventive care. Managed care plans encourage preventive care and the attainment of healthier lifestyles.
- risk sharing. Managed care plans are most successful if providers share in the financial consequences of medical decisions. Newer managed care plans have contractual guarantees to encourage cost-effective care. For example, a physician who minimizes diagnostic tests may receive a bonus. Ideally, such an arrangement will eliminate unnecessary tests, but not discourage tests that should be performed.
- high-quality care. A managed care plan will not be well received and selected by participants if there is a perception of inferior or inconvenient medical care. In the past, too little attention was paid to this aspect of cost containment. Newer managed care plans not only select providers more carefully but also monitor the quality of care on a continuing basis.

health maintenance organizations (HMOs)
preferred-provider organizations (PPOs)
point-of-service (POS) plans

Within this framework, three general types of managed care arrangements have developed: *health maintenance organizations (HMOs), preferred-provider organizations (PPOs),* and *point-of-service (POS) plans.*

HMOs. HMOs were the first type of managed care plan to be widely used. They are generally regarded as organized systems of health care that provide a comprehensive array of medical services on a prepaid basis to voluntarily enrolled persons living within a specified geographic region. HMOs act like insurance companies in that they finance health care. However, unlike insurance companies, they also deliver medical services. HMOs can be either profit or not-for-profit organizations. They may be sponsored or owned by insurance companies, Blue Cross and Blue Shield plans, consumer groups, physicians, hospitals, labor unions, or private investors.

HMOs have several characteristics that distinguish them from traditional medical expense contracts:

- comprehensive care. HMOs offer their subscribers a comprehensive package of health care services, generally including benefits for outpatient services as well as for hospitalization. Subscribers usually get these services at no cost except the periodically required premium. However, in some cases a copayment, such as $10 or $15 per physician's visit, may be imposed for certain services. HMOs emphasize preventive care and provide such services as routine physicals and immunizations.
- delivery of medical services. HMOs provide for the delivery of medical services, which in some cases are performed by salaried physicians and other personnel employed by the HMO who accept the HMOs reimbursement as payment in full. Although this approach is in contrast to the traditional fee-for-service delivery system of medical care, some HMOs do contract with providers on a fee-for-service basis. Providers deal directly with the HMO for reimbursement, eliminating the need for subscribers to file claims.
  - Subscribers are required to obtain their care from providers of medical services who are affiliated with the HMO. Since HMOs may operate in a geographic region no larger than a single metropolitan area, this requirement may result in limited coverage for subscribers if treatment is received elsewhere. Most HMOs do have "out-of-area coverage" but only in the case of medical emergencies.
  - HMOs emphasize treatment by primary care physicians to the greatest extent possible and subscribers must usually select a primary care physician to whom they will go for medical treatment. These practitioners fulfill a gatekeeper function and historically have controlled access to specialists. The traditional HMO covers services provided by a specialist only if the primary care physician recommends the specialist, who may be a fellow employee in a group-practice plan or a physician who has a contract with the HMO. The subscriber has little or no say regarding the specialist selected. This has been one of the more controversial aspects of HMOs and one that has discouraged larger enrollment. In response to consumer concerns, many HMOs now make the process of seeing a specialist easier.

- cost control. HMOs emphasize control of medical expenses. By providing and encouraging preventive care, HMOs attempt to detect and treat medical conditions at an early stage, thereby avoiding expensive medical treatment in the future.
    - The use of salaried employees by many HMOs may also result in lower costs since the physician or other care provider has no financial incentive to prescribe additional, and possibly unnecessary, treatment. In fact, the physicians and other medical professionals in some HMOs may receive bonuses if the HMO operates efficiently and has a surplus.

PPOs. PPOs have evolved as a middle ground between the tight controls of HMOs over health care and the lack of controls by traditional major medical plans. Most are owned by insurance companies, but some are owned by HMOs to diversify their health plan portfolios. Still others are owned by private investors, physicians, hospitals, and third-party benefit administrators.

A PPO is a benefit plan that contracts with preferred providers to obtain lower costs for plan members. PPOs typically differ from HMOs in several respects. First, the preferred providers are generally paid on a fee-for-service basis as their services are used. However, fees are usually subject to a schedule that is the same for all similar providers under PPO contracts and providers may have an incentive to control utilization through bonus arrangements. Second, employees and their dependents are not required to use the practitioners or facilities that contract with the PPO; rather, a choice can be made each time medical care is needed, and benefits are also paid for care provided by nonnetwork providers. Employees are offered incentives to use network providers; these incentives include lower or reduced deductibles and copayments as well as increased benefits, such as preventive health care. Third, most PPOs do not use a primary care physician as a gatekeeper; employees do not need referrals to see specialists.

The basic benefit structure of a PPO is very similar to that of the traditional major medical contract. The most significant difference is that PPOs include a higher level of benefits for care received from network providers than for care received from nonnetwork providers. Many PPOs have extensive networks of preferred providers, particularly in the geographic areas in which they operate; hence there is little reason to seek care outside the network. However, other PPOs have more limited networks, so their subscribers' need for treatment from nonnetwork providers is greater.

A PPO may have annual deductibles that apply separately to network and nonnetwork charges—for example, $100 and $250, respectively.

However, many PPOs have no deductible for network charges or waive this deductible for certain medical services, such as emergency or preventive care. Small copayments are usually required for physicians visits and prescription drugs.

POS Plans. A newer and fast-growing type of managed care arrangement is the point-of-service (POS) plan. A POS plan is a hybrid arrangement that combines aspects of a traditional HMO and a PPO. With a POS plan, participants in the plan elect, at the time medical treatment is needed, whether to receive treatment within the plan's tightly managed network, usually an HMO, or outside the network. Expenses received outside the network are reimbursed in the same manner as described earlier for nonnetwork services under PPO plans.

There are two basic types of POS plans: the open-ended HMO and the gatekeeper PPO. An open-ended HMO is by far the most common form and is the HMO industry's response to the demand for more consumer flexibility in the choice of providers, even though it increases costs somewhat. It essentially consists of traditional HMO coverage with an endorsement for nonnetwork coverage. It can take the basic form of any of the HMOs previously described. However, at any time a subscriber can elect to go outside the HMO network of medical care providers.

It can be argued that any PPO is actually a POS plan. However, the normal usage of the term POS implies a higher degree of managed care than is found in most PPOs. A gatekeeper PPO requires the PPO participant to elect a primary care physician in the manner of an HMO participant. This physician acts as a gatekeeper to control utilization and refer members to specialists within the PPO network. However, at any time care is needed, a covered person can elect to go outside the network.

Under some POS plans, a covered person can go outside the plan's network without informing the plan of this fact. In other POS plans, the person must notify the gatekeeper that such treatment will be sought.

A Comparison of Plan Types. While variations within each type of medical expense plan exist, some generalizations can be made. These are summarized in table 3-1. The degree of managed care increases as one moves from left to right in the table. However, the cost of the plans, on the average, decreases as the degree of managed care increases. In addition, a higher degree of managed care is generally associated with lower annual premium increases by a plan.

TABLE 3-1
Comparison of Health Insurance Plans

	Traditional Major Medical Contracts	PPOs	POS Plans	HMOs
Provider Choice	Unlimited	Unlimited, but benefits are greater if network provider is used	Unlimited, but benefits are greater if network provider is used	Network of providers must be used; care from nonnetwork providers covered only in emergencies
Use of Gatekeeper	None	None	Used for care of network specialists	Used for access to specialists
Out-of-pocket Costs	Deductibles and percentage participation	Deductibles and percentage participation, which are lower if network providers are used; may have small copayment for network services	Small copayments for network services; deductibles and percentage participation for nonnetwork services	Small copayments for some services
Utilization Review	Traditionally little, but a few techniques are likely to be used now	More than traditional plans, but less than HMOs; network provider may be subject to some controls	Like HMOs for network services; like PPOs for nonnetwork services	Highest degree of review, including financial incentives and disincentives for providers
Preventive Care	Little covered other than that required by law	Usually more coverage than traditional major medical plan but less coverage than HMOs and POS plans	Covered	Covered
Responsibility for Claims Filings	Covered person	Plan providers for network services; covered person for nonnetwork services	Plan providers for network services; covered person for nonnetwork service	Plan providers

Chapter 3 Employee Benefits Planning

Plan Provisions

Medical expense plans have numerous provisions that concern financial advisors. This section briefly looks at eligibility, covered expenses, coordination of benefits, and cost sharing.

Eligibility. Typically, the same medical expense benefits that are provided for an employee are also available for that employee's dependents. The term dependents most commonly refers to an employee's spouse who is not legally separated from the employee and any unmarried dependent children (including stepchildren, adopted children, and children born out of wedlock) under the age of 19. However, coverage is usually provided for children to age 23 or 26 if they are full-time students. In addition, coverage may also continue (and is required to be continued in some states) for children who are incapable of earning their own living because of a physical or mental infirmity.

Over the last few years, an increasing number of employers are including domestic partners in the definition of dependent.

Covered Expenses. Most medical expense plans today provide very comprehensive coverage. However, there are certain exclusions and limitations.

The following are common exclusions:

- care provided by family members or when no charge would be made for the care received in the absence of the insurance contract
- cosmetic surgery, except as required for breast reconstruction by the Women's Health and Cancer Rights Act or unless such surgery is to correct a condition resulting from either an accidental injury or a birth defect
- convalescent, custodial, or rest care
- dental care except for (1) treatment required because of injury to natural teeth and (2) hospital and surgical charges associated with hospital confinement for dental surgery
- eye refraction, or the purchase or fitting of eyeglasses or hearing aids.
- expenses either paid or eligible for payment under Medicare or other federal, state, or local medical expense programs
- experimental services

preexisting condition

Most major medical plans also contain an exclusion for preexisting conditions. A *preexisting condition* is typically defined as any illness or injury for which a covered person received medical care during the 3-month period prior to the person's effective date of coverage. Usually, the condition is no longer considered preexisting after the earlier of (1) a period of 3 consecutive months during which no medical care is received for the condition or (2) 12 months of coverage under the contract by the individual.

It is not unusual, particularly with large employers, for the preexisting-conditions clause to be waived for newly hired employees. In addition, the Health Insurance Portability and Accountability Act (HIPAA) limits the use of preexisting-conditions provisions with respect to newborn or adopted children. Preexisting-conditions provisions also cannot apply to pregnancy. HIPAA also requires the preexisting conditions period to be reduced by the time a new employee had coverage under a prior employer-provided or individual medical expense plan as long as the gap in coverage was less than 63 days.

Limitations also exist for certain types of benefits. Some examples that may be found include

- hospital room charges limited to the cost of semi-private accommodations
- dollar limits on benefits (if available) for extended care facilities, home health care, and hospice care
- 50 percent percentage participation for infertility treatment
- limitations on the number of days of treatment or higher cost sharing for treatment of mental illness, alcoholism, and drug addition

Coordination of Benefits. In recent years, the percentage of individuals having duplicate group medical expense coverage has increased substantially and is estimated to be about 10 percent.

In the absence of any provisions to the contrary, group medical expense plans are obligated to provide benefits in cases of duplicate coverage as if no other coverage exists. However, to prevent individuals from receiving benefits that exceed their actual expenses, most group medical expense plans contain a *coordination-of-benefits (COB) provision,* under which priorities are established for the payment of benefits by each plan covering an individual.

coordination-of-benefits (COB) provision

As a general rule, coverage under multiple policies will allow a person to receive benefits equal to 100 percent of his or her medical expenses. The coverage determined to be primary will pay as if no other coverage exists. If some expenses are not reimbursed (because, for example, of deductibles, copayments, or policy limitations), the secondary coverage will pick up the balance as long as it is less than what that coverage would have paid if it were the only coverage in existence.

While the rules are complex, a few generalizations can be made:

- Coverage as an employee is usually primary to coverage as a dependent.
- Coverage as an active employee is primary to coverage as a retiree.
- If children live in a two-parent household, the plan of the parent whose birthday falls earlier in the calendar year is primary.
- If children do not live with both parents, a court order may spell out which parent's plan is primary. In the absence of such an order, the plan of the parent with custody is primary; the plan of a stepparent who lives with the custodial parent is secondary; and the plan of the parent without custody is tertiary.

Cost Sharing. Many employers pay the majority of an employee's medical expense coverage. In addition, a share of dependent coverage is often paid by the employer.

defined-contribution medical expense plan

The beginning of the new decade has seen considerable interest in the concept of the *defined-contribution medical expense plan.* A definition of a defined-contribution plan is difficult because the term has been used in many different ways. However, the common thread is that the employer makes a fixed contribution, which the employee can use to "purchase" his or her own coverage. This practice enables an employer to control costs because the amount of the contribution can remain level from year to year or increase at any rate an employer chooses.

Even though some defined-contribution approaches for medical expense plans are in their infancy or still in the proposal stage, defined-contribution medical expense plans have actually been used for some time. For example, many employers make several medical expense plans available to their employees, such as an HMO, a PPO, and a traditional major medical plan. The employer contribution to the cost of coverage for each plan may be a dollar amount that is pegged to a fixed percentage of the cost of the HMO plan. Therefore, an employee who elects a more expensive PPO or major medical plan will need to make a greater out-of-pocket contribution for his or her coverage than if the HMO had been selected.

Newer types of defined-contribution medical expense plans, often referred to as consumer-directed health care, have features other than just fixed employer contributions. At a minimum, these approaches force employees to make financial decisions involving their health care. For example, an employer provides employees with a high-deductible health plan (HDHP) that has a $5,000 per year deductible. The employer also contributes up to $2,900 (as indexed for 2008) per year to a health savings account (HSA), from which the employee can make withdrawals to pay medical expenses that are not covered because of the high deductible. The employee can carry forward any unused amount in the account and add it to next year's employer contribution. Such a plan gives the employee an immediate incentive to purchase medical care wisely because, if the amount in the account is exceeded, the employee will have to pay medical expenses out of his or her own pocket until the deductible is satisfied. The plan may incorporate one or more preferred-provider type networks to give employees choices in how their account balances are spent.

Additional Benefits for Executives

Some employers have plans that provide additional medical (and dental) benefits for executives. While this group of employees is most likely to be able to pay for the expenses covered by such plans, these supplemental benefits are frequently viewed as a way of attracting and retaining key employees.

From a purely administrative standpoint, it would be relatively easy to self-fund these benefits, but the benefits, as explained later under the section on federal taxation, would most likely represent taxable income to employees. As a result, these additional executive benefits are usually insured as either a separate coverage or as a rider to the plan covering other employees.

This type of plan usually covers the executives and their dependents. Benefits almost always include coverage to provide reimbursement for deductibles, percentage participation, and copayments under the employer's plan that applies to all covered employees. It is also common to find coverage for annual physicals and the extra cost of private hospital rooms. In addition, there frequently is extra coverage, though possibly limited to an annual maximum such as $10,000, for expenses such as mental or emotional treatment, hearing care, vision care, and dental work.

Taxation

Employer contributions for an employee's or dependents medical expense coverage do not create any income tax liability for an employee. Moreover, benefits are not taxable to an employee except when they exceed any medical expenses incurred. The amount of any employer contribution for an employee's domestic partner, however, typically represents taxable income to the employee since the employee's domestic partner generally would not qualify under IRS rules as the employee's dependent.

One major difference between group medical expense coverage and other forms of group insurance is that a portion of an employee's contribution for coverage may be tax deductible as a medical expense if that individual itemizes his or her income tax deductions. Under the Internal Revenue Code, individuals are allowed to deduct certain medical care expenses (including dental expenses) for which no reimbursement was received. This deduction is limited to expenses (including amounts paid for insurance) that exceed 7.5 percent of the person's adjusted gross income.

The tax situation may be different if an employer provides medical expense benefits through a self-funded plan (referred to in the Internal Revenue Code as a self-insured medical reimbursement plan), under which employers either (1) pay the providers of medical care directly or (2) reimburse employees for their medical expenses. If a self-funded plan meets certain nondiscrimination requirements for highly compensated employees, the employer can deduct benefit payments as they are made, and the employee will have no taxable income. If a plan is discriminatory, the employer will still receive an income tax deduction. However, all or a portion of the benefits received by highly compensated employees, but not by other employees, will be treated as taxable income.

Coverage after Termination of Employment

A concern of any employee is the effect of termination of employment on his or her medical expense coverage—whether it be by voluntarily quitting a job, being fired or laid off, or retiring. There are many provisions in medical expense plans that address these issues. They include COBRA, conversion, portability, and postretirement coverage.

COBRA

COBRA. The Consolidated Omnibus Budget Reconciliation Act of 1985 (*COBRA*) requires that group health plans allow employees and dependents covered under the plans to elect to have their current health insurance coverage extended at group rates for up to 36 months following a "qualifying event." The COBRA definition of group health plans is broad enough to include medical expense plans, dental plans, and vision care plans, regardless of whether benefits are self-funded or provided through other entities such as insurance companies or managed care organizations.

The act applies only to employers who had the equivalent of 20 or more full-time employees on a typical business day during the preceding calendar year; however, certain church-related plans and plans of the federal government are exempt from the act.

Under the act, each of the following is a qualifying event if it results in the loss of coverage by an employee or dependent:

- the death of the covered employee
- the termination of the employee for most any reason. This includes quitting, retiring, or being fired for anything other than gross misconduct.
- a reduction of the employee's hours so that the employee or dependent is ineligible for coverage

- the divorce or legal separation of the covered employee and his or her spouse
- for spouses and children, the employee's eligibility for Medicare
- a child's ceasing to be an eligible dependent under the plan

The act specifies that a person losing coverage is entitled to elect continued coverage without providing evidence of insurability. Coverage can continue until the earliest of the following:

- 18 months for employees and dependents when the employee's employment has terminated or coverage has been terminated because of a reduction in hours. This period is extended to 29 months if the Social Security Administration determines that the beneficiary was or became totally disabled at any time during the first 60 days of COBRA coverage.
- 36 months for other events
- the date the plan terminates for all employees
- the date the person subsequently becomes entitled to Medicare or becomes covered (as either an employee or dependent) under another group health plan, provided the group health plan does not contain an exclusion or limitation with respect to any preexisting condition

The cost of the continued coverage may be passed on to the employee or dependent, but the cost cannot exceed 102 percent of the cost to the plan for a similarly situated active employee. The one exception to this rule occurs for months 19 through 29 if an employee is disabled, in which case the premium can then be as high as 150 percent.

Conversion. Medical expense plans often contain a conversion provision, whereby most covered persons whose group coverage terminates are allowed to purchase individual medical expense coverage without evidence of insurability and without any limitation of benefits for preexisting conditions. Covered persons commonly have 31 days from the date of termination of the group coverage to exercise this conversion privilege, and coverage is then effective retroactively to the date of termination.

A person who is eligible for both the conversion privilege and the right to continue the group insurance coverage under COBRA has two choices when eligibility for coverage terminates. He or she can either elect to convert under the provisions of the policy or elect to continue the group coverage. If the latter choice is made, the COBRA rules specify that the person must again be eligible to convert to an individual policy after the maximum continuation-of-coverage period ceases.

The use of the word conversion is often a misnomer. In actuality, a person whose coverage terminates is only given the right to purchase a contract on an individual basis at individual rates. Some plans offer a conversion policy that is written by another entity. For example, an HMO or self-funded plan might enter into a contractual arrangement with an insurance company.

Portability. The Health Insurance Portability and Accountability Act (HIPAA) makes it easier for individuals who lose employer-provided medical expense coverage to find alternative coverage in the individual marketplace. The purpose of the federal legislation is to encourage states to adopt their own mechanisms to achieve this goal and most states have complied. The federal rules apply in a state only if the state does not have its own plan. The state alternative must provide a choice of health insurance coverage to all eligible individuals and impose no preexisting-conditions restrictions.

Postretirement Coverage. Many employers continue coverage on retired employees. Although coverage can also be continued for retirees' dependents, it is often limited only to spouses. Retired employees under age 65 usually have the same coverage as the active employees have. However, coverage for employees aged 65 or older (if included under the same plan) may be provided under a Medicare carve-out or a Medicare supplement.

With a Medicare carve-out plan, benefits are reduced to the extent that benefits are payable under Medicare for the same expenses. As an alternative, some employers use a Medicare supplement that provides benefits for certain specific expenses not covered under Medicare. These include (1) the portion of expenses that is not paid by Medicare because of deductibles, percentage participation, or copayments and (2) certain expenses excluded by Medicare, such as prescription drugs. Such a supplement may or may not provide benefits similar to those available under a carve-out plan.

Because of changes in accounting rules for retiree medical expense coverage and increasing benefit costs, many employers have lowered or eliminated retiree benefits or are considering such a change. However, there are legal uncertainties as to whether benefits that have been promised to retirees can be eliminated or reduced. Many employers also feel that there is a moral obligation to continue these benefits. As a result most employers are not altering plans for current retirees or active employees who are eligible to retire. Rather, the changes apply to future retirees only. These changes, which seem to be running the gamut, include the following:

- the elimination of benefits for future retirees
- the shifting of more of the cost burden to future retirees by reducing benefits. Such a reduction may be accomplished by providing lower benefit maximums, covering fewer types of expenses, or increasing copayments.
- adding or increasing retiree sharing of premium costs after retirement
- shifting to a defined-contribution approach to funding retiree benefits. For example, an employer might agree to pay $5 per month toward the cost of coverage after retirement for each year of service by an employee.

Life Insurance

With the exception of paid holidays and vacations, life insurance is the most commonly provided employee benefit. Approximately 95 percent of the coverage in force is *group term life insurance*. This is yearly renewable term insurance that provides death benefits only and no build up of cash values. Because death benefits paid under a self-funded life insurance plan are taxable to beneficiaries, life insurance plans are almost always fully insured. The ways in which this group coverage differs from individually purchased policies are discussed with respect to benefit schedule, termination of coverage, and taxation. Additional coverages that can be added to group term life insurance are also described. Finally, there is a brief discussion of group universal life insurance.

*Marginal note: **group term life insurance***

Benefit Schedule

The benefits under a life insurance plan may be based on a multiple of earnings or specified dollar amount. Benefits are also typically reduced for older employees.

Multiple-of-Earnings Schedules. The majority of group term life insurance plans use an earnings schedule under which the amount of life insurance is determined as a multiple (or percentage) of each employee's earnings. For example, the amount of life insurance for each employee may be twice (200 percent of) the employee's annual earnings. Most plans use a multiple between one and two, but higher and lower multiples are occasionally used. The amount of insurance may be subject to a maximum benefit, such as $200,000. For purposes of the benefit schedule, an employee's earnings usually consist of base salary only and do not include additional compensation like overtime pay or bonuses.

Specified-Dollar-Amount Schedules. There are numerous types of benefit schedules that base benefits on specified dollar amounts. They include flat-benefit schedules and schedules that vary by earnings or position.

By far the most common type of specified-dollar-amount schedule is the flat-benefit schedule, under which the same amount of life insurance is provided for all employees regardless of salary or position. This type of benefit schedule is commonly used in plans covering hourly paid employees, particularly when benefits are negotiated with a union.

Some employers use schedules that have brackets based on income or position. Everyone within the bracket receives the same flat amount of coverage, but the amount varies by bracket, usually in a way that benefits higher-paid employees. For example, employees earning less than $30,000 might receive $20,000 of life insurance; employees earning between $30,000 and $69,999 might receive $75,000 of life insurance, and employees earning $70,000 or more might receive $200,000 of life insurance.

Reduction in Benefits. Group life insurance plans often provide for a reduction in benefits for active employees who reach a certain age, commonly 65 to 70. Such a reduction, which is due to the high cost of providing benefits for older employees, is specified in the benefit schedule of a plan. Any reduction in the amount of life insurance for active employees is subject to the provisions of the Age Discrimination in Employment Act.

Benefit reductions fall into three categories: (1) a reduction to a flat amount of insurance; (2) a percentage reduction, such as to 65 percent of the amount of insurance that was previously provided; or (3) a gradual reduction over a period of years (for example, a 10 percent reduction in coverage each year until a minimum benefit amount is reached).

Termination of Coverage

The termination of group life insurance coverage is usually accompanied by a conversion provision. In some cases the coverage is also portable.

Conversion. All group term insurance contracts covering employees contain a conversion privilege that gives any employee whose coverage ceases the right to convert to an individual insurance policy without evidence of insurability. The conversion policy, however, must usually be a cash value policy rather than term insurance and the conversion is at attained-age rates.

Portability of Term Coverage. A few, but an increasing number of, insurers issue contracts with a portability provision that allows employees whose coverage terminates to continue coverage at group rates in much the same manner as is found in voluntary employee-pay-all plans. The rates are age based and will continue to increase as an insured person ages.

Added Coverages

Group term insurance contracts often provide additional insurance benefits in the form of (1) supplemental life insurance, (2) accidental death and dismemberment insurance, and (3) dependent life insurance. These added benefits which are also forms of term insurance can be provided for all employees insured under the basic group term contract or may be limited to certain classes of employees.

Supplemental Life Insurance. The majority of group life insurance plans enable all or certain classes of employees to purchase additional amounts of life insurance. Generally, the employer provides a basic amount of life insurance to all eligible employees on a noncontributory basis. Although the employee may pay the entire cost of the supplemental coverage, either state laws that require employer contributions or insurance company underwriting practices often result in the employer's paying a portion of the cost.

The amount of supplemental coverage available is specified in a benefit schedule. Under some plans, an employee must purchase the full amount of coverage; under other plans, an employee may purchase a portion of the coverage. Table 3-2 is an example of a benefit schedule for a basic-plus-supplemental life insurance plan.

Because giving employees the right to choose their benefit amounts leads to adverse selection, stringent underwriting requirements usually accompany supplemental coverage. These often include requiring individual evidence of insurability, except possibly when the additional coverage is modest. Higher rates may be charged for the supplemental insurance than for the basic coverage.

TABLE 3-2
Benefit Schedule for a Basic-Plus-Supplemental Life Plan

Type of Coverage	Amount of Life Insurance
Basic insurance	1 times salary
Supplemental insurance	1/2, 1, 1 1/2, or 2 times salary, subject to a maximum (including basic insurance) of $250,000

> **FOCUS ON ETHICS**
> **Focusing on the Client's Need**
>
> One of the charges frequently made against financial advisors is that whole life policies are often proposed when additional insurance in the form of supplemental group term coupled with a basic amount of employer-provided group term would have provided better results for the client. The logic of this criticism is based on the fact that the advisor earns a commission on whole life and, therefore, emphasizes it in his or her planning.
>
> The real issue is the importance of clearly focusing on the client's need. Consider a single earner family with young children and a limited budget. Their primary life insurance need is to replace the breadwinner's income in case of premature death. The amount of the insurance need is calculable and the funds available are limited. If a financial advisor encourages purchase of an insufficient amount of cash value whole life insurance instead of a sufficient amount of lower-cost supplemental group term insurance, that advisor has ignored the client's need. The advisor would then have traded compassion, integrity, and professionalism for commissions.
>
> If a client died and was underinsured because the advisor had failed to focus on the client's need, the result would be more than an ethical lapse. It would be a financial catastrophe for an entire family.

accidental death and dismemberment (AD&D) insurance

Accidental Death and Dismemberment Insurance. Many group life insurance contracts contain an *accidental death and dismemberment (AD&D) insurance* provision that gives additional benefits if an employee dies accidentally or suffers certain types of injuries.

Under the usual form of AD&D insurance, an employee eligible for group life insurance coverage (and electing the life insurance coverage if it is contributory) automatically has the AD&D coverage if the employer adds it or if the insurer includes it as a standard part of its group term life insurance contract. Under the typical AD&D rider, the insurance company pays an additional amount of insurance that is equal to the amount of coverage under the basic group life insurance contract (referred to as the principal sum) if an employee dies as a result of accidental bodily injuries while he or she is covered under the policy. In addition to an accidental death benefit, the benefit schedule shown in table 3-3 is often used for certain specific types of injuries.

In some cases, the AD&D rider is written to provide the same benefits for any accident covered under the contract. However, it is not unusual to have a higher level of death benefits (for example, three times the principal sum) for accidents that occur while the employee is traveling on business for the employer.

Death benefits are paid in accordance with the beneficiary provision of the group life insurance contract, and dismemberment benefits are paid to the employee.

TABLE 3-3
Benefit Schedule for Dismemberment Injuries

Type of Injury	Benefit Amount
Loss of (including loss of use of):	
Both hands or both feet	The principal sum
The sight of both eyes	The principal sum
One hand and sight of one eye	The principal sum
One foot and sight of one eye	The principal sum
One foot and one hand	The principal sum
One hand	One-half the principal sum
One foot	One-half the principal sum
The sight of one eye	One-half the principal sum

For competitive reasons, some insurers make available a number of additional benefits for purchase by the employer if an employee is injured or killed in a covered accident. Some of these additional benefits include

- a benefit to help cover the costs of the employer to make worksite adaptations that are necessitated by the Americans with Disabilities Act to accommodate a disabled employee
- a benefit to return an injured employee or the body of a deceased employee home if death or disability occurs elsewhere
- rehabilitation benefits for an injured employee
- monthly income benefits for an employee who is permanently disabled
- monthly income benefits for an employee who becomes a paraplegic or quadriplegic

dependent life insurance

Dependent Life Insurance. Some group life insurance contracts provide insurance coverage on the lives of employees' dependents. *Dependent life insurance* has been viewed as a method of giving the employee resources to meet the funeral and burial expenses associated with a dependent's death. Consequently, the employee is automatically the beneficiary. The employee also elects and pays for this coverage if it is contributory.

For purposes of dependent life insurance coverage, dependents are usually defined as an employee's spouse who is not legally separated from the employee and an employee's unmarried dependent children (including stepchildren and adopted children) who are over 14 days of age and younger than some specified age, commonly 19 or 21. To prevent adverse selection, an employee usually cannot select coverage on individual dependents. A few policies do allow an employee to elect coverage for the spouse only or for children only. If dependent coverage is selected, all dependents fitting the definition are insured. When dependent coverage is in effect for an employee, any new eligible dependents are automatically insured.

The amount of coverage for each dependent is usually quite modest. Employer contributions used to purchase more than $2,000 of coverage on a dependent result in the entire amount of coverage being taxable to the employee for purposes of federal taxation. However, amounts in excess of $2,000 may be purchased with employee contributions without adverse tax consequences. In some cases, the same amount of coverage is provided for all dependents; in other cases, a larger amount is provided for the spouse than for the children. Table 3-4 is an example of a benefit schedule under dependent coverage.

TABLE 3-4
Benefit Schedule for Dependent Coverage

Class	Amount of Insurance
Spouse	50% of the employee's insured amount, subject to a maximum of $5,000
Dependent children: at least 14 days old but less than 6 months 6 months or older	$ 500 $1,000

A single premium applies to the dependent coverage for each employee and is unrelated to the number of dependents. In some cases, the premium may vary, depending on the age of the employee (but not the dependents), but more commonly it is the same amount for all employees regardless of age.

Taxation

Section 79

Section 79 of the Internal Revenue Code (Sec. 79) gives favorable tax treatment to life insurance plans that qualify as group term insurance, and most employer plans are established to meet these requirements.

General Tax Rules. Under Sec. 79, the cost of the first $50,000 of employer-provided coverage is not taxed to the employee. The cost of coverage in excess of $50,000, minus any employee contributions for the entire amount of coverage, represents taxable income to the employee. For purposes of Sec. 79, the cost of this excess coverage is determined by a government table called the Uniform Premium Table I (table 3-5).

TABLE 3-5	
Uniform Premium Table I	
Age	Cost per Month per $1,000 of Coverage
24 and under	$ .05
25–29	.06
30–34	.08
35–39	.09
40–44	.10
45–49	.15
50–54	.23
55–59	.43
60–64	.66
65–69	1.27
70 and over	2.06

To calculate the cost of an employee's coverage for one month of protection under a group term insurance plan, the Uniform Premium Table I cost shown for the employee's age bracket (based on the employee's attained age at the end of the tax year) is multiplied by the number of thousands in excess of 50 of group term insurance on the employee. For example, if an employee aged 57 (whose Table I monthly cost is $.43 per $1,000 of coverage) is provided with $150,000 of group term insurance, the employee's monthly cost (assuming no employee contributions) is calculated as follows:

Coverage provided	$150,000
Minus Sec. 79 exclusion	– 50,000
Amount subject to taxation	$100,000

Monthly cost = $.43/$1,000 x $100,000 = $43

The monthly costs are then totaled to obtain an annual cost. Assuming no change in the amount of coverage during the year, the annual cost is $43 x 12, or $516. Any employee contributions for the entire amount of coverage are deducted from the annual cost to determine the taxable income that an employee must report. If an employee contributes $.25 per month ($3 per year) per $1,000 of coverage, the employee's total annual contribution for $150,000 of coverage is $450. This reduces the amount reportable as taxable income from $516 to $66. Note that if the employee contribution is

$.30 rather than $.25 per month, the annual employee contribution in this example is $540. Because $540 exceeds the Table I cost, there is no imputed income.

Nondiscrimination Rules. Any plan that qualifies as group term insurance under Sec. 79 is subject to nondiscrimination rules, and the $50,000 exclusion is not available to key employees if a plan is discriminatory. Such a plan favors key employees in either eligibility or benefits. In addition, the value of the full amount of coverage for key employees, minus their own contributions, are considered taxable income, based on the greater of actual or Table I costs.

Taxation of Proceeds. In most instances, the death proceeds under a group term insurance contract do not result in any taxable income to the beneficiary if they are paid in a lump sum. If the proceeds are payable in installments over more than one taxable year, only the interest earnings attributable to the proceeds are included in the beneficiary's income for tax purposes.

Treatment of Added Coverages. If an employer contributes to the cost of supplemental life insurance, the amount of coverage provided is added to all other group term insurance for purposes of calculating the Uniform Premium Table I cost. Any premiums the employee pays for the supplemental coverage are included in the deduction used to determine the final taxable income.

Premiums paid for AD&D insurance are considered to be health insurance premiums rather than group term insurance premiums. Benefits paid to an employee under the dismemberment portion of the coverage are treated as benefits received under a health insurance contract and are income tax free. Death benefits received under the coverage are treated like death benefits received under group term life insurance.

Employer contributions for dependent life insurance do not result in taxable income to an employee as long as the value of the benefit is de minimis. This means that the value is so small that it is administratively impractical for the employer to account for the cost on a per-person basis. Dependent coverage of $2,000 or less on any person falls into this category. The IRS considers amounts of coverage in excess of $2,000 on any dependent to be more than de minimis. If more than $2,000 of coverage is provided for any dependent from employer contributions, the cost of the entire amount of coverage for that dependent (as determined by Uniform Premium Table I rates) is considered taxable income to the employee.

Group Universal Life Insurance

A small amount of group life insurance is written under plans that provide cash value life insurance—usually group universal life insurance. The nature of this form of life insurance is discussed in chapter 2.

Coverage Available. Under group universal life insurance plans, employees pay the full cost of their coverage and can generally elect amounts of pure insurance equal to varying multiples of their salaries, which typically start at one-half or one and range as high as three or five. There may be a minimum amount of coverage that must be purchased, such as $10,000. The maximum multiple an insurance company offers is influenced by such factors as the size of the group and the amount of insurance provided under the employer's basic employer-pay-all group term insurance plan. The initial premium, which is a function of an employee's age and death benefit, is frequently designed to accumulate a cash value at age 65 equal to approximately 20 percent of the total death benefit.

Options at Retirement and Termination. Several options are available to the retiring employee. First, the employee can continue the group insurance coverage like an active employee. However, if premium payments are continued, the insurance company bills the employee, probably on a quarterly basis. Because of the direct billing, the employee may also be subject to a higher monthly expense charge. Second, the employee can terminate the coverage and completely withdraw his or her accumulated cash value. Third, the employee can elect one of the policy settlement options for the liquidation of the cash value in the form of annuity income. Finally, some insurers allow the retiring employee to decrease the amount of pure insurance so that the cash value is adequate to keep the policy in force without any more premium payments. In effect, the employee then has a paid-up policy.

The same options are generally available to an employee who terminates employment prior to retirement.

Taxation. Group universal life insurance products are not designed to be policies of insurance under Sec. 79. Therefore, the tax treatment is the same to employees as if they had purchased a universal life insurance policy in the individual insurance marketplace.

Disability Income Insurance

The purpose of disability income insurance is to partially (and sometimes totally) replace the income of employees who are unable to work because of sickness or accident. Employers are less likely to provide employees with disability income benefits than with either life insurance or medical expense benefits. It is difficult to estimate the exact extent of disability coverage because often benefits are not insured and workers are sometimes covered under overlapping plans. However, a reasonable estimate would be that at least 75 percent of all employees have some form of short-term employer-provided protection, and only about 40 percent have protection for long-term disabilities.

Disability income protection consists of two distinct types of benefits:

- short-term disability income plans, which provide benefits for a limited period of time, usually 6 months or less. Benefits may be provided under uninsured sick-leave plans or under insured plans.
- long-term disability income insurance, which provides extended benefits (possibly for life) after an employee has been disabled for a period of time, frequently 6 months

Short-Term Plans

sick-pay plans

The majority of short-term disability income plans are uninsured and generally replace 100 percent of lost income for a limited period of time. These are commonly referred to as *sick-pay plans*.

Several approaches are used in determining the duration of benefits. The most traditional approach credits eligible employees with a certain amount of sick leave each year, such as 10 days. The majority of plans using this approach allow employees to accumulate unused sick leave up to some maximum amount, which rarely exceeds 6 months (sometimes specified as 180 days or 26 weeks). A variation of this approach is to credit employees with an amount of sick leave, such as one day, for each month of service.

In general, the employee's word is accepted for disabilities that last a week or less. Most plans have a provision that benefits for longer periods are paid only if the employee is under the care of a physician, who certifies that the employee is unable to work.

Some short-term plans are insured, either from the onset of an employee's disability or after an initial period of benefits under an employer's sick-pay plan. Benefits under insured plans vary from 50 to 100 percent of pay. In addition, there tends to be a more formal process of verifying that an employee is unable to perform his or her job.

Long-Term Plans

Long-term disability income plans are often limited to salaried employees, and have probationary periods of 3 months to one year. Most long-term disability contracts use a dual definition of disability. Under such a definition, benefits are paid for some period of time (usually 24 or 36 months) as long as an employee is unable to perform his or her regular occupation. After that time, benefits are paid only if the employee is unable to engage in any occupation for which he or she is qualified by reason of training, education, or experience.

A more recent definition of disability found in some long-term contracts contains an occupation test and an earnings test. Under the occupation test, a person is totally disabled if he or she meets the definition of disability as described in the previous paragraph. However, if the occupation test is not satisfied, a person is still considered disabled as long as an earnings test is satisfied. This means that the person's income has dropped by a stated percentage, such as 20 percent, because of injury or sickness. This newer definition makes a group insurance contract similar to an individual disability income policy that provides residual benefits.

Benefits. Long-term plans typically provide benefits that range from 50 to 70 percent of earnings, with 60 and 66 2/3 being the most prevalent percentages. Some plans also use a sliding scale, such as 66 2/3 percent of the first $4,000 of monthly earnings and 40 percent of earnings in excess of $4,000.

It is common for plans that determine benefits as a percentage of earnings to also place a maximum dollar amount on the benefit that is provided, regardless of earnings. For example, a plan may provide benefits equal to 66 2/3 percent of earnings, but might be subject to a monthly maximum that may vary from $3,000 or $4,000 for some small employers to as much as $6,000 to $10,000 for large employers. The purpose of such a maximum is to prevent the absolute benefit from being so high that an employee, by adjusting his or her lifestyle, could live comfortably on the disability income benefit and thus have no financial incentive to return to work.

Long-term disability income benefits may be paid for as short a period as 2 years or as long as the lifetime of the disabled employee. In a few cases, the length of the benefit period may differ, depending on whether the disability was a result of an accident or a sickness. At one time, it was common for long-term disability income benefits to stop at age 65, but this is no longer permissible under the Age Discrimination in Employment Act. Several different approaches are now used for older employees. The most common approach is to use a schedule such as the one in table 3-6.

TABLE 3-6
Disability Benefit Duration Schedule

Age at Commencement of Disability	Benefit Duration
59 and younger	To age 65
60–64	5 years
65–69	To age 70
70–74	1 year
75 and older	6 months

To minimize the possibility that an employee will receive total benefits higher than his or her predisability earnings, disability income plans commonly stipulate that benefits be integrated with other sources of disability income. The effect of this integration is to reduce (either totally or partially) the benefits payable under the disability income plan to the extent that certain other benefits are available. In general, the insurance laws or regulations of most states allow such reductions to be made as a result of benefits from social insurance programs (such as Social Security) and group insurance or retirement plans provided by the employer, but not as a result of benefits from individual disability income contracts unless they were purchased by the employer.

Supplemental Benefits. It is becoming increasingly common to find long-term disability income plans that provide employees with a base of employer-paid benefits and that allow each covered employee to purchase additional coverage at his or her own expense. For example, a plan may provide basic benefits of 50 percent of earnings and an option for an employee to increase this amount to 55, 66, or 70 percent of earnings. These buy-up (or supplemental) plans are becoming more popular, because employers feel the need to control the costs of benefits by shifting a greater burden of the cost to employees.

Some plans are also designed to "carve out" benefits for certain employees, frequently key executives. For example, an employer might design one plan to cover most of its employees, but top executives might be covered with another group plan that provides enhanced benefits in the form of a larger percentage of earnings and a more liberal definition of disability. Another variation of a carve-out plan would provide the executives with a lower benefit percentage than other employees receive, but it could provide supplemental benefits in the form of individual disability income policies. In addition to more favorable policy provisions, an individual policy carve-out plan might offer better rate guarantees and an overall higher benefit than a group plan could offer. Furthermore, the portability of the individual policy might be attractive to executives.

Taxation

Employer contributions for disability income insurance result in no taxable income to an employee. However, the payment of benefits under an insured plan or sick-leave plan may or may not result in the receipt of taxable income. To make this determination, it is necessary to look at whether the plan is fully contributory, noncontributory, or partially contributory.

Under a fully contributory plan, the entire cost is paid by employee contributions and benefits are received free of income taxation. Under a noncontributory plan, the employer pays the entire cost and benefits are included in an employee's gross income. However, the Internal Revenue Code provides a tax credit to persons who are permanently and totally disabled. The amount of the credit varies with filing status and phases out for persons with more than modest income, including nontaxable disability benefits.

Under a partially contributory plan, benefits attributable to employee contributions are received free of income taxation. Benefits attributable to employer contributions are includible in gross income, but employees may be eligible for the tax credit described previously.

Dental Insurance

dental insurance

Since the early 1970s, *dental insurance* has been one of the fastest-growing employee benefits. It has been estimated that in the past 25 years the percentage of employees who have dental coverage has grown from about 5 percent to more than 60 percent. More than 90 percent of firms with 500 or more employees make coverage available.

To a great extent, dental insurance plans have been patterned after medical expense plans, and they contain many similar, if not identical, provisions. Like medical expense plans, however, dental insurance has many variations. Dental plans may be limited to specific types of expenses, or they may be broad enough to cover virtually all dental expenses. In addition, coverage can be obtained from various types of providers, and benefits can be in the form of either services or cash payments.

Managed care has significantly affected the evolution of group dental insurance plans. However, this evolution has been somewhat different from that of medical expense plans. Group dental plans are more likely to provide benefits on a traditional fee-for-service basis. However, these traditional plans are also more likely to take a managed care approach to providing benefits. The most common example of this is the emphasis on providing a higher level of benefits for preventive care. It is interesting to note that as group dental plans have become more prevalent, the percentage of persons receiving preventive care has continued to increase. As a result, the percentage of persons needing care for more serious dental problems has continued to decrease.

Benefits

Most dental insurance plans pay for almost all types of dental expenses, but a particular plan may provide more limited coverage. One characteristic of dental insurance that is seldom found in medical expense plans is the inclusion of benefits for both routine diagnostic procedures (including oral examinations and X rays) and preventive dental treatment (including teeth cleaning and fluoride treatment). In fact, a few dental plans actually require periodic oral examinations as a condition for continuing eligibility.

In addition to benefits for diagnostic and preventive treatment, benefits for dental expenses may be provided for these categories of dental treatment:

- restoration (including fillings, crowns, and other procedures used to restore the functional use of natural teeth)
- oral surgery (including the extraction of teeth as well as other surgical treatment of diseases, injuries, and defects of the jaw)
- endodontics (treatment for diseases of the dental pulp within teeth, such as root canals)
- periodontics (treatment of diseases of the surrounding and supporting tissues of the teeth)
- prosthodontics (the replacement of missing teeth and structures by artificial devices, such as bridgework and dentures)
- orthodontics (the prevention and correction of dental and oral anomalies through the use of corrective devices, such as braces and retainers)

Most dental plans usually cover any expenses that arise from the first five categories listed above, and they may include benefits for orthodontics. Whatever benefits are provided may be on a scheduled basis, on a nonscheduled basis, or on some combination of the two.

Scheduled Plans. A scheduled dental plan provides benefits up to the amount specified in a fee schedule. Most scheduled dental plans provide benefits on a first-dollar basis and contain no deductibles or percentage participation. However, benefit maximums are often lower than reasonable-and-customary charges, thereby forcing employees to bear a portion of the costs of their dental services.

Although once common, scheduled dental plans are now used less frequently than either nonscheduled plans or combination plans.

Nonscheduled Plans. Nonscheduled dental plans, often called comprehensive dental plans, are the most common type of dental coverage. They resemble major medical expense contracts because dental expenses are paid on a reasonable-and-customary basis, subject to any exclusions or limitations in the contract.

Nonscheduled dental plans usually have both deductibles and percentage participation provisions. Although a single deductible and a single percentage participation percentage may apply to all dental services, the more common practice is to treat different classes of dental services in different ways. The typical nonscheduled dental plan breaks dental services into three broad categories: diagnostic and preventive services, basic services (such as fillings, oral surgery, periodontics, and endodontics), and major services (such as inlays, crowns, dentures, and orthodontics).

Diagnostic and preventive services are typically covered in full and are not subject to a deductible or percentage participation. (They are, however, subject to any other contract limitations.) The other two categories, however, are generally subject to an annual deductible (usually between $25 and $100 per person). In addition to the deductible, the cost of basic services may be subject to a low percentage participation (most often 20 percent), while major services are subject to a higher percentage (most often 50 percent).

Combination Plans. Combination plans contain features of both scheduled and nonscheduled plans. The typical combination plan covers diagnostic and preventive services on a reasonable-and-customary basis but uses a fee schedule for other dental services.

Taxation

The federal taxation of dental insurance premiums and benefits is the same as the taxation that is described earlier in this chapter for medical expense premiums and benefits.

Vision Insurance

More than half of the persons covered under employer-provided medical expense plans have some type of vision coverage provided by insurance companies, Blue Cross and Blue Shield plans, plans of state optometric associations, closed-panel HMO–type plans established by local providers of vision services, vision care PPOs, or third-party administrators. In most cases, however, the *vision benefit plan* is separate from the medical expense

vision benefit plan

plan. Despite concerns with rising benefit costs in recent years, vision care is one type of benefit that employers continue to add. Routine eye exams can result in better overall health care because certain other types of health problems—such as high blood pressure, diabetes, and kidney problems—are first discovered during the course of such routine exams. Proper vision correction can also result in fewer accidents and greater productivity by minimizing eyestrain and headaches.

Benefits are occasionally provided on a reasonable-and-customary basis or are subject to a flat benefit per year that may be applied to any covered expenses. Normally, however, a benefit schedule will be used that specifies the type and amounts of certain benefits and the frequency with which they will be provided. Table 3-7 is an example of one such schedule.

TABLE 3-7
Vision Care Benefit Schedule

Type of Benefit	Maximum Amount
Any 12-month Period	
Eye examination	$ 45
Lenses, pair	
single vision	45
bifocal	75
trifocal	125
lenticular	200
contact (when medically necessary)	300
contact (when not medically necessary)	125
Any 24-month Period	
Frames	60

Vision care plans do not pay benefits for necessary eye surgery or treatment of eye diseases because these are covered under the regular coverage of a medical expense plan. However, many vision plans make benefits available for elective procedures to improve vision, such as LASIK surgery. The benefit is usually in the form of a discounted fee from a provider who has a relationship with the plan.

Voluntary Insurance Benefits

As previously mentioned, voluntary benefit plans make benefits available through the workplace. However, the employer does not share in the cost. Even though an employee must pay the full cost of his or her own coverage, these plans have several characteristics that are popular with employees. These include

- payment through payroll deduction
- more liberal underwriting than for similar coverage in the individual insurance marketplace
- lower cost than in the individual marketplace. It is estimated that voluntary benefits on the average are about 10 percent less expensive than coverage purchased outside the employment relationship. Each individual's situation is unique, and it should not be assumed that a voluntary benefit plan will always be the least expensive way to purchase insurance. However, it is an alternative that should be evaluated.
- portability of coverage. Many voluntary benefit plans allow employees to continue coverage on a direct bill basis when they leave their employment.

Many of the insurance products previously described are also made available as voluntary benefits. In some cases, the voluntary benefits supplement a basic amount of employer-paid coverage. As already mentioned, additional life insurance coverage may be available on a voluntary basis. In addition, an employer may pay for a group long-term disability income plan that provides benefits equal to 50 percent of salary. Voluntary benefits then allow employees to purchase additional protection. Or the employer may pay for short-term disability income protection only and make long-term protection available under a voluntary plan. While many employers pay some or all of the cost of dental and vision benefits, other employers offer these benefits only as a voluntary benefit.

Some types of insurance are most commonly offered as voluntary benefits. Four of these benefits—legal expense insurance, long-term care insurance, supplemental medical expense insurance, and property and liability insurance—are briefly discussed.

Legal Expense Insurance

legal expense insurance

Legal expense insurance is designed to provide coverage for the legal services needed by employees. In many cases, this is a voluntary benefit that is provided through a contract purchased from an insurer, bar association, or group of attorneys. The cost of such coverage is often relatively small and frequently falls in the range of $55 to $70 per month per employee. Some employers, however, provide the legal services on a self-insured basis and provide the benefits at no cost to employees.

Some legal expense plans merely provide referrals to attorneys and discounts from their regular fees. However, most legal expense plans are referred to as comprehensive plans. In addition to telephone consultation, comprehensive plans cover in-office and trial work of attorneys. The term comprehensive may be a slight misnomer because most plans are not designed to cover 100 percent of a plan member's potential legal services; 80 to 90 percent is probably a better figure.

Comprehensive plans usually contain a list of covered services. While there are significant variations among plans, most cover at least the following:

- document review and preparation
- name changes
- adoptions
- purchase or sale of primary residences
- eviction defense
- civil actions
- driver's license suspension
- juvenile court proceedings
- consumer protection
- bankruptcy
- IRS audits
- debt collection
- child custody and support
- divorce, but possibly only for the covered employee and not dependents

If a particular legal service that is required is not on the list of covered services, there may be some limited coverage as long as the service is not otherwise excluded. This limited service, for example, may be in the form of telephone consultation or a limited amount of work by the attorney, such as 2 to 4 hours per family per year.

Legal expense plans have exclusions, and common exclusions include the following:

- business activities or transactions
- preparation of tax returns
- class-action suits
- actions involving the legal expense plan
- actions involving the employer
- actions involving the union that bargained for the coverage
- cases that have contingent fees

Comprehensive plans take three approaches to the method by which a plan member may select an attorney. Many plans use a closed-panel approach, under which a panel of attorneys has agreed to provide covered services at a predetermined fee or hourly rate for which they bill the plan. The plan member selects the attorney, and benefits are generally available at little or no additional cost. However, plans may limit some benefits to a scheduled maximum (such as $500) and usage limitation (such as 4 hours). A few plans also have deductibles and copayments.

Other plans are open-panel. A plan member can choose any licensed attorney; however, benefits are usually subject to scheduled dollar maximums.

Many plans are modified-panel plans. Under such plans, a plan member may choose either a panel attorney as in a closed-panel plan or select his or her own attorney. The election of a panel attorney often results in benefits being paid in full, while the election of a nonpanel attorney results in the use of benefit maximums.

Taxation. An employer has no tax implications from a legal expense plan if it is a voluntary benefit. Employees, however, have taxable income to the extent of any employer payments. If the plan is prefunded, the employee is taxed on his or her share of the premium paid and benefits are received tax free. If a plan is self-funded by the employer, the employee's taxable income is the value of the benefits paid by the plan.

Long-Term Care Insurance

Since the late 1980s, it has become increasingly common for employers to make long-term care insurance available as an employee benefit. For the most part, the coverage is voluntary and its tax treatment is identical to the individual policies that were described in chapter 2. However, there are a few differences. Employees tend to have fewer choices with respect to benefit amounts, benefit duration, and the length of the elimination period. In addition to spouses being able to obtain coverage, eligibility is also often made available to other persons, such as children, parents, and parents-in-law.

Taxation. Employer-provided long-term care insurance plans are designed to be tax-qualified for IRS purposes. This means that, as with individually purchased policies, a portion of the premium cost paid by an employee may be tax deductible, and benefits are generally received free of income taxation.

A few employers pay some or all of the cost of the long-term care insurance premiums for employees. When this is the case, these premium payments typically are tax deductible to the employer and do not result in taxable income to employees.

Supplemental Medical Expense Insurance

There are three types of voluntary medical expense insurance that are designed to supplement an employee's primary medical expense plan by providing benefits that can be used for (1) out-of-pocket medical expenses not covered by even a comprehensive medical plan and/or (2) associated medical expenses such as travel, lodging, meals, child care, and lost income.

This type of insurance includes

- hospital indemnity insurance, which provides the insured with a fixed daily cash benefit (such as $150) during a covered hospitalization. There is also a maximum benefit duration, such as 90 days.
- specified (dread) disease insurance, which provides benefits to the insured upon the diagnosis of, or medical events related to the treatment of, a disease named in the policy. The list of diseases includes cancer and as many as 20 or 30 more diseases. Benefits may be based on expenses incurred, a fixed amount per day, or a lump sum.
- critical illness insurance, which provides a lump sum cash benefit upon the first diagnosis of a condition or specified surgical treatment. These policies usually cover such illnesses as Alzheimer's disease, heart attacks, organ transplants, paralysis, kidney failure, and strokes.

These supplemental policies are no substitute for adequate medical expense insurance and disability income insurance. And if medical expense and disability income coverages are adequate, there are many financial advisors who question whether these supplemental policies are necessary, particularly if a person has appropriate financial reserves for emergencies.

Property and Liability Insurance

A small number of employers make property and liability insurance coverage available to employees. Most plans offer automobile insurance, and a few also offer other coverages, such as homeowners insurance and umbrella liability insurance. Employees usually have the same choices regarding the amount and type of coverage that they would have in the individual marketplace, and the contracts offered are usually identical. However, modifications that attempt to decrease the cost of the coverage are sometimes made. These include larger deductibles and provisions in the automobile insurance policy that eliminate coverage for medical expenses to the extent that they are paid under the employer's medical expense plan.

Taxation. As with individual property and liability insurance, an employee cannot deduct property and liability premiums for income tax purposes, and benefits received are tax free. In the rare situation when an employer pays a portion of the premium, employees must report as taxable income any contributions made in their behalf.

Miscellaneous Fringe Benefits

The employee benefits previously discussed all fall into the broad category of insurance. However, employees often receive numerous other types of "fringe" benefits. Some of these *miscellaneous fringe benefits* that are important in the financial planning process are discussed here: education assistance, adoption assistance, dependent care assistance, and family leave.

miscellaneous fringe benefits

Education Assistance

The Internal Revenue Code provides favorable tax treatment to employees for the first $5,250 of annual education assistance received from their employers. In order for benefits to be tax free, the employer's plan cannot discriminate with respect to eligibility in favor of officers, shareholders, highly compensated employees, or their dependents. In addition, no more than 5 percent of the benefits may be paid to shareholders or owners (or their dependents) who are more-than-5-percent owners of the firm.

Eligible benefits include tuition, fees, and books for undergraduate or graduate students. The costs of supplies and equipment are also included as long as they are not retained after completion of the course. Reimbursements for meals, lodging, and transportation associated with educational expenses cannot be received tax free. In addition, courses involving sports, games, or hobbies are ineligible for favorable tax treatment.

Many employers provide reimbursement for certain educational expenses that do not qualify for favorable tax treatment under the Code. While such reimbursements result in taxable compensation for an employee, the employee may be eligible for a federal income tax deduction (subject to the 2 percent-of-adjusted-gross-income floor on miscellaneous itemized deductions) if he or she itemizes deductions. The deduction is allowed for educational expenses that are incurred (1) to maintain or improve a skill required in employment or (2) to meet the express requirements of the employer as a condition for retaining employment. Other types of educational expenses, such as costs incurred to qualify the employee for a new trade or business, are not deductible.

Adoption Assistance

While many types of benefits have long been available to natural parents because of the birth of a child, comparable benefits historically have not been available to adoptive parents. Over the last few years, this disparity has begun to change. Even before the passage of family-leave legislation, many employers had established comparable leave policies for natural parents and adoptive parents. For example, if an employer allowed maternity leave (either paid or unpaid) for a new mother, no distinction was made between natural mothers and adoptive mothers. Leave may also be available for time involved in qualifying for the adoption and taking possession of the child.

A smaller number of employers provide reimbursement for some or all of the expenses associated with adoption. Reimbursements are generally available only to employees who have satisfied some minimum service requirement, most commonly one year. Amounts typically range from $1,000 to $3,000 per adoption, but higher amounts may be paid for adoptions involving handicapped children or children from a foreign country. There may also be a lifetime cap, such as $6,000.

Employer payments of up to $11,650 (as indexed for 2008) per child for qualified adoption expenses are excludible from an employee's gross income if an employer has an adoption-assistance program that satisfies IRS requirements.

The program however cannot discriminate in favor of highly compensated employees or their dependents, and no more than 5 percent of the benefits under the plan can be paid to shareholders or owners (or their dependents) who are more-than-5-percent owners of the firm.

Qualified adoption expenses include reasonable and necessary adoption fees, court costs, attorney's fees, travel expenses, and other expenses directly related to the legal adoption of an eligible child. An eligible child is defined as a child who is under age 18 or who is incapable of caring for himself or herself. Expenses incurred in adopting a spouse's child or carrying out a surrogate parenting arrangement are not qualified adoption expenses, nor are expenses that are reimbursed from other sources. In addition, expenses to adopt a child with special needs are not qualified adoption expenses unless the adoption becomes final.

The full $11,650 (as indexed for 2008) exclusion from gross income is available to employees with a modified adjusted gross income of $174,730 (as indexed for 2008) or less, and married couples must file joint returns to obtain the exclusion. For employees with higher gross incomes, the exclusion is gradually phased out until it is eliminated when modified adjusted gross income reaches $214,730 (as indexed for 2008).

In addition to the $11,650 exclusion, there is also a tax credit for the same amount available to all taxpayers for adoption expenses. This credit, however, is not available for expenses that were paid by employer-provided adoption assistance regardless of whether the employer paid the expenses through an adoption-assistance program. The credit can only be used for expenses not reimbursed by an employer's plan, although a taxpayer can take both a credit and an exclusion since the dollar limit applies separately to each.

Dependent Care Assistance

Changes in society and the workforce often create changing needs for both employers and employees. When the workforce was largely male and most families had two parents, caring for children and older parents frequently was the female spouse's responsibility. As the number of families headed by two wage earners or by single parents has increased, so has the need for dependent care. This change in demographics has also created problems for employers. Caring for family members can lead to increased absenteeism, tardiness, turnover, and time taken as family leave. Workplace morale can also suffer if the employer is viewed as insensitive to employee responsibilities.

The nature of employee benefit plans has changed as employers have increasingly responded to the need for dependent care. Child-care benefits are increasingly common, and a small but growing number of firms also make eldercare benefits available. Firms that have dependent-care assistance plans generally feel that such plans alleviate the problems cited in the previous paragraph. Furthermore, the availability of the benefit often makes it easier to hire new employees.

In addition to a formal dependent-care assistance plan, there are other ways in which employers can respond to employee needs to care for family members. These include flexible work schedules, part-time employment, job sharing, salary reduction options under cafeteria plans, and family-leave policies that are more liberal than those required by federal and state laws.

Child-Care Plans. Several alternative types of benefits can be provided under child-care plans. A few employers maintain on-site day-care centers, and the number is growing. Some employers provide benefits by supporting a limited number of off-site child-care centers. The employer may make arrangements to reserve spaces for employees' children at these centers and/or arrange for corporate discounts for employees. Probably the most common approach is to provide reimbursements to employees who make their own arrangements for child care, either at child-care centers or in their own home or the home of a caregiver. Reimbursement is sometimes tied to pay levels, with lower-paid workers receiving higher reimbursements.

Eldercare Benefits. Benefits to care for elderly dependents are much less prevalent than benefits for child care, but the need for them continues to grow as parents live longer. Although eldercare benefits may take a variety of forms, frequently they are much like those provided under child-care plans. Within limits, the employer may pay for costs associated with home care for elderly dependents or care at adult day-care facilities for the elderly.

Taxation of Benefits. Under the Internal Revenue Code, dependent care is a tax-free benefit to employees up to statutory limits as long as certain requirements are met. The amount of benefits that can be received tax free is limited to $5,000 for single persons and married persons who file jointly and to $2,500 for married persons who file separately. The benefits must be for care to a qualifying individual—a child under age 13 for whom the employee is allowed a dependency deduction on his or her income tax return and a taxpayer's spouse or other dependent who is mentally or physically incapable of caring for himself or herself. Although benefits must generally be for dependent care only, educational expenses at the kindergarten or preschool level can also be paid.

Dependent-care benefits are subject to a series of nondiscrimination rules. If the rules are not met, highly compensated employees are taxed on the amount of benefits received. However, the benefits for other employees still retain their tax-free status.

Even if an employer does not provide assistance for dependent care, other tax-saving options may be available to employees. Under the Code, a tax credit (subject to limits) is available for child-care expenses. In addition, the employer may have the opportunity to make before-tax contributions to a cafeteria plan that includes dependent care as an option.

Family Leave

Over the last two decades, an increasing number of employers have voluntarily begun to allow employees to take time off without pay. Reasons for such leave may include active military duty, extended vacations, honeymoons, education, the birth or adoption of a child, and the illness of a family member. Usually, such time off has been subject to the approval of the employer. Family leave is becoming more and more common as many states and the federal government adopt family-leave legislation.

State Laws. In recent years, the legislatures of almost every state have considered family-leave legislation, and many of these states have enacted such legislation. As a general rule, these laws allow an employee to take an unpaid leave of absence for such reasons as the birth or adoption of a child and the illness of a family member. The length of leave allowed varies considerably among states but usually ranges from 3 to 6 months. When the family leave is completed, the employer is required to allow the employee to return to the same or a comparable job.

At a minimum, most family-leave laws allow an employee to continue medical expense coverage at his or her own cost. Some laws require all employee benefits to be made available.

Federal Law. In 1993, the first federal family-leave legislation—the Family and Medical Leave Act—became effective. The legislation applies only to employers who have more than 50 employees within a 75-mile radius.

With some exceptions, a worker must be allowed to take up to 12 weeks of unpaid leave in any 12-month period for the birth or adoption of a child; to care for a child, spouse, or parent with a serious health condition; or for the worker's own serious health condition that makes it impossible to perform a job.

The act applies to both full-time and part-time employees. The latter must be allowed to take leave on a basis that is proportional to that given to full-time employees. However, leave can be denied to anyone who has not worked for the employer for at least one year and worked at least 1,250 hours during that period.

An employer is allowed to substitute an employee's accrued paid leave for any part of the 12-week period of family leave. In addition, an employer can deny leave to a salaried employee within the highest-paid 10 percent of its workforce if the leave would create a substantial and grievous injury to the organization's operations.

During the period of leave, an employer has no obligation to continue an employee's pay or most benefits, and the employee is ineligible for unemployment compensation. However, an employer must continue to provide medical and dental benefits during the leave as if the worker were still employed. The employee must continue to pay any required plan contributions and must be given a 30-day grace period for such payments. The employer is allowed to recover the cost of premiums paid by the employer during the leave if the employee does not return to work for reasons other than (1) the continuance, recurrence, or onset of a serious health condition affecting the employee or the employee's spouse, parent, or child or (2) other circumstances beyond the employee's control.

Upon returning from leave, an employee must be given his or her former job or one that is equivalent. The employee must also be permitted to regain any benefits that he or she enjoyed prior to the leave without having to meet any requalification requirements.

Other Benefits

There are numerous other types of employee benefits that will not be discussed in detail in this chapter. However, they are of significance in evaluating an employee's overall benefit package. Some of them include

- vacations. Significant variations exist in the number of paid vacation days given to employees and how the number increases over time.
- holidays. Most employers provide somewhere between 6 and 12 paid holidays to employees.
- no additional-cost services and employee discounts. Employers in many service industries provide their employees with free or discounted services. Examples include telephone service to employees of phone companies, airline tickets to employees of airlines, and educational courses to employees (and their dependents) of educational institutions. Similarly, many manufacturers and retailers sell their merchandise to employees at a discount. As long as these services and discounts are provided in accordance with certain IRS rules, the benefits are tax free.
- wellness programs. Employers are increasingly aware that the well-being of employees increases productivity and lowers medical expense. Wellness programs may involve medical screening, such as tests for high blood pressure or high cholesterol, or life-style management programs to promote physical fitness or discourage smoking.
- work/life benefits. These include onsite ATMs, convenience stores, travel agencies, and dry cleaning pick-up. A few employers make dental clinics and pharmacies available.
- employee-assistance programs. These include treatment for alcohol or drug abuse, counseling for family and marital problems, legal advice, referrals for child care or eldercare, and crisis intervention.
- preretirement counseling and financial planning. The former is often made available to all employees, while the later is frequently limited to executives.
- transportation and free parking. Under provisions of the Internal Revenue Code, an employer can provide significant tax-free benefits in the form of transit passes, van pools, and reimbursement for parking expenses.
- company vehicles. In addition to using a vehicle for business purposes, an employee is often able to use a company vehicle for personal purposes. However, an employee who drives a company

vehicle for personal use must include the value of the use in his or her taxable income.
- subsidized eating facilities. In addition to convenience, this benefit can also be offered on a tax-free basis if there are inadequate facilities in the area for employees to obtain meals within a reasonable period of time.

CAFETERIA PLANS

cafeteria plans

Many organizations have benefit programs in which all (or almost all) of the employees can design their own benefit packages by purchasing benefits with a prespecified amount of employer dollars from a number of available options. Generally, these *cafeteria plans* (often referred to as flexible benefit plans or cafeteria compensation plans) also allow additional benefits to be purchased on a payroll-deduction basis. Today, the number of employees with full-fledged cafeteria plans continues to grow.

Nature

In its purest sense, a cafeteria plan can be defined as any employee benefit plan that allows an employee to have some choice in designing his or her own benefit package by selecting different types or levels of benefits that are funded with employer dollars. At this extreme, a benefit plan that allows an employee to select an HMO as an option to a traditional major medical expense plan can be classified as a cafeteria plan. However, the more common use of the term cafeteria plan denotes something much broader—a plan that is designed to comply with Section 125 of the Internal Revenue Code (Sec. 125).

Prior to the addition of Sec. 125 to the Code, the use of cafeteria plans had potentially adverse tax consequences for an employee. If an employee had a choice among benefits that were normally nontaxable (such as medical expense insurance or disability income insurance) and benefits that were normally taxable (such as life insurance in excess of $50,000 or cash), then the doctrine of constructive receipt would result in an employee's being taxed as if he or she had elected the maximum taxable benefits that could have been obtained under the plan.

Sec. 125 allows employees to choose between two or more benefits consisting of (1) qualified benefits and (2) cash. Qualified benefits essentially include any welfare benefits excluded from taxation under the Internal Revenue Code except contributions to Archer medical savings accounts (MSAs), long-term care insurance, scholarships and fellowships, transportation benefits, educational assistance, no-additional-cost services, employee discounts, and de minimis fringe benefits. Thus, medical expense benefits and contributions to health savings accounts (HSAs), disability benefits, accidental death and dismemberment benefits, COBRA premiums, adoption assistance, paid time off, and dependent-care assistance (such as day-care centers) can be included in a cafeteria plan. The Code also allows group term life insurance to be included, even in amounts exceeding $50,000. In general, a cafeteria plan cannot include benefits that defer compensation except for a qualified Section 401(k) or similar plan.

The term cash is actually broader than it would otherwise appear. In addition to the actual receipt of dollars, a benefit is treated as cash as long as (1) the cost of the benefit is paid by the employee with after-tax dollars on a payroll-deduction basis or (2) employer dollars are used to obtain the benefit, but the employer reports the cost of the benefit as taxable income for the employee. This rule allows the inclusion of group automobile insurance or long-term care insurance in a cafeteria plan but not on a tax-favored basis.

As long as a benefit plan offering choice meets the definition of a cafeteria plan, the issue of constructive receipt does not apply. Employees have taxable income only to the extent that normally taxable benefits—group term life insurance in excess of $50,000 and cash—are elected.

Sec. 125 requires that benefit elections under a cafeteria plan be made prior to the beginning of a plan year. These elections cannot be changed for that plan year except under certain specified circumstances. Some of these circumstances, which are spelled out in IRS regulations, include such circumstances as a change in legal marital status, a change in the number of dependents, and increases or decreases in the cost of benefits under the plan.

Types

Under some cafeteria plans, employees are allowed to allocate only a predetermined employer contribution for benefits. Other cafeteria plans are designed so that employees can obtain additional benefits with optional payroll deductions or salary reductions.

Many cafeteria plans that provide a wide array of benefits allow an employee to elect an after-tax payroll deduction to obtain additional benefits. For example, under a cafeteria plan an employee might be given $300 per month with which to select varying types and levels of benefits. If the benefits the employee chooses cost $340, the employee has two options—either to decrease the benefits selected or to authorize a $40 payroll deduction. Even though the payroll deduction is on an after-tax basis, the employee gains to the extent that the additional benefits are selected at a lower cost through a group arrangement than in the individual marketplace.

premium-conversion plan
flexible spending account (FSA)

Sec. 125 also allows employees to purchase certain benefits on a before-tax basis through the use of a *premium-conversion plan* and/or a *flexible spending account (FSA)*. Premium-conversion plans or FSAs, both of which are technically cafeteria plans, can be used by themselves or incorporated into a more comprehensive cafeteria plan. They are most commonly used alone by small employers who are unwilling to establish a broader plan, primarily for cost reasons. The cafeteria plans of most large employers contain one or both of these arrangements as an integral part of the plan.

A premium-conversion plan (also called a premium-only plan, or POP) allows an employee to elect a before-tax salary reduction to pay his or her premium contribution to any employer-sponsored health or other welfare benefit plan. For example, an employer might provide medical expense coverage to employees at no cost but make a monthly charge for dependent coverage. Under a premium-conversion plan, the employee can pay for the dependent coverage with a before-tax salary reduction. As a rule, premium-conversion plans are established for medical and dental expenses only.

An FSA allows an employee to fund certain benefits on a before-tax basis by electing to take a salary reduction, which can then be used to fund the cost of any qualified benefits included in the plan. However, FSAs are used almost exclusively for medical and dental expenses not covered by the employer's plan and for dependent-care expenses.

The amount of any salary reduction is, in effect, credited to an employee's reimbursement account, and benefits are paid from this account when an employee properly files for such reimbursement. Reimbursements are typically made on a monthly or quarterly basis, although many employers allow employees to use debit cards to pay for eligible services from approved health care providers. The use of debit cards permits employees to deduct payment from their FSA accounts at the time the services are provided. However employees who use debit cards must be willing to substantiate FSA reimbursements if requested.

The amount of the salary reduction must be determined prior to the beginning of the plan year. Once the amount is set, changes are allowed only under the specified circumstances previously mentioned for benefit elections. A separate election must be made for each benefit, and the funds are accounted for separately. Monies from a salary reduction for one type of expense (such as medical and dental bills) cannot be used as reimbursement for another type of expense (such as dependent care). If the monies in the FSA are not used during the plan year, they are forfeited unless the FSA has a grace period. An FSA can provide for a grace period of up to 2 ½ months after the end of the plan year. Any eligible expenses incurred in that period can be paid from any monies left in the FSA at the end of the previous year. However, once the grace period expires, any remaining monies will be forfeited.

Cafeteria plans can take many forms, but the most common type of full-fledged cafeteria plan is one that offers a basic core of benefits to all employees, plus a second layer of optional benefits that permits an employee to choose which benefits he or she will add to the basic benefits. These optional benefits can be "purchased" with dollars, or credits, that are given to the employee as part of the benefit package. If these credits are inadequate to purchase the desired benefits, an employee can make additional purchases with after-tax contributions or with before-tax salary reductions under a premium-conversion plan and/or an FSA.

Example: All employees receive a minimum level of employer-paid benefits, called basic benefits, as follows:

- term life insurance equal to one-half of salary
- travel accident insurance (when traveling on employer business)
- disability income insurance
- 2 to 4 weeks' vacation

Employees are also given flexible credits, equal to between 3 and 6 percent of salary (depending on length of service, with the maximum reached after 10 years), which can be used to purchase additional or "optional" benefits. There is a new election of benefits each year, and no carryover of any unused credits is allowed. The optional benefits are the following:

- an array of medical expense options. Although there is no charge for HMO coverage, a charge is made for coverage under other options, and additional flexible credits are given if a person elects no medical expense coverage.
- additional life insurance, up to 4 1/2 times salary
- accidental death insurance when the basic travel accident insurance does not apply
- dental insurance for the employee and dependents
- up to 2 weeks' additional vacation time
- cash

If an employee does not have enough flexible credits to purchase the desired optional benefits, additional amounts may be contributed on a payroll-deduction basis for all but more vacation time. In addition, a salary reduction may be elected for contributions to an FSA that provides dependent-care-assistance benefits.

THE FINAL WORD

In 2007, the average payment by employers for employee benefits was equal to 42.7 percent of payroll. This translated into each employee receiving an average of $21,527 in benefits. In addition to employer costs, employee payroll deductions for benefits amounted to 16.9 percent of payroll, with 7.5 percent of these deductions covering Social Security and Medicare taxes, 5.6 percent covering contributions to retirement and savings plans, and 3.8 percent covering medically related benefits, including life insurance premiums. These amounts show just how much individuals and their families rely on benefits provided and/or available to them because of their employment. Consequently, financial advisors need to understand these benefits, because these benefits are the foundation upon which advisors will develop financial plans for their clients.

CHAPTER SUMMARY

The narrowest definition of employee benefits includes only employer-provided benefits for situations involving death, accident, sickness, retirement, or unemployment. On the other hand, the broadest definition of employee benefits includes all benefits and services, other than wages for time worked, that employees receive in whole or in part from their employers. This chapter follows a broad definition of employee benefits, although not all types of employee benefits are covered here. Many employee benefits are covered in other chapters.

While employee benefits currently comprise a significant portion of overall employee compensation, this has not always been the case. The growth of employee benefits over the last 80 years stems from several factors that include industrialization, the influence of organized labor, wage controls, cost advantages, inflation, and legislation.

This significant growth in employee benefits calls for increasingly complex decisions. Whether these decisions are made by employers providing benefits, unions negotiating for benefits, or employees selecting benefit options, the need for proper benefit planning is crucial. Therefore, it is important to look at the benefit planning process for employers. This process is a dynamic process that must continually be reviewed and modified in order to meet the needs of employees in a changing environment.

Furthermore, it is important that financial advisors be aware of the employee benefits provided to and used by employees, since these benefits will almost certainly form the basis for the financial plans they develop for their clients.

Employee benefit plans are very precise in their definition of what constitutes an eligible person for coverage purposes. In general, an employee must be in a covered classification and work full-time. In addition, any requirements concerning probationary periods, insurability, premium contributions, and termination must be satisfied.

Employee benefit plans fall into three basic categories. The first category is traditional group insurance plans, for which the employer typically pays the majority of the cost of an employee's coverage. These plans provide medical expense insurance, life insurance, disability income insurance, dental insurance, and vision insurance. The second category of employee benefits is voluntary benefit plans. These plans make benefits available through the workplace, but the employer does not share in the cost. Available coverages often include legal expense insurance, long-term care insurance, supplemental medical insurance, and property and liability insurance. Finally, the third category of benefits is miscellaneous fringe benefits. These benefits take the form of payments for time not worked, payments to employees, and payments to cover the costs of specific services to employees.

While the taxation of benefits to an employee is not consistent from benefit to benefit and may or may not be affected by nondiscrimination rules, the cost of providing benefits to the employee is almost always tax deductible for the employer, as long as the overall compensation of the employee is reasonable.

In its purest sense, a cafeteria plan can be defined as any employee benefit plan that allows an employee to have some choice in designing his or her own benefit package by selecting different types or levels of benefits that are funded with employer dollars. Following this definition, a benefit plan that allows an employee to select an HMO as an option to a traditional major medical expense plan can be classified as a cafeteria plan. However, the more common use of the term cafeteria plan denotes something much broader—a plan that is designed to comply with Section 125 of the Internal Revenue Code.

Sec. 125 allows employees to choose between two or more benefits consisting of (1) qualified benefits and (2) cash. Qualified benefits essentially include medical expense benefits and HSAs (but not Archer MSAs and long-term care insurance), disability benefits, accidental death and dismemberment benefits, COBRA premiums, adoption assistance, paid time off, and dependent-care assistance (such as day-care centers). In addition, the code also allows group term life insurance to be included, even in amounts exceeding $50,000. However, a cafeteria plan cannot include benefits that defer compensation, except for a Section 401(k) or similar plan.

Besides the actual receipt of cash, a benefit is treated as cash as long as (1) the cost of the benefit is paid by the employee with after-tax dollars on a payroll-deduction basis or (2) employer dollars are used to obtain the benefit, but the employer reports the cost of the benefit as taxable income for the employee. This rule allows the inclusion of group automobile insurance or long-term care insurance in a cafeteria plan but not on a tax-favored basis.

As long as a benefit plan offering choice meets the definition of a qualified plan, the issue of constructive receipt does not apply. Employees have taxable income only to the extent that normally taxable benefits—group term life insurance in excess of $50,000 and cash—are elected.

CHAPTER REVIEW

Key Terms and Concepts are explained in the Glossary. Answers to the Review Questions and Self-Test Questions are found in the back of the book in the Answers to Questions section.

Key Terms and Concepts

employee benefits
buy-up plan
voluntary benefit plans
major medical plans
managed care plan
health maintenance organizations (HMOs)
preferred-provider organizations (PPOs)
point-of-service (POS) plans
preexisting condition
coordination of benefits (COB) provision
defined-contribution medical expense plan

COBRA
group term life insurance
accidental death and dismemberment (AD&D) insurance
dependent life insurance
Section 79
sick-pay plans
dental insurance
vision benefit plan
legal expense insurance
miscellaneous fringe benefits
cafeteria plans
premium-conversion plan
flexible spending account (FSA)

Review Questions

3-1. Identify the five categories of employee benefits.

3-2. Identify six reasons for the growth of employee benefits over the last 75 years.

3-3. What are the steps in the benefit-planning process for employers?

3-4. Explain why financial advisors should be aware of employee benefits.

3-5. Describe six requirements that employee benefit plans may use to determine who is an eligible person for coverage purposes.

3-6. What are the five basic characteristics of a true managed care plan?

3-7. Describe three ways that PPOs differ from HMOs?

3-8. What is the basic concept or "common thread" of defined-contribution medical expense plans?

3-9. Identify six qualifying events for which employees or their dependents can extend medical expense coverage under the provisions of COBRA.

3-10. Explain how benefits under a group life insurance plan are determined.

3-11. Describe two possible options that an employee may have for the continuation of life insurance coverage if he or she terminates employment.

3-12. Bruce is age 25 and works for the ABC Company, which pays the total premium for his $100,000 of group term insurance coverage. If the Uniform Premium Table I rate for a person aged 25 is $.06 per month per $1,000 of coverage, what monthly amount will be reportable as taxable income to Bruce?

3-13. Explain the tax treatment to employees under a noncontributory group long-term disability income insurance plan.

3-14. Identify four characteristics of voluntary benefit plans that make them popular with employees.

3-15. According to Sec. 125 of the Internal Revenue Code, what benefits are excluded from the definition of qualified benefits?

Self-Test Questions

Instructions: Read chapter 3 first, then answer the following questions to test your knowledge. There are 10 questions. Circle the correct answer, then check your answers with the answer key in the back of the book.

3-1. In 2007, a study by the U.S. Chamber of Commerce found that the average payment by employers for employee benefits was equal to what percent of payroll?

(A) 16.9 percent
(B) 24.0 percent
(C) 42.7 percent
(D) 50.0 percent

3-2. Employer contributions for dependent life insurance are considered de minimis (by the IRS) and not taxable to the employee if the amount of the coverage on the dependent does not exceed

(A) $ 2,000
(B) $ 5,000
(C) $ 7,000
(D) $10,000

3-3. The cost of continuing coverage under COBRA may be passed on to the employee or dependent but cannot exceed what percent of the cost to the plan for a similarly situated active employee?

(A) 100 percent
(B) 102 percent
(C) 105 percent
(D) 108 percent

3-4. Comprehensive legal expense insurance plans typically provide coverage for which of the following types of legal services?

(A) cases that have contingent fees
(B) actions involving the employer
(C) class-action suits
(D) civil actions

3-5. Characteristics that distinguish HMOs from traditional medical expense contracts include which of the following?

I. HMOs provide for the delivery of medical services.
II. HMOs emphasize control of medical expenses.

(A) I only
(B) II only
(C) Both I and II
(D) Neither I nor II

3-6. Which of the following statements concerning the tax treatment of employees under a partially contributory group long-term disability income insurance plan is (are) correct?

　　　I.　Employer contributions result in no taxable income to the employees.
　　　II.　Benefits attributable to employer contributions are received tax free by employees.

　　(A)　I only
　　(B)　II only
　　(C)　Both I and II
　　(D)　Neither I nor II

3-7. Which of the following statements concerning point-of-service (POS) plans is (are) correct?

　　　I.　The typical POS plan provides for a lower degree of managed care than most PPOs.
　　　II.　A POS plan is a hybrid arrangement that combines aspects of a traditional HMO and a PPO.

　　(A)　I only
　　(B)　II only
　　(C)　Both I and II
　　(D)　Neither I nor II

3-8. All the following statements concerning flexible spending accounts (FSAs) are correct EXCEPT:

　　(A)　FSAs allow employees to fund certain benefits on a before-tax basis by electing to take a salary reduction.
　　(B)　FSAs can be used for medical and dental expenses not covered by the employer's plan and for dependent-care expenses.
　　(C)　FSAs can be used by themselves or incorporated into a more comprehensive cafeteria plan.
　　(D)　FSA funds not used during the year or grace period are returned to the employees or credited to next year.

3-9. Group medical expense plans containing coordination-of-benefits (COB) provisions have established all the following priorities for determining which plans pay benefits EXCEPT:

(A) Coverage as a retired employee is primary to coverage as an active employee.
(B) Coverage as an employee is usually primary to coverage as a dependent.
(C) If a child lives in a two-parent household, the plan of the parent whose birthday falls earlier in the calendar year is primary.
(D) If a child does not live with both parents, the plan of the parent with custody of the child is primary in the absence of a court order specifying otherwise.

3-10. Group term insurance contracts often provide additional insurance benefits in the form of all the following coverages EXCEPT

(A) supplemental life insurance
(B) accidental death and dismemberment insurance
(C) dependent life insurance
(D) long-term disability income insurance

NOTE

1. U.S. Chamber of Commerce, The 2007 Employee Benefits Study

4

Investment Planning

Walt J. Woerheide
C. Bruce Worsham

Learning Objectives

An understanding of the material in this chapter should enable you to

4-1. Explain the meaning of investment and contrast investing with speculating.

4-2. Explain both expected return and risk as they relate to investments.

4-3. Explain the relationship of financial risk tolerance to asset allocation models and asset selection.

4-4. Describe the categories of investment assets and the sources of investment risk.

4-5. Explain the importance of liquidity, marketability, taxation, and diversification to building a portfolio.

4-6. Describe three methods for comparing the investment returns from different investments.

4-7. Describe several investment principles, strategies, and techniques used by successful investors.

4-8. Explain the major types of markets where investment trading occurs, and describe the major federal laws and regulations that affect investments.

Chapter Outline

THE MEANING OF INVESTMENT   4.3
    Investment versus Speculation   4.3
    Expected Return and Risk   4.4
    Basic Investment Theorems   4.7
SERVICE TO THE CLIENT   4.7
    Determining Risk Tolerance   4.9

Asset Allocation Models 4.10
CATEGORIES OF INVESTMENT ASSETS 4.11
    Cash Equivalents 4.11
    Long-Term Debt Instruments 4.13
    Equity Securities 4.15
    Real Estate and Other Investments 4.20
SOURCES OF INVESTMENT RISK 4.21
    Purchasing Power Risk 4.21
    Interest Rate Risk 4.23
    Business Risk 4.25
SPECIAL PORTFOLIO CONSIDERATIONS 4.25
    Liquidity 4.26
    Marketability 4.27
    Taxation 4.27
    Diversification 4.30
INVESTMENT RETURNS 4.31
    Current Yield 4.32
    Holding-Period Return (HPR) 4.33
    Approximate Yield 4.34
INVESTMENT PRINCIPLES, STRATEGIES, AND TECHNIQUES 4.35
    Meeting Emergency and Protection Needs First 4.36
    Matching Investment Instruments with Investment Goals 4.36
    Holding Periods for Equity Investments 4.37
    Tax-Saving Rationale 4.37
    Understanding the Investment 4.37
    Using a Consistent Pattern of Investing 4.38
    The Power of Compounding 4.39
    High-Pressure Sales Tactics 4.39
    Avoiding Discretionary Power 4.40
    Applying Control through the Financial Planning Process 4.40
INVESTMENT MARKETS AND REGULATION 4.41
    Investment Markets 4.41
    Regulation of the Markets 4.43
THE FINAL WORD 4.45
CHAPTER SUMMARY 4.46
CHAPTER REVIEW 4.48

This chapter begins with a brief discussion on the meaning of investment and compares investing with speculating. There is then an in-depth look at expected return and risk as they relate to investments. The importance of understanding a client's financial risk tolerance is examined in the context of making asset-allocation decisions. Next, the chapter focuses on the various categories of investments, before proceeding to the sources of investment risk and several portfolio considerations. Three quick methods for comparing the investment returns from different investments are reviewed, as well as some investment principles, strategies, and techniques used by successful investors. Finally, the chapter covers the major types of markets where investments trading occurs and concludes with the major federal laws and regulations affecting investments.

THE MEANING OF INVESTMENT

personal assets
investment assets

The assets that consumers buy can be thought of as being of two types: *personal assets* and *investment assets*. Personal assets are bought primarily for the creature comforts that they provide. These include such items as homes, cars, and clothes. Investment assets are those acquired for the purpose of investing, which is defined as the purchase of an asset with the expectation that said asset will provide a return commensurate with its risk. Returns are in the form either of price appreciation, income, or some combination of the two. Income is usually in the form of dividends (when the asset is stock), interest (when the asset is a bond), or rents (when the asset is a rental property).

From the above descriptions, it should be obvious that the distinction between personal and investment assets is not always clear. For example, the purchase of an antique car may be for pleasure, in which case it is a personal asset. It might be for investment purposes (price appreciation), in which case it is an investment asset. Or, it may be for both pleasure and investment purposes. Jewelry is another obvious example of where the categorization of the asset is illusive. In cases where there is ambiguity, the ultimate distinction is based on the intent of the buyer. The exact same asset may be a personal asset for one person, and an investment asset for another person. Fortunately, the categorization of most assets held by consumers is clear and unambiguous.

Investment versus Speculation

In chapter 2 risk was divided into (1) pure risks, which involve only the possibility of financial loss, and (2) speculative risks, which involve not only the possibility of financial loss, but also the possibility of financial gain. The distinction between pure risks and speculative risks is an important one, because normally only pure risks are insurable. Speculative risks, on the other hand, are what people encounter when they purchase investment assets hoping to receive some form of return.

investing

speculating

The term speculative risk is perhaps an unfortunate one because both investment and speculation involve speculative risk. This is true, despite the connotation that the term speculative risk is only associated with speculating. However, even though both investment and speculation involve speculative risk, there is a very clear difference between them. *Investing* is based on a reasoned consideration of expected return and the risk associated with that return. *Speculating* occurs when a person buys an asset in the hopes of receiving some form of return, without consideration or knowledge of the expected return or risk, or both. It may also be the purchase of an asset in which the buyer expects to lose some or all of his or her purchase price, but which might have some huge payoff. One of the best examples of speculation is the purchase of a lottery ticket. A lottery may sell $10,000,000 worth of tickets, and have as a prize $1,000,000. Thus, the average ticket buyer will receive back ten cents for each dollar paid for the lottery tickets. In actuality, one person will receive $1,000,000 and everyone else will receive nothing. A rational analysis of expected return and risk would result in no one buying lottery tickets. However, most lotteries are successful. Many people buy lottery tickets. There is nothing wrong with buying lottery tickets, but the buyer should bear in mind that he or she is speculating, not investing.

Another example of speculation is the purchase of what are known as penny stocks. These are common stocks that trade for pennies a share. In most cases, these are stocks of companies that are about to become worthless. On a rare occasion, something happens to one of these companies and it becomes quite valuable. Like lotteries, most buyers of penny stocks lose some, if not all, of their entire purchase price, while a few buyers get lucky and hit it big. Again, this is speculating, not investing.

Expected Return and Risk

Expected return and risk are usually thought of in quantitative terms. Measurement of these two values can be quite complex for some securities. To obtain a feel for these concepts, let us consider the following example:

Example: Imagine that a local bank offers a deal to its depositors. Because the city's football team is playing in the Super Bowl, the bank says that between now and the day of the game, customers can buy a one-year certificate of deposit (CD) that will pay 4 percent interest if the local team wins, but only 3 percent if the local team loses. The rate of interest a depositor expects to receive is dependent on the expected outcome of the football game. In national betting, the game is rated a toss-up, meaning it is equally likely that either team could win. Thus, there is a 50 percent probability that the depositor will receive 4 percent interest, and a 50 percent probability that he or she will receive 3 percent interest.

expected return

One way that an *expected return* is calculated is to multiply the probability of each outcome occurring by the value of that outcome, and add the products together. So in the example, the 50 percent probability of receiving 4 percent is multiplied by the value of 4 percent, and the 50 percent probability of receiving 3 percent is multiplied by the value of 3 percent. The first product is 2 percent (.50 x 4%), the second is 1.5 percent (.50 x 3%), and the sum is 3.5 percent. Thus, the expected return on this investment is 3.5 percent. Note that in this case, the actual return will be either 4 percent or 3 percent. It cannot be 3.5 percent. So it is not necessary that the expected return be one of the possible actual returns. The expected return serves as a proxy for the return one would expect if he or she were to compare the one-year CD, or any specific investment for that matter, to other investments.

As previously mentioned, risk can be divided into (1) pure risks, which involve only the possibility of financial loss, and (2) speculative risks, which involve not only the possibility of financial loss, but also the possibility of financial gain. Individuals typically handle their pure risks by purchasing insurance. Insurance is not, however, designed to protect individuals against losses arising out of speculative risks. With few exceptions, individuals assume speculative risks because of the possibility of financial gain. To insure these risks against the possibility of financial loss would require a premium in an amount that would substantially reduce or eliminate the extent of gain that encouraged the assumption of the risk in the first place.

In applying the definition of speculative risk to the world of investments, it is important to recognize, as pointed out in chapter 2, that there are two ways a financial loss can occur. The first and most obvious way is when there is a reduction in the value of something that an individual already possesses—for example, the loss of one's investment in the common stock of a firm that fails. The second and most common way is when there is a reduction in the value of something that an individual expects to receive in the future. This second type of financial loss is illustrated by the following example:

Example: Tom Jones has just inherited $10,000. He talks with his stockbroker about investment opportunities. His broker offers two choices. One is the purchase of a U.S. government bond that matures in one year and provides a 5 percent rate of return. As the chances of the United States government defaulting on this bond are virtually zero, this would be considered a risk-free investment. The broker offers as an alternative investment some common stock in a local company, which is described as having an expected return of 10 percent. However, the broker goes on to say that the actual return could range anywhere from plus 30 percent to minus 10 percent over the coming year. If Tom picks the stock and ends up with a rate of return of one percent for the year, he will have made money. However, Tom ends up making less than he would have made had he bought the government bond, which would have been a virtually certain 5 percent return. Tom has suffered what is known as an opportunity loss. This loss is real to Tom, although he has not lost money, per se.

The definition of speculative risk works quite well in the investment world when it is used to describe the risk people face when making an investment. However, it presents mathematical problems for the advisor if he or she wants to quantify an estimate of an investment's risk. To be able to do this, the advisor has to define investment risk differently. For this purpose, investment risk typically is measured by the dispersion of potential variation in possible returns.

Because most people would agree that the probability of doing worse than expected is usually about equal to the probability of doing better than expected, the range of possible returns may well be described as symmetrical. *Investment risk* is measured by the likelihood that realized returns will differ from those that are expected. An asset with a wide range of possible returns is considered risky, while an asset with a narrow range of possible returns is considered more secure.

investment risk

The range of returns is generally measured in terms of the distance or dispersion from the mean or expected (per-period) return. An asset's expected return is the average of its possible returns weighted by their respective likelihoods. Thus, the probabilities of below-expectation and above-expectation returns balance out. The actual yields of risky assets almost always differ from the market's expectations. The owner of a relatively risky asset whose return is expected to be between 2 percent and 18 percent bears the "risk" that the actual return could be anywhere within this range. The investor who owns a relatively secure asset with a 99+ percent probability of earning exactly 7.5 percent has little risk about which to be concerned. Simply stated, investment risk refers to the magnitude of the range of possible returns. In other words, the greater the range of possible returns, the riskier the investment.

Basic Investment Theorems

When engaged in investment planning, there are two theorems that the financial advisor must always keep in mind. The first is that all investors are greedy! Everyone would like a risk-free investment with an incredibly high rate of return. The second is that there is no free lunch! This means that there is a well-established relationship in the world of investments between risk and expected return. Low-risk investments have low expected returns, and high-risk investments have high expected returns. When an investment offers too low an expected return to justify its risk, the asset's price will fall, thus increasing its expected return. This adjustment process will continue until the market views the asset's expected return is in line with its risk. The higher the price people are willing to pay for an asset means that the rate of return they receive will be lower because people are willing to pay more for investments with less risk. Conversely, no one will willingly hold a high-risk investment unless there is a strongly felt expectation of a rate of return that will, on average, compensate him or her for the risk.

This relationship between risk and expected return is known as the positive risk-expected return tradeoff. In the end, some high-risk investments will have low or even negative rates of return. This is what is meant by risk. However, other high-risk investments will have rates of return greater than expected. On average, high-risk investments will provide returns greater than low-risk investments. But it is critical to remember these two words: on average. A person who holds many different high-risk investments has a better chance of achieving this average than someone who holds only one high-risk investment.

SERVICE TO THE CLIENT

When engaged in investment planning for a client, the single most important service that a financial advisor can perform is to ascertain the client's financial risk tolerance, and then make sure that the riskiness of the client's investment holdings is consistent with this tolerance level, as well as with his or her financial ability to handle the risk. Performing this service is never an easy task. It requires ascertaining the client's tolerance for risk and his or her ability to handle it. Investment planning is made much easier when these two items are consistent with each other. However, there are two cases when they are not consistent.

First, consider the case where the client has a high financial risk tolerance, but a low ability to deal with it. This case is demonstrated by the following example:

Example: Winston is 84 years old. His portfolio is worth approximately $500,000. His only sources of retirement income are Social Security, a small pension, and investment income. Based on his current level of expenses at his assisted-living facility, his investment income is critical in meeting his annual expenses. Winston has been addicted to the stock market his entire life. He has made and lost large amounts of money in the stock market over the years. He always believes the market will do better in the future, and wants an aggressive portfolio to increase his wealth for his old age.

In this scenario, Winston has a high tolerance for risk. In fact, he would almost seem to be addicted to gambling. The fact that his investment income is critical to his annual expenses would suggest, however, that he has a low ability to handle financial risk. If he sustained any substantive losses, he might have to dramatically and unsatisfactorily change his standard of living. At his age and with his health, Winston has no ability to resume working to rebuild any portfolio losses by additional savings. So, despite Winston's desire to hold risky investments (that is, his financial risk tolerance is high), he should be advised to hold a low-risk portfolio.

Now, consider the case where the client has a low financial risk tolerance, but a high ability to handle financial risk. This case is depicted in the following example:

Example: Edgar is 55 and has been a successful business leader his whole life. He is worth $15 million. However, Edgar's wife fixes him a brown-bag lunch every day, as he abhors the idea of spending a few dollars for lunch. He spends vacations at home because he finds the cost of vacations to be too expensive. He has a comfortable income, and as owner and president of his own company, he plans to continue working for many years.

In Edgar's case, he clearly has the ability to take on a substantial amount of financial risk. His assets are large enough to afford a well-diversified portfolio. He appears to have a good income and to save prolifically. He also appears to be a miser who would find any loss (even a small one) extremely upsetting. Edgar most likely should be advised to hold conservative (that is, not very risky) investments, not because he cannot afford to handle the risk, but because he psychologically is not equipped to deal with it.

Determining Risk Tolerance

Although understanding the risk tolerance of a client is so critically important to proper investment planning, there is no simple formula, tool, or technique that allows an advisor to identify the client's financial risk tolerance and then relate it to an investment portfolio. The fact that measurement of financial risk tolerance is not perfect does not mean it cannot or should not be done. For this reason, many companies have developed risk tolerance questionnaires.[1] These range from a few questions (5 to 10) to an extensive questionnaire requiring substantial time to complete.

Whether engaged in single-purpose, multiple-purpose, or comprehensive financial planning, a financial advisor should make the use of one of these risk tolerance questionnaires a top priority in data gathering (step 2, determine goals and gather data, in the financial planning process or FPP). This type of information is necessary in order for an advisor to develop a financial and/or investment plan (step 4, develop and present a plan, in the FPP) for his or her client. When the questionnaire has been completed and analyzed (step 3, analyze and evaluate the data, in the FPP), it provides the advisor with information that can help in assessing the client's risk tolerance. Information about risk tolerance, however, is not intended to be a substitute for the advisor's professional judgment about the client's ability to sustain a financial loss.

The advisor is under a legal and an ethical obligation to help clients make investment choices that are suitable for their particular circumstances. Determining suitability requires consideration of the client's goals (as determined in step 2, determine goals and gather data, in the FPP), his or her ability to sustain a financial loss, and his or her psychological attitudes toward risk taking. Developing a suitable financial and/or investment plan for the client should lead to a lasting and profitable relationship with the client. Not only will the client be happy, but the advisor will come away with a sense of personal satisfaction and professional pride from having fulfilled the client's expectations. Conversely, extreme client dissatisfaction with an inappropriate plan can result in an unsuitability lawsuit. In such disputes, the charge is that the financial advisor knew—or should have known—that the plan was inappropriate for the client. Knowing and understanding the client helps to determine whether a plan is appropriate or not.

Asset Allocation Models

After information about the client's financial risk tolerance has been gathered (step 2 in the FPP) and analyzed (step 3 in the FPP), the next step in the investment planning process (step 4, develop and present a plan, in the FPP) is for the advisor to translate his or her knowledge about the client's risk tolerance into a portfolio recommendation. As previously mentioned, there is no simple formula, tool, or technique that allows an advisor to define the optimal portfolio, even if he or she has obtained a perfect measure of the client's risk tolerance. To help deal with this step in the investment planning process, advisors often develop their plans by constructing recommended investment portfolios for different levels of financial risk tolerance. These portfolios will be based on categories of assets, rather than specific assets. For example, for extremely conservative investors, a recommended portfolio might consist of the following: 15 percent in relatively risk-free, cash equivalent investments, 25 percent in U.S. government bonds, 30 percent in corporate bonds, 10 percent in preferred stocks, and 20 percent in common stocks. For investors with the highest degree of risk tolerance, the recommended portfolio might be 70 percent in common stocks.

asset allocation models

asset selection

Portfolio recommendations such as these are known as *asset allocation models*. The emphasis is on the different categories of assets and the percentage to be placed in each category. The client's level of risk tolerance needs to be known to properly determine both the categories and the appropriate percentages for the client. This leads to the next step in the investment planning process known as *asset selection,* whereby specific assets are recommended and purchased (step 5, implement the plan, in the FPP). Thus, in the case of a conservative client who is looking to put 20 percent of his or her portfolio into common stocks, the final question then is what specific stocks to buy.

Most people new to the world of investing think that the investment planning process works in the reverse order. That is, they think that asset selection precedes asset allocation. They focus on the selection of specific assets by looking for something that will have a high return with little or no risk, and end with seeing if the client is comfortable with the selection. However, investment research has consistently shown that correct asset allocation will do far more to benefit a client than asset selection.[2] It is far more important that a financial advisor make sure that a client holds an asset allocation that is consistent with his or her risk tolerance and ability to handle risk, than that the advisor occasionally "picks a few winners."

CATEGORIES OF INVESTMENT ASSETS

Now that the importance of asset allocation has been established, let us look at some of the categories of assets. Basically, there are only two types of investment assets: debt and equity. Debt is any investment in which the individual loans money to someone, receives interest during the life of the loan, and expects repayment of the money at the end of the loan. Equity is any investment in which the individual is the owner of the assets that generate the income.

There are three critical characteristics to any debt investment: the maturity of the loan, the risk of default on the loan, and the liquidity of the loan (that is, the ability to sell the investment or otherwise cash it out prior to maturity). The debt instruments with the shortest maturity, highest degree of safety with regard to default, and the most liquidity are known as cash equivalents. The more common types of cash equivalents include savings accounts, negotiable and nonnegotiable certificates of deposit, Treasury bills, commercial paper, money market deposit accounts, and money market mutual funds. The next category of debt instruments is government bonds, which have no default risk and good liquidity, but longer maturities. The last category of debt instruments is always corporate debt, which may contain substantial default risk, have long maturities, and lack liquidity.

The primary equity investment is always common stock. Common stockholders are the owners of the corporation. Another form of equity is preferred stock. There are many equity investments in which investors do not own common stock directly but own a claim on common stock. These include American Depositary Receipts and investment companies. Other investment opportunities like real estate are also classified as equity investments; they just are not referred to in this manner. Let us consider these debt and equity investments in more detail.

Cash Equivalents

cash equivalents

To satisfy the need to make transactions and to have readily accessible money in case of an emergency, many individuals use instruments that are known as *cash equivalents*. Typically, cash equivalents either have no specified maturity date or have one that is one year or less in the future. Investments in this category often provide only a modest current income and typically have little or no potential for capital appreciation.

Bank Deposits

The most widely known and used types of cash-equivalent investments are savings accounts and nonnegotiable certificates of deposit (CDs) at banks, savings and loans, and credit unions. Because these investments are usually insured to a limit of $250,000 by the Federal Deposit Insurance Corporation (FDIC), they have minimal risk. In addition, few restrictions are placed on withdrawals of deposits in savings accounts.

CDs, which are deposits for a specified period of time such as 3, 6, or 12 months (although maturities of up to 10 years are available), generally impose a loss of a portion of the interest earnings as a penalty for a withdrawal before maturity. Because of the time commitment made by the investor and the early-withdrawal penalty, the interest rate earned on CDs exceeds that earned on savings accounts.

Another characteristic of savings accounts and CDs is their ease of acquisition and disposal. Both can be opened or closed at any office of the issuer with little delay and at no cost. Savings accounts can be increased or decreased in virtually any desired sum. CDs can be acquired in sufficiently varied dollar amounts and with staggered maturities to allow the depositor to match maturity to future cash needs. At maturity, CDs can be automatically reinvested for an equivalent time period without the investor having to take any action.

Money Market Instruments

money market deposit accounts (MMDAs)
money market mutual funds (MMMFs)

Money market deposit accounts (MMDAs) and *money market mutual funds (MMMFs)* are other popular cash equivalents. For both types of investments, minimum initial dollar amounts are typically required to open the account. In the case of MMDAs offered by banks, virtually any amount can be added to the account. MMDAs typically are insured like savings accounts and CDs. MMDAs allow withdrawals at the bank window or by check. However, a limit is imposed on the number of checks that are allowed at little or no cost per month, and additional checks can be costly. The earnings rate obtained from these instruments often increases depending on the size of the investor's account.

In contrast, MMMFs frequently require minimum dollar deposits, and they are not FDIC insured. MMMFs provide access by check, by wire transfer, and, in some cases, by phone. MMMFs are mutual funds, and investments therein are used to buy shares in the fund. Because MMMFs often belong to a commonly managed family of funds, these MMMF shares can be readily redeemed for shares in other funds within the family with little or no delay or transaction cost.

Both MMDAs and MMMFs hold portfolios of short-term obligations of the federal government and its agencies, of state and local governments, and of businesses. The securities usually have maturity dates averaging under 60 days.

Treasury Bills

U.S. Treasury bills (T-bills)

Another popular cash-equivalent investment is *U.S. Treasury bills (T-bills)*. These short-term obligations of the U.S. government are issued with a term of one year or less, and they are backed by the full taxing authority of the government. With this backing, T-bills are the safest investment available and, thus, pay investors the lowest interest rate of the various money market instruments. When the term risk-free investment is used, it refers to T-bills. In this context, risk free means no possible risk of default on paying interest or principal when due. These instruments are sold at a discount from face value and do not pay interest before maturity. The interest is the difference between the purchase price of the bill and the amount that is paid either at maturity (the face amount) or when the T-bill is sold prior to maturity. T-bills require a minimum purchase of $1,000, making them readily available for clients of modest means. They can be acquired by bidding directly at the nearest Federal Reserve Bank's weekly auction, or by bidding through brokers, dealers, or financial institutions. Also, they can be readily sold and converted to cash at a modest cost to meet client needs.

Many other investments have the characteristics of cash equivalents, such as the short-term obligations of state and local governments (for example, tax anticipation notes) and of businesses (for example, commercial paper) and the long-term debt obligations of governments and businesses that are to mature within one year. Some of the characteristics of these long-term securities are described below.

long-term debt instruments

notes

Long-Term Debt Instruments

Long-term debt instruments are those whose term to maturity is one year or more. Some people refer to bonds with maturities of one to 10 years as being intermediate term. When bonds are issued with maturities of one to 10 years, they are frequently referred to as *notes*.

Bond issues of state and local governments (both of which are referred to as municipals) and of businesses typically are rated by Standard and Poor's Corporation (S&P) and/or Moody's Investors Service as to the likelihood that the issuer will default on the timely payment of interest or principal. Based on a financial analysis of the issuer, a letter grade is assigned to each bond issue. Bonds rated at the top of the B grade (BBB for S&P, Baa for Moody's) or higher are considered to be "investment quality." Lower ratings are assigned for bonds assessed as "speculative." These rating organizations evaluate the bond when it is issued and continue to monitor the issuer during the bond's life. The lower the quality rating, the greater is the risk of default and the higher will be the yield that the investor will expect to earn if the issuer does not default.

Governmental Debt Securities

Governmental debt includes securities of the federal, state, and local governments, and their agencies. Some federal bonds are backed by the full faith and credit of the U.S. government. For example, all U.S. Treasury obligations have such backing. Bonds issued by federal agencies or organizations, such as the Tennessee Valley Authority, are not direct obligations of the U.S. Treasury. These bonds, known collectively as *agency bonds,* provide investors with returns greater than that available on U.S. Treasury bonds although the difference in return is quite small. A few of these agency bonds have guarantees that effectively place the full faith and credit of the U.S. Treasury behind the bonds.

agency bonds

general obligations

revenue bonds

Some state and local government bonds, known as *general obligations,* are backed by the taxing power of the state or local government. Others, usually issued by agencies of a state or local government, are known as *revenue bonds.* They are guaranteed by the revenues earned from such ventures as turnpikes, airports, and sewer and water systems. Without the taxing authority behind them, these revenue bonds are viewed as riskier and pay investors a somewhat higher interest rate than do general obligation bonds.

Typically, interest earned on debt issues of the federal government, although subject to federal income taxation, is exempt from income taxation by state and local governments. Exceptions to the exemption from state and local income taxation include mortgage-backed securities issued by federal agencies such as the Government National Mortgage Association (Ginnie Mae) or the Federal National Mortgage Association (Fannie Mae). Interest earned on most, but not all, state and local obligations is exempt from federal income taxation and income taxation by the state in which they originate. In contrast, most states generally tax the interest earned on state and local obligations issued in other states.[3]

Corporate Debt Securities

Businesses are major issuers of debt instruments. These securities have various characteristics, which are detailed in the indenture. The indenture is the legal contract associated with a bond issue, written by the issuer, that specifies the rights and protections afforded to the bond investor. Some of the more frequently encountered characteristics include the following:

- secured—a promise backed by specific assets as further protection to the bondholder should the corporation default on payment of interest or principal
- debenture—an unsecured promise, based only on the issuer's general credit status, to pay interest and principal
- callable—an option exercisable at the discretion of the issuer to redeem the bond prior to its maturity date at a specified price
- convertible—an option exercisable by the bondholder to exchange the bond for a predetermined number of common or preferred shares of stock

For bonds of the same quality rating, these features affect the interest rate paid to the investor. If the feature provides a benefit to the bondholder, such as being secured or convertible, a lower interest rate is paid. If the feature provides a benefit to the issuer, such as the presence of a call feature, the interest rate is higher.

junk bonds

The market often assigns labels to securities. One label frequently heard in the news is *junk bonds,* now more commonly called high yield bonds. These bonds have weak quality ratings from S&P or Moody's and are risky because the firm either has a large amount of debt outstanding relative to its equity base or has suffered financial reverses and may be headed for serious trouble or bankruptcy. Because the risk is high, the return on junk bonds also is high if the issuer does not default.

Note: The term junk bonds can also apply to certain municipal bonds if the government or agency tax or revenue base sharply deteriorates.

Equity Securities

Equity investments represent an ownership position in a business. As such, they represent a higher risk for the investor than do the debt investments. Although an equity interest can be as the sole owner of a proprietorship or as one of several partners in a partnership, this discussion will focus on equity as evidenced by shares of stock issued by a corporation.

Corporations acquire equity funds by selling ownership shares to either a few individuals or to the public. In the former case, the individuals often agree not to sell the shares to others, hence keeping the firm closely held and the shares not marketable. When equity shares are sold to the public, a market for their resale emerges if enough shares are publicly held, and the ownership interest then can be readily sold or purchased. Corporations can and often do offer different types of ownership interests of which the two most popular are common and preferred stock.

Common Stock

Investors in common stock have the ultimate ownership rights in the corporation. They elect the board of directors that oversees the management of the firm. Each common share receives an equal portion of the dividends distributed as well as any liquidation proceeds. If the firm is unsuccessful, losses will occur that can lead to a cessation of any dividend payments and, if losses continue, to an eradication of the common equity ownership and eventual bankruptcy.

preemptive right

The payment of dividends to the shareholder is at the sole discretion of the board of directors. The board is under no legal obligation to make dividend payments and may instead retain the profits within the business. The owners of common stock typically vote on issues such as mergers and stock splits. Common stockholders sometimes have a *preemptive right,* which is the right to maintain their relative voting power by purchasing shares of any new issues of common stock of the corporation. This is accomplished by the free distribution of securities known as rights when a company wants to raise cash via the sale of new shares of common stock. The rights have an expiration date, and can either be used to buy the new shares at a price below the current market price, or be sold to others who would like to exercise the rights.

Preferred Stock

Preferred stockholders usually have two privileges that provide them with a preferential position relative to common stockholders. The first privilege is the right to receive dividends before any dividends are paid to the common shareholders. This preference is usually limited to a specified amount per share each year. As previously stated, dividends are payable only if declared by the board. If the preferred shares are noncumulative and no dividend is paid to the preferred shares in any one year, the dividend is skipped and does not ever have to be paid. In the next year, the corporation can pay the specified annual preferred dividend and then pay a large dividend to the common shareholders. To prevent this from happening, many preferred stocks have a cumulative provision associated with the issue. This provision requires the corporation to pay all the skipped preferred dividends as well as the current year's preferred dividend before any dividends can be paid to the common shareholders.

The second privilege of preferred stockholders is the right to receive up to a specified amount for each share (plus current or cumulative dividends) at the time of liquidation. This liquidation value must be paid to the preferred stockholders in full before anything can be paid to the common stockholders.

In exchange for these two preferences, preferred stockholders surrender the basic rights of common shareholders, which were previously described.

Occasionally, preferred stocks may have callable or convertible provisions such as those for bonds. The effect of these features on the amount of the preferred dividend is the same as on the bond interest rate. The preferred's stated dividend is higher if the feature favors the corporation or lower if it benefits the shareholder. In some cases, preferred stockholders elect some or all members of the board of directors if dividends have not been paid to them for a specified number of years.

American Depositary Receipts (ADRs)

Many investors desire to own shares in foreign corporations. These shares can be purchased abroad in the same way that domestic corporation shares are purchased in the United States. However, inconvenient trading hours due to time differences and large transaction fees make these transactions undesirable. To overcome these problems, some U.S. banks have acquired shares in foreign corporations and hold these shares in trust in one of their foreign branches. Then they sell negotiable instruments, called American Depositary Receipts (ADRs), that represent a specified number of shares in a foreign company. ADRs are the equivalent of ownership of the stock, trade as such in domestic markets, and have rights and privileges as are accorded common shareholders in the country of issue.

Investment Companies

Investment companies can be distinguished in several ways. For example, there is a distinction between closed-end and open-end investment companies.

closed-end investment company

At formation, a *closed-end investment company* issues a given number of shares. Rarely, if ever, are additional shares issued. These shares are traded in the stock markets in exactly the same manner as those of traditional corporations, such as General Motors. That is, the forces of demand and supply for the stock determine the share price.

The closed-end investment company uses the proceeds from the initial sale of its stock to acquire a portfolio of securities. The market value of this portfolio influences, but does not directly determine, the market price of the closed-end company's shares. Theoretically, the value of a share in a closed-end investment company should equal the net asset value of the portfolio. The net asset value (NAV) is as follows:

$$\text{Net asset value} = \frac{\text{Total assets} - \text{total liabilities}}{\text{Number of shares outstanding}}$$

However, the shares of most closed-end investment companies sell at a discount to their net asset values. When stock market prices in general are buoyant, the discount, as a percentage of net asset value, typically declines. The reverse occurs during periods when general stock market prices decline. Occasionally the shares of some closed-end funds trade at a premium, that is, a market price that is higher than the NAV.

open-end investment company

An *open-end investment company*, popularly called a mutual fund, continually sells and redeems its shares at net asset value. Hence, the shares are not traded in the stock market. Similar to closed-end companies, mutual funds acquire a portfolio of securities in which each of the fund's shares owns a proportionate interest. As sales and redemptions of the fund's shares take place, the size of the fund's total portfolio changes, increasing when additional shares are issued and decreasing when shares are redeemed.

The nature of the acquisition fees is another distinguishing characteristic among investment companies. Buyers of closed-end shares, because the shares are traded on securities markets, are subject to normal stock-brokerage commissions for both purchase and sale transactions. Some mutual funds charge a sales fee and are called load funds. The loading is regulated, and it can be as high as 8.5 percent of the value of the investment. If no sales fee is levied, the fund is called a no-load fund.

Technically, this load versus no-load distinction should refer not only to an initial sales fee but also to other fees that carry different names but are used to compensate individuals for selling and marketing efforts. One of these fees is the 12-b(1) fee, which is an annual charge against the net assets of the fund that typically ranges from 0.1 to 1.0 percent. A fund may call itself a no-load fund as long as its 12-b(1) fee does not exceed one-quarter of one percent. About 60 percent of all funds now charge 12-b(1) fees. A second type of marketing fee is called an exit fee, deferred-sales charge, or back-end load. This is not a modest charge simply to cover the expenses of processing a redemption. Rather, the exit fee is sometimes as high as 4 or 5 percent of the dollar value of the shares being redeemed and is used to pay the marketing and selling costs. Some individuals believe that a true no-load fund assesses investors neither a front-end, a 12-b(1), nor a deferred sales fee, because these are all forms of marketing and selling costs. Regardless of whether the fund is load or no-load, the shareholders must pay the administrative, transactions, and investment advising expenses incurred by the fund. These expenses are deducted from the interest, dividend, and capital-gain fund income prior to distributing fund income to the shareholders.

Under the federal laws that regulate security transactions, a prospectus (a document that gives a potential buyer the relevant information about a newly issued security) must be delivered to security buyers before a purchase takes place. The initial material of the prospectus includes required tables showing the amount of all loads and other expenses associated with the purchase, holding, and sale of the fund's shares. Therefore, the magnitude of these additional fees can be determined by the investor.

Investment companies can also be differentiated on the basis of their portfolio objectives. The more than 10,000 open-end and closed-end investment companies in existence at the end of 2006 can be segregated into several broad categories and subcategories based on their portfolio objectives.[4] These major categories are as follows:

- money market mutual funds—These funds own a portfolio of short-term interest-bearing securities. As mentioned earlier, they are used by investors as an alternative to cash. They operate only as open-end funds. Subcategories include funds that focus mainly on nontaxable securities or federal securities only or on diversified portfolios.
- index funds—These funds own a portfolio of common stock that replicates a major market index, such as the S&P 500. They operate only as open-end funds.
- bond funds—These companies own a portfolio of bonds. Subcategories include some that invest only in U.S. government issues, municipal issues, corporate issues, and low-quality (junk) bonds. Further subcategories can be short-term (up to 4 or 5 years), intermediate-term (5 to 10 years), or long-term (10 or more years duration) bond funds.
- common stock funds—These companies hold a portfolio of common stocks and perhaps a small number of preferred stocks. Subcategories include those that invest primarily in conservative or *defensive stocks*, *growth stocks*, *value stocks*, *large cap stocks*, *small cap stocks*, and foreign stocks.
- mixed portfolio funds—These companies own a portfolio of bonds, stocks, and other investment instruments. Subcategories include balanced funds and income funds.
- specialty funds—These companies have very specialized portfolios designed for investors who seek special investment opportunities. The most common is the sector fund, which specializes in stocks from a single industry or country.

defensive stocks
growth stocks
value stocks
large cap stocks
small cap stocks

In some cases, an investment company is a totally separate organization that has no links to any other business venture. More often, to enable the fund sponsors to meet a wide range of client preferences, a fund is a part of a family of funds representing several of the above categories or subcategories of portfolio objectives. This feature permits investors to move their investments from stocks to bonds to money market instruments as conditions change. Small fees are sometimes charged when a switch is made within the family of funds. Every time a switch is made, there is an income tax consequence because a sale, and then a purchase transaction, occurred.

Several reasons have been advanced to explain the current popularity of investment companies. The first is that each share in an investment company benefits from the pooled diversification of the portfolio. In addition, the professional management that selects and continuously monitors the securities and the appropriate securities markets should provide better overall portfolio performance than can the typical individual investor. A third reason is that many investors lack the time to properly select securities and can better delegate this responsibility to others. A fourth reason is that the wide diversity of investment companies allows an investor to select the diversified portfolio that best suits his or her investment objective. The tax and record keeping provided by the fund management is another reason for the popularity of investment companies. Last, as more companies institute 401(k) plans for their employees, shares of different mutual funds frequently are some of the permitted choices suitable for participants. The major disadvantage of funds is that, on average, they underperform market averages by an amount equal to their annual fees.

Real Estate and Other Investments

Real Estate

Many forms of real estate ownership are available to investors. One such form is the purchase of property directly, either as an individual or as a managing partner in a partnership. One way that requires less active management by the investor is owning shares in a real estate investment trust (which is similar to an investment company but the trust either owns property it manages or owns a portfolio of real estate mortgages). A second way is by owning a limited-partnership interest in a general partnership. This limited-partnership interest has no active role in the firm's management. Real estate investments usually involve more complexities than the previous investment categories because of

- the uniqueness of each property
- the differing rights associated with ownership of each property
- the absence of organized markets for the ready sale and purchase of the property or ownership interest
- the complexity of the federal taxation of the income and appreciation from real estate (other than the investor's primary residence)

Before embarking into real estate for investment purposes, most such investors should remember that they probably already have a major investment in real estate: their own home.

Other Investments

Virtually any asset can be used for investment purposes. Over the years, such activities as cattle feeding (usually a farming or feed lot operation) or oil-and-gas drilling and exploration activities have been used as limited-partnership tax-advantaged investments. The growth of the options, futures, and commodities markets has spawned investment instruments that offer different objectives. In addition, the federal government's granting permission for U.S. citizens to own gold was instrumental in expanding markets for investment instruments such as gold bullion, gold coins, gold futures, and gold-mining stocks. Moreover, although coins along with stamps have long been collectibles, other types of collectibles have become popular because of the strong economic performance of coins and stamps. Art, ceramics, and china have captured the fancy of many individuals due to the appreciation of selected items. For most collectibles, the spread between the current purchase price and the amount of the sales proceeds an investor receives from a dealer is sizable.

Similar to real estate, each of these investments is a specialty field unto itself. Any technical treatment of the characteristics of these investments is beyond the scope of this introductory discussion.

SOURCES OF INVESTMENT RISK

Both the concept of speculative risk and the definition of investment risk as the magnitude of the range of possible returns were discussed earlier in this chapter. Let us now consider the sources of risk.

Purchasing Power Risk

purchasing power risk

One major source of risk is always *purchasing power risk*, sometimes called inflation risk. Inflation is the increase in the general level of prices. It is estimated by the Bureau of Labor Statistics, and is based on the concept of what it would take to buy the basket of goods and services typically purchased by a family of four living in an urban community. Although inflation rates are published with great precision, they are always, at best, an approximation because of the fact that not everyone buys this same basket of goods and services, and that changes in the quality of goods and services are difficult to incorporate into this calculation.

real rate of return

nominal rate of return

The impact of inflation is popularly misunderstood. Suppose someone had $100,000 to invest, and this person earned a 5 percent rate of return over the course of a year. If over that same year, the rate of inflation turned out to be 3 percent, then we would say that this person's *real rate of return* is approximately 2 percent. The rate actually earned, 5 percent, is referred to as the *nominal rate of return*, and the real rate can always be approximated as the nominal rate less the inflation rate. A more precise measure of the real rate of return is as follows:

$$\text{Real rate of return} = \frac{(1 + \text{nominal rate of return})}{(1 + \text{current rate of inflation})} - 1$$

Both the nominal rate of return and the current rate of inflation must be expressed as decimals in this formula.

Thus, the real rate of return in the above example would be calculated as follows:

$$\text{Real rate of return} = \frac{(1 + .05)}{(1 + .03)} - 1$$
$$= 1.019 - 1$$
$$= .019 \text{ or } 1.9\%$$

The key point to understand is that even if this investor had taken the $100,000 and put it under a mattress, the inflation rate would still have been 3 percent, and he or she would still have lost purchasing power. So, the investor did not lose purchasing power as a result of investing the money, the loss of purchasing power would have occurred whether or not the money was invested. However, investing the money reduced the impact of inflation.

Besides inflation's effect on purchasing power, another risk from inflation lies in the fact that inflation will actually affect the performance of some investments. Consider as an example the stocks of two companies, A and B. If Company A has the flexibility to raise the prices of its products as other prices rise, particularly the prices it pays for raw materials, then its stock's price should be relatively unaffected by inflation. However, if Company B is not able to raise the prices of its products despite the fact that the costs of its raw materials are rising, its profits and, thus, its stock's price will almost certainly be harmed by inflation. Moreover, some companies may actually benefit from inflation if they can raise the prices of their products faster than the rate of inflation without affecting sales, or if they are able to hold down the prices they pay for raw materials. Thus, different companies, depending on the nature of their businesses and how they operate, will be affected differently by inflation.

Looking at another example, suppose the impact of inflation is not uniform across all products and that there is a tremendous jump in the price of oil, while the prices of coal and natural gas remain relatively stable. In this situation, companies that use oil for energy will be hurt, but companies that use coal and natural gas for energy will be relatively unaffected.

Interest Rate Risk

interest rate risk

Another major source of risk for investors is *interest rate risk*. Due to many forces at work in the economy, such as actions by the Federal Reserve System to control money supply, changes in the demand for borrowed funds, and/or movements of foreign exchange rates, interest rates will change over time. The result of these changing interest rates is that the value of securities, the income earned on securities, or both will also change over time. This effect, known as interest rate risk, has two segments: price risk and reinvestment rate risk.

price risk

Price risk results from the fact that any change in market interest rates typically leads to an opposite change in the value of investments. When interest rates rise (fall), the value of an investment declines (increases). This inverse relationship is most pronounced for debt instruments, such as bonds, mortgages, and U.S. Treasury bills that have a contractually specified rate of interest or return and a specified time to maturity. The longer the time until maturity, the greater will be the resulting change in market price. For other instruments, such as common stock or real estate, the relationship is not as pronounced, but it is nonetheless present. In fact, not only do changes in interest rates affect the valuation of securities, they also affect the profitability of many companies. When interest rates rise, some businesses, such as banks, tend to become more profitable.

The following example will illustrate why the value of an investment changes when interest rates change. Suppose that an investor purchased a bond when the market interest rate for the bond's risk was 8 percent and that this $1,000 face-amount bond has a maturity date one year hence and pays interest of $80 annually. Next assume that on the following day the market interest rate for bonds of this same risk and maturity rises to 9 percent. Of course this investor would now like to sell this bond for $1,000. However, the investor will not be able to do so because a potential buyer can obtain $90 interest (instead of $80) by purchasing a newly issued, one-year maturity bond. However, a price can be determined that would make the total return, both interest income and appreciation in the market price of the 8 percent bond, such that a potential buyer would be virtually indifferent to either the existing 8 percent or a newly issued 9 percent bond. This price would have to be somewhat less than $1,000 so that the buyer's total return would be 9 percent. Alternatively, if the market interest rate had fallen to 7 percent, the value of the

8 percent bond would rise above its $1,000 face amount so that the total return to the buyer would be equal to 7 percent.

Rather than the one-year maturity used in the previous example, suppose the security had a 10-year maturity. With a 9 percent market interest rate, a buyer would have $10 less interest each year for 10 years if he or she buys the 8 percent debt instrument. Therefore, the resulting market price change for this 8 percent security with a 10-year maturity date must be greater than for the one-year maturity in the previous example. This potential change in the market price of debt securities takes on importance if a sale of the security is anticipated prior to its stated maturity date. The longer the time remaining until maturity, the greater will be the resulting market price change.

How can a financial advisor make use of this relationship between the interest rate and the market price of debt securities? If it is anticipated that the forces affecting interest rates are working to increase them, the advisor should counsel the investor to sell the debt instruments in his or her portfolio. If interest rates do in fact rise, securities similar to those that were disposed of can be repurchased at lower prices. If interest rates are expected to decrease, the investor should be advised to purchase debt securities that, after interest rates decrease, can be sold at a gain.

reinvestment rate risk

Reinvestment rate risk is the risk associated with reinvesting investment income at unknown future interest rates. Suppose an investor buys $100,000 worth of 10-year bonds that pay $5,000 in interest annually. At maturity, the investor would expect to receive back his or her $100,000 in principal, plus to have accumulated $50,000 in interest payments (10 years x $5,000 per year), plus interest income from reinvesting the interest payments during that 10-year period. If interest rates rise during the 10 years, the investor will be able to reinvest the interest payments for a higher rate of return than anticipated. If interest rates fall during the 10 years, the investor will have to be satisfied with reinvesting the interest payments at a lower rate of return than anticipated. The level of interest rates over the 10-year period will have a substantial impact on the investor's final accumulation.

The important feature about price risk and reinvestment rate risk is that they work in opposite directions. For an investor holding a bond, there is always both good news and bad news when interest rates change, regardless of the direction of change. When interest rates rise, interest payments can be reinvested at higher rates, but the price of the bond falls. When interest rates fall, reinvested interest payments receive lower rates of return, but the price of the bond rises. The task for the investor when interest rates are changing is to have the opposing effects from price risk and reinvestment rate risk exactly offset each other so that the news from price risk, whether it be good or bad, exactly offsets the news from reinvestment rate risk.

It should be noted that purchasing power or inflation risk and interest rate risk are related because the rate of inflation is the major determinant of the level of interest rates. In almost all instances when the rate of inflation increases, interest rates rise, and vice versa for decreases in the rate of inflation.

Business Risk

business (default) risk

Investors must consider the *business (default) risk* for each of their investments. For whatever reason, whether it be changes in consumer preference away from a particular good or service, ineffective management, law changes, or foreign competition, some enterprises will experience financial difficulties and will be unable to repay bond principal or make interest payments on a timely basis. Consequently, investors in the bonds of these defaulting organizations may not receive interest payments, or worse yet, may even lose some or all of their principal. And this unfortunate situation can happen to investors in either profit-seeking businesses or nonprofit institutions such as municipalities.

Because the debts of bankrupt corporations in the process of being liquidated must be paid in full before any funds can flow to their stockholders, rarely is anything left for the owners of profit-seeking firms that have failed. (There is no equity ownership in nonprofit or governmental organizations.) Of course, this business (default) risk is not associated with debt instruments of the U.S. Treasury, which are backed by the full faith, credit, and taxing power of the federal government.

An investment strategy designed to minimize the business (default) risk is to purchase only bonds that are issued by organizations having a high credit rating. As mentioned earlier, both Moody's and Standard & Poor's provide assessments of the investment quality of various bond issues. Obtaining this type of information for other forms of investments, such as limited partnerships, requires a diligent investigation by the financial advisor or the investor.

SPECIAL PORTFOLIO CONSIDERATIONS

There are several concerns a financial advisor needs to worry about when selecting securities for a portfolio. Two key aspects of investment planning, namely ascertaining the client's financial risk tolerance and then making an appropriate asset allocation decision, have already been discussed. Other issues that need to be dealt with are liquidity, marketability, taxation, and diversification.

Liquidity

An asset is said to be liquid if it can be converted to cash (sold) quickly at any time with little or no loss of principal. Every portfolio should have some *liquidity* in it because it allows clients the flexibility to quickly obtain cash for emergency purposes. There are two different ways to obtain liquidity. One is to own liquid assets. Liquid assets were discussed earlier, and they include such investments as savings accounts, MMDAs, MMMF's, and Treasury bills.

There is, of course, a drawback to owning liquid assets, which is that they tend to have the lowest expected rates of return. Although there is negligible risk in owning liquid assets, there is also negligible return. Put another way, there are often substantial *opportunity costs* to owning liquid assets.

An alternative way to have liquidity is to have readily available opportunities for borrowing money. Consider the following example:

Example: John Robbins has a portfolio worth about $500,000. The portfolio is mostly common stocks with a few bonds. It is held in a margin account, but there currently is no borrowing against this account. There are no money market securities in the account. John suddenly needs $20,000 to buy a new car. What are his choices?

John's first choice is to sell some securities, but this may trigger taxes and will certainly generate some transaction fees. A second choice for John is to borrow the cash from the brokerage firm. A margin account permits an investor to either borrow money from a brokerage firm to buy securities or pledge currently held securities as collateral for a loan. The amount that can be borrowed or pledged depends on the type and amount of securities held and the borrowing rules set by the Federal Reserve Board, which permit loans up to 50 percent of the value of an investor's portfolio. So John can borrow up to $250,000 against his portfolio, although he needs to borrow only $20,000 for a new car. The interest rate on a $20,000 margin account loan to John would be his cost for obtaining liquidity. In the meantime, John would have minimized his opportunity costs by not holding any low yielding money market securities in his portfolio.

> Interest expense accruing on margin account debt typically is tax deductible as investment interest if used to buy taxable securities. It would not be tax deductible for money borrowed to buy a new car. Thus, any interest expense on a $20,000 margin account loan to John to buy a new car would be considered nondeductible personal interest even though the debt would be secured by his investment portfolio.
>
> Perhaps a better way for John to have some liquidity is for him to establish a home equity line of credit. Interest on up to $100,000 of home equity indebtedness typically is tax deductible even if the loan proceeds are used for personal expenditures, such as buying a new car

The key point to all of this discussion is that everyone needs liquidity, and there are two ways to have liquidity. One is to own liquid assets, and the other is to own assets that allow for quick and convenient loans.

Marketability

marketability

Marketability is a little different than liquidity, but the two are frequently confused. Marketability refers to the ability to sell an asset quickly. Thus, liquid assets are marketable, but not all marketable assets are liquid. Stock is a classic example of a marketable asset that is not liquid. If a stock is listed on a major exchange, it can be sold in a matter of seconds. However, there is no certainty as to the price at which the stock can be sold. It is important that portfolios have marketable assets, but this is not a substitute for liquidity. Also, this does not mean that it is inappropriate to hold some nonmarketable assets. For example, homes are nonmarketable assets. It often takes weeks and even months to sell a typical home, and the transaction fees can be substantial. Jewelry is another such asset.

Taxation

Financial advisors must pay careful attention to their clients' tax situations when making investment recommendations. The main reason is that different tax rates apply to different forms of income, and the timing of when the taxes are due can be quite different. The first critical feature to understand is that taxation of ordinary income varies depending on income level. The federal income tax is a progressive tax, and this means that higher tax rates apply to incremental income as the individual's total income increases.

Example: Suppose that a financial advisor has two clients with different income levels. The first client, Robert Roe, is a bank teller and has a taxable income of $20,000, placing him squarely in the 15 percent income tax bracket. The second client, Sally Jo, is an executive vice president with a large firm and has a taxable income of $400,000, placing her in the top 35 percent income tax bracket. They each ask the advisor to help them invest $100,000 in bonds, and the advisor offers them two choices. They are Park District bonds, which pay an annual interest rate of 4 percent, and First National Bank bonds, which pay an annual interest rate of 5 percent. The Park District bonds have the lower interest rate because, as municipal bonds, they are exempt from federal income taxes. Both Robert and Sally say they do not enjoy paying income taxes, and thus, want to buy Park District bonds. Is this a good choice for both of them?

A $100,000 investment in Park District bonds would produce interest income of $4,000 per year ($100,000 principal x 4 percent interest rate), while a $100,000 investment in First National bonds would produce interest income of $5,000 per year ($100,000 principal x 5 percent interest rate). For Robert, the purchase of First National bonds would provide an extra $5,000 of taxable income each year and would bring his total taxable income up to $25,000 per year. The extra $5,000 would still be taxed to Robert at the rate of 15 percent because his now larger taxable income of $25,000 would not be large enough to move him up to the next higher (25 percent) tax bracket. Thus, Robert's taxes on the $5,000 of interest income would be $750 ($5,000 x 15 percent). After the payment of taxes, he would still have $4,250 left. This is greater than the interest income from the tax-exempt bonds. Consequently, Robert should clearly invest in the First National bonds, even though he prefers not having to pay taxes.

In Sally's case, the purchase of First National bonds would require her to pay $1,750 in taxes ($5,000 x 35 percent), leaving her with $3,250. Clearly, Sally would be better off buying the Park District tax-exempt bonds even though the total interest paid is only $4,000 (versus $5,000 for the First National bonds)

The following formula converts a tax-exempt yield to an equivalent taxable yield:

$$\text{Equivalent fully taxable yield} = \frac{\text{tax-exempt yield}}{(1 - \text{MRT})}$$

where: MRT is the investor's marginal income tax rate

A second formula converts a fully taxable yield to an equivalent tax-exempt yield:

$$\text{Equivalent tax-exempt yield} = \text{fully taxable yield} \times (1 - \text{MRT})$$

To use these formulas, the tax-exempt yield or the fully taxable yield must be expressed as a percentage, while the marginal tax rate must be expressed as a decimal.

Another aspect to the taxation of investment income is that long-term capital gains traditionally have been taxed at a lower rate than interest or dividend income. However, under the Jobs and Growth Tax Relief Reconciliation Act (JGTRRA) of 2003, qualified dividends received by individual shareholders from domestic (and qualified foreign) corporations generally are taxed at the same rates that apply to long-term capital gains. A long-term capital gain occurs whenever an asset held for more than 1 year is sold for more than was paid for it. Not only that, but taxes on a long-term capital gain are due only when the asset is sold.

Example: Frank Kasper bought some stock when he was 25 years old for $1,000. He is now 75 years old and still holds that stock. Even though the company has never paid dividends, the stock is now worth $46,902. How much has Frank had to pay in taxes from this investment?

The answer, of course, is zero, because the company has never paid dividends (hence, no taxes were payable on dividend income), and Frank still owns the stock (hence, no capital gains taxes are due).

Another interesting aspect to the tax treatment of investments is that a person who dies can leave a certain amount of assets to his or her children without incurring any federal estate tax liability. The amount of assets exempted from estate taxation in 2008 is $2 million and is scheduled to increase to $3.5 million for 2009. Moreover, a person's assets transferred at his or her death will acquire a new basis in the hands of the beneficiaries equal to fair market value. Therefore, if Frank from our previous example were to suddenly die and leave the stock to his children, not only would he never have paid income and/or capital gains taxes on the stock while he was alive, but his children could immediately sell the stock for its current value of $46,902 without incurring any capital gains taxes. In addition, if all the assets (including the stock) in Frank's estate do not put it over the exemption amount, no federal estate taxes will be payable either.

The key point of this section is that investors who are in high tax brackets can enhance the after-tax returns of their portfolios by investing in stocks of domestic (and qualified foreign) corporations, tax-exempt bonds, and/or assets with a large potential for capital appreciation. On the other hand, investors who are in low tax brackets can benefit by focusing their investment activity on assets that provide the largest amount of current taxable income. However, regardless of the tax bracket that investors are in, their investments must be commensurate with their financial risk tolerances.

Diversification

diversification

The importance of *diversification* in a client's portfolio can never be overemphasized. Asset allocation among a variety of investments is a first step in the diversification process. For example, a portfolio with a goal of asset allocation as shown below already has a good first round of diversification.

10%	Cash equivalents
10%	Intermediate term government bonds
10%	Long-term government bonds
20%	Long-term corporate bonds
20%	Large cap stocks
20%	Value stocks
<u>10%</u>	Sector mutual funds
100%	

However, within each of these categories, an investor has to be sure there is not excessive concentration within an industry. For example, the large cap stocks category should not have large holdings of both General Motors and Ford. Similarly, there should not be concentration across categories. If the investor holds stock in General Motors, he or she should not also hold General Motors bonds. Finally, the investor should be cautious about investing too heavily in investments that are closely aligned with his or her occupation. For example, if the investor is a software engineer for an internet firm, his or her portfolio should not be too heavily concentrated in internet stocks. The reason is that if the internet industry collapses (as it did in 2000), then not only would there be a drop in the value of the investor's portfolio, but he or she also might be out of a job. It is tempting for people to want to invest in industries with which they are familiar, but it should be done with caution. The principle of diversification should always be adhered to no matter how strong the temptation to do otherwise. The financial advisor should monitor his or her clients' portfolios to make sure they are and will remain diversified.

INVESTMENT RETURNS

As indicated earlier, the returns on an investment come in two forms: current income and capital appreciation. Not all investments produce both forms of return. Some investments, such as savings accounts, produce only current (interest) income. Others, such as undeveloped land, produce only capital appreciation (unless the land can be farmed or rented). Still others, such as borrowing to purchase common stock when the annual interest expense from borrowing is greater than the dividends being paid, produce negative current income. However, in the case of common stock, there is always the potential for capital appreciation or depreciation, regardless of whether current income is positive or negative.

Despite varying combinations of current income and capital appreciation, a method for comparing the investment returns from different investments is an absolute necessity. Over the years and before computers or calculators, three quick methods for measuring an investment's return acquired widespread acceptance within the investment community. Still widely used, these three methods of measuring return are the (1) current yield, (2) holding-period return (HPR), and (3) approximate yield.

Current Yield

current yield

The *current yield* is perhaps the most widely used of the three methods for measuring an investment's return. It is calculated by dividing an investment's current annual income by its current market price as follows:

$$\text{Before-tax current yield} = \frac{\text{current annual income}}{\text{current market price}}$$

For example, assume that an investor purchases a corporate bond for $1,050 and that it will pay him or her an annual interest income of $98. Under these circumstances, the investor's before-tax current yield from the bond would be calculated as follows:

$$\text{Before-tax current yield} = \frac{\$98}{\$1,050}$$
$$= .0933 \text{ or } 9.33\%$$

One advantage of the current yield is that it provides a quick way to compare different investments being considered for purchase, retention, or sale. The current yield is particularly important when an investor needs a certain amount of annual income from his or her portfolio. For example, if an investor has a portfolio worth $500,000 and wants an income of $20,000 per year from the portfolio, the portfolio must produce a current yield of 4 percent ($20,000/$500,000) each year.

The major shortcoming of the current yield is that it fails to look beyond the present moment. The investments being compared may have different potentials for future increases or decreases in their income streams or market prices. This possibility is not considered when calculating the current yield. A second shortcoming is that the calculation is made on a before-tax basis. To calculate an after-tax current yield, the above formula must be modified so that the current annual income is reduced by the investor's marginal rate of tax (MRT). The following formula makes this adjustment:

$$\text{After-tax current yield} = \frac{\text{current annual income} \times (1 - \text{MRT})}{\text{current market price}}$$

where: MRT is the investor's marginal income tax rate

As previously mentioned, qualified dividends received by individuals following the passage of the JGTRRA are taxed at the same rates that apply to long-term capital gains. Consequently, an investor's MRT depends on the type of income being received (qualified dividends versus interest) as well as the different tax rates imposed by the taxing authorities (state versus federal).

If a 28 percent marginal income tax rate applies to the investor in the previous example, his or her after-tax current yield would be calculated as follows:

$$\text{After-tax current yield} = \frac{\$98 \times (1 - .28)}{\$1,050} = \frac{\$98 \times .72}{\$1,050} = \frac{\$70.56}{\$1,050}$$

$$= .067 \text{ or } 6.7\%$$

Alternatively, the investor's before-tax current yield of 9.33 percent shown above can be multiplied by one minus the investor's marginal tax rate to obtain the after-tax current yield of 6.7 percent [9.33% x (1 – .28)].

Holding-Period Return (HPR)

holding-period return (HPR)

Although the name *holding-period return (HPR)* may imply that the method is used to measure an investment's return over any holding period, it is most appropriate for investment periods of one year[5]. This is because no consideration is given to the timing of investment returns and, therefore, to the time value of money. The HPR is calculatd by dividing the total amount of current income plus the total amount of capital appreciation by the beginning dollar valuc of the investment. The following formula shows this relationship for a before-tax HPR for a one-year period as follows:

$$\text{Before-tax HPR} = \frac{\text{total current income} + \text{total capital appreciation}}{\text{total initial investment}}$$

For example, assume that an investor in the 28 percent income tax bracket purchased common stock one year ago for $800 and that he or she wants to know what the HPR return is on the stock. During the onc-year holding period, the investor received $50 of dividend income, and the stock's market price increased from $800 to $840. Based on this information, the before-tax HPR for the stock investment would be calculated as follows:

$$\text{Before-tax HPR} = \frac{\$50 + (\$840 - \$800)}{\$800}$$

$$= \frac{\$90}{\$800}$$

$$= .1125 \text{ or } 11.25\%$$

If an after-tax HPR is desired, the formula is as follows:

$$\text{After-tax HPR} = \frac{[TCI \times (1 - MRT)] + [TCA \times (1 - TCG)]}{\text{total initial investment}}$$

where: TCI is the investor's total current income
MRT is the investor's marginal income tax rate
TCA is the investor's total capital appreciation
TCG is the investor's tax rate for capital gains

However, because the investor's MRT for qualified dividends under JGTRRA is 15 percent, the same as his or her TCG under JGTRRA, his or her after-tax HPR return would be calculated as follows:

$$\text{After-tax HPR} = \frac{\$50(1 - .15) + [(\$840 - \$800)(1 - .15)]}{\$800}$$

$$= \frac{\$50(.85) + \$40(.85)}{\$800}$$

$$= \frac{\$42.5 + \$34}{\$800} = \frac{\$76.5}{\$800}$$

$$= .0956 \text{ or } 9.56\%$$

Approximate Yield

The true yield of an investment can be described as the rate of interest or discount rate (called the internal rate of return) that makes the present value of the benefits derived from the investment exactly equal to the present value of the cost to purchase the investment. This calculation can be fairly complex, so investors often calculate a quick approximation. The most common approximation is known as the *approximate yield*, and it is found by using the following formula:

approximate yield

$$\text{Before-tax approximate yield} = \frac{\text{annual income} + \dfrac{\text{future price} - \text{current price}}{\text{number of years}}}{\dfrac{\text{future price} + \text{current price}}{2}}$$

For example, assume that an investor is interested in buying a particular stock that is currently selling for $50 a share but is expected to increase in value to $68 a share by the end of 3 years. The annual dividends from the stock are expected to average $3 for each of the next 3 years. Based on this information, the investor's approximate yield for the 3-year holding period would be calculated as follows:

$$\text{Before-tax approximate yield} = \frac{\$3 + \dfrac{\$68 - \$50}{3}}{\dfrac{\$68 + \$50}{2}}$$

$$= \frac{\$3 + \$6}{\$59} = \frac{\$9}{\$59}$$

$$= .1525 \text{ or } 15.26\%$$

If there is no difference in the tax rates applied to the two types of income (as is the case for qualified dividends and long-term capital gains following the passage of JGTRRA), the after-tax approximate yield can be computed by multiplying the before-tax approximate yield by one minus the investor's appropriate tax rate (that is, TCG if the investment involves both qualified dividends and capital appreciation, although long-term capital gains taxes will be payable only if the asset has actually been sold). However, in situations where the MRT and TCG differ, then each segment of the numerator must be multiplied by one minus the investor's appropriate tax rate for that type of income.

The approximate-yield method can provide a meaningful estimate of an investment's yield over both short and long holding periods. Applications of this method include (1) estimating the yield over a planned holding period, as shown in the previous example, (2) determining the yield from the date of acquisition to the present on a currently owned investment, and (3) determining what the yield was for an investment that has been sold. Only the purpose of the calculation changes; the formula remains unchanged.

Whenever the rate of inflation exceeds the after-tax rate of return obtained over a holding period, an investor will realize a negative real after-tax rate of return. This was the situation for many investors during the late 1970s and early 1980s when inflation rates in the United States neared and even exceeded 10 percent and the before-tax return on some investments was 5 percent.

INVESTMENT PRINCIPLES, STRATEGIES, AND TECHNIQUES

Now that the types of investments frequently used and various investment risks and returns have been examined, this section will describe some of the investment principles, strategies, and techniques recommended by financial advisors and used by successful investors. Not all are appropriate in all situations, but collectively, they provide the advisor with some guidelines that he or she can follow when advising clients.

Meeting Emergency and Protection Needs First

No investments should be undertaken unless the investor has first set aside some funds for emergency purposes. Obviously, a large portion of the investor's emergency funds could be placed in investments that provide a current return. However, the choices for these investments are limited to cash equivalents, such as bank savings accounts or MMDAs. These types of investments are highly liquid as required to be for emergency situations, but typically they do not provide much in the way of a return.

Besides preparing for possible emergency situations, an investor should also take steps prior to undertaking an investment program to protect himself or herself from the various pure risks (which can be categorized as personal risks, property risks, and liability risks) identified in chapter 2. As indicated in chapter 2, insurance is the primary technique, and for many people the only meaningful technique, for dealing with most of the pure risks that people face in their everyday lives.

Matching Investment Instruments with Investment Goals

The investment must be appropriate for the personal financial goal that is being sought. For example, individual retirement accounts (IRAs) accumulate interest on a tax-free basis until the monies are withdrawn. Therefore, using tax-free municipal bonds as an IRA funding instrument is not a prudent course of action, since the IRA already provides for the benefit of tax deferral regardless of the type of funding instrument used. A better course of action would be to fund the IRA with investments that provide a higher rate of return commensurate with the client's financial risk tolerance and retirement goals.

When funds are being accumulated for purposes that are not deferrable, it is essential to have virtually the precise amount available at the needed time. For example, investments whose market price fluctuates sharply or investments that are not readily salable would not be appropriate for funding a child's expected education expenses. For this type of goal, the proper approach would be to match the investment's maturity with the date the funds are needed.

In yet another example, a young client who is funding for retirement should not use short-term investments, because these usually do not provide for very high returns and offer little opportunity for appreciation over the planning horizon. Instead, investments that have long-term capital growth as their objective are more likely to offset the inflation that is expected to occur over the next 10, 20, or 30 years.

Holding Periods for Equity Investments

planned holding period

Investments in common stocks that are owned individually or through investment companies should generally have a *planned holding period* of at least 5 years. Any period shorter than 5 years subjects the stocks to increased risk. The problem of market timing, or when to buy or sell, and the transactions costs of the purchase and sale combine to make success quite difficult with shorter-term holding periods.

In addition, the behavior of the stock market favors at least a 5-year holding period. Combined with the dividends earned on a portfolio of common stocks, the ups and downs of the market typically are such that only a few 5-year holding periods fail to provide positive returns. However, many shorter holding periods, such as one year or less, have produced negative total returns.

Other equity investments, such as real estate, require even longer planned holding periods due to their relatively higher transactions costs and their general lack of marketability. Indeed, for some limited partnerships that invest in real estate, financial advisors often advocate at least a 10-year planned holding period.

Tax-Saving Rationale

Investment analysis and decision making should focus on the underlying economic facts. Sometimes financial advisors who recommend investments focus on the tax benefits that will accrue to the client rather than on the economic soundness of the venture. Frequent tax legislation over the past two decades stands as a monument to the fact that government can drastically change the tax rules. Many investments that were made solely on the basis of tax considerations have generated problems and losses for their owners. Certainly tax considerations influence investment decisions, and their effect must be analyzed. However, tax considerations are only one of many factors that determine the economic soundness of an investment.

Understanding the Investment

Selecting and managing some types of investments require little or no knowledge, facilities, or time commitment. For instance, an investor need not be an expert on short-term debt securities to understand the relevant characteristics (risk, expected return, liquidity, marketability, and tax treatment) of Treasury bills and similar securities. However, individuals who invest in real estate, collectibles, soybean futures, or mink farms need special knowledge, talent, and/or facilities. Similarly, some types of investments may be maintained with little or no effort (bonds), whereas others require constant management (an apartment complex). Accordingly, financial advisors and/or investors need to carefully consider the expertise, talent, facilities, and time required to assemble and manage a particular type of investment portfolio. A financial advisor should never recommend an investment to a client that is not fully understood by both the advisor and the client.

Using a Consistent Pattern of Investing

Attempts to outguess the market or to predict the start of the next downturn or upturn and, thus, achieve superior returns through market timing for each and every investment are never worth the effort. For example, one study showed that if $5,000 was invested every year in a particular stock mutual fund from 1975 to 1995, the 20 $5,000 investments along with the reinvestment of all dividends and capital gains would have grown to a value of $484,521 in 20 years for an average annual total return of 13.5 percent. Suppose this investor had perfect knowledge (or with perfect hindsight) and the purchases were made each year at the lowest net asset value per share of this fund. How much better would the return have been? The accumulated value would have been $500,249 and the average annual total return would have been 14.1 percent over the 20-year period. Either the 13.5 percent or the 14.1 percent return is quite acceptable. And how many individuals can accurately predict the lowest point of the market in any one year, let alone in every year for 20 years?

Another study, using the Standard and Poor's 500 Stock Index for the years 1968 to 1988, returned 18.5 percent per year if the purchases were made at the lowest point and 16.6 percent if the purchases were at the peak of the market each year. The biggest loss to investors who attempt to engage in market timing is the opportunity losses associated with not being invested when a big jump in prices occurs.

dollar cost averaging

To avoid the necessity of trying to time the market, an investor can engage in *dollar cost averaging*. This method requires the investment of a fixed amount of dollars at specified time intervals. Investing a fixed amount of dollars at set intervals means that the investor buys more shares when prices are low and fewer shares when prices are high. Unless the market goes into a persistent decline, dollar cost averaging works fairly well, and it establishes a consistent pattern of investing. Moreover, the overall cost of investing using dollar cost averaging is lower than it would be if a constant number of shares were bought at set intervals.

The Power of Compounding

Compound interest, or interest earned on interest, is a powerful force in determining the size, at some future time, of an accumulation of funds. The importance of this concept should not be ignored in a client's investment program. Many investments provide easy reinvestment of current income that results in the benefit of compounding. Some of the more frequently encountered examples are as follows:

- passbook savings accounts—The interest is automatically added to the account, and the investor must take specific action by withdrawing the interest to prevent compounding from occurring.
- certificates of deposit—Small CDs typically do not distribute interest during the life of the instrument. Rather, the interest is automatically reinvested, most often at the same rate being earned on the principal amount invested in the CD.
- mutual funds—Most mutual funds allow for the automatic purchase of additional shares whenever current income or capital gains are credited to a shareholder's account.
- common stocks—Many large corporations permit the investor to reinvest dividends in additional shares of that corporation's common stock. Often no brokerage charges are levied, and in rare cases the corporation subsidizes the purchase by providing up to a 5 percent discount from the average market price of its stock over the past 3 months.
- zero coupon bonds—Bonds that do not make an annual interest payment to the bondholder, such as U.S. government Series EE bonds and selected issues of corporate, government, and municipal bonds, have a built-in automatic compounding of interest over their life.

High-Pressure Sales Tactics

Many marketers possess persuasive skills, which sometimes border on pressure selling. Unfortunately, marketers of investment products are no exception. Frequently tales of high-pressure, boiler-room, telephone solicitations receive widespread coverage in the news media. These are the blatant examples. Although caution on the part of financial advisors and their clients might lead to missed opportunities, the frequency of this occurring is far less than implied by the solicitations and does not outweigh the benefits of careful investigation.

Avoiding Discretionary Power

Many clients prefer to have others perform the necessary work of managing their portfolios and grant broad managerial powers to accomplish this end. Although this may be an indication of trust in the judgment of the person receiving this power, conflict is likely to develop. Portfolio performance that does not meet a client's expectations, such as a sharp decline in market prices that generates portfolio losses, can precipitate this conflict. To avoid this problem, financial advisors may want to obtain prior approval from the client before any action is taken.

FOCUS ON ETHICS
Understanding Investment Risk

In the 1980s many headlines were written concerning junk bonds. Both the yields and the name of these securities implied high risk. Many families suffered financial loss directly or indirectly through investments in securities bearing a level of risk well above what their portfolios warranted.

In the early 1990s, the same thing happened with derivatives, hybrid securities that few really understand. Although derivatives have valid uses in hedging and speculation, their high level of risk makes them a poor choice for all but the most sophisticated investors.

It is the financial advisor's responsibility to comprehend and effectively communicate the risk associated with alternative investments. To do otherwise is an ethical, professional, and potentially legal error that can lead to disastrous results.

Applying Control through the Financial Planning Process

Investment planning typically is focused on selecting investments that will help a client achieve the financial goals (step 2, determine goals and gather data, in the financial planning process or FPP) set forth in his or her financial plan. However, before selecting any investments, the client's advisor should construct a recommended investment portfolio or asset allocation model (step 4, develop and present a plan, in the FPP) that is tailored to the client's level of risk tolerance and ability to handle risk (as determined in step 2, determine goals and gather data, and step 3, analyze and evaluate the data, in the FPP). This asset allocation model outlines the client's investment strategy within the context of his or her overall financial plan. The emphasis of an asset allocation model is on the different categories of assets and the percentage to be placed in each category. Once the client has an asset allocation model tailored to his or her unique circumstances, the next step is to actually select investments (step 5, implement the plan, in the FPP) that fit within the parameters of the model.

The client's asset allocation model in conjunction with his or her financial goals determine the performance standards by which selected investments are evaluated. Evaluating the performance of the individual investments in the client's portfolio (step 6, monitor the plan, in the FPP) provides the data with which to compare their performance with the standards. If an investment is not meeting the standards, then it needs to be replaced with one that will meet them. Of course, this whole process of monitoring the performance of the client's portfolio is just another adaptation of the financial planning process.

INVESTMENT MARKETS AND REGULATION

Many types of markets exist for investments. This section will first describe major types of markets where investments trading occurs on a regular basis. These markets are (1) true-auction markets, (2) negotiated markets, (3) dealer markets, and (4) organized-securities markets. Following this material, the purpose and thrust of the major federal laws and regulations affecting investments will be covered.

Investment Markets

True-Auction Markets

In true-auction markets, investment assets such as artwork, collectibles, or real estate are offered for sale to the highest bidder. The bidding continues until no one exceeds the last bid price. When this occurs, the sale is consummated. Since the advent of telecommunications, potential buyers need not attend these trading sessions. Normally, only a small number of potential buyers participate in true-auction markets for several reasons. First, buyers might not be aware that such an auction is being held. Second, buyers often prefer first-hand evaluation of the asset, and the cost of attending these auctions can be high. Third, for some of these assets (such as a particular painter's artwork) only a relatively few potential purchasers exist either regionally, nationally, or internationally. Lastly, the unit price of some of these investments dictates that only a handful of bidders will have the financial resources.

A variant of this form of auction market is used by the Treasury Department to sell T-bills. To buy T-bills at more than 150 auctions held throughout the year, investors must place bids. These bids may be entered on either a competitive or a noncompetitive basis. All noncompetitive bids are accepted by the Treasury, and buyers who enter these bids agree to pay the price (yield) that corresponds to the lowest price (highest yield) of all the competitive bids that are accepted. Buyers entering competitive bids state a price (yield) they are willing to pay and the Treasury accepts these bids, taking the highest prices (lowest yields) first until the issue is sold out. However, the price (yield) that all buyers who have accepted competitive bids actually pay is the same as the price (yield) that noncompetitive buyers pay. In other words, once the lowest price (highest yield) that the Treasury is willing to accept is determined, then all buyers (both competitive and noncompetitive) pay that same price (receive that yield). Investors who do not consider themselves expert securities traders usually bid noncompetitively.

Negotiated Markets

Negotiated markets predominate for the trading of real estate and similar investment assets. In these markets, sellers list their offerings with brokers who then seek to attract buyers through various advertising and other marketing methods. After a buyer has been located, negotiations determine the price.

Large institutional investors such as pension funds and mutual funds often employ brokers to locate buyers or sellers of large blocks of bonds or stocks. When these transactions involve listed securities (see subsequent treatment of organized-securities market), this negotiated market is called the *fourth market* because the transaction does not take place on the floor of an organized exchange. This market has many of the same characteristics as the true-auction market such as the lack of general awareness that the asset is available for purchase and sale. Also, as in auction markets, there is often a need for physical examination of the asset, especially a piece of real estate. Lastly, the high unit cost that restricts the number of participants in auction markets may have the same effect in negotiated markets.

fourth market

Dealer Markets

For many securities, one or more dealers make an active market by offering to buy (at a bid price) and sell (at an ask price) as much of a particular security as desired by investors. The difference between the bid and ask price is the dealer's spread, or compensation, for making the market and bearing the risk of holding an inventory of the security. The dealer makes the market. When demand for the security rises, the dealer raises his or her bid and ask prices; when demand falls, the dealer lowers these prices. Similar adjustments are made for changes in supply.

over-the-counter market

The *over-the-counter market*, which is a network of securities dealers, includes over 30,000 different securities issues. A numerical majority, but not the dollar-value majority, of all stocks are traded on this market. In addition to the stocks of operating corporations, this market also includes shares of some closed-end investment companies and most government and corporate bonds.

Organized Securities Markets

Formal trading locations and markets exist for securities listed on one or more of the national or regional exchanges. The most noted, the New York Stock Exchange, lists the securities of approximately 1,500 firms and actively maintains trading in these corporations' common and preferred stocks and their bonds. Each security is assigned a trading post on the floor of the exchange where commission brokers, employed by the various stock-brokerage firms, meet to engage in auction trading for the buy and sell orders transmitted to them. Each listed security is assigned to a specialist who makes a continuous, fair, and orderly market for the issue. The specialist performs this job by buying or selling the particular issue to offset any imbalance that develops in the number of buy and sell orders coming to the security's trading post from the commission brokers. The specialist maintains records of special orders brought to the market and accommodates members of the exchange for transactions that are less than the standard amount, which for stocks is 100 shares.

All exchanges have membership requirements for individuals trading on the floor of the exchange. Also exchanges maintain listing requirements that must be met by a corporation before any trading of its securities can take place on the exchange. The New York Stock Exchange has the most stringent requirements, including a national rather than local interest in the security, a minimum number of shareholders and publicly traded shares, and a minimum dollar amount of profits, assets, and market value of the corporation's common stock. Other exchanges, such as the American Stock Exchange, the Pacific Stock Exchange, and the Philadelphia Stock Exchange, tend to pattern their membership and listing requirements after those of the New York Stock Exchange except that their requirements are not as stringent.

Regulation of the Markets

Both state and federal regulations govern trading terms, conditions, and practices in all four markets. Federal laws dominate the organized securities and dealer markets whereas state laws are of greater importance in the true-auction and negotiated markets. The focus of this discussion centers on the most important federal laws and briefly describes the main purpose of each.

Securities Act of 1933

The Securities Act of 1933 requires issuers of new securities to file a registration statement with the Securities and Exchange Commission (SEC).

The issuing corporation may not sell the security until the SEC verifies that the information contained in the registration statement is complete and is not false or misleading. Once approval is obtained, a prospectus is prepared that contains a summary of information from the registration statement. Then the securities can be sold to the public if a copy of the prospectus is made available to all interested buyers. In any event, the SEC makes no attempt to evaluate the investment merits of a proposed offering.

The 1975 amendments to this act called for development of a national competitive system for trading securities, which resulted in the consolidated tape and the end of fixed brokerage commission rates.

Securities Exchange Act of 1934

As the name implies, the emphasis of the Securities Exchange Act of 1934 is to regulate the various securities markets. Its scope includes the organized securities exchanges, the over-the-counter markets, all stockbrokers and dealers, and the securities traded in these markets. In addition to requiring registration with the SEC, this act requires these institutions, individuals, and issuing corporations to file periodic updated data with the SEC.

Further, this regulation extends to many practices that occur in the market that the SEC believes are detrimental or misleading. When this occurs, the SEC develops and promulgates, after public hearings and comments, rules and procedures that must be followed. Examples of such include methods of calculating and comparing mutual fund performance between funds, advertising of returns earned on funds, and trading practices of dealers who purchase for their own account.

Maloney Act of 1938

The Maloney Act of 1938 permits the establishment of trade associations for the purpose of self-regulation of a segment of the securities industry. The only self-regulating organization (SRO) that has formed is the Financial Industry Regulatory Authority (FINRA, formerly NASD)[6]. This SRO regulates the securities firms, their owners, and stockbrokers, and establishes rules of practice to which members must adhere. Securities firms that are not members of the FINRA are regulated by the SEC.

Investment Company Act of 1940

The Investment Company Act of 1940 established rules and regulations that apply to all investment companies with respect to their dealings with and on behalf of their shareholders. This act is designed to require investment companies (1) to provide adequate disclosure to shareholders and (2) to refrain from paying excessive advisory, management, or brokerage fees. Significant amendments to this act, which were passed in the 1970s, regulate fees associated with contractual purchase plans entered into by individual investors.

Investment Advisors Act of 1940

The Investment Advisors Act of 1940, as amended by the Investment Advisors Supervision Coordination Act of 1996, requires that advisors register with either the SEC or state regulatory authorities, depending primarily on the amount of assets under an advisor's management. Registration does not guarantee the competence of any advisor; rather, it provides a modest degree of protection from fraudulent or unethical practices, principally by requiring that the advisor provide full disclosure to clients.

Securities Investor Protection Act of 1970

As part of the Securities Investor Protection Act, Congress set up the Securities Investor Protection Corporation (SIPC). It is patterned after the Federal Deposit Insurance Corporation (FDIC), with the objective of protecting customer property. Customers are insured by the SIPC for up to $500,000, not more than $100,000 of which may be in cash that is left on deposit incidental to transactions. The SIPC is a nonprofit, nongovernmental, membership corporation funded by member brokers/dealers, although it does have the privilege of borrowing from the SEC if its own funds are inadequate for meeting its obligations.

THE FINAL WORD

The intent of this chapter has been to provide a basic overview of the investment planning process. It always starts with understanding the investment needs of the client and his or her financial risk tolerance. The overall riskiness of the portfolio should never exceed the client's risk tolerance. It is more important that the financial advisor identify the appropriate asset allocation for the client than that the advisor pick a few "hot tips." Making the appropriate asset allocation recommendations requires an understanding of the various assets available.

Finally, the financial advisor then has to worry about such issues as purchasing power risk, interest rate risk, business risk, liquidity, marketability, taxation, and diversification.

CHAPTER SUMMARY

The assets that consumers buy are of two types—personal assets and investment assets. Personal assets are bought primarily for the creature comforts they provide, while investment assets are those acquired for the purpose of investing. The distinction, however, between personal and investment assets is not always clear. The exact same asset may be a personal asset for one person and an investment asset for another person.

Pure risks involve only the possibility of financial loss, while speculative risks involve not only the possibility of financial loss but also the possibility of financial gain. The distinction between pure risks and speculative risks is important, because normally only pure risks are insurable. Speculative risks, on the other hand, are what people encounter when they purchase investment assets hoping to receive some form of return.

Expected return and risk are usually thought of in quantitative terms. An asset's expected return is the average of its possible returns weighted according to their respective likelihoods. An asset with a wide range of possible returns is considered risky, while an asset with a narrow range of possible returns is considered more secure. The range of returns is generally measured in terms of the distance or dispersion from the expected returns. The relationship between risk and expected return is known as the positive risk/expected return tradeoff. Low-risk investments have low expected returns, and high-risk investments have high expected returns.

When engaged in investment planning for a client, the single most important service that a financial advisor can perform is to ascertain the client's financial risk tolerance, and then make sure that the riskiness of the client's investment holdings is consistent with this tolerance level, as well as with his or her financial ability to handle the risk. Although understanding the risk tolerance of a client is so critically important to proper investment planning, there is no simple formula, tool, or technique that allows an advisor to identify the client's financial risk tolerance and then relate it to an investment portfolio. However, the fact that measurement of financial risk tolerance is not a perfect science does not mean it cannot or should not be done. For this reason, many companies have developed risk tolerance questionnaires that can help in assessing a client's risk tolerance.

After information about a client's risk tolerance has been gathered, the advisor can use this information to develop portfolio recommendations known as asset allocation models. The emphasis of these models is on the different categories of assets and the percentage of assets to be placed in each category. The client's level of risk tolerance needs to be known to properly determine both the categories and the appropriate percentages for the client.

Because of the importance of asset allocation, several categories of investment assets need to be considered, the most important of which are the major categories of cash equivalents (short-term debt instruments), long-term debt instruments, and equity securities. These major categories can then be subdivided into several smaller more homogeneous categories.

The major sources of investment risk are purchasing power risk, interest-rate risk, and business risk. The first of these sources is purchasing power risk, also known as inflation risk. Inflation is the increase in the general level of prices. The second major source of risk for investors is interest-rate risk, which has two segments: price risk and reinvestment rate risk. Price risk results from the fact that any change in market interest rates typically leads to an opposite change in the value of investments. Reinvestment rate risk, on the other hand, is the risk associated with reinvesting investment income at unknown future interest rates. The important feature about price risk and reinvestment rate risk is that they work in opposite directions. Finally, investors must consider the business (default) risk for each of their investments. This risk exists because some businesses are unable to repay bond principals or make interest payments on a timely basis.

There are several concerns besides financial risk tolerance and asset allocation that a financial advisor needs to worry about when selecting securities for a portfolio. These other concerns are liquidity, marketability, taxation, and diversification. An asset is said to be liquid if it can be converted to cash (sold) quickly at any time with little or no loss of principal. Marketability is a little different than liquidity. It refers to the ability to sell an asset quickly. Thus, liquid assets are marketable, but not all marketable assets are liquid. Taxation is also important because different tax rates apply to different forms of income, and the timing of when the taxes are due can be quite different. Lastly, the importance of diversification in a client's portfolio can never be overemphasized.

The returns on an investment come in two forms: current income and capital appreciation. Despite varying combinations of these two types of returns, a method for comparing the investment returns from different investments is an absolute necessity. Three quick methods for measuring an investment's return are widely used. These three methods are (1) the current yield, (2) the holding-period return (HPR), and (3) the approximate yield. All three of these methods can be used to calculate an investment's return on either a before-tax or an after-tax basis.

There are several investment principles, strategies, and techniques recommended by financial advisors and used by successful investors. These include meeting emergency and protection needs first, matching investment instruments with investment goals, holding equity investments for periods of at least 5 years, focusing on the underlying economic soundness of investments rather than on just their tax benefits, understanding the investments, using a consistent pattern of investing, using the power of compounding, the infrequent use of high-pressure sales tactics, avoiding discretionary power, and applying control through the financial planning process. While not all these principles, strategies, and techniques are appropriate in all situations, collectively they provide an advisor with some guidelines that he or she can follow when advising clients.

The major types of markets where investments trading occurs on a regular basis are (1) true-auction markets, (2) negotiated markets, (3) dealer markets, and (4) organized-securities markets. In true-auction markets, investments are offered for sale to the highest bidder. The bidding continues until no one exceeds the last bid price. When this occurs, the sale is consummated. In negotiated markets, sellers list their offerings with brokers, who then seek to attract buyers. After a buyer has been located, negotiations determine the price. In dealer markets, dealers make an active market by offering to buy (at a bid price) and sell (at an ask price) as much of a particular security as desired by investors. The difference between the bid and ask price is the dealer's spread, or compensation, for making the market and bearing the risk of holding an inventory of the security. In organized-securities markets, formal trading locations and markets exist for listed securities. Each listed security is assigned to a specialist who makes a continuous, fair, and orderly market for the security.

Both state and federal regulations govern trading terms, conditions, and practices in all four markets. Federal laws dominate the organized-securities and dealer markets, whereas state laws are of greater importance in the true-auction and negotiated markets. The most important of the federal laws are (1) the Securities Act of 1933, (2) the Securities Exchange Act of 1934, (3) the Maloney Act of 1938, (4) the Investment Company Act of 1940, (5) the Investment Advisors Act of 1940, as amended by the Investment Advisors Supervision Coordination Act of 1996, and (6) the Securities Investor Protection Act of 1970.

CHAPTER REVIEW

Key Terms and Concepts are explained in the Glossary. Answers to the Review Questions and Self-Test Questions are found in the back of the book in the Answers to Questions section.

Key Terms and Concepts

personal assets
investment assets
investing
speculating
expected return
investment risk
asset allocation models

asset selection
cash equivalents
money market deposit accounts
   (MMDAs)
money market mutual funds
   (MMMFs)
U.S. Treasury bills (T-bills)

long-term debt instruments
notes
agency bonds
general obligations
revenue bonds
junk bonds
preemptive right
closed-end investment company
open-end investment company
defensive stocks
growth stocks
value stocks
large cap stocks
small cap stocks
purchasing power risk
real rate of return

nominal rate of return
interest rate risk
price risk
reinvestment rate risk
business (default) risk
liquidity
opportunity costs
marketability
diversification
current yield
holding-period return (HPR)
approximate yield
planned holding period
dollar cost averaging
fourth market
over-the-counter market

Review Questions

4-1. Describe the two types of assets that consumers buy.

4-2. Explain the difference between investing and speculating.

4-3. Explain what is meant by investment risk.

4-4. What are the two most basic theorems of investment?

4-5. Explain what is meant by asset allocation models.

4-6. Explain what is meant by a common stockholder's preemptive right.

4-7. What two privileges do preferred stockholders usually have that provide them with a preferential position relative to common stockholders?

4-8. Explain what is meant by price risk.

4-9. Explain the difference between liquidity and marketability.

4-10. Jack owns some tax-exempt municipal bonds that provide him with a 3 percent current yield. If Jack is in the 33 percent marginal income tax bracket, what is his equivalent fully taxable yield?

4-11. Joe purchased some stock one year ago for $50 per share. The stock just paid an annual dividend of $4 per share and is now selling for $60 per share. Joe is in the 28 percent marginal income tax bracket. On the basis of this information, calculate Joe's after-tax holding-period return.

4-12. Sally is investing in commercial real estate that costs $100,000. She expects that it will generate $5,000 of annual rental income and that in 5 years it will be worth $200,000. Sally is in the 28 percent marginal income tax bracket. What would Sally's after-tax approximate yield be from this investment for the 5-year holding period?

4-13. What two things should an investor do prior to beginning an investment program?

4-14. Explain how dollar cost averaging establishes a consistent pattern of investing.

4-15. Describe the principal characteristics of each of the following types of securities markets:
a. negotiated markets
b. dealer markets

4-16. What is the primary purpose of each of the following federal statutes?
a. Securities Act of 1933
b. Maloney Act of 1938

Self-Test Questions

Instructions: Read chapter 4 first, then answer the following questions to test your knowledge. There are 10 questions; circle the correct answer, then check your answers with the answer key in the back of the book.

4-1. Jack owns some tax-exempt municipal bonds that provide him with a current yield of 5 percent. If Jack is in the 28 percent marginal income tax bracket, what is his equivalent fully taxable yield from the bonds?

(A) 4.91 percent
(B) 5.50 percent
(C) 6.12 percent
(D) 6.94 percent

$\dfrac{5\%}{1-.28}$

4-2. Which of the following statements concerning the Securities Investor Protection Act of 1970 is correct?

(A) It requires advisors to register with either the SEC or the state, depending on the amount of assets under management.
(B) It sets up a corporation that is patterned after the FDIC, with the objective of protecting customer property.
(C) It is designed to regulate the various securities markets, as well as the securities traded in these markets.
(D) It is designed to require investment companies to provide adequate disclosure to their shareholders.

Chapter 4 Investment Planning   4.51

4-3. Which of the following major categories of investment companies operate only as open-end funds?

(A) index funds
(B) bond funds
(C) common stock funds
(D) mixed portfolio funds

4-4. Bill owns stock that currently sells for $60 per share and pays an annual dividend of $4 per share. If Bill is in the 28 percent marginal income tax bracket, what is his after-tax current yield from the stock?

(A) 3.4 percent
(B) 3.9 percent
(C) 4.8 percent
(D) 5.6 percent

4-5. Components of the interest rate risk include which of the following?

 I. Business (default) risk
 II. Reinvestment rate risk

(A) I only
(B) II only
(C) Both I and II
(D) Neither I nor II

4-6. Which of the following statements concerning an open-end investment company is (are) correct?

 I. Its shares are traded in the stock market like those of large corporations.
 II. It issues a given number of shares at formation and rarely, if ever, issues additional shares.

(A) I only
(B) II only
(C) Both I and II
(D) Neither I nor II

4-7. Which of the following statements concerning holding periods for common stock investments is (are) correct?

 I. Short holding periods, such as one year or less, may produce negative total returns.
 II. Individually owned stocks should generally have planned holding periods of at least 10 years.

 (A) I only
 (B) II only
 (C) Both I and II
 (D) Neither I nor II

4-8. All the following statements concerning the ownership of liquid assets are correct EXCEPT:

 (A) Liquid assets tend to have the lowest expected rates of return.
 (B) Owning liquid assets provides flexibility for emergency purposes.
 (C) There are often substantial opportunity costs to owning liquid assets.
 (D) There typically is a sizable risk in owning liquid assets.

4-9. Reasons for the popularity of investment companies include all the following EXCEPT:

 (A) Each share in an investment company benefits from the pooled diversification of the portfolio.
 (B) The wide diversity of investment companies allows an investor to select the portfolio that best suits his or her objectives.
 (C) Investment companies typically perform better than the market averages because they have no fees.
 (D) Investment companies have professional managers that select and continuously monitor the portfolio's securities.

4-10. All the following are considered cash equivalents EXCEPT

 (A) American Depositary Receipts (ADRs)
 (B) nonnegotiable certificates of deposit (CDs)
 (C) money market deposit accounts (MMDAs)
 (D) U.S. Treasury bills (T-bills)

NOTES

1. Survey of Financial Risk Tolerance, The American College, Bryn Mawr, PA, 1992.
2. Gary P. Brinson, Brian D. Singer, and Gilbert L. Beebower, "Determinants of Portfolio Performance," *Financial Analysts Journal*, July/August, 1986. Updated in *Financial Analysts Journal*, May/June, 1991, pp.40–48. This study shows that correct asset allocation will do far more to benefit a client than asset selection.
3. On May 19, 2008, the U.S. Supreme Court reversed the Kentucky Court of Appeals decision in *Department of Revenue of Kentucky v. Davis*. The Supreme Court held 7-2 that Kentucky did not unconstitutionally discriminate against interstate commerce by taxing income from out-of-state bonds while exempting in-state municipal bond earnings. Consequently, a state may continue to exempt in-state obligations from taxation while taxing out-of-state obligations.
4. See the 2007 Investment Company Institute Fact Book at www.ici.org.
5. When holding-period returns (HPRs) are calculated for an investment period of one year, they are typically referred to as per-period returns (PPRs), which generally are expressed for standard periods of 1 year's length.
6. FINRA, the largest nongovernmental regulator for all securities firms doing business in the United States, was created in July 2007 through the consolidation of the National Association of Securities Dealers (NASD) and the member regulation, enforcement, and arbitration functions of the New York Stock Exchange (NYSE). FINRA oversees nearly 5,100 brokerage firms, about 173,000 branch offices, and more than 676,000 registered securities representatives.

5

Income Tax Planning

Jim F. Ivers III
C. Bruce Worsham

Learning Objectives

An understanding of the material in this chapter should enable you to

5-1. Explain the purpose of income tax planning, and describe the concept of gross income.

5-2. Explain the difference between exclusions and deductions, and distinguish above-the-line deductions from below-the-line deductions.

5-3. Distinguish the standard deduction from itemized deductions, and explain how the depreciation deduction differs from most other deduction

5-4. Describe the structure of federal income tax rates.

5-5. Explain why a tax credit is more valuable than a tax deduction of an equal amount.

5-6. Describe the nature and purpose of the alternative minimum tax (AMT).

5-7. Explain the concept of the taxable year, and describe the two most popular tax accounting methods.

5-8. Describe the doctrines of economic benefit, fruit and tree, and constructive receipt.

5-9. Explain the use of several basic income tax planning techniques.

5-10. Identify several different types of taxable entities.

Chapter Outline

THE PURPOSE OF INCOME TAX PLANNING 5.3
THE PRINCIPLE OF GROSS INCOME 5.3
EXCLUSIONS FROM GROSS INCOME 5.5
DEDUCTIONS 5.5
    Adjusted Gross Income 5.5

Taxable Income 5.6
The Standard Deduction or Itemized Deductions 5.6
Categories of Deductions 5.7
Depreciation: A Special Type of Deduction 5.9
PERSONAL AND DEPENDENCY EXEMPTIONS 5.11
TAX RATES AND BRACKETS 5.11
TAX CREDITS 5.14
THE ALTERNATIVE MINIMUM TAX (AMT) 5.14
TAX PERIODS AND ACCOUNTING METHODS 5.15
THREE IMPORTANT ISSUES 5.16
The What Question: The Economic Benefit Doctrine 5.16
The To Whom Question: The Fruit and Tree Doctrine 5.17
The When Question: The Constructive Receipt Doctrine 5.18
BASIC INCOME-TAX-PLANNING CONCEPTS 5.19
Income and Deduction Shifting 5.19
Avoiding Limitations on Deductions 5.20
Deferral and Acceleration Techniques 5.22
The Passive-Loss Rules 5.23
Tax-Exempt Transactions 5.24
Nonrecognition Transactions 5.24
Transactions That Result in a Taxable Loss 5.26
Ordinary versus Capital Gain and Loss 5.27
TAXABLE ENTITIES 5.30
THE FINAL WORD 5.30
CHAPTER SUMMARY 5.31
CHAPTER REVIEW 5.34

This chapter begins by discussing the purpose of income tax planning and the concept of gross income. It then briefly reviews exclusions from gross income before focusing on the various types of deductions. The chapter then looks at personal and dependency exemptions, tax rates and brackets, and personal tax credits. Next, it examines the alternative minimum tax (AMT) system in addition to tax periods and accounting methods. To help gain a better understanding of the income tax system, the chapter then follows with a discussion of the doctrines of economic benefit, assignment of income, and constructive receipt. Several basic tax planning techniques are then used to illustrate how financial advisors think in their efforts to help clients. Finally, the chapter concludes with a brief treatment of taxable entities.

THE PURPOSE OF INCOME TAX PLANNING

It is said that the only things certain in life are death and taxes. Although death would seem to be more certain than anything, it is likely that even Houdini would have had trouble defying Uncle Sam. At the least, it would take a highly accomplished escape artist to evade both the federal income tax and a jail cell.

In any event, such extremes are not advisable for a variety of legal, ethical, and moral reasons. Yet, it is perfectly acceptable (and perhaps even commendable) to use every legal means to minimize and/or avoid the payment of federal income taxes.

This chapter will outline the most important basic concepts of our federal income tax law. It will not deal with advanced tax planning. It will provide, however, a firm grasp of fundamental concepts—always an excellent foundation to build upon. More advanced texts present planning techniques that are available to avoid paying taxes. Some tax-avoidance techniques (many call them loopholes) must be left to the experienced tax professional to recommend and implement.

Even though there are several planning techniques that can be utilized to minimize and/or avoid paying taxes, tax relief may not be the only goal of income tax planning. The best tax plan is one that accurately reflects the client's overall financial goals. This requires that various tax strategies be explained to the client so that he or she can understand their limitations and benefits. With this knowledge and the recommendations of the financial advisor, the client can choose those tax strategies that best fit into and become a part of his or her multiple-purpose or comprehensive financial plan. A tax plan that focuses on *tax minimization* and/or *tax avoidance* is a poor plan if it is inconsistent with the client's other financial goals. Nevertheless, almost all clients want to minimize and/or avoid paying taxes.

tax minimization
tax avoidance

A working knowledge of the tax law will enable the financial advisor to help clients, as well as to help himself or herself know when to ask for the assistance of a tax expert. Therefore, the purpose of this chapter is both to explain basic income tax concepts to the advisor, and to introduce the advisor to the ways in which he or she can help a client plan for tax minimization and/or tax avoidance within the context of the client's financial plan.

THE PRINCIPLE OF GROSS INCOME

gross income

For the advisor to learn about the federal income tax law, it is important to begin with an understanding of the term *gross income*. Basically, gross income includes every item of value, whether consisting of money or other property, that is either made available to or comes into the possession of the taxpayer. In other words, anything of value is considered to be gross income for income tax purposes unless—and this qualification is very important—the Internal Revenue Code contains a specific provision that excludes a particular item from the taxpayer's gross income.

This is why the provision in the Internal Revenue Code that provides the gross income rule is referred to as a "shotgun" clause. Although the provision lists 15 different items that are includible in a taxpayer's gross income, the provision states that gross income includes, but is not limited to, these items. Gross income means "all income from whatever source derived."

However, certain items of money or other property are not includible in a taxpayer's gross income. These items include gifts, income from tax-exempt bonds, workers' compensation benefits, and many other items. Such items are called exclusions from gross income. It is important to remember that the reason such items are excluded from a taxpayer's gross income is that there is a specific section in the Internal Revenue Code that says so. In other words, no item of money or other property can be excluded from gross income unless there is a code provision stating that it is to be excluded. Therefore, it is fairly simple in most cases to determine whether an item is includible in the taxpayer's gross income.

exclusion
deduction

It is also important to distinguish the concept of an *exclusion* from that of a *deduction* for tax purposes. As noted above, an exclusion is an item of value that the taxpayer receives that is not includible in the taxpayer's gross income. A deduction, on the other hand, is an item of expense (not an item of receipt) that reduces the amount of income that is subject to tax.

Example: Cheryl has the following items of income and expense for the current year: a $35,000 salary from her job as a paralegal, a $5,000 gift from her aunt, and an alimony payment of $3,000 to her former husband. The $35,000 salary is includible in Cheryl's gross income. The $5,000 gift is not includible in her gross income because there is a provision in the Internal Revenue Code that says that gifts are not includible in the recipient's gross income. The $3,000 alimony payment is deductible from Cheryl's gross income in determining how much of Cheryl's income will actually be taxed, because the Internal Revenue Code contains a provision that states that alimony payments are generally deductible.

EXCLUSIONS FROM GROSS INCOME

There are many items that the Internal Revenue Code states are excludible from a taxpayer's gross income. Among these items are the following:

- gifts and inheritances
- income from certain bonds issued by states and municipalities
- workers' compensation benefits
- life insurance proceeds
- benefits paid from medical expense insurance policies
- social security benefits (for taxpayers below certain income levels)
- amounts received under certain dependent-care-assistance programs and educational assistance programs
- certain qualified scholarships

The specific rules determining how and to what extent these items are excludible from gross income are beyond the scope of this chapter. The point of this discussion is that it is important for the advisor to, at least, understand the concept of an exclusion, and how exclusions are used in the overall process of computing an individual's tax liability. An item that is excludible generally does not have to be reported in any way on the taxpayer's return.

DEUCTIONS

adjusted gross income (AGI)
taxable income

As previously stated, a deduction is an item of expense that reduces the amount of the taxpayer's income that is subject to tax. There are many different items that are deductible for federal income tax purposes. However, before some of these items are listed and explained, the concepts of *adjusted gross income (AGI)* and *taxable income* should be understood.

Adjusted Gross Income

Adjusted gross income is an intermediate calculation that is made in the process of determining an individual's income tax liability for a given year. Why is such an intermediate calculation necessary or useful? For purposes of the tax law, adjusted gross income is used as a base amount to determine how the taxpayer must treat certain other items for tax purposes. For example, adjusted gross income is used to calculate the maximum amount of charitable contributions that may be deducted by an individual in a given year (generally 50 percent of the individual's adjusted gross income).

Taxable Income

Taxable income is the amount of income that will actually be subject to tax in a given year. How does taxable income differ from adjusted gross income? Taxable income is the taxpayer's adjusted gross income, reduced by certain deductions that are taken only after the individual's adjusted gross income has been computed. In other words, in the computation of an individual's tax liability, there are two basic types of deductions. The first type consists of those deductions that are subtracted from gross income to determine adjusted gross income. The second type consists of those deductions that are subtracted from adjusted gross income to determine taxable income. The first type is known as *above-the-line deductions*, while the second type is known as *below-the-line deductions*.

above-the-line deductions
below-the-line deductions

What is the significance of this distinction? There are two basic reasons why the distinction is important. The first is that above-the-line deductions will change how certain other items on the individual's return are treated. This is so because, as previously stated, adjusted gross income is used as a base for defining or limiting how and to what extent certain other items may be excluded or deducted on the individual's return. The second reason relates to the concept of the *standard deduction*.

standard deduction

FOCUS ON ETHICS
The Ethics of "Playing the Odds"

Every year at tax time the media highlights the probability that certain categories of taxpayers will be audited. Usually the likelihood is quite low, and this can cause some clients to suggest "liberally interpreting" the tax law for their own financial gain. Among the myriad of possible approaches are deducting personal travel expenses by suggesting that they were business related, showing phony charitable donations, and failing to report cash income.

Financial advisors have a responsibility to assist clients in legally minimizing their taxes, and tax counseling can be one of the most significant contributions a financial advisor can make. However, it is obvious that advisors must never participate in or condone fraudulent behavior. Regardless of the odds, an improper action could be disastrous to the client financially and legally, not to mention the impact on reputation. The same is true for the financial advisor.

The Standard Deduction or Itemized Deductions

itemized deductions

The standard deduction is a fixed amount that the individual may claim in lieu of claiming *itemized deductions* on Schedule A of Form 1040. Itemized deductions, or deductions taken on Schedule A, include charitable contributions, deductions for interest payments, taxes, casualty losses, certain business expenses of employees, and other items. The amount of the standard deduction depends on whether the individual is filing the return as a single taxpayer, an unmarried head of household, a married taxpayer filing jointly, or a married taxpayer filing separately.

If the individual is entitled to claim itemized deductions that, when added together, are more than the amount of his or her standard deduction, then the individual will deduct his or her itemized deductions and not claim the standard deduction. The standard deduction amounts are indexed annually for inflation.

All itemized deductions are below-the-line deductions (deductions taken in calculating taxable income). However, if these items were above-the-line deductions (deductions taken in determining adjusted gross income rather than taxable income), the taxpayer would deduct these items regardless of whether he or she claims the standard deduction. The standard deduction can be taken in addition to other deductions. This is the second important difference between above-the-line and below-the-line deductions. The first type are deductible regardless of whether the individual claims the standard deduction. The second type may be claimed only in lieu of the standard deduction.

Categories of Deductions

Before we discuss the various types of deductions that are allowable under federal tax law, it is important to remember that a deduction may be claimed only if there is a specific provision in the Internal Revenue Code that allows it. If there is no provision in the Code regarding a given item, no deduction may be claimed for that item.

Stated broadly, there are three basic categories of deductions allowable to individual taxpayers. The first category includes deductions for expenses that are incurred in the course of carrying on a trade or business. For example, the cost of employees' salaries or advertising would fall into this category. These are referred to as business deductions. The second basic category includes deductions for expenses that are incurred in the course of an activity that is not a trade or business, but is engaged in for the purpose of producing income and making a profit. An example of a deduction falling into this category is an expense incurred in connection with the maintenance of a taxpayer's investments, such as a fee for investment advice. The third basic category includes deductions for expenses that are simply personal, family, or living expenses. Although the Code provides as a general rule that these expenses are nondeductible, there are several important exceptions to the general rule. Personal expenses that are deductible within limitations include charitable contributions, medical expenses, interest payments for home mortgages, and student loan interest. However, many of these personal deductions are subject to limitations as to what and how much can be deducted.

business expense
expense for the production of income
personal expense

Whenever the client or advisor is determining whether a given item of expense is deductible, certain questions should always be asked. Obviously, the first and most basic question is whether the Code allows a deduction for the item. A second important question is what basic category the expense falls under; in other words, whether it is a *business expense*, an *expense for the production of income*, or a *personal expense*. A third question is whether the deduction is an above-the-line or below-the-line deduction. It is always important for tax planning purposes to know where an item will appear on the individual's tax return.

A fourth question that should be asked is whether there is a particular restriction or limitation on the deductibility of the item. For example, certain deductions such as the medical expense deduction and the casualty loss deduction are subject to a floor. This floor is based on a percentage of the taxpayer's adjusted gross income. If the taxpayer's expenses in a given category are less than the applicable floor, no deduction will actually be allowed for the expenses.

Example: Trish has medical expenses of $5,000 this year. Medical expenses are deductible, but only to the extent they exceed 7.5 percent of the taxpayer's adjusted gross income. Trish's adjusted gross income this year is $70,000. Although Trish has $5,000 of medical expenses, her deduction for these expenses is zero because the amount of the expenses ($5,000) is less than 7.5 percent of her adjusted gross income ($5,250).

Other types of restrictions may apply to particular deduction items. For example, cash contributions to a public charity are generally deductible, but only up to a maximum of 50 percent of an individual's adjusted gross income for any given year. Contributions in excess of that amount must be carried over to future taxable years. In the case of charitable contributions, the individual's adjusted gross income provides a ceiling for the deduction, rather than a floor.

Under present law, there is also an overall limitation on an individual's total itemized deductions. The overall limitation applies to all itemized deductions except medical expenses, casualty and theft losses, and investment interest expenses. The overall limitation is also based on adjusted gross income. It applies to individuals with adjusted gross income above a specified amount that is adjusted annually for inflation. Itemized deductions are disallowed or "phased out" to the extent of the individual's adjusted gross income in excess of the specified amount multiplied by 3 percent. Up to 80 percent of a taxpayer's itemized deductions can be disallowed under this rule. It applies after all other limitations and restrictions on the deductions have been taken into account.

Another type of restriction that may apply to a deduction is a dollar-amount restriction. An example of this restriction is the rule for deducting interest payments on a taxpayer's first mortgage on his or her principal residence. Generally such payments are deductible, but only with respect to a maximum of $1 million of loan principal. If the first mortgage exceeds $1 million, a corresponding portion of the interest deduction is disallowed. Note that in the case of the deduction for home mortgage interest, the dollar amount limitation is based on the amount of the loan principal, not the amount of the interest expense itself. Another example of a dollar-amount limitation is the limitation on deductible contributions to a traditional individual retirement account (IRA) that may be available to individuals who are not covered by employer-provided retirement plans and by certain other individuals whose income falls within specified ranges.

Yet another type of restriction on the deductibility of certain expenses is a percentage limitation. For example, business entertainment expenses are generally deductible, but the deduction is limited to 50 percent of the actual expenses. There are many other ways in which the Internal Revenue Code limits the claiming of deductions.

Depreciation: A Special Type of Deduction

paper deductions

Not all tax deductions represent actual out-of-pocket expenses. Some deductions are allowable even though they represent no corresponding cash outlay. These are often referred to as *paper deductions,* because they represent or are related to some entry on the books of a taxpayer's business or investment activity, but they are not a cash-flow item.

What is the nature of these items? And why are they allowable as deductions against a taxpayer's income? What these items represent is a measure of a gradual decrease in the value or usefulness of property owned by the taxpayer. But they are only an arbitrary measure of such a decrease in value or usefulness. They are not a real-life measure of such a decrease.

depreciation deduction

The most important noncash deduction is the deduction for depreciation. The *depreciation deduction* allows a taxpayer to recover the cost of certain property for tax purposes by allowing the taxpayer to deduct a specified portion of the cost of the property each year against the taxpayer's income. The reason why such a deduction is allowed is that the cost of property that is used in business or for income-producing purposes should be deductible, but the deduction should be spread out over the useful life of the property.

Generally capital expenditures, such as those made for the purchase of a building or piece of equipment, are not deductible in full for income tax purposes in the year the asset is acquired. This is so because a capital expenditure is not considered to be an operating expense of a business, but a more long-term investment in an asset. As such, the capital expenditure would normally be recovered for tax purposes only when the asset is sold. In other words, the amount of the capital expenditure becomes the taxpayer's tax basis in the asset. This basis will be subtracted from the amount realized when the asset is sold to determine how much of the sale proceeds should be taxed.

But the depreciation deduction allows the taxpayer to deduct portions of the capital expenditure before the asset is sold, that is, on an annual basis. The theory is that the asset experiences wear and tear while it is being used by the taxpayer, and therefore, there should be a deduction allowed for such wear and tear. However, in reality, the asset might actually be appreciating in real economic terms in spite of the wear and tear it is experiencing. This can happen with many types of assets, but is particularly common with real estate. In such a situation, the taxpayer is receiving a tax deduction, which is supposed to represent a decrease in the property's value, while the property is actually increasing in value.

income tax basis

Any depreciation deductions claimed with respect to an asset are subtracted from the taxpayer's *income tax basis* in the asset. This means that when the asset is sold later, the amount of depreciation deducted is, in effect, recouped by the government because the portion of the sales proceeds that is taxable will be increased. But, in the meantime, the taxpayer has enjoyed the economic benefit of the tax deductions for depreciation. The concept of basis will be discussed in more detail later in this chapter.

Because depreciation is a deduction that often does not represent economic reality, there is an element of social policy behind its presence in the tax law. That policy is to stimulate investment in business assets and assets held for the production of income.

What types of assets are eligible for this cost recovery that results from the depreciation deduction? There are two basic requirements. The first is that the asset must be used either in the taxpayer's business or in some other activity intended to produce income for the taxpayer. Assets held for personal use are not eligible for the deduction. The second requirement is that the asset must have a limited useful life in order to qualify. This requirement explains why land, for example, does not qualify for a depreciation deduction. Land is considered to be an asset that does not wear out.

There are some fairly complicated rules that determine how much of a qualifying asset's cost can be claimed each year as a depreciation deduction. These rules are based on two factors: the number of years over which the cost of the asset will be deducted, and the percentage of the cost of the asset that will be deducted each year. The details are beyond the scope of this chapter. In summary, however, it is fair to say that the depreciation deduction is especially beneficial to taxpayers because it allows them to save tax dollars without a corresponding cash outlay in the year of the tax saving.

PERSONAL AND DEPENDENCY EXEMPTIONS

personal exemption

Each individual taxpayer is allowed to claim a *personal exemption* for himself or herself. A married couple filing jointly may claim an exemption for each spouse. The amount of the exemption or exemptions is subtracted from adjusted gross income in the process of computing taxable income. Personal exemptions are not itemized deductions claimed on Schedule A of Form 1040, however. Therefore, either the standard deduction or itemized deductions may be claimed in addition to the taxpayer's exemptions.

dependency exemption

Individual taxpayers are also permitted to claim a *dependency exemption* for each dependent individual who is supported by the taxpayer. There are strict rules regarding whom a taxpayer may claim as a dependent and under what circumstances. The exemption amount changes annually by way of an inflation adjustment.

In addition, under current law taxpayers at certain income levels lose a portion of their personal and/or dependency exemption amounts. The amount lost is equal to 2 percent of the applicable personal and/or dependency exemption amount for every $2,500 (or any fraction thereof) by which the taxpayer's adjusted gross income exceeds a specified threshold amount. The threshold amounts are based on filing status and are adjusted annually for inflation. This phaseout of exemption amounts applies simultaneously to all of the taxpayer's personal and dependency exemptions, rather than sequentially or "one-by-one." For 2008 and 2009, the percentage of each exemption amount that is lost by the phaseout is multiplied by one-third to recalculate the phaseout percentage. This additional step lessens the detrimental effect of the phaseout rule, which is scheduled to be completely eliminated by 2010.

TAX RATES AND BRACKETS

Once the taxpayer's gross income has been determined, all deductions allowable in determining adjusted gross income are subtracted from gross income. Next, all deductions and exemptions allowable in determining taxable income are subtracted from adjusted gross income. The resulting figure is the taxpayer's taxable income. This is the figure to which the income tax rates are applied to determine the amount of income tax payable for the year.

Under the 2003 Jobs and Growth Tax Relief Reconciliation Act, income tax for ordinary income purposes (and not for capital gain purposes) is imposed under a six bracket system with the lowest bracket's rate being 10 percent. The next four brackets' rates are 15 percent, 25 percent, 28 percent, and 33 percent, respectively. The highest bracket's rate is 35 percent. The tax

marginal tax rate

rate applicable to each income bracket is called the *marginal tax rate*. The

filing status

tax bracket

amount of taxable income subject to each marginal tax rate for each *filing status* is referred to as a *tax bracket*. The brackets are indexed annually for inflation.

Example: Gary and Karen Smith are married taxpayers filing jointly. Their taxable income for 2008 is $380,700. Their tax due is $104,820, computed as follows:

- Their taxable income not over $16,050 is taxed at a rate of 10 percent, which results in a tax of $1,605.
- Their taxable income over $16,050 but not over $65,100 (or $49,050) is taxed at a rate of 15 percent, which results in a tax of $7,357.50, with the total tax accumulating to $8,962.50 (that is, $1,605 plus $7,357.50).
- Their taxable income over $65,100 but not over $131,450 (or $66,350) is taxed at a rate of 25 percent, which results in a tax of $16,587.50, with the total tax accumulating to $25,550 (that is, $8,962.50 plus $16,587.50).
- Their taxable income over $131,450 but not over $200,300 (or $68,850) is taxed at a rate of 28 percent, which results in a tax of $19,278, with the total tax accumulating to $44,828 (that is, $25,550 plus $19,278).
- Their taxable income over $200,300 but not over $357,700 (or $157,400) is taxed at a rate of 33 percent, which results in a tax of $51,942, with the total tax accumulating to $96,770 (that is, $44,828 plus $51,942).
- Their taxable income over $357,700 is taxed at a rate of 35 percent. Because the Smiths' taxable income is $380,700, this amount is $23,000, which results in a tax of $8,050, with the total tax for the Smiths accumulating to $104,820 (that is, $96,770 plus $8,050).

As shown, the tax computed under each of the tax brackets is added together for a total tax of $104,820 (that is, $1,605 from the 10 percent bracket,

effective tax rate

$7,357.50 from the 15 percent bracket, $16,587.50 from the 25 percent bracket, $19,278 from the 28 percent bracket, $51,942 from the 33 percent bracket, and $8,050 from the top 35 percent bracket). This tax gives the Smiths' an *effective tax rate* of about 28 percent (that is, the tax of $104,820 divided by their taxable income of $380,700). Except when a taxpayer is in the lowest tax bracket, a taxpayer's effective tax rate will always be lower than his or her marginal tax rate because of the progressive structure of the federal income tax system. A taxpayer in the lowest tax bracket has both an effective tax rate and a marginal tax rate equal to 10 percent.

As indicated above, the brackets of taxable income to which the various marginal tax rates apply depend on the individual's filing status. As previously described, an individual taxpayer files his or her tax return under one of four filing status categories: a single taxpayer, an unmarried head of household, a married taxpayer filing jointly, and a married taxpayer filing separately. The amount of taxable income that will fall into each tax bracket depends upon the individual's filing status (see table 5-1).

TABLE 5-1
Tax Rate Schedules for Individuals in 2008

	If Taxable Income is:	**The Tax is:**
Single Taxpayer	Not over $8,025 Over $8,025 but not over $32,550 Over $32,550 but not over $78,850 Over $78,850 but not over $164,550 Over $164,550 but not over $357,700 Over $357,700	10% of taxable income $802.50 plus 15% of the amount over $8,025 $4,481.25 plus 25% of the amount over $32,550 $16,056.25 plus 28% of the amount over $78,850 $40,052.25 plus 33% of the amount over $164,550 $103,791.75 plus 35% of the amount over $357,700
Unmarried Head of Household	Not over $11,450 Over $11,450 but not over $43,650 Over $43,650 but not over $112,650 Over $112,650 but not over $182,400 Over $182,400 but not over $357,700 Over $357,700	10% of taxable income $1,145 plus 15% of the amount over $11,450 $5,975 plus 25% of the amount over $43,650 $23,225 plus 28% of the amount over $112,650 $42,755 plus 33% of the amount over $182,400 $100,604 plus 35% of the amount over $357,700
Married Taxpayer Filing Jointly	Not over $16,050 Over $16,050 but not over $65,100 Over $65,100 but not over $131,450 Over $131,450 but not over $200,300 Over $200,300 but not over $357,700 Over $357,700	10% of taxable income $1,650 plus 15% of the amount over $16,050 $8,962.50 plus 25% of the amount over $65,100 $25,550 plus 28% of the amount over $131,450 $44,828 plus 33% of the amount over $200,300 $96,770 plus 35% of the amount over $357,700
Married Taxpayer Filing Separately	Not over $8,025 Over $8,025 but not over $32,550 Over $32,550 but not over $65,725 Over $65,725 but not over $100,150 Over $100,150 but not over $178,850 Over $178,850	10% of taxable income $802.50 plus 15% of the amount over $8,025 $4,481.25 plus 25% of the amount over $32,550 $12,775 plus 28% of the amount over $65,725 $22,414 plus 33% of the amount over $100,150 $48,385 plus 35% of the amount over $178,850

effective marginal tax rate

It should be noted that an upper-income taxpayer's *effective marginal tax rate* may be higher than his or her statutory marginal rate. This can happen as a result of the phaseout rules that reduce the taxpayer's itemized deductions and personal and/or dependency exemption amounts as his or her adjusted gross income increases. The effective marginal rate for an upper-income taxpayer depends on the level of his or her adjusted gross income, the amount of his or her itemized deductions, and the number of personal and/or dependency exemptions that he or she can claim. The calculation of the effective marginal rate for an upper-income taxpayer is beyond the scope of this chapter.

TAX CREDITS

tax credits

Once the tax rates have been applied to an individual's taxable income, the resulting figure is the individual's tentative tax. However, this tentative tax can be reduced if the individual is eligible to claim any income *tax credits*.

It is important to understand the difference between a tax credit and a tax deduction. A tax credit is a dollar-for-dollar reduction of the actual tax payable. As explained earlier, a deduction is an item of expense that only reduces the amount of the taxpayer's income that is subject to taxation. It produces a net tax benefit equal to the taxpayer's marginal tax rate multiplied by each dollar deducted. For example, a taxpayer whose top marginal tax rate is 28 percent would receive a benefit equal to 28 cents for each deductible dollar. Therefore, although deductions are certainly beneficial, a tax credit, if available, is of more value to the taxpayer than a deduction of an equal amount.

There are several personal tax credits available for individual taxpayers. The main ones are the credit for children, the dependent-care credit, the credit for the elderly or the permanently and totally disabled, the adoption credit, and the two credits for higher education expenses. All personal tax credits reflect Congress's concern with providing tax incentives for individual taxpayers' socially beneficial or economically necessary activities. Each tax credit has its own set of rules for eligibility, availability based on the taxpayer's income level, and credit amounts. Knowledge of how tax credits operate is essential to a fundamental understanding of the income tax law.

THE ALTERNATIVE MINIMUM TAX (AMT)

alternative minimum tax (AMT)

The *alternative minimum tax (AMT)* is a separate and parallel system of income taxation to the regular system. It applies to any taxpayer whose tax liability under the parallel system is greater than the liability for that year under the regular income tax system. In other words, the taxpayer pays the AMT amount if the AMT is greater than the regular tax. Therefore, it follows that the computational process for determining the AMT is a different process from that used in determining the regular tax. The deduction rules are different. The credit rules are different. The tax rates are different.

The purpose of the AMT is to make certain that taxpayers who enjoy certain tax benefits will not be permitted to reduce their tax liability below a minimum amount by claiming certain tax deductions. For example, one thing that the AMT rules do is to add back certain deductions for AMT purposes that are allowable to the taxpayer for regular tax purposes. These items that are deductible for the regular tax, but face different rules under the AMT, are referred to as *tax preference items*. These items generally produce no benefit to the taxpayer under the AMT system as they would under the regular system.

tax preference items

The tax rate under the AMT system is applied to income subject to the AMT. For individuals, there are two ordinary income brackets with rates of 26 percent and 28 percent, respectively. For corporations, it is a flat rate of 20 percent. Certain small corporations are not subject to AMT. Note that although the AMT tax rates for individuals are lower than the tax rates in the top brackets in the regular system, the tax payable may be greater. If so, the AMT must be paid instead of the regular tax.

For purposes of this chapter, the financial advisor should simply be aware that the AMT tax system exists, and that certain taxpayers with certain types of deductions will be subject to it. The details for calculating the AMT and the various rules for determining what goes in and out of the AMT tax base are found in more advanced texts. For the advisor engaged in a tax practice or in comprehensive financial planning, it will be necessary to acquire a basic understanding of these rules.

TAX PERIODS AND ACCOUNTING METHODS

Individuals file tax returns on an annual basis. For the vast majority of individuals, income tax is calculated based upon a calendar-year period. However, many partnerships and corporations (as well as a small number of individuals) report their tax liability based upon a 12-month period that does not coincide with the calendar year. Such a period is referred to as a fiscal year. In the past, the use of a fiscal year for tax purposes by a business entity provided an opportunity for deferring taxable income. This was accomplished by paying or crediting income to a partner or shareholder in the beginning of a calendar year that was actually earned by the business during its fiscal year, which began several months before the onset of the calendar year. However, such techniques have been virtually eliminated by strict rules governing the election of a fiscal year for tax purposes.

taxable year

Taxable income must be computed not only on the basis of a fixed accounting period—that is, a *taxable year*—but also in accordance with a method of tax accounting that clearly reflects income. Most financial advisors and their clients use the *cash-basis method*, which means that they report income and pay taxes on the income only if it is received during the taxable year. Almost all individual taxpayers who do not own a trade or business (and many who do) use this method of accounting.

cash-basis method

However, there is an exception to the general rule that income is reported by a cash-basis taxpayer only when it is actually received. The exception is known as the constructive receipt doctrine, which is designed to prevent taxpayers from unilaterally determining the tax year when an item of income is "received by" them for federal income tax purposes. More about this doctrine later.

accrual method

The other popular method of accounting is the *accrual method*, which typically is used by C corporations. Under this method, income is accounted for when the right to receive it comes into being, that is, when all the events that determine the right have occurred. It is not the actual receipt but the right to receive that governs.

THREE IMPORTANT ISSUES

The preceding material has been an overview of the process by which an individual's tax liability is computed. To more fully understand the income tax system, it is helpful to think about three basic issues in addition to understanding the computation process. These three issues are (1) what is taxed? (2) to whom is it taxed? and (3) when is it taxed? There are important tax law doctrines that clarify each of these issues.

The What Question: The Economic Benefit Doctrine

The question of what is taxed has already been discussed in the section of this chapter that describes the concept of gross income. In general, anything of value received by the taxpayer is taxed. Any event or transaction that confers an economic benefit on the taxpayer will result in gross income to the taxpayer, as long as the economic benefit is certain and can be measured. For example, suppose the Carroll Corporation sets up a trust for one of its key employees, Toby. The terms of the trust provide that in 2 years Toby will receive $20,000 a year for a 10-year period. Toby's right to the money is nonforfeitable and the trust assets are not otherwise available to the Carroll Corporation in any way. Even though Toby is not receiving any money currently, the Carroll Corporation has conferred an economic benefit upon

Toby that is certain and can be measured using time-value-of-money calculations. Therefore, Toby will be taxed currently on the present value of the payments to be made in the future. Note that the result would be different if the payments were contingent on the rendering of future services by Toby, or if the assets of the trust were available to the Carroll Corporation or its creditors for use other than to pay Toby. This is an example of the *economic benefit doctrine*, which holds that a taxpayer must pay tax whenever an economic benefit has been conferred on the taxpayer, regardless of whether the taxpayer has actually received any cash or property. Another example of the application of this doctrine is the case in which an employer pays life insurance premiums on a policy covering the life of an employee who has the right to name the beneficiary under the policy. The employer in such a case has conferred an economic benefit upon the employee (life insurance coverage) that is subject to income tax.

economic benefit doctrine

The To Whom Question: The Fruit and Tree Doctrine

There are many types of assets that produce income that is taxed. The asset producing the income may be a corporate bond that pays interest. Or it may be a piece of real estate that generates rental income. Or it may be an individual, whose knowledge or expertise generates income from sales or services. In any event, the tax principle that applies is this: Income is to be taxed to the person who earns it, or to the person who owns the asset that produces it. In other words, for income tax purposes, the "fruit" comes from the "tree" that produced it, and must be taxed accordingly. This is known as the *fruit and tree doctrine*.

fruit and tree doctrine

Example: Sandra owns a $1,000 bond issued by the Merlin Corporation. Sandra clips the interest coupons from the bond and gives them to her son, Brett. Brett receives the interest income. Sandra retains ownership of the bond itself. In spite of the fact that Brett has received the income, Sandra is still taxed on it because she owns the asset that produced the income.

Similarly, income from personal services is taxed to the person who earns it. The fruits of an individual's labor cannot be assigned to another individual for tax purposes. For example, assume an insurance advisor irrevocably assigns in writing to his or her daughter the right to future commissions from a policy that he or she sold to a client. Will the daughter be taxed on the income? The answer is no. The advisor who earned the income must be taxed on it. This principle is often referred to as the *assignment of income doctrine*.

assignment of income doctrine

The When Question: The Constructive Receipt Doctrine

The current use of money is valuable. Therefore, if taxation can be deferred, the taxpayer gains a monetary benefit through the use of tax money until it is paid to the government later. As a result, taxpayers may try to use techniques that defer the receipt of income until a later tax year in order to defer the payment of tax on the income. An important doctrine that limits the use of such techniques is referred to as the *constructive receipt doctrine*. Were it not for this doctrine, cash-basis taxpayers could shift, at will, the year in which they report an item of income merely by not taking any steps to reduce that income to possession.

constructive receipt doctrine

Under the doctrine of constructive receipt, a cash-basis taxpayer is deemed to have received income for tax purposes when it is either credited to the taxpayer's account, set apart for the taxpayer, or otherwise made available to be taken into the taxpayer's possession.

Example: John, an insurance advisor, filed a policy application with his company in November of last year. In December, the policy was issued, and a commission check was made out to John. John did not pick up the check until January of this year, even though he could have easily picked it up in December. John must report this income on last year's tax return under the doctrine of constructive receipt, even though John did not actually receive the income until this year.

It is important to know, however, that if there is any condition or restriction that limits the taxpayer's right to receive the income, the doctrine of constructive receipt will not apply.

Example: Natalie is a financial advisor with a real estate license. In November of last year, her client signed an agreement to purchase a home that Natalie listed. The sale is closed on January 2 of this year. Although Natalie was fairly certain in November that she would receive her commission, the client still had to go through with the closing in order for

Natalie's rights to her money to become unconditional. Therefore, the constructive receipt doctrine does not apply to Natalie and she will be taxed on the commission in the year she actually receives it.

BASIC INCOME-TAX-PLANNING CONCEPTS

Despite repeated efforts to simplify the tax law, much complexity remains in the understanding and application of the Internal Revenue Code. Because of this complexity, many highly intelligent people devote their professional lives to the process of trying to figure out how the Code can be analyzed (and, in some cases, manipulated) to save some tax money for their clients. This is fine and good, as long as the tax is saved through tax avoidance (that is, a reasonable interpretation of the tax laws), and not through *tax evasion* (that is, ignoring or flouting the tax laws).

tax evasion

As previously stated, sophisticated tax planning is not the subject of this chapter. However, it is important, as well as helpful, to outline some of the basic concepts that are used in tax planning to illustrate how tax lawyers and other tax advisors think in their efforts to help clients both minimize and/or avoid taxes.

Income and Deduction Shifting

The purpose behind income-shifting techniques is this: Get taxable income into the hands of a taxpayer who is in a lower tax bracket than the taxpayer who would otherwise have to report the income. The result is that less tax is paid on the income. For example, a taxpayer in the top 35 percent marginal tax bracket will pay $3,500 in tax on $10,000 of additional income. However, a taxpayer in the 15 percent bracket will pay only $1,500 of tax on the same $10,000 of income. Clearly, income shifting can provide substantial tax savings.

What, then, are some of the income-shifting techniques that are available? Perhaps the simplest one is an outright gift of property. As previously discussed, income is taxed to the person who owns the asset that produces the income. If the asset is transferred by gift, the donee will be taxed on income generated by the asset. However, the gift tax consequences of giving away property to shift the income tax burden must always be considered.

For planning purposes, the converse of income shifting is deduction shifting. Deduction shifting is a simple, yet frequently overlooked, planning technique. Here, the idea is to shift deductions to a taxpayer who is in a higher tax bracket than the taxpayer who would otherwise claim the deduction. As a result, the deduction is taken against income that would be taxed in a higher bracket, thereby resulting in a greater tax savings.

Example: Marjorie is ill and must enter the hospital for an extended stay. The cost of her care is only partially covered by insurance. Although Marjorie has some assets, she is not working and does not have much income. Her mother, Ruth, is in the 28 percent tax bracket and also has enough medical expenses of her own this year to claim a medical expense deduction. Marjorie is Ruth's dependent for tax purposes, and therefore, Ruth can deduct medical expense payments she makes for Marjorie's care. If Ruth pays for Marjorie's care, there will be a tax savings of 28 cents for every dollar of expense. If, on the other hand, Marjorie pays for her own expenses, there will be little or no tax savings.

Avoiding Limitations on Deductions

deduction floor

miscellaneous itemized deductions

As was explained earlier in this chapter, although many types of expenses are deductible for income tax purposes, there may be limitations on how much of a given expense may actually be deducted. One common way that the law limits deductions is through the use of a *deduction floor*. You will recall that the taxpayer is allowed to deduct items that are subject to the floor, but only to the extent those items exceed a specified percentage of income (specifically, adjusted gross income in most cases).

For example, there is an entire group of deductions that are claimed by individual taxpayers on Schedule A of Form 1040 that are referred to as *miscellaneous itemized deductions*. This group of deductions includes unreimbursed employee expenses, fees for safe deposit boxes, tax preparation fees, and several other items. First, all of the taxpayer's deductions that fall within this group are added together. Then, the taxpayer's adjusted gross income is multiplied by 2 percent. The resulting figure is subtracted from the total of the items in the group to determine how much the taxpayer can actually deduct. The result is that the taxpayer is permitted to deduct miscellaneous itemized deductions only to the extent they exceed this 2 percent floor.

How can taxpayers avoid this floor? With respect to some deductions that fall within this category, it is impossible to avoid the floor itself. However, if adjusted gross income can be reduced in a year in which the taxpayer has these items, a greater portion of the items will be deductible, since the floor will be less. How, then, can adjusted gross income be reduced? By maximizing above-the-line deductions, as previously discussed. If a taxpayer has miscellaneous itemized deductions and wishes to minimize the effect of the 2 percent floor, it may be appropriate to bunch the taxpayer's above-the-line deductions into a given year to reduce adjusted gross income. Conversely, it may also be helpful to bunch a greater number of the miscellaneous itemized deductions subject to the floor into one year. The result of this technique would be that some deductions that would be lost under the floor if claimed in next year's return can actually be deducted if taken this year, because the floor has already been exceeded.

Other deductions that are subject to a floor include the medical expense deduction (7.5 percent of adjusted gross income) and the deduction for personal casualty and theft losses (10 percent of adjusted gross income). However, in the case of casualty and theft losses, while the floor is applied to the total amount of such losses, it is applied only after each separate loss that makes up the total is first reduced by $100.

Example: Lynn accidentally rinses her diamond ring down the drain this year. Lynn's husband paid $10,100 for the ring as an anniversary present. Assume Lynn and her husband file a joint return and are in the 25 percent tax bracket. The ring is not insured. Lynn and her husband have an adjusted gross income of $83,000 for the year. Therefore, $8,400 of their $10,100 casualty loss will be lost as a deduction, after first subtracting $100 from the loss and then applying the 10 percent floor [$10,100 − $100 = $10,000 − ($83,000 x .10) = $10,000 − $8,300 = $1,700]. The result is a $1,700 deduction for their $10,100 casualty loss. Since Lynn and her husband are in the 25 percent tax bracket, their tax savings from the $1,700 deduction will be $425 ($1,700 x .25 = $425).

However, if both Lynn and her husband are each eligible to contribute $4,000 to their IRAs (an above-the-line deduction), the couple's adjusted gross income for the year would be reduced to $75,000 ($83,000 − $8,000 = $75,000). As a result of the reduced adjusted gross income, the 10 percent floor applied to the couple's casualty loss will be reduced from $8,300 to $7,500. This means that after first subtracting $100 from the loss and then applying the 10 percent floor, the deduction for their

> casualty loss would increase from $1,700 to $2,500. Their tax savings for the $2,500 deduction would be $625 ($2,500 x .25 = $625), an increase of $200 over the $425 tax savings for the $1,700 deduction. The increased casualty loss deduction and tax savings resulting from the IRA contributions are in addition to the tax benefits produced by the IRA contributions themselves.

The same technique (reducing adjusted gross income) is also helpful in avoiding the overall limitation or "phaseout" of itemized deductions, mentioned earlier.

Deferral and Acceleration Techniques

Deferral of income and acceleration of deductions are basic and common tax planning techniques. These techniques are based on the time value of money. If income can be deferred to a later year, the tax payable on the income is also deferred and the taxpayer has the use of that money for a longer time. Similarly, if deductible expenses are accelerated into an earlier tax year, the tax saving from those deductions is realized sooner, thereby giving the taxpayer the use of that money sooner. However, it is important to note that most tax deductions are attributable to actual out-of-pocket expenses. Therefore, the expense itself involves the loss of use of money, which over the same time period will be greater than the benefit realized by the tax savings. The point here is to not let the tax "tail" wag the overall financial "dog."

What, then, is the potential benefit of accelerating deductions? The benefit lies in a differential with respect to the comparative time periods. For example, if a taxpayer makes a deductible expense in December of this year rather than in January of next year, the taxpayer has only lost the use of the money spent for one additional month. However, the tax savings generated by the expense gives the taxpayer the use of the tax savings for an entire additional year, as compared to making the expense in January. In such a situation, the taxpayer does in fact gain a net benefit from accelerating the expense.

> *Example:* Harry makes a $10,000 deductible business expense in December of this year. Assume Harry's marginal tax bracket is 35 percent. By making the expenditure in December of this year rather than January of next year, Harry postpones the payment of $3,500 in

taxes ($10,000 x .35) for one year. Assume Harry can invest money for one year at 6 percent annual interest. Harry will have $210 ($3,500 x .06) that he would not have if he had deferred the expense until next year. However, by paying the $10,000 in December instead of January, Harry loses one month's interest on the $10,000. This amount is $50 [($10,000 x .06) ÷ 12]. But note that Harry is still ahead $160 ($210 − $50) by accelerating the deductible expense and, in effect, deferring the payment of taxes on $10,000 of income for one year.

The Passive-Loss Rules

passive losses

There are special limitations on the deductibility of so-called *passive losses*. These tax losses are typically generated by activities in which the taxpayer has an ownership interest, but does not participate in the activity of the business. For example, suppose a taxpayer owns an interest in a limited partnership that invests in rental real estate. Assume that the depreciation deductions and other deductions generated by the partnership properties exceed the income generated by the properties. Therefore, for tax purposes, the partnership generates losses.

Under tax laws in effect before the Tax Reform Act of 1986, there were few limitations on the deductibility of such items by taxpayers owning interests in limited partnerships and other activities in which the taxpayer did not participate. Because these investments allowed taxpayers to write off the tax losses against salary and other types of income, they were referred to as *tax shelters*. Tax shelters were a very important weapon in the tax-avoidance arsenal.

tax shelters

Under current law, however, there are strict limitations on the deductibility of losses generated by tax-shelter investments. These rules are intended to prevent taxpayers from investing in activities merely for tax purposes, as distinguished from the actual economics of the investment. There are complicated rules and definitions as to what constitutes a passive activity that will be subject to the strict deduction rules. The basic rule, however, is that tax losses generated by passive activities can be deducted only against income generated by the taxpayer's passive activities, and not against salary or other income of the taxpayer.

There are qualifications, exceptions, and certain significant loopholes to these rules. This is one of those areas of the tax law that is a specialty in itself. In fact, some specialists in this area have trouble understanding the rules, which are complicated by hundreds of pages of Treasury regulations. For purposes of this chapter, the reader should simply be aware that if a taxpayer invests in an activity in which the taxpayer does not participate, and the activity generates tax losses, the deductibility of those losses is limited by some very strict rules. Activities deemed to be passive include most rental activities in which the taxpayer owns an interest. However, investments in publicly traded stocks and bonds are not covered by these rules, because these are not the type of investments that usually produce tax losses on an annual basis.

Tax-Exempt Transactions

Perhaps one of the best types of tax planning techniques is that of creating a transaction that produces a monetary benefit without the taxpayer being taxed on that transaction. Within this general category there are two basic types of transactions. The first is where taxation is altogether eliminated, and the second is where taxation of the transaction is merely deferred. The first type can be described as a tax-exempt transaction. Such transactions are generally based on some specific exclusion from gross income.

An example of a tax-exempt transaction is the receipt of income from a public-purpose municipal bond. The income from such bonds is excludible from the taxpayer's gross income for federal income tax purposes. As previously discussed, however, all income is includible in gross income unless there is a provision in the Code that specifically excludes it. There is such an exclusion for certain municipal bond income (IRC Sec. 103).

Financial market forces generally dictate that unless the taxpayer is subject to a high marginal income tax rate, the interest rate on such bonds will not be greater than the after-tax rate on taxable obligations. Therefore such investments are generally of interest only to upper-bracket taxpayers.

Another example of a tax-exempt monetary gain is the exclusion of the first $250,000 ($500,000 if married, filing jointly) of gain on the sale of a personal residence if certain requirements are met.

Nonrecognition Transactions

nonrecognition transactions

There are many types of transactions in which taxation is merely deferred rather than eliminated. These transactions may generally be referred to as *nonrecognition transactions*. Typically, such a transaction involves the sale or exchange of property at a gain realized by the taxpayer. However, because of a provision in the Internal Revenue Code, the realized gain is not currently recognized (reportable on Form 1040).

How do such transactions merely defer, rather than eliminate, taxable gain? In order to understand the mechanics of the nonrecognition transaction, the basic tax treatment of a sale or exchange of property must be understood.

Computation of Gain or Loss

When property is sold, it is necessary to determine what portion of the sale proceeds will be subject to taxation. In general, the gain realized from a sale of property is equal to the total amount realized from the sale, minus the taxpayer's basis in the property.

What does the term basis mean? Broadly stated, basis is the amount that the taxpayer has invested in the property. Therefore, basis is generally the amount that the taxpayer paid for the property, plus the cost of improvements to the property, if any. Stated another way, the basis of property is generally equal to its cost. As a result, the gain realized from a sale of property is the sales price minus the taxpayer's cost.

Example: Nancy bought 1,000 shares of stock in Cleanseco, Inc., a household cleanser manufacturer, 2 years ago. She paid $5,000 for the stock. This year, she sells the Cleanseco stock for $10,000. The amount realized from the sale is $10,000. Nancy's basis is $5,000. Therefore, the realized gain from the sale is $5,000 ($10,000 – $5,000)

The fact that the portion of the sales price that represents a recovery of the taxpayer's basis is not taxable illustrates a basic principle of tax law, namely, that money received that represents a return of capital is not treated as gross income. The Internal Revenue Code contains many provisions which reflect this basic principle. It is really a matter of common sense: Getting back money that the taxpayer has invested in property should not result in taxation, because there has been no profit returned to the taxpayer, only the original investment.

How Nonrecognition Transactions Differ from Taxable Transactions

Some sales and exchanges are governed by specific provisions in the Internal Revenue Code, which provide that the gain realized shall not be recognized (that is, reported on Form 1040 and taxed). It has been stated above that the purpose of these transactions is not to eliminate taxation, but merely to defer it. How is this accomplished?

The answer to this question relates to the taxpayer's basis in property. Generally, a taxpayer's basis in property is equal to the cost of the property. In the case of an exchange of property, the taxpayer's cost for the property received in the exchange is really the fair market value of the property surrendered in the exchange. However, if the exchange is one in which gain is not recognized, the taxpayer's basis in the new property will generally be the same as the taxpayer's basis in the old property. This preserves the unrecognized gain and allows that gain to be taxed when the new property is later sold in a taxable transaction.

Example: Robert owns a condominium that he holds as a rental property. He paid $100,000 for the property and added $20,000 worth of improvements. The value of the property is now $180,000. Robert exchanges the property for another condominium in a transaction that qualifies for nonrecognition treatment under the Internal Revenue Code. The property received in the exchange is also worth $180,000. Robert's realized gain is $60,000 ($180,000 value of property received minus $120,000 basis in property given up). Robert's recognized gain is zero because the exchange qualifies for nonrecognition treatment. However, Robert's basis in the new property will be the same as his basis in the old property ($120,000). As a result, if the new property is sold later, the gain that would have been recognized if the exchange was taxable earlier will be recognized later, when the new property is sold. On the other hand, if the exchange was taxable, Robert would pay tax currently on the $60,000 of gain, but he would have a basis of $180,000 in the new property.

Clearly, the deferral of taxation in such a transaction has significant value. Moreover, the deferred gain may never be taxed if the taxpayer does not sell the property received in the exchange at a later date. The intent of the nonrecognition provisions is merely to defer taxation. But there is no assurance that Uncle Sam will ever get his tax money, particularly if the taxpayer keeps the new property until death.

The example above is just one type of transaction that qualifies for nonrecognition. Other examples include exchanges of insurance policies and involuntary conversions. These transactions, and the specific rules that govern their tax treatment, are beyond the scope of this chapter.

Transactions That Result in a Taxable Loss

Some sales of property will result in a loss rather than a gain to the selling taxpayer. This will happen when the amount received for the property is less than the taxpayer's basis in the property. In such cases, the amount of the loss will generally be deductible for income tax purposes if the property sold is either business property or property held for the production of income. If the property is held for personal use, the loss resulting from a sale of the property is generally nondeductible.

Example: Alexandra owns stock in the Hi-Five Corporation, a publicly traded corporation that sells sneakers. Alexandra paid $5,000 for the stock 2 years ago. This year, she sells the stock for $3,500. Alexandra has a realized loss of $1,500 ($5,000 basis minus $3,500 amount realized). Alexandra may deduct the $1,500 loss on her tax return this year.

Ordinary versus Capital Gain and Loss

Some different rules apply to sales of a taxpayer's assets, depending on whether the gain or loss is treated as an ordinary gain or loss or a capital gain or loss.

Capital Gain versus Ordinary Income

As most financial advisors know, one of the most important pieces of the federal tax law puzzle is the broad scope of social policy considerations. In other words, what politicians perceive to be a policy that will get them elected or reelected often finds its way into the tax laws. One of the policy issues that is a continuous source of controversy and change is the question of whether *capital gain* should be taxed at the same rates as *ordinary income.*

capital gain
ordinary gain

What is the difference between capital gain and ordinary income? Basically, capital gain is income that is realized through the sale or exchange of a capital asset. The definition of a capital asset does appear in the Internal Revenue Code, although the Code defines a capital asset by stating what it is not rather than what it is. In any event, a capital asset can generally be described as any property held by the taxpayer other than property held for sale by the taxpayer, or intellectual or artistic property created by the taxpayer. Special tax rules apply to the sale of property used by a taxpayer in a trade or business. These rules will be discussed below.

The social policy issue surrounding the sale of capital assets is this: Should the sale of such assets receive a tax break relative to other kinds of income? Those who answer yes argue that capital-gain tax relief encourages savings and investment. They also argue that full taxation of capital gain subjects taxpayers to what is really a tax on inflation, rather than one on real economic gains.

How does a capital-gain tax break favor savings and investment? Stocks, bonds, real estate, and other investment-type assets generally are treated as capital assets. When an investor sells such an asset, a greater portion of the amount realized from the sale will remain in the investor's pocket if favorable tax treatment applies to the realized gain. Therefore, the investor has a higher rate of return on the investment, which presumably provides an incentive to save rather than spend.

In addition, it is argued that a portion of the increase in value of an investment-type asset is attributable to inflation, rather than to real economic appreciation. Therefore, the argument goes, taxing the full amount of gain when the asset is sold is confiscatory, because the portion of the gain attributable to inflation has conferred no real economic benefit upon the taxpayer who is paying tax on it.

These theories have helped to introduce varying legislative measures over the years that provide relief for the taxation of capital gain. For example, through the use of an exclusion from gross income for a specified percentage of an individual's capital gain or a lower tax rate on capital gain, a lower tax bill on the overall gain results.

Under the 2003 Jobs and Growth Tax Relief Reconciliation Act, the maximum rate applicable to capital gains on assets held by individual taxpayers for more than 12 months is generally 15 percent, as opposed to the much higher maximum marginal tax rate of 35 percent that is applicable to ordinary income. Gains from collectibles and real estate gains attributable to "unrecaptured" depreciation are taxed at the higher rates of 28 percent and 25 percent, respectively.

What are the arguments against favorable tax treatment for capital gain? The principal argument is that a preferential treatment for capital gain favors wealthy taxpayers at the expense of the average citizen. The theory goes that most stocks and bonds and other investment assets are owned by the rich, and that by taxing gains from the sale of these investments at a lower effective rate, the government is playing Robin Hood in reverse: stealing from the poor to feed the rich.

Draw your own conclusions.

Qualified Dividends Taxed at Long-Term Capital Gains Rates

Dividends represent income that has already been taxed at the corporate level before being distributed to individual stockholders. Under the 2003 Jobs and Growth Tax Relief Reconciliation Act, dividends paid to individual stockholders typically are designated as qualified dividends, which are taxed at the same rates that apply to long-term capital gains. Beginning in 2008 (and continuing through 2010), taxpayers in the 10 percent or 15 percent tax bracket pay a 0 percent rate of tax on qualified dividends. Taxpayers in the tax brackets above 15 percent pay a 15 percent rate of tax on qualified dividends. (In 2011, long-term capital gains rates and tax rates for qualified dividends are scheduled to revert to pre-2003 levels unless Congress extends the lower rates.) Even though the tax rates that apply to qualified dividends are the same as those applicable to long-term capital gains, qualified dividends are classified as ordinary income (as opposed to capital gains). The tax treatment of qualified dividends applies for purposes of both the regular tax and the alternative minimum tax (AMT).

Tax Treatment of Capital Losses

When a capital asset is sold at a loss rather than at a gain, special rules apply. Basically, capital losses can be deducted only against the taxpayer's capital gains. In other words, a taxpayer cannot deduct capital losses against ordinary income (such as his or her wages for the year). Moreover, even though qualified dividends are taxed at long-term capital gains rates, capital losses cannot be deducted against qualified dividends either. However, in the special case of individual taxpayers, capital losses can be deducted against ordinary income (including qualified dividends) in an amount up to $3,000 per year. Capital losses in excess of $3,000 can be carried over to future tax years.

Sec. 1231 Assets: Depreciable Property and Real Property Used in a Trade or Business

This class of assets receives different tax treatment, depending on whether the asset is sold at a gain or at a loss. If the asset is sold at a gain, the gain is treated as a capital gain. If the asset is sold at a loss, the loss is treated as an ordinary loss, not as a capital loss.

What is the significance of this hybrid form of tax treatment? The most important thing is that the sale of an asset falling into this category is not subject to the limitations that apply to the deductibility of capital losses. Therefore, if such an asset is sold at a loss, the loss can be deducted against the taxpayer's salary or other income.

If the asset is sold at a gain, the gain will be treated as capital gain. Even though there is currently no partial exclusion or other preferential treatment available for capital gains, capital-gains treatment can provide a benefit for taxpayers who have capital losses for the year. Why? Because the capital losses can be deducted against capital gains, but not against ordinary income.

| *Example:* | Pat sells a piece of machinery this year that is used in his business. The machinery is sold at a gain of $40,000. Pat also has a capital loss of $40,000 this year from a sale of stock from his investment |

portfolio. Because the gain from the sale of the machinery is treated as capital gain and not ordinary income, Pat can deduct his stock losses in full against the gain from the sale of the machinery.

The assets that receive this hybrid form of tax treatment include all depreciable property plus land that is used in the taxpayer's business (land is not depreciable for tax purposes). These so-called Sec. 1231 assets provide the best of both worlds for taxpayers, and the rules that govern them are designed to stimulate investment in assets that are used in the conduct of a business.

TAXABLE ENTITIES

Most of the discussion in this chapter has focused on the individual taxpayer who receives income from salary, investment, or a sole proprietorship. However, the individual is not the only taxpayer under the federal income tax system. Trusts, estates, and corporations also are subject to the federal income tax. However, certain corporations can make an election to have their shareholders taxed on the corporation's taxable income. This is called a subchapter S election. The effect of such an election is to have the corporation treated for tax purposes very much like a partnership. Like a partnership, a corporation that makes an S election is not subject to income tax at the entity level. Rather, the owners of the business pay the taxes. Partnerships and *S corporations* are often referred to as pass-through entities, because the responsibility for paying their taxes is passed through the entity to the owners of the entity.

S corporations

C corporations

However, trusts, estates, and *C corporations* (that is, corporations other than S corporations) do pay taxes. There are special rules that apply to each of these entities that do not apply to individual taxpayers. In addition, each of these entities has a tax rate structure that is different from the rate structure applicable to individual taxpayers.

THE FINAL WORD

This chapter has outlined basic income tax concepts and planning techniques that should be familiar to financial advisors. However, there is much more that can be learned about each of these topics. If a financial advisor is going to be a tax specialist or offer comprehensive financial planning for his or her clients, then it will become necessary for him or her to study more advanced tax sources. Besides, income tax planning is still a crucial component of financial planning despite the fact that legislation has closed many tax loopholes under prior law.

CHAPTER SUMMARY

Even though there are several planning techniques that can be utilized to minimize and/or avoid paying taxes, tax relief may not be the only goal of income tax planning. The best tax plan is one that accurately reflects the client's overall financial goals. A tax plan that focuses on tax minimization and/or tax avoidance is a poor plan if it is inconsistent with the client's other financial goals. Therefore, the purpose of this chapter is to introduce the advisor to the ways that he or she can help a client plan for tax minimization and/or tax avoidance within the context of the client's financial plan.

For an advisor to learn about federal income tax law, it is important to begin with an understanding of the term gross income. Basically, gross income includes every item of value, whether consisting of money or other property, that is either made available to or comes into the possession of the taxpayer. In other words, anything of value is considered to be gross income for income tax purposes unless the Internal Revenue Code contains a specific provision that excludes a particular item from the taxpayer's gross income.

It is also important to distinguish the concept of an exclusion from that of a deduction for tax purposes. An exclusion is an item of value that the taxpayer receives that is not includible in the taxpayer's gross income, while a deduction is an item of expense (not an item of receipt) that reduces the amount of income subject to taxation. However, before some deductions can be explained, the concepts of adjusted gross income and taxable income should be understood.

Adjusted gross income is an intermediate calculation that is made in the process of determining an individual's income tax liability for a given year. It is used as a base amount to determine how the taxpayer must treat certain other items for tax purposes. Taxable income, on the other hand, is the amount of income that will actually be subject to taxation in a given year. It is calculated by deducting certain items from the taxpayer's adjusted gross income.

In the computation of an individual's tax liability, there are two basic types of deductions. The first type consists of deductions that are subtracted from gross income to determine adjusted gross income. The second type consists of deductions that are subtracted from adjusted gross income to determine taxable income. The first type is known as above-the-line deductions, while the second type is known as below-the-line deductions.

The standard deduction is a fixed amount that the individual may claim in lieu of claiming itemized deductions on Schedule A of Form 1040. The amount of the standard deduction depends on the taxpayer's filing status—

single taxpayer, unmarried head of household, married filing jointly, or married filing separately. If the individual is entitled to claim itemized deductions that, when added together, are more than his or her standard deduction, then the individual should deduct his or her itemized deductions instead of claiming the standard deduction. With either claim, the itemized deductions—or the alternative standard deduction—are considered below-the-line deductions, that is, deductions taken in calculating taxable income.

There are three basic categories of deductions allowable to individual taxpayers. These are business expenses, expenses for the production of income, and personal expenses. Whenever the client or advisor is determining whether a given item of expense is deductible, certain questions should be asked. The first is whether the Code allows a deduction for the item. The second is which basic category the expense falls under. The third is whether the deduction is an above-the-line or below-the-line deduction. The fourth and final question is whether there is a particular restriction or limitation on the deductibility of the item, such as a floor, a ceiling, a percentage limitation, or an overall limitation.

Not all tax deductions represent actual out-of-pocket expenses. Some deductions are allowable even though they represent no corresponding cash outlay. These are referred to as paper deductions, because they represent or are related to some entry on the books of the taxpayer's business or investment activity, but they are not a cash-flow item. The most important of these noncash deductions is the deduction for depreciation.

Each individual taxpayer is allowed to claim a personal exemption for himself or herself. A married couple filing jointly may claim an exemption for each spouse. In addition, individual taxpayers are also permitted to claim a dependency exemption for each dependent supported by the taxpayer. The amount of these exemptions is subtracted from adjusted gross income in the process of computing taxable income. Since these exemptions are not itemized deductions, either itemized deductions or the alternative standard deduction may be claimed in addition to the taxpayer's exemptions.

Once the taxpayer's gross income has been determined, all deductions allowable in determining adjusted gross income are subtracted from gross income. Next, all deductions and exemptions allowable in determining taxable income are subtracted from adjusted gross income. The resulting figure is the taxpayer's taxable income. This is the figure to which the income tax rates are applied to determine the amount of income tax payable for the year. Currently, there are six income tax rates, and they are 10, 15, 25, 28, 33, and 35 percent. The tax rate applicable to each income bracket is called the marginal tax rate. Once the tax rates have been applied to an individual's taxable income, the resulting figure is the individual's tentative tax. This tentative tax, however, can be reduced if the individual is eligible to claim any income tax credits.

It is important to understand the difference between a tax credit and a tax deduction. A tax credit is a dollar-for-dollar reduction of the actual tax payable. A deduction, on the other hand, is an item of expense that only reduces the amount of the taxpayer's income that is subject to taxation. Therefore, although deductions are certainly beneficial, a tax credit, if available, is of more value to the taxpayer than a deduction of an equal amount.

The alternative minimum tax (AMT) is a separate and parallel system of income taxation to the regular system. It applies to any taxpayer whose tax liability under the parallel system is greater than the liability for that year under the regular income tax system. The purpose of the AMT is to make certain that taxpayers who enjoy certain tax benefits are not permitted to reduce their tax liability below a minimum amount by claiming certain tax deductions.

Individuals file tax returns on an annual basis. For the vast majority of individuals, income tax is calculated based upon a calendar-year period. However, many business entities and some individuals report their tax liability based upon a 12-month period other than the calendar year. Such a period is referred to as a fiscal year.

Taxable income must be computed not only on the basis of a fixed accounting period—that is, a taxable year—but also in accordance with a method of tax accounting that clearly reflects income. Most financial advisors and their clients use the cash-basis method, which means that they report income and pay taxes on the income only if it is received during the taxable year. The other popular method of accounting is the accrual method, which typically is used by C corporations. Under this method, income is accounted for when the right to receive it comes into being, that is, when all the events that determine the right have occurred. It is not the actual receipt but the right to receive that governs.

In addition to understanding the computation process, to more fully understand the income tax system, it is helpful to consider three basic issues. These three issues are (1) what is taxed, as clarified by the economic benefit doctrine, (2) to whom is it taxed, as clarified by the fruit and tree doctrine, and (3) when is it taxed, as clarified by the constructive receipt doctrine.

While sophisticated tax planning is not the subject of this chapter, it is nevertheless helpful to outline some of the basic concepts that are used in tax planning to minimize and/or avoid taxes. These include techniques for income and deduction shifting, avoiding limitations on deductions, deferral of income and acceleration of deductions, limitations on the deductibility of passive losses, participating in both tax-exempt and nonrecognition transactions, participating in transactions that result in a taxable loss, and distinguishing ordinary income from capital gain and loss tax treatment.

Individuals are not the only taxpayers under the federal income tax system. Trusts, estates, and corporations also are subject to federal income tax. Certain corporations, however, can make a subchapter S election to have their shareholders taxed on the corporation's taxable income. Like a partnership, a corporation that makes an S election is not subject to income tax at the entity level. Rather, the owners of the business pay the taxes.

CHAPTER REVIEW

Key Terms and Concepts are explained in the Glossary. Answers to the Review Questions and Self-Test Questions are found in the back of the book in the Answers to Questions section.

Key Terms and Concepts

tax minimization
tax avoidance
gross income
exclusion
deduction
adjusted gross income (AGI)
taxable income
above-the-line deductions
below-the-line deductions
standard deduction
itemized deductions
business expense
expense for the production of income
personal expense
paper deductions
depreciation deduction
income tax basis
personal exemption
dependency exemption
marginal tax rate
filing status
tax bracket

effective tax rate
effective marginal tax rate
tax credits
alternative minimum tax (AMT)
tax preference items
taxable year
cash-basis method
accural method
economic benefit doctrine
fruit and tree doctrine
assignment of income doctrine
constructive receipt doctrine
tax evasion
deduction floor
miscellaneous itemized deductions
passive losses
tax shelters
nonrecognition transactions
capital gain
ordinary income
S corporations
C corporations

Review Questions

5-1. Explain what is considered to be gross income for income tax purposes.

5-2. Explain the difference between an exclusion from gross income and a deduction from gross income.

5-3. Explain the difference between an above-the-line deduction and a below-the-line deduction.

5-4. Explain what is meant by the standard deduction.

5-5. Describe the three basic categories of deductions allowable to individual taxpayers.

5-6. This year George has medical expenses totaling $9,500. If George has an adjusted gross income of $80,000 and he itemizes deductions, how much of these medical expenses will he be allowed to deduct for income tax purposes?

5-7. Describe the concept of phasing out a taxpayer's itemized deductions.

5-8. Explain the difference between a taxpayer's marginal tax rate and his or her effective tax rate.

5-9. Compare the effect on the amount of federal income tax payable of a $10,000 tax deduction versus a $10,000 tax credit.

5-10. Explain the nature and purpose of the alternative minimum tax (AMT).

5-11. Explain the meaning of each of the following federal income tax doctrines:
   a. the economic benefit doctrine
   b. the doctrine of the fruit and tree
   c. the doctrine of constructive receipt

5-12. Distinguish between federal income tax avoidance and federal income tax evasion.

5-13. Contrast the basic purpose of income-shifting techniques with that of deduction shifting techniques.

5-14. Explain how bunching of above-the-line deductions and below-the-line deductions can be used to minimize the impact of the floor on certain types of deductions.

5-15. a. Explain the meaning of the term passive losses.
   b. What is the general effect of the current federal income tax treatment of passive losses?
   c. Explain how a nonrecognition transaction may result in more than simply a deferral of federal income taxes on the transaction.
   d. Briefly describe the social policy issue surrounding taxation of the sales of capital assets.

5.16. a. Why might the federal income tax treatment of the sale of a Sec. 1231 asset be termed a hybrid form of tax treatment?

   b. What is the importance of the hybrid form of taxation of the sale of a Sec. 1231 asset?

Self-Test Questions

Instructions: Read chapter 5 first, then answer the following questions to test your knowledge. There are 10 questions; circle the correct answer, then check your answers with the answer key in the back of the book.

5-1. The floor for casualty loss deductions is set at what percentage of the taxpayer's adjusted gross income (AGI)?

(A) 2 percent
(B) 7.5 percent
(C) 10 percent
(D) 12 percent

5-2. During the past taxable year, Susan sold some common stock she had held for several years and incurred a capital loss of $6,000. Susan had no capital gains during the year, and her other income for the year was $60,000. How much of the capital loss can Susan deduct for the taxable year?

(A) None
(B) $3,000
(C) $5,000
(D) $6,000

5-3. Which of the following tax law doctrines is most useful in determining when an item of income is taxable?

(A) Shotgun doctrine
(B) Assignment of income doctrine
(C) Constructive receipt doctrine
(D) Economic benefit doctrine

Chapter 5 Income Tax Planning

5-4. Which of the following statements concerning tax credits is (are) correct?

    I. A $100 tax credit provides the taxpayer the same benefit as a $100 deduction.
    II. A $200 tax credit is worth more to a taxpayer in the 35 percent bracket than to one in the 15 percent bracket.

(A) I only
(B) II only
(C) Both I and II
(D) Neither I nor II

5-5. Which of the following statements concerning federal income tax rates is (are) correct?

    I. The highest marginal tax rate for an individual taxpayer is 35 percent.
    II. An individual taxpayer's effective tax rate is always higher than his or her marginal tax rate.

(A) I only
(B) II only
(C) Both I and II
(D) Neither I nor II

5-6. Which of the following types of business entities is (are) considered a pass-through entity under the federal income tax laws?

    I. a partnership
    II. an S corporation

(A) I only
(B) II only
(C) Both I and II
(D) Neither I nor II

5-7. All the following statements concerning the standard deduction are correct EXCEPT:

(A) The amount of the standard deduction depends on the taxpayer's filing status.
(B) The standard deduction is classified as an above-the-line deduction.
(C) The taxpayer may choose to itemize deductions instead of taking the standard deduction.
(D) The standard deduction amounts are indexed annually for inflation.

5-8. All the following statements concerning the alternative minimum tax (AMT) for individual taxpayers are correct EXCEPT:

(A) The taxpayer pays the AMT amount if the AMT is greater than the regular tax.
(B) It is a separate and parallel income tax system to the regular system.
(C) The computational process for determining the AMT is different from that used in determining the regular tax.
(D) It permits taxpayers to deduct the same items that they deduct for regular tax purposes.

5-9. All the following statements concerning personal and dependency exemptions are correct EXCEPT:

(A) A taxpayer may claim the standard deduction in addition to his or her exemptions.
(B) The amount of the exemption(s) is subtracted from gross income in the process of determining adjusted gross income.
(C) The exemption amount changes annually by way of an inflation adjustment.
(D) A taxpayer is permitted to claim a dependency exemption for each qualified individual he or she supports.

5-10. All the following assets may be treated as Sec. 1231 assets for federal income tax purposes EXCEPT

(A) common stock in the taxpayer's investment portfolio
(B) machinery used in the taxpayer's business
(C) the building in which the taxpayer's business is located
(D) land used in the taxpayer's business

6

Retirement Planning

David A. Littell
Kenn B. Tacchino

Learning Objectives

An understanding of the material in this chapter should enable you to

6-1. Explain why clients need to start retirement planning when they are young.

6-2. Explain the role of the retirement advisor, and describe the holistic approach to retirement planning.

6-3. Describe the responsibilities of the retirement advisor, and explain how retirement planning parallels the financial planning process.

6-4. Explain why financial planning for retirement is more art than science.

6-5. Explain why clients are never too old to plan for retirement, and describe several roadblocks to saving for retirement.

6-6. Explain the difficulties in estimating client financial needs during retirement, and describe two methods for determining how much retirement income may be needed.

6-7. Describe the potential sources of retirement income available to clients to meet their financial goals during retirement.

6-8. Describe several strategies that clients can use to overcome their having inadequate retirement resources.

Chapter Outline

STARTING RETIREMENT PLANNING WHEN YOUNG 6.2
THE ROLE OF THE RETIREMENT ADVISOR 6.4
    Holistic Retirement Planning 6.4
    Responsibilities of the Retirement Advisor 6.8
    Retirement Planning and the Financial Planning Process 6.9

THE ART OF FINANCIAL PLANNING FOR RETIREMENT 6.11
    Older Clients Still Need to Plan for Retirement 6.12
    Overcoming Roadblocks to Retirement Saving 6.13
DEVELOPING A RETIREMENT PLAN 6.16
    Replacement Ratio Method 6.17
    Expense Method 6.19
    The Effects of Inflation 6.19
POTENTIAL SOURCES OF RETIREMENT INCOME 6.25
    Tax-Advantaged Qualified Plans 6.26
    Other Tax-Advantaged Plans 6.39
    Nonqualified Plans 6.42
    IRAs 6.43
OVERCOMING INADEQUATE RETIREMENT RESOURCES 6.48
    Trading Down to a Less Expensive Home 6.48
    Obtaining a Reverse Mortgage 6.48
    Postretirement Employment 6.49
    Pension Maximization 6.50
THE FINAL WORD 6.51
CHAPTER SUMMARY 6.51
CHAPTER REVIEW 6.54

This chapter begins by discussing why clients need to start retirement planning when they are young. It then looks at the role of the retirement advisor and describes the holistic approach to retirement planning. The chapter then explains the responsibilities of the retirement advisor and how retirement planning parallels the financial planning process. The art of financial planning for retirement is reviewed along with why clients are never too old to plan for retirement. Next, several roadblocks to saving for retirement are examined before discussing the difficulties in estimating client financial planning needs during retirement. Two methods for determining how much retirement income may be needed are analyzed and potential sources of retirement income are surveyed. Finally, the chapter concludes with a brief treatment of strategies that clients can use to overcome their having inadequate retirement resources.

STARTING RETIREMENT PLANNING WHEN YOUNG

Not too long ago retirement meant being given a gold watch and then quietly living out one's remaining few years with family. But changing lifestyles, increased longevity, and improved expectations have drastically altered the nature of retirement. Today, people anticipate active, vibrant retirements in which they enjoy life and economic self-sufficiency. They see retirement not as the short final phase of life but as the reward phase of life—the icing on the cake. Moreover, a significant percentage of the population has become increasingly interested in achieving the financial independence currently associated with retirement. Put another way, the so-called graying of America has resulted in a maturing retirement planning movement.

However, instead of waiting until one turns gray to start planning for retirement, it is best if people start the planning process when they are relatively young. Getting young people to take retirement planning seriously, however, often requires some convincing. With this in mind, financial advisors may be able to motivate their younger clients to act by sharing the following information with them:

- Starting early can mean the difference between success and failure. Assuming a 10 percent rate of return, saving $225 a month beginning at age 40 will result in an accumulation of $300,000 by age 65. With a start at age 50, only $93,750 is accumulated.
- Americans are saving less than ever.
- As companies switch to defined-contribution type plans, more responsibility for retirement planning falls on employees. In many cases, participants must decide how much to save, when to start doing so, and how the company retirement money is invested.
- Careful planning requires preparing for contingencies. Realistic possibilities include Social Security cutbacks, reduction in or elimination of company pension benefits, periods of high inflation, and forced early retirement.
- In the future, retiring at age 65 or earlier may not be so easy. Those individuals born in 1938 or later will not be entitled to full Social Security benefits at age 65.
- Retirement may last longer than planned, because life expectancies continue to rise. From 1981 to 1995, the life expectancy for a 65-year old increased by almost a full year.
- To be sure funds are not depleted too early, clients need to plan on beating the odds and living beyond the average life expectancy.
- For most people today, maintaining the preretirement standard of living requires 60 to 80 percent of pretirement earnings.
- Working with a financial advisor can help an individual focus on the right issues, prepare a retirement plan, and follow through with it. The advisor provides expertise, a dispassionate viewpoint, and motivation.

Retirement planning is no easy process, however. Financial advisors who engage in retirement planning must be prepared to answer some tough questions. Several of these questions concern their role as retirement advisors, the amount of income their clients will need for retirement, the sources of retirement income available to their clients, and strategies for maximizing their clients' retirement incomes. This chapter will examine these questions in the hopes of providing financial advisors with the knowledge and tools they need to properly serve their clients' retirement needs.

THE ROLE OF THE RETIREMENT ADVISOR

Retirement planning is a multidimensional field. As such it requires that the advisor be schooled in the nuances of many financial planning specialties as well as other areas. Unfortunately, many so-called advisors approach retirement planning from only one point of view (investments, for example). This perspective, the perspective offered by specializing in just one field, is too limited for dealing with the diversified needs of the would-be retiree. A client is better served by a team of advisors who have specialized but complementary backgrounds or by a single advisor who is experienced in a variety of important retirement topics.

Holistic Retirement Planning

holistic retirement planning

Whether the retirement team or the multitalented individual is the vehicle, the holistic approach to retirement planning is the only means by which a client's needs can be fully and adequately met. Under *holistic retirement planning*, the advisor is required to communicate with clients concerning such topics as

- the effect of financial well-being on the quality of life
- employer-provided retirement plans
- Social Security considerations
- personal savings and investments
- income tax issues
- insurance coverage
- IRAs and Roth IRAs
- Medicare choices
- tax planning for distributions and other distribution issues
- health insurance planning including medigap insurance and long-term care insurance
- wealth accumulation for retirement
- selecting a retirement community or another living arrangement
- relocation possibilities and reverse mortgages

- asset allocation and risk
- wellness, nutrition, lifestyle choices, and other gerontological issues
- assessment of current savings needed to achieve retirement goals

Because the advisor must be conversant in so many disciplines, he or she must be somewhat of a renaissance person. Nevertheless, the role of the financial advisor engaged in a retirement planning practice is complicated not only because of the broad-based knowledge needed for the job, but also because the advisor must be able to integrate retirement planning strategies with other financial planning needs such as tax, estate planning, and investment goals.

A word of caution is in order at this point. Understanding how to plan for a client's retirement is much more art than science. There is no one-size-fits-all approach to retirement planning. For example, an attempt to describe the average retiree is like trying to describe the average book—even if it could be done, the information would not be very useful. Retirees are wealthy and poor, male and female, old and not-so-old. They are single, married, and widowed; they have children and do not have children. They are healthy and unhealthy, happy and miserable, active and sedentary, and sophisticated and naïve.

A further complication is that retirement planning does not always begin early enough in the financial life cycle. While the old axiom "it's never too early or too late to plan for retirement" is true, it is a completely different job to plan for a client's retirement when it is too late to influence the client's ability to retire with financial security. Conversely, planning at a relatively young age for clients opens up a multitude of opportunities and presents different planning challenges.

Because client situations are like snowflakes—there are no two alike—the advisor must be able to meet a variety of situations creatively and cannot rely on a "formula approach" to solve their clients' problems.

Some examples will help to demonstrate just how varied the topics are that may be discussed while retirement planning.

Example 1: Adam, aged 65, is retired and he and his wife receive $30,000 in pension income and $10,000 in Social Security income. Adam would like to know how he will be taxed for federal tax purposes. Adam and his wife file jointly.

The general rule that applies to all retirees, including Adam, is that pension income is fully taxable. However, a taxpayer filing a joint return can exclude all Social Security benefits from income for tax purposes if provisional income is $32,000 or less. (Provisional income is defined as adjusted gross income plus tax-exempt interest plus half of Social Security benefits.) For provisional income from $32,001 to $44,000, as much as 50 percent of Social Security benefits are taxable. If provisional income exceeds $44,000, as much as 85 percent of Social Security benefits are taxable.

In this case, Adam's provisional income is calculated by adding his $30,000 pension to one-half of his $10,000 Social Security benefit ($5,000). Since a provisional income of $35,000 ($30,000 + $5,000) exceeds the base amount of $32,000 by $3,000, Adam will have to pay tax on a portion of his Social Security benefit, in addition to his $30,000 pension. (The exact amount of the taxable Social Security benefit is determined by complex formulas that are beyond the scope of this discussion.) However, Adam can take heart in the fact that married taxpayers age 65 and over are each entitled to an additional standard deduction of $1,050 (as indexed for 2008) over their regular standard deduction of $10,900. (The additional amount is $1,350 for single taxpayers aged 65 and older over the regular amount of $5,450.)

Example 2: Barbara, aged 58, has questions about investing for retirement. Barbara is currently heavily concentrated in aggressive growth equities. Barbara's advisor told her that she should become less growth oriented and begin to be more concerned with a portfolio that provides enough income for retirement needs. Also, it is appropriate to make the portfolio less volatile because now there is less time to recover losses should the higher-risk growth stocks suffer reverses.

Barbara's advisor should not, however, offer her one-time advice to change portfolio strategies, but should help her to implement his or her recommendations while continuing to offer her investment advice. Moving toward more current income and less volatility usually means taking less risk, which does have the impact of reducing the long-term total return each year from the portfolio. This factor does have to be taken into consideration in any long term retirement planning.

Today, advisors have a number of strategies to accomplish the above goals. Traditional approaches include changing the asset allocation mix to include fewer stocks and more bonds, and/or to change the stock portfolio to include more income producing stocks.

Example 3: Charlie and his wife, Ann, have heard about long-term care insurance from a friend and wonder if it would be right for them. Charlie, aged 65, has recently retired and his personal disability income policy has just expired. Ann, also retired with no personal disability income policy, is slightly older than Charlie and has a family history of poor health. Charlie and Ann have a retirement income of $95,000 per year and are not in a position to spend down (that is, shed income and qualify for Medicaid to pay for nursing home care). Charlie and Ann are covered by Medicare but their advisor informs Charlie that nursing home stays are not covered by Medicare to any significant degree.

Charlie and Ann are good candidates for long-term care insurance. As pointed out in chapter 2, the majority of newer long-term care policies pay benefits on a reimbursement basis. These contracts reimburse the insured for actual expenses up to the specified policy limit every day that the insured utilizes nursing home facilities. Without a long-term care insurance policy, the costs of a nursing home would quickly deplete Charlie and Ann's assets.

Charlie and Ann are uncertain about what level of benefits to purchase. The average annual cost for a nursing home stay in a semiprivate room is approximately $69,000[1], but the facilities that Charlie and Ann would be comfortable with cost over $80,000 per year. Charlie's financial advisor informs him that premiums for, say, a $100 a day policy ($36,500 annually) would be approximately $1,800 per year each ($3,600 total). The additional

> cost of a nursing home (beyond $36,500) would have to be absorbed by Charlie and Ann's income, unless they each purchase a more expensive long-term care policy that covers up to $220 or more of costs per day.

Responsibilities of the Retirement Advisor

In addition to being a "Jack of all trades," a financial advisor engaged in a retirement planning practice must undertake several responsibilities that may not have been a part of his or her traditional financial practice. These aspects of a retirement planning practice include doing the following:

- incorporating retirement planning as a segment of comprehensive financial planning. This means the use of financial planning techniques such as fact finding, budgeting, income flow regulating, and the rendering of investment advice.
- dealing with other professionals who advise the client. These professionals include the client's lawyer, accountant, banker, investment advisor, and insurance advisor. By communicating with this group, the advisor can gain many advantages, including a better understanding of the client's needs, a team approach for motivating the client to save for retirement, and referral sources for future business.
- dealing with relatively young clients. One common mistake is to start retirement planning only after a client has satisfied his or her other long-term responsibilities, such as buying a home or educating a child. Retirement planning is best, however, if clients start saving for retirement at a relatively young age.
- monitoring and/or updating the client's plan. Whether it is part of a comprehensive or multiple-purpose financial plan or is a single purpose plan, the advisor needs to continually monitor and/or update the client's retirement plan because of changes in family circumstances (such as job changes, births, deaths, divorces, and the acquisition of inheritances) and/or changes in the tax and economic environment.
- being familiar with available resources. The advisor should be familiar with the various resources available in the retirement planning field. These resources include the National Council on Aging, the American Society on Aging, and the Financial Planning Association, all of which offer a forum that provides newsletters, conferences, and a chance for interaction with other advisors. In addition, advisors should make their

clients aware of the American Association of Retired Persons (AARP), an organization that provides information on services for the elderly and is a valuable resource for retirement information. Advisors may also want to check the numerous retirement planning websites on the Internet.

Retirement Planning and the Financial Planning Process

As one of the major planning areas that should be part of any comprehensive financial plan, retirement planning follows the same six step process used in financial planning.

Step 1: Establish and Define the Advisor-Client Relationship

The first step is to establish and define the advisor-client relationship. This normally starts at the first client meeting, where advisors begin building trust with their clients by explaining to them how they work and the types of products and/or services they provide. They also must explain the financial planning process and how that process is used to plan for retirement. In addition, they need to disclose their background, philosophy, and method of compensation, whether that be fee-only, commission, or a fee and commission. Lastly, advisors must clarify not only what their responsibilities for the relationship are but also what is expected from their clients.

Step 2: Determine Goals and Gather Data

After having established and defined the advisor-client relationship, it is time to move on to step 2 of the process. Advisors begin this step by listening to their clients' goals and expectations for retirement. Listening skills are important because it is easy for advisors to impose their personal views of retirement on clients or to assume that what they believe to be important is also important to their clients and vice versa. Clients have a variety of goals that range from never having to work again to working full-time during retirement. Clearly, advisors have their work cut out for them as they deal with a plethora of client expectations and, in some cases, help frame these expectations through the education process.

After sorting through their clients' goals and expectations for retirement, advisors must gather a considerable amount of information about their clients. They must focus on conducting a financial inventory of retirement assets and an assessment of the strategies that clients have available to them. For example, advisors must account for all their clients' resources allocated to retirement, and they must note all opportunities that clients have available to them, such as, being able to contribute to a Roth IRA or being able to participate in a 401(k) plan at their place of work.

Step 3: Analyze and Evaluate the Data

In this step, the advisor looks at the client's current situation as well as his or her future goals in order to evaluate the appropriate strategies for that particular client. This includes the performance of a retirement needs analysis as well as an analysis of the client's financial risk tolerance, risk management strategies, and risk exposures. For example, does the client have adequate disability insurance and long-term care insurance? Does the client's current asset allocations adequately achieve his or her financial and/or retirement goals? Is the client currently saving enough for retirement? What tax planning and distribution strategies are available to the client and do they make sense for the client's situation? Advisors need to analyze and evaluate current retirement plan exposures (for example, the penalty tax for premature distributions), current retirement plans, Social Security benefits, and current retirement strategies.

Step 4: Develop and Present a Plan

The advisor should develop a client-specific retirement plan tailored to meet the client's goals and expectations, commensurate with the client's values, attitudes, temperament, and financial risk tolerance. In addition to the client's current financial position, the plan should include the client's projected retirement status under the status quo as well as projected status if the advisor's recommendations are followed. The advisor should also provide a current asset allocation model along with strategy recommendations. Investments should be summrized, and the advisor should recommend an investment policy. The retirement plan should also include an assessment of distribution options and tax strategies. Finally, the plan should include a list of prioritized action items and address issues such as housing and health care.

After developing the plan, the advisor should present the plan to the client and review it with him or her. The advisor should collaborate with the client to ensure that the plan meets the goals and expectations of the client.

Step 5: Implement the Plan

The advisor should assist the client in implementing the recommendations. Often this requires coordinating with other professionals, such as accountants, attorneys, real estate advisors, investment advisors, stock brokers, and insurance advisors.

Step 6: Monitor the Plan

After the plan is implemented, the advisor should periodically monitor and evaluate the soundness of his or her recommendations and review the progress of the plan with the client. The advisor should also discuss and evaluate changes in the client's personal circumstances such as family births or deaths, illness, divorce, or change in job status. Any relevant changes in tax laws, benefit and pension options, and the economic environment should be reviewed and evaluated before the advisor recommends revisions to the plan to accommodate new and/or changing circumstances.

THE ART OF FINANCIAL PLANNING FOR RETIREMENT

A successful financial advisor must not only have a working knowledge of a large variety of financial planning and retirement-related topics but also know how to apply the knowledge to a client's particular situation. This requires understanding the client's goals, attitudes, and personal preferences. For example, an advisor should be prepared to help a client meet the important goals of maintaining his or her preretirement standard of living during retirement, becoming economically self-sufficient, minimizing taxes on retirement distributions, adapting to the retirement lifestyle, and taking care of a dependent parent or dealing with special health needs. In addition, the advisor should be prepared to deal with a variety of attitudes on how long the client wants to work, what the client's prospects are for health and longevity, whether the client can be disciplined enough to save for retirement, and to what extent the client accepts investment risk. It is this application of a broad range of knowledge to a diverse group of clients that makes financial planning for retirement more art than science.

For the financial advisor, the primary responsibility in the "art of financial planning for retirement" is to make clients aware that they are making choices about their retirement every day. For example, should the client take an expensive vacation or take a moderately priced vacation and save the difference for retirement? The advisor cannot force the client to make lifestyle choices that will provide an adequate source of retirement funds. The advisor can, however, make the client aware of the large amount of funds needed for retirement and point out that a spendthrift lifestyle (one that uses the full after-tax income to support the current standard of living) during the client's active working years hurts him or her upon retirement in two ways.

First, a spendthrift lifestyle minimizes the client's ability to accumulate savings that will produce an adequate income stream to complement his or her employer pension and Social Security. These three elements—private savings, employer pensions, and Social Security—are considered essential for a secure retirement. If any leg on this "three-legged stool" is missing, the client is in danger of falling short of an economically secure retirement. Second, the client becomes accustomed to an unnaturally high standard of living. By living below his or her means before retirement, the client establishes a lifestyle that is more easily maintained in the retirement years.

Forcing clients to think about financial planning for retirement and lifestyle choices is a primary responsibility of the financial advisor. However, two other important facets to financial planning for retirement exist. First, the advisor must devise different retirement strategies for clients who are prepared for retirement than for those who are not, and second, the advisor must overcome roadblocks to retirement saving.

Older Clients Still Need to Plan for Retirement

Advisors new to the financial planning for retirement field soon find out that clients are never too old or too young to plan for retirement. Retirement planning, however, takes on different characteristics for different age groups, and advisors must deal with clients of all ages. Starting young, however, can mean all the difference in the world. (See table 6-1.)

Unfortunately, some clients do not begin to save for retirement until the time to retire is upon them. As a result, they loose the ability to set aside savings on a systematic basis and to let compound interest work for them. Nevertheless, retirement planning can still be conducted for these clients. Important decisions must be made about distributions from qualified plans, liquidation of personal assets, and investment of private savings. Developing retirement plans for clients who have procrastinated involves determining what funds are available for retirement and creating strategies, even if the funds are inadequate.

One such strategy calls for the advisor to suggest that the client postpone retirement. The combined effect of lengthening the accumulation period and shortening the retirement period is financially desirable. If delaying retirement from his or her current job is not feasible, the client can achieve similar results by working for another employer after forced retirement. A second strategy is to recommend that the client move to an area with a lower cost of living. This strategy will enable the client to stretch his or her retirement dollars. Moreover, by freeing up some of the equity in his or her home, the client can make assets available for investment purposes.

After recommending these strategies, the advisor needs to help the client change his or her expectations about retirement. By forcing the client to look realistically at the lifestyle he or she will be able to afford, the advisor can save the client from overspending during the early retirement years and avoid becoming financially destitute in the later retirement years.

TABLE 6-1
IRA Funding Plans: The Advantages of Starting Young[*]

Plan One			Plan Two		
Age start	18		Age start	27	
Age end	26		Age end	65	
Amount per year	$3,000		Amount per year	$3,000	
Rate of return	8%		Rate of return	8%	
Value at age 65	$753,572		Value at age 65	$713,823	
Total amount contributed	$27,000		Total amount contributed	$114,000	
Age	**Amount**	**Value**	**Age**	**Amount**	**Value**
18	$3,000	$ 3,240	18	0	0
19	3,000	6,739	19	0	0
20	3,000	10,518	20	0	0
21	3,000	14,600	21	0	0
22	3,000	19,008	22	0	0
23	3,000	23,768	23	0	0
24	3,000	28,910	24	0	0
25	3,000	34,463	25	0	0
26	3,000	40,459	26	0	0
27	0	43,696	27	$3,000	$ 3,240
28	0	47,192	28	3,000	6,739
29	0	50,967	29	3,000	10,518
30	0	55,044	30	3,000	14,600
.	.	.	.	.	.
.	.	.	.	.	.
.	.	.	.	.	.
60	0	512,869	60	3,000	472,880
61	0	553,898	61	3,000	513,950
62	0	598,210	62	3,000	558,306
63	0	646,067	63	3,000	606,211
64	0	697,752	64	3,000	657,947
65	0	753,572	65	3,000	713,823

[*] This comparison is hypothetical; no guarantees are implied for specific investments. The interest rate is assumed to remain unchanged for the entire period.

Overcoming Roadblocks to Retirement Saving

Perhaps the biggest roadblock to retirement planning is the tendency of many working people to use their full after-tax income to support their current standard of living. These people will not have any private savings to supplement Social Security and pension funds. Many of them also may have experienced adversities like unemployment that pushed them into debt. In other cases, a lifestyle that incurs debt can stem from a spendthrfit attitude or from the desire to emulate or improve upon their parents' standard of living. Whatever the reason for their lack of retirement savings, clients must follow a budget that allows them to live within their means and that also provides for retirement savings. Advisors should make their clients aware that a spending ratio of no higher than 90/10 is generally desired. Under a 90/10 spending ratio, 90 percent of the client's earnings are directed toward the current standard of living, and 10 percent is directed toward other long-term financial goals, such as funding the children's education and the client's own retirement. For example, a family with a gross annual income of $50,000 should allocate no more than $45,000 (including taxes) of its total income to current standard-of-living and lifestyle items, leaving $5,000 or more for long-term goals. Furthermore, financial advisors should recommend that as income rises, the percentage spent on the current standard of living should decline.

A second impediment to retirement saving is unexpected expenses, including uninsured medical bills; repairs to a home, auto, or major appliance; and periods of unemployment. The client should set up an emergency fund to handle these inevitable problems. Usually 6 to 9 months' income is set aside for this purpose. If a client's salary is stable and other income, such as dividends, is part of the individual's income flow, then a 6 months' income level in the emergency fund can be sufficient. However, if the main source of income is commissions that fluctuate between pay periods, 9 months' income held for emergencies is more appropriate.

Inadequate insurance coverage is a third impediment to retirement saving. Regardless of whether it is life, disability, health, home, or auto, many individuals continue to remain uninsured or underinsured. Because the client cannot always recover economically from such losses, one important element of retirement planning is protection against catastrophic financial loss that would make future saving impossible. Advisors should conduct a thorough review of their clients' insurance needs to make sure they are adequately covered. Two frequently overlooked areas are disability insurance and umbrella liability insurance. Make sure your client is adequately protected with both coverages.

A fourth roadblock to saving for retirement occurs in the case of a divorced client. Divorce often leaves one or both parties with little or no accumulation of pension benefits or other private sources of retirement income. These clients may have only a short time to accumulate any retirement income and may not be able to earn significant pension or Social Security benefits. If the marriage lasted 10 years or longer, however, divorced persons are eligible for Social Security based on their former spouse's earnings record. In addition, a spouse may be entitled to a portion of the former spouse's retirement benefits if the divorce decree includes a

qualified domestic relations order (QDRO)

qualified domestic relations order (QDRO). QDROs are judgments, decrees, or orders issued by state courts that allow a participant's retirement plan assets to be used for marital property rights, child support, or alimony payments to a former spouse or dependent.

Another common retirement planning problem is the lack of a retirement plan at the place of employment. In fact, only 59 percent of workers expect to receive employer-provided retirement benefits from defined-benefit plans. More encouraging, however, is the fact that 74 percent of workers expect to receive employer-provided benefits from retirement savings plans.[2] Nevertheless, these figures indicate that there are still a large number of workers who do not expect to receive any employer-provided retirement benefits because their employers do not sponsor any type of retirement plan.

Workers who have frequently changed employers also face the problem of arriving at retirement with little or no pension. Statistics show that employees today are unlikely to remain with one employer for their working life and will, typically, hold seven full-time jobs during their career. Generally, these people will not accumulate vested pension benefits because they never stayed with an employer long enough to become vested. Even if they did become vested, they may have received a distribution of their accumulated pension fund upon leaving the job and probably spent this money rather than investing it or rolling it over for retirement. Advisors should recommend to clients who change jobs to roll over vested benefits into an IRA or into their new qualified plan to preserve the tax-deferred growth of their retirement funds. They should also advise clients who have recently changed jobs that if they do not meet the participation requirements of their new employer's plan, they can make annual tax-deductible contributions to an IRA until they do meet the requirements, regardless of their salary.

Another problem that inhibits people from saving for retirement is a lack of financial literacy. Many employees have never been properly schooled about investments and finance. For this reason, investment education has replaced health care as the top concern for employee benefit professionals and employees.

A final impediment to the acquisition of adequate retirement savings involves other long-term goals that clients desire to fund. The down payment on a primary residence and/or vacation home and the education of their children can consume any long-term savings that people have managed to accumulate. Because these goals tend to have a greater urgency for completion than retirement, they supplant retirement as a saving priority. Although these other accumulation goals are worthy, it is important to remind clients that savings must be carved out for retirement purposes in addition to other long-term goals.

DEVELOPING A RETIREMENT PLAN

Another important task in financial planning for retirement is determining how much the client will need to save in order to achieve his or her retirement goals. Estimating a client's financial needs during retirement is like trying to predict the future: Such estimates are fraught with complicating factors and clouded by unknown variables. For example, the advisor and client must establish what standard of living is desired during retirement, when retirement will begin, what inflation assumptions should be made before and after retirement, and what interest can be earned on invested funds. In addition, for the client who is forced by economic necessity to liquidate his or her retirement nest egg during retirement, the advisor and client must estimate the life expectancy over which liquidation will occur. Many of these variables can dramatically change overnight and without warning. The following are examples of how variables could change:

- The client may be planning to retire at age 65 but health considerations, or perhaps a plant shutdown, force retirement at age 62.
- A younger client may be planning on a relatively moderate retirement lifestyle but business success may lead to a higher retirement income expectation.
- Forecasters may predict that long-term inflation will result in an annual 4 percent increase in the cost of living when in reality 6 percent increases occur. (Even a one percentage point disparity can make a significant difference.)
- Clients may hope for an after-tax rate of return of 7 percent when in fact investment returns are adversely affected by a bear market, or the real after-tax rate of return is suppressed by rising tax rates.
- Clients may plan on a short life expectancy and have the "misfortune" of living longer.

While it is important to understand that planning is, at best, an educated guess, it still beats the alternative. Moreover, changing variables can be overcome if the retirement plan is monitored and evaluated periodically. Once the advisor has explained to his or her client the tentative nature of the plan and the need for hands-on monitoring, then the task of setting out a plan for the client begins.

As previously indicated, in step 2 (determine goals and gather data) of the financial planning process (FPP), the advisor needs to ascertain the standard of living the client expects during retirement. Once having done this, the advisor must then determine where the client stands financially for retirement purposes. This involves adding up the client's existing resources.

These may include the amount of any Social Security benefits due; the amount of any pension benefits due; any private savings the client has accumulated to date, including IRAs and personally owned life insurance; and any other sources of retirement income, such as the proceeds from the sale of a home.

Once a financial inventory of possible sources of retirement income has been taken, step 3 (analyze and evaluate the data) of the FPP requires the advisor to determine how much annual income will be needed in the first year of retirement to achieve the client's goals. There are two common ways of determining this, the *replacement ratio method* and the *expense method*.

replacement ratio method
expense method

Replacement Ratio Method

The replacement ratio method of determining retirement income assumes that the standard of living enjoyed during the years just prior to retirement will be the determining factor for the standard of living during retirement. For clients at or near retirement, it is much easier to define the target. For example, if a 64-year old near-retiree is earning $102,000, then his or her retirement income should maintain most of the current purchasing power that he or she has. However, if a younger client is involved, growth estimates should be made to approximate what his or her salary will be at retirement.

Note that the entire final salary is not needed for determining the proper amount of purchasing power. In general, a 60 to 80 percent replacement ratio of a client's final average salary is typically used for individual retirement planning purposes. Support for this range rests upon the elimination of some employment-related taxes and some expected changes in spending patterns that reduce the retiree's need for income (see figure 6-1).

Reduced Taxes

Retirees can assume that a lower percentage of their income will go toward paying taxes in the retirement years because, in many cases, there is an elimination or a reduction of certain taxes that they previously had to pay. Tax advantages for the retiree include the elimination of the Social Security wage base tax, an increased standard deduction depending on the retiree's age and filing status, the exclusion of all or part of the amount of the Social Security benefit from gross income, reductions in state and local income taxes, a reduction in property taxes if the retiree moves to a more modest residence, and an increased ability to use deductible medical expenses.

FIGURE 6-1
Justification of a 60 to 80 Percent Replacement Ratio

In 2008, Joe Jones, who is aged 64 and single, has a fixed salary of $102,000 and is in the 28 percent marginal tax bracket. He would like to maintain his current purchasing power when he retires next year. If Joe has no increased retirement-related expenses, he can do this by having a retirement income of 68 percent of his final salary as illustrated below. If Joe has increased retirement- related expenses, a somewhat higher figure should be used. (Note that postretirement inflation will be accounted for later.)

Working salary			$102,000
less annual retirement savings		$18,000.00	
less Social Security taxes		7,803.75	
less reduction in federal taxes	(extra standard deduction of $1,350 for being 65)	378.00	
	(no tax on portion of Social Security received)	1,063.00	
less annual commuting expenses to work		864.00	
less mortgage expenses	(mortgage expires on retirement date)	4,492.00	
Reductions subtotal			32,600
Total purchasing power needed at 65			$ 69,400
Percentage of final salary needed			68%

Reduced Living Expenses

Retirees face a variety of changes in spending patterns after retirement, and some of these changes will reduce their living expenses. These reductions often include the elimination of work-related expenses; the elimination of home-mortgage expenses; the elimination of dependent care, that is, child-rearing expenses; the elimination of long-term savings obligations; and a reduction in automotive expenditures.

Additional Factors

It is not all good news for retirees, however. Retirees also face several factors that tend to increase the amount of income they will need during the retirement period. These may include increases in long-term inflation, in medical expenses, in travel expenses, and in other retirement-related expenses. On the other hand, it is also true that retirees typically start to spend less later in their retirement when travel and other activities become more difficult to manage.

Expense Method

The expense method of determining retirement income focuses on the projected expenses that the retiree will have. As with the replacement ratio method, it is much easier to define the potential expenses for those clients who are at or near retirement. For example, if the 64-year-old near-retiree expects to have $5,783.33 in monthly bills ($69,400 annually), then the retirement income for that retiree should maintain approximately $69,400 worth of purchasing power in today's dollars. If, however, a younger client is involved, more speculative estimates of retirement expenses must be made (and periodically revised).

A list of expenses that should be considered includes expenses that may be unique to the particular client as well as other more general expenses.

Some expenses that tend to increase for retirees include the following:

- utilities and telephone
- medical/dental/drugs/health insurance
- house upkeep/repairs/maintenance/property insurance (until a move occurs)
- recreation/entertainment/travel/dining (during the early years of retirement)

On the other hand, some expenses tend to decrease for retirees:

- mortgage payments
- food
- clothing
- income taxes
- property taxes (if a move occurs)
- transportation costs (car maintenance/insurance/other)
- debt repayment (charge accounts/personal loans)
- child support/alimony
- household furnishings

The Effects of Inflation

Both the replacement ratio method and the expense method can be used to determine the income level a retiree will need at age 65. They do not, however, calculate the amount of savings that the client must accumulate in order to achieve a consistent level of financial security throughout retirement. The amount that the client needs to save to achieve his or her goals is a function of two opposing factors, both of which are influenced by inflation. The first factor is the savings that the client currently has (as determined in step 2 of the FPP), while the second is the income that the client will need (as determined in steps 3 and 4 of the FPP). In order to better understand the effects of inflation over time, consider the loss of purchasing power that occurs in the following example.

Example: Al Edwards, aged 65, is retiring this year and needs $50,000 of retirement income to maintain his current standard of living. If the inflation rate is 4 percent per year over Al's retirement period, he will need to have an increasing amount of retirement income each year of retirement. Table 6-2 illustrates the amount of annual income Al will need at specified intervals to maintain a consistent amount of purchasing power.

To calculate the true retirement income needed, the financial advisor must provide inflation protection both before and after retirement for all the client's resources. In order to accomplish this, the advisor must decide which of the client's resources are subject to a decline in purchasing power due to the effects of inflation.

TABLE 6-2
Retirement Income Al Edwards Needs to Maintain a Consistent Amount of Purchasing Power (Assuming a 4 Percent Rate of Inflation)

Al's Age	Income Needed
65	$ 50,000
70	60,833
75	74,012
80	90,047
90	133,292
100	197,304

Any Social Security that the client might receive will not be subject to a decline in purchasing power, because Social Security is indexed each year to reflect inflation. Therefore, the advisor will not have to provide inflation protection for a client's Social Security benefit. The advisor cannot, however, generally assume any inflation protection for pension benefits. For this reason, the client will need to fund for an amount that can be used to bolster a non-inflation-protected pension benefit during retirement.

Another item that will be affected by inflation is the retirement income deficit itself. The retirement income deficit is any shortfall that exists between what the client has and what the client needs. This is not inflation-proof before or after retirement. The advisor will, therefore, need to calculate an inflation factor that protects the client's purchasing power for this amount.

The next step (step 4, develop and present a plan, of the FPP) in mapping a client's retirement needs is to calculate the target amount of savings needed. In order to do this, work sheets, such as those in figures 6-2 and 6-3, are helpful. The first work sheet (figure 6-2), based on the replacement ratio method, produces the estimated income gap between the desired retirement income and the available retirement benefits. That gap is then adjusted for inflation. The amount of additional capital needed to fill the gap and to supplement the pension benefit (inflation-unprotected) is then computed. Finally, the funding pattern that will be used to generate the needed new capital is calculated.

The second work sheet (figure 6-3), based on the expense method, calls for an estimate of the client's current monthly and annual living expenses. The total of these expenses (line 10, figure 6-3) is then adjusted for inflation to reflect the expected total at retirement date. Next, a capital sum is calculated (lines 15–19, figure 6-3) that will be sufficient, together with interest earnings, to provide an inflation-adjusted income during the estimated number of years in the retirement period.

FIGURE 6-2
Replacement Ratio Method Work Sheet

1.	Current annual gross salary	$_____
2.	Retirement-income target (multiply line 1 by 0.8) (80 percent target)	$_____
3.	Estimated annual benefit from pension plan, not including IRAs, 401(k)s, or profit-sharing plans [1]	$_____
4.	Estimated annual Social Security benefits [1]	$_____
5.	Total retirement benefits (add lines 3 and 4)	$_____
6.	Income gap (subtract line 5 from line 2)[2]	$_____
7.	Adjust gap to reflect inflation (multiply line 6 by factor A, below)	$_____
8.	Capital needed to generate additional income and close gap (multiply line 7 by 16.3)[3]	$_____
9.	Extra capital needed to offset inflation's impact on pension (multiply line 3 by factor B, below)	$_____
10.	Total capital needed (add lines 8 and 9)	$_____
11.	Total current retirement savings (includes balances in IRAs, 401(k)s, profit-sharing plans, mutual funds, CDs)	$_____
12.	Value of savings at retirement (multiply line 11 by factor C, below)	$_____
13.	Net capital gap (subtract line 12 from line 10)	$_____
14.	Annual amount in current dollars to start saving now to cover the gap (divide line 13 by factor D, below)[4]	$_____
15.	Percentage of salary to be saved each year (divide line 14 by line 1)[5]	_____%

(continued)

FIGURE 6-2 (continued)
Replacement Ratio Method Work Sheet

Capital Calculation Factors

(Assume 4 percent inflation before and after retirement and 8 percent annual return before and after retirement.)

Years to Retirement	Factor A	Factor B	Factor C	Factor D
10	1.5	7.0	2.2	17.5
15	1.8	8.5	3.2	35.3
20	2.2	10.3	4.7	63.3
25	2.7	12.6	6.9	107.0
30	3.2	15.3	10.1	174.0

[1] Lines 3 and 4: Employers can provide annual estimates of your projected retirement pay; estimates of your Social Security benefits are available from the Social Security Administration at 1-800-772-1213, or on your Social Security Statement. Both figures will be stated in current dollars, not in the higher amounts that you will receive if your wages keep up with inflation. The work sheet takes this into consideration.

[2] Line 6: Even if a large pension lets you avoid an income gap, proceed to line 9 to determine the assets you may need to make up for the erosion of a fixed pension payment by inflation.

[3] Line 8: This calculation includes a determination of how much capital you will need to keep up with inflation after retirement and assumes that you will deplete the capital over a 25-year period.

[4] Line 14: Amount includes investments earmarked for retirement and payments by employee and employer to defined-contribution retirement plans such as 401(k)s. The formula assumes you will increase annual savings at the same rate as inflation.

[5] Line 15: Assuming earnings rise with inflation, you can save a set percentage of gross pay each year, and the actual amount you stash away will increase annually.

Source: Reprinted with permission of *U.S. News & World Report,* August 14, 1989, p. 62, Volume 107, and Issue No. 7.

FIGURE 6-3
Expense Method Work Sheet

Estimated Retirement Living Expenses and Required Capital (in current dollars)

	Monthly x 12 = Annual
	$ _____ $ _____
1. Food	_____ _____
2. Housing:	
a. Rent/mortgage payment	_____ _____
b. Homeowners insurance (if not included in a.)	_____ _____
c. Property taxes (if not included in a.)	_____ _____
d. Utilities	_____ _____
e. Maintenance (if you own)	_____ _____
f. Management fee (if a condominium)	_____ _____
3. Clothing and Personal Care:	
a. Wife	_____ _____
b. Husband	_____ _____
c. Dependents	_____ _____
4. Medical Expenses:	
a. Doctor	_____ _____
b. Dentist	_____ _____
c. Medicines	_____ _____
d. Medical insurance to supplement Medicare	_____ _____
5. Transportation:	
a. Car payments	_____ _____
b. Gas	_____ _____
c. Auto insurance	_____ _____
d. License fees	_____ _____
e. Car maintenance (tires and repairs)	_____ _____
f. Other transportation	_____ _____
6. Miscellaneous Expenses:	
a. Entertainment	_____ _____
b. Travel	_____ _____
c. Hobbies	_____ _____
d. Club fees and dues	_____ _____
e. Other	_____ _____
7. Insurance (other than auto and homeowners)	_____ _____
8. Gifts and Contributions	_____ _____
9. Income Taxes (if any)	_____ _____

(continued)

> **FIGURE 6-3 (continued)**
> **Expense Method Work Sheet**
>
> | | | |
> |---|---|---|
> | 10. | Total Annual Expenses (current dollars) | $ _____ |
> | 11. | Inflation Rate until Retirement (I) | _____ |
> | 12. | Total Years until Retirement (N) | _____ |
> | 13. | Inflation Adjustment Factor $(1 + I)^N$ | x _____ |
> | 14. | Total Annual Expenses (future dollars) | = $ _____ |
> | 15. | Inflation Rate Postretirement (i) | _____ |
> | 16. | After-tax Rate of Return (r) | _____ |
> | 17. | Anticipated Duration of Retirement (n) | _____ |
> | 18. | Inflation-Adjusted Discount Factor | _____ |
>
> $$a = \frac{1 + i}{1 + r}$$
>
> | | | |
> |---|---|---|
> | 19. | Capital Required at Retirement to Fund Retirement Living Expenses | $ _____ |
>
> $$\text{line } 14 \times \frac{1 - a^n}{1 - a}$$
>
> | | | |
> |---|---|---|
> | 20. | One-Time Expenses | + $ _____ |
> | 21. | Total Capital Need at Retirement | = $ _____ |

POTENTIAL SOURCES OF RETIREMENT INCOME

Understanding how much a client will need for retirement is only one part of sound financial planning for retirement. Knowing the potential sources of retirement income is another crucial function with which the financial advisor must be familiar. For purposes of this discussion, the various types of tax-advantaged retirement plans can be divided into those that are qualified and those that are not. Qualified plans are those plans subject to Code Sec. 401(a) and include defined-benefit pension plans, cash-balance pension plans, money-purchase pension plans, target-benefit pension plans, profit-sharing plans, 401(k) plans, stock bonus plans, and ESOPs. All qualified plans can be sponsored by for-profit and nonprofit employers.

Three other types of tax-advantaged plans are not qualified. These are SEPs, SIMPLEs. and 403(b) plans. Like qualified plans, SEPs and SIMPLEs can also be sponsored by both for-profit and nonprofit employers. 403(b) plans, on the other hand, can only be sponsored by public school systems and those nonprofit organizations qualifying for Code Sec. 501(c)(3) tax-exempt status. Whether or not qualified, all of these employer-sponsored tax-advantaged plans share some characteristics.

Another very different type of employer-sponsored retirement planning vehicle is the nonqualified plan. Most advisors use this term to refer to deferred compensation plans other than the tax-advantaged plans identified above. Unlike the tax-advantaged plans, nonqualified plans are generally for only a few key people and have few design restrictions regarding the benefit structure, vesting requirements, and coverage. However, in exchange for the added flexibility in plan design, the tax rules are not as kind to nonqualified plans.

Another type of retirement plan is the individual retirement account (IRA). As its name implies, this type of plan is generally established by individuals, not by employers. At times, a businessowner or employee will be faced with the choice of participating in a company-sponsored plan or establishing an IRA. In some cases, the individual can choose to participate in both.

The final source of retirement income is Social Security. Retirement benefits under Social Security are based more on social adequacy than on individual equity. Under the principle of social adequacy, benefits are designed to provide a minimum floor of income to all recipients regardless of their economic status. Above this floor, clients are expected to provide additional sources of retirement income from their own individually established plans and from employer-sponsored plans. Because Social Security provides the foundation upon which individually-established and employer-sponsored retirement plans are built, it is important for the advisor to thoroughly understand this government program. Consequently, Social Security is covered separately in chapter 8. The remainder of this section discusses employer-sponsored and individually-established retirement plans in the following order:

- tax-advantaged qualified plans
- other tax-advantaged plans
- nonqualified plans
- IRAs

Tax-Advantaged Qualified Plans

qualified plan

Perhaps the most valuable way to save for retirement is through a tax-advantaged *qualified plan*. The advantageous nature of a qualified plan stems from the fact that, even though the employer is able to take a tax deduction when contributions are made, contributions to the plan are made on a before-tax basis. In other words, the employee does not have to pay income tax on those contributions when they are made. Instead, the employee pays income tax when plan funds are distributed to him or her some years later. In addition, investment earnings on plan assets are also tax-deferred. This combination of tax-deferred contributions and tax-deferred earnings is like receiving an interest-free loan from the government, thus permitting the employee to invest funds for retirement that otherwise would be lost to taxation.

A final tax advantage applicable to qualified plans is that distributions from these plans can be rolled into an IRA or other tax advantaged plan with taxation continuing to be deferred until the funds are finally withdrawn as retirement income.

Tax-advantaged qualified plans can be categorized in several ways, and one method for categorizing them looks at what the employer provides. Under this method of categorizing, one type of plan focuses on the employer's promise to pay an annual retirement benefit (a defined-benefit plan), while a second type of plan focuses on the employer's annual contribution to an employee's individual account (a defined-contribution plan). A second method for categorizing qualified plans distinguishes plans primarily geared to sharing employer profits (profit-sharing plans) from those geared to providing retirement benefits (pension plans).

In addition to categorizing plans as defined-benefit or defined-contribution, or as pension or profit-sharing, a third method for categorizing qualified plans focuses on the type of business organization served by the plan. Today all types of businesses choose from the same group of qualified plans. However, historically, that was not always true. At one time, plans for partnerships and self-employed persons were governed by separate statutory provisions, and plans for such organizations were referred to as Keogh plans. Unfortunately, the name still sticks—generally providing more confusion than information. Over the years, however, the rules for Keogh and corporate plans have evolved so that only a few minor distinctions exist between the two types of plans.[3] Today, a sole proprietor does not establish a Keogh plan; he or she establishes a profit-sharing, defined-benefit, or other plan from the array of tax-advantaged retirement plans. Therefore, only the differences between defined-benefit/defined-contribution plans and pension/profit-sharing plans are examined in the following paragraphs.

Defined-Benefit versus Defined-Contribution Plans

defined-benefit plan
defined-contribution plan

All qualified plans are either defined-benefit or defined-contribution plans. One way to look at these dissimilar approaches is to say that a *defined-benefit plan* provides a fixed predetermined benefit for the employee but has an uncertain cost to the employer, whereas a *defined-contribution plan* has a predetermined cost to the employer but provides an uncertain benefit for the employee. Let us examine each of these two types of plans more closely.

Under a defined-benefit plan, the required employer contributions vary depending on what is needed to pay the promised benefits. The maximum annual benefit that can be provided to a retired employee from a defined-benefit plan must not exceed the lesser of $185,000 (as indexed for 2008) or 100 percent of the employee's average compensation for his or her 3 consecutive years of highest pay while an active participant in the plan. A defined-benefit plan usually uses a benefit formula to stipulate a promised retirement benefit. This promised benefit is typically a percentage of the employee's salary (for example, 50 percent of the employee's final salary or 50 percent of the employee's final-average salary, such as the average of the final 3 to 5 years' salary or the average of the highest 3 to 5 years consecutive salary).

Defined-contribution plans, on the other hand, do not promise to pay a specified retirement benefit; instead, they specify the contribution that annually can be made to an employee's individual account. The maximum annual contribution that can be made to a defined-contribution plan on behalf of an employee must not exceed the lesser of $46,000 (as indexed for 2008) or 100 percent of the employee's compensation. Annual contributions include both employer and employee contributions, as well as any forfeitures allocated to the employee's account. By their nature, defined-contribution plans base an employee's benefit on the employee's entire career earnings and not the employee's final or final-average salary. Because defined-contribution plans allocate contributions to the accounts of individual employees, they are sometimes called individual account plans.

Clients covered by defined-contribution plans may find themselves short of retirement income if investment results are unfavorable. This is because, unlike a defined-benefit plan, the employer's obligation begins and ends with making the annual contribution. If plan investments are poor in a defined-contribution plan, the employee suffers the loss and may have inadequate retirement resources. In a defined-benefit plan, the benefits are promised and the employer has to make additional contributions to compensate for poor investment performance.

A second problem with defined-contribution plans is that contributions are based on participants' salaries for each year of their careers, rather than on their salaries at retirement as in most defined-benefit plans. Consequently, if inflation increases sharply in the years just prior to retirement, the chances of a participant achieving an adequate income-replacement ratio are diminished because most of the annual contributions would have been based on his or her salary paid prior to the inflationary spiral. In contrast, if the participant had been covered by a final-average defined-benefit plan, the employer would have had to make significant contributions to account for the higher final-average salary due to the increased inflation.

Another instance where either a defined-benefit plan or a defined-contribution plan may provide inadequate retirement income occurs when a client joins a plan late in his or her career. In this situation, since the years to retirement are few, a defined-contribution plan may not provide enough time to accumulate an adequate amount of assets. A defined-benefit plan, where the benefit is based in part on length of service, would also provide a relatively small benefit because these plans are geared to provide adequate replacement ratios for long-service employees only. (Table 6-3 provides a summary of some of the differences between these two types of plans.)

TABLE 6-3
Differences Between Defined-Benefit and Defined-Contribution Plans

Defined-Benefit Plans	Defined-Contribution Plans
Defines the benefit; the law specifies the maximum allowable benefit payable from the plan—the lesser of 100 percent of salary or $185,000 per year (as indexed for 2008)	Defines the employer's contribution; the law specifies the maximum allowable annual contribution—the lesser of 100 percent of salary or $46,000 (as indexed for 2008)
Contributions not attributed to specified employees	All contributions allocated to individual employee accounts
Employer assumes risk of preretirement inflation, investment performance, and the adequacy of retirement income	Employee assumes risk of preretirement inflation, investment performance, and the adequacy of retirement income
Unpredictable costs	Predictable costs

Pension versus Profit-Sharing Plans

Under a pension plan, the employer is committed to making annual contributions to the plan, since the main purpose of the plan is to provide a retirement benefit or at least provide for deferral of income until termination of employment. Under a profit-sharing plan, however, the employer can retain the flexibility necessary to avoid funding the plan annually. Moreover, a profit-sharing plan is not necessarily intended to provide a retirement benefit as much as to provide tax deferral of present compensation. To this end, the law generally allows that profit-sharing plans may be written to permit distributions during employment. The plan can distribute funds accumulated under the plan after a fixed number of years, with the attainment of a stated age, or upon the occurrence of certain events such as layoff, illness, financial hardship, disability, retirement, death, or severance of employment. The IRS has interpreted "a fixed number of years" to mean that:

- Distributions can be made of any contributions that have been held in the plan for 2 years or more.
- Any participant who has 5 or more years of plan participation can receive a distribution of his or her entire account balance.

Three important factors should be kept in mind if a client has a profit-sharing plan: First, the financial advisor should closely monitor the funding of the plan. It would be an easy mistake to assume that the employer is making scheduled payments to the plan when in actuality the employer is not contributing as expected because employer contributions are discretionary. It would also be an easy mistake to assume that the employee is allowing the funds to accumulate for retirement when in actuality the employee is depleting the account by taking withdrawals.

The second factor concerning profit-sharing plans is that the ability to withdraw funds prior to retirement under some profit-sharing plans opens up some interesting planning possibilities for the client and his or her advisor. For example, the client may want to gradually take money out while employed (starting after age 59 1/2 to avoid the 10 percent penalty tax) in order to reposition assets or take advantage of an excellent investment opportunity. In addition, the client may want to prepay any debt that would carry over into retirement, such as prepaying a mortgage or reducing interest expenses on a major capital purchase.

As previously indicated, pension plans, unlike profit-sharing plans, are meant to provide retirement income or at least provide for deferral of income until termination of employment. Because of this principle, for many years pension plans could only allow distributions upon termination of employment or attainment of normal retirement age. The Pension Protection Act of 2006 amended this rule somewhat in recognition of a recent trend in older workers choosing to cut back the number of hours employed without leaving the workforce. Since this group may need to begin receiving retirement benefits prior to retiring, the law now allows pension plans to begin payments as early as age 62.

A final factor concerning profit-sharing plans is their ability to invest in company stock. Profit-sharing plans have no restrictions on investing in employer stock; all plan assets can be used to purchase employer stock (although this seldom occurs). Pension plans, on the other hand, can invest only up to 10 percent of plan assets in employer stock. Table 6-4 provides a summary of some of the differences between pension and profit-sharing plans.

TABLE 6-4
Differences between Pension and Profit-Sharing Plans

Characteristic	Pension Plan	Profit-Sharing Plan
Employer commitment to annual funding	Yes	No
Withdrawal flexibility for employees	None	After 2 years
Investment in company stock	Limited to 10%	Unlimited

Types of Tax-Advantaged Qualified Plans

Once the financial advisor understands the basic characteristics of each category of qualified plans, he or she is well on the way to understanding the specific type of plan that a client has. For example, if a client has a plan that is both a defined-contribution and a pension plan, the advisor knows that employer contributions are mandatory but that the employee assumes the risks associated with investment performance and preretirement inflation.

The final component that the advisor needs to understand is the plan's benefit or contribution formula. These formulas are unique to the specific type of plan involved.

unit-benefit formula

Defined-Benefit Pension Plans. As its name implies, a defined-benefit pension plan is both a defined-benefit plan and a pension plan. The employer's contributions under this type of plan are determined actuarially on the basis of the benefits expected to become payable. These benefits are determined under a benefit formula and there are several different types of defined-benefit formulas. The most common type, the *unit-benefit formula*, directly accounts for both the participant's service with the employer and his or her salary in determining the pension benefit. An example of how a unit-benefit formula might read is as follows:

Example: Each plan participant will receive a monthly pension commencing at the normal retirement age and paid in the form of a life annuity equal to 2 percent of final-average monthly salary (annual salary considered in the benefit formula is limited to a maximum amount of $230,000 as indexed for 2008) multiplied by the participant's years of service.

Normal retirement age in this plan is defined as the later of age 65 or 5 years of plan participation. Service is limited to a maximum of 30 years.

Under this unit-benefit formula, an employee with 20 years of service and a $260,000 final-average annual salary will receive $7,666.67 per month in the form of life annuity payments [.02 x $19,166.67 (not $21,666.67 because of the compensation limit) x 20].

flat-percentage-of-earnings formula

There are a number of less common formulas that are also used. One of these is a *flat-percentage-of-earnings formula* under which the benefit is tied to salary. Length of service, however, is also a factor, albeit indirect. To prevent discrimination in favor of participants hired later in their careers, the IRS passed regulations that required this type of formula to have a 25-year minimum period of service in order for the participants to receive the full benefits promised. For those with less service, the benefits are proportionately reduced. An example of a flat-percentage-of-earnings formula is as follows:

Example: Each plan participant will receive a monthly pension commencing at the normal retirement age of 65 and paid in the form of a life annuity equal to 40 percent of the participant's final-average monthly salary. (Annual salary taken into account is capped at $230,000 as indexed for 2008.) However, to receive the full benefit promised, the participant must have at least 25 years of service. If the participant has less service, the benefit is proportionately reduced.

Debbie, a plan participant, has a final-average salary of $100,000 and 10 years of service. Under the plan, Debbie's benefit would be $16,000 (40 percent of $100,000 x 10/25).

Understanding the benefit formula is just the beginning of understanding how much a client will receive from a defined-benefit plan. Every element of a benefit formula affects the ultimate benefit. In the unit-benefit formula previously discussed, the benefit is tied to four factors: final-average salary, years of service, the timing of when benefits begin, and the form of the benefit. In a defined-benefit plan, compensation can be defined inclusively to cover all wages paid or it can be limited to only base salary, excluding bonuses, overtime, or other extraordinary pay. Final-average salary is usually defined to include the highest 3-to-5 years of salary, although this also can vary. In any event, compensation is capped at $230,000 (as indexed for 2008), meaning that compensation used for a particular year in the formula cannot exceed that year's compensation cap.

The definition of years of service can also vary from plan to plan. Some plans exclude years prior to plan participation, and some exclude part-time service or give only partial credit for part-time service. For an early retiree, the timing of when benefits begin is a key element. For example, a plan may provide for full retirement benefits to begin at age 65, but allow early retirement at age 62 with actuarially reduced benefits to reflect the longer payout period. What this should point out to the advisor is that helping a client determine what benefits he or she is eligible to receive can be tricky, especially if the client is going to retire early, late, or has an unusual employment history with the company.

cash-balance pension plan

Cash-Balance Pension Plans. A *cash-balance pension plan* is a defined-benefit plan that is designed to look like a defined-contribution plan. As a defined-benefit plan, it has some level of funding flexibility, but its defined-contribution like design means that its benefit formula is more easily explained.

The heart of the cash-balance pension plan is the benefit formula. As in a defined-contribution plan, the benefit is stated as an account balance that increases with contributions and investment experience. However, in the cash-balance plan the account is fictitious. Contributions are a bookkeeping credit only—no actual contributions are allocated to participants' accounts. Investment credits are also hypothetical. Nonetheless, to the participants, this plan looks like a traditional defined-contribution individual account plan. An example of how a cash-balance formula might read is as follows:

Example: The participant is entitled to a single-sum benefit that is based on a credit of 5 percent of compensation each year. The credited amounts will accumulate with interest. Interest will be credited annually using the 30-year treasury rate on that date. Actual investment experience will not affect the value of the benefit.

From the employer's perspective, a cash-balance pension plan is still a defined-benefit plan, and as in any defined-benefit plan, the employer is ultimately responsible for making the contributions necessary to pay promised benefits—meaning that the sponsor is "on the hook" for the plan's investment experience. If plan assets earn a higher rate of return than expected, then future contributions can be reduced, and vice versa.

money-purchase pension plan

Money-Purchase Pension Plans. A *money-purchase pension plan* is a type of defined-contribution plan. It is also, as its name states, a pension plan. Under a money-purchase pension plan, the employer's annual contributions are mandatory and are specified in the plan. For example, a money-purchase contribution formula may require annual contributions equal to 10 percent of each participant's compensation. The definition of compensation will vary from plan to plan. In some cases, it will include overtime, bonuses, and the like; in other cases, it will be restricted to base salary. In either case, compensation considered in the contribution formula is limited to a maximum amount of $230,000 (as indexed for 2008). In order to accurately estimate the amount of retirement savings that a client will be able to accumulate in his or her plan, the advisor must understand how the plan defines compensation. Plan benefits for each participant are the amounts that can be provided by the sums contributed to the participant's individual account plus investment earnings.

target-benefit pension plan

Target-Benefit Pension Plans. A *target-benefit pension plan*, like a money-purchase pension plan, is both a defined-contribution plan and a pension plan. Because of this, target-benefit plans have many of the same characteristics as money-purchase plans. Despite the similarities, however, target benefit plans are a unique form of defined-contribution plan because they have some of the features associated with traditional defined-benefit plans. One of these features is that a defined-benefit formula is used to determine the annual contribution.

At the inception of a target-benefit plan, an actuary takes into account final-average salary assumptions, age, mortality, interest earnings, and other assumptions in order to project the annual level contribution for each participant. While the employer hopes to provide a specific benefit (the target) at retirement, the employer does not guarantee that the targeted benefit will be paid. The investment risk falls on the participants, and an amount less than or greater than the target may be available, depending on the investment performance of the participants' accounts.

For a comparison of target-benefit plans and cash-balance plans, see table 6-5.

Profit-Sharing Plans. A profit-sharing plan is also a type of defined-contribution plan. Under a profit-sharing plan, there are two parts to the contribution formula. One part relates to how much the employer contributes to the plan and the other relates to how the contribution is allocated among the participants.

In most profit-sharing plans, employer contributions are made on a discretionary basis. The employer decides whether a contribution will be made and how much that contribution will be. Typically, contributions are geared to profits, although the employer can make contributions even if there are no profits. However, a profit-sharing plan can also be written to require a specified contribution. One way to do this is to state the required contribution as a specified percentage of profits or some other objective formula stated in the plan. This approach is appropriate when the employer wants employees to feel that they have a clear and determinable stake in the performance of the company.

TABLE 6-5
Hybrid Plans: Mirrors of Each Other

Target-Benefit Pension Plan	Cash-Balance Pension Plan
Defined-contribution plan	Defined-benefit plan
Participant entitled to vested account balance	Participant entitled to promised benefit, regardless of actual plan assets
Feels like a defined-benefit plan because contributions target a monthly benefit at retirement	Feels like a defined-contribution plan because promised benefit is based on an accumulated hypothetical account balance
Contribution is fixed based on the contribution formula	Contribution is variable based on the actuarial determination

The heart of a profit-sharing plan is the method of allocating the employer contribution among the participants. This formula must be definite and predetermined. The most common type of allocation formula is one that allocates the total contribution so that each participant receives a contribution that is the same percentage of compensation, for example, 3 percent or 5 percent. This allocation formula is popular, in part, because it satisfies the requirement that contributions or benefits cannot discriminate in favor of highly compensated employees. Another way to allocate contributions is to integrate the formula with Social Security so that employees who earn more than the Social Security taxable wage base receive a higher portion of the employer's contribution. Newer approaches that allocate even a larger portion of the contribution to the older, more highly compensated employees, include the age-weighted and cross-tested allocation methods. However, even a brief explanation of these newer approaches is beyond the scope of this introductory chapter on retirement planning.

401(k) plan

401(k) Plans. One of the most popular types of qualified plans is the 401(k) defined-contribution profit-sharing plan. A *401(k) plan* allows employees to elect to defer current salary, which is contributed to the plan on a pretax basis. In addition to the salary deferral feature, a 401(k) plan can contain a traditional profit-sharing feature, an employer matching contribution feature, or both. The plan may even allow for employee after-tax contributions. This means the plan can be as simple as a stand-alone plan (salary deferrals only) or as complex as a plan that allows both pretax and after-tax employee contributions, employer matching contributions, and employer profit-sharing contributions. In today's market, many employers, even those that already have defined-benefit or money-purchase pension plans, opt to sponsor 401(k) plans. From a retirement planning perspective, 401(k) plans are an excellent way for employees to save for retirement, and in most cases clients should be encouraged to take full advantage of them.

Salary Deferral Contributions. The heart of a 401(k) plan is the salary deferral feature that employees may elect. The amount of elective deferrals can never exceed a specified limit. For 2008, the limit is $15,500 (as indexed). In addition, the maximum salary deferral is increased for those individuals who have attained age 50 by the end of the current year. For 2008, the additional allowable contribution is $5,000.

In addition to encouraging clients to participate in 401(k) plans and elect to defer part of their salaries, financial advisors should also be aware of the following factors that apply to 401(k) salary deferrals:

- 401(k) salary reductions are immediately 100 percent vested and cannot be forfeited, but matching contributions can be subject to a vesting schedule.
- Participants may have limited access to salary deferral contributions while still employed. The law only allows in-service withdrawals upon a severe financial hardship or the attainment of age 59 1/2. However, some plans allow additional access through loans.

Beginning in 2006, 401(k) plans (as well as 403(b) plans) may allow participants to treat some or all of their salary deferral contributions as Roth IRAs at the time of distribution. If the election is made, the contributions are made on an after-tax basis and are subject to the same treatment as Roth IRAs at the time of distribution. This means that the participant has the option to forgo tax deferral in exchange for tax-free treatment upon distribution.

Plan participants who like the tax treatment of the Roth IRA may be very interested in having this feature added to their own 401(k) or 403(b) plan for two reasons. First, the 401(k) plan salary deferral limit ($15,500 in 2008) is significantly higher than the Roth IRA limit ($5,000 in 2008). Second, a Roth 401(k) does not have the income phaseout rules necessary for eligibility for a Roth IRA. Individuals at all income levels can contribute to a Roth 401(k).

Employer Contributions. In addition to salary deferrals by participating employees, most employers make additional contributions to the plan. The employer that wants to make additional contributions can choose how to spend those dollars—as matching or as profit-sharing contributions. A common practice today is to choose a matching contribution feature in which the employer agrees to match employee contributions to a certain extent. For example, the employer might agree to contribute 50 cents to the plan for each dollar the employee contributes up to the first 6 percent of the employee's salary. In this example, the maximum employer match is 3 percent of the employee's salary.

Both the matching percentage and the maximum match must be carefully chosen to meet the employer's objectives and budget. The primary reason for the match is to stimulate plan participation through the offer of an instant return on the participant's contributions. Another goal is to create a retirement planning partnership between the employer and the participants. Under this philosophy, an employer is committed to contribute toward an employee's funds for retirement, but only if the employee is willing to save for retirement.

To meet specific employer objectives, the design of the matching contribution can be as straightforward as described above, or more complex—such as a graded formula in which the matching contribution rate varies for different levels of salary deferrals. Under a typical graded formula, the employer contributes 50 cents for each dollar contributed by an employee up to 4 percent of the employees salary, plus 25 cents for each dollar contributed over 4 percent up to a maximum of 6 percent of the employee's salary. Matching contributions can also be made on a discretionary basis. However, because the uncertainty of a discretionary employer contribution might discourage plan participation, it is more common to provide a small, guaranteed matching contribution, which can be made larger at the discretion of the employer.

A profit-sharing feature in a 401(k) plan works the same way as in a traditional profit-sharing plan. Contributions are made for eligible participants, regardless of whether they make salary deferral contributions. When a 401(k) plan is the only plan offered by an employer, it is not uncommon—in a good year—for the employer to make both matching contributions and profit-sharing-type contributions.

stock bonus plan
employee stock ownership plan (ESOP)

Stock Bonus Plans and ESOPs. Both a *stock bonus plan* and an *employee stock ownership plan (ESOP)* are variations of profit-sharing plans and are, therefore, similar in many ways:

- Stock bonus plans, ESOPs, and profit-sharing plans are all defined-contribution plans and fall into the profit-sharing (not pension) category.
- Contributions need not be fixed and need not be made every year.
- The allocation formulas used under a profit-sharing plan may be used under either a stock bonus plan or an ESOP.
- Contributions for all three types of plans are usually based on profits, although they are not required to be.

Stock bonus plans and ESOPs differ from profit-sharing plans, however, in three important ways:

- Both stock bonus plans and ESOPs typically invest plan assets primarily in the employer's stock (in fact, an ESOP is required to invest primarily in employer stock). Profit-sharing plans, on the other hand, are usually structured to diversify investments and do not concentrate investments in employer stock (even though they are legally permitted to do so).
- Both stock bonus plans and ESOPs are chosen because they provide a market for employer stock. This, in turn, generates capital for the corporation and is a method to finance a company's growth. Profit-sharing plans, however, are not viewed as a way to finance company operations but are more concerned with providing tax-favored deferred compensation that can be used for retirement purposes.
- Stock bonus plans and ESOPs allow distributions to participants in the form of employer stock. Profit-sharing plans generally do not. This creates a distinct advantage for participants in a stock bonus plan or an ESOP, because they receive a tax break inasmuch as any unrealized appreciation (gain in value) in the stock is not taxed until the stock is sold.

Despite the many similarities between stock bonus plans and ESOPs, there is one major difference. An ESOP allows the plan to borrow to purchase employer stock. Under this technique, the employer guarantees repayment of the loan, and the plan repays the loan with employer contributions to the ESOP.

Other Tax-Advantaged Plans

In this section, three types of tax-advantaged retirement plans, other than qualified plans, are briefly discussed. These are the simplified employee pension (SEP), the savings incentive match plan for employees (SIMPLE), and the 403(b) plan. What is noteworthy about these plans is that each has its own unique set of rules.

SEPs

simplified employee pension (SEP)

A *simplified employee pension (SEP)* is a retirement plan that uses an individual retirement account (IRA) or an individual retirement annuity (IRA annuity) as the receptacle for contributions. As it name implies, this type of plan is simpler than a qualified retirement plan, making it, in many cases, attractive to the small businessowner.

From a design perspective, a SEP is quite similar to a profit-sharing plan—that is, employer contributions are made on a discretionary basis, although the plan can require specified employer contributions. What makes the SEP different from a profit-sharing plan is that contributions must be allocated to participants in a way that provides a benefit as a level percentage of compensation. (For example, all employees receive an allocation of 5 percent of compensation.) The only exception to the level-percentage-of-compensation rule is that the allocation formula may be integrated with Social Security in the same manner as in other defined-contribution plans. This provides highly compensated employees with contributions that are slightly larger (as a percentage of pay) than those for the rank-and-file employees. All employer contributions to a SEP must be immediately and 100 percent vested.

SIMPLEs

savings incentive match plan for employees (SIMPLE)

Since 1997, employers have had another plan option available, referred to as the *savings incentive match plan for employees (SIMPLE)*. Like SEPs, a SIMPLE plan is funded with individual retirement accounts, which means that the following requirements apply to the SIMPLE:

- Participants must be fully vested in all benefits at all times.
- Assets cannot be invested in life insurance or collectibles.
- No participant loans are allowed.

Any type of business entity can establish a SIMPLE; however, the business cannot have more than 100 employees (only counting those employees who earned $5,000 or more of compensation). If the employer grows beyond the 100-employee limit, the law does allow the employer to sponsor the plan for an additional 2-year grace period. Also note that to be eligible, the sponsoring employer cannot maintain any other qualified plan, 403(b) plan, or SEP at the same time it maintains the SIMPLE.

Salary Deferral Contributions. In a SIMPLE, all eligible employees have the opportunity to make elective pretax contributions of up to $10,500 (as indexed for 2008). As with the 401(k) plan, participants who have attained age 50 before the end of the year can make additional contributions to a SIMPLE. For 2008, the additional amount is $2,500.

Employer Contributions. Unlike the 401(k) plan, there is no nondiscrimination testing, meaning that highly compensated employees can make contributions without regard to the salary deferral elections of the nonhighly compensated employees.

However, in exchange, the SIMPLE has a mandatory employer contribution requirement. This contribution can be made in one of two ways:

1. The employer can make a dollar-for-dollar matching contribution on the first 3 percent of compensation that the individual elects to defer, or
2. The employer can make a 2 percent nonelective contribution for all eligible employees.

These employer contribution amounts are both the minimum required and the maximum allowed. In other words, if the employer elects the matching contribution, 3 percent is the maximum match, and nonelective contributions are not allowed. If the employer elects the nonelective contribution, then the 2 percent contribution is the maximum, and matching contributions are not allowed.

403(b) Plans

403(b) plan

The plans we have studied up to this point are not limited to any particular type of industry. For the most part, they are available to any organization. In contrast to other retirement plans, a *403(b) plan* can be sold only to tax-exempt organizations and public schools. Despite these limitations, 403(b) plans represent a separate and lucrative opportunity for financial advisors, particularly those who sell annuity products. A 403(b) plan, which is also referred to as a tax-sheltered annuity (TSA) or a tax-deferred annuity (TDA), is similar to a 401(k) plan. Like the 401(k) plan, the 403(b) plan

- allows deferrals in the form of a salary reduction that is chosen by the employee

- allows before-tax employer contributions to be made to the employee's individual account
- can be used in conjunction with, or in lieu of, most other retirement plans

However, 403(b) plans are distinguishable from 401(k) plans both in the market they serve and in their makeup.

Salary Deferral Contributions. The maximum salary reduction contribution that can be made by an individual is subject to the same dollar limitations that apply to 401(k) plans. For 2008, the dollar limit is $15,500 (as indexed). Also, as with the 401(k) plan, additional contributions can be made by individuals who have attained age 50 by the end of the current year. For 2008, the additional allowable contribution is $5,000.

Also, it is important to note that the dollar limit applies to all contributions made by the individual to any 403(b) plan, 401(k) plan, simplified employee pension (SEP), or savings incentive match plan for employees (SIMPLE). This is true even if the individual is covered by plans of unrelated employers. For example, a 40-year old participant deferring $6,000 in a 403(b) plan for 2008 would only be able to defer a maximum of $9,500 under a 401(k) arrangement for 2008.

On top of the normal limit (including the additional contribution allowed by participants over age 50), another special "catch-up" election applies to 403(b) plans. Individuals who have completed at least 15 years of service with most qualified sponsors are eligible for the catch-up election. The otherwise applicable limit ($15,500 for 2008) is increased for such eligible individuals by the smallest of the following amounts:

- $3,000 (which makes the limit $18,500 for 2008)
- $15,000, reduced by increases to the regular limit the individual was allowed during earlier years because of this rule
- $5,000 times the number of years of service with the organization, minus the total elective deferrals made under the plan for the individual during earlier years

As with 401(k) plans, 403(b) plans may allow participants to treat some or all of their salary deferral contributions as Roth contributions. If the election is made, the contributions are made on an after-tax basis and are subject to the same tax treatment as Roth IRAs at the time of distribution. This means that the participant has the option to forgo tax deferral in exchange for tax-free treatment upon distribution.

Employer Contributions. Employers may use 403(b) plans as a means of providing additional retirement benefits for their employees. Including employer contributions drastically changes the nature of the plan, subjecting it to ERISA and placing additional fiduciary responsibility on the plan sponsor. Also, a significant number of additional tax rules—which make the 403(b) plan more like a qualified plan—will apply.

As in a 401(k) plan, employer contributions can be made as matching contributions based on employee elections to defer compensation.

Another alternative is to make contributions on a nonelective basis, as in a profit-sharing plan or money-purchase pension plan. Typically, such plans provide contributions as a uniform percentage of compensation; however, some flexibility is available in determining the allocation formula.

Nonqualified Plans

nonqualified plan

Another very different type of employer-sponsored retirement planning vehicle is a *nonqualified plan.* In the case of nonqualified plans, the tax savings are not attributable to Uncle Sam but instead stem from the fact that, in most cases, the employer defers his or her business deduction so that specifically chosen employees will not be deemed to be in constructive receipt of deferred compensation promised them. These plans are primarily given to highly compensated executives and managers. In some plans, the employer provides an additional benefit, while other plans are similar to 401(k) plans, allowing participants the right to defer salary.

Financial advisors must be wary of certain potential problems for clients covered by nonqualified plans. One trap awaiting clients covered by these plans is that they have somewhat inflexible withdrawal provisions. In qualified plans, distributions can generally be rolled over into an IRA, with taxable withdrawals occurring as needed. Nonqualified benefits cannot be rolled over to an IRA. Also the participant generally is not given a choice of distribution options at retirement time. The distribution options are generally quite limited, and the option desired typically must be selected (to avoid tax problems) at the time participation begins.

A second trap awaiting clients covered by nonqualified plans is that promised benefits are typically subject to loss for a variety of reasons. For example, a nonqualified plan may contain a forfeiture provision stipulating that benefits will be forfeited if certain conditions are not met. In many circumstances, the client may be either unwilling or unable to meet his or her part of the commitment. A second way nonqualified benefits can be lost is if the employer sponsoring the plan goes bankrupt. Nonqualified plan funds are typically held as corporate assets that are subject to the claims of corporate creditors in bankruptcy. This is in sharp contrast to the funds in a qualified or tax-advantaged plan that are held in a trust or insurance contract separate from business assets and that are not subject to forfeiture in case of bankruptcy.

A final insecurity associated with nonqualified plans is the threat of immediate taxation to the employee that would result in a lower overall retirement accumulation. For example, despite employer contentions to the contrary, some plans are construed by the IRS as providing an immediate economic benefit to the employee, or the employee may be deemed to be in constructive receipt of the income. In either case, the prefunded benefit will be taxable while the client is still employed and the advantages of tax deferral will be lost.

Despite all these problems, nonqualified plans have an important role in retirement planning for executive clients. The major reason is that qualified and tax-advantaged plan rules limit plan benefits and a nonqualified plan may be necessary to ensure that the executive will have an adequate income replacement ratio.

IRAs

One of the most important sources of retirement income that financial advisors can counsel their clients about is an individual retirement account (IRA). There are three types of IRAs: traditional IRAs, Roth IRAs, and education IRAs (now known as Coverdell Education Savings Accounts). Since education IRAs are not really intended as retirement savings vehicles, they are not covered here. Traditional IRAs are similar to qualified plans in many respects. Both encourage retirement savings by allowing contributions to be made with pretax dollars (if the taxpayer is eligible) and earnings to be tax deferred until retirement, at which time all withdrawals are taxable. In contrast, Roth IRA contributions are not deductible, but qualifying withdrawals are not subject to income tax.

Traditional IRAs and Roth IRAs are subject to certain limitations. The most important are the maximum contribution limits. Total contributions to either a traditional IRA or a Roth IRA may not exceed $5,000 a year (for 2008) or 100 percent of compensation, whichever is smaller. In addition, an owner of either type of IRA who has attained age 50 before the end of the taxable year can contribute an additional $1,000. Other rules include the following:

- Traditional IRA contributions may not be made during or after the year in which the client reaches age 70 1/2, but Roth IRA contributions may continue during and after that year.
- IRA funds may not be commingled with the client's other assets; the funds may contain only IRA contributions and rollover contributions.

- IRA funds may not be used to buy a life insurance policy.
- Funds contributed to an IRA may not be invested in collectibles.
- No loans may be taken from IRA accounts.

Traditional IRAs

traditional IRA

Any person under age 70 1/2 who receives $5,000 in compensation (either salary or self-employment earned income) may make a $5,000 contribution to a *traditional IRA*. In addition, if a person is married, even if he or she does not work, that person can contribute $5,000 as long as the spouse's salary is at least $10,000 (then each spouse can make a $5,000 contribution).

The contribution, however, is only deductible if certain eligibility requirements are satisfied. The contribution will be deductible if neither the taxpayer nor the taxpayer's spouse is an active participant in an employer-maintained retirement plan. If the taxpayer is an active participant, then the contribution is deductible only if his or her modified adjusted gross income falls below prescribed limits (designed to approximate a middle-class income). If an individual is not an active participant, but his or her spouse is, then the contribution is deductible for the spouse who is not an active participant if the couple's income is less than a different higher income threshold.

Active Participant. The first eligibility issue concerns whether the client is an active participant in an employer-maintained plan. Employer-maintained plans include every type of qualified plan, as well as all federal, state, and local government plans. Not included, however, are nonqualified plans.

The term active participant has a special meaning that depends on the type of plan involved. Generally, a person is an active participant in a defined-benefit plan unless excluded under the eligibility provision of the plan for the entire year. This is true even if the person elects not to participate in the plan. In the case of any type of defined-contribution plan, a person is an active participant if the plan specifies that employer contributions must be allocated to the individual's account. This category also includes SEPs, 403(b) plans, and SIMPLEs. In a profit-sharing or stock plan where employer contributions are discretionary, the participant must actually receive some contribution for active-participant status to be triggered. Furthermore, mandatory contributions, voluntary contributions, and contributions made pursuant to a salary reduction SEP, 403(b) plan, SIMPLE, or 401(k) arrangement will also trigger active-participant status.

Monetary Limit. The second issue of IRA deductibility is the taxpayer's income. If a taxpayer is an active participant, fully deductible contributions are allowed only if the taxpayer has a modified adjusted gross income (AGI) that falls below a specified level (see table 6-6). The level for unreduced contributions depends on the taxpayer's filing status. For 2008, married couples filing a joint return will get full IRA deductions if their modified AGI is $85,000 or less. Married persons filing separately cannot get a full IRA deduction. Single taxpayers and taxpayers filing as heads of households will get a full IRA deduction if their modified AGI is $53,000 or less. For taxpayers whose modified AGI falls between the no-deduction level and the full-deduction level, their reduced deduction is determined on a pro rata basis. For example, in 2008, a single taxpayer who is an active participant and has a modified AGI of $58,000 can make only a $2,500 deductible contribution.

TABLE 6-6
2008 Modified AGI* Limits for Deductible IRA Contributions

Filing Status	Full IRA Deduction	Reduced IRA Deduction	No IRA Deduction
Individual or head of household	$53,000 or less	$53,000.01–$62,999.99	$63,000 or more
Married filing jointly	$85,000 or less	$85,000.01–$104,999.99	$105,000 or more
Married filing separately	Not available	$0.01–$9,999.99	$10,000 or more

* Explaining how AGI is modified is beyond the scope of this introductory chapter.

Special Spousal Rule. If a married taxpayer and his or her spouse are both active participants, then the deduction rules just described apply to both IRAs. However, the rules are different when only one spouse is an active participant. In this case, a $5,000 deductible IRA contribution is allowed for the nonactive participant spouse as long as the couple's modified AGI does not exceed $159,000. The deduction is phased out if the couple's joint modified AGI exceeds $159,000 and will be gone entirely if their modified AGI is $169,000 or more. A deductible contribution is not available for the nonactive participant spouse if the couple files separate tax returns.

Example: In 2008, Joe and Jane Morgan are considering establishing IRAs for themselves. Joe works but Jane does not because she stays home with the children. Joe is an active participant in a retirement plan and Jane, of course, is not. They file a joint return and have a modified AGI of $110,000. Consequently, Joe cannot make a deductible IRA contribution on his own behalf because the couple's modified AGI exceeds $105,000. However, Joe can make a $5,000 deductible IRA contribution for Jane because their joint modified AGI is less than $159,000.

Distributions. Taxpayers can withdraw all or part of their IRAs any time they wish. Unless the participant has made nondeductible contributions, which can be withdrawn tax free on a pro rata basis, distributions are treated as ordinary income for federal income tax purposes. If distributions are taken prior to age 59 1/2, however, they are also subject to the 10 percent penalty on early withdrawals unless an exception applies. Exceptions are made for

- payments on account of the participant's death
- payments on account of the participant's disability
- the payment of certain medical expenses
- substantially equal periodic payments over the remaining life of the participant and a chosen beneficiary
- payments for qualified higher education expenses for the participant, spouse, or any child or grandchild of the participant or spouse at an eligible educational institution
- payments to cover qualified first-time homebuyer expenses for the participant, spouse, or any child, grandchild, or ancestor of the participant or spouse. However, this exception has a $10,000 lifetime limit per IRA participant.

Traditional IRAs are also subject to the rules that control the maximum length of the tax-deferral period. These are the minimum-distribution rules that generally require that distributions begin when the participant attains age 70 1/2 and also require specified payments at the death of the participant.

Roth IRAs

Roth IRA

Individuals have a choice between contributing to a traditional IRA or to a *Roth IRA* each year. The Roth IRA is tied to the old rules in that total contributions for the year (to either type of IRA) cannot exceed $5,000 (and spousal IRAs are allowed). Contributions to a Roth IRA are not deductible, but distributions are tax free as long as certain eligibility requirements are satisfied. The maximum contribution to a Roth IRA is phased out for single taxpayers with a modified AGI of at least $101,000 but less than $116,000 (a pro rata reduction over a $15,000 income spread) and for married joint filers with a modified AGI of at least $159,000 but less than $169,000 (a pro rata reduction over a $10,000 income spread). For purposes of this calculation, the AGI is modified under the same procedure as that used for traditional IRAs and is beyond the scope of this introductory chapter.

Unlike traditional IRAs, the owner of a Roth IRA can make contributions even after he or she attains age 70 1/2. Moreover, the minimum distribution rules that apply to traditional IRAs do not apply to a Roth IRA while the owner is alive. The owner of a Roth IRA is not required to take distributions at any age. However, after the death of a Roth IRA owner, certain of the minimum distribution rules that apply to traditional IRAs also apply to Roth IRAs.

For distributions to be "qualified distributions" that are entirely tax free, they have to meet two requirements. First, the distribution must be made more than 5 years after the Roth IRA was established. Second, the distribution must be made after one of the four following events has occurred:

- The owner has attained age 59 1/2.
- The distribution is paid to a beneficiary because of the owner's death.
- The owner has become disabled.
- The withdrawal is made to pay qualified first-time homebuyer expenses for the owner, his or her spouse, or any child, grandchild, or ancestor of the owner or spouse. As previously stated, however, there is a $10,000 lifetime limit per IRA owner for these expenses.

If these requirements are not satisfied, the distribution is referred to as a nonqualifying distribution. However, even nonqualifying distributions receive somewhat favorable tax treatment. Contributions can be withdrawn first, without having to pay any taxes. Once all contributions have been withdrawn, amounts representing earnings can then be withdrawn but are subject to income tax and the 10 percent penalty on early withdrawals.

OVERCOMING INADEQUATE RETIREMENT RESOURCES

In addition to determining how much income clients will need in order to retire, a financial advisor should also help clients produce as much retirement income as possible from their existing resources. The final part of this chapter addresses four strategies that the advisor can recommend to accomplish this goal:

- trading down to a less expensive home
- obtaining a reverse mortgage
- postretirement employment
- pension maximization

Trading Down to a Less Expensive Home

If a client can be persuaded to sell his or her home and relocate to a smaller, less expensive residence, the money made available from the transaction can be a valuable source of retirement income. For example, if a retiree sells his or her home for $200,000 and buys a new residence for $100,000, the $100,000 gain can be used to produce an extra $6,000 a year in income (assuming a 6 percent interest rate). This is very desirable from a financial perspective, because it enables retirees to capitalize on what for many of them is their single most important financial asset—their home. In addition, the Internal Revenue Code allows taxpayers to exclude up to $250,000 of gain ($500,000 on a joint return in most situations) from the sale or exchange of their homes if the following restrictions are met:

- During the prior 5 years, the house must have been owned and used by the taxpayer as his or her principal residence for periods aggregating 2 years or more.
- The taxpayer may not have excluded a gain from the sale of his or her principal residence in the prior 2 years.

Obtaining a Reverse Mortgage

reverse mortgage

If a client would like to take some equity out of his or her home, but is reluctant to move to a less expensive one, an alternative that is available is a *reverse mortgage*. A reverse mortgage is a loan against an individual's home that requires no repayment as long as the individual continues to live in the home. In other words, a reverse mortgage is a strategy that allows a client to live in his or her home while withdrawing substantial amounts of money from its built up equity. This money can be used for current needs, and there is no need to repay it. A reverse mortgage is typically available only when all of the owners are aged 62 or older and when the home is the principal residence. Also, the home must either have no debt or only a small debt that can be paid off with part of the reverse mortgage loan.

The federally sponsored Home Equity Conversion Mortgage (HECM) program is the most popular type of reverse mortgage. The FHA insures HECM loans to protect lenders against loss if amounts withdrawn exceed equity when the property is sold. Any lender authorized to make HUD-insured loans, such as banks, mortgage companies, and savings and loan associations, can participate in the HECM program. There are also a number of other privately sponsored programs.

The amount of loan payments made to the client depends on the client's age (or clients' joint ages), the amount of equity the home currently has or is expected to have, the interest rate and fees that are being charged, and which reverse mortgage program is used. In many cases, the HECM program pays the largest amount; however, in some cases, certain special needs loans offered by a state or local government program may be more favorable. For very expensive homes, a privately sponsored program may be more favorable. Payment options vary depending on the specific program, but generally they fall within a number of categories, including an immediate lump sum payment, a credit line account, or a specified monthly amount for a specific number of years.

The amount of the debt grows based on the amount paid and accumulated interest. Typically, the loan only has to be repaid when the last surviving borrower either dies, sells the home, or permanently moves away. Most loans are nonrecourse, meaning the maximum amount that has to be repaid is the value of the home. If property values erode, the borrower receives a windfall and the lender ends up with a loss. Because these programs are truly loans, if the retiree wants or needs to sell the home, any equity that exceeds the loan balance is the property of the retiree. If the property is sold after the borrower dies, his or her heirs receive any remaining equity after the loan is repaid.

Postretirement Employment

A third strategy that can be used to provide the retiree with extra cash is a part-time job during the retirement years. Many retirees find that working on a scaled-back basis not only meets their financial needs but also helps them adapt psychologically to the changes that retirement brings. This is especially true for retirees whose self-esteem and sense of self-worth were tied to their careers.

Working after retirement poses a potential problem for retirees who have begun receiving Social Security retirement benefits but who have not yet attained the full retirement age (age 66 for those retiring in 2008) if they have work wages that exceed a specified level. As will be discussed in chapter 8, Social Security beneficiaries under the full retirement age are allowed earnings of $13,560 in 2008. If a beneficiary earns more than that, his or her Social Security benefit is reduced $1 for every $2 of excess earnings. A different formula applies for the calendar year in which an individual attains the full retirement age. For that year, the reduction is only $1 for every $3 of excess earnings and counts only earnings before the month the individual reaches full retirement age. Also, for that year the threshold is higher, $36,120 in 2008.

Once an individual reaches the full retirement age, the problem goes away. At that point the individual can earn any amount without it resulting in a reduction of Social Security retirement benefits.

Pension Maximization

The final strategy that we will discuss is so-called pension maximization. Qualified plans typically stipulate the type of distribution that your client will receive. The normal form of benefit for a married client is a joint and survivor benefit that pays not less than 50 percent nor greater than 100 percent of the joint benefit amount to the survivor. One strategy available for the married client is to have him or her elect a different payment option by electing out of the normal benefit form with the spouse's written consent. If a married client who would otherwise be locked into a joint and survivor annuity elects to have his or her benefit paid in the form of a life annuity, he or she can increase retirement income significantly. If at the same time life insurance is purchased (or kept in force) on the life annuitant, the spouse's future also remains secure.

Example:	Joe Jones, aged 65, and his wife Sally, aged 62, are eligible to receive a $1,500 joint and survivor benefit from the $200,000 they have in Joe's retirement plan. (This is a qualified joint and survivor benefit that pays 100 percent of the joint benefit amount to the survivor.) If they elect to receive a life annuity based on Joe's life, they will receive $325 more each month ($1,825). The extra $3,900 a year represents a 22 percent increase in annual income for them. If they can purchase (or keep in force) enough life insurance on Joe to provide for Sally at a premium that is less than the $3,900 a year, they will stretch their retirement savings and take a big step toward their financial security goals.

> **FOCUS ON ETHICS**
> **Who Is the Client?**
>
> One of retirement planning's unique challenges is determining and focusing on the actual client. This needs further explanation.
>
> Current law requires married retirees to accept a joint and survivor annuity rather than a single-life annuity (in the absence of a spousal waiver). Obviously, the monthly check is lower for the joint and survivor payout.
>
> What should the financial advisor do if the client wants the higher single-life benefit and tries to talk the spouse into signing a waiver? Should the pension holder die first, this could leave the spouse with little or no income. The ethical issue is whether the advisor should defend the welfare of the vulnerable spouse. This is more easily done when the client is viewed as the couple, as opposed to only the pension-receiving spouse.

THE FINAL WORD

Retirement planning is no easy process. Financial advisors who engage in retirement planning must be prepared to answer some tough questions. Their biggest challenge, however, is convincing clients to start saving for retirement as early in their careers as possible. Starting early allows clients to take advantage of the magic of compound interest. Nevertheless, clients are never too old to plan for retirement. Developing retirement plans for clients who have procrastinated involves determining what funds are available for retirement and creating strategies, even if the funds are inadequate.

Even when financial advisors convince clients to start saving for retirement when they are relatively young, the advisors still must provide inflation protection both before and after retirement for their clients' resources. If advisors do nothing to help their clients combat the effects of inflation, many clients will discover when they retire that their resources are still inadequate, despite having started saving for retirement early in their careers.

CHAPTER SUMMARY

Instead of waiting until they turn gray to start planning for retirement, it is best if people start the planning process when they are relatively young. Starting young can mean the difference between success and failure. Getting young people to take retirement planning seriously, however, often requires some convincing.

Retirement planning is a multidimensional field. As such it requires that the advisor be schooled in the nuances of many financial planning specialties, as well as in other areas. Specializing in just one field is too limited for dealing with the diversified needs of the would-be retiree. A client is best served by a team of advisors who have specialized, but complementary, backgrounds or by a single advisor who is experienced in a variety of important retirement topics.

Whether a retirement team or a multitalented individual is the vehicle, the holistic approach to retirement planning is the only means by which a client's needs can be fully and adequately met. Under holistic retirement planning, the advisor is required to be conversant with clients in many disciplines. Because of this, the advisor must be a bit of a renaissance person. In addition, the role of an advisor engaged in a retirement planning practice is complicated, not only because of the broad-based knowledge needed for the job, but also because the advisor must be able to integrate retirement planning strategies with other financial planning needs—such as tax planning, estate planning, and meeting investment goals.

A word of caution is in order at this point. Understanding how to plan for a client's retirement is more art than science. There is no one-size-fits-all approach to retirement planning. Because client situations are like snowflakes—no two are alike—the advisor must be able to handle a variety of situations creatively and cannot rely on a "formulaic approach" to solving his or her clients' problems.

Besides being a "Jack of all trades," a financial advisor engaged in a retirement planning practice must undertake several responsibilities that may not have been a part of his or her traditional financial practice. These aspects of a retirement planning practice include incorporating retirement planning as a segment of comprehensive financial planning, dealing with other professionals who advise the client, dealing with relatively young clients, monitoring and/or updating the client's plan, and being familiar with available resources. In addition, the retirement planning advisor must also follow the same six step process used in financial planning.

Another responsibility of the financial advisor is to show clients that they are making choices about their retirement every day. While the advisor cannot force the client to make lifestyle choices that will provide an adequate source of retirement funds, he or she can make clients aware of the large amount of funds needed for retirement and point out that a spendthrift lifestyle during their working years hurts them upon retirement.

Besides a spendthrift lifestyle, clients face several other impediments to saving for retirement. These include unexpected expenses, inadequate insurance coverage, divorce, the lack of a retirement plan at the place of employment, frequently changing employers, a lack of financial literacy, and other long-term goals that need funding.

Estimating a client's financial needs during retirement is like trying to predict the future. Such estimates are fraught with complicating factors and clouded by unknown variables. For example, the advisor and client must establish what standard of living is desired during retirement, when retirement will begin, what inflation assumption should be made before and after retirement, and what interest can be earned on invested funds. Moreover, many of these variables can dramatically change overnight and without warning.

There are two common methods for determining how much annual income will be needed in the first year of retirement. The first method, the replacement-ratio method, assumes that the standard of living enjoyed during the years just prior to retirement will be the determining factor for the standard of living during retirement. In general, a 60 to 80 percent replacement ratio of a client's final average salary is used to estimate the amount of retirement income needed. The second method, the expense method, focuses on the projected expenses that the retiree will have during retirement. Neither of these methods, however, considers the effects of inflation. To calculate the true retirement income needed, the advisor must determine which of the client's potential sources of retirement income are affected by inflation.

Understanding how much a client will need for retirement is only one part of sound financial planning for retirement. Knowing the potential sources of retirement income is another crucial function with which the financial advisor must be familiar. For purposes of the discussion in this chapter, the various types of tax-advantaged employer-sponsored retirement plans can be divided into those that are qualified and those that are not. Qualified plans include defined-benefit plans, cash-balance plans, money-purchase plans, target-benefit plans, profit sharing plans, 401(k) plans, stock bonus plans, and ESOPs. The tax-advantaged plans that are not qualified include SEPs, SIMPLEs, and 403(b) plans.

In addition to the various types of tax-advantaged plans, another very different type of employer-sponsored retirement planning vehicle is a nonqualified plan. These plans are primarily given to highly compensated executives and managers. The tax savings from these plans are not attributable to Uncle Sam but stem from the fact that the employer, in most cases, defers his or her business deduction so that specifically chosen employees will not be deemed to be in constrictive receipt of deferred compensation promised them.

Another source of retirement income that advisors can counsel their clients about is IRAs. Traditional IRAs are similar to qualified plans in many respects. Both encourage retirement savings by allowing contributions to be made with pretax dollars and earnings to be tax deferred until retirement, at which time all withdrawals are taxable. In contrast, Roth IRA contributions are not deductible, but qualifying withdrawals are not subject to income tax.

In addition to determining how much income clients will need in order to retire, a financial advisor should also help clients produce as much retirement income as possible from their existing resources. The final part of this chapter addresses four strategies that the advisor can recommend to accomplish this goal. These strategies are trading down to a less expensive home, obtaining a reverse mortgage, postretirement employment, and pension maximization with the help of life insurance.

CHAPTER REVIEW

Key Terms and Concepts are explained in the Glossary. Answers to the Review Questions and Self-Test Questions are found in the back of the book in the Answers to Questions section.

Key Terms and Concepts

holistic retirement planning
qualified domestic relations order (QDRO)
replacement ratio method
expense method
qualified plan
defined-benefit plan
defined-contribution plan
unit-benefit formula
flat-percentage-of-earnings formula
cash-balance pension plan
money-purchase pension plan
target-benefit pension plan

401(k) plan
stock bonus plan
employee stock ownership plan (ESOP)
simplified employee pension (SEP)
savings incentive match plan for employees (SIMPLE)
403(b) plan
nonqualified plan
traditional IRA
Roth IRA
reverse mortgage

Review Questions

6-1. Describe two ways in which a spendthrift lifestyle during a client's active working years makes retirement planning more difficult for him or her.

6-2. Explain how each of the following may constitute important roadblocks preventing the client from accumulating adequate retirement saving:
   a. inadequate insurance coverage
   b. divorce
   c. frequent changes of employer

6-3. Explain how several of the variables affecting the amount a client will need to save in order to achieve his or her retirement goals can change due to forces largely beyond the client's control.

6-4. Distinguish between the replacement ratio method and the expense method of determining how much income a client will need in the first year of retirement in order to achieve his or her goals.

6-5. Identify several factors that make it likely that clients will have a lower annual federal tax burden after retirement than before retirement.

6-6. Identify several categories of general living expenses that for most retirees will be
a. lower after retirement than before retirement
b. higher after retirement than before retirement

6-7. Distinguish between the following:
a. a defined-benefit plan and a defined contribution plan
b. a pension plan and a profit-sharing plan

6-8. Describe several factors associated with a defined-contribution plan that may result in inadequate retirement income for a client.

6-9. Describe two important factors that the retirement advisor should keep in mind if his or her client is a participanat in a profit-sharing plan.

6-10. Present a typical benefit formula of each of the following types that might be found in a qualified defined-benefit pension plan.
a. unit-benefit formula
b. flat-percentage-of-earnings formula

6-11. Describe the principal characteristics of 401(k) plans.

6-12. Identify several potential retirement planning problems that participation in a nonqualified plan may pose for a client.

6-13. Describe the principal characteristics of traditional IRAs with respect to
a. limitations on contributions
b. eligibility for deductible contributions

6-14. Describe the principal characteristics of Roth IRAs with respect to
a. deductibility of contributions
b. taxability of distributions

6-15. Explain how each of the following strategies can be used to maximize a client's retirement income.
a. trading down to a less expensive home
b. obtaining a reverse mortgage
c. postretirement employment

Self-Test Questions

Instructions: Read chapter 6 first, then answer the following questions to test your knowledge. There are 10 questions; circle the correct answer, then check your answers with the answer key in the back of the book.

6-1. Which of the following correctly describes the unit-benefit formula found in defined-benefit pension plans?

  (A) It directly ties the participant's pension benefit to both service and salary.
  (B) It bases the participant's pension benefit on final-average salary only.
  (C) It provides each participant with the same pension benefit.
  (D) It provides each participant with a flat benefit amount for each year of service.

6-2. Which of the following types of retirement plans is qualified?

  (A) a SIMPLE plan
  (B) a 401(k) plan
  (C) a SEP plan
  (D) a 403(b) plan

6-3. Which of the following types of retirement plans is a defined-benefit plan designed to look like a defined-contribution plan?

  (A) a target-benefit pension plan
  (B) a stock bonus plan
  (C) an ESOP
  (D) a cash-balance pension plan

6-4. Which of the following statements concerning a 403(b) plan is (are) correct?

  I. It allows deferrals in the form of a salary reduction chosen by the employee.
  II. It can be used in conjunction with most other retirement plans.

  (A) I only
  (B) II only
  (C) Both I and II
  (D) Neither I nor II

6-5. Which of the following statements concerning a Roth IRA is (are) correct?

   I. Contributions can be made even after the owner attains age 70 1/2.
   II. Distributions must begin no later than when the owner attains age 70 1/2.

   (A) I only
   (B) II only
   (C) Both I and II
   (D) Neither I nor II

6-6. Which of the following statements concerning a money-purchase pension plan is (are) correct?

   I. A money-purchase pension plan is a type of defined-benefit plan.
   II. Compensation considered in the contribution formula is limited to a maximum of $100,000.

   (A) I only
   (B) II only
   (C) Both I and II
   (D) Neither I nor II

6-7. Which of the following statements concerning qualified plans is (are) correct?

   I. Distributions can be rolled into an IRA.
   II. A SEP is a qualified plan that uses an IRA.

   (A) I only
   (B) II only
   (C) Both I and II
   (D) Neither I nor II

6-8. All the following statements concerning SIMPLE plans are correct EXCEPT:

   (A) Assets cannot be invested in life insurance or collectibles.
   (B) Participants are allowed to borrow from their accounts.
   (C) Participants must be fully vested in all benefits at all times.
   (D) Any type of business entity can establish a SIMPLE plan.

6-9. All the following statements concerning defined-benefit plans are correct EXCEPT:

(A) Plan contributions are not allocated to individual employee accounts.
(B) The employer assumes the risk of preretirement inflation and investment performance.
(C) The costs associated with a defined-benefit plan are unpredictable.
(D) The law specifies the maximum allowable annual contribution that can be made for an employee.

6-10. All the following statements concerning a reverse mortgage are correct EXCEPT:

(A) It typically is available only when the home is the borrower's principal residence.
(B) If property values erode, the lender may end up with a loss.
(C) It typically is available regardless of the borrower's age.
(D) It does not have to be repaid as long as the borrower lives in the home.

NOTES

1. The MetLife Market Survey of Nursing Home & Assisted Living Costs, October 2007, The MetLife Mature Market Institute, p.4.
2. Employee Benefit Research Institute and Matthew Greenwold & Associates, Inc., 2008 Retirement Confidence Survey, figure 6.
3. Except for one remaining distinction between plans for sole proprietorships and partnerships and those for corporations, the rules are entirely the same and the same considerations regarding plan choice and plan design apply. The one remaining distinction is that a self-employed person's contribution or benefit is based on net earnings instead of salary. This creates some complications whose solutions are beyond the scope of this chapter. See David A. Littell and Kenn Beam Tacchino, *Planning for Retirement Needs*, 9th edition (Bryn Mawr, PA: The American College Press, 2007) pp. 3.15–3.17.

7

Estate Planning

Ted Kurlowicz
Constance J. Fontaine
C. Bruce Worsham

Learning Objectives

An understanding of the material in this chapter should enable you to

7-1. Describe both the narrow view and the broader view of estate planning, and explain why the client needs to answer the who, how, and when questions.

7-2. Describe several different types of property interests.

7-3. Explain the significance of wills, trusts, durable powers of attorney, and advance medical directives in developing a cohesive estate plan.

7-4. Explain why knowledge of how property is transferred at death is necessary to plan an estate.

7-5. Describe the various federal and state taxes imposed on transfers of wealth.

7-6. Describe several planning techniques for preserving a client's wealth.

Chapter Outline

THE GOALS OF ESTATE PLANNING 7.2
STARTING THE PROCESS 7.3
TYPES OF PROPERTY INTEREST 7.5
    Individual Ownership of Property 7.5
    Joint Concurrent Ownership of Property 7.6
    Other Property Rights 7.8
ESTATE PLANNING DOCUMENTS 7.9
    Wills 7.10
    Trusts 7.11
    Durable Powers of Attorney 7.13
    Advance Medical Directives 7.15
TRANSFERS AT DEATH 7.16

The Probate Estate 7.16
The Nonprobate Estate 7.17
TAXES IMPOSED ON TRANSFERS OF WEALTH 7.19
Federal Transfer Taxes 7.19
State Death Taxes 7.29
PRESERVING THE CLIENT'S WEALTH 7.31
The Advantages of Lifetime Gifts 7.31
Federal Estate Tax Planning 7.35
Life Insurance in the Estate and/or Financial Plan 7.42
THE FINAL WORD 7.45
CHAPTER SUMMARY 7.45
CHAPTER REVIEW 7.48

This chapter starts with a brief discussion of the goals of estate planning and then focuses on the client's need to answer who, how, and when questions. Next, the chapter examines several types of property interests before discussing four basic estate planning documents. The means through which property is transferred at death is then reviewed, along with the kinds of taxes imposed on wealth transfers. Finally, the chapter concludes with several planning techniques for preserving a client's wealth.

THE GOALS OF ESTATE PLANNING

Planning the client's estate is an essential step in the ongoing process of life-cycle financial planning. The narrow view of estate planning is that the process merely involves the conservation and distribution of a client's estate. The broader view of estate planning, however, is that it is an integral part of financial planning, and the role of the financial advisor is to maximize the distributable wealth of the client and transfer that wealth to the client's beneficiaries in an appropriate fashion. Following this broader view, the estate plan should reflect life-cycle financial planning strategies that lead to increases in the client's distributable wealth, in addition to planning for the disposition of such wealth. Such an estate plan is not independent from a comprehensive financial plan and must also take into consideration the other major planning areas (that is, insurance planning, employee benefits planning, investment planning, income tax planning, and retirement planning) that make up a comprehensive plan.

Because the other major planning areas in a comprehensive financial plan are thoroughly covered in other chapters, the discussion in this chapter will follow the narrow view and focus on planning for the conservation and distribution of a client's estate. Nonetheless, it is essential for the financial advisor to bear in mind that a client's estate plan typically is broader because it is an integral part of a comprehensive financial plan for the client.

Selecting the appropriate alternatives in estate planning involves answering the "who," "how," and "when" questions. The client must determine who will be the recipients of his or her property. The "who" question is generally the easiest for the client to answer and will often be determined without significant professional advice.

The client must also determine how his or her beneficiaries will receive the property. For example, the property can be distributed outright to the beneficiaries. Alternatively, the property could be left to the beneficiaries in trust with various restrictions on their enjoyment rights. Or, beneficiaries could receive a partial interest in property. One example of a partial interest is a life estate.

The client generally can only answer the "how" question with significant professional advice. The financial advisor should be able to determine the client's goals and design a transfer mechanism that both meets the goals and complies with state property law.

The transfer taxes imposed on a specific transfer of property often depend on the form of the property transfer. Planning for the resolution of the "how" question will often focus on the minimization of these transfer taxes within the framework of the client's goals.

Finally, it must be determined "when" a client's estate will be distributed. Typically, distributions will not be made from the client's property until his or her death. However, it may be appropriate to transfer specific items of a client's wealth during his or her lifetime. The reasons for lifetime gifts are numerous, but the primary estate planning purpose of lifetime giving is the reduction of the client's estate tax base. Systematic, planned lifetime giving is often recommended for wealthy clients to reduce the amount of death taxes payable on testamentary dispositions.

Three Primary Questions in Estate Planning

- Who should receive the client's property?
- How should beneficiaries receive the property?
- When should beneficiaries receive the property?

STARTING THE PROCESS

The estate planning process (a subset of the financial planning process) begins early in the client's financial life cycle with the financial advisor helping the client establish his or her goals and gathering relevant data from the client. Data gathering is usually accomplished by interviewing the client and completing a fact finder. Although the estate plan should be an integral part of the client's comprehensive financial plan, estate planning concerns generally gain prominence later in the client's financial life cycle. Other than having a simple will to direct the disposition of assets, the client typically is well on the way toward reaching his or her wealth accumulation and retirement planning goals before estate planning becomes paramount. Nonetheless, as part of the financial planning process, the financial advisor needs to gather data early in the client's financial life cycle in order to help the client determine appropriate responses to the "who," "how," and "when" questions and to ensure that both the advisor and the client have a full understanding of the client's asset inventory as revealed on the completed fact finder form. An accurate asset inventory will indicate the composition and magnitude of the client's assets available for distribution. This data will help the client and advisor determine whether the assets are in the appropriate form for distribution and whether their total value is adequate to provide the desired distributions to the client's beneficiaries. Planning to convert the assets into the appropriate form and/or to accumulate additional wealth could follow.

After the client's goals have been established and data gathered, the financial advisor analyzes the data and develops a dispositive plan to distribute the client's assets. In other words, once the client answers the "who" questions, the advisor is then in a position to assist the client by developing a dispositive plan that answers the how and when questions. In many cases, answering the who question is fairly easy for the client. For example, a married individual may want to leave all of his or her wealth to a surviving spouse. In other cases, however, the "who" decision is more difficult and will require some soul-searching by the client. The advisor should be aware that the client may not be able to answer the "who" question immediately. For example, the client may want to disinherit some children or to ensure that children from a prior marriage are provided for.

Once having determined who should receive the property, the client, with the aid of the advisor, must determine both how and when the property will be distributed. In doing this, both the client and the advisor should be aware that some beneficiaries may not have the acumen to handle outright distributions of property. Moreover, the client may wish to restrict the ultimate right of some beneficiaries to dispose of any property they receive from the client. This is why the advisor needs to make the client aware of the alternative forms of property transfers and the benefits and risks associated with each. This will assist the client in determining how and when his or her property should be distributed and will permit the advisor to draft a more complete estate plan to recommend to the client.

The interview as a form of data gathering is often an uncomfortable event for the client. Many clients feel uneasy talking about issues associated with their death and personal family matters. Moreover, it is not unusual for a client to modify his or her initial goals during the estate planning process. The alternative distribution choices discussed with the advisor will often raise issues that the client had failed to contemplate initially. It may also be necessary to interview spouses separately if an estate plan is being drawn up for a marital unit. This is particularly true if the goals of the spouses are not congruent. Nonetheless, a thorough interview with appropriate follow-up will result in the greatest probability that the financial advisor will receive an accurate picture of the client's goals and enable the advisor to design a plan that will satisfy the client.

TYPES OF PROPERTY INTEREST

The asset inventory of a client as indicated in his or her completed fact-finder form may or may not provide a complete financial picture for the advisor. The manner in which the client owns the property may also be a factor. It is important for the advisor to determine the form of property ownership and inquire about any additional property rights held by the client that are not indicated on the asset inventory form. Some forms of property ownership provide for less than full use and enjoyment and may have been ignored by the client in completing the fact finder. Knowledge of the various forms of property ownership is essential for the advisor if he or she wants to determine all of the possible property rights that a client can hold and the possible types of dispositions that a client can make to beneficiaries.

Individual Ownership of Property

Fee Simple Estate

fee simple estate

The most complete interest in property is a *fee simple estate* (outright ownership of property). The individual who holds such an unlimited interest in property owns all the rights associated with the property, including the current possessory rights and the ability to transfer the property at any point during his or her lifetime or at death. In planning a client's estate, property that is held outright is an obvious asset to be considered in the dispositive scheme. If the estate being planned is that of a married couple, it is possible that either spouse might own substantial property individually.

Life Estate

The life estate is a common form of property ownership and provides the life tenant with the right to possess and enjoy the property for a time period measured by the life of an individual (typically the life tenant). The life estate gives the life tenant the absolute right to possess, enjoy, and receive current income from the property until the life estate terminates.

Term Interest

A term interest provides the current tenant with the right to possess, enjoy, and receive income from the property during a specified term. The interest of the current tenant terminates at the end of the specified term.

Future Interest

A future interest in property is the current right to future enjoyment of the property. A future interest in property could either be vested or contingent on the occurrence of some future event. The future interest holder has no immediate right to use and enjoy the property. One type of future interest is a remainder interest, which is an interest that takes effect immediately on the expiration of another interest in the same property. For example, a remainder interest might take effect on the termination of a life estate or a term interest. A remainder interest is often held by one individual, the remainderperson, on property contained in a trust that currently benefits another individual—for example, a life income beneficiary.

Another type of future interest is a reversionary interest. The reversionary interest occurs when the current property owner transfers current possessory rights to another. The reversionary interest gives the transferor the right to the return of the property at the end of the possessory term of the transferee. For example, a parent could create a trust for a child for a term of years and retain a reversionary interest in the trust property following the child's interest.

Joint Concurrent Ownership of Property

Current possessory rights to property may be held by more than one individual. Such a partial current interest in property is often generically referred to as joint ownership of property.

Tenancy in Common

Two or more individuals may hold current possessory rights to property without survivorship rights. Such individuals, known as tenants in common, each hold an undivided interest in the property and may transfer their interest during their lifetime or at their death. Both related and unrelated individuals may hold property by tenancy in common.

Joint Tenancy with Right of Survivorship

Two or more individuals may hold property jointly with their survivors ultimately receiving the entire interest in the property. Both related and unrelated individuals may hold property jointly with rights of survivorship. Because this property interest transfers automatically at the death of a joint tenant to his or her surviving tenants, the property is not subject to disposition by a joint tenant at his or her death. Usually, a joint tenant may transfer his or her interest during life without the consent of the other joint tenants. Such a transfer will generally sever the joint tenancy and destroy the survivorship rights of the joint tenants.

Tenancy by the Entirety

A tenancy by the entirety is a property interest restricted solely to spouses. It is joint ownership of the property by the spouses with rights of survivorship. A tenancy by the entirety creates a unique situation with respect to disposition of the property. Property is transferred automatically to the surviving spouse at the death of his or her spouse. Thus, the property is not subject to disposition by will of the deceased spouse. In addition, the property cannot be transferred during the lifetime of the spouses unless both tenants consent. Tenancy by the entirety is severed automatically upon divorce. A financial advisor must know the laws within his or her state jurisdiction with respect to joint property since property held jointly by spouses may or may not be presumed to be held with such rights of survivorship.

Community Property

Nine states—Arizona, California, Idaho, Louisiana, Nevada, New Mexico, Texas, Washington, and Wisconsin—have some form of community-property law with respect to spousal property. Property in such states is treated as either separate or community property. Generally speaking, property acquired during marriage is treated as community property and is equally owned by the spouses. Although community property is not technically jointly held, the law limits the ability of each spouse to transfer community property to individuals other than his or her spouse. In addition to the above mentioned nine community-property states, Alaska allows a statutory election for certain property to be treated as community property.

Types of Property Interest

• Individual ownership of property
    Fee simple estate
    Life estate
    Term Interest
    Future Interest
• Joint concurrent ownership of property
    Tenancy in common
    Joint tenancy with right of survivorship
    Tenancy by the entirety
    Community property

Other Property Rights

Other property interests may be held by a client and used as a vehicle for the transfer of the client's wealth. These other rights generally provide varying restrictions on the ability of the holder to enjoy or transfer the property. These forms of property ownership should be used when the restrictions are appropriate for the goals and objectives of the client.

Beneficial Interests

Certain property interests may provide one individual with a beneficial interest in property, such as the right to current income or principal distributions. An example of a beneficial interest is the interest owned by the beneficiary of a trust. The trust is created by a grantor who transfers title to the trust property to a trustee. The trustee's function is to hold legal title to and administer the trust property for the benefit of the beneficiary. The trustee's ability to make distributions to the beneficiary is determined by the terms of the trust. The trustee may be required to make specific distributions or may be given broad discretion as to the size and/or timing of distributions and to the identity of the beneficiaries. Thus, the trustee could possibly be left with substantial dispositive decisions. Trust beneficiaries themselves are generally limited in their ability to transfer their interests until trust distributions are actually received.

Powers

Certain powers to make property decisions may be held by (or transferred by) the client.

Power of Appointment. A *power of appointment* provides the holder of the power with the ability to transfer the property subject to the power. The holder may have a broad power to transfer the property to virtually any recipient. This is known as a *general power of appointment.* Or the holder may have a *special power of appointment*, which typically provides the holder with a limited class of potential recipients of the property. Any powers of appointment held by a client should be considered in his or her dispositive plans. In addition, a client may wish to grant a power of appointment to another, thereby delegating the ability to transfer his or her property.

power of appointment

general power of appointment
special power of appointment

Power of Attorney. Another power that can be held or granted by a client is a *power of attorney.* A power of attorney gives the holder of the power (the attorney-in-fact) the ability to stand in the place of or represent the grantor of the power (the principal) in various transactions. Among the possible transactions is the ability of the attorney-in-fact to transfer property for the principal. The advantages of using a power of attorney will be discussed later in this chapter.

power of attorney

> **Other Property Rights**
>
> - Beneficial interests
> - Powers
>   Power of appointment
>   General power of appointment
>   Special power of appointment
>   Power of attorney

ESTATE PLANNING DOCUMENTS

An estate plan (a subset of a comprehensive financial plan) is a roadmap that directs how a client's wealth will be assembled and disposed of during the client's life and/or at his or her death. The estate plan itself is useless unless the documents of the plan have been drafted appropriately. The documents must be drafted carefully to avoid hidden traps and to provide direction to the appropriate personal representatives, *fiduciaries*, and beneficiaries of the client. These directions must be drafted according to the principles of state law and should unambiguously state the intent of the client. Because these documents necessarily involve compliance with state law, they should be prepared by an attorney who specializes in estate planning in the local jurisdiction.

fiduciaries

Wills

Despite the importance of a will in a client's estate plan, it is estimated that seven out of ten Americans die without a valid will. Unfortunately, these individuals have left the disposition of their estates to the provisions of state *intestacy* law. In addition, the estates of these individuals will be handled by a court-appointed administrator. In many cases, the estate will be subject to unnecessary taxes and administration expenses. In any event, a valid will is necessary for the implementation of a cohesive estate plan, whether that plan is the result of single purpose, multiple purpose, or comprehensive financial planning.

intestacy

Requirements for a Valid Will

Although the requirements for wills are provided by the laws of the various states, several items are universal. With some minor exceptions for rare circumstances, the following are required for a valid will:

- The will must be in writing.
- The testator, or creator of the will, must sign the will at the end of the document, usually in the presence of witnesses.
- A number of witnesses (generally two or three) must sign the will after the testator's signature. The witnesses are attesting that the signature of the testator is in fact his or her signature.

What Can a Valid Will Accomplish?

The client's will is the centerpiece of the estate plan. Although its primary function is to direct the disposition of the client's wealth, it serves other purposes as well. A properly drafted will can accomplish the following objectives:

probate

- Direct the disposition of the client's *probate* assets.
- Nominate the personal representative of the testator, known as the executor, who will handle the administration of the client's estate.
- Nominate the guardians of any minor children of the testator.
- Create testamentary trusts that will take effect at the testator's death to hold the property of the testator for the benefit of named beneficiaries.
- Name the trustee of any trust created under the will.

- Provide directions to the executor and/or trustees named in the will indicating how these fiduciaries will manage assets contained in the estate or testamentary trust. (The directions could be quite specific or provide broad powers to the fiduciaries.)
- Provide directions for payment of the estate's taxes and expenses. (Care should be taken in naming the components of the estate that will be responsible for taxes and expenses. Incorrect designation of the component obligated to pay such expenses could result in increased death taxes or inappropriately diminished shares of specific beneficiaries.)
- Establish the compensation of executors and/or trustees named in the will.

Trusts

grantor

A trust is a relationship (generally in the form of a written document) that divides the ownership of property. Legal title to the trust is held by one party, known as a trustee. The beneficial or equitable interest in the trust property is owned by the beneficiaries of the trust. The trustee has the duty to manage the trust property provided by the *grantor* of the trust for the benefit of the beneficiaries. The trust is used to provide for beneficiaries when, for one reason or another, they are unable to administer the trust assets for themselves. For example, a trust may be created to provide for minor beneficiaries. Minor beneficiaries are incapable under state law of holding property in their own name and perhaps lack the necessary experience and financial acumen to manage the trust property. The trust is an excellent tool for handling and/or consolidating accumulations of wealth.

The trustee manages the trust property under the terms of the trust. The trust terms are the directions and intentions of the grantor with respect to the management of the trust. For example, there may be directions with respect to the investment of trust assets. More importantly, there are directions with respect to providing for the beneficiaries of the trust. The trust terms may be restrictive and provide the trustee with very little discretion. For example, the terms may provide for specified distributions of income and/or principal to designated beneficiaries at various points in time. Or, the trustee may be provided with "sprinkle" powers, permitting the trustee to determine when distributions of either income or principal are appropriate for the various beneficiaries. The trustee has the legal obligation to manage the trust prudently and, to the extent the trustee has discretionary powers, to act impartially with respect to the beneficiaries.

> **FOCUS ON ETHICS**
> **Trusts, "Don't Trusts," and Loss of Trust**
>
> Financial planning often includes the use of trusts to save taxes. An equally important goal is to control wealth distribution. Because of the desire of clients to retain control, even from the grave, trusts might more appropriately be called "don't trusts."
>
> Estate planning is fraught with moral and ethical pitfalls. For example, a divorced and remarried person may elect to leave his or her entire estate to the second spouse with no provision for the children of the first marriage. Another example is a client who, anticipating an irrevocable life insurance trust, applies for coverage before establishing the trust. Informed that this premature application invalidates gift tax advantages of the trust, the client may want to redate legal documents or simply claim the tax benefit anyway, hoping never to be audited. Financial advisors must not succumb to this pressure.
>
> To decline business because of moral, ethical, or legal objections may be financially painful in the short run. However, in the long run, the financial advisor with an unquestioned reputation attracts more and higher quality business. That same advisor also has a clear conscience and the knowledge that the likelihood of legal, ethical, and malpractice problems is dramatically reduced.

Because the trust terms describe the intentions of the grantor, a trust should be drafted carefully under the direction of an attorney who specializes in such matters. In addition, the grantor should select the trustee, whether a private individual or a corporate trustee, with great care.

Living (Inter Vivos) Trust

living trust

A trust that is created during the lifetime of a grantor is called a *living trust* or, using the Latin, an *inter vivos* trust. It could be created for several reasons. The trust could hold property and operate prior to the death of the grantor. Or, it could be created during the lifetime of the grantor simply to receive assets at the grantor's death. Such a trust is known as a *pour-over trust*.

pour-over-trust

revocable trust

A trust could be either revocable or irrevocable. A *revocable trust* is created when a grantor transfers property to a trust but reserves the power to alter or revoke the agreement. Because a revocable trust is an incomplete transfer, the creation of a revocable trust has no effect on a client's income, gift, or estate tax situation. A revocable trust gives a grantor the ability to observe the management of the trust assets without relinquishing ultimate control of the assets. Thus, the grantor can reclaim the trust assets at any time. A revocable trust becomes irrevocable only when the grantor modifies the trust to become irrevocable or dies and, therefore, is no longer able to modify the trust.

The revocable trust has gained popularity in recent times as an estate plan in itself. This occurs when it is drafted to provide the dispositive directions normally contained in a client's will. The client then transfers all appropriate assets to the trustee to be retitled in the trustee's name. At the grantor's death, the trust becomes irrevocable and all property contained in the trust is managed or disposed of under the terms of the trust. The revocable trust has become popular as an estate plan because property disposed of by a revocable trust avoids the publicity, delay, and some expenses associated with the probate process.

irrevocable trust

A living trust can also be designated as irrevocable by the grantor. Because a transfer to an *irrevocable trust* is a completed gift, it will affect the grantor's income, gift, and/or estate tax situation. A properly designed irrevocable trust can receive property from the grantor that avoids inclusion in the grantor's estate at his or her death. In addition, funds placed in an irrevocable trust become the property of its trustee and are exempt from the claims of the grantor's creditors. The irrevocable trust is an effective estate and financial planning tool for older grantors who face substantial estate tax burdens.

Testamentary Trust

testamentary trust
testator

A *testamentary trust* is created under the will of a *testator*. Because the will can be changed as long as the testator retains legal capacity, the testamentary trust is never irrevocable until the client's death (or permanent legal disability). A testamentary trust does not receive property until a client dies and the proceeds are transferred to the trust by the executor. Since the trust is contained in the client's will, it is subject to probate. In a fairly simple estate plan, testamentary trusts are often drafted to provide for the testator's children should the spouses die in a common disaster. In a more complex estate plan, testamentary trusts are often the vehicles for the A or marital trust and B or family trust described later in this chapter.

Durable Powers of Attorney

attorney-in-fact

A power of attorney is a written document that enables the client, known as the principal, to designate an agent, known as the *attorney-in-fact*, to act on the client's behalf. The agent has the power to act on behalf of the client only with respect to powers specifically enumerated in the document.

conventional power of attorney

Under a general or *conventional power of attorney*, the client authorizes the agent to act on his or her behalf. The client may choose anyone to act as the agent but most often selects a trusted relative or friend. The power may be quite limited, perhaps permitting the agent only to make deposits to the client's bank account. Or the power can be broad, authorizing the agent to engage in nearly any transaction that the client could perform. However, no matter how limited or broad the power, a conventional power becomes inoperative if the client is incapacitated. In short, it becomes useless at the time it is needed most.

durable power of attorney

Enter the *durable power of attorney.* Unlike a conventional power, a durable power of attorney remains valid and operative despite any subsequent incapacity of the client. A durable power belongs with a client's will as an integral part of his or her estate or comprehensive financial plan.

A durable power of attorney takes effect immediately upon execution—though it may not be needed until much later, if ever. Some clients, however, are reluctant to grant another person wide powers to act when they themselves are still mentally and physically capable. Such clients might prefer a *springing durable power of attorney.* Recognized in several jurisdictions, a springing power lies dormant and ineffective until it is needed. A determination that the client has become incapacitated would trigger the springing power.

springing durable power of attorney

Since family members may dispute whether a disability has properly triggered the springing power, clear language is necessary in the instrument defining incapacity and in the mechanism for determining whether it has occurred.

Because a power of attorney provides the agent with the potential to abuse the privileges granted by the document, these documents are construed very narrowly in transactions with third parties. The agent must look to the legal document for scope of authority and may not go beyond, or deviate from, the power of attorney. For the sake of expediency, an attorney drafting a power of attorney often will use standard powers, instead of taking the time to draft the document for the specific powers needed. But drafting the document so that the powers granted the agent are very specific helps persuade third parties to enter into transactions with the agent. Third parties typically are not eager to assume risks by implying powers that are not specifically expressed in the document. Therefore, the more specific the language, the more likely it is that third parties will honor the power.

Many potential uses for a durable power of attorney arise during estate or financial planning. However, while the durable power can be a useful management arrangement during a person's lifetime, it constitutes only one part of an estate or comprehensive financial plan and cannot serve as the primary planning vehicle. In addition, a durable power may be difficult to use if it is dated long before it is operative. Banks, brokers, and health care personnel may be reluctant to accept a document executed years ago that grants broad powers to an agent.

As indicated above, a power of attorney should be drafted prudently for the specific circumstances of the client. Care should be taken as to the choice of the agent and the powers granted to him or her. And like other estate and financial planning documents, it should be reviewed and updated periodically.

The advantages of a durable power of attorney include the following:

- An older client can execute a durable power of attorney and avoid the necessity of having a guardian or a conservator appointed should the client lose legal capacity.
- The agent can be given the power to manage the client's assets should the client suffer a permanent or temporary loss of legal capacity. This is particularly important for owners of a closely held business.
- The durable power can replace or complement a revocable trust. The agent can manage a client's assets subsequent to the client's legal disability and, if empowered, continue the client's dispositive scheme. For example, the agent could continue to make annual gifts or charitable contributions after the client's legal disability but prior to the client's death.
- Most states allow a durable power of attorney for health care in which the agent can make medical care decisions on behalf of the client.

Advance Medical Directives

durable power of attorney for health care
living will

Either a *durable power of attorney for health care* or a *living will* is referred to as an advance medical directive. These documents are receiving more attention, because advances in medical technology that prolong life have increased fears of lengthy artificial life support and family financial disaster. Modern medicine can keep a person alive by artificial mechanisms even though the individual is unconscious and essentially nonfunctional. Life-sustaining procedures are used in cases of accident or terminal illness where death is imminent and recovery highly improbable. Advance medical directives have evolved in response to these situations. Preparing advance directives lets the physician and other health care providers know the kind of medical care a client wants, or does not want, if he or she becomes incapacitated. Usually, directives will go into effect only in the event that the client cannot make and communicate his or her own health care decisions.

Estate Planning Documents
• Wills
• Trusts
• Durable powers of attorney
• Advance medical directives

By executing a durable power of attorney for health care, clients are giving authority to others to carry out their health care instructions. A durable power of attorney for health care is a signed and witnessed legal document that names the person the client wishes to make medical decisions about his or her care. Other than the person named, it relieves family and friends of the responsibility for making decisions regarding life-prolonging actions. The other type of advance medical directive is a living will. It describes the types of medical treatment a client wishes to receive and also the types of medical treatment the client does not want to receive. The existence of a living will lets others know of the client's medical wishes, should he or she become terminally ill and lie in a persistent vegetative state, unable to communicate. Although a living will makes the client's medical wishes known, it does not guarantee that those wishes will be followed. Someone still has to make the necessary medical decisions regarding whether or not to continue treatment. That someone typically is the person named in a durable power of attorney for health care to carry out the client's medical wishes as expressed in a living will. Together, these two types of advance medical directives are an important part of any estate or comprehensive financial plan.

TRANSFERS AT DEATH

Knowledge of how property is transferred at death under the laws of the jurisdictional state is necessary to plan an estate. A common misconception is that the client's will determines the distribution of the estate at his or her death. Under most circumstances, the will actually affects the distribution of only a small portion of the client's property. This fact does not minimize the importance of a carefully drafted will, but merely emphasizes the importance of coordinating all of the client's testamentary transfers, including those transfers affected by his or her will, in the estate and financial planning process.

The Probate Estate

Transfers through Will Provisions

Many misconceptions exist with respect to the various goals associated with the estate and financial planning process. Popular opinion is that a primary goal of the process is to reduce the size of the probate estate. The probate estate includes all assets passing by will or intestacy. Probate property is owned outright by the deceased and is not transferred by operation of law or contract, as discussed later. For married individuals, probate property is generally limited to the individually owned property of a deceased spouse. Thus, the probate estate is often minimized by the usual form of property ownership between spouses—tenancy by the entirety.

Probate (which technically means the process of proving the validity of the will) begins when the original will is deposited in the court with jurisdiction over the deceased's estate. The probate court oversees matters involving the settlement of the estate, distribution of probate property, appointment and supervision of fiduciaries, and disputes concerning the deceased's will. If a valid will exists, the probate court will ensure that the probate property is distributed according to the terms of the will after all estate settlement costs are paid. Although the court has jurisdiction solely over probate property, the state and federal taxing authorities may have the statutory authority to collect any unpaid taxes from nonprobate property if probate assets are insufficient.

Transfers by Intestacy

intestate succession
intestate laws

If a client dies without a valid will, all probate property passes under the laws of *intestate succession* of the jurisdiction state. The *intestate laws* are deemed to replace the intent of the deceased client in the distribution of his or her probate property. The default mechanism provided by the intestate laws may be of little significance since the probate assets in the typical estate are not substantial.

States vary with respect to intestate laws. Distribution under these laws depends on which relatives survive a deceased client. A deceased client's spouse receives primary consideration and will receive the entire probate estate if the deceased is not also survived by children or parents. If the deceased client is survived by both a spouse and children, the surviving spouse and children will generally each receive 50 percent of the estate. The parents of a deceased client with a surviving spouse will generally get a share only if the deceased client is not also survived by children. If the client is not survived by a spouse, children, or parents, then the next closest surviving relatives will inherit.

State intestacy laws also apply to a transfer under a will or contract that is deemed invalid.

The Nonprobate Estate

Transfers by Operation of Law

The nature of certain ownership interests in property causes the property to pass automatically at the death of a client. Such property is not subject to the laws of probate and does not pass under the will or intestacy rules. The most significant example of property that is transferred by operation of law is property held jointly with rights of survivorship. The survivorship provisions cause such property to automatically pass to the surviving joint tenant(s). As discussed earlier, property held as tenants by the entirety is also an example of an operation-of-law transfer. Many married clients own property acquired during their marriage in this fashion. For example, the family home, automobile, and significant investments are often held jointly by spouses. At the death of one spouse, the property automatically passes to the surviving spouse outside the jurisdiction of the probate court.

As previously noted, living trusts can be effective tools in estate and financial planning. Recall that only irrevocable living trusts have an effect on the grantor's income, gift and/or estate tax situation. However, both revocable and irrevocable living trusts are methods of transferring property by operation of law, thus avoiding some of the expense, publicity, and delay of probate.

In addition, it is quite common for elderly parents to reduce their probate estates by creating operation-of-law transfers to their descendants. One such transfer is the establishment of joint bank and/or securities accounts with their children and/or grandchildren with survivorship rights. A similar vehicle for transfer by operation of law is the Totten trust. A Totten trust occurs when an individual client (generally a parent or grandparent) opens up a bank account in trust for a named beneficiary (generally a child or grandchild). At the death of the client, the account will pass automatically by operation of law to the named beneficiary. It should be noted that these kinds of transactions are incomplete gifts and, while effective in reducing probate, have no impact on the taxable estate.

Transfers by Operation of Contract

Another form of nonprobate transfer is transfer by contract. The most common form of transfer by contract involves the transfer of life insurance or employee benefits to a named beneficiary. For example, life insurance policy death benefits are distributed to the policy's designated beneficiary. The same result occurs if an employee has named beneficiaries to receive various employment benefits, such as death benefits from a retirement plan. These benefits pass by operation of contract and will not become part of a deceased client's probate estate unless they are made payable to the estate's executor (or the estate) in lieu of named beneficiaries.

> **Transfers at Death**
>
> Probate estate:
> - Fee simple ownership
> - Nonterminating ownership interests (certain life estates, term interests, future interests, beneficial interests, and powers that do not terminate at the client's death)
> - Tenancy in common
>
> Nonprobate estate:
> - Transfers by operation of law
>   - Joint tenancy with right of survivorship
>   - Tenancy by the entirety
>   - Community property (in community property states)
>   - Living trusts
>   - Totten trusts
> - Transfers by operation of contract
>   - Life insurance proceeds payable to a named beneficiary (rather than to the client's estate or executor)
>   - Retirement plan death benefits payable to a named beneficiary
>   - Payable at death investment accounts

TAXES IMPOSED ON TRANSFERS OF WEALTH

The most significant costs of transferring wealth are the various transfer taxes imposed at the federal and state levels. The tax rates applicable to affected transfers can be quite high. The relatively large impact of these transfer taxes makes tax reduction a primary focus in the estate and financial plan with respect to the conservation of a client's wealth. By optimizing the solutions to the "who," "how," and "when" questions, the client may be able to implement a plan that will achieve his or her stated goals and hold the reduction in the size of his or her estate by transfer taxes to a minimum. The primary focus of this discussion will be the federal gift and estate transfer taxes, but the federal generation-skipping transfer tax (GSTT) and state death taxes will also be discussed.

Federal Transfer Taxes

The federal transfer tax system consists of three components—gift taxation, estate taxation, and generation-skipping taxation. Two of these components, the gift tax and the estate tax, are unified in that they share one progressive set of tax rates. Nonetheless, there are several differences between them that make lifetime gifts attractive.

Gift taxes are imposed only if transfers exceed various exemptions, exclusions, deductions, and credits. The initial gifts made by a client will be exempt from taxation due to the exclusions and/or credits. Once gift taxes become payable, they are imposed by a progressive tax rate structure, with marginal rates ranging from 41 to 45 percent for 2008 and 2009 (see table 7-1). Paying gift taxes at the lower bracket rates is advantageous because the estate tax return is cumulative, and a deceased client's estate is subject to the highest bracket rate for the size of the gross estate (at the time of death) plus the amount of adjusted taxable gifts made (after 1976) while the client was alive (see chart 7-1, step 3(10): This includes taxable gifts made after 1976 that are not includible in the deceased's gross estate. The term taxable in this context means either that gift tax liability occurred or that the applicable exclusion amount applied to the gift).

As indicated above, even though the gift tax and the estate tax share one progressive set of tax rates, the estate tax is quite different from the gift tax in several regards. First, there is no exclusion for the estate tax return that is analogous to the gift tax annual exclusion. Second, all appreciation on property included in the gross estate is subject to estate tax. Third, estate taxes are paid at the highest marginal rate imposed on the deceased client's transfers due to the nature of the estate tax calculation. Fourth, the estate tax is a tax-inclusive system—that is, estate taxes are imposed on all property included in the gross estate, including the estate assets used to pay the estate taxes. Fifth, the estate tax is scheduled to be repealed (for one year only) in 2010, while the gift tax is not. Finally, the estate tax applicable exclusion amount (which corresponds to an applicable credit amount) is scheduled to increase in 2009 (see table 7-2 for the 2009 increase) prior to 2010, while the gift tax applicable exclusion amount is frozen at $1 million.

TABLE 7-1
Federal Gift and Estate Tax Rate Schedule: 2008 through 2009

If the amount with respect to which the tentative tax is to be computed is...	The tentative tax is...
Not over $10,000	18% of such amount
Over $10,000 but not over $20,000	$1,800, plus 20% of excess of such amount over $10,000
Over $20,000 but not over $40,000	$3,800, plus 22% of excess of such amount over $20,000
Over $40,000 but not over $60,000	$8,200, plus 24% of excess of such amount over $40,000
Over $60,000 but not over $80,000	$13,000, plus 26% of excess of such amount over $60,000
Over $80,000 but not over $100,000	$18,200, plus 28% of excess of such amount over $80,000
Over $100,000 but not over $150,000	$23,800, plus 30% of excess of such amount over $100,000
Over $150,000 but not over $250,000	$38,800, plus 32% of excess of such amount over $150,000
Over $250,000 but not over $500,000	$70,800, plus 34% of excess of such amount over $250,000
Over $500,000 but not over $750,000	$155,800, plus 37% of excess of such amount over $500,000
Over $750,000 but not over $1,000,000	$248,300, plus 39% of excess of such amount over $750,000
Over $1,000,000 but not over $1,250,000	$345,800, plus 41% of excess of such amount over $1,000,000
Over $1,250,000 but not over $1,500,000	$448,300, plus 43% of excess of such amount over $1,250,000
Over $1,500,000	$555,800, plus 45% of excess of such amount over $1,500,000

CHART 7-1
Illustrative Chart Showing the Steps for Computing Federal Estate Tax
(Actual Computations are Beyond the Scope of This Book)

	STEP 1	(1)	Gross estate		$_____
minus					
		(2)	Funeral and administration expenses (estimated as _____% of _____)	$_____	
		(3)	Debts and taxes	_____	
		(4)	Losses	_____	(−) _____
equals					
	STEP 2	(5)	Adjusted gross estate		$_____
minus					
		(6)	Marital deduction	$_____	
		(7)	Charitable deduction	_____	
		(8)	State death tax deduction[1]	_____	(−) _____
equals					
	STEP 3	(9)	Taxable estate		$_____
plus					
		(10)	Adjusted taxable gifts (taxable portion of post-1976 lifetime taxable transfers not included in gross estate)		+ _____
equals					
		(11)	Tentative tax base (total of taxable estate and adjusted taxable gifts)		$_____
compute					
		(12)	Tentative tax (see table 7-1)		$_____
minus					
		(13)	Gift taxes payable on post-1976 gifts[2]		(−) _____
equals					
	STEP 4	(14)	Estate tax payable before credits		$_____
minus					
		(15)	Tax credits		
			(a) Applicable credit amount	$_____	
			(b) Allowable state death tax credit[3]	_____	
			(c) Credit for foreign death taxes[4]	_____	
			(d) Credit for gift tax for pre-1977 gifts[5]	_____	
			(e) Credit for tax on prior transfers[6]	_____	(−) _____
equals					
	STEP 5	(16)	Net federal estate tax payable		$_____

1. 2005 through 2009 (replaces Step 4(15)(b)).
2. Once the tentative tax is determined, gift taxes generated by taxable gifts made after 1976 in excess of the applicable credit amount are subtracted from it (see table 7-2 for applicable credit amounts from previous years).
3. Repealed in 2005 and replaced with a deduction in 2005 through 2009 as shown in Step 2(8).
4. This credit is not discussed in this book.
5. Credit still exists for gift taxes paid by a deceased on taxable gifts made before 1977 if the property is included in the gross estate. This credit is not discussed in this book.
6. To avoid double taxation on double transfers of property occurring within a reasonably short time period (that is, 10 years before or 2 years after the deceased's death), a credit is allowed against the federal estate tax paid by the deceased as a result of his or her inheriting property that is included in the gross estate. This credit varies from 100 percent down to 20 percent depending on the period of time before the deceased's death.

TABLE 7-2
Federal Gift and Estate Tax Credit and Exclusion Amounts Schedule

The applicable credit amount applies to both gratuitous lifetime (gift) transfers and testamentary (after-death) transfers. The credit amount is first used to offset gift taxes with any remaining credit to be applied against federal estate taxes. The following table shows the applicable credit amount and the applicable exclusion amount (that is, the value of the gross estate sheltered from taxation) for each year from 1982 through 2009.

Year	Applicable Credit Amount	Applicable Exclusion Amount (Size of Estate Sheltered)
1982	$ 62,800	$ 225,000
1983	79,300	275,000
1984	96,300	325,000
1985	121,800	400,000
1986	155,800	500,000
1987 to 1998	192,800	600,000
1998	202,050	625,000
1999	211,300	650,000
2000 and 2001	220,550	675,000
2002 and 2003	345,800*	1,000,000*
2004* and 2005	555,800	1,500,000
2006, 2007, and 2008	780,800	2,000,000
2009	1,455,800	3,500,000

* The applicable credit and exclusion amounts for gratuitous lifetime transfers (that is, gifts) are fixed at the 2002 levels of $345,800 and $1 million respectively for gifts through 2009, while for testamentary (after-death) transfers both amounts increase in step-rate fashion until they reach the 2009 levels.

The requirement to file an estate tax return has been adjusted upward to reflect increases in the applicable credit amount. Executors of estates (including lifetime adjusted taxable gifts) having a gross value that is less than the applicable exclusion amount shown in the right column above are not required to file federal estate tax returns. Only estates having values exceeding the applicable exclusion amount are potentially subject to the federal estate tax.

Certain transfers, whether made by lifetime gift or at the client's death, are subject to the generation-skipping transfer tax (GSTT). Generally, the GSTT applies to outright transfers that skip a generation in the client's family and are taxable under either the gift tax or the estate tax. Transfers subject to the GSTT are taxed at the maximum gift and estate tax rates, currently 45 percent for 2008 and 2009. The GSTT, like the estate tax, is scheduled for repeal (for one year only) in 2010.

Federal Gift Tax

The federal gift tax applies only if the following two elements are present:

- There is a completed transfer and acceptance of the property.
- The transfer of the property is for less than full and adequate consideration.

These two essential elements of a taxable gift are premised on several facts. First, only property transfers are subject to gift taxation. A transfer of services by a client is not a taxable gift. Second, all completed transfers including direct and indirect gifts of property are taxable. Finally, for transfer tax purposes, the less than full and adequate consideration requirement generally does not contain an element of intent. Therefore, it is not necessary that the grantor intends to make a gift. It is merely required that the transfer be for less than full and adequate consideration. However, such transfers between unrelated individuals in a business setting typically are treated as "bad bargains" and are not treated as taxable gift transfers.

Exempt Transfers. Certain transfers are exempt from the gift tax base by statute. First, a transfer of property pursuant to a divorce or property settlement agreement is deemed to be for full and adequate consideration under some circumstances. Second, transfers directly to the provider of education or medical services on behalf of an individual are not taxable gifts to the recipient of the services. Third, gifts that are disclaimed by the donee in a qualified disclaimer are not treated as taxable gifts. Finally, transfers of money or other property to a political organization are exempt from the gift tax if the transfer is for the use of the political organization. However, contributions to individual politicians do not come within this exemption.

Gift Tax Annual Exclusion. Much of the design and complexity involved in gift tax planning involves the gift tax annual exclusion. In 2008, qualifying gifts of up to $12,000 (indexed for inflation beginning in 1999) may be made by a donor to each of any number of donees without gift tax. This annual exclusion was instituted to eliminate the need for a taxpayer donor to keep an account of or report numerous small gifts. Moreover, the $12,000 exempt amount can be increased to $24,000 (also indexed) if the donor is married and the donor's spouse elects to split the gift with the donor. However, in the case of a split gift, the election by the donor's spouse must be made on a gift tax return for the donor filed in a timely fashion, even though the gift will be exempt from gift taxation.

To qualify for the annual exclusion, a gift must provide the donee recipient with a present interest. Outright interests or current income interests in a trust will provide the beneficiary with a present interest. Trust provisions giving beneficiaries current withdrawal powers can be used to qualify gifts to a trust for the annual exclusion, even if the trust provides for deferred benefits. Use of the gift tax annual exclusion in the estate and financial planning process is discussed later in this chapter.

Deductions from the Gift Tax Base. Two types of gifts are fully deductible from the transfer tax base. First, the marital deduction provides that unlimited qualifying transfers made by a donor to his or her spouse are fully deductible from the gift tax base. The marital deduction will prove quite useful if it is necessary to rearrange ownership of marital assets in the implementation of an estate or financial plan. As shown later in this chapter, this deduction is similar to the marital deduction used in computing the federal estate tax.

The charitable deduction provides that qualifying transfers to a legitimate charity will be deductible against the gift tax base. Thus, all qualifying transfers made to charity will avoid transfer taxation.

Applicable Credit Amount. A cumulative credit is currently available against federal gift and/or estate taxes due on taxable transfers. For 2008 and 2009, the applicable credit amount for gift tax purposes is $345,800, and it applies to both gratuitous lifetime transfers (gifts) and testamentary (after-death) transfers (see table 7-2). This credit amount is first used to offset gift taxes, with any remaining credit being applied against estate taxes.

Under the current structure of the federal gift and estate tax system, the applicable credit amount provides a dollar-for-dollar reduction in transfer taxes otherwise payable for lifetime and/or testamentary transfers. The credit amount can be used against each dollar of transfer tax until it is exhausted. The 2008 and 2009 gift tax credit amount of $345,800 shelters $1 million of taxable transfers from federal gift and/or estate taxation. Since no taxes are due in 2008 or 2009 until aggregate lifetime and/or testamentary transfers exceed $1 million, the first tax bracket applicable to a transfer that is actually subject to tax is 41 percent (see table 7-1).

Starting in 2004 (see table 7-2), the applicable credit amount used to offset estate taxes diverged from the amount being used to offset gift taxes. The gift tax credit was frozen at its 2002 amount of $345,800 through 2009, while the estate tax credit increased in step-rate fashion from its 2002 amount of $345,800 to $780,800 for 2008 and $1,455,800 for 2009. As indicated above, the applicable credit amount is first used to offset gift taxes up to $345,800. Any remaining portion of the $345,800 limit can then be applied against estate taxes. For 2008, the $435,000 excess credit amount over the $345,800 limit for gift taxes ($780,800 – $345,800) can only be applied against estate taxes. Likewise for 2009, the $1,110,000 excess credit amount over the $345,800 limit for gift taxes ($1,455,800 – $345,800) can only be applied against estate taxes.

Federal Estate Tax

Often the most difficult task in calculating the estate tax is determining the assets that are included in a deceased client's estate tax base. Some of the included assets are obvious, such as individually owned property. However, the estate tax rules often cause the inclusion of property in surprising circumstances. For example, property previously transferred by the client can be brought back to his or her estate tax base.

The Gross Estate. The starting point in the estate tax calculation is determining the property included in the gross estate (see chart 7-1, Step 1 (1)). The gross estate not only includes the property included in the client's probate estate, but it also includes property transferable at the client's death by other means. The client's gross estate includes

- property individually owned by the client at the time of death
- (some portion of) property held jointly by the client at the time of death
- the proceeds of any insurance on the client's life if either (1) incidents of ownership are held by the client within 3 years of death or (2) the proceeds are deemed payable to the estate
- pension or IRA payments left to survivors
- property subject to general powers of appointment held by the client at the time of death
- property transferred by the client during his or her lifetime if he or she retained (1) a life interest in the property, (2) a reversionary interest valued greater than 5 percent of the property at the time of death, or (3) rights to revoke the transfer at the time of death

As the list above indicates, the gross estate of the client is defined much more broadly than the probate estate, and consequently, a reduction in the size of the probate estate will often have little effect on the amount of the federal estate tax paid.

Items Deductible from the Gross Estate. Analogous to the federal gift tax rules, certain items are deductible from the gross estate to determine the adjusted gross estate for estate tax calculation purposes. First, legitimate debts of the deceased client are deductible from the gross estate if they are obligations of the gross estate. Second, reasonable funeral expenses and other death costs of the deceased client are deductible from the gross estate. Third, the costs of estate settlement, such as the executor's commission and attorney fees, are deductible to the extent such fees are reasonable.

Marital Deduction. As with the gift tax, qualifying transfers to a surviving spouse are deductible under the marital-deduction rules (see chart 7-1, Step 2 (6)). Because the marital deduction is unlimited, the usual dispositive scheme (100 percent to the surviving spouse) will result in no estate taxes for a married couple until the death of the surviving spouse. As a client's wealth increases, sophisticated planning is needed to make optimal use of the marital deduction. Planning for the marital deduction is discussed later in this chapter.

Charitable Deduction. The federal estate tax charitable deduction provides that transfers at death to qualifying charities will be fully deductible from the estate tax base (see chart 7-1, Step 2 (7)). The charitable deduction is an excellent device to reduce the gross estate of a wealthy client. As discussed later in this chapter, the transfer of a remainder interest or current term income interest to charity can substantially reduce the estate tax burden of a wealthy client without significantly disrupting his or her dispositive goals.

Applicable Exclusion Amount. The applicable exclusion amount shows the size of the gift or estate that is being sheltered by the corresponding applicable credit amount. As shown on table 7-2, the 2008 estate tax credit amount of $780,800 corresponds to a $2 million applicable exclusion amount. Likewise, the $1,455,800 estate tax credit amount for 2009 corresponds to a $3.5 million exclusion amount.

As previously indicated, the applicable credit amount for gift tax purposes is frozen at the $345,800 amount through 2009, which means that its corresponding exclusion amount also remains frozen at the $1 million level. If the applicable $345,800 credit is not exhausted by sheltering lifetime gifts, any remaining amount is available against transfers made at the client's death. The optimal use of this credit in conjunction with the marital deduction is discussed later in this chapter.

State Death Tax Credit. The state death tax credit provided a dollar-for-dollar reduction against the federal estate tax due for any state death taxes paid by the estate. However, the state death tax credit was limited, and the maximum state death tax credit available to a particular estate was set forth in a progressive credit schedule. The size of the credit against the federal estate tax was equal to the lesser of the state death tax actually paid or the maximum state death tax allowable under the progressive credit schedule. If a state's death tax was less than the maximum amount allowed as a credit against the federal estate tax, it typically was increased to equal the maximum amount. In any event, the credit for state death taxes was available only when the property subject to the state death tax was actually included in the deceased client's gross estate for federal estate tax purposes.

The passage of the Economic Growth and Tax Relief Reconciliation Act (EGTRRA) in 2001 made some significant changes to state death taxation. Under EGTRRA, the state death tax credit was reduced by 25 percent for 2002, 50 percent for 2003, and 75 percent for 2004. Beginning in 2005, the state death tax credit was fully repealed and replaced with a deduction for the actual amount of state death taxes paid. This new federal approach has encouraged states to review and modify their state death tax rules.

Generation-Skipping Transfer Tax (GSTT)

The GSTT was created (by the Tax Reform Act of 1986) to prevent the federal government from losing transfer tax revenue when clients transfer property to a generation that is more than one generation below their own generation (for example, when grandparents make gifts of property to their grandchildren). Although the GSTT is designed to prevent clients from finding a transfer tax loophole in the federal gift tax or estate tax, it is different from those taxes in many ways. The GSTT is applied at a flat rate equal to the highest current gift or estate tax rate on every taxable generation-skipping transfer. Thus, in 2008 or 2009, any taxable transfer is subject to a 45 percent rate if the GSTT applies. Moreover, if the GSTT applies, it is in addition to any gift or estate tax that also applies to the transfer. This means that in 2008 or 2009 a generation-skipping transfer could easily be subject to a tax rate of 90 percent. Obviously, planning to avoid the GSTT is of paramount importance for wealthy clients.

Federal Transfer Taxes

- Federal gift tax
- Federal estate tax
- Generation-skipping transfer tax (GSTT)

direct skip

Types of Transfers. The GSTT applies to three different types of transfers. First, the GSTT applies to a *direct skip*. A direct skip can be an outright transfer during life or at death to a skip person, an individual who is two generations or more younger than the transferor client. Or, it can be a transfer in trust for the benefit of a skip person. A transfer in trust will be treated as a direct skip if (1) the trust benefits only one skip person, (2) no portion of the trust property may be distributed to anyone else during the skip person's lifetime, and (3) the trust property will be included in the skip person's estate if he or she dies before the termination of the trust.

To be a direct skip, the transfer to the skip person must also be subject to gift or estate tax. Transfers that are not subject to gift tax because of the gift tax annual exclusion or the exemption for direct payment of medical and/or tuition expenses are not subject to the GSTT. Moreover, for all types of transfers, if the parent of the skip person is deceased at the time of the transfer, the transfer is not subject to the GSTT. In this instance, the GSTT is eliminated because the grandchild is the natural recipient of the grandparent's wealth if the grandchild's parent is deceased.

taxable termination

The second type of transfer that the GSTT applies to is a *taxable termination*. A taxable termination occurs when an interest in property held in trust for a skip person is terminated by an individual's death, lapse of time, release of a power, or otherwise and the trust property is either held for or distributed to the skip person. If a transfer subject to gift or estate tax occurs at the time of the termination, the transfer is not a taxable termination, but it could be a direct skip. Also, the transfer is not a taxable termination if a nonskip person has an interest in the trust immediately after the termination. In this case, the transfer would be a taxable distribution.

taxable distribution

The third type of transfer subject to the GSTT is a *taxable distribution*. A taxable distribution is any distribution from a trust to a skip person that is not a taxable termination or a direct skip. As indicated above, a taxable distribution can occur even if a nonskip person still holds a current beneficial interest in the trust after the trustee makes a distribution to a skip person.

Lifetime Exemption and Annual Exclusion. A lifetime exemption can protect generation-skipping transfers during life or at death from the GSTT. Thus, in 2008, individual taxpayers receive a lifetime exemption that shields $2 million in generation-skipping transfers from the GSTT. In 2009, the GSTT exemption amount increases to $3.5 million, before being repealed (for one year) in 2010. The increase in the GSTT exemption amount parallels that for the federal estate tax applicable exclusion amount as shown in table 7-2.

It is important to note that for lifetime transfers the exemption must be allocated affirmatively by the donor client to specific transfers on a timely filed gift tax return. A lifetime allocation is particularly appropriate because the exemption is leveraged. That is, the exemption will be applied to the value of the property at the time of the transfer, and any post transfer appreciation will not be subject to the GSTT and need not be sheltered by part of the exemption. Consequently, wealthy clients can make lifetime transfers of appreciating property that will eventually grow into substantial wealth at a huge total transfer tax savings. Any exemption not used at the time of the taxpayer client's death and not made by his or her executor will be allocated according to the default rules.

Similar to the gift tax annual exclusion discussed earlier in this section but with specific rules of its own, a $12,000 (as indexed for 2008) exclusion from the GSTT is available for direct skips. As previously indicated, a direct skip is either an outright gift to a skip person or certain gifts in trust providing a present interest to a skip person.

State Death Taxes

Frequently, the subject of state death taxes is overshadowed by the attention given to the federal estate tax. Although the emphasis on federal estate taxation is warranted for estates that have a value of more than the applicable exclusion amount, statistically the federal tax affects a relatively small percentage of all estates settled. On the other hand, most estates are within reach of the death taxes levied by states. Therefore, state death tax planning should not be ignored since taxable transfers for state purposes can often be avoided by simple planning that might otherwise be ineffective (and thus disregarded) for federal estate tax planning purposes. For example, many states exempt life insurance benefits paid to a named beneficiary.

State Inheritance Tax

state inheritance tax

A *state inheritance tax* is a tax imposed on a beneficiary's right to inherit property from a deceased person's estate. The tax rate is based on the amount of property received by each beneficiary and is often based on the relationship of the beneficiary to the deceased. An inheritance received by a close relative is generally subject to a lower tax rate than an inheritance received by a more distant relation. In many cases, the inheritance tax on property received by relatives outside the deceased's immediate family (surviving spouse and children) is subject to a tax that exceeds the federal state death tax credit. In many instances, the state inheritance tax could be more significant than any federal estate tax due. Despite the fact that inheritance taxes are imposed on the right to receive property, payment of these taxes is usually the responsibility of the estate.

State Estate Tax

state estate tax

A *state estate tax* is similar in nature to the federal estate tax. It differs from an inheritance tax in that an inheritance tax is imposed on a beneficiary's right to inherit, while an estate tax is imposed on a deceased person's right to transfer or pass property to beneficiaries.

Credit Estate Tax (Prior to 2005)

credit estate tax

Prior to 2005, states imposed a *credit estate tax*. This tax was referred to as a sponge, slack, or gap tax, and it supplemented a state's inheritance or estate tax. Its objective was to boost the amount of state death taxes up to the maximum amount of paid state death taxes allowed to be credited against the federal estate tax payable. Thus, if a state's death tax was less than the amount allowed as a credit against the federal estate tax payable, the credit estate tax allowed the state to pick up the difference for the state coffers, instead of that amount going to the federal government. In fact, as a credit, the amount of the credit estate tax was applied dollar-for-dollar against the federal estate tax payable, thereby reducing it. As previously noted, however, the state death tax credit was fully repealed by EGTRRA beginning in 2005 and replaced with a deduction for the actual amount of state death taxes paid. These changes to the federal rules have encouraged states to review and modify their state death tax rules. A detailed analysis of individual state rules, however, is beyond the scope of this discussion.

Types of State Death Taxes

- State inheritance tax
  - tax on the right of a beneficiary to receive estate property
- State estate tax
  - tax on the right of a deceased individual to leave property to beneficiaries
- Credit estate tax (prior to 2005)
  - tax to bring state death tax up to credit amount allowed by federal law

---

Planning for State Death Taxes

As indicated, a detailed analysis of each state's death tax rules is beyond the scope of this discussion. However, there are some peculiarities in the state death tax base that a financial advisor should be aware of in the state where his or her clients are located. First, as mentioned earlier, some portion of jointly held property is included in the client's federal estate tax base. However, there are some states that do not tax property held jointly by an individual at the time of his or her death. Therefore, without affecting federal estate taxes, an individual in one of these states can avoid state death taxes by transferring property to joint ownership prior to his or her death.

In addition, some states provide for no marital deduction for individually owned property transferred to a surviving spouse. Therefore, severing a joint ownership of property with a surviving spouse may create state death taxes even if that property is transferred to the surviving spouse in a transfer deductible for federal estate tax purposes.

Finally, life insurance owned individually by an insured at the time of his or her death is often not taxable at the state level if payable to a named beneficiary.

PRESERVING THE CLIENT'S WEALTH

There are many techniques that can be used to reduce the transfer tax burden associated with transferring a client's wealth to his or her heirs. The appropriate answer to the "who" question may be used to reduce estate taxes. For example, qualifying transfers to a surviving spouse are fully deductible from the client's gross estate. The optimal resolution of the "how" question could also reduce estate taxes. For example, transferring assets to a family trust takes advantage of the applicable credit against federal estate taxes. Finally, if the "when" question is answered appropriately, the gross estate of a client can be substantially reduced through a systematic lifetime gifting program, and substantial wealth can be transferred free of all transfer taxes.

The Advantages of Lifetime Gifts

Nontax Advantages of Lifetime Gifts

Clients give away property during their lifetime for many reasons. The nontax advantages of making lifetime gifts are as follows:

- The donor client can provide for the support, education, and welfare of the donee beneficiary.
- The donor client gets the pleasure of seeing the donee beneficiary enjoy the gift.
- The donor client avoids the publicity and administrative costs associated with a probate transfer at death.
- The donated property is protected from the claims of the donor client's creditors.

Tax Advantages of Lifetime Gifts

Although the federal gift tax and estate tax share the same set of progressive tax rates, there are some distinctions that make lifetime gifts more favorable from a tax standpoint. These tax advantages of lifetime gifts are as follows:

- The gift tax annual exclusion for gifts of $12,000 (as indexed for inflation) or less provides a complete loophole from federal transfer taxes. In 2008, any number of gifts can be made by clients ($24,000 if their spouses join with them) to reduce their transfer tax bases.
- The gift tax is imposed on the value of the gift at the time a completed transfer is made. Thus, any posttransfer appreciation in the property avoids all transfer tax.
- The gift tax payable on gifts made more than 3 years prior to the donor client's death is excluded from his or her estate tax base.
- The income produced by gifted property is shifted from the donor client to the donee beneficiary for income tax purposes. In other words, lifetime gifting may be used to move taxable income from a high-bracket donor client to a lower-bracket donee beneficiary. (This advantage is somewhat limited by special tax rules related to unearned income of children under age 19 or 24 for full-time students.)
- Unlimited qualifying transfers can be made between spouses without incurring gift taxes. Spouses can advantageously shift assets between themselves to meet the needs of the estate and financial plan of each spouse.

Opportunities Created by the Gift Tax Annual Exclusion

As discussed earlier, the annual exclusion allows a donor client to give up to $12,000 (as indexed) tax free to any number of donee beneficiaries in 2008. If the donor client's spouse elects to split gifts with the donor client for the tax year, the annual exclusion is increased to $24,000 per donee beneficiary. If the donor client has a substantial estate and several individuals to benefit, the systematic use of annual exclusion gifts can cause the transfer of substantial wealth free of transfer tax.

Example: Tom Taxplanner, a retired widower, has two children and four grandchildren. In 2008, Tom can give up to $72,000 of qualifying transfers to his heirs without ever subjecting the transfers to federal transfer taxes. If Tom lives an additional 16 years (his actual life expectancy), he can give away $1,152,000 (assuming no increase in the annual exclusion) and save up to $518,400 of estate tax (assuming the maximum 45 percent bracket for 2008 remains in effect for the period). The actual tax savings are even greater because the appreciation on the property transferred also escapes transfer taxes.

The annual exclusion is available only for gifts that provide the donee beneficiary with a present interest. For example, an outright transfer of property provides a present interest. Because an outright transfer is often unfavorable (for example, the donee beneficiary is a minor), significant planning is often necessary to design gifts that restrict the donee beneficiary's current access to the funds while still qualifying for the annual exclusion.

Gifts to Minors

Quite often annual exclusion gifts will be made to minor children or grandchildren as part of the financial and estate plan of a wealthy client. This creates problems for the donor client and the minor beneficiaries. First, there are restrictions on the ability of minors to hold or otherwise deal with property under state law. In addition, the donor client will naturally be concerned about the safety of the funds if the minors have significant access rights. Fortunately, there are several methods for making annual exclusion gifts to minors that restrict their access to the property.

Transferring Assets to Minors: Techniques That Restrict Access
• Uniform Gifts to Minors Act (UGMA) • Uniform Transfers to Minors Act (UTMA) • Sec. 2503(b) trust • Sec. 2503(c) trust • Irrevocable trust with current withdrawal powers

Uniform Gifts to Minors Act (UGMA) or Uniform Transfers to Minors Act (UTMA). The UGMA and UTMA statutes are model laws that have been adopted in various forms in individual states. They permit the transfer of funds to a custodial account for the benefit of a minor. The custodian of an UGMA or an UTMA account manages the property under the rules provided by state law. There are restrictions on the type of property permissible as an investment for these purposes. The original UGMA model law has been expanded in many states to increase the types of permissible investments. In a majority of states, the newer UTMA model law has been adopted, and relatively few restrictions exist in these states on the permissible investments. An UGMA or an UTMA transfer is particularly favorable for smaller gifts because it provides for the protection of the assets without the expense of administering a trust. The provisions for distribution from an UGMA or UTMA are provided under the various state laws. Generally speaking, UGMA or UTMA funds can be accumulated during the minority of the donee beneficiary, but the custodial assets must be distributed to the beneficiary when he or she reaches the age specified in the relevant statute—generally 18 or 21.

Sec. 2503(b) Trust. A Sec. 2503(b) trust is an irrevocable trust created by a donor client during his or her lifetime to receive annual exclusion gifts for a minor beneficiary. The trust principal should be invested in income-producing property because the trust's income must be distributed at least annually to (or for the benefit of) the minor beneficiary. The trust principal does not have to be distributed at the majority of the beneficiary. It can be distributed to the beneficiary whenever the trust agreement specifies. Also, the gift tax annual exclusion is limited to the present-interest gift value of the income interest provided by the trust to the beneficiary. In some respects, a Sec. 2503(b) trust is less favorable than an UGMA/UTMA gift because the trust's income cannot be accumulated. However, the trust's income can be distributed to (that is, deposited in) an UGMA/UTMA custodial account and used for the benefit of the minor or left to accumulate in the custodial account until the minor reaches majority.

Sec. 2503(c) Trust. A Sec. 2503(c) trust is another type of irrevocable trust designed to receive annual exclusion gifts for a minor beneficiary. This type of trust requires that both income and principal be distributed to the minor at age 21. However, the trust is allowed to accumulate current income prior to the termination of the trust.

Irrevocable Trust with Current Withdrawal Powers. A donor client often wishes to make gifts to a minor in trust for the purpose of accumulation. If the trust provides for accumulation and does not currently benefit the minor beneficiary, the gift tax annual exclusion would normally be forfeited. Provisions of the law, however, permit the annual exclusion if current beneficial rights are given to the beneficiary. These rights, known as *Crummey powers*, provide the beneficiary with temporary withdrawal rights to the funds contributed to the trust. Under these rules, a gift to a trust will qualify for the annual exclusion if the beneficiary has the noncumulative, temporary (for example, 30 days) right to demand up to the annual exclusion amount from his or her share of the amount contributed to the trust by the donor client.

Crummey powers

Irrevocable trusts with Crummey withdrawal powers are often used for the purpose of holding a life insurance policy on the life of the grantor.

Because the life insurance premiums are paid with annual contributions to the trust, it is intended that these contributions remain in the trust and that no distributions will be made until the death of the grantor. Therefore, if each trust beneficiary is provided with the ability to withdraw a pro rata share of the annual premium contributions to the trust for a short period of time (even though he or she is not expected to exercise the withdrawal right), the premium contributions will qualify for the gift tax annual exclusion. Thus, an irrevocable life insurance trust can be created without gift tax costs. The estate tax advantage of a life insurance trust will be discussed later in this chapter.

Federal Estate Tax Planning

Despite the advantages of systematic annual gifting, most individuals desire to retain a significant portion of their wealth until death. To the extent this wealth is included in their gross estates at death, it will be part of their estate tax calculations. Due to the deductions and credits provided by the estate tax laws, a properly designed estate and financial plan can distribute significant wealth to a deceased client's heirs while minimizing or deferring federal estate taxes.

Planning for the Marital Deduction

The marital deduction provides that certain transfers at death from a deceased spouse to a surviving spouse are fully deductible from the gross estate for federal estate tax purposes. This deduction is unlimited as long as the property is included in the gross estate of the deceased spouse and is transferred to the surviving spouse in a qualifying manner.

Through maximum use of the marital deduction, a married couple can, at their option, eliminate all federal estate taxes due at the first death of the two spouses. The estate and financial plan of the marital unit making full use of the marital deduction merely defers the estate taxes until the second spouse dies. The marital deduction will be available at the death of the surviving spouse only if he or she remarries and transfers the property to the new spouse. Thus, a married couple can avoid all federal estate taxes on the first death of the two spouses by making a qualifying transfer of all property included in the deceased spouse's gross estate (both probate and nonprobate property) to the surviving spouse.

Simply answering the "who" question in favor of the surviving spouse will not necessarily qualify such transfers for the marital deduction. The tax laws provide that only qualifying transfers will be eligible for the marital deduction. Thus, the "how" question must also be answered appropriately.

Outright Transfers. The simplest and most common method of transferring property to a surviving spouse—the unrestricted transfer—is eligible for an unlimited marital deduction. This includes all property included in the deceased spouse's gross estate that passes directly to the surviving spouse. Therefore, outright transfers of probate assets by will or intestacy qualify for the marital deduction. In addition, transfers by operation of contract or law that pass outright to the surviving spouse at death similarly qualify. Thus, life insurance proceeds payable to the surviving spouse or jointly held property received by the surviving spouse qualify for the marital deduction.

Property transfers that place restrictions on the surviving spouse's use or enjoyment of the property may or may not qualify for the marital deduction. The marital deduction was designed to prevent a substantial first-death tax to a married couple if the usual dispositive scheme (100 percent to the spouse) was followed. However, Congress intended that federal estate taxes would be payable at the second death of the two spouses. Thus, a general rule of thumb is that the marital deduction is available only for transfers to a surviving spouse that would cause the ultimate inclusion of the property in the surviving spouse's gross estate. Property transferred to a surviving spouse typically will not qualify for the marital deduction if the interest is terminable at the death of the surviving spouse.

An interest in property left to a surviving spouse will be nondeductible if

- it terminates on the occurrence of an event or a contingency, such as death, and
- a third party gains possession of the property after the surviving spouse's interest terminates.

A common example of a nondeductible terminable interest is the transfer of a life estate to a surviving spouse with the remainder interest being paid to the couple's children under the terms of the deceased spouse's will. Such a transfer would not create a second-death tax because the surviving spouse's interest terminates and, therefore, would not be included in his or her estate. However, a first-death tax would be payable because the life estate transferred to the surviving spouse would not qualify for the marital deduction.

Congress recognized that many married individuals prefer leaving property in trust for the surviving spouse. The transferor spouse may want to leave the property in trust because of concern that the surviving spouse would be unable to properly manage the property if left outright to him or her. Also, even when property is left in trust to a surviving spouse, the transferor spouse may want to further protect the property by limiting the invasion rights of the surviving spouse. In fact, the transferor spouse may even want to control the ultimate disposition of the property to make sure that it goes to his or her children. This is particularly true if the transferor spouse has children from a prior marriage. Fortunately, there are several trust arrangements that provide the transferor spouse with varying degrees of control over the disposition of property after his or her death but still qualify for the marital deduction.

Estate Trust. A transfer to a surviving spouse through an estate trust qualifies for the marital deduction. Under this arrangement, a deceased spouse leaves a life estate in trust to the surviving spouse. The surviving spouse's estate is the remainderperson of the trust. Income from the estate trust can either accumulate or be paid to the surviving spouse at the discretion of the trustee. Because the remainder interest is transferred to the surviving spouse's estate, the property will be included in the surviving spouse's gross estate, and a second-death federal estate tax may be payable at that time.

Power-of-Appointment Trust. Another common marital-deduction trust is the power-of-appointment trust. This trust is designed to distribute income to the surviving spouse during his or her life and to provide the surviving spouse with a general power of appointment over the trust property. The general power of appointment may be exercisable by the surviving spouse in all events, or it may be exercisable only at the death of the surviving spouse. Because the surviving spouse has a general power of appointment over the trust property, it is included in his or her gross estate for federal estate tax purposes.

QTIP Marital-Deduction Trust. A special provision of the tax law provides for a marital deduction if qualifying terminable interest property (QTIP) is left to a surviving spouse. Under these rules, a terminable property interest can be transferred to a surviving spouse with the interest qualifying for the marital deduction. The QTIP deduction is available if the executor of the deceased spouse's estate elects QTIP treatment on the estate tax return. The QTIP trust can be funded by probate assets or other types of testamentary dispositions. The surviving spouse must have the right to all income annually from the QTIP trust for life. At the death of the surviving spouse, the QTIP election provides that the trust property will be included in the surviving spouse's gross estate.

The primary advantage of a QTIP trust for the transferor spouse is the ability to control the ultimate disposition of his or her assets. This is determined by the terms of the QTIP trust as specified by the transferor spouse. Thus, a QTIP trust permits a transferor spouse to provide income for his or her surviving spouse, while also protecting the interests of his or her children in the trust property.

Transfers Qualifying for the Marital Deduction

• Outright transfers
   By will or intestacy
   By operation of law
   By operation of contract
• Estate trust
• Power-of-appointment trust
• QTIP trust

Planning for the Gift and Estate Tax Applicable Credit Amount

The applicable credit against gift and/or estate taxes is designed to eliminate the payment of transfer taxes on moderate-sized estates. Starting in 2002, as previously noted, a credit amount of $345,800 is available to shelter up to $1 million of property transfers from gift taxes during a transferor's lifetime. However, if this credit is not exhausted sheltering gifts, any remaining portion (of the $345,800 credit) is available to shelter transfers made at death. Moreover, there is an additional $435,000 of credit (that is, the 2008 estate tax credit of $780,800 minus the gift tax credit of $345,800) amount that is also available in 2008 to shelter property transfers from estate taxes at the transferor's death. This additional credit amount increases to $1,110,000 in 2009 (that is, the 2009 estate tax credit of $1,455,000 minus the gift tax credit of $345,800). In other words, if no taxable gifts have been made, there is a $780,800 credit in 2008 (increasing to $1,455,800 in 2009) that can be used to shelter up to $2 million ($3.5 million in 2009) of property transfers from estate taxes at the transferor's death.

However, before any of the available credit can be used to offset gift or estate taxes, there must first be a property transfer that creates gift or estate taxes. Thus, the applicable credit amount cannot be used when a property transfer is already exempt or deductible from the tax base as a result of other federal transfer tax rules. For example, if a transfer is already exempt from tax because of the gift tax annual exclusion or from gift or estate tax because of the marital deduction, the transferor's credit cannot be used.

Coordination of the Marital Deduction and the Applicable Credit Amount

The typical dispositive scheme for most married couples makes maximum use of the federal estate tax marital deduction. This occurs when all property is left to the surviving spouse either outright or in another manner that qualifies for the marital deduction. Because no estate tax is payable under these circumstances, the applicable credit amount that is available at the first spouse's death is wasted.

With appropriate planning each spouse can make maximum use of the applicable credit. In fact, the marital unit as a whole can shelter up to $4 million in marital wealth from federal estate taxes in 2008 (increasing to $7 million in 2009). This shelter can only be accomplished if each spouse makes maximum use of the applicable credit amount. As previously mentioned, the typical marital dispositive scheme does not take advantage of the applicable credit amount available at the first spouse's death. Thus, all assets transferred to the surviving spouse under the marital deduction will be sheltered only by the applicable credit amount available at the surviving spouse's death (that is, $2 million in 2008 and $3.5 million in 2009).

The typical dispositive scheme can be altered to make maximum use of each spouse's applicable credit amount and optimal use of the marital deduction. Again, this requires appropriate answers to the "who" and "how" questions. With some restrictions, all the objectives of the typical dispositive scheme can be accomplished without wasting the applicable credit amount of either spouse. This maximum estate tax shelter is accomplished by designing each spouse's estate and financial plan to transfer property to two separate trusts, an A or "marital trust" and a B or "family" trust. This two trust arrangement is commonly referred to as an AB trust arrangement. The AB trust arrangement is designed to operate as follows (see chart 7-2):

- The A or marital trust is some form of marital-deduction trust. This trust receives assets in a manner that qualifies them for the federal estate tax marital deduction and provides for maximum use of these assets by the surviving spouse. The remainder of the assets transferred by the deceased client are placed into the B or family trust.
- The B or family trust is designed not to qualify for the marital deduction. Instead, the B trust may be funded with transfers valued at approximately the applicable exclusion amount of $2 million in 2008 (increasing to $3.5 million in 2009) and will be part of the client's taxable estate since the transfers are not deductible under the marital deduction. However, the $2 million transferred in 2008 (or $3.5 million in 2009) to the B or family trust can be sheltered from estate taxes by the applicable exclusion amount.

> **CHART 7-2**
> **Characteristics of the AB Trust Arrangement (under which both spouses create two testamentary trusts)**
>
> | A or Marital Trust | B or Family Trust |
> |---|---|
> | • Surviving spouse is beneficiary
• Receives all assets not placed in B trust
• Qualifies for marital deduction
• Subject to estate taxation at death of surviving spouse | • Surviving spouse receives no more than life income interest and limited invasion powers; children may receive current and/or remainder interest.
• Can receive up to $2 million of assets in 2008 ($3.5 million in 2009)
• Does not qualify for marital deduction; makes use of the applicable credit amount
• Escapes estate taxation at death of surviving spouse |

The "how" question must be answered by designing the transfer to the B or family trust in a nonqualifying manner for the marital deduction. Therefore, the surviving spouse's interest in the B trust must be limited to a life estate, perhaps with some limited invasion rights. Because the B or family trust is designed as a nonqualifying terminable interest, the assets in the B trust will not be included in the surviving spouse's gross estate and the remainder interest can be reserved for the children.

The "who" question must be answered with respect to the B or family trust, also referred to as a credit-shelter trust, or bypass trust. The B trust can be used to provide substantial rights to the surviving spouse but must fail to qualify for the marital deduction. If the marital couple is extremely wealthy, the B or family trust could entirely avoid benefiting the surviving spouse and just focus on benefiting other family members at the first death.

The AB trust arrangement makes maximum use of each spouse's applicable credit, and since the A or marital trust qualifies for the marital deduction and the B or family trust is sheltered entirely by the applicable credit, no estate tax will be paid at the first spouse's death. Thus, the AB trust arrangement does not change the usual first-death tax results. However, the second-death taxes are reduced since the applicable credit amount is used at the time of the first death. Thus, the surviving spouse's estate is reduced in size by the amount of property transferred to the B or family trust at the first death of the two spouses. The increase in the applicable credit and exclusion amounts for 2009 requires careful planning with respect to funding AB trust arrangements.

Planning Charitable Contributions

Qualifying gifts of property to charities may generate deductions against federal income, gift, and estate taxes. Although some limitations exist for the charitable deduction for income tax purposes, qualifying gifts of property are deductible in full against either the federal gift or estate tax base.

Charitable contributions are deductible for federal income, gift, and estate tax purposes only if made to qualified organizations. Generally speaking, an organization is qualified if it is operated exclusively for religious, charitable, scientific, literary, or educational purposes. In addition, the charity must hold such qualified status under the rules of the Internal Revenue Service (IRS). A list of qualified charities is published by the IRS and may be inspected by individuals interested in making a charitable contribution.

Advantages of Gifts to Charity. The value of property gifted to a qualified charity is fully deductible from the federal gift or estate tax base. In addition, the value of property gifted to charity will be deductible from the federal income tax base of the donor client. (Some limitations exist on the size of the income tax deduction, but they are not discussed here.) Thus, a donor client can reduce current income taxes and the eventual size of his or her taxable estate. Quite simply, any property gifted to charity will remove the property (including any postcontribution appreciation) from the transfer-tax base of the donor. Because the gift tax charitable deduction is unlimited, charitable contributions can be even more effective than gifts to noncharitable donees in reducing the size of the gross estate of a wealthy client. The estate tax charitable deduction is similarly unlimited for testamentary bequests to charities. Through the techniques discussed below, charitable contributions can significantly reduce a deceased client's estate tax liability without completely divesting other heirs of the donated property.

charitable remainder trust

Gifts of Remainder Interests to Charity. One disadvantage of an outright lifetime contribution of property to charity is that the donor client loses the current enjoyment of the property. Fortunately, there are methods to take advantage of the tax benefits provided by charitable contributions while retaining the donor client's use or enjoyment of the property. A certain type of trust arrangement, known as a *charitable remainder trust*, can be employed to retain the current enjoyment of the property for the life of the donor client (or lives of the donor's family members) while providing income, gift, and estate tax advantages. The charitable remainder trust can be established during the donor client's lifetime or at his or her death. The charitable remainder trust permits the donor client to retain the current income for the client or his or her family. The income from the trust's assets will be retained for a time period (usually measured by the life of the donor client or lives of selected family members) with the charitable institution holding the remainder interest. The current charitable deduction is measured by the present value of the remainder interest held by the charity. Thus, the donor client (or possibly members of the client's family) receives not only the current enjoyment of the trust property but also a current tax deduction, while the charity receives outright ownership of the property sometime in the future when the remainder interest is distributed by the trust. To prevent abuses of the transfer tax system, tax rules carefully specify the types of charitable remainder trusts eligible for such tax benefits.

Donating Income Interests to Charity. Under some circumstances, a donor client may give a current income interest to charity instead of a remainder interest. To accomplish this, a type of trust known as a *charitable lead trust* is established to provide the charity with a current term income interest. At the end of the term period, the property either reverts to the donor client or passes to a member of his or her family. The donor client gets an immediate income and gift or estate tax deduction for the present value of the lead income interest donated to the charity. However, careful planning is required with this type of trust because even though the donor client receives a charitable tax deduction, all trust income is still taxable to the client.

charitable lead trust

Charitable lead trusts generally are used for testamentary dispositions. If the current income interest bequeathed to the charity is substantial, the estate will receive a tax deduction in an amount equal to a large portion of the value of the property placed in trust. Thus, the taxable estate will be significantly reduced while the family retains ultimate control of the trust property through its remainder interest. The charitable lead trust is an excellent planning tool for extremely wealthy clients who have a substantial amount of other assets that they can leave to their heirs currently, since the assets placed in the charitable lead trust may not be available for several years.

Life Insurance in the Estate and/or Financial Plan

Life insurance can serve either as an estate enhancement or estate liquidity tool. The most appropriate use of life insurance in an estate and/or financial plan depends on the age, family circumstances, and financial status of the particular client.

Life Insurance for Estate Enhancement

Life insurance is generally used for estate enhancement by (1) younger clients, (2) clients with dependent family members, and (3) clients with small to moderate-sized estates. Clients in these categories generally cite protection as their primary need for life insurance. They want to protect their families from the loss of future earnings needed for support. These clients are either in or are headed toward their peak earning years, and their families are relying on these future earnings to maintain their standard of living, educate the children, and accumulate retirement assets.

The death taxes facing younger clients with small to moderate-sized estates are relatively minor. The applicable credit amount and marital deduction will generally remove the danger of federal estate taxes for these individuals. Thus, estate liquidity is not their primary concern. Nonetheless, it is highly improbable that these clients can accumulate enough wealth to replace their future incomes. This is where life insurance plays a role. It is the perfect estate enhancement tool for replacing some or all of the lost earnings resulting from a client's premature death.

Life Insurance for Estate Liquidity

For older clients with larger estates, estate liquidity becomes their primary focus in the use of life insurance. Older clients with families generally have completed or nearly completed the heaviest support and educational expense years for dependent children. These clients are usually well along in their funding for retirement and have fewer years of employment ahead of them.

Because older clients may have accumulated substantial wealth, the protection offered by the applicable exclusion amount and the marital deduction may be inadequate to shelter their estates from taxation. Although the marital deduction will generally shelter all of the estate from tax at the death of the first spouse, the second death can create a substantial tax problem. As noted earlier, with optimal planning the marital unit can shelter up to $4 million of total family wealth from taxes in 2008, increasing to $7 million in 2009. Consequently, marital wealth in excess of these amounts will be subject to taxation and may well create liquidity problems for these large estates as they struggle with how best to pay the taxes. Besides, the client's accumulated wealth may not be in a form that is liquid and available for paying taxes. For example, an interest in a closely held family business is often assigned a high value for federal estate tax purposes. However, the reality is that the business interest may be unmarketable to purchasers outside the family group. If the heirs are to remain in the business, they must discover a method to pay any estate taxes due.

The one method that can guarantee the availability of sufficient funds to pay estate taxes at the exact time the funds are needed is life insurance. Life insurance can provide the funds with which to pay estate settlement costs, including any federal estate taxes. Without the liquidity provided by life insurance, illiquid and often unmarketable estate assets may have to be sold at a fraction of their value to cover the settlement costs.

The estate tax treatment of the life insurance on the client is critical. Because an affluent client is hoping to solve liquidity problems rather than add to a tax burden, the life insurance should be purchased and owned in a manner that keeps the death proceeds out of the client's gross estate, if possible. Thus, wealthy clients often make arrangements for using life insurance that provide them with no incidents of ownership. This can be accomplished by having either their spouses or children apply for and own the policies. Or, as discussed below, a trust can be designed to own the insurance. In either case, the estate or the executor should never be the beneficiary of the policy because this designation would place the proceeds in the client's gross estate for estate tax purposes.

Life Insurance Trusts

Revocable Life Insurance Trusts. A revocable life insurance trust is designed to own and/or be the beneficiary of life insurance on the grantor client's life. This type of trust, however, serves no estate tax planning purposes. Because the trust is revocable, the client is treated as the owner of the policy and the death proceeds will be included in his or her gross estate. The revocable life insurance trust is ordinarily used when a specific, perhaps temporary, protection need exists.

The revocable life insurance trust is an excellent method of providing protection for young children. If the client dies, the trust becomes irrevocable and the children can be provided for out of the proceeds paid into the trust. The revocable life insurance trust is also an excellent method of providing protection for children following a divorce.

Irrevocable Life Insurance Trusts. An irrevocable life insurance trust is generally used by older clients who have a more stable family and financial situation. It can be designed to provide life insurance benefits for a client's heirs that will not be included in the client's gross estate. In addition, contributions to the trust can be designed to avoid gift and generation-skipping taxes. Thus, an irrevocable life insurance trust is a perfect tool for the estate liquidity needs of older, wealthy clients without adding to their tax burden. Because the trust is irrevocable, the client should be certain of his or her beneficial intent at the time the trust is drafted.

THE FINAL WORD

Although the drafting of estate planning documents suggests a certain finality, the process should be ongoing. The financial advisor should never be satisfied that a client has an approved plan because change is the one constant that is guaranteed. The advisor and the client should take the necessary steps to coordinate the estate plan with the other components of the client's comprehensive financial plan.

In addition, all appointed individuals, such as executors, trustees, and attorneys-in-fact, should be informed of their roles and the intentions of the client. In many cases, members of the client's family will be relied upon to make responsible decisions with respect to the estate plan. These family members should be informed, to the extent necessary, of the client's dispositive intentions.

Finally, periodic follow-up is necessary for all the components of a comprehensive financial plan. Many aspects of the estate plan component will be revocable, although such flexibility may provide additional opportunities for both the advisor and the client. Changes in tax law should be monitored and may necessitate new planning steps as a result. The failure to follow up would probably result in client dissatisfaction and perhaps malpractice claims against the advisor.

CHAPTER SUMMARY

Planning the client's estate is an essential step in the ongoing process of life-cycle financial planning. The narrow view of estate planning is that the process merely involves the conservation and distribution of the client's estate. In contrast, the broader view of estate planning is that it is an integral part of financial planning, and the role of the financial advisor is to maximize the distributable wealth of the client and transfer that wealth to the client's beneficiaries in an appropriate fashion. The discussion in this chapter follows the narrow view since the other major planning areas that make up a comprehensive financial plan are covered in other chapters.

Selecting the appropriate alternatives in estate planning involves answering "who," "how," and "when" questions. The client must determine "who" will be the recipients of his or her property, as well as "how" those recipients will receive the property. Generally, the "how" questions can only be answered with significant professional advice. Finally, the client must determine "when" his or her property will be distributed, whether that be during lifetime, at death, or—as typically happens—both during lifetime and at death.

Although the estate plan should be an integral part of the client's comprehensive financial plan, estate planning concerns generally gain prominence later in the client's financial life cycle. With the exception of preparing a simple will to direct the disposition of assets, wealth planning typically does not become paramount until the client is well on the way toward reaching his or her wealth accumulation and retirement planning goals. Nonetheless, as part of the financial planning process, the financial advisor needs to gather data early in the client's financial life cycle in order to help the client determine appropriate responses to the "who," "how," and "when" questions.

Knowledge of the various forms of property ownership is essential for the advisor if he or she wants to determine all of the possible property rights that a client can hold and the possible types of dispositions that a client can make to beneficiaries. The most complete interest in property is a fee simple estate, which provides for the outright individual ownership of property. Another common form of individual ownership of property is the life estate. It provides the life tenant with the right to possess and enjoy the property for a time period measured by the life of an individual (typically the life tenant). Other forms of individual ownership of property are term interests and future interests. A term interest provides the current tenant with the right to possess, enjoy, and receive income from the property during a specified term, while a future interest in property is the current right to future enjoyment of the property.

Current possessory rights to property may be held by more than one individual. Such a partial current interest in property is generically referred to as joint ownership of property. These types of ownership interest include tenancy in common, joint tenancy with right of survivorship, tenancy by the entirety, and community property.

Other types of property interests that can play a role in the transfer of the client's wealth include beneficial interests and powers. Beneficial interests (such as the rights to current income or principal distributions given to the beneficiaries of a trust) and powers (such as those embodied in powers of appointment and powers of attorney) are types of property interests that should be used by the client when they can help to achieve his or her goals and objectives.

An estate plan (a subset of a comprehensive financial plan) is a roadmap that directs how a client's wealth will be assembled and disposed of during the client's life and/or at his or her death. The estate plan itself is useless unless the documents of the plan have been drafted appropriately. These documents should include a valid will to serve as the centerpiece of the estate plan. Also important for carrying out a client's estate plan are trusts, either living trusts, testamentary trusts, or both. In addition, another important estate planning document is a durable power of attorney. Unlike a conventional power, a durable power remains valid and operative despite any subsequent incapacity of the client. Even better in many situations is a springing durable power of attorney, which lies dormant and ineffective until such time as it may be needed. Finally, advance medical directives are an important part of any estate plan. The person named in a durable power of attorney for health care is the person designated by the client to carry out the client's medical wishes, as expressed in a living will, should the client become incapacitated.

Knowledge of how property is transferred at death under the laws of the jurisdictional state is necessary to plan an estate. A common misconception is that the client's will determines the distribution of the estate at his or her death. Under most circumstances, the will actually affects the distribution of only a small portion of the client's property. If a valid will exists, the probate court will ensure that the probate property is distributed according to the terms of the will. If the client dies without a valid will, all probate property passes under the laws of intestate succession of the jurisdiction state.

The nature of certain property ownership interests causes the property to pass automatically at the death of the client. Such property is not subject to the laws of probate and does not pass under the will or intestacy rules. The most significant example of property that is transferred by operation of law is property held jointly with rights of survivorship. Another form of nonprobate transfer is transfer by contract. The most common form of transfer by contract involves the transfer of life insurance proceeds or employee benefits to a named beneficiary.

The most significant costs of transferring wealth are the various transfer taxes imposed at the federal and state levels. The federal transfer tax system consists of three components—gift taxation, estate taxation, and generation-skipping taxation. Two of these components, the gift tax and the estate tax, are unified in that they share one progressive set of tax rates, although there are several important differences between them. Moreover, certain transfers, whether made by lifetime gift or at the client's death, are subject to the generation-skipping transfer tax (GSTT). Generally, the GSTT applies to outright transfers that skip a generation in the client's family and are taxable under either the gift tax or the estate tax.

The subject of state death taxes frequently is overshadowed by the attention given to the federal estate tax. State death tax planning, however, should not be ignored since taxable transfers for estate purposes can often be avoided by simple planning that might otherwise be ineffective (and thus disregarded) for federal estate tax planning purposes. For example, many states exempt life insurance benefits paid to a named beneficiary.

There are many techniques that can be used to reduce the transfer tax burden associated with transferring a client's wealth to his or her heirs. The appropriate answer to the "who" question may be used to reduce estate taxes. For example, qualifying transfers to a surviving spouse are fully deductible from the client's gross estate. Optimal resolution of the "how" question could also reduce estate taxes. For example, transferring assets to a family trust takes advantage of the applicable credit against federal estate taxes. Finally, if the "when" question is answered appropriately, the gross estate of a client can be substantially reduced through a systematic lifetime gifting program, and substantial wealth can be transferred free of all transfer taxes.

CHAPTER REVIEW

Key Terms and Concepts are explained in the Glossary. Answers to the Review Questions and Self-Test Questions are found in the back of the book in the Answers to Questions section.

Key Terms and Concepts

fee simple estate	durable power of attorney
power of appointment	springing durable power of attorney
general power of appointment	durable power of attorney for health care
special power of appointment	
power of attorney	living will
fiduciaries	intestate succession
intestacy	intestate laws
probate	direct skip
grantor	taxable termination
living trust	taxable distribution
pour-over trust	state inheritance tax
revocable trust	state estate tax
irrevocable trust	credit estate tax
testamentary trust	Crummey powers
testator	charitable remainder trust
attorney-in-fact	charitable lead trust
conventional power of attorney	

Review Questions

7-1. Of what value to a financial advisor doing estate planning is the inventory of assets section of a fact finder form?

7-2. Why might an interview by a financial advisor gathering information for a client's estate plan be an uncomfortable event for the client?

7-3. Explain each of the following ways in which an individual might have an ownership interest in property.
  a. life estate
  b. term interest
  c. future interest

7-4. Explain each of the following ways in which two individuals might have a joint concurrent ownership interest in property.
   a. tenancy in common
   b. joint tenancy with right of survivorship
   c. tenancy by the entirety

7-5. Explain the difference between a general power of appointment and a special power of appointment.

7-6. a. Describe the requirements for a valid will.
   b. What objectives can be accomplished by a properly drafted will?

7-7. Explain the difference between a conventional power of attorney and a durable power of attorney.

7-8. Briefly describe the process of probating an estate.

7-9. Briefly describe the typical distribution system provided by state intestacy laws.

7-10. Describe the types of gratuitous transfers that are exempt from the gift tax base by statute.

7-11. Identify the types of property that are includible in the gross estate of a deceased for federal estate tax purposes.

7-12. a. Describe the purpose of the federal generation-skipping transfer tax (GSTT) system.
   b. Identify the three types of transfers that are subject to the GSTT.

7-13. Explain the difference between a state inheritance tax and a state estate tax.

7-14. a. Describe several nontax advantages from making lifetime gifts.
   b. Describe several tax advantages from making lifetime gifts.

7-15. Describe each of the following techniques for making gifts to minors that will not be subject to federal gift taxes:
   a. UGMA or UTMA gifts
   b. irrevocable trusts

7-16. Explain how each of the following trusts may be used to qualify property left by a deceased to his or her spouse for the federal estate tax marital deduction:
   a. an estate trust
   b. a power of appointment trust
   c. a QTIP marital-deduction trust

7-17. Explain how an AB trust arrangement can make maximum use of each spouse's applicable credit amount while also making optimal use of the marital deduction.

7-18. Explain how a charitable remainder trust can be used advantageously in planning a client's estate.

7-19. Describe the type of client for whom life insurance may be particularly appropriate for purposes of estate enhancement.

7-20. Explain why a revocable life insurance trust is not a very useful device for estate tax planning purposes.

Self-Test Questions

Instructions: Read chapter 7 first, then answer the following questions to test your knowledge. There are 10 questions; circle the correct answer, then check your answers with the answer key in the back of the book.

7-1. The most complete ownership interest one can have in property is a

(A) fee simple estate
(B) life estate
(C) tenancy by the entirety
(D) future interest

7-2. A life insurance policy death benefit paid to a named beneficiary is an example of a transfer of property by operation of

(A) will
(B) law
(C) contract
(D) intestacy

7-3. A power of appointment over property that gives the holder the broad power to transfer the property to virtually any recipient is referred to as a

(A) special power of appointment
(B) general power of appointment
(C) legal power of appointment
(D) reversionary power of appointment

7-4. Which of the following statements concerning the gift tax annual exclusion is (are) correct?

    I. It is available only for gifts to close relatives of the donor.
    II. It is available only for gifts that provide the donee with a future interest.

(A) I only
(B) II only
(C) Both I and II
(D) Neither I nor II

7-5. Which of the following statements concerning the use of charitable lead trusts is (are) correct?

    I. They allow donor clients to give remainder income interests to charities.
    II. They provide donor clients with immediate income and gift or estate tax deductions for their donations.

(A) I only
(B) II only
(C) Both I and II
(D) Neither I nor II

7-6. Which of the following trusts created to receive annual exclusion gifts for minors require(s) income to be distributed at least annually to (or for the use of) the minor?

    I. A Sec. 2503(b) trust
    II. A Sec. 2503(c) trust

(A) I only
(B) II only
(C) Both I and II
(D) Neither I nor II

7-7. The federal gift tax applies only if which of the following elements is (are) present?

   I. There is a completed transfer and acceptance of the property.
   II. The transfer of the property is for less than full and adequate consideration.

   (A) I only
   (B) II only
   (C) Both I and II
   (D) Neither I nor II

7-8. The generation-skipping transfer tax (GSTT) applies to all the following types of transfers EXCEPT a(n)

   (A) taxable termination
   (B) direct skip
   (C) taxable distribution
   (D) indirect skip

7-9. All the following statements concerning a revocable trust are correct EXCEPT:

   (A) The creation involves a transfer that is a completed gift.
   (B) It avoids the publicity, delay, and expense of probate.
   (C) It becomes irrevocable at the grantor's death.
   (D) Its creation has no effect on the grantor's gross estate.

7-10. All the following statements concerning a durable power of attorney are correct EXCEPT:

   (A) It takes effect immediately upon execution.
   (B) It can be designed for use in making medical care decisions.
   (C) It becomes inoperative if the principal is incapacitated.
   (D) It can replace or complement a revocable trust.

8

Social Security, Medicare, and Medicare Supplements

Burton T. Beam, Jr.

Learning Objectives

An understanding of the material in this chapter should enable you to

8-1. Explain both the importance of and the extent of coverage under the Social Security and Medicare programs, and describe how the programs are financed.

8-2. Explain the requirements for eligibility under Social Security, and describe the types and amounts of benefits available.

8-3. Explain the requirements for eligibility under Medicare, and describe the benefits available under Parts A and B.

8-4. Explain the options available to beneficiaries under Parts C and D of Medicare.

8-5. Explain how Medicare supplement coverages fill some of the gaps in Medicare benefits, and describe the eligibility requirements for buying a medigap policy.

Chapter Outline

SOCIAL SECURITY AND MEDICARE 8.2
    The Importance, Coverage, and Financing of Social Security and Medicare 8.3
    Eligibility for Social Security 8.4
    Social Security Benefits 8.6
    Social Security Benefit Amounts 8.9
    Eligibility for Medicare 8.15
    Medicare Part A: Hospital Benefits 8.16

Medicare Part B: Medical Insurance 8.20
Medicare Part C: Medicare Advantage 8.22
Medicare Part D: Prescription Drug Coverage 8.25
COVERAGE TO SUPPLEMENT MEDICARE 8.31
Employer Plans to Supplement Medicare 8.31
Individual Medigap Policies to Supplement Medicare 8.31
THE FINAL WORD 8.36
CHAPTER SUMMARY 8.36
CHAPTER REVIEW 8.39

This chapter begins with a brief discussion of why Social Security and Medicare are important to the financial advisor, the extent of coverage under the programs, and the way these programs are financed. The discussion then shifts to the eligibility requirements and benefits of each separate program. The last part of the chapter is devoted to explaining the various types of coverages designed to supplement Medicare.

SOCIAL SECURITY AND MEDICARE[1]

OASDHI

In a broad sense, the term Social Security can be used to refer to several of the programs resulting from the Social Security Act of 1935 and its subsequent amendments. Taken together, these programs constitute the old-age, survivors, disability, and health insurance *(OASDHI)* program of the federal government. This program is often separated into two broad parts. The first part is the old age, survivors, and disability insurance (OASDI) program. Over the years, OASDI has become synonymous with Social Security, which is the term used in this chapter. The remainder of the OASDHI program is called Medicare.

Although the Social Security and Medicare programs could have been covered in earlier chapters as subparts of one of the major planning areas, they are dealt with separately in this chapter because of their importance to the financial advisor as a foundation upon which he or she can develop comprehensive financial plans for clients. The following discussion about Social Security and Medicare begins with a brief explanation of why they are important, how many people they cover, and how they are financed. The discussion then continues by focusing on the eligibility requirements and benefits of each separate program.

The Importance, Coverage, and Financing of Social Security and Medicare

Importance of Programs

The Social Security and Medicare programs are important to financial advisors and their clients for at least two reasons. First, the most significant insurance expense for most individuals is their contributions to Social Security and Medicare. For many persons, this contribution will exceed the combined cost of all other types of insurance purchased directly by the individual. Second, these programs form the foundation on which employee benefit plans and individual insurance plans are built. In fact, nearly one-quarter of the dollars employers spend on benefits for their employees is used to make legally required payments to these programs. Moreover, it is impossible to do a proper job of personal insurance planning, or financial planning for that matter, without taking Social Security and Medicare benefits into consideration.

Extent of Coverage

Over 95 percent of the workers in the United States are in covered employment under the Social Security program and over 98 percent under the Medicare program. This means that these workers have wages (if they are employees) or self-employment income (if they are self-employed) on which Social Security and Medicare taxes must be paid.

Tax Rates and Wage Bases

All the benefits of the Social Security program and Part A of Medicare are financed through a system of payroll and self-employment taxes paid by all persons covered under the programs. In addition, employers of covered persons are also taxed. (These taxes are often referred to as FICA taxes because they are imposed under the Federal Insurance Contributions Act.) Part B of Medicare is financed by a combination of monthly premiums paid by persons eligible for benefits and contributions from the federal government.

In 2008, an employee and his or her employer pay a tax of 7.65 percent each on the first $102,000 of the employee's wages. Of this tax rate, 6.2 percent is for Social Security, and 1.45 percent is for Part A of Medicare. The Part A tax rate of 1.45 percent is also levied on all wages in excess of $102,000. The tax rates are currently scheduled to remain the same after 2008, but the $102,000 wage base is adjusted annually for changes in the national level of wages. Therefore, if wage levels increase by 4 percent in a particular year, the wage base for the following year will also increase by 4 percent. The tax rate for the self-employed is 15.3 percent on the first $102,000 of self-employment income and 2.9 percent on the balance of any self-employment income. This is equal to the combined employee and employer rates.

Paying for Social Security and Medicare

- Social Security—Employees pay 6.20 percent of the first $102,000 (2008) of earnings. Employers pay the same. Self-employed persons pay 12.40 percent of first $102,000 (2008) of self-employment income.
- Medicare Part A—Employees pay 1.45 percent of all earnings. Employers pay the same. Self-employed persons pay 2.9 percent of all self-employment income.
- Medicare Part B—Covered persons pay at least a $96.40 (2008) monthly premium. Single persons with annual incomes exceeding $82,000 and married couples with annual incomes exceeding $164,000 pay higher monthly premiums. General revenues of the federal government cover the remainder (about 75 percent) of the program's cost.

Over the years, both the tax rates and wage bases have risen dramatically to finance increased benefit levels under Social Security and Medicare as well as new benefits that have been added to the program. In 1950, a tax rate of 1.5 percent was levied on the first $3,000 of wages. These figures increased to 4.8 percent and $7,800 in 1970, and 7.65 percent and $51,300 in 1990. Starting in 1991, a two-tier program was introduced with a tax of 7.65 percent (6.2 percent for Social Security and 1.45 for Medicare) on the first $53,400 of wages and a Medicare tax of 1.45 percent on the next $71,500. By 1994, all wages were subject to the Medicare tax.

The adequacy of the current funding structure to pay for Social Security and Medicare benefits continues to be a source of public concern and political debate.

Eligibility for Social Security

quarters of coverage

To be eligible for benefits under Social Security, an individual must have credit for a minimum amount of work under the program. This credit is based on *quarters of coverage*. For 2008, a worker receives credit for one quarter of coverage for each $1,050 in annual earnings on which Social Security taxes were paid. However, credit for no more than 4 quarters of coverage may be earned in any one calendar year. Consequently, a worker who pays Social Security taxes on as little as $4,200 ($1,050 x 4) at any time during the year will receive credit for the maximum 4 quarters of coverage. As in the case of the wage base, the amount of earnings necessary for a quarter of coverage is adjusted annually for changes in the national level of wages.

Quarters of coverage are the basis for establishing an insured status under Social Security. The three types of insured status are fully insured, currently insured, and disability insured.

Fully Insured

fully insured

A person is *fully insured* under Social Security if either of two tests is met. The first test requires credit for 40 quarters of coverage. Once a person acquires such credit, he or she is fully insured for life even if covered employment under Social Security ceases.

Under the second test, a person who has credit for a minimum of 6 quarters of coverage is fully insured if he or she has credit for at least as many quarters of coverage as there are years elapsing after 1950 (or after the year in which age 21 is reached, if later) and before the year in which he or she dies, becomes disabled, or reaches age 62, whichever occurs first. Therefore, a worker who reached age 21 in 1996 and who died in 2008 would need credit for only 11 quarters of coverage for his or her family to be eligible for survivors benefits.

Currently Insured

currently insured

If a worker is not fully insured, certain survivors benefits are still available if a *currently insured* status exists. To be currently insured, it is only necessary that a worker have credit for at least 6 quarters of coverage out of the 13-quarter period ending with the quarter in which his or her death occurs.

Disability Insured

disability insured

In order to receive disability benefits under Social Security, it is necessary to be *disability insured*. At a minimum, a disability-insured status requires that a worker (1) be fully insured and (2) have a minimum amount of work under Social Security within a recent time period. In connection with the latter requirement, workers aged 31 or older must have credit for at least 20 of the last 40 quarters ending with the quarter in which disability occurs; workers aged 24 through 30 must have credit for at least half the quarters of coverage from the time they turned 21 and the quarter in which disability begins; and workers under age 24 must have credit for 6 out of the last 12 quarters, ending with the quarter in which disability begins. A special rule for the blind considers them disability insured as long as they are fully insured.

Social Security Benefits

As its name implies, the Social Security program provides three principal types of benefits: retirement (old-age) benefits, survivors benefits, and disability benefits.

Retirement Benefits

A worker who is fully insured under Social Security is eligible to receive monthly retirement benefits as early as age 62. However, the election to receive benefits prior to the full Social Security retirement age results in a permanently reduced benefit. Full retirement benefits are payable when a participant attains *full retirement age*.

full retirement age

Full retirement age (sometimes referred to as normal retirement age), or the age at which nonreduced retirement benefits are paid, was 65 for workers born in 1937 or before. This age, however, is in the process of transitioning to age 67. Individuals born from 1943 through 1954 will have a full retirement age of 66; those born from 1955 through 1959 will have a full retirement age of 66 plus some number of months, and those born in 1960 and later will have a full retirement age of 67. As shown in table 8-1, a gradually increasing full retirement age applies to workers born in 1938 and later.

TABLE 8-1
Retirement Age for Nonreduced Benefits

Year of Birth	Full Retirement Age
1937 and before	65 years
1938	65 years, 2 months
1939	65 years, 4 months
1940	65 years, 6 months
1941	65 years, 8 months
1942	65 years, 10 months
1943–54	66 years
1955	66 years, 2 months
1956	66 years, 4 months
1957	66 years, 6 months
1958	66 years, 8 months
1959	66 years, 10 months
1960 and later	67 years

In addition to the retired worker, the following dependents of persons receiving retirement benefits are also eligible for monthly benefits:

- a spouse aged 62 or older. However, benefits are permanently reduced if this benefit is elected prior to the spouse's reaching full retirement age. This benefit is also available to a divorced spouse under certain circumstances if the marriage lasted at least 10 years.
- a spouse of any age if the spouse is caring for at least one child of the retired worker as long as the child is (1) under age 16 or (2) disabled and entitled to a child's benefit as described below. This benefit is commonly referred to as a *mother's/father's benefit*.

mother's/father's benefit

- dependent, unmarried children under 18. This child's benefit will continue until age 19 as long as a child is a full-time student in elementary or secondary school. In addition, disabled children of any age are eligible for benefits as long as they were disabled before reaching age 22.

It is important to note that retirement benefits, as well as all other benefits under Social Security and Medicare, are not automatically paid upon eligibility but must be applied for.

Survivors Benefits

All categories of survivors benefits are payable if a worker is fully insured at the time of death. However, three types of benefits are also payable if a worker is only currently insured. The first is a lump-sum death benefit of $255, payable if there is a surviving spouse or dependent child who meets certain requirements.

Two categories of persons are eligible for income benefits as survivors if a deceased worker was either fully or currently insured at the time of death:

- dependent, unmarried children under the same conditions as previously described for retirement benefits
- a spouse (including a divorced spouse) caring for a child or children under the same conditions as described for retirement benefits

The following categories of persons are also eligible for benefits, but only if the deceased worker was fully insured:

- a widow or widower aged 60 or older. However, benefits are reduced if taken prior to full retirement age. This benefit is also payable to a divorced spouse if the marriage lasted at least 10 years. In addition, the widow's or widower's benefit is payable to a disabled spouse at

age 50 as long as the disability commenced no more than 7 years after the (1) worker's death, or (2) end of the year in which entitlement to a mother's or father's benefit ceased.
- a parent age 62 or over who was a dependent of the deceased worker at the time of death

blackout period

No survivors benefits are payable to the surviving spouse of a deceased covered worker from the time the youngest child reaches age 16 (or is no longer disabled in certain cases) until the surviving spouse is 60. This period of time is called the *blackout period.*

Disability Benefits

A disabled worker under full retirement age is eligible to receive benefits under Social Security as long as he or she is disability insured and meets the definition of disability under the law. The definition of disability is very rigid and requires a mental or physical impairment that prevents the worker from engaging in any substantial gainful employment ($940 per month in 2008). The disability must also have lasted (or be expected to last) at least 12 months or be expected to result in death. A more liberal definition of disability applies to blind workers who are aged 55 or older. They are considered disabled if they are unable to perform work that requires skills or abilities comparable to those required by the work they regularly performed before reaching age 55 or becoming blind, if later.

Disability benefits are subject to a waiting period and are payable beginning with the sixth full calendar month of disability. In addition to the benefit paid to a disabled worker, the other categories of benefits available are the same as those described under retirement benefits.

As previously mentioned, certain family members not otherwise eligible for Social Security benefits may be eligible if they are disabled. Disabled children are subject to the same definition of disability as workers. However, disabled widows or widowers must be unable to engage in any gainful (rather than substantial gainful) employment.

Eligibility for Dual Benefits

In many cases, a person is eligible for more than one type of Social Security benefit. Probably the most common situation occurs when a person is eligible for both a spouse's benefit and a worker's retirement or disability benefit based on his or her own Social Security record. In this and any other case when a person is eligible for dual benefits, only an amount equal to the higher benefit is paid.

Termination of Benefits

Monthly benefits to any Social Security recipient cease upon his or her death. When a retired or disabled worker dies, the family members' benefits that are based on the worker's retirement or disability benefits also cease, but the family members are then eligible for survivors benefits.

Disability benefits for a worker technically terminate at full retirement age but are then replaced by comparable retirement benefits. Any benefits payable because of disability cease at an earlier date if medical or other evidence shows that the definition of disability is no longer satisfied. However, the disability benefits continue during a readjustment period that consists of the month of recovery and 2 additional months. As an encouragement for them to return to work, disabled beneficiaries for whom there is no evidence that their disability has otherwise terminated are allowed a 9-month trial work period during which benefits are not affected regardless of how much the beneficiary earns. At the end of that period, a beneficiary's earnings are evaluated to determine if the earnings are substantial, that is, $940 per month in 2008. If earnings then exceed this amount for 3 months, benefits are suspended but can be reinstated during the next 36 months without starting a new application process should the earnings fall below this level.

As long as children are not disabled, benefits usually terminate at age 18 but may continue until age 19 if the child is a full-time student in elementary or secondary school.

A surviving spouse's benefit terminates upon remarriage unless remarriage takes place at age 60 or later.

Social Security Benefit Amounts

Calculating Benefits

primary insurance amount (PIA)

With the exception of the $255 lump-sum death benefit, the amount of all Social Security benefits is based on a worker's *primary insurance amount (PIA)*. When a beneficiary is eligible for benefits, his or her actual PIA is calculated by the Social Security Administration using a complex formula that is heavily weighted in favor of lower-income workers.

The PIA is the amount a worker receives if he or she retires at full retirement age or becomes disabled, and it is the amount on which benefits for family members are based. In 2008, the average PIA for a retired worker is $1,079. A worker who has continually earned the maximum income subject to Social Security taxes can expect to have a PIA for retirement purposes of about $2,150 if he or she retires at age 66 in 2008.

The maximum PIA in 2008 for purposes of disability and survivors benefits ranges from approximately $2,100 to $2,300. The higher PIA results for workers who are disabled or who die at younger ages. Table 8-2 shows the Social Security Administration's estimated average monthly benefit that various categories of beneficiaries receive in 2008.

TABLE 8-2
Estimated Average Monthly Social Security Benefits, 2008

Category of Beneficiary	Amount
All retired workers	$1,079
Aged couple, both receiving benefits	$1,761
Widowed mother and two children	$2,243
Aged widow(er) alone	$1,041
Disabled worker spouse, and one or more children	$1,690
All disabled workers	$1,004

If a worker is retired or disabled, these benefits are paid to family members, as shown in table 8-3. If the worker dies, survivors benefits are paid to family members, as shown in table 8-4.

However, the full benefits described above may not be payable because of a limitation imposed on the total benefits that may be paid to a family. This family maximum is again determined by a formula and is usually reached if three or more family members (including a retired or disabled worker) are eligible for benefits.

If the total amount of benefits payable to family members exceeds the family maximum, the worker's benefit (in the case of retirement and disability) is not affected, but the benefits of other family members are reduced proportionately.

TABLE 8-3
Benefits for Family Members of a Disabled or Retired Worker

Family Member	Percentage of Worker's PIA
Spouse at full retirement age	50%
Spouse caring for disabled child or child under 16	50%
Child under 18 or disabled	50% each

TABLE 8-4
Survivors Benefits for Family Members of a Deceased Worker

Family Member	Percentage of Worker's PIA
Spouse at full retirement age	100%
Spouse caring for disabled child or child under 16	75%
Child under 18 or disabled	75% each
Dependent parent	82.5% for one 75% each for two

Example: Sam Chen died leaving a spouse aged 42 and three children. All four family members are eligible for 75 percent of Sam's PIA of $1,200. Ignoring the family maximum, the benefits total $3,600 ($900 for each family member). However, the family maximum, using the prescribed formula[2] for 2008 is $2,155.02. Therefore, each family member has his or her benefit reduced to $539 (rounded to the next higher dollar). When the first child loses benefits at age 18, the other family members' benefits increase to $718 (rounded to the next lower dollar and ignoring any automatic benefit increases, including the family maximum).

When a second family member loses eligibility, the remaining two family members each receive the full benefit of $900 because the total benefits the family receives are now less than the family maximum of $2,155.02 calculated by the formula.

Other Factors Affecting Benefits

Benefits Taken Early. If a worker elects to receive retirement benefits prior to full retirement age, benefits are permanently reduced by 5/9 of one percent for each of the first 36 months that the early retirement precedes full retirement age and 5/12 of one percent for each month in excess of 36. For example, in the case of a worker who retires at exactly age 62 in 2008, the monthly benefit is 25 percent less than that worker's PIA at the full retirement age of 66. If the worker waits one year and retires at exactly age 63, his or her monthly benefit will only be 20 percent less than his or her PIA at the full retirement age of 66. A spouse who elects retirement benefits prior to full retirement age has benefits reduced by 25/36 of one percent per month, for each of the first 36 months and 5/12 of one percent for each month in excess of 36. A widow or widower has benefits reduced proportionately from 100 percent at full retirement age to 71.5 percent at age 60. If the widow or widower elects benefits prior to age 60 because of disability, there is no further reduction.

Many Americans retire before the age at which they are eligible for nonreduced Social Security benefits. In some cases, an individual may need the Social Security benefit to meet regular living expenses. In other cases, however, an individual may have income or investments to bridge the gap until full retirement age. Then the decision becomes: Do I elect early benefits at a reduced amount for a longer period of time or larger benefits that will start later? There is no absolute answer. As a general rule, if a person expects to live to 78 years or older, the better decision is to wait until full retirement age. However, the "break-even age" will vary according to such factors as when early benefits start, gender, the category of Social Security benefits, and the interest rate at which funds can be invested.

Delayed Retirement. Workers who delay applying for benefits until after full retirement age are eligible for an increased benefit. Benefits are increased for each month of late retirement until age 70. For persons born in 1943 or later, the increase is 2/3 of 1 percent per month, which equals 8.0 percent for delaying application for benefits for one full year. To encourage later retirement, the monthly percentage gradually increases. Table 8-5 shows the percentage for each month of deferral, as well as the maximum percentage increase that is available if the worker postpones retirement until age 70.

TABLE 8-5
Increase for Delayed Retirement

Year of Birth	Monthly Percentage Increase	Maximum Percentage Increase
1937	13/24	132 1/2
1938	13/24	131 5/12
1939	7/12	132 2/3
1940	7/12	131 1/2
1941	15/24	132 1/2
1942	15/24	131 1/4
1943–54	2/3	132
1955	2/3	130 2/3
1956	2/3	129 1/3
1957	2/3	128
1958	2/3	126 2/3
1959	2/3	125 1/3
1960 and later	2/3	124

The increases in benefits shown in table 8-5 apply to a worker's PIA as determined at the time he or she applies for retirement benefits. Therefore, if a person continues to work during the period of delayed retirement and covered wages are sufficiently high, it is quite possible for the worker's PIA at the time of his or her delayed retirement to exceed what his or her PIA would have been at full retirement age. If this happens, the increased monthly retirement benefit from working past full retirement age will likely be greater than the percentages shown in table 8-5.

earnings test

Earnings Test. The *earnings test* applies to beneficiaries who are under full retirement age. It determines whether a beneficiary's income benefits should be reduced because his or her earned income exceeds a specified amount. The beneficiary is allowed earnings of up to $13,560 in 2008, and this figure is subject to annual indexing for later years. If the beneficiary earns more than this amount, his or her Social Security benefit is reduced by $1 for each $2 of excess earnings. There is one exception to the test: The reduction is $1 for every $3 of earnings in excess of $36,120 (in 2008) in the calendar year a worker attains the full retirement age, for earnings in months prior to such age attainment. Once the beneficiary reaches full retirement age, any amount can be earned without a Social Security reduction.

Social Security Earnings Test

- Beneficiaries who have reached full retirement age—no loss of benefits regardless of annual wages
- Beneficiaries who are under full retirement age—$1 of benefits lost for every $2 of annual wages in excess of $13,560 (2008). A more liberal test applies in the calendar year a worker attains the full retirement age.

The reduction in a retired worker's benefits resulting from excess earnings is charged against the entire benefits that are paid to a family and based on the worker's Social Security record. If large enough, this reduction may totally eliminate all benefits otherwise payable to the worker and family members. In contrast, excess earnings of family members are charged against their individual benefits only. For example, a widowed mother who holds a job outside the home may lose her mother's benefit, but any benefits her children receive are unaffected.

Cost-of-Living Adjustments. Social Security benefits are increased automatically each January as long as there has been an increase in the

Consumer Price Index (CPI) for the one-year period ending in the third quarter of the prior year. The increase is the same as the increase in the CPI since the last cost-of-living adjustment, rounded to the nearest 0.1 percent. Benefits do not automatically decrease if the CPI declines.

Offset for Other Benefits. Disabled workers under full retirement age who are also receiving workers' compensation benefits from certain other federal, state, or local disability programs will have their Social Security benefits reduced to the extent that the total benefits received (including family benefits) exceed 80 percent of their average current earnings at the time of disability. In addition, the monthly benefit of a spouse or surviving spouse is reduced by two-thirds of any federal, state, or local government pension that is based on earnings not covered under Social Security on the last day of employment.

FOCUS ON ETHICS
Understanding the OASDHI Program

It is important that a financial advisor have a good understanding of government programs. In order to do comprehensive financial planning for clients, the advisor must be knowledgeable about Social Security and Medicare so that any plan he or she develops can build upon the foundation provided by these programs. To discount the importance of these programs is to ignore that for most people their contributions to Social Security and Medicare exceed the combined cost of all other types of insurance purchased directly by them. The advisor who does not properly take these programs into account when developing plans for his or her clients is guilty of malpractice at worst and unethical behavior at best.

Requesting Benefit Information

Social Security Statement

Each year the Social Security Administration sends a *Social Security Statement* to all persons aged 25 or older who have covered employment under Social Security and are not currently receiving monthly benefits. The statement enables a worker to verify his or her contributions to the Social Security and Medicare programs. It also contains an estimate of benefits that will be available upon retirement, disability, or death, as well as a reminder of the right to request corrections of omissions or errors. As a general rule, such requests must be made within 3 years, 3 months, and 15 days following the year in which wages were paid or self-employment income was earned. However, clerical or fraudulent errors can be corrected after that time.

Eligibility for Medicare

Part A, the hospital portion of Medicare, is available to any person aged 65 or older as long as the person is entitled to monthly retirement benefits under Social Security or the railroad retirement program. Civilian employees of the federal government aged 65 or older are also eligible. It is not necessary for these workers to actually be receiving retirement benefits, but they must be fully insured for purposes of retirement benefits. The following persons are also eligible for Part A of Medicare at no monthly cost:

- persons aged 65 or older who are dependents of fully insured workers aged 62 or older
- survivors aged 65 or older who are eligible for Social Security survivors benefits
- disabled persons at any age who have been eligible to receive Social Security benefits for 2 years because of their disability. This includes workers under age 65, disabled widows and widowers aged 50 or over, and children 18 or older who were disabled prior to age 22.
- workers who are either fully or currently insured and their spouses and dependent children with end-stage renal (kidney) disease who require renal dialysis or kidney transplants. Coverage begins either the first day of the third month after dialysis begins or earlier for admission to a hospital for kidney-transplant surgery.

Most persons aged 65 or over who do not meet the previously discussed eligibility requirements may voluntarily enroll in Medicare. However, they must pay a monthly Part A premium and also enroll in Part B.

Any person eligible for Part A of Medicare is also eligible for Part B. However, a monthly premium must be paid for Part B. The minimum premium ($96.40 in 2008) is adjusted annually and represents only about 25 percent of the cost of the benefits provided. The general revenues of the federal government finance the remaining cost of the program. As a result of the Medicare Prescription Drug, Improvement, and Modernization Act, the Part B premium will continue to equal 25 percent of Part B benefit costs, but only for beneficiaries with a modified adjusted gross income of $82,000 or less for a single person and $164,000 or less for a couple (in 2008 and subject to indexing). Higher-income persons pay a larger premium that increases with income.

Persons who receive Social Security or railroad retirement benefits are automatically enrolled in Medicare if they are eligible. If they do not want Part B, they must reject it in writing. Other persons eligible for Medicare must apply for benefits. As a general rule, anyone who rejects Part B or who does not enroll when initially eligible may later apply for benefits during a general enrollment period that occurs between January 1 and March 31 of each year. However, the monthly premium is increased by 10 percent for each 12-month period during which the person was eligible but failed to enroll.

Medicare secondary rules make employer-provided medical expense coverage primary to Medicare for certain classes of individuals who are over 65, who are disabled, or who are suffering end-stage renal disease. These persons (and any other Medicare-eligible persons still covered as active employees under their employers' plans) may not wish to elect Medicare because it largely constitutes duplicate coverage. When their employer-provided coverage ends, these persons have a 7-month special enrollment period to elect Part B coverage, and the late enrollment penalty is waived.

Medicare is also secondary to benefits received by persons (1) entitled to veterans' or black lung benefits, (2) covered by workers' compensation laws, or (3) whose medical expenses are paid under no-fault insurance or liability insurance.

Medicare Part A: Hospital Benefits

Medicare Part A provides benefits for expenses incurred in hospitals, skilled-nursing facilities, and hospices. Some home health care benefits are also covered. In order for benefits to be paid, the facility or agency providing benefits must participate in the Medicare program. Virtually all hospitals are participants, as are most other facilities or agencies that meet the requirements of Medicare.

Part A of Medicare, along with Part B, provides a high level of benefits for medical expenses. However, as is described in the next few pages, deductibles and copayments are also high and will, no doubt, become even higher as they are adjusted annually to reflect increasing costs. Moreover, certain benefits that were previously provided under employer-provided plans may be excluded or limited under Medicare. For this reason, persons without supplemental retiree coverage from prior employment may wish to consider the purchase of a Medicare supplement (medigap) policy in the individual marketplace.

Hospital Benefits

Part A pays for inpatient hospital services for up to 90 days in each benefit period (also referred to as a spell of illness). A benefit period begins the first time a Medicare recipient is hospitalized and ends only after the recipient has been out of a hospital or skilled-nursing facility for 60 consecutive days. A subsequent hospitalization then begins a new benefit period.

In each benefit period, covered hospital expenses are paid in full for 60 days, subject to an initial deductible ($1,024 in 2008). This deductible is adjusted annually to reflect increasing hospital costs. Benefits for an additional 30 days of hospitalization are also provided in each benefit period, but the patient must pay a daily copayment ($256 in 2008) equal to 25 percent of the initial deductible amount. Each recipient also has a lifetime reserve of 60 additional days that may be used if they exhaust the regular 90 days of benefits. However, once a reserve day is used, it cannot be restored for use in future benefit periods. When using reserve days, patients must pay a daily copayment ($512 in 2008) equal to 50 percent of the initial deductible amount.

There is no limit on the number of benefit periods a person may have during his or her lifetime. However, there is a lifetime limit of 190 days of benefits for treatment in psychiatric hospitals.

Covered inpatient expenses include the following:

- room and board in semiprivate accommodations. Private rooms are covered only if required for medical reasons.
- nursing services (except private-duty nurses)
- use of regular hospital equipment, such as oxygen tents or wheelchairs
- drugs and biologicals ordinarily furnished by the hospital
- diagnostic or therapeutic items or services
- operating room costs
- blood transfusions after the first three pints of blood. Patients must pay for the first three pints of blood unless they get donors to replace the blood.

There is no coverage under Part A for the services of physicians or surgeons.

Skilled-Nursing Facility Benefits

In many cases, a patient may no longer require continuous hospital care but may not be well enough to go home. Consequently, Part A provides benefits for care in a skilled-nursing facility if a physician certifies that skilled-nursing care or rehabilitative services are needed for a condition that was treated in a hospital within the last 30 days. In addition, the prior hospitalization must have lasted at least 3 days. Benefits are paid in full for 20 days in each benefit period and for an additional 80 days with a daily copayment ($128 in 2008) that is equal to 12.5 percent of the initial hospital deductible. Covered expenses are the same as those described for hospital benefits.

A skilled-nursing facility may be a separate facility for providing such care or a separate section of a hospital or nursing home. The facility must have at least one full-time registered nurse, and nursing services must be provided at all times. Every patient must be under the supervision of a physician, and a physician must always be available for emergency care.

One very important point should be made about skilled-nursing facility benefits. Custodial care is not provided under any part of the Medicare program unless skilled-nursing or rehabilitative services are also needed and covered. Older individuals often need custodial care to help them with such personal needs as walking, bathing, dressing, or taking medication. This care may be short-term in nature, but often it is long-term and a major health care expense. Long-term care insurance is discussed in chapter 2.

Home Health Care Benefits

If a patient can be treated at home for a medical condition, Medicare pays the full cost for an unlimited number of home visits by a home health agency. To receive these benefits, a person must be confined at home and be treated under a home health plan set up by a physician. The care needed must include skilled-nursing services, physical therapy, or speech therapy. In addition to these services, Medicare also pays for the cost of part-time home health aides, medical social services, occupational therapy, and medical supplies and equipment provided by the home health agency. There is no charge for these benefits other than a required 20 percent copayment for the cost of such durable medical equipment as oxygen tanks and hospital beds. Medicare does not cover home services that are furnished primarily to assist people in activities of daily living (ADLs) such as housecleaning, preparing meals, shopping, dressing, or bathing.

If a person has only Part A of Medicare, all home health care benefits are covered under Part A. If a person has both Parts A and B, Part A covers the first 100 visits that commence within 14 days of a hospital stay of at least 3 days. Part B covers all other home health visits.

Hospice Benefits

Hospice benefits are available under Part A of Medicare for beneficiaries who are certified as being terminally ill with a life expectancy of 6 months or less. Although a hospice is thought of as a facility for treating the terminally ill, Medicare benefits provided by a Medicare-approved hospice are available primarily to patients in their own homes. However, a hospice can provide inpatient care if the patient needs it. In addition to including the types of benefits described for home health care, hospice benefits include drugs, bereavement counseling, and inpatient respite care when family members need a break from caring for the ill person.

To qualify for hospice benefits, a Medicare recipient must elect such coverage in lieu of other Medicare benefits, except for the services of the attending physician or services and benefits that do not pertain to the terminal condition. There are modest copayments for some services. A beneficiary may cancel the hospice coverage at any time (for example, to pursue chemotherapy treatments) and return to regular Medicare coverage. The beneficiary can elect hospice benefits again but must be recertified as terminally ill.

Exclusions

There are some circumstances under which Part A of Medicare does not pay benefits. In addition, there are times when Medicare acts as the secondary payer of benefits. Exclusions under Part A include the following:

- services outside the United States and its territories or possessions. However, there are a few exceptions to this rule for qualified Mexican and Canadian hospitals.
- elective luxury services, such as private rooms or televisions
- hospitalization for services that are not necessary for the treatment of an illness or injury, such as custodial care or elective cosmetic surgery

Under the following circumstances, Medicare is the secondary payer of benefits:

- when there is primary coverage under an employer-provided medical expense plan for (1) an employee or spouse aged 65 or older or (2) a disabled beneficiary
- when medical care can be paid under any liability policy or policies that provide no-fault benefits for vehicle accidents
- in the first 30 months for end-stage renal disease when an employer-provided medical expense plan provides coverage. By law, employer plans cannot specifically exclude this coverage during this period.

Medicare pays only if complete coverage is not available from these sources and then only to the extent that benefits are less than would otherwise be payable under Medicare.

Medicare Part B: Medical Insurance

Benefits

Medicare Part B provides benefits for most medical expenses not covered under Part A. These include

- physicians' and surgeons' fees. Under certain circumstances, benefits are also provided for the services of chiropractors, podiatrists, and optometrists.
- diagnostic tests
- x rays
- physical therapy
- blood transfusions
- drugs and biologicals that cannot be self-administered
- radiation therapy
- medical supplies, such as surgical dressings, splints, and casts
- rental of medical equipment, such as oxygen tents, hospital beds, and wheelchairs
- prosthetic devices, such as artificial heart valves or lenses after a cataract operation
- ambulance service if a patient's condition does not permit the use of other methods of transportation
- mammograms and Pap smears
- diabetes glucose monitoring and education
- diabetic screening for persons at risk of diabetes
- screening blood test for early detection of heart disease
- colorectal cancer screening
- bone mass measurement
- prostate cancer screening
- pneumococcal vaccination and flu shots
- dilated eye examinations for beneficiaries at high risk for glaucoma
- home health care services as described for Part A when a person does not have Part A coverage or when Part A benefits are not applicable

Exclusions

Although the preceding list of benefits may appear to be comprehensive, there are numerous medical products and services Part B does not cover, some of which represent significant expenses for the elderly. These exclusions include

- most drugs and biologicals that can be self-administered except drugs that are used for osteoporosis, oral cancer treatment, and immunosuppressive therapy under specified circumstances. However, benefits are now available under Part D, which is discussed later.
- most routine physical, eye, and hearing examinations except those previously mentioned. However, as part of the Medicare Prescription Drugs, Improvement, and Modernization Act, all Medicare beneficiaries are eligible for a one-time physical examination within 1 year of enrolling in Part B.
- routine foot care
- immunizations except pneumococcal vaccinations or immunization required because of an injury or immediate risk of infection
- cosmetic surgery unless it is needed because of an accidental injury or to improve the function of a malformed body part
- dental care unless it involves jaw or facial bone surgery or setting fractures
- custodial care
- eyeglasses, hearing aids, or orthopedic shoes

In addition, benefits are not provided to persons eligible for workers' compensation or to those treated in government hospitals. Benefits are provided only for services received in the United States, except for physicians' services and ambulance services rendered for a hospitalization that is covered in Mexico or Canada under Part A. Part B is also a secondary payer of benefits under the same circumstances described for Part A.

Amount of Benefits

The benefits available under Part B are subject to a number of different payment rules. A few charges are paid in full without any cost sharing. These include (1) home health services, (2) pneumococcal vaccinations and flu shots, (3) certain outpatient surgical procedures that are performed in lieu of hospitalization, (4) outpatient diagnostic preadmission tests performed within 7 days prior to hospitalization, (5) mammograms, (6) Pap smears, and (7) a one-time physical examination.

For other charges, there is a calendar-year deductible ($135 in 2008). When the deductible is satisfied, Part B pays 80 percent of approved charges for most covered medical expenses other than professional charges for mental health care and outpatient services of hospitals and mental health centers. Medicare pays only 50 percent of approved charges for the mental health services of physicians and other mental health professionals. There is a separate payment system under which Medicare determines a set payment for each type of service for outpatient services of hospitals and mental health centers. This amount varies across the country to reflect factors such as the level of hospital wages. For some services, Medicare patients are required to pay an amount equal to 20 percent of the set payment amount, and Part B pays 80 percent. For other services, there is a fixed copayment that may be more or less than 20 percent of the set payment amount. In no case can the amount a Medicare patient pays for a single service exceed a dollar figure equal to the Part A hospital deductible ($1,024 in 2008).

The approved charge for doctors' services covered by Medicare is based on a fee schedule issued by the Centers for Medicare & Medicaid Services, the federal agency that administers Medicare. A patient will be reimbursed for only 80 percent of the approved charges above the deductible—regardless of the doctor's actual charge. Most doctors and other suppliers of medical services accept an assignment of Medicare benefits and, therefore, are prohibited from charging a patient more than the fee schedule. They can, however, bill the patient for any portion of the approved charges that Medicare does not pay because of the annual deductible and/or 20 percent copayment for which the beneficiary is responsible. They can also bill for any services that Medicare does not cover.

If a doctor does not accept assignment, the patient will receive a reimbursement directly from Medicare. However, this reimbursement is only 95 percent of what Medicare would have paid to a participating doctor. Doctors who do not accept an assignment of Medicare benefits cannot charge a Medicare patient more than 115 percent of this amount. The effect is that a doctor who does not accept assignment of Medicare benefits can charge a fee that is only 9.25 percent greater than if an assignment had been accepted (115 percent x 95 percent = 109.25 percent). As a result, some doctors either do not see Medicare participants or limit the number of such patients they treat.

The previous limitation on charges does not apply to providers of medical services other than doctors. Although a provider that does not accept assignment can charge any fee, Medicare pays only what it would have paid if the provider accepted assignment. For example, if the approved charge for medical equipment is $100 and the actual charge is $190, Medicare reimburses $80 (.80 x $100), and the Medicare recipient must pay the balance.

Medicare Part C: Medicare Advantage

In 1985, Congress amended the Medicare program to allow a beneficiary to elect coverage under a health maintenance organization (HMO) as an alternative to the traditional Medicare Parts A and B, which are usually referred to as original Medicare. At first, the number of persons who elected this option was relatively small. However, HMO coverage for Medicare beneficiaries grew rapidly in the mid- to late 1990s.

In 1999, Part C of Medicare (originally called Medicare+Choice) went into effect. It expanded the choices available to most Medicare beneficiaries by allowing them to elect health care benefits through one of several alternatives to the original Medicare, as long as the providers of these alternatives enter into contracts with the Centers for Medicare & Medicaid Services. Although beneficiaries must still pay Part B premiums, these alternatives are private insurance plans. Some of these plans market directly to Medicare beneficiaries. Others use agents or brokers to sell their products.

While these alternative plans must provide all benefits available under Parts A and B of Medicare, they typically include broader benefits as part of their basic coverage at no additional cost or for an additional premium. These broader benefits include coverage for the deductibles, copayments, and percentage participation of original Medicare. They may also include some benefits for vision, hearing, or dental care as well as some wellness benefits. As a result, beneficiaries with one of these alternative plans generally have little or no reason to have a Medicare supplement policy. In fact, they are ineligible to purchase one, although they still have a need for Medicare prescription drug coverage.

The initial reaction to Medicare+Choice was less than overwhelming. Few new providers of alternative coverage entered the marketplace, and the enrollment in alternatives to the original Medicare program decreased after several years of growth.

Medicare Advantage

The situation, however, changed in 2005 as a result of provisions in the Medicare Prescription Drug, Improvement, and Modernization Act. The act changed the name of Medicare+Choice to *Medicare Advantage*, and all materials for such plans must now use this terminology. The act made numerous administrative changes to the program aimed at increasing participation. Consequently, about one out of every seven Medicare beneficiaries is now enrolled in a Medicare Advantage plan. About 85 percent of these enrollees are in HMO plans; the remainder are scattered among the other types of plans. Beneficiaries are generally able to enroll in a Medicare Advantage plan or switch plans (including reenrollment in Parts A and B) from November 15 to December 31.

Types of Plans

There are currently five types of Medicare Advantage plans. It is important to emphasize that if one of these options is selected, a beneficiary is still technically covered by Medicare. However, benefits are paid by the Medicare Advantage plan, not original Medicare. Any medical expenses not covered by the Medicare Advantage plan are the responsibility of the plan member. The five types of plans are

- health maintenance organizations (HMOs). As with HMOs for persons who are not eligible for Medicare, beneficiaries typically must select a primary care physician from the plan's network. Usually, this physician must make referrals for specialty care. Some Medicare Advantage HMOs have a point-of-service option, under which a beneficiary can elect to go outside the plan's network, but the beneficiary will pay a portion of the cost of these services.
- preferred-provider organizations (PPOs). Medicare Advantage PPOs are essentially like the PPOs described in chapter 3. Beneficiaries can elect out-of-network care if they are willing to pay the additional cost for such care, which can be substantial.
- private fee-for-service (PFFS) plans. Beneficiaries can go to any provider who agrees to accept the payment rates determined by the plan, but they may be required to pay a portion of these rates in the form of cost sharing. If a provider does not accept the PFFS plan rates, the beneficiary is responsible for the entire balance above what the plan pays. PFFS plans are similar to traditional major medical plans. Although not widely purchased until recently, PFFS plans are becoming increasingly common as more insurers are marketing such products.
- Medicare medical savings account (MMSA) plans. A beneficiary has a high-deductible policy, with the size of the deductible varying from plan to plan. Medicare then puts an annual amount into a medical savings account that can be used for unreimbursed medical costs. MMSA plans are not yet widely purchased and are offered by only a small number of insurers in limited parts of the country.
- special needs plans (SNPs). SNPs are designed primarily to meet the needs of beneficiaries who are eligible for both Medicare and Medicaid (or who have certain chronic conditions) and who live in institutions such as nursing homes or continue to live at home but need the level of care provided by such institutions. These plans help manage and coordinate the many services and providers needed by such beneficiaries. These plans are available only in limited geographic regions.

Is a Medicare Advantage Plan an Appropriate Option?

It is clear from the earlier part of this chapter that the original Medicare program provides less-than-complete protection for medical expenses. As a result, many retirees have some type of medical expense coverage to provide additional benefits. Some retirees have this coverage under employer-provided postretirement medical expense plans; other retirees purchase a Medicare supplement (medigap) policy. However, the selection of a Medicare Advantage plan is often a viable option that may provide broad coverage at a relatively modest cost, although this type of plan is not available in all parts of the country. Moreover, most Medicare Advantage plans are structured as HMOs. For a retiree who was covered by an HMO plan while working, the nature of the coverage will be familiar, and the HMO plan may even be with the same insurer that provided coverage previously. For other retirees, the inherent nature of such plans may be less than desirable.

Other Medicare Alternatives

In addition to Medicare Advantage plans, there are three other types of health plans that are part of the Medicare program. Each is available only in limited parts of the country.

The first is referred to as a Medicare cost plan, which is a type of HMO. Unlike a Medicare Advantage HMO, which receives a set amount of money for each beneficiary, the plan is reimbursed for its reasonable costs by Medicare. The plan pays benefits only if a beneficiary uses a network provider. If services are received outside the plan's network, they are covered by original Medicare. Medicare cost plans predate Medicare+Choice plans and are no longer common. A person eligible for Medicare can enroll at any time as long as such a plan is accepting new members and may return to original Medicare at any time.

Medicare has also approved special projects in some parts of the country that are referred to as demonstration/pilot programs. The purpose of these programs is to test improvements in Medicare coverage, payment, and quality of care for specific groups of people. For example, one program is for persons who have been diagnosed with end-stage renal disease.

The final plan is PACE (programs of all-inclusive care for the elderly). PACE combines medical, social, and long-term care services for frail, elderly beneficiaries who live in and get care in the community. These are joint Medicare and Medicaid programs available in a few states that have chosen to offer them as an optional Medicaid benefit.

Medicare Part D: Prescription Drug Coverage

Along with numerous other changes to Medicare, the Medicare Prescription Drug, Improvement, and Modernization Act added a very complex prescription drug program to Medicare—Medicare Part D.

Part D has been a subject of considerable controversy. Some members of Congress argue that it does not go far enough in meeting the needs of beneficiaries. Other members of Congress contend that its cost will saddle the government with another major entitlement. Part D is also viewed by some as a boon to the pharmaceutical industry that will cost $400–$700 billion over the next 10 years. As with any new program of this magnitude and complexity, there will undoubtedly be factors that come to light during its infancy that will result in the need for changes. Consequently, advisors need to keep abreast of current developments so they can better advise their clients.

Eligibility

Medicare prescription drug plans

Part D is a voluntary prescription drug benefit available to all Medicare beneficiaries enrolled in original Medicare (either Part A and/or Part B) or in any of the various Medicare Advantage plans. Each enrollee must pay a monthly premium. No one can be denied coverage because of income level or for health reasons. Hereafter, Part D benefits are referred to as *Medicare prescription drug plans*.

Types of Plans

Medicare prescription drug plans are private plans offered by insurance companies, managed care plans, and other organizations. These sponsors typically contract with pharmacy benefit managers to design plan formularies. The plans must meet certain standards and be approved by the Secretary of Health and Human Services. Like Medicare Advantage plans, Medicare prescription drug plans may be marketed directly to Medicare beneficiaries or sold by agents or brokers.

There are two basic types of Medicare prescription drug plans. One type of plan is for persons enrolled in the majority of Medicare Advantage plans. As long as the Medicare Advantage plan has a prescription drug program, members can obtain their prescription drug coverage only through that program. The other type of plan, referred to as a stand-alone plan, is available to persons enrolled in original Medicare or in Medicare Advantage plans without prescription drug programs. The main differences between these two types of plans are in the process of enrollment and premium payment.

Standard Benefit Structure

The act provides for a standard prescription drug plan but also allows for alternative plans to be approved if certain requirements are met and the plans are at least as generous as the standard plan. Most plans that are now available provide broader coverage than the standard plan.

Chapter 8 Social Security, Medicare, and Medicare Supplements

**coverage gap
(doughnut hole)**

The standard prescription drug program has an initial annual deductible of $275 in 2008. This amount, and other dollar figures mentioned below, will increase in later years if the expenditures for prescription drugs by Medicare beneficiaries increase.

After the deductible has been satisfied, the plan will pay 75 percent of the next $2,235 of prescription drug costs covered by the plan. Benefits then cease until a beneficiary's total drug costs (including the deductible) reach $5,726.25. This range where no benefits are paid is often referred to as the *coverage gap* (or *doughnut hole*). Once the $5,726.25 amount is reached, the beneficiary will have had out-of-pocket costs of $4,050 (often referred to as *TROOP* or true out-of-pocket costs) in addition to the annual premium. For covered drug costs in excess of $5,726.25, for each prescription the beneficiary will then pay the greater of (1) 5 percent of the cost of the prescription or (2) a modest copay of $2.25 for a generic or $5.60 for a brand name drug. For all but inexpensive drugs, this means that the plan will pay 95 percent of the cost to fill a prescription.

It is important to point out that all of the above limits apply to drug costs covered by the plan. If a beneficiary purchases a drug that is not covered by the plan, the beneficiary must pay the full cost for the drug and cannot apply this amount toward the initial deductible or use it to satisfy the previously mentioned limits. In addition, certain other drug costs do not count toward the limits. These include the cost of drugs purchased outside the United States, the cost of drugs specifically excluded by Medicare, and any payments made by most other private or government drug programs. However, drug costs paid by family members and certain state assistance programs count toward these limits.

The following example shows that beneficiaries with $755 or less in annual prescription drug expenditures will receive no net benefit from a Medicare prescription drug plan, assuming the prescription drug premium is $30 per month. Approximately half of Medicare beneficiaries fall into this category and will need to decide whether they should purchase coverage. The negative side of choosing not to sign up when initially eligible is that there will be a financial penalty for enrollment at a later date, when a beneficiary might have significantly higher drug costs.

Example: Bryan incurs $755 in covered drug costs during the year.

Payment by drug plan	
[.75 x ($755 – $275 deductible)]	$360
Minus premium ($30/month)	–360
Net benefit from plan	0
Percentage of drug costs paid by Bryan	100%

The next example shows that Medicare beneficiaries with $5,726.25 or less in annual prescription drug expenditures will also pay a significant percentage of their drug costs.

Example: Wendy and her husband Keith have annual prescription drug costs of $2,600 and $5,726.25 respectively. (Wendy's costs are about the same as the average prescription drug costs for Medicare recipients.)

Wendy and Keith will each receive $1,676.25 under their Medicare prescription drug plans. This amount equals 75 percent of the first $2,235 in drug costs exceeding the deductible. In Wendy's case, she will have out-of-pocket costs equal to $1,283.75, or slightly more than 49 percent of her expenditures. This $1,283.75 figure is calculated as follows:

Payment ($30/month)	$ 360.00
Deductible	275.00
25% of first $2,235 above deductible	558.75
100% of expenses in excess of $2,510	90.00
	$1,283.75

In Keith's case, his expenses above $2,510 are $3,216.25, and his total out-of-pocket costs and premium are nearly $4,410, or 77 percent of his drug expenditures.

The percentage of drug costs that a beneficiary pays drops as costs exceed $5,726.25 because Part D plans pay 95 percent of this excess amount. For example, a beneficiary with annual drug costs of $50,000 will pay about 12 percent of this amount, and a beneficiary with annual drug costs of $100,000 will be responsible for about 9 percent.

Covered Drugs

Each Medicare prescription drug plan has a formulary, which is a list of approved drugs that the plan will cover. Formularies do not need to cover every prescription drug. Moreover, plans are allowed to make approved formulary changes during the year. By law, however, they must include at least two drugs in every therapeutic class. (There are 146 therapeutic classes.) Most plans cover more than the minimum required number of drugs.

Medicare prescription drug plans are required to cover a majority of drugs in certain classes. These classes include antidepressant, antipsychotic, anticonvulsant, antiretroviral, anticancer, and immunosuppressant drugs.

Some drugs are excluded from Medicare coverage by law. These include nonprescription drugs, prescription vitamins and minerals, certain barbiturates and benzodiazepines, and drugs for anorexia, weight loss or weight gain, fertility, cosmetic purposes, hair growth, and relief of such symptoms of cold as cough and stuffy nose. Plans may provide enhanced benefits and cover some of these excluded drugs. However, charges for the excluded drugs will not count towards meeting out-of-pocket limits.

Plan Variations

Very few Medicare prescription drug plans are exactly like the standard benefit plan. In fact, fewer than 15 percent of persons with Medicare prescription drug coverage have such plans. There are several major ways most plans provide more comprehensive benefits, the details of which vary significantly for each plan.

Formulary Drugs. Most, if not all, plans have more drugs on their formularies than required by law. In some cases, the additional drugs are mostly generics; in other cases, there are both generic and brand name drugs.

Reduced Deductibles. Although many drug plans have an annual calendar-year deductible of $275, the majority of drug plans have no initial deductible. A small number of plans have a deductible that is less than $275 (often $100).

Tiered Copayments. In lieu of paying 75 percent of the cost of each drug after meeting the deductible, most plans have a tiered copayment structure. This is acceptable as long as the average amount paid by the plan for the initial level of benefits is at least 75 percent.

Benefits in the Coverage Gap. A small number of plans provide benefits in the coverage gap, when drug costs exceed $2,510 ($275 + $2,235) but are less than $5,726.25. Some plans cover generic drugs only; in other cases, both generic and brand name drugs are covered.

When there is coverage in this gap, the full cost of the drugs is used to calculate whether the $5,726.25 threshold has been met.

Where Prescriptions Can Be Filled

Prescription drug plans use a network of pharmacies to dispense drugs. Some plans operate on a national basis; others operate within defined regions. In some cases, the network may include many local pharmacies; in other cases, it may consist of a single large retail chain. In any event, all plans must include walk-in pharmacies, although most plans also fill prescriptions through mail-order pharmacies that can be accessed by mail, telephone, fax, or Internet.

Beneficiaries are allowed to use out-of-network pharmacies only if they cannot reasonably be expected to use a network pharmacy and they do not regularly get their drugs from the out-of-network pharmacy.

Cost

The federal government pays a significant subsidy out of general tax revenue to each Medicare prescription drug plan. On average, this subsidy is about 75 percent of the cost for a plan with the standard benefit structure. There are, however, significant variations in the premiums that a beneficiary must pay. Nationally, the premiums average less than $30 per month, but some stand-alone plans cost less and others significantly more. Premiums for drug coverage under Medicare Advantage drug plans are generally somewhat lower, and a few plans even offer the benefit at no extra cost.

These variations are a function of several factors, including drugs covered, deductibles, copays, pharmacies used, and the plan's ability to negotiate with manufacturers of drugs. Some lower-cost plans are also attempting to buy market share.

Subsidies in the form of waiver of premiums and copayments are available to beneficiaries who have low incomes and limited assets.

Enrollment

The initial enrollment period for a person who becomes eligible for Medicare is a 7-month period that includes the month of eligibility and the 3 months before and after that date. This is the same as the enrollment period for Part B of Medicare. In addition, there are also special enrollment periods for certain events, such as moving out of a plan's service area or returning to original Medicare from a Medicare Advantage plan.

creditable prescription drug coverage

If an individual fails to enroll in a Medicare prescription drug plan at the time of initial eligibility, there is a penalty unless the person had prior *creditable prescription drug coverage.* Creditable coverage includes prescription drug coverage under another plan that is at least as good as Medicare. These other plans, such as employer or union plans, must certify the actuarial equivalency of their plan benefits with Medicare.

An individual may change prescription drug plans, without evidence of insurability, during an annual election period that runs from November 15 until December 31 of each year. The new plan is effective on the following January 1.

COVERAGE TO SUPPLEMENT MEDICARE

This section of chapter 8 is devoted to explaining the various types of coverages designed to supplement original Medicare.

Employer Plans to Supplement Medicare

Precise statistics are difficult to obtain, but the majority of individuals have some type of coverage to supplement Medicare. About 30 percent of Medicare beneficiaries are still fortunate enough to have retiree benefits provided by their former employers, but this percentage is shrinking. Employer-provided coverage for retirees may take the form of a Medicare carve-out or a Medicare supplement. With a Medicare carve-out, the employer-provided group benefits are reduced to the extent that benefits are payable under Medicare for the same expenses. As an alternative, some employers use a group Medicare supplement plan that provides benefits for certain expenses not covered by Medicare. Note that the term Medicare supplement in the group market is applied generically to any supplemental medical expense plan. These plans are not subject to the rules that apply to individual Medicare supplement policies, as described later in this chapter. The extent to which employer-provided coverage includes benefits for prescription drugs varies.

Another 30 to 40 percent of Medicare beneficiaries are covered under Medicare Advantage plans (previously discussed) or have individually purchased Medicare supplement policies. However, even with such coverage, some people may still need coverage for the cost of prescription drugs. This coverage, as previously discussed, can be obtained with Medicare prescription drug coverage.

Individual Medigap Policies to Supplement Medicare

medigap insurance

Medicare supplement insurance in the individual marketplace is frequently referred to as *medigap insurance*. As the name implies, its objective is to fill some of the gaps left after Medicare benefits have been exhausted. When originally developed, Medicare supplement plans were as diverse as the companies that sold them. This led to confusion in the marketplace and to questionable sales practices and duplications of coverage. As a result, the federal government enacted legislation to address the structure and marketing of Medicare supplement plans.

In 1990, the Medicare supplement market became directly subject to federal regulation when Congress directed the National Association of Insurance Commissioners (NAIC) to develop a group of standardized Medicare supplement policies. Congress mandated several other features, including a 6-month open-enrollment period, limited preexisting-conditions exclusions, prohibition of the sale of duplicate coverage, and increased loss ratios. Furthermore, when describing the benefits of each of the Medicare supplement policies, insurance companies must use the same format, language, and definitions. They also are required to use a uniform chart and outline of coverage to summarize the benefits in each plan. These requirements are intended to make it easier for beneficiaries to compare policies and to choose among them based on service, reliability, and price.

Federal laws have also generated several restrictions on the markets to which Medicare supplement policies may be sold. Under these restrictions, known as antiduplication provisions, it is generally illegal for an insurance company to sell a Medicare supplement policy to the following:

- a current Medicare supplement policyowner, unless that person states in writing that the first policy will be cancelled
- a Medicaid recipient
- an enrollee in a Medicare Advantage plan

Violation of these provisions is subject to criminal and/or civil penalties under federal law.

Basic Benefits

basic benefits

The NAIC adopted 10 standard Medicare supplement plans; all 10 required the inclusion of a core of specified *basic benefits*. States may approve, and insurers may offer, fewer than the 10 standard plans, but all states must permit the basic benefits to be sold alone (plan A). Most states permit the sale of all 10 plans, but a few limit the types sold, and a few states are not affected by the mandate because alternative standardized programs were already in place prior to the federal legislation. There are now two additional plans that contain consumer-directed health plan features. These two plans differ somewhat from the original 10 plans, which are discussed first.

Note that the following rules for standardized policies apply to the individual marketplace. Group Medicare supplements that employers offer to their retirees are not considered Medicare supplement policies and may differ. In addition, three states—Massachusetts, Minnesota, and Wisconsin—had Medicare supplement programs prior to the NAIC standards. These programs were allowed to continue and the policies issued are somewhat different from the 10 standard plans. However, they are required to contain the basic benefits available in all other states.

The basic benefits that all 10 original plans must contain are:

- hospitalization—the copayment or cost sharing of Part A benefits for the 61st through the 90th day of hospitalization and the 60-day

lifetime reserve. In addition, coverage is extended for 365 additional days after Medicare benefits end.
- medical expenses—the Part B percentage participation for Medicare-approved charges for physicians' and medical services after a beneficiary has satisfied the Part B deductible
- blood—the payment for the first three pints of blood each year

Additional Benefits

The 10 original Medicare supplement plans that can be sold include, in addition to the basic benefits, an array of benefits for services that Medicare covers only in part or not at all. These benefits include paying

- the Part A copayment for the 21st through the 100th day of skilled-nursing facility care
- the hospital inpatient Part A deductible for each benefit period
- the Part B deductible
- charges for physicians' and medical services that exceed the Medicare-approved amount (either 80 or 100 percent of these charges)
- 80 percent of the charges for emergency care in a foreign country (with several limitations)
- an at-home provider to give assistance with activities of daily living (ADLs) while a beneficiary qualifies for Medicare home health care benefits. Coverage is limited to seven visits per week and a maximum benefit of $40 per visit and $1,600 per year.
- limited annual amounts for preventive care (annual shots, physicals, certain screening tests, and so forth)

The 10 plans are illustrated in table 8-6. The policies available in the individual marketplace must be identified by the letters A through J. Insurers can offer plans F and J as high-deductible policies with a deductible that is set annually by the federal government. The 2008 deductible is $1,900.

The most widely available Medicare supplement plans are A, C, D, and F. Plan A generally represents less than 5 percent of Medicare supplement sales, however. Plan F represents more than half, while plans C and D make up approximately a third of total sales. Plans K and L and Medicare SELECT policies (also described later), which are generally less available, represent no more than 10 percent of total Medicare supplement sales.

Plans H, I, and J were originally designed to pay 50 percent of outpatient prescription drug charges after a $250 deductible up to an annual $1,250 or $3,000 calendar limit. Beginning in 2006, insurance companies may no longer issue these policies to new insureds with a drug benefit included. Persons already insured under these policies have several options. They may continue to renew the policies with drug benefits included as long as they do not enroll in a Medicare prescription drug plan (Part D). However, they will then probably be subject to the penalty for late enrollment if they later enroll in a Part D plan because the benefits under their Medicare supplement policies are not likely to qualify as creditable coverage. If they choose to enroll in a Medicare prescription drug plan, they may keep their existing Medicare supplement policies in force but with the drug benefit eliminated and the premium adjusted accordingly. Alternatively, they can switch to another available Medicare supplement policy that has no drug benefit. Such a switch is allowed without evidence of insurability or a penalty for preexisting conditions as long as it occurs during the initial Part D enrollment period.

TABLE 8-6
Medicare Supplement (Medigap) Policies

Benefits	A	B	C	D	E	F	G	H	I	J
Basic	X	X	X	X	X	X	X	X	X	X
Skilled-nursing facility (days 21–100)			X	X	X	X	X	X	X	X
Part A deductible		X	X	X	X	X	X	X	X	X
Part B deductible			X			X				X
Part B excess charges						100%	80%		100%	100%
Foreign travel emergency			X	X	X	X	X	X	X	X
At-home recovery				X			X		X	X
Preventive medical care					X					X
Prescription drugs								$1,250*	$1,250*	$3,000*

*Not available with newly sold policies; can be eliminated by an already insured person who enrolls in a Medicare prescription drug plan.

Other Plans

With two exceptions, insurance companies cannot offer policies that provide benefits that differ from those under plans A through J. The first exception is that the companies can now offer two plans with consumer-directed features. Called plans K and L, these plans include the same basic hospital benefits as plans A through J and pay 100 percent of these amounts. In addition, these plans cover the following benefits:

- the Part A deductible
- the daily copayment for the 21st through the 100th day of skilled-nursing facility care
- the first three pints of blood
- the percentage participation for Part B services
- hospice and respite care cost sharing (not covered under plans A through J)

Under plan K, the insured must pay 50 percent of the amounts for these additional benefits except for Part B preventive services, which are covered at 100 percent. When the insured's out-of-pocket payments plus the Part B deductible equal $4,400 (in 2008 and subject to indexing), plan K will pay 100 percent of the self-responsible amounts (any required copayments and percentage participation for Medicare services other than prescription drugs) for the rest of the calendar year. However, provider charges that exceed Medicare-approved amounts (excess charges) do not count toward the annual out-of-pocket limit.

Plan L is identical to plan K except that the percentage the insured must pay is 25 percent, rather than 50 percent. In addition, the out-of-pocket limit is $2,220 (in 2008).

Because of the more limited benefits and cost sharing, plans K and L are significantly less expensive than plans A through J.

Medicare SELECT policy

The second exception is for policies issued under the Medicare SELECT program, which has been in existence since 1994. A *Medicare SELECT policy* is one of the 12 standard Medicare supplement policies (plans A through L), but it can exclude or limit benefits (except in emergencies) for medical services if they are not received from network providers. Medicare SELECT policies are issued by insurance companies as PPO products and by some HMOs. As a general rule, the cost of a Medicare SELECT policy is 15 to 25 percent less than the cost of a comparable policy that does not use such preferred-provider networks. An insured who has a Medicare SELECT policy has the right to switch to a regular Medicare supplement policy the same company sells, as long as the new policy has equal or less coverage than the Medicare SELECT policy.

Eligibility

Persons aged 65 or older and anyone else eligible for Medicare may buy any available Medicare supplement policy, regardless of health status, at any time during the 6-month period after initial enrollment for Medicare Part B benefits. Insurance companies are allowed to exclude benefits for no more than 6 months because of preexisting conditions, but this period is reduced or eliminated by prior creditable coverage. Some policies, however, immediately provide benefits for preexisting conditions or have an exclusion period shorter than 6 months.

If a person initially elects a Medicare Advantage plan in lieu of original Medicare benefits, he or she will be eligible to purchase a Medicare supplement policy, without evidence of insurability, if he or she leaves the Medicare Advantage plan during the first 12 months of coverage and returns to original Medicare benefits. Similarly, a person who drops Medicare supplement coverage and elects a Medicare Advantage plan can regain Medicare supplement coverage if he or she decides to drop the Medicare Advantage plan during the first 12 months of coverage.

In addition, a person can obtain a Medicare supplement policy without evidence of insurability because of the termination of an employer-provided plan that supplements Medicare or because a Medicare Advantage plan no longer provides coverage or because the person loses eligibility by moving out of the plan's service area. Policies also have a free-look period and are guaranteed renewable.

THE FINAL WORD

Many of the Social Security and Medicare numbers change every year and, consequently, are difficult to learn. It is not, however, as important to memorize these numbers as it is to understand that they do change every year. Both Social Security (www.ssa.gov) and Medicare (www.medicare.gov) have websites that display the updated numbers every year when they are available. In addition, the Centers for Medicare & Medicaid Services (www.cms.gov) also has a website. Together, these websites provide a lot of useful information about programs. They are worth investigating if only to sift through the wealth of information located there.

CHAPTER SUMMARY

In a broad sense, the term Social Security can be used to refer to several of the programs resulting from the Social Security Act of 1935 and its subsequent amendments. Taken together, these programs constitute the old-age, survivors, disability, and health insurance (OASDHI) program of the federal government. This program is often separated into two broad parts. The first part is the old-age, survivors, and disability insurance (OASDI) program called Social Security. The second part is the health insurance (HI) program called Medicare.

The Social Security and Medicare programs are important to financial advisors and their clients for at least two reasons. First, the most significant insurance expense for most individuals is their contributions to Social Security and Medicare. Second, these programs form the foundation on which employee benefit plans and individual insurance plans are built.

All the benefits of the Social Security program and Part A of Medicare are financed through a system of payroll and self-employment taxes paid by all persons covered under the programs. In addition, employers of covered persons are also taxed. Part B of Medicare is financed by a combination of monthly premiums paid by persons eligible for benefits and contributions from the federal government.

To be eligible for benefits under Social Security, an individual must have credit for a minimum amount of work under the program. This credit is based on quarters of coverage, which are the basis for establishing an insured status under Social Security. The three types of insured status are fully insured, currently insured, and disability insured.

The Social Security program provides three principal types of benefits: retirement benefits, survivors benefits, and disability benefits. A worker who is fully insured is eligible to receive monthly retirement benefits as early as age 62. However, the election to receive benefits prior to full retirement age results in a permanently reduced benefit. All categories of survivors benefits are payable if a worker is fully insured at the time of death. However, three types of survivors benefits are also payable if a worker is only currently insured. A disabled worker under full retirement age is eligible to receive disability benefits as long as he or she is disability insured and meets the definition of disability. In any event, monthly benefits to any Social Security recipient cease upon his or her death.

With the exception of the small lump-sum death benefit of $255, the amount of all Social Security benefits is based on a worker's primary insurance amount (PIA). When a beneficiary is eligible for benefits, his or her actual PIA is calculated by the Social Security Administration. The PIA is the amount a worker receives if he or she retires at full retirement age or becomes disabled, and it is the amount on which benefits for family members are based.

Part A, the hospital portion of Medicare, is available to any person aged 65 or older as long as the person is entitled to monthly Social Security retirement benefits. Any person eligible for Part A is also eligible for Part B, the medical insurance portion of Medicare. However, a monthly premium must be paid for Part B. Persons who receive Social Security retirement benefits are automatically enrolled in Medicare if they are eligible. If they do not want Part B, they must reject it in writing.

Medicare Part A provides benefits for expenses incurred in hospitals, skilled-nursing facilities, and hospices. Some home health care benefits are also covered. Medicare Part B provides benefits for most medical expenses not covered under Part A. While both Parts A and B provide a high level of benefits for medical expenses, deductibles and copayments are also high and will, no doubt, become even higher as they are adjusted annually to reflect increasing costs.

Medicare Part C is an alternative to the traditional Medicare Parts A and B. Part C expands the choices available to most Medicare beneficiaries by allowing them to elect health care benefits through one of several alternatives known as Medicare Advantage plans. Although Medicare Advantage plans are private insurance plans, their beneficiaries are still technically covered by Medicare and must pay Part B premiums.

The Medicare Prescription Drug, Improvement, and Modernization Act added a prescription drug program to Medicare—Medicare Part D. Part D is a voluntary prescription drug benefit available to all Medicare beneficiaries enrolled in Part A and/or Part B or in any of the various Medicare Advantage plans. The benefits of Part D are provided through private plans called Medicare prescription drug plans.

The act provides for a standard prescription drug plan but also allows for alternative plans to be approved if they meet certain requirements and are at least as generous as the standard plan. Most plans that are now available provide broader coverage than the standard plan. Nationally, plan premiums average less than $30 per month, but there are significant variations. These variations depend on the drugs covered, the deductibles, the copays, the pharmacies used, and the plan's ability to negotiate with manufacturers of drugs.

Although precise statistics are difficult to obtain, the majority of individuals have some type of coverage to supplement Medicare. About 30 to 40 percent of Medicare beneficiaries are covered under Medicare Advantage plans (discussed previously) or have individually purchased Medicare supplement policies. Another 30 percent of Medicare beneficiaries are fortunate enough to have benefits provided by their former employers, but this percentage is shrinking. Employer-sponsored plans are not subject to the rules that apply to individual Medicare supplement policies.

Medicare supplement insurance in the individual marketplace is frequently referred to as medigap insurance. As the name implies, its objective is to fill some of the gaps left after Medicare benefits have been exhausted. When originally developed, Medicare supplement plans were as diverse as the companies that sold them. This led to confusion in the marketplace and to questionable sales practices and duplications of coverage. As a result, the Medicare supplement market became directly subject to federal regulation when Congress directed the NAIC to develop a group of standardized Medicare supplement policies. In addition, Congress also generated several restrictions on the markets to which Medicare supplement policies may be sold.

As directed by Congress, the NAIC adopted 10 standard Medicare supplement plans, each of which is required to include a core of specified basic benefits. These 10 plans must be identified by the letters A through J. The most widely available plans are A, C, D, and F, with plan F accounting for more than half of total sales.

Insurance companies cannot offer policies that provide benefits that differ from those under plans A through J with two exceptions. The first exception is that insurers can now offer plans K and L with consumer-directed health features. The second exception is for policies issued under the Medicare SELECT program. A Medicare SELECT policy is one of the 12 standard Medicare supplement policies (plans A through L), but it can exclude or limit benefits for medical services (except for emergencies) if they are not received from network providers. Consequently, the cost of a Medicare SELECT policy is 15 to 25 percent less than the cost of a comparable policy that does not use a preferred-provider network.

CHAPTER REVIEW

Key Terms and Concepts are explained in the Glossary. Answers to the Review Questions and Self-Test Questions are found in the back of the book in the Answers to Questions section.

Key Terms and Concepts

OASDHI
quarters of coverage
fully insured
currently insured
disability insured
full retirement age
mother's/father's benefit
blackout period
primary insurance amount (PIA)
earnings test

Social Security Statement
Medicare Advantage
Medicare prescription drug plans
coverage gap (doughnut hole)
creditable prescription drug
 coverage
medigap insurance
basic benefits
Medicare SELECT policy

Review Questions

8-1. How are the Social Security and Medicare programs financed?

8-2. As of this year, Evelyn Grey, aged 38, had 28 quarters of coverage under Social Security. Twenty-four of these quarters were earned prior to the birth of her first child 11 years ago. Four quarters have been earned since she reentered the labor force one year ago.
   a. Is Grey fully insured? Explain.
   b. Is Grey currently insured? Explain
   c. Is Grey disability insured? Explain

8-3. Explain when a worker is eligible to receive retirement benefits under Social Security.

8-4. What categories of persons are eligible for Social Security survivors benefits?

8-5. What is the definition of disability under Social Security?

8-6. a. Explain the relationship between a worker's PIA and the benefits available for dependents and survivors.
   b. What happens if the total benefits for a family exceed the maximum family benefit?

8-7. Explain how a worker's retirement benefits under Social security will be affected if that person elects early or delayed retirement.

8-8. Describe the earnings test applicable to the Social Security program.

8-9. Describe the automatic cost-of-living adjustment provision under Social Security as it relates to benefit amounts.

8-10. With respect to Part A of Medicare:
   a. Describe the types of benefits that are available.
   b. Explain the extent to which deductibles and copayments are required.
   c. Identify the major exclusions.

8-11. With respect to Part B of Medicare:
   a. Describe the types of benefits that are available.
   b. Explain the extent to which copayments are required.
   c. Identify the major exclusions.

8-12. Identify five types of Medicare Advantage plans available under Part C of Medicare.

8-13. Explain who is eligible to receive Medicare Part D prescription drug coverage.

8-14. Besides the basic benefits that must be included in all medigap (Medicare supplement) policies, what other features did Congress mandate for medigap (Medicare supplement) insurance?

8-15. What are the eligibility criteria for medigap (Medicare supplement) insurance?

Self-Test Questions

Instructions: Read chapter 8 first, then answer the following questions to test your knowledge. There are 10 questions; circle the correct answer, then check your answers with the answer key in the back of the book.

8-1. As of this year, Brad, aged 35, has 36 quarters of coverage under the Social Security program. These quarters were all earned in the last 40 quarters. What is Brad's insured status under the program?

 (A) He is currently, fully, and disability insured.
 (B) He is disability insured, but neither fully nor currently insured.
 (C) He is currently and fully insured, but not disability insured.
 (D) He is currently insured, but neither fully nor disability insured.

8-2. Which of the following statements concerning Social Security disability benefits is correct?

 (A) Benefits are subject to a waiting period and commence one year after a disability begins.
 (B) Benefits are payable as long as the disabled worker is unable to perform his or her regular job.
 (C) Benefits are payable as long as the disabled worker is considered to be currently insured.
 (D) Benefits cease at full retirement age but are replaced by comparable Social Security retirement benefits.

8-3. Which of the following persons will have his or her Social Security benefits reduced or terminated because of the earnings test?

(A) A widow, aged 39, who receives survivors benefits and has annual income of $24,000 from a full-time job.
(B) A child, aged 12, who receives survivors benefits and has a monthly annuity income of $1,000 from a settlement option of her father's life insurance policy.
(C) A retired worker, aged 73, who earns $14,000 annually from part-time employment.
(D) A retired worker, aged 64, who receives $18,000 annually from investment income.

8-4. Which of the following statements concerning monthly Social Security benefits for the family members of a 67-year-old retiree receiving full retirement benefits is correct?

(A) The 60-year-old spouse of the retired worker is eligible to receive 75 percent of the worker's PIA.
(B) The 15-year-old daughter of the retired worker is eligible to receive 50 percent of the worker's PIA.
(C) The 22-year-old son of the retired worker is eligible to receive 75 percent of the worker's PIA if he stays in college.
(D) The 87-year-old mother of the retired worker is eligible to receive 50 percent of the worker's PIA if she is a dependent.

8-5. Which of the following statements concerning insured status under Social Security is (are) correct?

   I. A currently insured worker must have credit for at least 4 quarters of coverage out of the last 12-quarter period.
   II. A fully insured worker must be currently insured and have credit for at least 50 quarters of coverage over his or her work life.

(A) I only
(B) II only
(C) Both I and II
(D) Neither I nor II

8-6. Which of the following statements concerning Social Security benefits is (are) correct?

    I. Social Security benefits are increased automatically in accordance with increases in the CPI.
   II. If a person is eligible for more than one type of Social Security benefit, only the higher benefit is paid.

(A) I only
(B) II only
(C) Both I and II
(D) Neither I nor II

8-7. Which of the following statements concerning the financing of Social Security is (are) correct?

    I. The Social Security tax rate for self-employed persons is one-half of the combined tax rate for employees and employers.
   II. The Social Security wage base on which taxes are paid increases annually based on changes in the national level of wages.

(A) I only
(B) II only
(C) Both I and II
(D) Neither I nor II

8-8. Part A of Medicare provides benefits for all the following types of expenses EXCEPT

(A) inpatient hospital services
(B) hospice care
(C) physicians' and surgeons' fees
(D) home health care visits

8-9. All the following are types of Medicare Advantage plans used with Part C of Medicare EXCEPT

(A) preferred-provider organization (PPO) plans
(B) private fee-for-service (PFFS) plans
(C) health maintenance organization (HMO) plans
(D) supplementary (medigap) insurance plans

8-10. Basic benefits required to be in all medigap insurance policies include all the following EXCEPT the

(A) Part A copayment for the 61st through the 90th day of hospitalization
(B) Part A copayment for the 21st through the 100th day of skilled-nursing facility care
(C) Part B percentage participation for Medicare-approved charges for physicians' and medical services
(D) payment for the first 3 pints of blood each year

NOTES

1. For a comprehensive treatment of Social Security and Medicare, see Thomas P. O'Hare and Burton T. Beam, Jr., *Individual Health Insurance Planning*, (Bryn Mawr, PA: The American College Press, 2008), chapter 10, and Burton T. Beam, Jr. and Eric A. Wiening, *Fundamentals of Insurance Planning,* chapter 7.
2. The family maximum benefit for 2008 is calculated using the following formula:
    (1) 150% of the 1st $909 of the worker's PIA, plus
    (2) 272% of the worker's PIA over $909 through $1,312, plus
    (3) 134% of the worker's PIA over $1,312 through $1,711, plus
    (4) 175% of the worker's PIA over $1,711

Appendix A

Topic List for CFP® Certification Examinations*

The following topics, based on the 2004 Job Study Analysis, are the basis for CFP® Certification Examinations.

TOPIC	TOPIC	TOPIC
GENERAL PRINCIPLES OF FINANCIAL PLANNING	32. Stock plans	67. Distribution rules, alternatives, and taxation
1. Financial planning process	33. Non-qualified deferred compensation	**ESTATE PLANNING**
2. CFP Board's *Code of Ethics and Professional Responsibility and Disciplinary Rules and Procedures*	**INVESTMENT PLANNING**	68. Characteristics and consequences of property titling
	34. Characteristics, uses and taxation of investment vehicles	69. Methods of property transfer at death
3. CFP Board's *Financial Planning Practice Standards*	35. Types of investment risk	70. Estate planning documents
	36. Quantitative investment concepts	71. Gifting strategies
4. Financial statements	37. Measures of investment returns	72. Gift tax compliance and tax calculation
5. Cash flow management	38. Bond and stock valuation concepts	73. Incapacity planning
6. Financing strategies	39. Investment theory	74. Estate tax compliance and tax calculation
7. Function, purpose, and regulation of financial institutions	40. Portfolio development and analysis	75. Sources for estate liquidity
	41. Investment strategies	76. Powers of appointment
8. Education planning	42. Asset allocation and portfolio diversification	77. Types, features, and taxation of trusts
9. Financial planning for special circumstances	43. Asset pricing models	78. Qualified interest trusts
10. Economic concepts	**INCOME TAX PLANNING**	79. Charitable transfers
11. Time value of money concepts and calculations	44. Income tax law fundamentals	80. Use of life insurance in estate planning
	45. Tax compliance	81. Valuation issues
12. Financial services regulations and requirements	46. Income tax fundamentals and calculations	82. Marital deduction
13. Business law	47. Tax accounting	83. Deferral and minimization of estate taxes
14. Consumer protection laws	48. Characteristics and income taxation of business entities	84. Intra-family and other business transfer techniques
INSURANCE PLANNING AND RISK MANAGEMENT	49. Income taxation of trusts and estates	85. Generation-skipping transfer tax (GSTT)
15. Principles of risk and insurance	50. Basis	86. Fiduciaries
16. Analysis and evaluation of risk exposures	51. Depreciation/cost-recovery concepts	87. Income in respect of a decedent (IRD)
17. Property, casualty and liability insurance	52. Tax consequences of like-kind exchanges	88. Postmortem estate planning techniques
18. Health insurance and health care cost management (individual)	53. Tax consequences of the disposition of property	89. Estate planning for non-traditional relationships
19. Disability income insurance (individual)	54. Alternative minimum tax (AMT)	
20. Long-term care insurance (individual)	55. Tax reduction/management techniques	**ADDENDUM**
21. Life insurance (individual)	56. Passive activity and at-risk rules	The following topics are an addendum to the Topic List for CFP® Certification Examination.
22. Income taxation of life insurance	57. Tax implications of special circumstances	
23. Business uses of insurance	58. Charitable contributions and deductions	1. Client and planner attitudes, values, biases and behavioral characteristics and the impact on financial planning.
24. Insurance needs analysis	**RETIREMENT PLANNING**	
25. Insurance policy and company selection	59. Retirement needs analysis	
26. Annuities	60. Social Security (Old Age, Survivor, and Disability Insurance, OASDI)	2. Principles of communication and counseling
EMPLOYEE BENEFITS PLANNING	61. Types of retirement plans	
27. Group life insurance	62. Qualified plan rules and options	
28. Group disability insurance	63. Other tax-advantaged retirement plans	
29. Group medical insurance	64. Regulatory considerations	
30. Other employee benefits	65. Key factors affecting plan selection for businesses	
31. Employee stock options	66. Investment considerations for retirement plans	

---

*An outline of the topics on the Topic List for CFP®Certification Examinations. The complete topic list with all the subparts can be found on the Certified Financial Planner Board of Standards, Inc. website at: http://www.cfp.net/become/topiclist.asp. This outline list is used with permission. All rights reserved by the Certified Financial Planner Board of Standards, Inc.

Appendix B

RISK IDENTIFICATION QUESTIONNAIRE
(Individual Form)

_____
(Name)
_____
(Mailing Address)
_____

_____
_____
(Phone Number)
_____
(E-Mail Address)

REAL PROPERTY

Address of principal residence _____

_____

This is a single family dwelling _____ duplex _____ apartment unit _____ condominium _____

other (describe) _____

Address of all additional locations:

Seasonal residence _____

Farm _____

Income property _____

Vacant land _____

Other property interests _____

Property Owned	Principal Residence	Other (identify)	
Residence—square ft.			
Number of stories			
Type of construction			
Year built			
Original building cost			
Date purchased			
Purchase price			
Actual cash value			
Replacement cost (excl. land value)			
Current mortgage			

Describe detached garage or other buildings on the same premises.
_____

If any of these properties were rented rather than owned, what amount of rent would probably be charged?
_____

If any occupied property would become untenantable because of damage or destruction, what monthly expenses over and above current living expenses would be incurred? _____
_____

Provide a copy of the latest appraised value excluding land or property. _____

Appendix B B.3

Property Rented

Single family dwelling _____ duplex _____ apartment _____

Monthly rent _____

Lease termination date _____

If premise becomes untenantable because of damage or destruction, does lease require continuation of rent?
_____

Income Property	**Location 1**	**Other**
Number of units		
Type of commercial use		
Rental income—annual		
Monthly rates		

If all leases could be cancelled and rewritten today, what change would there be in annual rental income and rate per unit? _____

Land	**Farm**	**Vacant Land**
Number of acres		

General

Occupation and other business pursuits (describe duties) _____
_____

Amount of largest personal check likely to be drawn _____

Number of credit cards _____ Number of fund transfer cards _____

Number of full-time servants _____ part-time _____

Number of caretakers or other household employees _____

PERSONAL PROPERTY

	Principal Residence		Secondary Residence	
Estimated Value of	Actual Cash Value	Replacement Cost	Actual Cash Value	Replacement Cost
a. Silverware, pewter				
b. Linens (including dining and bedroom)				
c. Clothing (men's, women's, children's)				
d. Rugs (including floor coverings and draperies)				
e. Books				
f. Musical instruments (including pianos)				
g. Television sets, radios, record players, and records				
h. Paintings, etchings, pictures and other objects of art				
i. China, glassware (including bric-a-brac)				
j. Cameras, photographic equipment				
k. Golf, hunting, fishing, and other sports equipment				
l. Refrigerators, washing machines, stoves, electrical appliances, and other kitchen equipment				
m. Bedding (including blankets, comforters, covers, pillows, mattresses, and springs)				
n. Furniture (including tables, chairs, sofas, desks, beds, chests, lamps, mirrors, and clocks)				
o. Business property				
p. All other personal property (including wines, liquors, foodstuffs, garden and lawn tools and equipment; trunks, traveling bags; children's playthings; and miscellaneous articles in basement and attic)				
Total Estimated Value				

Special Items

Jewelry and watches:

    a. Describe each item _____

    b. Original cost of each _____

    c. Appraised value (obtain appraisal) _____

    d. Where kept (safe-deposit box) _____

Furs:

    a. Describe each article of fur _____

    b. Original cost of each _____

    c. Appraised value (obtain appraisal) _____

    d. Where stored (limit of liability per receipt) _____

Describe and value other items of unusual value:

    a. Stamp collections _____

    b. Fine arts _____

    c. Paintings _____

    d. Antiques _____

    e. Securities _____

Boats or marine equipment:

    a. Length and type of boat _____

    b. Size of motor _____

Miscellaneous Items

Dogs, saddle horses, and other pets (pedigreed) _____

_____

Contents of barns, sheds, and other outbuildings _____

_____

Value of children's property away at school _____

_____

Airplanes, motorcycles, and motorized scooters _____

_____

Location, nature, and value of property in storage warehouses: furs in storage, sports equipment at clubs, silver in safe-deposit vaults, etc. _____

_____

Cash on hand _____

Automobiles

	#1	#2	#3
Year and make			
Body style/model			
Identification number			
Name of registered owner			
Purchase date (new/used)			
Purchase price			
Actual cash value (current)			
Use of automobile			
Distance to work			
Where garaged (if other than principal residence)			
Trailers—Type			
Weight			
Axles			

Describe all recreational vehicles _____
_____

_____

Do you ever rent an automobile? _____ Length of typical rental period _____

Describe your use of company-owned vehicles _____
_____

PREMATURE DEATH

	If You Die	If Spouse Dies
Lump-Sum Cash Needs of the Survivor(s)		
Cleanup fund. Includes unpaid last illness expenses, burial costs, federal and state taxes, probate costs, and other unpaid bills or debts	$	$
Mortgage. The remaining balance, (Assumes that preference is to pay off mortgage. If not, mortgage payments should be included in income needs.)	$	$
Education fund. Estimated present value of future costs to educate children	$	$
Emergency fund. Used for unexpected expenses not readily payable from current income	$	$
Other	$	$
Totals	$	$
Income Needs of the Survivor(s)		
Level of income desired for each category (based on current purchasing power)		
Survivors		
Lifetime monthly income to surviving spouse	$	$
Additional monthly income to family during child-raising years (dependency period)	$	$
Monthly income during first 2 years after death (readjustment period)	$	$

DISBILITY INCOME

	You	Spouse
Estimated monthly income needed if disability occurs today	$	$

MEDICAL EXPENSES

	For You and/or Your Family
Estimated cost of major illness requiring extended hospitalization and physician care	$

LONG-TERM CARE EXPENSES

Estimated cost of long-term care expenses	$

RETIREMENT INCOME

Desired monthly income at retirement	$

Glossary

above-the-line deductions • deductions taken from gross income in determining adjusted gross income

accidental death and dismemberment (AD&D) insurance • insurance that pays benefits if an employee dies accidentally or suffers certain types of injuries. Coverage is commonly provided as a rider to a group life insurance contract but may also be provided through a separate group insurance contract.

accrual method • a tax accounting method that C corporations typically use. Under this method, income is accounted for when the right to receive it comes into being, that is, when all the events that determine the right have occurred. It is not the actual receipt but the right to receive that governs.

actual cash value • replacement cost less a reduction for depreciation and obsolescence

adjusted gross income (AGI) • for income tax purposes, gross income minus all allowable above-the-line deductions. It is an intermediate calculation that is made in the process of determining an individual's income tax liability for a given year.

adverse selection • the tendency of persons with a higher-than-average chance of loss to seek insurance at standard (average) rates. Because this is selection against the insurer, it will result in higher-than-expected losses if it is not controlled by underwriting.

agency bonds • bonds issued by federal agencies or organizations, such as the Tennessee Valley Authority. They are not direct obligations of the U.S. Treasury, and thus they provide investors with returns greater than that available on U.S. Treasury bonds, although the difference in return is quite small.

alternative minimum tax (AMT) • a separate and parallel method of calculating income tax liability. The reason for using this method is to prevent the taxpayer from reducing his or her tax liability below reasonable levels through the use of certain tax benefits targeted by the AMT rules.

approximate yield • a method that provides the investor with a quick approximation of an investment's internal rate of return. It is found by using the following formula:

$$\text{before-tax approximate yield} = \frac{\text{annual income} + \dfrac{\text{future price} - \text{current price}}{\text{number of years}}}{\dfrac{\text{future price} + \text{current price}}{2}}$$

The after-tax approximate yield can be computed by multiplying the before-tax approximate yield by one minus the investor's appropriate marginal rate of tax. This method can provide meaningful estimates of an investment's yield over both short and long holding periods.

asset allocation models • portfolio recommendations developed by financial advisors to divide wealth among different types of assets. The emphasis is on the different categories of assets and the percentage to be placed in each category. A person's level of risk tolerance needs to be known to properly determine both the categories and the appropriate percentages.

asset selection • the step in the investment planning process that follows the development of asset allocation models. This occurs when specific assets are recommended and purchased.

attorney-in-fact • someone who is authorized to act as an agent for another under a power of attorney, which may be general or limited in scope

baby boom generation • the generation of people born between 1946 and 1964

basic benefits • the core of specified benefits that must be included in all medigap insurance plans. These basic benefits are designed to supplement the Medicare coverage for hospitalization, medical expenses, and blood.

below-the-line deductions • deductions taken from adjusted gross income in determining taxable income

blackout period • the period of time from whenever the youngest child of a deceased worker reaches age 16 (or is no longer disabled in certain cases) until the surviving spouse is aged 60. It is called the blackout period because the surviving spouse of a deceased worker is not eligible for monthly benefits during this time.

business (default) risk • risk that is based on the degree to which a firm's performance is subject to all potential risk factors such as a change in consumer preference away from a particular good or service, ineffective management, law change, or foreign competition. Because of the impact of these risk factors, some firms will be unable to repay bond principal or make interest payments on a timely basis. Because every firm has its own set of risk factors and degree of exposure, business risk is unique for each firm.

business expense • for income tax purposes, an expense paid or incurred during the taxable year in carrying on any existing trade or business. This type of expense is allowable as a deduction to an individual taxpayer.

buy-up plan • a benefit plan under which a covered person can purchase additional coverage at his or her own expense

C corporation • a regular corporation that is treated as a separate taxable entity, distinct and apart from the owners of its stock. The result is that a C corporation must compute its own income and deductions, file its own tax return, and pay its own tax at the applicable corporate rates.

cafeteria plans • flexible benefit plans that allow employees to purchase additional benefits on a payroll-deduction basis. Under these plans, employees can design their own benefit packages by purchasing benefits with a prespecified amount of employer dollars from a number of available options.

capital gain • income that is realized through the sale or exchange of a capital asset. A capital asset is any property the taxpayer holds other than property held for sale, or intellectual or artistic property the taxpayer creates.

cash equivalents • instruments that either have no specified maturity date or have one that is one year or less in the future. Investments in this category often provide only a modest current income and typically have little or no potential for capital appreciation. They usually are of such high liquidity and safety that they are virtually as good as cash.

cash-balance pension plan • a defined-benefit plan that is designed to look like a defined-contribution plan. As a defined-benefit plan, it has some level of funding flexibility, but the employer is ultimately responsible for making the contributions necessary to pay promised benefits.

cash-basis method • a tax accounting method that reflects income actually received during the taxable year. The one exception is the constructive receipt doctrine that is designed to prevent taxpayers from unilaterally determining the tax year when an item of income is received by them for federal income tax purposes. Almost all individual taxpayers who do not own a trade or business use this method of accounting.

charitable lead trust • a type of trust established to provide a charity with a current term income interest. At the end of the term period, the property either reverts to the donor or passes to a member of the donor's family. The donor gets an immediate income and gift or estate tax deduction for the present value of the lead income interest donated to the charity.

charitable remainder trust • a trust designed to take advantage of the tax benefits provided by charitable contributions while retaining the donor's use or enjoyment of the property. A charitable remainder trust permits the donor to retain the current income for himself or herself or for his or her family. The income will be retained for a time period (measured by the life of the donor or lives of selected family members) with a charitable institution holding the remainder interest. The current charitable deduction is measured by the present value of the remainder interest held by the charity.

closed-end investment company • an investment company that issues a given number of shares at its formation. These shares are traded in the stock markets in exactly the same manner as those of traditional corporations. That is, the forces of demand and supply for the stock determine the share price. Rarely if ever does this type of investment company issue additional shares.

COBRA • the Consolidated Omnibus Budget Reconciliation Act of 1985 (COBRA). This act requires that group health plans allow employees and dependents covered under the plans to elect to have their current health insurance coverage extended at group rates for up to 36 months following a qualifying event that results in a loss of coverage. The act applies only to employers with 20 or more full-time employees.

collision • an automobile insurance term that refers to the upset of an auto or its impact with another vehicle or object

comprehensive approach • the approach to financial planning that occurs when an advisor follows the financial planning process to develop a comprehensive financial plan that solves a client's financial problems. The plan considers all aspects of a client's financial position, which typically includes financial problems from all the major planning areas. In addition, the plan usually encompasses several integrated and coordinated planning strategies that can be used to help solve the client's problems and achieve his or her goals.

constructive receipt doctrine • a doctrine stating that a cash-basis taxpayer is deemed to have received income for tax purposes when it is either credited to the taxpayer's account, set apart for the taxpayer, or otherwise made available to be taken into the taxpayer's possession. It is important to know, however, that if there is any condition or restriction that limits the taxpayer's right to receive the income, the doctrine of constructive receipt will not apply.

Consumer Price Index (CPI) • the index that measures the change in consumer prices as determined by a monthly survey of the U.S. Bureau of Labor Statistics. It is also referred to as the cost-of-living index.

conventional power of attorney • a general power of attorney that authorizes another to act on behalf of the principal. However, no matter how limited or broad the power, it becomes inoperative if the principal is incapacitated.

conversion provision • a provision found in term life insurance that allows the policyowner insured to replace the term coverage with (permanent) whole life insurance without having to show evidence of insurability

coordination of benefits (COB) provision • a provision in most group medical expense plans under which priorities are established for the payment of benefits if an individual is covered under more than one plan

coverage gap (doughnut hole) • under Medicare prescription drug plans, the range in which the beneficiary must pay the full cost of prescription drugs

creditable prescription drug coverage • prescription drug coverage under other plans that is deemed to be equivalent to or better than the standard benefit plan for Medicare prescription drug coverage

credit estate tax • a tax imposed by a state to take full advantage of the amount allowed as a credit against the federal estate tax. It is also referred to as a sponge, slack, or gap tax.

Crummey powers • temporary rights granted to the beneficiaries of an irrevocable trust that allow them to demand all or a portion of the grantor's contributions to the trust. With these temporary withdrawal rights given to the beneficiaries, gifts (contributions) to the trust qualify for the gift tax annual exclusion.

current assumption whole life • nonpar whole life policies under which premium rates or cash values are redetermined periodically based on current assumptions as to mortality, interest, and expenses

current yield • perhaps the most widely used method for measuring an investment's return. It is calculated by dividing an investment's current annual income by its current market price. This calculation provides the investor with a before-tax current yield. To calculate an after-tax current yield, the investor's current annual income is reduced by his or her marginal rate of tax. The major shortcoming of the current yield is that it fails to look beyond the present moment.

currently insured • an insured status under Social Security. This status requires a person to have credit for at least six quarters of coverage out of the 13-quarter period ending with the quarter in which death occurs.

deduction floor • one common way in which the law limits deductions. A taxpayer is allowed to deduct items that are subject to the floor, but only to the extent those items exceed a specified percentage of income (which is, in most cases, adjusted gross income).

deduction • for income tax purposes, an item of expense (not an item of receipt) that reduces the amount of income that is subject to tax

defensive stocks • stocks that are more stable than average and provide a safe return on an investor's money. When the stock market is weak, defensive stocks tend to decline less than the overall market.

deferred annuities • annuities that begin to pay periodic benefits at a specified future time. They can be purchased with a single premium or on an installment premium basis. A deferred life annuity provides a tool for accumulating financial resources before retirement.

defined-benefit plan • a retirement plan that specifies the benefits that each employee receives at retirement. The employer is responsible for making the contributions necessary to pay the promised benefits. In other words, this type of plan provides a fixed predetermined benefit for each of the employees but has an uncertain cost for the employer.

defined-contribution medical expense plan • a type of medical expense plan under which an employer makes a fixed contribution with which an employee can purchase his or her own coverage. This practice enables an employer to control costs because the amount of the contribution can remain level from year to year or change at any rate the employer chooses.

defined-contribution plan • a retirement plan in which employer contributions are allocated to the participants' accounts. The participants' benefits are based on their account balances, which consist of the employer's contributions and investment experience. In other words, this type of plan involves a predetermined cost for the employer but provides uncertain benefits for the employees.

dental insurance • insurance that may be limited to specific types of dental expenses or broad enough to cover virtually all dental expenses. In addition, coverage can be obtained from various types of providers, and benefits can be in the form of either services or cash payments.

dependency exemption • an exemption that an individual taxpayer is allowed to claim for his or her support of a dependent. There are strict rules regarding whom a taxpayer may claim as a dependent and under what circumstances. The exemption amount changes annually by way of an inflation adjustment.

dependent life insurance • group life insurance on the lives of eligible dependents of persons covered under a group life plan. Amounts of coverage are usually limited, and the employee is automatically the beneficiary.

depreciation deduction • the most important noncash deduction. It permits a taxpayer to recover for tax purposes the cost of certain property by allowing the taxpayer to deduct a specified portion of the cost of the property each year against the taxpayer's income.

depreciation • a function of the age of an asset, its use, its condition at the time of loss, and any other factor causing deterioration. In addition, anything that causes the property to become obsolete is also included. Depreciation as a factor in measuring actual cash value differs from depreciation in an accounting sense.

direct skip • one of the three different types of transfers that the generation-skipping transfer tax applies to. A direct skip can be an outright transfer during life or at death to a skip person (an individual who is two generations or more younger than the transferor) or a transfer in trust for the benefit of a skip person.

disability income insurance • insurance that partially replaces the income of a person unable to work because of disability resulting from an accident or illness. It is most efficiently used in dealing with the possibility of a person experiencing a long-term, total disability.

disability insured • an insured status under Social Security. This status requires that a worker (1) be fully insured and (2) have a minimum amount of work under Social Security within a recent period.

diversification • the technique of spreading an investment portfolio over different industries, companies, and investment types for the purpose of reducing risk

dollar cost averaging • a method that requires the investment of a fixed amount of dollars at specified time intervals. Investing a fixed amount of dollars at set intervals means that the investor buys more shares when prices are low and fewer shares when prices are high. However, the overall cost of investing using dollar cost averaging is lower than it would be if a constant number of shares were bought at set intervals.

durable power of attorney • a power of attorney that remains valid and operative despite any subsequent incapacity of the principal.

durable power of attorney for health care • a durable power of attorney that gives authority to another to make medical decisions about the principal's care.

earnings test • the process for determining whether income benefits of Social Security beneficiaries who are under full retirement age should be reduced because of wages that exceed a specified level. The earnings threshold at which benefits are reduced changes annually on the basis of changes in national wage levels.

economic benefit doctrine • a doctrine stating that a taxpayer must pay tax whenever an economic benefit has been conferred on him or her regardless of whether the taxpayer has actually received any cash or property

effective marginal tax rate • for an upper income taxpayer this rate depends on the level of his or her adjusted gross income, the amount of his or her itemized deductions, and the number of personal and/or dependency exemptions that he or she can claim. It should be noted that an upper income taxpayer's effective marginal tax rate may be higher than his or her statutory marginal rate. This can happen as a result of the phaseout rules that reduce the taxpayer's itemized deductions and personal and/or dependency exemption amounts as his or her adjusted gross income increases.

effective tax rate • the rate at which the individual would be taxed if his or her taxable income were taxed at a constant rate rather than progressively. This rate is computed by determining what percentage the taxpayer's tax liability is of his or her total taxable income.

elimination (waiting) period • a period of time that a person must be disabled before benefits commence under disability income insurance, Social Security disability benefits, and workers compensation insurance

employee benefits • all benefits and services, other than wages for time worked, that employees receive in whole or in part from their employers. A narrower definition includes only employer-provided benefits for situations involving death, accident, sickness, retirement, or unemployment.

employee stock ownership plan (ESOP) • a variation of a defined-contribution profit-sharing plan. However, unlike a traditional profit-sharing plan, it is required to invest primarily in employer stock, thus providing a market for the stock. It also permits distributions to participants in the form of employer stock. In addition, it allows the plan to borrow to purchase employer stock. The loan is then repaid with employer contributions to the plan.

exclusion • for income tax purposes, an item of value that the taxpayer receives that is not includible in his or her gross income under a specific provision of tax law

expected return • the most likely return. It typically is calculated as the arithmetic average of possible returns weighted by their respective likelihoods.

expense for the production of income • for income tax purposes, expenses incurred in the course of an activity that is not a trade or business but is engaged in for the purpose of producing income and making a profit. This type of expense is allowable as a deduction to an individual taxpayer.

expense method • a method of determining retirement income. It focuses on the projected expenses that a retiree will have. A list of expenses that should be considered includes general expenses as well as expenses unique to the particular individual. As with the replacement ratio method, it is much easier to define the potential expenses for individuals who are at or near retirement.

fact-finder form • a form that needs to be completed by a financial advisor engaged in financial planning for a client. It typically includes both quantitative and qualitative information that the advisor needs in order to develop a financial plan for the client.

fee simple estate • the most complete interest in property. The individual who holds such an unlimited interest in property owns all the rights associated with the property. They include the current possessory rights and the ability to transfer the property at any point during his or her lifetime or at death.

fiduciaries • people who occupy a legally defined position of trust. They are charged with the responsibility of managing and investing money wisely for beneficiaries. Some examples of fiduciaries are executors of wills and estates, trustees, and those who administer the assets of underage or incompetent beneficiaries.

filing status • the taxpayer's filing selection (that is, single taxpayer, unmarried head of household, married taxpayer filing jointly, or married taxpayer filing separately). The filing status has a significant impact on taxable income. For each filing status, the amount of taxable income subject to each marginal tax rate varies considerably.

financial capacity • a technique insurers rely on to handle the risk that continues to exist after the operation of the law of large numbers. Insurers hold at least minimum amounts of required surplus (net worth) to, among other things, absorb underwriting losses that are not covered by investment gains.

financial life cycle • the five distinct phases in an individual's financial life or career. The five phases are (1) early career, (2) career development, (3) peak accumulation, (4) preretirement, and (5) retirement. Together the five phases span a person's entire financial life. Starting at a relatively young age, a career-minded person typically will pass through four phases en route to phase 5 and his or her retirement.

financial plan • a plan designed to carry a client from his or her present financial position to the attainment of financial goals. Since no two clients are alike, the plan must be designed for the individual, with all the advisor's recommended strategies tailored to each particular client's needs, abilities, and financial goals.

financial planning • a process that focuses on ascertaining a client's financial goals and then developing a plan to help the client achieve those goals

financial planning process • a six-step process that financial advisors must follow when they are engaged in financial planning. The steps are (1) establish and define the advisor-client relationship, (2) determine goals and gather data, (3) analyze and evaluate the data, (4) develop and present a plan, (5) implement the plan, and (6) monitor the plan.

financial planning pyramid • a widely accepted approach for developing a comprehensive financial plan over a period of time. It prioritizes financial goals by categorizing them into three levels. Level 1 goals provide protection against uncertainties, level 2 goals focus on growing investments, and level 3 goals address retirement and estate concerns.

financial risk tolerance • a client's psychological attitude toward his or her willingness to expose financial assets to the possibility of loss for the chance to achieve greater financial gain. It is measured along a continuum with individuals who are very risk tolerant at one end and those who are very risk averse at the other.

flat-percentage-of-earnings formula • a benefit formula in which the plan's retirement benefit is directly tied to salary. Because the IRS passed regulations that require this type of formula to have a 25-year minimum period of service in order for the participants to receive the full benefits promised, length of service with the employer is also a factor, albeit an indirect one.

flexible spending account (FSA) • a cafeteria plan in which an employee can elect to fund certain benefits on a before-tax basis by taking a salary reduction to pay the cost of any qualified benefits included in the plan. Benefits are paid from an employee's account as expenses are incurred, but any money remaining in the account is forfeited if not used by the end of the plan year.

401(k) plan • a type of defined-contribution profit-sharing plan that gives participants the option of reducing their taxable salary and contributing the salary reduction on a tax-deferred basis to an individual account for retirement purposes. In addition to the salary deferral feature, a 401(k) plan can contain a traditional profit-sharing feature, an employer-matching contribution feature, or both.

403(b) plan • a retirement plan that can be sold only to tax-exempt organizations and public schools. It is similar to a 401(k) plan in that it allows salary deferral contributions and before-tax employer contributions to be made to the employee's individual account. Employer contributions can be made as matching contributions based on employee elections to defer compensation.

fourth market • a market in which large institutional investors employ brokers to locate buyers or sellers of large blocks of stocks or bonds. When these transactions involve listed securities, this negotiated market is called the fourth market because the transaction does not take place on the floor of an organized exchange.

fruit and tree doctrine • a doctrine stating that income is to be taxed to the person who earns it or to the person who owns the asset that produces it. In other words, the fruits of an individual's labor cannot be assigned to another individual for tax purposes.

full retirement age • the age at which nonreduced Social Security retirement benefits are paid

fully insured • an insured status under Social Security. This status requires one of the following: (1) 40 quarters of coverage or (2) credit for at least as many quarters (but a minimum of six) of coverage as there are years elapsing after 1950 (or after the year in which age 21 is reached, if later) and before the year in which a person dies, becomes disabled, or reaches age 62, whichever occurs first.

general obligations • state and local government bonds that are backed by the taxing power of the state or local government

general power of appointment • a power over the disposition of property exercisable in favor of any person whom the donee of the power may select including the donee, the donee's estate, the donee's creditors, or the creditors of the donee's estate

grantor • the individual who creates a trust. A grantor is also referred to as a settler, creator, or trustor.

gross income • for income tax purposes, all income from whatever source derived minus allowable exclusions. In other words, anything of value is considered gross income unless the Internal Revenue Code contains a specific provision that excludes a particular item.

group term life insurance • yearly renewable term life insurance that provides death benefits only and no buildup of cash values. The coverage is bought for and provided to a group instead of an individual.

growth stocks • stocks of corporations that have exhibited faster-than-average gains in earnings over the recent past and are expected to continue to show high levels of profit growth. They also tend to outperform slower-growing stocks but are riskier because they typically have higher price/earnings ratios and pay little or no dividends to stockholders.

guaranteed renewable • a continuance provision in an insurance contract that gives the insured the right to renew the coverage at each policy anniversary date, usually up to a stated age. Under this provision, the coverage cannot be terminated during the policy term, and renewal is guaranteed up to the stated age. However, unlike a noncancelable contract, the insurer has the right to raise the premium rate for broad classes of insureds.

health maintenance organizations (HMOs) • a managed system of health care that provides a comprehensive array of medical services on a prepaid basis to voluntarily enrolled persons living within a specific geographic region. HMOs both finance health care and deliver health services. There is an emphasis on preventive care as well as cost control.

health savings account (HSA) • a type of tax-favored account to which an individual (or employer) contributes each year and from which the individual (or employee) can make withdrawals to pay medical expenses that are not covered by insurance because of the deductible under an underlying high-deductible health plan (HDHP). The individual (or employee) can carry forward any unused amount in the account and add it to the following year's contribution to the account. Such a plan gives the individual (or employee) an immediate incentive to purchase medical care wisely because if the amount in the account is exceeded, the individual (or employee) will have to pay medical expenses out of his or her own pocket until the HDHP's deductible is satisfied.

high-deductible health plan (HDHP) • a medical expense plan that uses insurance policies with high deductibles, often as much as $5,000 or more. They are commonly used with health savings accounts (HSAs).

holding-period return • a method most appropriately used for measuring an investment's return over a period of one year. This is because it gives no consideration to the timing of investment returns and therefore to the time value of money. It is calculated by dividing the total amount of current income plus the total amount of capital appreciation by the beginning dollar value of the investment. This calculation provides the investor with a before-tax holding-period return (HPR). An after-tax HPR can also be calculated by reducing each component of the numerator by the investor's appropriate marginal rate of tax.

holistic retirement planning • a way of looking at retirement planning that considers all aspects of the person, not just his or her financial picture

homeowners insurance • insurance that provides a package of coverages for a family's home, personal possessions, and liability that arises out of the many activities of family members. There are several homeowners insurance forms that provide varying degrees of coverage for different types of homeowners and tenants.

human-life-value method • a method for determining the amount of life insurance a person should carry. It is based on the proposition that a person should carry life insurance in an amount equal to the present value of the portion of the person's estimated future earnings that will be used to support his or her dependents.

immediate annuity • an annuity that must be purchased with a single premium because it begins to pay periodic benefits at the end of the first payment period (such as one month) following the purchase date

income tax basis • an amount designed to reflect the taxpayer's capital investment in property for income tax purposes. It is used to determine any gains or losses on disposition of the property.

insurance • a risk financing technique that involves the transfer of the financial burden of risk to an insurer, who pools together a large number of similar risks in an effort to make losses more predictable and thus, reduce risk. A technique for handling pure risk must have both of these features—risk transfer and pooling of similar risks—in order to be insurance.

interest rate risk • the risk that changes in interest rates will adversely affect the value of debt securities. In other words if interest rates rise, the value of debt securities, especially long-term ones, will fall.

internal limits • special limits of coverages on certain types of property. Some of these internal limits can be increased for an additional premium.

intestacy • the state or condition of dying without having made a valid will. The estates of these individuals are distributed according to the state's intestate laws.

intestate laws • a state's laws that provide for the disposition of a person's probate estate if he or she dies without a valid will

intestate succession • a disposition of probate property that occurs when the deceased has left no will or when the will has been revoked or annulled as irregular

investing • what occurs when a person buys an asset with the expectation that it will provide a return commensurate with its risk. Investing is distinguished from speculating, which occurs when a person buys an asset hoping to receive some form of return without consideration of the expected return or risk or both.

investment assets • assets acquired for the purpose of investing, which is defined as the purchase of an asset with the expectation that it will provide a return. However, the distinction between investment assets and personal assets is not always clear and is based on the buyer's intent. The exact same asset may be an investment asset for one individual and a personal asset for another.

investment risk • risk measured by the likelihood that realized returns will differ from those that are expected. An asset with a wide range of possible returns is considered risky, while an asset with a narrow range of possible returns is considered more secure.

irrevocable trust • a trust created when the grantor permanently transfers property to the trustee and cannot alter, amend, revoke, or terminate the arrangement or reclaim the property

itemized deductions • a limited group of expenditures by individuals that can be deducted from adjusted gross income (in lieu of the standard deduction) in determining taxable income. They typically include interest, taxes, medical expenses, and charitable contributions, subject to

junk bonds • bonds that have weak quality ratings from S&P or Moody's. Junk bonds are risky because the firm either has a large amount of debt outstanding relative to its equity base or has suffered financial reverses and may be headed for serious trouble or bankruptcy. Because the risk is high, the return on them also is high if the issuer does not default.

large cap stocks • stocks with a large capitalization (number of shares outstanding times the price of a share). They typically have at least $5 billion in outstanding market value. There are numerous mutual funds that specialize in these stocks.

law of large numbers • a concept that embodies a mathematical principle stating that as the number of independent trials or events (that is, exposures) increases, the more closely will actual results approach the probable results expected from an infinite number of trials or events (exposures)

legal expense insurance • insurance designed to provide coverage for the legal services sometimes needed by employees. Most plans usually contain a list of covered services, although there may be limited coverage for a service that is not on the list as long as it is not specifically excluded.

liability risks • pure risks that involve the possibility of loss from damaging or destroying the property of others or from causing physical or personal injuries to others

life annuities • annuities whose benefit payments continue for the duration of a designated life

life-cycle financial planning • a financial planning process that is ongoing and occurs throughout a client's financial life. The advisor who monitors this type of planning is practicing life-cycle financial planning.

liquidity • the ease with which an investment can be converted to cash with little or no loss of principal. Every portfolio should have some liquidity in it because it allows the investor the flexibility to quickly obtain cash for emergency purposes. There are two ways to obtain liquidity. One is to own liquid assets, and the other is to have readily available opportunities for borrowing money.

living trust • a trust that is created and operates before the death of the grantor

living will • a document in which the principal specifies the types of medical treatment he or she wishes to receive and does not wish to receive. Its existence lets others know of the principal's medical wishes, should he or she become terminally ill and lie in a persistent vegetative state, unable to communicate.

loan provision • a provision in cash value life insurance that allows the policyowner to borrow cash. The amount borrowed is charged interest at either a fixed or variable rate as stated in the policy. A variation of this provision can be used to automatically pay the premium when the policyowner, for whatever reason, fails to pay it.

long-term care insurance • insurance that provides coverage for custodial care, intermediate care, and skilled-nursing care. Benefits may also be available for home health care, adult day care, and assisted living. Benefits are usually limited to a specified dollar amount per day.

long-term debt instruments • debt instruments whose term to maturity is one year or more. Some people, however, refer to bonds with maturities of one to 10 years as being intermediate term.

loss control • one category of techniques available to handle pure risks. Loss control is concerned with activities that reduce both the frequency and severity of losses. Loss control techniques typically available include risk avoidance, loss prevention, and loss reduction.

loss financing • one category of techniques available to handle pure risks. Loss financing is concerned with how to finance the losses that do occur despite ongoing loss control activities. Loss financing techniques commonly used are retention and insurance.

loss prevention • a risk control technique that involves activities designed to reduce the frequency of loss associated with inescapable risks by preventing the occurrence of loss

loss reduction • a risk control technique that involves activities designed to reduce the severity of losses that do occur

major medical plans • a plan in which medical coverage is designed to provide substantial protection against catastrophic medical expenses. There are few exclusions and limitations, but deductibles and coinsurance are commonly used.

managed care plans • a plan that delivers cost-effective health care without sacrificing quality or access. Common characteristics include controlled access to providers, comprehensive case management, preventive care, risk sharing, and high-quality care.

marginal tax rate • the tax rate applicable to each income bracket. In the U.S. progressive income tax system, the marginal tax rate increases as income rises. It is the rate of tax applied to the last dollar of income.

marketability • the ability to sell an asset quickly. Although marketability and liquidity are often confused, they are not the same. Liquid assets are marketable, but not all marketable assets are liquid. Stock is a classic example of a marketable asset that is not liquid. It is important that portfolios have marketable assets, but they are not a substitute for liquidity.

medical expense insurance • insurance that provides protection against financial losses that result from medical bills because of an accident or illness.

Medicare Advantage • the program administered by the Centers for Medicare & Medicaid Services that allows Medicare beneficiaries to enroll in certain HMOs, PPOs, and other approved options as alternatives to receiving their benefits under the original Medicare program. *Also known as* Medicare Part C and originally called Medicare+Choice.

Medicare prescription drug plans • private prescription drug plans in which Medicare participants can voluntarily enroll. The plans must meet certain standards established by Medicare, and beneficiaries must pay a monthly premium.

Medicare SELECT policy • one of the 12 standard Medicare supplement policies (plans A through L). It can exclude or limit benefits (except in emergencies) for medical services if they are not received from network providers. Medicare SELECT policies are issued by insurance companies as PPO products and by some HMOs. An insured who has a Medicare SELECT policy has the right to switch to a regular Medicare supplement policy sold by the same company, as long as the new policy has equal or less coverage than the Medicare SELECT policy.

medigap insurance • individual Medicare supplement insurance. As the name implies, its objective is to fill some of the gaps left after Medicare benefits have been exhausted. There currently are 12 standard medigap plans, including the 10 original plans (A through J) and 2 additional plans (K and L).

miscellaneous fringe benefits • fringe benefits that do not fall into the broad category of insurance. They typically include education assistance, adoption assistance, dependent care assistance, and family leave.

miscellaneous itemized deductions • a group of deductions that includes employee business expenses, fees for safe deposit boxes, and fees for investment and individual tax advice, to name but a few. All of the taxpayer's deductions that fall within this group are subject to the 2 percent deduction floor. The result is that the taxpayer is permitted to deduct miscellaneous itemized deductions only to the extent they exceed the 2 percent floor.

money market deposit accounts (MMDAs) • a popular cash equivalent. MMDAs are offered by banks and permit virtually any amount to be deposited in the accounts. They usually are insured like savings accounts and CDs and allow withdrawals at the bank window or by check.

money market mutual funds (MMMFs) • a popular cash equivalent. MMMFs frequently require minimum dollar deposits and are not insured. They provide access by check, wire transfer, and in some cases by phone. Because they are mutual funds, investments in them are used to buy shares in the funds.

money-purchase pension plan • a type of defined-contribution pension plan. Under this type of plan, the employer's annual contributions are mandatory and are specified in the plan. Plan benefits for each participant are the amounts that can be provided by the sums contributed to the participant's individual account plus investment earnings.

mother's/father's benefit • the spouse of a person receiving retirement benefits is eligible for monthly benefits regardless of age if he or she is caring for at least one child of the retired worker who is (1) under age 16 or (2) disabled and entitled to a child's benefit. This benefit is also available to the surviving spouse (as well as a divorced spouse) of a deceased worker who was either fully or currently insured at the time of death if the surviving spouse is caring for at least one child of the deceased worker under the same conditions as for the retired worker.

multiple-purpose approach • the approach to financial planning that occurs when an advisor follows the financial planning process to develop a plan that solves two or more financial problems for a client. The plan may focus on solving several problems from one of the major planning areas, or it may focus on problems from two major planning areas.

named-perils approach • a way of insuring property that lists the specific perils for which coverage is provided. If the peril is not listed in the policy, it is not covered.

needs analysis • a process for dealing with pure risks involving the loss of income-earning ability resulting from death, disability, or old age. It involves steps similar to those in the financial planning process that is used to identify and solve a client's financial problems. The needs analysis steps are (1) identify the client's needs in the event of death, disability, and/or retirement; (2) collect information on the client's current financial situation; (3) determine the types and amounts of resources required and available and then subtract the available resources from those required in order to determine the gaps to be filled by additional resources; (4) develop a plan for filling the resource gaps; (5) buy additional insurance and increase saving; and (6) monitor for changes in the client's needs.

nominal rate of return • the current rate of return unadjusted for inflation

noncancelable • a continuance provision in an insurance contract that gives the insured the right to renew the coverage at each policy anniversary date, usually up to a stated age. Under this provision, the coverage cannot be terminated during the policy term, renewal is guaranteed up to the stated age, and the premium rate is guaranteed in the contract.

nonforfeiture option • a set of choices available to a life insurance policyowner regarding the use of the policy's cash value. The choices include surrendering the policy for cash, buying a reduced amount of paid-up whole life insurance, or buying extended term insurance. For long-term care insurance, the most common option is a paid-up policy with a shortened benefit period. Another option is the return of a portion of the premium if the policy had been in force for a specified number of years.

nonparticipating (nonpar) policies • policies that do not pay policyowner dividends

nonqualified contracts • long-term care insurance contracts that do not meet the requirements of the Health Insurance Portability and Accountability Act

(HIPAA). They are believed to not be eligible for the tax benefits provided under tax-qualified policies as defined by HIPAA.

nonqualified plan • a flexible retirement plan that is established primarily for executives but is not eligible for the special tax benefits available for qualified or other tax-advantaged retirement plans

nonrecognition transactions • transactions in which taxation is merely deferred rather than eliminated. These transactions involve the sale or exchange of property at a gain realized by the taxpayer. However, because of a provision in the Internal Revenue Code, the realized gain is not currently recognized for tax purposes.

notes • bonds issued with maturities of one to 10 years

OASDHI • the old age, survivors, disability, and health insurance program of the federal government, commonly known as Social Security and Medicare

open-end investment company • an investment company that is popularly called a mutual fund and continually sells and redeems its shares at net asset value. Hence the shares are not traded in the stock market. This type of company acquires a portfolio of securities in which each of the company's shares owns a proportionate interest.

open-perils approach • a way of insuring property that covers all types of losses except those that are specifically excluded by the policy's terms. If the peril is not specifically excluded in the policy, it is covered.

opportunity costs • the implicit cost of an activity or course of conduct based on forgone opportunities. In other words, it is the highest price or rate of return an alternative course of action would provide.

ordinary income • gain from the sale or exchange of property that is neither a capital asset nor a Section 1231 asset. In addition, income other than from actual or constructive sales or exchanges (such as rents or wages) is also generally referred to as ordinary income.

other than collision • (formerly referred to as comprehensive) an automobile insurance term that refers to physical damage to a vehicle that is not caused by collision

over-the-counter market • a market in which securities transactions are conducted through a network connecting dealers in stocks and bonds rather than on the floor of an exchange. This market deals in unlisted securities and off-board trading in listed securities.

paper deductions • allowable deductions even though they represent no corresponding cash outlay. Paper deductions represent or are related to some entry on the books of a taxpayer's business or investment activity, but they are not a cash-flow item.

partial disability • the inability to perform some stated percentage of job duties or to need a longer-than-normal amount of time to complete job duties

participating (par) policies • life insurance policies that provide for, but do not guarantee, the payment of dividends to the policyowner. The dividends reflect the insurer's past experience with respect to mortality, interest, and expenses.

passive losses • tax losses generated by activities in which the taxpayer has an ownership interest but does not participate in the activity of the business. The basic rule with respect to tax losses generated by passive activities is that they can be deducted only against income generated by the taxpayer's passive activities and not against the taxpayer's salary or other income.

per diem basis • the method of paying long-term care insurance benefits whereby the insured receives a specified daily or weekly benefit amount regardless of the actual cost of care

peril • an event that causes a loss. Examples include fire, earthquake, and flood.

personal assets • assets bought primarily for the creature comforts they provide. They include such items as homes, cars, and clothes. However, the distinction between personal assets and investment assets is not clear and is based on the buyer's intent. The exact same asset may be a personal asset for one individual and an investment asset for another.

personal exemption • an exemption that each individual taxpayer is allowed to claim for himself or herself. The amount of the exemption is subtracted from adjusted gross income in the process of computing taxable income. The exemption amount changes annually by way of an inflation adjustment.

personal expense • for income tax purposes, expenses that are simply personal, family, or living expenses. Although as a general rule the Code provides that these expenses are nondeductible, there are several important exceptions to the general rule. However, many of the personal expenses that are allowable as deductions are subject to limitations as to what and how much can be deducted.

personal risks • pure risks that involve the possibility of loss of income-earning ability because of premature death, disability, unemployment, or retirement. In addition, the extra expenses associated with accidental injuries, periods of sickness, and long-term care are types of personal risks.

planned holding period • the period of time that an investor should plan to own a common stock. Periods shorter than 5 years subject stocks to increased risks and often produce negative total returns. The problem of market timing, or when to buy or sell, and the transactions costs of the purchase and sale combine to make success quite difficult with shorter-term holding periods.

point-of-service (POS) plans • a hybrid arrangement that combines aspects of a traditional medical expense plan with an HMO or a PPO. At the time of medical treatment, a participant can elect whether to receive treatment within the plan's network or outside the network.

pool of money • an indirect method for determining the benefit period under a reimbursement type of long-term care policy. Under this approach, there is a pool of money from which benefit payments are made. When the pool is exhausted, the policy terminates. However, the pool of money may last well beyond the policy's specified benefit period if benefits are paid at a rate that is less than the policy's maximum daily benefit amount.

portfolio effect • a technique insurers rely on to handle the risk that continues to exist after the operation of the law of large numbers. This involves reducing risk by writing different lines of insurance whose financial results vary inversely over time.

pour-over trust • a trust created during the grantor's lifetime simply to receive assets at the grantor's death

power of appointment • a property right created by the donor of the power that enables the donee of the power to designate, within such limits as the donor has prescribed, who will be the transferees of the property

power of attorney • an instrument by which one person, the principal, appoints another as his or her agent and confers upon the agent the authority to perform certain specified acts or kinds of acts on behalf of the principal

preemptive right • the right that common stockholders sometimes have to maintain their relative voting power by purchasing shares of any new issues of common stock of the corporation

preexisting condition • an illness or injury for which a covered person received medical care during a specified period of time before becoming eligible for coverage. Usually the condition is no longer considered preexisting after the earlier of a period of 3 consecutive months during which no medical care is received for the condition or 12 months of coverage under the plan by the individual.

preferred-provider organizations (PPOs) • groups of health care providers who contract with employers, insurance companies, union trust funds, third-party administrators, or others to provide medical care services at a reduced fee. PPOs may be organized by the providers themselves or by such organizations as insurance companies, the Blues, or groups of employers.

premium-conversion plan • a cafeteria plan in which an employee can elect a before-tax salary reduction to pay his or her premium contribution to an employer-sponsored health or other welfare benefit plan. As a rule, these plans are established for medical and dental expenses only.

price risk • the risk of a bond's price changing in response to future interest rate changes. If rates increase after a bond is purchased, the bond's price in the secondary market will fall; if rates decrease, the bond's price will rise. Because the direction of future interest rates is unknown, there is uncertainty about the bond's future price.

primary insurance amount (PIA) • the amount a worker will receive under Social Security if he or she retires at full retirement age or becomes disabled. It is also the amount on which all other Social Security income benefits are based.

prime interest rate • the interest rate banks charge their most creditworthy customers. It is a key interest rate because loans to less creditworthy customers are often tied to the prime rate.

probate • the process of proving a will's validity in court and executing its provisions under the guidance of the court. The probate estate encompasses all property that passes under the terms of the will.

property risks • pure risks that involve the possibility of direct losses associated with the need to replace or repair damaged or missing property, and indirect (consequential) losses such as additional living expenses that are caused by a direct loss

purchasing power risk • sometimes called inflation risk. Purchasing power risk is based on the degree to which the purchasing power of an investment asset's future cash flows is affected by changes in the general level of prices in the economy.

pure risk • risk that involves the possibility of only financial loss. With pure risk, there is no possibility of financial gain. This type of risk has two outcomes—loss or no loss (that is, no change). With few exceptions, insurance is a technique for dealing with pure risk. Pure risks can be categorized as personal risks, property risks, and liability risks.

qualified domestic relations order (QDRO) • a court decree under state law that allows a participant's retirement plan assets to be used for marital property rights, child support, or alimony payments

qualified plan • a retirement plan that is rewarded with favorable tax status for meeting Internal Revenue Code Section 401(a) restrictions. There are eight types of qualified plans including defined-benefit pension plans, cash-balance plans, money-purchase pension plans, target-benefit plans, profit-sharing plans, 401(k) plans, stock bonus plans, and ESOPs.

quarters of coverage • the basis on which eligibility for benefits under Social Security is determined. Credit for up to four quarters of coverage may be earned in any calendar year.

real rate of return • the current or nominal rate of return minus the inflation rate. It provides investors in bonds and other fixed-rate instruments a way to see whether their returns will allow them to keep up with or beat the erosion in dollar values caused by inflation.

reimbursement basis • the method of paying long-term care insurance benefits that reimburses the insured for actual expenses incurred up to the specified benefit amount

reinsurance • a technique insurers rely on to handle the risk that continues to exist after the operation of the law of large numbers. This involves an insurer transferring part of its risk to other insurers (that is, insurance for insurance companies).

reinvestment rate risk • the risk associated with reinvesting interest income at unknown future interest rates. If interest rates fall, the investor will have to be satisfied with reinvesting the interest payments from current bonds at a lower rate of return than anticipated. If interest rates rise, the investor will be able to reinvest the interest payments from current bonds at a higher rate of return than anticipated. Because the direction of future interest rates is unknown, there is uncertainty about the rates at which interest income will be reinvested.

renewability provision • a provision frequently found in term life insurance that allows the policyowner insured to renew the policy for another period of protection without having to show evidence of insurability. Most insurers, however, do not permit renewals to carry coverage beyond a certain age.

replacement cost • the cost necessary to replace or repair damaged property. Depreciation is not factored into an asset's replacement cost.

replacement ratio method • a method of determining retirement income. It assumes that the standard of living enjoyed during the years just prior to retirement will be the determining factor for the standard of living during retirement. In general, a 60 to 80 percent replacement ratio of a person's final average salary is used for individual retirement planning purposes.

replacement-cost requirement • a provision that requires the insured to carry insurance equal to a specified percentage of the replacement cost of the dwelling. If the appropriate amount of insurance is carried, losses will be settled on a full replacement-cost basis.

residual disability • the replacement of lost earnings due to less-than-total disability. It is based on a person's reduction in earnings rather than his or her physical condition.

retention • a risk financing technique that involves financing or paying for one's own losses. In cases where retention is consciously practiced, an individual may set aside funds earmarked for a particular risk. However, most retention is practiced informally by covering losses with funds in a savings account, by borrowing, or by paying for the loss on an out-of-pocket basis.

revenue bonds • bonds issued by agencies of a state or local government. They are guaranteed by the revenues earned from such ventures as turnpikes, airports, and sewer and water systems. Without the taxing authority behind them, they are viewed as riskier and pay investors a somewhat higher interest rate than do general obligation bonds.

reverse mortgage • a loan against an individual's home that requires no repayment for as long as the individual continues to live in the house. It is available only when all of the owners are aged 62 or older and when the home is the principal residence.

revocable trust • a trust in which the grantor reserves the power to alter or revoke the agreement. Thus, the grantor can reclaim the trust assets at any time. It becomes irrevocable only when the grantor modifies the trust to become irrevocable or dies and, therefore, is no longer able to modify the trust.

risk avoidance • a risk control technique that involves avoiding situations that include certain types of risks

risk management • a process for handling pure risks involving possible damage or destruction of property or legal liability. It involves steps similar to those in the financial planning process that is used to identify and solve a client's financial problems. The risk management steps are (1) determine objectives; (2) identify the risks; (3) analyze the risks; (4) consider alternative risk treatment devices and select the device(s) believed to be best for treating the risk(s); (5) implement the decision; and (6) monitor the process.

risk • the possibility of financial loss (for insurance and financial planning purposes). Loss can occur as a result of the reduced value of something that an individual already possesses. Loss can also occur as a result of the reduced value of something that an individual does not possess but expects to receive in the future, such as earning only a 5 percent return on an investment that was expected to yield 10 percent.

Roth IRA • an individual retirement account plan in which an individual's contributions are not deductible, but qualifying withdrawals are not subject to income tax. Roth IRAs are subject to certain limitations, the most important of which is the maximum contribution limit. Unlike traditional IRAs, the owner of a Roth IRA can make contributions even after he or she attains age 70 1/2. Moreover, the minimum distribution rules that apply to traditional

IRAs do not apply to a Roth IRA while the owner is alive. The owner of a Roth IRA is not required to take distributions at any age.

S corporation • a corporation that is taxed similarly to a partnership under the provisions of the Internal Revenue Code. Like a partnership, an S corporation is not subject to tax at the entity level. Rather, the owners of the business pay the taxes. An S corporation is often referred to as a pass-through entity because the responsibility for paying its taxes is passed through the entity to the owners of the entity.

sandwiched generation • another name for the baby-boom generation. Many of its members are faced with financing their children's educations and aiding their parents while trying to save for their own retirement.

savings incentive match plan for employees (SIMPLE) • a retirement plan funded with individual retirement accounts. Any type of business entity can establish a SIMPLE, but the business cannot have more than 100 employees. Also the sponsoring employer cannot maintain any other qualified plan, 403(b) plan, or SEP at the same time it maintains the SIMPLE. In addition, all eligible employees are able to make elective salary deferral contributions.

Section 79 • Internal Revenue Code Section that gives favorable tax treatment to life insurance plans that qualify as group term insurance

sick-pay plans • a plan that is typically an uninsured arrangement to replace for a limited period of time lost income because of disability or illness

simplified employee pension (SEP) • a type of retirement plan that uses an individual retirement account (IRA) or an individual retirement annuity (IRA annuity) as the receptacle for contributions. Plan contributions must be allocated to participants in a way that provides a benefit as a level percentage of compensation. The only exception to this rule is that the allocation formula may be integrated with Social Security, providing highly compensated employees with contributions that are slightly larger (as a percentage of pay) than those for the rank-and-file employees.

single limit of liability • a limit used in automobile insurance. It specifies the maximum amount that will be paid under the policy for all damages involving bodily injury and property damage resulting from any one accident.

single-purpose approach • the approach to financial planning that occurs when an advisor follows the financial planning process to develop a plan that solves a single financial problem for a client. The plan may be as simple as selling a single financial product or service to the client in order to solve the problem.

small cap stocks • stocks that generally have a market capitalization (number of shares outstanding times the price of a share) of $500 million or less. They usually represent companies that are less well established but in many cases are faster growing than large cap stocks ($5 billion or more). Because they are often less well established, they are usually more volatile than Blue Chips.

Social Security Statement • an annual statement issued by the Social Security Administration that enables an individual to verify his or her contributions to the Social Security and Medicare programs. The statement also contains an estimate of benefits that will be available because of retirement, disability, or death. It is sent to each worker aged 25 or older who has worked in employment covered by Social Security and who is not currently entitled to monthly benefits.

special power of appointment • a power over the disposition of property in which the donor of the power limits the donee's appointment of the property to other than the donee, the donee's estate, or the donee's creditors

speculating • what occurs when a person buys an asset in the hopes of receiving some form of return without consideration or knowledge of the expected return or risk or both. Speculating is distinguished from investing, which occurs when a person buys an asset expecting that it will provide a return commensurate with its risk.

speculative risk • risk that involves not only the possibility of financial loss but also the possibility of financial gain. This type of risk has three possible outcomes—loss, gain, or no loss or gain (that is, no change). Speculative risk is the type of risk that investors face in their investment activities.

split limit of liability • a limit used in automobile insurance that is divided into three components. The first number specifies the maximum amount that will be paid for bodily injury to each person in an accident; the second specifies the maximum for all bodily injury in an accident; and the third specifies the maximum for all property damage in an accident.

springing durable power of attorney • a power of attorney that lies dormant and ineffective until it is needed. A determination that the principal has become incapacitated would trigger the springing power.

Standard & Poor's 500 Index • a broad-based measurement of changes in stock-market conditions based on the average performance of 500 widely held common stocks

standard deduction • a fixed amount that an individual may claim in lieu of claiming itemized deductions. The amount depends on the individual's filing status category.

state estate tax • a tax imposed on a deceased person's right to transfer or pass property to beneficiaries

state inheritance tax • a tax imposed on a beneficiary's right to inherit property from a deceased person's estate. The tax rate is often based on the beneficiary's relationship to the deceased.

stock bonus plan • a variation of a defined-contribution profit-sharing plan. However, unlike a traditional profit-sharing plan, it typically invests a large percentage of the plan's assets in the employer's stock, thus providing a market for the stock. It also permits distributions to participants in the form of employer stock.

target-benefit pension plan • a type of defined-contribution pension plan that has some of the features associated with a traditional defined-benefit plan. This hybrid plan uses a benefit formula like that of a defined-benefit plan and individual accounts like that of a defined-contribution plan. While the employer hopes to provide a specific benefit (the target) at retirement, the employer does not guarantee that the targeted benefit will be paid.

tax avoidance • a strategy that focuses on paying the least amount of tax possible through legal means. Some tax-avoidance techniques, or loopholes as they are often called, require the knowledge of an experienced tax professional to recommend and implement. Illegal strategies to avoid paying taxes is tax evasion.

tax bracket • the range of taxable income applicable to each marginal tax rate for each filing status

tax credits • a dollar-for-dollar reduction of the actual tax payable. There are several personal tax credits available for individual taxpayers. Each tax credit has its own set of rules for eligibility, availability based on the taxpayer's income level, and credit amounts.

tax evasion • any method of reducing taxes not permitted by law. It carries heavy penalties.

tax minimization • a strategy that focuses on minimizing (or avoiding) tax liability by analyzing the tax implications of various alternatives to find the one that best suits the individual within the context of his or her financial plan

tax preference item • items that are deductible for the regular tax but face different rules under the AMT. They generally produce no benefit to the taxpayer under the AMT system as they would under the regular system.

tax shelters • investments that allow taxpayers to write off tax losses against salary and other types of income. Under current law, however, there are strict limitations on the deductibility of losses generated by tax-shelter investments.

taxable distribution • one of the three different types of transfers that the generation-skipping transfer tax applies to. A taxable distribution is any distribution from a trust to a skip person (an individual who is two generations or more younger than the transferor) that is not a taxable termination or a direct skip.

taxable income • the amount of income that will actually be subject to tax in a given year. For individuals it is equal to adjusted gross income minus the standard or itemized deduction(s) and personal exemptions.

taxable termination • one of the three different types of transfers that the generation-skipping transfer tax applies to. A taxable termination occurs when an interest in property held in trust for a skip person (an individual who is two generations or more younger than the transferor) is terminated by an individual's death, lapse of time, release of a power or otherwise, and the trust property is either held for or distributed to the skip person.

taxable year • the annual accounting period during which taxable income or loss is determined for the taxpayer. For most individuals, it is simply the calendar year.

tax-qualified contracts • long-term care insurance contracts that meet the requirements of the Health Insurance Portability and Accountability Act and therefore are eligible for favorable tax treatment

term life insurance • a type of life insurance under which the death proceeds are payable if the insured dies during a specified period. If the insured survives to the end of the period, nothing is paid by the insurer.

testamentary trust • a trust created by the terms of a will. It does not receive property until the testator dies and the executor transfers the property to the trust.

testator • a person who leaves a will in force at death.

total disability • the condition of an insured person who is unable to work. One definition, typically called the any-occupation definition, states that the insured is totally disabled when he or she cannot perform the major duties of any gainful occupation for which he or she is reasonably suited by education, training, or experience. A less restrictive definition deems the insured to be totally disabled when he or she cannot perform the major duties of his or her regular occupation.

traditional IRA • an individual retirement account plan that allows an individual's contributions to be made with pretax dollars (if the taxpayer is eligible) and earnings to be tax deferred until retirement, at which time all withdrawals are taxable. Traditional IRAs are subject to certain limitations, the most important of which is the maximum contribution limit. In addition, contributions may not be made during or after the year in which the individual reaches age 70 1/2, and no loans may be taken from IRA accounts.

U.S. Treasury bills (T-bills) • a popular cash equivalent. T-bills are short-term obligations of the U.S. government issued with a term of one year or less. In addition, they are backed by the full taxing authority of the government and consequently are the safest investment available. Because of their safety, they pay investors the lowest interest rate of the various money market instruments.

unit-benefit formula • a benefit formula that directly accounts for both the participant's service with the employer and his or her salary in determining the plan's retirement benefit

universal life insurance • a type of whole life insurance with flexible premiums and adjustable death benefits that enables the policyowner to see how premiums are allocated to the protection and cash value elements of the policy

value stocks • stocks that typically have below average price/earnings ratios and regularly pay dividends to stockholders

variable life insurance • a whole life policy that permits the policyowner to allocate the funds generated by the policy among a variety of separate accounts. These policies shift the investment risk to the policyowner and provide no minimum guaranteed rate of return or guaranteed cash value. The rate of return credited to policy funds and thus the amount of the cash value depend on the investment success of the policyowner.

variable universal life • life insurance that is identical to universal life except that the cash value is invested by the policyowner in a variety of separate accounts rather than in the general assets of the insurer. In other words, it combines the premium flexibility features of universal life with the policyowner-directed investment aspects of variable life.

vision benefit plan • a plan that covers vision care expenses that usually are not covered under other medical expense plans. Benefits are provided for the cost of eye examinations and eyeglasses and/or contact lenses.

voluntary benefit plans • an arrangement in which the employer does not share in the cost of the benefit, but merely makes it available to an employee who pays the entire cost of coverage if he or she elects the benefit. The premiums are paid through payroll deductions by the employer.

whole life insurance • a type of life insurance under which the death proceeds are payable in the event of the insured's death regardless of when that occurs, provided the policy has been kept in force by the policyowner

Answers to Review Questions and Self-Test Questions

Chapter 1

Answers to Review Questions

1-1. The six steps in the financial planning process and their corresponding activities are as follows:
1. Establish and define the advisor-client relationship. Begin building trust with the client, ensuring client satisfaction, and creating a relationship with the client that will span the client's entire financial life. Explain the financial planning process and how that process is used to develop plans for clients. Disclose information about background, philosophy, and method of compensation.
2. Determine goals and gather data. Help the client set goals that are SMART and prioritize them. Gather client information through fact-finder forms, questionnaires, counseling, and examination of documents.
3. Analyze and evaluate the data. Identify the strengths and weaknesses in the client's present financial condition as they affect the ability to achieve the client's goals. Revise goals if necessary.
4. Develop and present a plan. Design a set of recommended strategies tailored to the client's circumstances and goals, including alternative ways of achieving those goals. Draw on other experts as needed. Obtain client approval.
5. Implement the plan. Motivate and help the client acquire all the necessary financial products and services to put the plan into action. Draw on other experts as needed.
6. Monitor the plan. Evaluate the performance of all implementation vehicles. Review changes in the client's circumstances and the financial environment. Revisit the steps when necessary.

1-2. a. The single-purpose approach to financial planning involves the sale to a client of a product to implement the recommendation of a plan developed according to the financial planning process and approved by the client.
 b. The multiple-purpose approach to financial planning involves solving multiple financial problems with financial products and/or services used to implement the recommendation of a plan developed according to the financial planning process and approved by the client.
 c. The comprehensive approach to financial planning considers all of a client's financial needs and objectives by developing a plan according to the financial planning process and approved by the client for fulfilling those needs and objectives.

1-3. At a minimum, the subjects that should be included in a comprehensive financial plan are

- financial planning principles
- insurance planning and risk management
- employee benefits planning
- investment planning
- income tax planning
- retirement planning
- estate planning

1-4. Financial planning is a process that should be ongoing throughout a client's financial life. Life-cycle financial planning occurs when an advisor actually engages in financial planning over a client's entire financial life cycle.

1-5. The financial planning pyramid illustrates how to develop a comprehensive financial plan in three stages or levels over a period of time. The advisor begins at the first or foundation level and concentrates on protecting the client against unexpected occurrences that could cause financial hardship. At the second or middle level, the advisor focuses on the clients wealth accumulation objectives. At the third and final level, the advisor addresses retirement and estate concerns.

1-6. The opportunities for financial planning advisors result from the
   a. rising median age—This results in more clients needing retirement planning and assistance in planning for the cost of their children's college educations.
   b. increasing number of dual-income families—These families typically have higher total incomes, pay higher income and Social Security taxes, and have less time to manage their finances, providing many opportunities for advisors to assist clients.
   c. volatility of financial conditions—With the possible exception of the bull markets of the late 1990s and mid 2000s when many investors felt they could do it themselves without the benefit of professional advice, volatile economic conditions generally create greater demand for financial planning services. They also emphasize the need for financial advisors to continuously monitor their client's financial circumstances and to adjust the plans as circumstances dictate.
   d. increasing use of sophisticated technology by the financial services industry—The revolution in technology has made possible the creation of many new financial products and has made it easier to tailor these products to individual client needs. Also, the technology has made possible improved analysis of the performance of these products by advisors with the skills to do so.

1-7. The top 10 reasons why people begin financial planning are
   1. building a retirement fund (82 percent of those surveyed)
   2. home purchase/renovation (41 percent)
   3. building an emergency fund (40 percent)
   4. managing/reducing current debt (34 percent)
   5. vacation/travel (34 percent)
   6. building a college fund (32 percent)
   7. accumulating capital (31 percent)
   8. providing insurance protection (29 percent)
   9. sheltering income from taxes (26 percent)

10. generating current income (25 percent)
1-8. Three important obstacles preventing households from gaining control of their own financial destinies are
- the natural human tendency to procrastinate
- the tendency to live up to, or beyond, their current income
- their lack of financial knowledge

Answers to Self-Test Questions
1-1. B
1-2. F
1-3. C
1-4. E
1-5. C
1-6. A
1-7. A
1-8. B
1-9. D
1-10. C

Chapter 2

Answers to Review Questions
2-1. For insurance and financial planning purposes, the term risk means the possibility of financial loss. However, risk is not the same as uncertainty. Risk exists as a state of the world, while uncertainty is a state of mind characterized by doubt. Although risk can give rise to uncertainty, risk is not uncertainty. Moreover, risk is not the probability of loss. While risk may be measurable in terms of probabilities, it need not be measurable to exist. This is the reason risk is defined as the possibility, not the probability, of financial loss.
2-2. The two categories of risk are
- pure risk, which involves only the possibility of financial loss or no loss
- speculative risk, which involves not only the possibility of financial loss, but also the possibility of financial gain
2-3. The three types of pure risk are
- personal risks, which involve the possibility of
  (a) loss of income-earning ability because of
    (1) premature death
    (2) disability
    (3) unemployment
    (4) retirement
  (b) extra expenses associated with accidental injuries, periods of sickness, or the inability to perform safely some of the activities of daily living
- property risks, which involve the possibility of

(a) direct losses associated with the need to replace or repair damaged or missing property
(b) indirect (consequential) losses, such as additional living expenses that are caused by a direct loss
- liability risks, which involve the possibility of
  (a) loss from damage to or destruction of others' property
  (b) loss from physical or personal injuries to others

2-4. The risk management process is used to deal with pure risks involving possible damage or destruction of property or legal liability, while the needs analysis process is used to deal with pure risks involving the loss of income-earning ability due to death, disability, or old age. However, the risk management and needs analysis processes not only contain steps similar to each other, but also contain steps similar to those of the financial planning process. In other words, all three processes are essentially different statements of the same professional approach for helping to identify and solve an individual's financial problem(s).

2-5. Actual cash value is defined as replacement cost less a reduction resulting from depreciation and obsolescence. This is expressed as: Actual cash value = Replacement cost − Depreciation. Replacement cost is that cost necessary to replace or repair the damaged asset. Depreciation is a function of the age of the asset, its use, its condition at the time of loss, and any other factor causing deterioration.

When used for real property, replacement cost is interpreted to mean the cost to rebuild the same type dwelling on the same site for the same type of occupancy and with materials of like kind and quality. It has become the more practical measure of the maximum possible loss associated with real property in pure-risk situations. Sometimes there is a temptation to use market value as the measurement of loss for real property, but market value is closely linked to supply and demand conditions and should be used with caution.

For insurance purposes, the measurement of loss for personal property such as furniture, clothing, and automobiles has traditionally been the item's actual cash value. However, the maximum possible loss for a particular item is its replacement cost.

2-6. No perfect method has been developed for measuring the maximum possible dollar loss that individuals can suffer from the liability exposure. An individual can enter into certain contractual arrangements that will limit the extent of liability, but in most cases the liability loss will depend upon the severity of the future accident and the amount the court awards to the injured parties (or the amount of the out-of-court settlement agreement).

2-7. Two methods of measuring the financial loss associated with premature death are the
- human-life-value method—This approach is based on the calculation of the present value of a given number of years at some assumed interest rate.
- needs analysis method—This approach involves (1) identifying and attaching a dollar amount to the specific financial needs of the survivors, (2) identifying and attaching a dollar amount to the resources currently available to meet those needs, and (3) determining the gaps between the survivors' needs and the resources available to meet them. These gaps must be filled with additional financial resources if the survivors' needs are to be fully met.

2-8. The two categories of techniques for handling pure risks are

- loss control, which is concerned with reducing the probability that events resulting in financial loss will occur and minimizing the magnitude of those losses that do occur
- loss financing, which is concerned with how to fund the losses that do occur

2-9. As insurers accept insureds, they pool those insureds with similar loss exposures, and the combination of many similar exposure units permits the operation of the law of large numbers. That is, as the number of exposure units increases, the deviation of actual experience from expected experience diminishes.

2-10. Participating (par) policies provide for, but do not guarantee, the payment of dividends to the policyowner. The dividends reflect the insurance company's past experience with respect to mortality, interest, and expenses. Favorable experience—lower mortality, lower expenses, and higher interest than expected—tends to increase the dividend scale, whereas unfavorable experience tends to have the opposite effect. In contrast to par policies, nonparticipating (nonpar) policies do not pay policyowner dividends.

2-11. The reserves (and, thus, cash values) of traditional whole life policies are invested in the general assets of the insurance company. Moreover, these policies contain a guaranteed interest rate that is the lowest rate with which policy funds can be credited. In contrast, variable life policies permit the policyowner to allocate the funds generated by the policy among a variety of separate accounts. In other words, these policies shift the investment risk to the policyowner and provide no minimum guaranteed rate of return or guaranteed cash value. The rate of return credited to policy funds and, thus, the amount of the cash value depend upon the investment success of the policyowner.

2-12. Definitions of disability in disability income policies are based on the ability of the insured to perform certain occupational tasks. One definition, typically called the any-occupation definition, states that insureds are considered to be totally disabled when they cannot perform the major duties of any gainful occupation for which they are reasonably suited by education, training, or experience.

A somewhat less restrictive definition is usually referred to as the own-occupation definition. With a pure own-occupation definition, insureds are deemed to be totally disabled when they cannot perform the major duties of their regular occupations. Because this definition would allow an insured to work in some other capacity and still be entitled to benefits, many insurers now use a modified own-occupation definition that also provides that benefits either will not be paid or will be reduced if the insured chooses to work in any other occupation.

Due to adverse claims experience, most companies no longer issue contracts of long benefit duration that have pure own-occupation definitions of disability for the contract duration. Instead, either a modified own-occupation definition or a dual definition of total disability is typically used in long-term disability income policies. With a dual definition, an own-occupation definition applies during the first few policy years after which it is replaced by an any-occupation definition.

2-13. a. Policies pay benefits in one of two basic ways—reimbursement or per diem. The majority of newer policies pay benefits on a reimbursement basis. These contracts reimburse the insured for actual expenses up to the specified policy limit. Some policies provide benefits on a per diem basis once care is actually being received. This means that benefits are paid regardless of the actual cost of care.

b. There are two ways that the benefit period is applied in the payment of benefits. Under one approach, benefit payments are made for exactly the benefit period chosen. If the client selects a benefit period of 4 years and collects benefits for 4 years, the benefit payments cease. The other approach, most commonly but not exclusively used with reimbursement policies, uses a pool of money. Under this concept, there is an amount of money that can be used to make benefit payments as long as the pool of money lasts. The client does not select the amount in the pool of money; it is determined by multiplying the daily benefit by the benefit period selected.

c. Most states require that a long-term care policy offer some type of automatic inflation protection. The client is given the choice to select this option, decline the option, or possibly select an alternative option. The cost of an automatic-increase option is built into the initial premium, and no additional premium is levied at the time of an annual increase. The automatic option found in almost all policies is a 5 percent benefit increase that is compounded annually over the life of the policy. Under such a provision, the amount of a policy's benefits increases by 5 percent each year over the amount of benefits available in the prior year. A common alternative that many insurers make available is based on simple interest, with each annual automatic increase being 5 percent of the original benefit amount. Another alternative offered by some insurers is to allow the policyowner to increase benefits without evidence of insurability on a pay-as-you-go basis at specified intervals, such as every one, 2, or 3 years.

2-14. a. Coverage A or dwelling coverage requires the selection of a limit or dollar amount of insurance coverage. For HO-2 and HO-3, this is the only part of Section I for which the client must choose a limit of coverage, and it should be chosen with care. If a loss should occur to the dwelling and at the time of loss the amount of insurance carried is equal to 80 percent or more of the full replacement cost of the dwelling, the loss will be settled on a full replacement-cost basis. If the current replacement cost of the dwelling is $200,000, a minimum limit of coverage on the dwelling of $160,000 and a maximum limit of $200,000 should be recommended. In most cases, it would be appropriate to recommend the selection of a limit closer to the top of the range, particularly if the client would need to replace the entire dwelling following a total loss.

b. Coverage B or coverage for other structures provides insurance on other structures located on the premises that are not attached to the dwelling. These include detached garages or tool-sheds and such things as fences, driveways, and retaining walls. Unless increased by the insured, the amount of coverage is 10 percent of the limit on the dwelling. Losses to these other structures are settled on a replacement-cost basis.

c. Coverage C or coverage on personal property includes the items normally contained in a dwelling, such as furniture, appliances, and clothing, and property stored in a garage, other structure, or outdoors. Unless increased, the limit of coverage on personal property for HO-2 and HO-3 is 50 percent of the dwelling limit. Personal property coverage is provided worldwide.

2-15. Coverage D, the loss-of-use coverage, provides insurance protection for certain indirect losses. The primary loss-of-use coverage is for additional living expenses—those increased costs necessary to maintain normal living standards when the insured's dwelling is uninhabitable because of damage caused by a covered cause of loss. The automatic limit for this coverage is a percent of the coverage applicable to the dwelling for HO-2 (30 percent), HO-3 (30 percent), HO-5 (30 percent), and HO-8 (10 percent), and a percent of the coverage applicable to personal property for HO-4 (30 percent) and HO-6 (50 percent). Payment is limited to the period required to repair or replace the damage or if the insured permanently relocates, to the period required to resettle the household.

2-16. a. Coverage E, personal liability coverage, provides protection for activities and conditions at the premises where the named insured maintains a covered residence and for personal activities of the named insured and members of his or her family anywhere in the world. All homeowners forms contain the same liability coverage.

Coverage E is similar to other liability insurance policies. Protection is provided for legal liability involving bodily injury or property damage, but not for personal injury. The latter includes such injuries as libel, slander, violation of privacy, malicious prosecution, and wrongful entry. These may be added by endorsement or covered under an umbrella liability policy.

Also, as with other liability policies, the insurer promises to defend the insured at the company's expense even if the suit is groundless, false, or fraudulent. The insurer may investigate and settle any claim that it feels is appropriate. The costs associated with investigating and defending a claim against an insured are paid in addition to the limit of liability.

Exclusions play an important role in liability insurance coverage, because the insurer is essentially promising to pay any claim involving bodily injury or property damage for which an insured is legally liable unless the particular situation is specifically excluded by the policy. Some of the exclusions found in homeowners policies should be expected, such as war and nuclear exposure. Others should be anticipated because the exposure can be covered with a different policy as in the case of motor vehicle, large and powerful watercraft, aircraft, workers' compensation, and business and professional service exposures. Liability arising out of the transmission of a communicable disease, sexual molestation or abuse, and the use, sale, manufacture, delivery, transfer, or possession of a controlled substance by an insured is also excluded. Finally, losses that are intentionally caused are not covered, nor is bodily injury to an insured.

b. Coverage F, medical payments to others, provides medical benefits to persons, other than the residents of the insured household, who suffer bodily injury at an insured location or who are injured because of an insured's activities away from the insured location. The basic limit for Coverage F is $1,000 per person. This amount is available for all necessary medical expenses incurred within 3 years of the date of the accident. Benefits under this coverage will be paid whether or not the insured is legally liable.

2-17. Under the medical payments coverage (Part B) of the PAP, the insurer will pay reasonable expenses incurred for necessary medical and funeral services because of bodily injury caused by an accident and sustained by an insured. Subject to certain exclusions, benefits are payable to the named insured and family members if injured while occupying any motor vehicle designed for public roads or if struck by a motor vehicle. This coverage differs from medical payments coverage under the homeowners policy where the named insured and members of the household are not covered, and coverage applies only to other persons injured on the premises or because of an insured's activities. In the PAP, medical expenses of other persons are also covered, but only while they are occupying a covered auto.

2-18. Uninsured motorists coverage (Part C of the PAP) provides that if an insured sustains bodily injury (some states also include property damage) in an auto accident where the other driver was operating an uninsured motor vehicle, the insured may recover from his or her own insurance company those sums he or she is legally entitled to recover from the owner or operator of the uninsured motor vehicle.

The limit of liability for uninsured motorists coverage is typically the required limit of the financial responsibility law in the insured's state. However, the policy can be endorsed to add underinsured motorists coverage, which increases this limit. The underinsured benefit provides payment when the at-fault driver or owner has liability insurance, but its limits are less than the limits purchased for the underinsured motorists coverage.

2-19. An umbrella liability policy provides excess liability limits over underlying liability coverage limits. The insured is required to carry certain underlying liability policies and limits—for example, a homeowners policy with a liability limit of $300,000 and an automobile liability policy with a single limit of $500,000. If the insured has an umbrella liability policy with a limit of $2,000,000, the first $500,000 of any claim arising out of an automobile accident would be payable under the automobile policy, and the balance (up to the policy limit) would be payable under the umbrella policy. Therefore, the insured would have total coverage amounting to $2,500,000.

2-20. The umbrella policy covers situations not covered by underlying homeowners policies, such as personal injury in the form of libel, slander, and invasion of privacy. When the umbrella policy does provide coverage in these cases, it drops down to provide primary coverage over the insured's retained limit. A retained limit is like a deductible that must be paid by the insured. This can be as low as $250, but is typically in the $500 to $1,000 range.

Answers to Self-Test Questions
- 2-1. B
- 2-2. D
- 2-3. C
- 2-4. A
- 2-5. A
- 2-6. D
- 2-7. C
- 2-8. B
- 2-9. C
- 2-10. B

Chapter 3

Answers to Review Questions

3-1. The five categories of employee benefits are
- legally required payments for government programs
- payments for private insurance and retirement plans
- payments for time not worked
- extra cash payments, other than wages and bonuses based on performance
- cost of services to employees

3-2. The growth of employee benefits over the last 75 years stems from the following six factors:
- industrialization and urbanization of society
- labor unions ability to negotiate for benefits
- wage controls during World War II and the Korean War
- inflationary pressures on benefit levels
- cost advantages of benefits compared to alternatives
- legislation favorable to benefits

3-3. The steps in the benefit-planning process for employers are the same as those in the financial planning process. The six steps are
1. establish and define the advisor-client relationship
2. determine goals and gather data
3. analyze and evaluate the data
4. develop and present a plan
5. implement the plan
6. monitor the plan

3-4. Financial advisors should be aware of employee benefits for the following reasons:
- Employee benefits form the basis for almost all financial plans.
- Many employees can purchase additional insurance and retirement benefits through employer-sponsored plans.
- Many executives can negotiate their own compensation packages, including employee benefits.

3-5. Requirements that employee benefit plans may use to determine who is an eligible person for coverage purposes include
- covered classifications
- full-time employment
- probationary periods
- evidence of insurability
- employee premium contributions
- termination of coverage

3-6. The five basic characteristics of a true managed care plan are
- controlled access to providers
- comprehensive case management
- preventive care

- risk sharing
- high-quality care

3-7. PPOs differ from HMOs in the following ways:
- Preferred providers are generally paid on a fee-for-service basis as their services are used.
- Employees are not required to use the practitioners or facilities that contract with the PPO.
- Most PPOs do not use a primary care physician as a gatekeeper; employees do not need referrals to see specialists.

3-8. The basic concept of a defined-contribution medical expense plan is that the employer makes a fixed contribution, which the employee can use to "purchase" his or her own coverage.

3-9. The qualifying events for which employees or their dependents can extend medical expense coverage under the provisions of COBRA are the loss of coverage because of
- the death of the covered employee
- the termination of the employee for almost any reason except for gross misconduct
- a reduction in the employee's hours so that the employee or dependent is ineligible for coverage
- the divorce or legal separation of the covered employee and his or her spouse
- the employee becoming eligible for Medicare with the spouse and children ceasing to be eligible under the plan
- a child's ceasing to be an eligible dependent under the plan

3-10. Benefits under a group life insurance plan are determined by one or more of the following:
- multiple-of-earnings schedule
- specified-dollar-amount schedule
- scheduled reduction in benefits for older employees

3-11. There are two possible options that an employee may have for the continuation of life insurance coverage if he or she terminates employment.
- Conversion allows an employee to convert to an individual cash value life insurance policy without evidence of insurability at attained-age rates.
- Portability of term coverage allows an employee to continue coverage at group rates in much the same manner as is found in voluntary employee-pay-all plans.

3-12. The monthly amount that will be reportable by Bruce as taxable income is calculated as follows:

Coverage provided	$100,000
Minus Sec. 70 exclusion	– 50,000
Amount subject to taxation	$ 50,000

Monthly cost – $0.06/$1,000 x $50,000 = $3.00

3-13. The tax treatment of employees under a noncontributory group long-term disability income insurance plan is that employer contributions result in no taxable income to employees. However, any disability benefits paid to employees are taxable income, but the Code provides for a tax credit to persons of modest means who are permanently and totally disabled.

3-14. Characteristics of voluntary benefit plans that make them popular with employees are
- payment through payroll deduction

- more liberal underwriting than for similar coverage in the individual insurance marketplace
- lower cost than in the individual marketplace
- portability of coverage

3-15. Benefits not considered qualified benefits under Code. Sec. 125 include contributions to Archer medical savings accounts, long-term care insurance, scholarships and fellowships, transportation benefits, educational assistance, no-additional-cost services, employee discounts, and *de minimis* fringe benefits.

Answers to Self-Test Questions

3-1. C
3-2. A
3-3. B
3-4. D
3-5. C
3-6. A
3-7. B
3-8. D
3-9. A
3-10. D

Chapter 4

Answers to Review Questions

4-1. The two types of assets that consumers buy are
- personal assets—which are bought primarily for the creature comforts they provide. Examples include homes, cars, and clothes.
- investment assets—which are acquired for the purpose of investing. Investing is defined as the purchase of an asset with the expectation that it will provide a return commensurate with its risk.

From the above descriptions, it should be obvious that the distinction between personal and investment assets is not always clear. For example, the purchase of an antique car may be for pleasure or it may be for investment purposes or it may be for both. In cases where there is ambiguity, the ultimate distinction is based on the intent of the buyer. The exact same asset may be a personal asset for one person and an investment asset for another person.

4-2. Investing is based on a reasoned consideration of expected return and the risk associated with that return. Speculating occurs when a person buys an asset in the hopes of receiving some form of return, without consideration or knowledge of the expected return or risk, or both.

4-3. Investment risk is measured by the likelihood that realized returns will differ from those that are expected. An asset with a wide range of possible returns is considered risky, while an asset with a narrow range of possible returns is considered more secure. The range of returns is generally measured in terms of the distance or dispersion from the mean or expected return.

Risk refers to the magnitude of the range of possible returns. The greater the range of possible returns, the riskier the investment.

4-4. The two most basic theorems of investment are as follows:
- All investors are greedy. Everyone would like a risk-free investment with an incredibly high rate of return.
- There is no free lunch. This means that there is a well-established relationship in the world of investments between risk and expected return. Low risk investments have low expected returns, and high-risk investments have high expected returns.

4-5. Asset allocation models are recommended investment portfolios for different levels of financial risk tolerance. These recommended portfolios are based on categories of assets and the percentage to be placed in each category. To properly determine both the categories and the appropriate percentages for a client, the client's level of risk tolerance needs to be known.

4-6. Common stockholders usually have a preemptive right, which is the right to maintain their relative voting power by purchasing shares of any new issues of common stock of the corporation.

4-7. Preferred stockholders usually have two privileges that provide them with a preferential position relative to common stockholders. The first privilege is the right to receive dividends before any dividends are paid to the common stockholders. This preference is usually limited to a specified amount per share each year. The second privilege is the right to receive up to a specified amount for each share at the time of liquidation. This liquidation value must be paid in full before anything can be paid to the common stockholders.

4-8. Price risk results from the fact that any change in market interest rates typically leads to an opposite change in the value of investments. When interest rates rise (fall), the value of an investment declines (increases). This inverse relationship is most pronounced for debt instruments that have a contractually specified rate of interest or return and a specified time to maturity. The longer the time until maturity, the greater will be the resulting change in market price.

4-9. An asset is said to be liquid if it can be converted to cash (sold) quickly at any time with little or no loss of principal. Marketability is a little different than liquidity, but the two are frequently confused. Marketability refers to the ability to sell an asset quickly. Thus, liquid assets are marketable, but not all marketable assets are liquid. Stock is a classic example of a marketable asset that is not liquid. If a stock is listed on a major exchange, it can be sold in a matter of seconds. However, there is no certainty as to the price at which the stock can be sold.

4-10. Jack's equivalent fully taxable yield is calculated as follows:

$$\text{equivalent fully taxable yield} = \frac{\text{tax-exempt yields}}{(1 - \text{MRT})}$$

$$\text{equivalent fully taxable yield} = \frac{.03}{1 - .33} = \frac{.03}{.67} = .0448$$

equivalent fully taxable yield = 4.48%

4-11. Joe's after-tax holding period return would be caculated as follows:

after-tax HPR = $\dfrac{[TCI \times (1 - MRT)] + [TCA \times (1 - TCG)]}{\text{total initial investment}}$

where: TCI is Joe's total current income
MRT is his marginal income tax rate
TCA is his total capital appreciation
TCG is his tax rate for capital gains

Under JGTRRA, however, qualified dividends are taxed the same as long-term capital gains, so the formula becomes

after-tax HPR = $\dfrac{[TCI \times (1 - TCG)] + [TCA \times (1 - TCG)]}{\text{total initial investment}}$

which reduces to

after-tax HPR = $\dfrac{(TCI + TCA) \times (1 - TCG)}{\text{total initial investment}}$

after-tax HPR = $\dfrac{\$14 (1 - .15)}{\$50} = \dfrac{\$14 \times .85}{\$50}$

after-tax HPR = $\dfrac{\$11.9}{\$50} = .238 = 23.8\%$

4-12. Sally's after-tax approximate yield for a 5-year holding period would be calculated as follows:

$$\text{before-tax approximate yield} = \dfrac{\text{annual income} + \dfrac{\text{future price} - \text{current price}}{\text{number of years}}}{\dfrac{\text{future price} + \text{current price}}{2}}$$

$$\text{before-tax approximate yield} = \dfrac{\$5{,}000 + \dfrac{\$200{,}000 - \$100{,}000}{5}}{\dfrac{\$200{,}000 + \$100{,}000}{2}} = \dfrac{\$5{,}000 + \dfrac{\$100{,}000}{5}}{\dfrac{\$300{,}000}{2}}$$

$$\text{before-tax approximate yield} = \dfrac{\$5{,}000 + \$20{,}000}{\$150{,}000}$$

To calculate the after-tax approximate yield, multiply each segment of the numerator by one minus Sally's appropriate tax rate where MRT is Sally's marginal income tax rate and TCG is her capital gains tax rate.

after-tax approximate yield $= \dfrac{\$5{,}000\,(1 - \text{MRT}) + \$20{,}000\,(1 - \text{TCG})}{\$150{,}000}$

after-tax approximate yield $= \dfrac{\$5{,}000 \times .72 + \$20{,}000 \times .85}{\$150{,}000}$

after-tax approximate yield $= \dfrac{\$3{,}600 + \$17{,}000}{\$150{,}000} = \dfrac{\$20{,}600}{\$150{,}000} = .1373$

after-tax approximate yield $= 13.73\%$

4-13. Prior to beginning an investment program, an investor should set aside some funds for emergency purposes. In addition, the investor should also take steps to protect himself or herself from several types of pure risks. This typically is done by purchasing the appropriate kinds of insurance.

4-14. Dollar cost averaging requires the investment of a fixed amount of dollars at specified time intervals. Investing a fixed amount of dollars at set intervals in the stock market means that the investor buys more shares when prices are low and fewer shares when prices are high. Unless the market goes into a persistent decline, this approach to investing works fairly well, and it establishes a consistent pattern of investing. Moreover, the overall cost of investing using dollar cost averaging is lower than it would be if a constant number of shares were bought at set intervals.

4-15. a. Negotiated markets are markets where sellers list their offerings with brokers who then seek to attract buyers through various advertising and other marketing methods. After a buyer has been located, negotiations determine the price. When these transactions involve listed securities, this negotiated market is called the fourth market because the transaction does not take place on the floor of an exchange.

b. For many securities, one or more dealers make an active market by offering to buy (at a bid price) and sell (at an ask price) as much of a particular security as desired by investors. The difference between the bid and ask price is the dealer's spread, or compensation, for making the market and bearing the risk of holding an inventory of the security. This network of securities dealers is called the over-the-counter market and includes over 30,000 different securities issues.

4-16. a. The Securities Act of 1933 requires issuers of new securities to file a registration statement with the Securities and Exchange Commission (SEC). The issuing corporation may not sell the security until the SEC verifies that the information contained in the registration statement is complete and is not false or misleading. Once approval is obtained, a prospectus is prepared that contains a summary of information from the registration statement. Then the securities can be sold to the public if a copy of the prospectus is made available to all interested buyers.

The 1975 amendments to this act called for development of a national competitive system for trading securities, which resulted in the consolidated tape and the end of fixed brokerage commission rates.

b. The Maloney Act of 1938 permits the establishment of trade associations for the purpose of self-regulation of a segment of the securities industry. The only self-regulating organization that has formed is the Financial Industry Regulating Authority (FINRA, formerly NASD), which regulates securities firms, their owners, and stockbrokers. FINRA establishes rules of practice to which members must adhere. Securities firms that are not members of FINRA are regulated by the SEC.

Answers to Self-Test Questions

4-1. D
4-2. B
4-3. A
4-4. C
4-5. B
4-6. D
4-7. A
4-8. D
4-9. C
4-10. A

Chapter 5

Answers to Review Questions

5-1. Gross income for income tax purposes includes every item of value, whether consisting of money or other property, that is either made available to or comes into the possession of the taxpayer. In other words, anything of value is considered to be gross income for income tax purposes unless the Internal Revenue Code contains a specific provision that excludes a particular item from the taypayer's gross income.

5-2. An exclusion from gross income is an item of value that a taxpayer receives that is not includible in his or her gross income. A deduction from gross income is an item of expense that reduces the amount of the taxpayer's income that is subject to tax.

5-3. An above-the-line deduction consists of those deductions that are subtracted from gross income to determine adjusted gross income. A below-the-line deduction consists of those deductions that are subtracted from adjusted gross income to determine taxable income.

5-4. The standard deduction is a specified amount, indexed annually for inflation, that a taxpayer who does not itemize deductions may claim in calculating taxable income. If the taxpayer is entitled to claim itemized deductions that, when added together, are less than the amount of his or her standard deduction, then the taxpayer will claim the standard deduction. The amount of the standard deduction depends on the taxpayer's filing status.

5-5. The three basic categories of deductions allowable to individual taxpayers are as follows:
- The first includes deductions for expenses that are incurred in the course of carrying on a trade or business.

- The second includes deductions for expenses that are incurred in the course of an activity that is not a trade or business but is engaged in for the purpose of producing income and making a profit.
- The third includes deductions for expenses that are simply personal, family, or living expenses. Although the Code provides a general rule that these expenses are nondeductible, there are several important exceptions to the general rule.

5-6. Medical expenses are deductible only to the extent that they exceed the floor of 7.5 percent of the taxpayer's adjusted gross income (AGI). Therefore, assuming George has medical expenses of $9,500, an AGI of $80,000, and he itemizes, he will be able to deduct $3,500 of his medical expenses, calculated as follows:
- 7.5 percent x George's $80,000 AGI = $6,000
- $9,500 of medical expenses − $6,000 = $3,500 of medical expenses that George can deduct

5-7. Itemized deductions are disallowed or phased out to the extent of a taxpayer's adjusted gross income (AGI) in excess of a specified amount multiplied by 3 percent. Up to 80 percent of the taxpayer's itemized deductions can be disallowed under this rule, which applies to all itemized deductions except medical expenses, casualty and theft losses, and investment interest expenses. The rule applies after all other limitations and restrictions on the deductions have been taken into account.

5-8. The tax rate applicable to each of the six income brackets is called a marginal tax rate. The six marginal tax rates are 10 percent, 15 percent, 25 percent, 28 percent, 33 percent, and 35 percent. Due to the progressive structure of these marginal rates, an additional dollar of income could be taxed at a higher rate than all previous income. An effective tax rate is the rate at which a taxpayer would be taxed if his or her taxable income were taxed at a constant rate rather than progressively. This rate is computed by dividing the total tax liability by taxable income. Except when a taxpayer is in the lowest marginal tax bracket, his or her effective tax rate will always be lower than his or her marginal rate because of the progressive structure of the income tax system. A taxpayer in the lowest tax bracket has both an effective tax rate and a marginal tax rate equal to 10 percent.

5-9. A $10,000 tax deduction will reduce the taxpayer's taxable income by $10,000 and the federal income tax payable by $10,000 multiplied by the taxpayer's marginal tax rate. A $10,000 tax credit, on the other hand, will reduce the taxpayer's federal income tax payable by $10,000.

5-10. The alternative minimum tax (AMT) is a separate and parallel system of income taxation to the regular system. It applies to any taxpayer whose tax liability under the parallel system is greater than the liability for that year under the regular income tax system. In other words, the taxpayer pays the AMT amount if the AMT is greater than the regular tax. The purpose of the AMT is to ensure that the taxpayer who enjoys certain tax benefits will not be permitted to reduce his or her tax liability below a minimum amount by claiming certain tax deductions.

5-11. a. The economic benefit doctrine holds that a taxpayer must pay tax whenever an economic benefit has been conferred on the taxpayer, regardless of whether the taxpayer has actually received any cash or property. In other words, any event or transaction that confers an economic benefit on the taxpayer will result in gross income to the taxpayer, as long as the economic benefit is certain and can be measured.

b. The doctrine of the fruit and tree holds that income is to be taxed to the person who earns it, or to the person who owns the asset that produces it. In other words, for income tax purposes, the fruit comes from the tree that produced it and must be taxed accordingly. The fruits of a person's labor cannot be assigned to another person for tax purposes.

c. The doctrine of constructive receipt holds that a cash-basis taxpayer is deemed to have received income for tax purposes when it is either credited to the taxpayer's account, set apart for the taxpayer, or otherwise made available to be taken into the taxpayer's possession. However, if there is any condition or restriction that limits the taxpayer's right to receive the income, the doctrine of constructive receipt will not apply.

5-12. Federal income tax avoidance involves a reasonable interpretation of the tax laws. It is perfectly acceptable (and perhaps even commendable) to use every legal means to avoid the payment of federal income taxes. Tax evasion, on the other hand, happens when the taxpayer either ignores the tax laws or flouts them.

5-13. The purpose behind income-shifting techniques is to get taxable income into the hands of taxpayers who are in lower tax brackets than the taxpayers who would otherwise have to report the income. The result is that less tax is paid on the income. Deduction shifting, on the other hand, is the converse of income shifting. The purpose behind deduction shifting is to shift deductions to taxpayers who are in higher tax brackets than the taxpayers who would otherwise claim the deductions. The result, again, is greater tax savings.

5-14. If a taxpayer has miscellaneous itemized deductions and wishes to minimize the effect of the 2 percent floor, the taxpayer can bunch his or her above-the-line deductions into a given year to reduce adjusted gross income and, thus, the size of the 2 percent floor. Conversely, the taxpayer can bunch a greater number of miscellaneous itemized deductions subject to the floor into one year. The result is that some deductions that would be lost under the floor if claimed in next year's return can actually be deducted if taken this year because the floor has already been exceeded.

5-15 a. For income tax purposes, passive losses are losses that typically are generated by activities in which the taxpayer has an ownership interest but does not participate in the activity of the business.

b. The basic rule is that tax losses generated by passive activities can be deducted only against income generated by passive activities and not against salary or other income. The rule is intended to prevent taxpayers from investing in activities merely for tax purposes, as distinguished from the actual economics of the investment.

c. The intent of the nonrecognition provisions is merely to defer taxation. However, the deferred gain may never be taxed if the taxpayer does not sell the property received in the exchange at a later date. In other words, there is no assurance that the government will ever get its tax money, particularly if the taxpayer keeps the new property until death when it receives a stepped-up basis in the hands of the beneficiary.

d. The social policy issue surrounding the sale of capital assets has two sides. Those people who believe that the sale of such assets should receive a tax break relative to other kinds of income argue that capital-gain tax relief encourages savings and investment. They also argue that full taxation of capital gain subjects taxpayers to what is really a tax on inflation, rather than one on real economic gains. These views have helped to introduce varying legislative measures over the years that provide relief for the taxation of capital gain. Those people who argue against favorable tax treatment for capital gain believe that preferential treatment for capital gain favors wealthy taxpayers at the expense of the average citizen because most stocks and other investment assets are owned by the rich.

5-16. a. The federal income tax treatment of the sale of Sec. 1231 assets might be termed a hybrid form of tax treatment because these assets receive different tax treatment, depending on whether they are sold at a gain or at a loss. If they are sold at a gain, the gain is treated as a capital gain. If they are sold at a loss, the loss is treated as an ordinary loss, not as a capital loss.
b. The importance of this hybrid form of tax treatment is that the sale of a Sec. 1231 asset is not subject to the limitations that apply to the deductibility of capital losses. If a Sec. 1231 asset is sold at a loss, the loss can be deducted against the taxpayer's salary or other income. This would not be the case if the sale of a Sec. 1231 asset at a loss was treated as a capital loss. Capital losses are deducted against capital gains; they generally cannot be deducted against ordinary income (except in the special case of individual taxpayers who are allowed to deduct up to $3,000 of capital losses against ordinary income each year).

Answers to Self-Test Questions
5-1. C
5-2. B
5-3. C
5-4. D
5-5. A
5-6. C
5-7. B
5-8. D
5-9. B
5-10. A

Chapter 6

Answers to Review Questions
6-1. A spendthrift lifestyle during a client's active working years makes retirement planning more difficult for him or her because it minimizes the client's ability to accumulate savings that will produce an adequate income stream to compliment his or her employer pension and Social Security. In addition, the client becomes accustomed to an unnaturally high standard of living. By living below his or her means before retirement, the client establishes a lifestyle that is more easily maintained in the retirement years.
6-2. Roadblocks preventing the accumulation of adequate retirement saving include
a. inadequate insurance coverage. Regardless of whether it is life, disability, health, home, or auto insurance, many individuals continue to remain uninsured or underinsured.

Because the client cannot always recover economically from these types of losses, one important element of retirement planning is protection against catastrophic financial loss that would make future saving impossible. Advisors should conduct a thorough review of their clients' insurance needs to make sure they are adequately covered.

b. divorce. Divorce often leaves one or both parties with little or no accumulation of pension benefits or other private sources of retirement income. These clients may have only a short time to accumulate any retirement income and may not be able to earn significant pension or Social Security benefits. Moreover, a spouse may be entitled to a portion of the former spouse's retirement benefits if the divorce decree includes a qualified domestic relations order (QDRO). QDROs allow a participant's plan assets to be used for marital property rights, child support, or alimony payments to a former spouse or dependent.

c. frequent changes of employer. Workers who have frequently changed employers also face the problem of arriving at retirement with little or no pension. Generally, these people will not accumulate vested pension benefits because they never stayed with an employer long enough to become vested. Even if they did become vested, they may have received a distribution of their accumulated pension fund upon leaving the job and probably spent this money rather than investing it or rolling it over for retirement. Advisors should recommend to clients who change jobs to roll over vested benefits into an IRA or into their new qualified plan to preserve the tax-deferred growth of their retirement funds. They should also advise clients who have recently changed jobs that if they do not meet the participation requirements of their new employer's plan, they can make annual tax-deductible contributions to an IRA until they do meet the requirements, regardless of their salary.

6-3. Many of the variables affecting the amount a client will need to save in order to achieve his or her retirement goals can dramatically change overnight and without warning. The following are examples of how variables could change.

- The client may be planning to retire at age 65 but health considerations, or perhaps a plant shutdown, force retirement at age 62.
- A younger client may be planning on a relatively moderate retirement lifestyle but business success may lead to a higher retirement income expectation.
- Forecasters may predict that long-term inflation will result in an annual 4 percent increase in the cost of living when in reality 6 percent increases occur. (Even a one percentage point disparity can make a significant difference.)
- Clients may hope for an after-tax rate of return of 7 percent when in fact investment returns are adversely affected by a bear market, or the real after-tax rate of return is suppressed by rising tax rates.
- Clients may plan on a short life expectancy and have the "misfortune" of living longer.

6-4. The replacement ratio method of determining retirement income assumes that the standard of living enjoyed during the years just prior to retirement will be the determining factor for the standard of living during retirement. The expense method, on the other hand, focuses on the projected expenses that the retiree will have. As with the replacement ratio method, it is much easier to define the potential expenses for those clients who are at or near retirement.

However, if a younger client is involved, more speculative estimates of retirement expenses must be made (and periodically revised).

6-5. Retirees can assume that a lower percentage of their income will go toward paying taxes in the retirement years because, in many cases, there is an elimination or a reduction of certain taxes that they previously had to pay. Tax advantages for the retiree include the elimination of the Social Security tax, an increased standard deduction depending on the retiree's age and filing status, the exclusion of all or part of the amount of the Social Security benefit from gross income, reductions in state and local income taxes, and an increased ability to use deductible medical expenses.

6-6. a. Retirees face a variety of changes in spending patterns after retirement, and some of these changes will reduce their living expenses. These reductions often include the elimination of work-related expenses, the elimination of home-mortgage expenses, the elimination of dependent care, that is, child-rearing expenses, the elimination of long-term savings obligations, and a reduction in automotive expenditures.

b. It is not all good news for retirees, however. Retirees also face several factors that tend to increase the amount of income they will need during the retirement period. These may include increases in long-term inflation, in medical expenses, in travel expenses, and in other retirement-related expenses. On the other hand, it is also true that retirees typically start to spend less later in their retirement when travel and other activities become more difficult to manage.

6-7. a. A defined-benefit plan provides a fixed predetermined benefit for the employee that has an uncertain cost to the employer. On the other hand, a defined-contribution plan has a predetermined cost to the employer but provides an uncertain benefit for the employee.

b. Under a pension plan, the employer is committed to making annual contributions to the plan, since the main purpose of the plan is to provide a retirement benefit. On the other hand, under a profit-sharing plan, the employer can retain the flexibility necessary to avoid funding the plan annually. Moreover, a profit-sharing plan is not necessarily intended to provide a retirement benefit as much as to provide tax deferral of present compensation. To this end, under certain profit-sharing plans, employees are permitted to withdraw funds after they have been in the plan for at least 2 years.

6-8. A defined-contribution plan may result in inadequate retirement income for a client if investment results are unfavorable. This is because the employer's obligation begins and ends with making the annual contribution. If plan investments are poor, the employee suffers the loss and may have inadequate retirement resources.

In addition, a second problem with a defined-contribution plan is that contributions are based on participants' salaries for each year of their careers, rather than on their salaries at retirement. Consequently, if inflation increases sharply in the years just prior to retirement, the chances of a participant achieving an adequate income-replacement ratio are diminished because most of the annual contributions would have been based on his or her salary paid prior to the inflationary spiral.

Another instance where a defined contribution plan may provide inadequate retirement income occurs when a client joins a plan late in his or her career. In this situation, since the years to retirement are few, the plan may not provide enough time to accumulate an adequate amount of assets.

6-9. Two important factors should be kept in mind if a client has a profit-sharing plan. First, the advisor should closely monitor the funding of the plan. It would be an easy mistake to assume that the employer is making scheduled payments to the plan when in actuality the employer is not contributing as expected because employer contributions are discretionary. It would also be an easy mistake to assume that the employee is allowing the funds to accumulate for retirement when in actuality the employee is depleting the account by taking withdrawals.

The second factor concerning profit-sharing plans is that the ability to withdraw funds prior to retirement under some profit-sharing plans opens up some interesting planning possibilities for the client and his or her advisor. For example, the client may want to gradually take money out while employed (starting after age 59 1/2 to avoid the 10 percent penalty tax) in order to reposition assets or take advantage of an excellent investment opportunity. In addition, the client may want to prepay any debt that would carry over into retirement, such as prepaying a mortgage or reducing interest expenses on a major capital purchase.

6-10. a. A unit-benefit formula might read as follows: Each plan participant will receive a monthly pension commencing at the normal retirement age and paid in the form of a life annuity equal to 2 percent of final-average monthly salary multiplied by the participant's years of service. Normal retirement age in this plan is defined as the later of age 65 or 5 years of plan participation. Service is limited to a maximum of 30 years.

b. A flat-percentage-of-earnings formula might read as follows: Each plan participant will receive a monthly pension commencing at the normal retirement age of 65 and paid in the form of a life annuity equal to 40 percent of the participant's final-average monthly salary. However, to receive the full benefit promised, the participant must have at least 25 years of service. If the participant has less service, the benefit is proportionately reduced.

6-11. A 401(k) plan allows employees to elect to defer current salary, which is contributed to the plan on a pretax basis. In addition to the salary deferral feature, a 401(k) plan can contain a traditional profit-sharing feature, an employer matching contribution feature, or both. The plan may even allow for employee after-tax contributions. This means the plan can be as simple as a stand-alone plan (salary deferrals only) or as complex as a plan that allows both pretax and after-tax employee contributions, employer matching contributions, and employer profit-sharing contributions. In today's market, many employers, even those that already have defined-benefit or money-purchase pension plans, opt to sponsor 401(k) plans.

6-12. One trap awaiting clients covered by nonqualified plans is that these plans have somewhat inflexible withdrawal provisions. For instance, distributions cannot be rolled over to an IRA. In addition, the client generally is not given a choice of distribution options at retirement. The options generally are quite limited, and the option desired typically must be selected (to avoid tax problems) at the time participation begins.

A second trap awaiting clients covered by nonqualified plans is that promised benefits are typically subject to loss for a variety of reasons. For example, a nonqualified plan may contain a forfeiture provision stipulating that benefits will be forfeited if certain conditions are not met. In many circumstances, the client may be either unwilling or unable to meet his or her part of the commitment. A second way nonqualified benefits can be lost is if the employer sponsoring the plan goes bankrupt. Nonqualified plan funds are typically held as corporate assets that are subject to the claims of corporate creditors in bankruptcy.

A final insecurity associated with nonqualified plans is the threat of immediate taxation to the employee that would result in a lower overall retirement accumulation. For example, despite employer contentions to the contrary, some plans are construed by the IRS as providing an immediate economic benefit to the employee, or the employee may be deemed to be in constructive receipt of the income. In either case, the prefunded benefit will be taxable while the client is still employed and the advantages of tax deferral will be lost.

6-13. a. There are limitations on contributions to a traditional IRA. Any person under age 70 1/2 who receives $5,000 in compensation in 2008 (either salary or self-employment earned income) may make a $5,000 contribution to a traditional IRA. In addition, if a person is married, even if he or she does not work, that person can contribute $5,000 as long as the spouse's salary is at least $10,000 (then each spouse can make a $5,000 contribution).

b. The contribution to a traditional IRA is only deductible if certain eligibility requirements are satisfied. The contribution will be deductible if neither the taxpayer nor the taxpayer's spouse is an active participant in any employer-maintained retirement plan. If the taxpayer is an active participant, then the contribution is deductible only if his or her modified adjusted gross income falls below prescribed limits (designed to approximate a middle-class income). If an individual is not an active participant, but his or her spouse is, then the contribution is deductible for the spouse who is not an active participant if the couple's income is less than a different higher income threshold.

6-14. a. Contributions to a Roth IRA are not deductible.

b. Distributions from a Roth IRA are tax free as long as two requirements are satisfied. First, the distribution must be made more than 5 years after the Roth IRA was established. Second, the distribution must be made after one of the four following events has occurred:

- The owner has attained age 59 1/2.
- The distribution is paid to a beneficiary because of the owner's death.
- The owner has become disabled.
- The withdrawal is made to pay for up to $10,000 of qualified first-time homebuyer expenses for the owner, his or her spouse, or any child, grandchild, or ancestor of the owner or spouse.

6-15. Strategies that can be used to maximize a client's retirement income include the following:

a. trading down to a less expensive home. If a client can be persuaded to sell his or her home and relocate to a smaller, less expensive residence, the money made available from the transaction can be a valuable source of retirement income. This is very desirable from a financial perspective, because it enables retirees to capitalize on what for many of them is their single most important financial asset—their home. In addition, the Internal Revenue Code allows taxpayers to exclude up to $250,000 of gain ($500,000 on a joint return in most situations) from the sale or exchange of their homes if certain conditions are met.

b. obtaining a reverse mortgage. If a client would like to take some equity out of his or her home, but is reluctant to move to a less expensive one, an alternative that is available is a reverse mortgage. A reverse mortgage is a loan against an individual's home that requires no repayment as long as the individual continues to live in the home. In other words, a reverse mortgage is a strategy that allows a client to live in his or her home while withdrawing substantial amounts of money from its built-up equity. This money can be used for current needs, and there is no need to repay it. A reverse mortgage is typically available only when all of the owners are aged 62 or older and when the home is the principal residence. Also, the home must either have no debt or only a small debt that can be paid off with part of the reverse mortgage loan.
c. postretirement employment. A part-time job during retirement can be used to provide a client with extra cash. Many clients find that working on a scaled-back basis not only meets their financial needs but also helps them adapt psychologically to the changes that retirement brings. This is especially true for clients whose self-esteem and sense of self-worth were tied to their careers.

Answers to Self-Test Questions

6-1. A
6-2. B
6-3. D
6-4. C
6-5. A
6-6. D
6-7. A
6-8. B
6-9. D
6-10. C

Chapter 7

Answers to Review Questions

7-1. An accurate asset inventory will indicate the composition and magnitude of the client's assets available for distribution. This data will help the client and advisor determine whether the assets are in the appropriate form for distribution and whether their total value is adequate to provide the desired distributions to the client's beneficiaries. Planning to convert the assets into the appropriate form and/or to accumulate additional wealth could follow.

7-2. An interview by a financial advisor gathering information for a client's estate plan may be an uncomfortable event for the client because he or she may feel uneasy talking about issues associated with death and personal family matters.

7-3. a. A life estate provides the life tenant with the right to possess and enjoy the property for a time period measured by the life of an individual (typically the life tenant). The life estate gives the life tenant the absolute right to possess, enjoy, and receive current income from the property until the life estate terminates.

b. A term interest provides the current tenant with the right to possess, enjoy, and receive income from the property during a specified term. The interest of the current tenant terminates at the end of the specified term.

c. A future interest in property is the current right to future enjoyment of the property. A future interest in property could either be vested or contingent on the occurrence of some future event. The future interest holder has no immediate right to use and enjoy the property. Two common types of future interest are a remainder interest and a reversionary interest. A remainder interest is an interest that takes effect immediately on the expiration of another interest in the same property, while a reversionary interest occurs when the current property owner transfers current possessory rights to another but retains the right to the return of the property at the end of the possessory term of the transferee.

7-4. a. A tenancy in common occurs when two or more individuals hold current possessory rights to property without survivorship rights. Such individuals, known as tenants in common, each hold an undivided interest in the property and may transfer their interests during their lifetimes or at their deaths. Both related and unrelated individuals may hold property by tenancy in common.

b. A joint tenancy with right of survivorship occurs when two or more individuals hold property jointly with their survivors ultimately receiving the entire interest in the property. Both related and unrelated individuals may hold property jointly with rights of survivorship.

Because this property interest transfers automatically at the death of a joint tenant to his or her surviving tenants, the property is not subject to disposition by a joint tenant at his or her death. Usually, a joint tenant may transfer his or her interest during life without the consent of the other joint tenants. Such a transfer will generally sever the joint tenancy and destroy the survivorship rights of the joint tenants.

c. A tenancy by the entirety is a property interest restricted solely to spouses. It is joint ownership of the property by the spouses with rights of survivorship. A tenancy by the entirety creates a unique situation with respect to disposition of the property. Property is transferred automatically to the surviving spouse at the death of his or her spouse. Thus, the property is not subject to disposition by will of the deceased spouse. In addition, the property cannot be transferred during the lifetime of the spouses unless both tenants consent. Tenancy by the entirety is severed automatically upon divorce.

7-5. A general power of appointment gives the holder of the power broad authority to transfer the property subject to the power to virtually any recipient. On the other hand, a special power of appointment typically limits who the holder of the power can transfer the property to.

7-6. a. With some minor exceptions for rare circumstances, the requirements for a valid will are as follows:
- The will must be in writing.
- The testator, or creator of the will, must sign the will at the end of the document, usually in the presence of witnesses.

- A number of witnesses (generally two or three) must sign the will after the testator's signature. The witnesses are attesting that the signature of the testator is in fact his or her signature.

b. A properly drafted will can accomplish the following objectives:
- Direct the disposition of the client's probate assets.
- Nominate the personal representative of the testator, known as the executor, who will handle the administration of the client's estate.
- Nominate the guardians of any minor children of the testator.
- Create testamentary trusts that will take effect at the testator's death to hold the property of the testator for the benefit of named beneficiaries.
- Name the trustee of any trust created under the will.
- Provide directions to the executor and/or trustees named in the will indicating how these fiduciaries will manage assets contained in the estate or testamentary trust. (The directions could be quite specific or provide broad powers to the fiduciaries.)
- Provide directions for payment of the estate's taxes and expenses. (Care should be taken in naming the components of the estate that will be responsible for taxes and expenses. Incorrect designation of the component obligated to pay such expenses could result in increased death taxes or inappropriately diminished shares of specific beneficiaries.)
- Establish the compensation of executors and/or trustees named in the will.

7-7. A conventional power of attorney authorizes the agent (otherwise known as an attorney-in-fact) to act on behalf of the principal with respect to the powers specifically enumerated in the document. The powers given the agent can be quite limited or very broad. However, no matter how limited or broad the powers, a conventional power becomes inoperative if the principal is incapacitated. A durable power of attorney is similar to a conventional power except that it does not become inoperative if the principal is incapacitated. Instead, it continues to operate during the incapacity of the principal when it is needed most.

7-8. The probate estate includes all assets passing by will or intestacy. Probate property is owned outright by the deceased and is not transferred by operation of law or contract. Probate technically means the process of proving the validity of the will. It begins when the original will is deposited in the court with jurisdiction over the deceased's estate. The probate court oversees the settlement of the estate, the distribution of probate property, appointment and supervision of fiduciaries, and settlement of disputes concerning the deceased's will. The probate court will ensure that probate property is distributed according to the terms of a valid will after all estate settlement costs are paid.

7-9. If an individual dies without a valid will, all probate property passes under the laws of intestate succession of the jurisdiction state. The intestate laws are deemed to replace the intent of the deceased individual in the distribution of his or her probate property. Distribution under these laws depends on which relatives survive the deceased. The deceased individual's spouse receives primary consideration and will receive the entire probate estate, if the deceased is not also survived by children or parents. If the deceased is survived by both a spouse and children, the surviving spouse and children will generally each receive 50 percent of the estate. The parents of a deceased individual will generally get a share only if the deceased individual is not also survived by children. If the deceased individual is not survived by a spouse, children, or parents, the next closest surviving relatives will inherit.

7-10. Certain transfers are exempt from the gift tax base by statute. First, a transfer of property pursuant to a divorce or property settlement agreement is deemed to be for full and adequate consideration under some circumstances. Second, transfers directly to the provider of education or medical services on behalf of an individual are not taxable gifts to the recipient of the services. Finally, gifts that are disclaimed by the donee in a qualified disclaimer are not treated as taxable gifts.

7-11. The types of property includible in a deceased's gross estate are as follows:
- property individually owned by the deceased at the time of death
- (some portion of) property held jointly by the deceased at the time of death
- the proceeds of any insurance on the deceased's life if either (1) incidents of ownership are held by the deceased within 3 years of death or (2) the proceeds are deemed payable to the estate
- pension or IRA payments left to survivors
- property subject to general powers of appointment held by the deceased at the time of death
- property transferred by the deceased during his or her lifetime if he or she retained (1) a life interest in the property, (2) a reversionary interest valued greater than 5 percent of the property at the time of death, or (3) rights to revoke the transfer at the time of death

7-12. a. The GSTT was created to prevent the federal government from losing transfer tax revenue when individuals transfer property to a generation that is more than one generation below their own generation (for example, when grandparents make gifts of property to their grandchildren). In other words, the GSTT is designed to prevent people from finding a transfer tax loophole in the federal gift tax or estate tax.

b. The GSTT applies to the following three types of transfers:
- It applies to a direct skip, which is an outright transfer during life or at death to a skip person. A skip person is an individual who is two generations or more younger than the transferor.
- It applies to a taxable termination, which occurs when an interest in property held in trust for a skip person is terminated by an individual's death, lapse of time, release of a power, or otherwise and the trust property is either held for or distributed to the skip person.
- It applies to a taxable distribution, which is any distribution from a trust to a skip person that is not a taxable termination or a direct skip.

7-13. A state inheritance tax is a tax imposed on a beneficiary's right to inherit property from a deceased person's estate, while a state estate tax is imposed on a deceased person's right to transfer or pass property to beneficiaries.

7-14. a. The nontax advantages from making lifetime gifts are as follows:
- The donor can provide for the support, education, and welfare of the donee beneficiary.
- The donor gets the pleasure of seeing the donee beneficiary enjoy the gift.

- The donor avoids the publicity and administrative costs associated with a probate transfer at death.
- The donated property is protected from the claims of the donor's creditors.

b. The tax advantages from making lifetime gifts are as follows:
- The gift tax annual exclusion for gifts of $12,000 (as indexed for 2008) or less provides a complete loophole from federal transfer taxes. Each year any number of $12,000 gifts can be made by donors ($24,000 if their spouses join with them) to reduce their transfer tax bases.
- The gift tax is imposed on the value of the gift at the time a completed transfer is made. Thus, any posttransfer appreciation in the property avoids all transfer tax.
- The gift tax payable on gifts made more than 3 years prior to the donor's death is excluded from his or her estate tax base.
- The income produced by gifted property is shifted from the donor to the donee beneficiary for income tax purposes. In other words, lifetime gifting may be used to move taxable income from a high-bracket donor to a lower-bracket donee beneficiary. (This advantage is somewhat limited by special tax rules related to unearned income of children under age 19 or 24 for full-time students.)
- Unlimited qualifying transfers can be made between spouses without incurring gift taxes. Spouses can advantageously shift assets between themselves to meet the needs of the estate and financial plan of each spouse.

7-15. a. The UGMA and UTMA statutes are model laws that have been adopted in various forms in individual states. They permit the transfer of funds to a custodial account for the benefit of a minor. The custodian of an UGMA or an UGMA account manages the property under the rules provided by state law. There are restrictions on the type of property permissible as an investment for these purposes. The original UGMA model law has been expanded in many states to increase the types of permissible investments. In a majority of states, the newer UTMA model law has been adopted, and relatively few restrictions exist in these states on the permissible investments. An UGMA or an UGMA transfer is particularly favorable for smaller gifts because it provides for the protection of the assets without the expense of administering a trust. The provisions for distribution from an UGMA or UTMA are provided under the various state laws. Generally speaking, UGMA or UTMA funds can be accumulated during the minority of the donee beneficiary, but the custodial assets must be distributed to the beneficiary when he or she reaches the age specified in the relevant statute—generally 18 or 21.

b. A donor often wishes to make gifts to a minor in trust for the purpose of accumulation. If the trust provides for accumulation and does not currently benefit the minor beneficiary, the gift tax annual exclusion would normally be forfeited. Provisions of the law, however, permit the annual exclusion if current beneficial rights are given to the beneficiary. These rights, known as Crummey powers, provide the beneficiary with temporary withdrawal rights to the funds contributed to the trust. Under these rules, a gift to a trust will qualify for the annual exclusion if the beneficiary has the noncumulative, temporary (for example, 30 days) right to demand up to the annual exclusion amount from his or her share of the amount contributed to the trust by the donor.

7-16. a. A transfer to a surviving spouse through an estate trust qualifies for the marital deduction. Under this arrangement, a deceased spouse leaves a life estate in trust to the surviving spouse. The surviving spouse's estate is the remainderperson of the trust. Income from the estate trust can either accumulate or be paid to the surviving spouse at the discretion of the trustee. Because the remainder interest is transferred to the surviving spouse's estate, the property will be included in the surviving spouse's gross estate, and a second-death estate tax may be payable at that time.

b. Another common marital-deduction trust is the power-of-appointment trust. This trust is designed to distribute income to the surviving spouse during his or her life and to provide the surviving spouse with a general power of appointment over the trust property. The general power of appointment may be exercisable by the surviving spouse in all events, or it may be exercisable only at the death of the surviving spouse. Because the surviving spouse has a general power of appointment over the trust property, it is included in his or her gross estate for federal tax purposes.

c. A special provision of the tax law provides for a marital deduction if qualifying terminable interest property (QTIP) is left to a surviving spouse. Under these rules, a terminable property interest can be transferred to a surviving spouse with the interest qualifying for the marital deduction. The QTIP deduction is available if the executor of the deceased spouse elects QTIP treatment on the estate tax return. The QTIP trust can be funded by probate assets or other types of testamentary dispositions. The surviving spouse must have the right to all income annually from the QTIP trust for life. At the death of the surviving spouse, the QTIP election provides that the trust property will be included in the surviving spouse's gross estate.

7-17. The typical dispositive scheme for most married couples makes maximum use of the marital deduction. This occurs when all property is left to the surviving spouse either outright or in another manner that qualifies for the marital deduction. Because no estate tax is payable under these circumstances, the applicable credit amount that is available at the first spouse's death is wasted.

However, the typical dispositive scheme can be altered to make maximum use of each spouse's applicable credit amount while also making optimal use of the marital deduction. This maximum estate tax shelter is accomplished by designing each spouse's estate and financial plan to transfer property to two separate trusts, an A or marital trust and a B or family trust. This two trust arrangement is commonly referred to as an AB trust arrangement. The AB trust arrangement is designed to operate as follows:

- The A or marital trust is some form of marital-deduction trust. This trust receives assets in a manner that qualifies them for the federal estate tax marital deduction and provides for maximum use of these assets by the surviving spouse. The remainder of the assets transferred by the deceased are placed into the B or family trust.
- The B or family trust is designed not to qualify for the marital deduction. Instead, the B trust may be funded with transfers valued at approximately the applicable exclusion amount of $2 million in 2008 (increasing to $3.5 million in 2009) and will be part of the individual's taxable estate since the transfers are not deductible under the marital deduction. However, the $2 million transferred in 2008 (or $3.5

million in 2009) to the B or family trust can be sheltered from estate taxes by the applicable exclusion amount.

The AB trust arrangement makes maximum use of each spouse's applicable credit, and since the A or marital trust qualifies for the marital deduction and B or family trust is sheltered entirely by the applicable credit, no estate tax will be paid at the first spouse's death. Thus, the AB trust arrangement does not change the usual first-death tax results. However, the second-death taxes are reduced since the applicable credit amount is used at the time of the first death. Thus, the surviving spouse's estate is reduced in size by the amount of property transferred to the B or family trust at the first death of the two spouses.

7-18. A charitable remainder trust can be employed to retain the current enjoyment of the property for the life of the donor client (or lives of the donor's family members) while providing income, gift, and estate tax advantages. The charitable remainder trust can be established during the donor client's lifetime or at his or her death. The charitable remainder trust permits the donor client to retain the current income for his or her use or the use of his or her family. The income from the trust's assets will be retained for a time period (usually measured by the life of the donor client or lives of selected family members) with the charitable institution holding the remainder interest. The current charitable deduction is measured by the present value of the remainder interest held by the charity. Thus, the donor client (or possibly members of the client's family) receives not only the current enjoyment of the trust property but also a current tax deduction, while the charity receives outright ownership of the property sometime in the future when the remainder interest is distributed by the trust.

7-19. Life insurance is generally used for estate enhancement by (1) younger clients, (2) clients with dependent family members, and (3) clients with small to moderate-sized estates. Clients in these categories generally cite protection as their primary need for life insurance. They want to protect their families from the loss of future earnings needed for support. These clients are either in or are headed toward their peak earning years, and their families are relying on these future earnings to maintain their standard of living, educate the children, and accumulate retirement assets.

The death taxes facing younger clients with small to moderate-sized estates are relatively minor. The applicable credit amount and marital deduction will generally remove the danger of federal estate taxes for these individuals. Thus, estate liquidity is not their primary concern. Nonetheless, it is highly improbable that these clients can accumulate enough wealth to replace their future incomes. This is where life insurance plays a role. It is the perfect estate enhancement tool for replacing some or all of the lost earnings resulting from a client's premature death.

7-20. A revocable life insurance trust serves no estate tax planning purposes. Because the trust is revocable, the grantor insured is treated as the owner of the policy and the death proceeds will be included in his or her gross estate. The revocable life insurance trust is ordinarily used when a specific, perhaps temporary, protection need exists.

Answers to Self-Test Questions

7-1. A
7-2. C

7-3. B
7-4. D
7-5. B
7-6. A
7-7. C
7-8. D
7-9. A
7-10. C

Chapter 8

Answers to Review Questions

8-1. The Social Security program and Part A of Medicare are financed through a system of payroll and self-employment taxes paid by all persons covered under the programs. In addition, employers of covered persons are also taxed. (These taxes are often referred to as FICA taxes because they are imposed under the Federal Insurance Contributions Act.)

In 2008, an employee and his or her employer pay a tax of 6.2 percent each on the first $102,000 of the employee's wages for Social Security. The employee and employer also pay the Medicare tax rate of 1.45 percent on employee wages. The tax rates are currently scheduled to remain the same after 2008, but the wage base is adjusted annually for changes in the national level of wages.

Part B of Medicare if financed by a combination of monthly premiums paid by persons eligible for benefits and contributions from the federal government.

8-2. a. Evelyn does not meet the first test, as she has not earned credit for 40 quarters. However, she does qualify as fully insured under the second test. Evelyn is 38 in 2008, so she was born in 1970. She was age 21 in 1991, so would require 15 quarters from 1992 to 2007 to be fully insured, and she has 28 quarters.
b. Because Evelyn is fully insured, she is also currently insured.
c. Although Evelyn is fully insured, she is not disability insured because she does not have the minimum number of quarters within a recent time period.

8-3. A worker who is fully insured under Social Security is eligible to receive monthly retirement benefits as early as age 62. However, the election to receive benefits prior to the full retirement age results in a permanently reduced benefit. Starting with workers born in 1937, the age at which full benefits are payable will increase in gradual steps from age 65 to age 67. Workers born in 1960 or later will wait until age 67 for their full retirement benefits.

8-4. If the deceased worker was either fully or currently insured at the time of death, the following categories of persons are eligible for survivor benefits:
- dependent, unmarried children under age 18. This child's benefit will continue until age 19 as long as a child is a full-time student in elementary or secondary school. In addition, disabled children of any age are eligible for benefits as long as they were disabled before reaching age 22.

- a spouse (including a divorced spouse) of any age if the spouse is caring for at least one child of the deceased worker who is (1) under age 16 or (2) disabled and entitled to a child's benefit.

If the deceased worker was fully insured at the time of death, the following categories of persons are also eligible for survivor benefits:

- a widow or widower aged 60 or older. However, benefits are reduced if taken prior to full retirement age. This benefit is also payable to a divorced spouse if the marriage lasted at least 10 years. The widow's or widower's benefit is payable to a disabled spouse at age 50 as long as the disability commenced no more than 7 years after the (1) worker's death or (2) end of the year in which entitlement to a mother's or father's benefit ceased.
- a parent aged 62 or over who was a dependent of the deceased worker at the time of death

8-5. The definition of disability requires a mental or physical impairment that prevents the worker from engaging in any substantial gainful employment. The disability must also have lasted (or be expected to last) at least 12 months or be expected to result in death. A more liberal definition of disability applies to blind workers who are aged 55 or older. They are considered disabled if they are unable to perform work that requires skills or abilities comparable to those required by the work they regularly performed before reaching age 55 or becoming blind, if later.

8-6. a. The primary insurance amount (PIA) is the amount a worker receives if he or she retires at full retirement age or becomes disabled, and it is the amount on which benefits for family members are based. If a worker is retired or disabled, benefits are paid to family members as follows:

- The spouse at full retirement age, or a spouse at any age caring for a disabled child or a child under 16 receives 50 percent of the worker's PIA.
- Each child under 18 or disabled receives 50 percent of the worker's PIA.

If a worker dies, benefits are paid to family members as follows:

- The spouse at full retirement age receives 100 percent of the worker's PIA.
- A spouse at any age caring for a disabled child or a child under 16 receives 75 percent of the worker's PIA.
- Each child under 18 or disabled receives 75 percent of the worker's PIA.
- A sole dependent parent receives 82.5 percent, while two dependent parents receive 75 percent each.

However, the full benefits described above may not be payable because of a limitation imposed on the total benefits that may be paid to a family.

b. If the total amount of benefits payable to family members exceeds the family maximum, the worker's benefit (in the case of retirement and disability) is not affected, but the benefits of other family members are reduced proportionately.

8-7. If a worker elects to receive retirement benefits prior to full retirement age, benefits are permanently reduced by 5/9 of one percent each of the first 36 months that the early retirement precedes full retirement age and 5/12 of one percent for each month in excess of 36. Workers who delay applying for benefits until after full retirement age are eligible for an increased benefit for each month of late retirement until age 70.

8-8. Beneficiaries under full retirement age are allowed earnings of up to $13,560 in 2008, and this figure is subject to annual indexing for later years. If a beneficiary earns more than this amount, then his or her Social Security benefit is reduced by $1 for each $2 of excess earnings. There is one exception to the test: The reduction is $1 for every $3 of earnings in excess of $36,120 (in 2008) in the calendar year a worker attains the full retirement age, for earnings in months prior to such age attainment.

8-9. Social Security benefits are increased automatically each January if there was an increase in the CPI for the one-year period ending in the third quarter of the prior year. The increase is the same as the increase in the CPI since the last cost-of-living adjustment, rounded to the nearest 0.1 percent.

8-10. a. Hospital Benefits. Part A pays for inpatient hospital services for up to 90 days in each benefit period (also referred to as a spell of illness). A benefit period begins the first time a Medicare recipient is hospitalized and ends only after the recipient has been out of a hospital or skilled-nursing facility for 60 consecutive days. A subsequent hospitalization then begins a new benefit period.

Skilled-Nursing Facility Benefits. In many cases, a patient may no longer require continuous hospital care but may not be well enough to go home. Consequently, Part A provides benefits for care in a skilled-nursing facility if a physician certifies that skilled-nursing care or rehabilitative services are needed for a condition that was treated in a hospital within the last 30 days. In addition, the prior hospitalization must have lasted at least 3 days. Benefits are paid in full for 20 days in each benefit period and for an additional 80 days with a daily copayment charge.

Home Health Care Benefits. If a patient can be treated at home for a medical condition, Medicare will pay the full cost for an unlimited number of home visits by a home health agency. To receive these benefits, a person must be confined at home and be treated under a home health plan set up by a physician.

Hospice Benefits. Hospice benefits are available under Part A of Medicare for beneficiaries who are certified as being terminally ill with a life expectancy of 6 months or less.

b. Hospital Benefits. In each benefit period, covered hospital expenses are paid in full for 60 days, subject to an initial deductible ($1,024 in 2008). This deductible is adjusted annually to reflect increasing hospital costs. Benefits for an additional 30 days of hospitalization are also provided in each benefit period, but the patient must pay a daily copayment ($256 in 2008) equal to 25 percent of the initial deductible amount. Each recipient also has a lifetime reserve of 60 additional days that may be used if the regular 90 days of benefits have been exhausted. However, once a reserve day is used, it cannot be restored for use in future benefit periods. When using reserve days, patients must pay a daily copayment ($512 in 2008) equal to 50 percent of the initial deductible amount.

Skilled-Nursing Facility Benefits. Benefits are paid in full for 20 days in each benefit period and for an additional 80 days with a daily copayment ($128 in 2008) that is equal to 12.5 percent of the initial hospital deductible.

Home Health Care Benefits. There is no charge for these benefits other than a required 20 percent copayment for the cost of such durable medical equipment as oxygen tanks and hospital beds.

Hospice Benefits. There are modest copayments for some services.

   c. Exclusions under Part A of Medicare include the following:
- services outside the United States and its territories or possessions. However, there are a few exceptions to this rule for qualified Mexican and Canadian hospitals.
- elective luxury services, such as private rooms or televisions
- hospitalization for services not necessary for the treatment of an illness or injury, such as custodial care or elective cosmetic surgery

In addition to the exclusions, there are times when Medicare will act as the secondary payer of benefits.

8-11. a. Part B of Medicare provides benefits for most medical expenses not covered under Part A. These can include physicians' and surgeons' fees, diagnostic tests, x rays, physical therapy, blood transfusions, drugs and biologicals that cannot be self-administered, radiation therapy, medical supplies, rental of medical equipment, prosthetic devices, ambulance service, mammograms and Pap smears, diabetes glucose monitoring and education, diabetic screening for persons at risk of diabetes, screening blood tests for early detection of heart disease, colorectal cancer screening, bone mass measurement, prostate cancer screening, pneumococcal vaccination and flu shots, dilated eye examinations when at risk for glaucoma, and home health care services as described for Part A when a person does not have Part A coverage or when Part A benefits are not applicable.

   b. A few charges are paid in full without any cost sharing. These include (1) home health services, (2) pneumococcal vaccination and flu shots, (3) certain outpatient surgical procedures that are performed in lieu of hospitalization, (4) outpatient diagnostic preadmission tests performed within 7 days prior to hospitalization, (5) mammograms, and (6) Pap smears.

For other charges, there is a calendar-year deductible ($135 in 2008). When it is satisfied, Part B pays 80 percent of approved charges for most covered medical expenses other than charges for mental health care. Medicare pays only 50 percent of approved charges for mental health care.

   c. A list of exclusions includes most drugs and biologicals that can be self-administered, most routine examinations, routine foot care, most immunizations, most cosmetic surgery, most dental care, custodial care, eyeglasses, hearing aids, and orthopedic shoes.

8-12. The five types of Medicare Advantage plans available under Part C of Medicare are HMOs, PPOs, PFFS plans, MMSA plans, and SNPs.

8-13. Part D is a voluntary prescription drug benefit available to all Medicare beneficiaries enrolled in either Part A and/or Part B (original Medicare) or in any of the various Medicare Advantage plans. Each enrollee must pay a monthly premium. In addition, no one can be denied coverage because of income level or for health reasons.

8-14. Besides basic benefits, Congress mandated several other features for medigap (Medicare supplement) insurance including a 6-month open enrollment period, limited preexisting-conditions exclusions, prohibition of the sale of duplicate coverage, and increased loss ratios.

8-15. Persons aged 65 or older and anyone else eligible for Medicare may buy any available medigap (Medicare supplement) policy, regardless of health status, at any time during the 6-month period after initial enrollment for Medicare Part B benefits. If a person initially elects a Medicare Advantage plan in lieu of original Medicare benefits, he or she will be eligible to purchase a medigap policy, without evidence of insurability, if he or she leaves the Medicare Advantage plan during the first 12 months of coverage and returns to original Medicare benefits. Similarly, a person who drops a medigap policy and elects a Medicare Advantage plan can regain the medigap coverage if he or she decides to drop the Medicare Advantage plan during the first 12 months of coverage. Also, a person can obtain a medigap policy because of the termination of an employer-provided plan that supplements Medicare, or because a Medicare Advantage plan no longer provides coverage, or because the person loses eligibility by moving out of the plan's service area.

Answers to Self-Test Questions

8-1. A
8-2. D
8-3. A
8-4. B
8-5. D
8-6. C
8-7. B
8-8. C
8-9. D
8-10. B

Index

A

AB trust arrangement, 7.39, 7.40
Above-the-line deductions, 5.6
Accidental death and dismemberment (AD&D) insurance, 3.29
Accrual method, 5.16
Actual cash value, 2.12
Added coverages under group term, 3.28
    accidental death and dismemberment (AD&D) insurance, 3.29
    dependent life insurance, 3.30
    supplemental life insurance, 3.28
Adjusted gross income (AGI), 5.5
Advance medical directives, 7.15
    durable power of attorney for health care, 7.15
    living will, 7.15
Advantages of gifts to charity, 7.41
Advantages of lifetime gifts, 7.31
    gifts to minors, 7.33
    nontax advantages of lifetime gifts, 7.31
    opportunities created by the annual exclusion, 7.32
    tax advantages of lifetime gifts, 7.31
Adverse selection, 2.35
Advisor awareness of employee benefits, 3.8
    basis of a financial plan, 3.8
    buy-up plan, 3.8
    purchase of additional benefits, 3.8
    source for negotiating a compensation package, 3.9
    voluntary benefit plans, 3.8
Agency bonds, 4.14
Alternative minimum tax (AMT), 5.14
Alternatives to Medicare Advantage plans, 8.25
    Medicare cost plans, 8.25
    Medicare pilot programs, 8.25
    PACE, 8.25
American Association of Retired Persons (AARP) report, 1.33
Analyze and evaluate the data (step 3), 1.12, 2.11, 6.10
Annuities, 2.35
    deferred annuities, 2.36
    immediate annuity, 2.36
    life annuities, 2.35
Applicable credit amount, 7.24, 7.38
Applicable exclusion amount, 7.26
Applying control through the financial planning process, 4.40
Approaches to financial planning, 1.4, 1.17
    comprehensive approach, 1.18
    multiple-purpose approach, 1.18
    single-purpose approach, 1.17
Approximate yield, 4.34
Areas of specialization in financial planning, 1.19
Art of financial planning for retirement, 6.11
    older people need to plan for retirement, 6.12
    overcoming roadblocks to retirement saving, 6.13
Asset allocation models, 4.10
Asset selection, 4.10
Assignment of income doctrine, 5.18
Attorney-in-fact, 7.9, 7.13
Avoiding discretionary power, 4.40
Avoiding limitations on deductions, 5.20
    deduction floor, 5.20
    miscellaneous itemized deductions, 5.20

B

Baby boom generation, 1.27, 1.33

Bank deposits, 4.12
Basic benefits, 8.32
Basic investment theorems, 4.7
Basis for income tax purposes, 5.10, 5.25, 5.26
Below-the-line deductions, 5.6
Beneficial interests, 7.8
Benefit-planning for the employer, 3.6
Benefits under Medicare, 8.16, 8.20, 8.22, 8.25
    Part A, 8.16
    Part B, 8.20
    Part C, 8.22
    Part D, 8.25
Benefits under Social Security, 8.6
Blackout period, 8.8
Business (default) risk, 4.25
Business expense, 5.8
Buy-up plan, 3.8

C

C corporations, 5.30
Cafeteria plans, 3.52
Calculating Social Security benefits, 8.9
Capital gain, 5.27, 5.28, 5.29
Cash-balance pension plan, 6.33
Cash-basis method, 5.16
Cash equivalents, 4.11
    Bank deposits, 4.12
    Money market instruments, 4.12
    Treasury bills, 4.13
Categories of deductions, 5.7
    Business expense, 5.8
    Expense for the production of income, 5.8
    Personal expense, 5.8
Categories of investment assets, 4.11
    Cash equivalents, 4.11
    Equity securities, 4.15
    Long-term debt instruments, 4.13
    Real estate and other investments, 4.20

Centers for Medicare & Medicaid, 8.22, 8.23, 8.36
CFP certification examinations topic list, A.1
Charitable contributions, 7.41
Charitable deduction, 7.24, 7.26, 7.42
Charitable lead trust, 7.42
Charitable remainder trust, 7.41
Closed-end investment company, 4.17
COBRA, 3.23, 3.24
Collision, 2.57
Common stock, 4.16
Community property, 7.7
Compensation limit, 6.31, 6.32, 6.33, 6.34
Compounding power, 4.39
Comprehensive approach to financial planning, 1.18, 4.9
Comprehensive financial plan, 1.18, 1.20, 1.24
    approach, 1.18
    content, 1.20
    format, 1.24
Constructive receipt doctrine, 5.18
Consumer needs for financial planning, 1.30
Consumer Price Index (CPI), 1.22, 8.14
Content of a comprehensive financial plan, 1.20
Conventional power of attorney, 7.13
Conversion provision, 2.31
Coordination-of-benefits (COB) provision, 3.20
Coordination of the marital deduction and the applicable credit amount, 7.38
Corporate debt securities, 4.14
Cost-of-living adjustments under Social Security, 8.13
Coverage gap (doughnut hole), 8.27
Coverage to supplement Medicare, 8.31
Creditable prescription drug coverage, 8.30
Credit estate tax, 7.30
Critical illness insurance, 3.45
Crummey powers, 7.34
Current assumption whole life, 2.33
Currently insured, 8.5
Current yield, 4.32

D

Dealer markets, 4.42
Deduction, 5.4
Deduction floor, 5.20
Deductions, 5.5
    above-the-line deductions, 5.6
    below-the-line deductions, 5.6
    categories of deductions, 5.7
    depreciation deduction, 5.9
    itemized deductions, 5.6
    paper deductions, 5.9
    standard deduction, 5.6
Defensive stocks, 4.19
Deferral and acceleration techniques, 5.22
Deferred annuities, 2.36
Defined-benefit pension plans, 6.31
Defined-benefit plan, 6.27
Defined-benefit versus defined-contribution plans, 6.27
Defined-contribution medical expense plan, 3.21
Defined-contribution plan, 6.27
Definition of financial planning, 1.3
Delayed retirement under Social Security, 8.12
Dental insurance, 3.38
    benefits, 3.39
    taxation, 3.40
Dental insurance benefits, 3.39
    combination plans, 3.40
    nonscheduled plans, 3.40
    scheduled plans, 3.39
Dependency exemption, 5.11
Dependent care assistance, 3.48
    child-care plans, 3.48
    eldercare benefits, 3.49
    taxation of benefits, 3.49
Dependent life insurance, 3.30
Depreciation, 2.12, 2.13
Depreciation deduction, 5.9
Determine goals and gather data (step 2), 1.7, 2.8, 6.9
Develop and present a plan (step 4), 1.13, 2.18, 6.10

Developing a retirement plan, 6.16
    effects of inflation, 6.19
    expense method, 6.19
    replacement ratio method, 6.17
Direct skip, 7.27
Disability benefits under Social Security, 8.8
Disability income insurance (group plans), 3.34
    long-term plans, 3.35
    short-term plans, 3.35
    taxation, 3.38
Disability income insurance (individual policy), 2.37, 2.38
    benefit amount, 2.41
    benefit period, 2.40
    elimination (waiting) period, 2.39, 2.40
    partial disability, 2.39, 2.42
    residual disability, 2.39, 2.42
    Social Security supplement, 2.42
    terms of renewability, 2.41
    total disability definition, 2.39
Disability insured, 8.5
Diversification, 4.30
Dividends taxed as capital gains, 5.28
Dollar cost averaging, 4.38
Dual benefits under Social Security, 8.8
Durable power of attorney, 7.13, 7.14
Durable power of attorney for health care, 7.15

E

Early retirement under Social Security, 8.1
Earnings test, 6.50, 8.13
Economic benefit doctrine, 5.17
Educational funding, 1.22
Effective marginal tax rate, 5.14
Effective tax rate, 5.13
Effects of inflation on retirement savings, 6.19
Eligibility for a medigap policy, 8.36
Eligibility for employee benefits, 3.9
    covered classifications, 3.10
    full-time employment, 3.10

insurability, 3.10
premium contributions, 3.11
probationary periods, 3.10
termination of coverage, 3.11
Eligibility for Medicare, 8.15
Eligibility for Social Security, 8.4
currently insured, 8.5
disability insured, 8.5
fully insured, 8.5
Elimination (waiting) period, 2.39, 2.40, 2.45
Employee benefits, 3.2
growth of employee benefits, 3.4
meaning of employee benefits, 3.2
significance of employee benefits, 3.3
Employee stock ownership plan (ESPOP), 6.38
Employer plans to supplement Medicare, 8.31
Equity securities, 4.15
American Depositary Receipts (ADRs), 4.17
common stock, 4.16
investment companies, 4.17
preferred stock, 4.16
Establish and define the advisor-client relationship (step 1), 1.6, 2.6, 6.9
Estate planning documents, 7.9
advance medical directives, 7.15
durable powers of attorney, 7.13
trusts, 7.11
wills, 7.10
Estate planning process, 7.3
Estate trust, 7.37
Exclusion, 5.4
Exclusions from gross income, 5.5
Exclusions under Medicare, 8.19, 8.20
Part A, 8.19
Part B, 8.20
Exemptions from income, 5.11
dependency exemption, 5.11
personal exemption, 5.11
Exempt transfers for gift tax purposes, 7.23
Expected return, 4.4, 4.5
Expense for the production of income, 5.8
Expense method, 6.19

Expense method work sheet, 6.24

F

401(k) plan, 6.36
403(b) plan, 6.40
Fact-finder form, 1.11
Family leave, 3.49
federal law, 3.50
state laws, 3.49
Family trust, 7.39, 7.40
Federal estate tax, 7.25
applicable exclusion amount, 7.26
charitable deduction, 7.26
deductible items, 7.25
gross estate, 7.25
marital deduction, 7.26
state death tax credit, 7.26
Federal estate tax planning, 7.35
coordination of the marital deduction and the applicable credit amount, 7.38
planning charitable contributions, 7.41
planning for the gift and estate tax applicable credit amount, 7.38
planning for the marital deduction, 7.35
Federal gift tax, 7.22
annual exclusion, 7.23
applicable credit amount, 7.24
deductions from gift tax base, 7.24
exempt transfers, 7.23
Federal transfer taxes, 7.19
federal estate tax, 7.25
federal gift tax, 7.22
generation-skipping transfer tax (GSTT), 7.27
Fee simple estate, 7.5
Fiduciaries, 7.9
Filing status, 5.12
Financial ability to handle risk, 4.7, 4.9
Financial capacity, 2.23
Financial life cycle, 1.22
Financial plan, 1.13
Financial planning, 1.3

Financial planning areas of specialization, 1.19
Financial planning process, 1.3, 1.16, 2.6, 6.9
    compared to risk management and needs analysis, 2.6, 2.7
    steps in financial planning, 1.3, 6.9
Financial planning profession, 1.2
Financial planning pyramid, 1.8
Financial planning umbrella, 1.35
Financial risk tolerance, 1.11, 4.7, 4.9
Flat-percentage-of-earnings formula, 6.32
Flexible spending account (FSA), 3.54
Focus on ethics, 1.21, 2.10, 3.29, 4.40, 5.6, 6.51, 7.12, 8.14
Format of a comprehensive financial plan, 1.24
Fourth market, 4.42
Frequency of loss, 2.23, 2.24
Fruit and tree doctrine, 5.17
Full retirement age, 8.6
Fully insured, 8.5
Future interest, 7.6

G

General obligations, 4.14
General power of appointment, 7.9
Generation-skipping transfer tax (GSTT), 7.27
    annual exclusion, 7.28
    lifetime exemption, 7.28
    types of transfers, 7.27
Gifts of income interests to charity, 7.42
Gifts of remainder interests to charity, 7.41
Gifts to minors, 7.33
    irrevocable trust with current withdrawal powers, 7.34
    Section 2503(b) trust, 7.34
    Section 2503(c) trust, 7.34
    Uniform Gifts to Minors Act (UGMA), 7.33
    Uniform Transfers to Minors Act (UTMA), 7.33
Gift tax annual exclusion, 7.23, 7.32

Goals of estate planning, 7.2
Governmental debt securities, 4.14
    agency bonds, 4.14
    general obligations, 4.14
    revenue bonds, 4.14
Grantor, 7.11
Gross estate, 7.25
Gross income, 5.3
Group term life benefit schedules, 3.26
    multiple-of-earnings schedules, 3.26
    reduction in benefits, 3.27
    specified-dollar-amount schedules, 3.27
Group term life insurance, 3.26
    added coverages, 3.28
    benefit schedule, 3.26
    taxation, 3.31
    termination of coverage, 3.27
Group universal life insurance, 3.34
    coverage available, 3.34
    options at retirement and termination, 3.34
    taxation, 3.34
Growth of employee benefits, 3.4
    cost advantages, 3.5
    industrialization, 3.4
    inflation, 3.6
    legislation, 3.6
    organized labor, 3.5
    wage controls, 3.5
Growth stocks, 4.19
Guaranteed renewable, 2.41

H

Health insurance, 2.37
    disability income insurance, 2.37, 2.38
    long-term care insurance, 2.37, 2.43
    medical expense insurance, 2.37
Health insurance coverage after termination of employment, 3.23
    COBRA, 3.23, 3.24
    conversion, 3.24
    portability, 3.25
    postretirement coverage, 3.25

Health Insurance Portability and
 Accountability Act (HIPAA), 2.46,
 3.20, 3.25
Health maintenance organizations (HMOs),
 3.14, 3.17, 3.18, 3.21, 3.25
Health savings account (HSA), 2.38, 3.21
High-deductible health plan (HDHP), 2.38,
 3.21
High severity losses, 2.17, 2.18, 2.21, 2.23,
 2.24
Holding-period return, 4.33
Holding periods for equity investments, 4.37
Holistic retirement planning, 6.4
Home health care benefits under Medicare
 Part A, 8.18
Homeowners insurance, 2.49
  Coverage A dwelling, 2.50, 2.51, 2.52
  Coverage B other structures, 2.50, 2.51,
   2.52
  Coverage C personal property, 2.50, 2.51,
   2.52
  Coverage D loss of use, 2.50, 2.51, 2.53
  Coverage E personal liability, 2.51, 2.54
  Coverage F medical payments to others,
   2.51, 2.55
  internal limits, 2.53
  named-perils approach, 2.50
  open-perils approach, 2.50
  replacement-cost requirement, 2.52
Hospice benefits under Medicare Part A, 8.18
Hospital benefits under Medicare Part A, 8.16
Hospital indemnity insurance, 3.45
Human-life-value method, 2.15

I

Immediate annuity, 2.36
Implement the plan (step 5), 1.14, 2.27, 6.10
Importance of protection objectives, 2.2
Income and deduction shifting, 5.19
Income tax basis, 5.10, 5.25, 5.26
Income-tax-planning concepts, 5.19
  avoiding limitations on deductions, 5.20

  deferral and acceleration techniques, 5.22
  income and deduction shifting, 5.19
  nonrecognition transactions, 5.24
  ordinary versus capital gain and loss, 5.27
  passive-loss rules, 5.23
  tax-exempt transactions, 5.24
  transactions that result in a taxable loss,
   5.26
Individual health insurance, 2.37
  disability income insurance, 2.37, 2.38
  long-term care insurance, 2.37, 2.43
  medical expense insurance, 2.37
Individual ownership of property, 7.5
  fee simple estate, 7.5
  future interest, 7.6
  life estate, 7.6
  term interest, 7.6
Insurance, 2.19, 2.21, 2.25
Insured status for Social Security, 8.5
Interest rate risk, 4.23
  price risk, 4.23
  reinvestment rate risk, 4.24
Internal limits, 2.53
Intestacy, 7.10
Intestate laws, 7.17
Intestate succession, 7.17
Investing, 4.4
Investment assets, 4.3
Investment companies, 4.17
  closed-end investment company, 4.17
  open-end investment company, 4.18
Investment markets, 4.41
  dealer markets, 4.42
  negotiated markets, 4.42
  organized securities markets, 4.43
  true-auction markets, 4.41
Investment planning, 4.7
Investment principles, strategies, and
 techniques, 4.35
  applying control through the financial
   planning process, 4.40
  avoiding discretionary power, 4.40
  high-pressure sales tactics, 4.39

holding periods for equity investments, 4.37
matching investment instruments with investment goals, 4.36
meeting emergency and protection needs first, 4.36
power of compounding, 4.39
tax-saving rationale, 4.37
understanding the investment, 4.37
using a consistent pattern of investing, 4.38
Investment returns, 4.31
approximate yield, 4.34
current yield, 4.32
holding-period return, 4.33
Investment risk, 4.6
Investment versus speculation, 4.3
IRAs, 6.43
Roth IRAs, 6.46
traditional IRAs, 6.44
Irrevocable life insurance trusts, 7.34, 7.44
Irrevocable trust, 7.13, 7.34, 7.44
Crummey powers, 7.34
current withdrawal powers, 7.34
Itemized deductions, 5.6

J

Joint concurrent ownership of property, 7.6
community property, 7.7
joint tenancy with right of survivorship, 7.7
tenancy by the entirety, 7.7
tenancy in common, 7.6
Joint tenancy with right of survivorship, 7.7
Junk bonds, 4.15

L

Large cap stocks, 4.19
Law of large numbers, 2.21
Legal expense insurance, 3.42

Liability risks, 2.15, 2.49
Life annuities, 2.35
Life-cycle financial planning, 1.22, 1.24
Life estate, 7.6
Life insurance, 2.29, 3.26, 7.42
term life insurance, 2.29
universal life insurance, 2.34
whole life insurance, 2.31
Life insurance for estate enhancement, 7.43
Life insurance for estate liquidity, 7.43
Life insurance in the estate and/or financial plan, 7.42
life insurance for estate enhancement, 7.43
life insurance for estate liquidity, 7.43
life insurance trusts, 7.44
Life insurance trusts, 7.44
irrevocable life insurance trusts, 7.44
revocable life insurance trusts, 7.44
Liquidity, 4.26
Living trust, 7.12
Living will, 7.15
Load funds, 4.18
Loan provision, 2.32
Long-term care insurance, 2.37, 2.43, 3.44
benefit amounts, 2.44
eligibility for benefits, 2.46
elimination period, 2.45
inflation protection, 2.48
maximum duration of benefits, 2.48
nonforfeiture options, 2.47
nonqualified contracts, 2.46
per diem basis, 2.45
pool of money, 2.45
premiums, 2.47
reimbursement basis, 2.45
renewability, 2.47
tax-qualified contracts, 2.46
types of care covered, 2.44
Long-term debt instruments, 4.13
corporate debt securities, 4.14
governmental debt securities, 4.14
Long-term disability income plans, 3.35
benefits, 3.36
supplemental benefits, 3.37

Loss control, 2.18, 2.24
Loss financing, 2.19
Loss prevention, 2.19, 2.24
Loss reduction, 2.19, 2.20, 2.24
Low severity losses, 2.17, 2.18

M

Major medical plans, 3.12, 3.18
Major planning areas, 1.20
Managed care plan, 3.13
    comparison of plan types, 3.17
    health maintenance organizations (HMOs), 3.14
    point-of-service (POS) plans, 3.14, 3.17
    preferred-provider organizations (PPOs), 3.14, 3.16
Marginal tax rate, 5.11
Marital deduction, 7.24, 7.26, 7.35, 7.37, 7.38
Marital trust, 7.39, 7.40
Marketability, 4.27
Matching investment instruments with investment goals, 4.36
Maximum annual benefit, 6.28
Maximum annual contribution, 6.28
Medical expense insurance, 2.37, 3.12
    additional benefits for executives, 3.22
    coverage after termination of employment, 3.23
    plan provisions, 3.19
    taxation, 3.22
    types of plans, 3.12
Medical expense plan provisions, 3.19
    coordination-of-benefits (COB) provision, 3.20
    cost sharing, 3.21
    covered expenses, 3.19
    eligibility, 3.19
    preexisting condition, 3.19
Medicare, 8.2
Medicare Advantage, 8.22, 8.23
Medicare benefits, 8.16, 8.20
Medicare care-out plan, 8.31
Medicare+Choice, 8.23, 8.25
Medicare cost plan, 8.25
Medicare eligibility, 8.15
Medicare Part A benefits, 8.16
    exclusions, 8.19
    home health care benefits, 8.18
    hospice benefits, 8.18
    hospital benefits, 8.16
    skilled-nursing facility benefits, 8.17
Medicare Part B benefits, 8.20
    amount of benefits, 8.21
    benefits, 8.20
    exclusions, 8.20
Medicare Part C, 8.22
    is a Medicare Advantage plan an appropriate option, 8.24
    Medicare Advantage, 8.22, 8.23
    other Medicare alternatives, 8.25
    types of plans, 8.23
Medicare Part D, 8.25
    cost, 8.30
    covered drugs, 8.28
    eligibility, 8.26
    enrollment, 8.30
    plan variations, 8.29
    standard benefit structure, 8.26
    types of plans, 8.26
    where prescriptions can be filled, 8.29
Medicare pilot programs, 8.25
Medicare Prescription Drug, Improvement, and Modernization Act of 2003, 8.15, 8.23, 8.25
Medicare prescription drug plans, 8.26
Medicare SELECT policy, 8.33, 8.35
Medicare supplements, 8.31
    employer plans, 8.31
    individual medigap policies, 8.31
Medicare website, 8.36
Medigap basic benefits, 8.32
Medigap insurance, 8.31
    additional benefits, 8.33
    basic benefits, 8.32
    eligibility, 8.36
    other plans, 8.35

Meeting emergency and protection needs first, 4.36
Miscellaneous fringe benefits, 3.46
    adoption assistance, 3.47
    dependent care assistance, 3.48
    education assistance, 3.46
    family leave, 3.49
    other benefits, 3.51
Miscellaneous itemized deductions, 5.20
Money market deposit accounts (MMDAs), 4.12
Money market instruments, 4.12
Money market mutual funds (MMMFs), 4.12
Money-purchase pension plan, 6.34
Monitor the plan (step 6), 1.15, 2.28, 6.11
Mother's/father's benefit, 8.7
Multiple-purpose approach to financial planning, 1.18, 4.9
Mutual fund, 4.18

N

Named-perils approach, 2.50
Needs analysis, 2.6, 2.7, 2.15
Negotiated markets, 4.42
Net asset value, 4.17
No-load funds, 4.18
Nominal rate of return, 4.22
Noncancelable, 2.41
Nonforfeiture options, 2.32, 2.47
Nonparticipating (nonpar) policies, 2.33
Nonprobate estate, 7.17
    transfers by operation of contract, 7.18
    transfers by operation of law, 7.17
Nonqualified contracts, 2.46
Nonqualified plan, 6.42
Nonrecognition transactions, 5.24
    compared to taxable transactions, 5.25
    computation of gain or loss, 5.25
Nontax advantages of lifetime gifts, 7.31

O

OASDHI, 8.2
OASDI, 8.2
Obstacles confronting consumers, 1.34
Older people need to plan for retirement, 6.12
Open-end investment company, 4.18
Open-perils approach, 2.50
Opportunities created by the gift tax annual exclusion, 7.32
Opportunity costs, 4.26
Ordinary income, 5.27
Ordinary versus capital gain and loss, 5.27
    capital gain, 5.27
    ordinary income, 5.27
    Section 1231 assets, 5.29
    tax treatment of capital losses, 5.29
    tax treatment of dividends as capital gains, 5.28
Organized securities markets, 4.43
Other property rights, 7.8
    beneficial interests, 7.8
    powers, 7.8
Other than collision, 2.57
Other (than qualified) tax-advantaged plans, 6.39
    403(b) plans, 6.40
    SEPs, 6.39
    SIMPLEs, 6.39
Overcoming inadequate retirement resources, 6.48
    obtaining a reverse mortgage, 6.48
    pension maximization, 6.50
    postretirement employment, 6.49
    trading down to a less expensive home, 6.48
Overcoming roadblocks to retirement savings, 6.13
Over-the-counter market, 4.42

P

PACE, 8.25
Paper deductions, 5.9

Partial disability, 2.39
Participating (par) policies, 2.33
Passive losses, 5.23
Pattern of investing, 4.38
Paying for Social Security and Medicare, 8.4
Pension maximization, 6.50
Pension versus profit-sharing plans, 6.29
Per diem basis, 2.45
Peril, 2.4
Personal assets, 4.3
Personal auto insurance, 2.55
    collision, 2.57
    no-fault benefits, 2.58
    other- than collision, 2.57
    Part A liability coverage, 2.55
    Part B medical payments coverage, 2.57
    Part C uninsured motorists coverage, 2.57
    Part D coverage for damage to your auto, 2.57
    single limit of liability, 2.56
    split limit of liability, 2.56
Personal exemption, 5.11
Personal expense, 5.8
Personal risks, 2.15, 2.28
Phases of the financial life cycle, 1.22
Planned holding period, 4.37
Planning charitable contributions, 7.41
    advantages of gifts to charity, 7.41
    donating income interests to charity, 7.42
    gifts of remainder interests to charity, 7.41
Planning for state death taxes, 7.30
Planning for the gift and estate tax applicable credit amount, 7.38
Planning for the marital deduction, 7.35, 7.38
    estate trust, 7.37
    outright transfers, 7.36
    power of appointment trust, 7.37
    QTIP marital-deduction trust, 7.37
Plan variations under Medicare Part D, 8.29
    benefits in the coverage gap, 8.29
    formulary drugs, 8.29
    reduced deductibles, 8.29
    tiered copayments, 8.29
Point-of-service (POS) plans, 3.14, 3.17, 3.18

Pool of money, 2.45
Portfolio effect, 2.23
Postretirement employment, 6.49
Postretirement health insurance coverage, 3.25
Pour-over trust, 7.12
Power of appointment, 7.9, 7.37
    general power of appointment, 7.9
    special power of appointment, 7.9
Power of appointment trust, 7.37
Power of attorney, 7.9, 7.13, 7.15
Powers, 7.8
    power of appointment, 7.9
    power of attorney, 7.9, 7.13, 7.15
Preemptive right, 4.16
Preexisting condition, 3.19
Preferred-provider organizations (PPOs), 3.14, 3.16, 3.18
Preferred stock, 4.16
Premium conversion plan, 3.54
Price risk, 4.23
Primary insurance amount (PIA), 8.9
Prime interest rate, 1.28
Probate, 7.10
Probate estate, 7.16
    transfers by intestacy, 7.17
    transfers through will provisions, 7.16
Profit-sharing plans, 6.34
Property risks, 2.11, 2.12, 2.49
Protection objectives, 2.2
Purchasing power risk, 4.21
    nominal rate of return, 4.22
    real rate of return, 4.22
Pure risk, 2.3, 2.5, 2.6, 2.7, 2.13, 4.3, 4.5
Purpose of income tax planning, 5.3

Q

QTIP marital-deduction trust, 7.37
Qualified domestic relations order (QDRO), 6.15
Qualified plan, 6.26
Quarters of coverage, 8.4

Questions in estate planning, 7.3, 7.4, 7.31, 7.39
    how should the property be received, 7.3, 7.4, 7.39
    when should the property be received, 7.3, 7.4
    who should receive the property, 7.3, 7.4, 7.39

R

Real estate, 4.20
Real rate of return, 4.22
Regulation of securities markets, 4.43
    Investment Advisors Act of 1940, 4.45
    Investment Company Act of 1940, 4.44
    Maloney Act of 1938, 4.44
    Securities Act of 1933, 4.43
    Securities Exchange Act of 1934, 4.44
Reimbursement basis, 2.45
Reinsurance, 2.23
Reinvestment rate risk, 4.24
Renewability provision, 2.30
Replacement cost, 2.13
Replacement-cost requirement, 2.52
Replacement ratio method, 6.17
    additional factors, 6.18
    reduced living expenses, 6.18
    reduced taxes, 6.17
    replacement ratio method work sheet, 6.22
Replacement ratio method work sheet, 6.22
Requesting Social Security benefit information, 8.14
Residual disability, 2.39, 2.42
Responsibilities of the retirement advisor, 6.8
Retention, 2.19, 2.20, 2.24
Retirement age for nonreduced Social Security benefits, 8.6
Retirement benefits under Social Security, 8.6
Retirement planning and the financial planning process, 6.9
    Step 1: establish and define the advisor-client relationship, 6.9

    Step 2: determine goals and gather data, 6.9
    Step 3: analyze and evaluate the data, 6.10
    Step 4: develop and present a plan, 6.10
    Step 5: implement the plan, 6.10
    Step 6: monitor the plan, 6.11
Revenue bonds, 4.14
Reverse mortgage, 6.48
Revocable life insurance trusts, 7.44
Revocable trust, 7.12, 7.44
Risk, 2.2, 2.5, 2.6, 2.12, 4.3, 4.5, 4.6
Risk avoidance, 2.19, 2.24
Risk evaluation, 2.17
Risk identification, 2.11, 2.17
Risk identification questionnaire, B.1
Risk Impact Chart, 2.17, 2.18
Risk management, 2.6
Risk measurement, 2.12, 2.16
Risk treatment devices, 2.18
    insurance, 2.19, 2.21
    loss control, 2.18
    loss financing, 2.19
    loss prevention, 2.19
    loss reduction, 2.19, 2.20
    retention, 2.19, 2.20
    risk avoidance, 2.19
Roadblocks to retirement savings, 6.13
Role of the financial advisor, 1.21, 1.34
Role of the retirement advisor, 6.4
    holistic retirement planning, 6.4
    responsibilities of the retirement advisor, 6.8
    retirement planning and the financial planning process, 6.9
Roth IRA, 6.46

S

Sale or exchange of principal residence, 6.48
Sales tactics, 4.39
Sandwiched generation, 1.33
Savings incentive match plan for employees(SIMPLE), 6.39

S corporations, 5.30
Section 79 (group term life tax treatment), 3.31
    general tax rules, 3.31
    nondiscrimination rules, 3.33
    taxation of proceeds, 3.33
    tax treatment of added coverages, 3.33
Section 1231 assets, 5.29
Section 2503(b) trust, 7.34
Section 2503(c) trust, 7.34
Selecting techniques for handling pure risks, 2.23
Selling/planning process, 1.4
Severity of loss, 2.21, 2.23, 2.24
Short-term disability income plans, 3.35
Sick-pay plans, 3.35
Simplified employee pension (SEP), 6.39
Single limit of liability, 2.56
Single-purpose approach to financial planning, 1.17, 4.9
Skilled-nursing facility benefits under Medicare Part A, 8.17
Small cap stocks, 4.19
SMART goals, 1.8, 1.24, 1.25
Social Security and Medicare, 8.2
    extent of coverage, 8.3
    importance of programs, 8.3
    tax rates and wage bases, 8.3
Social Security and Medicare tax rates and wage bases, 8.3
Social Security benefit amounts, 8.9
    calculating benefits, 8.9
    cost-of-living adjustments, 8.13
    delayed retirement, 8.12
    early retirement, 8.11
    earnings test, 8.13
    offset for other benefits, 8.14
    requesting benefit information, 8.14
Social Security benefits, 8.6
    disability benefits, 8.8
    eligibility for dual benefits, 8.8
    retirement benefits, 8.6
    survivors benefits, 8.7
    termination of benefits, 8.9
Social Security benefits taken early, 8.11
Social Security cost-of-living adjustments, 8.13
Social Security delayed retirement, 8.12
Social Security earnings test, 6.50, 8.13
Social Security eligibility, 8.4
Social Security Statement, 8.14
Social Security website, 8.36
Sources of investment risk, 4.21
    business (default) risk, 4.25
    interest rate risk, 4.23
    purchasing power risk, 4.21
Sources of retirement income, 6.25
    IRAs, 6.43
    nonqualified plans, 6.42
    other tax-advantaged plans, 6.39
    tax-advantaged qualified plans, 6.26
Specialized areas in financial planning, 1.19, 1.21
Special power of appointment, 7.9
Specified (dread) disease insurance, 3.45
Speculating, 4.4
Speculative risk, 2.3, 4.3, 4.4
Split limit of liability, 2.56
Springing durable power of attorney, 7.14
Standard & Poor's 500 Index, 1.28
Standard deduction, 5.6
Standard medigap plans, 8.32
Standard prescription drug plan under Medicare Part D, 8.26
Starting retirement planning when young, 6.2
State death tax credit, 7.26
State death taxes, 7.29, 7.30
    credit estate tax, 7.30
    state estate tax, 7.29
    state inheritance tax, 7.29
State estate tax, 7.29
State inheritance tax, 7.29
Steps in financial planning, 1.3, 1.5, 6.9
    Step 1: establish and define the advisor-client relationship, 1.6, 2.6, 6.9
    Step 2: determine goals and gather data, 1.7, 2.8, 6.9
    Step 3: analyze and evaluate the data, 1.12, 2.11, 6.10

Step 4: develop and present a plan, 1.13, 2.18, 6.10
Step 5: implement the plan, 1.14, 2.27, 6.10
Step 6: monitor the plan, 1.15, 2.28, 6.11
Stock bonus plan, 6.38
Studies and surveys, 1.31, 1.33
    Allstate Corporation, 1.33
    American Association of Retired Persons, 1.33
    CFP Board Consumer Survey, 1.31
    Employee Benefit Research Institute, 1.31
Supplemental medical expense insurance, 3.45
    critical illness insurance, 3.45
    hospital indemnity insurance, 3.45
    specified (dread) disease insurance, 3.45
Survivors benefits under Social Security, 8.7

T

Target-benefit pension plan, 6.34
Taxable distribution, 7.28
Taxable entities, 5.30
    C corporations, 5.30
    S corporations, 5.30
Taxable income, 5.5
Taxable termination, 7.28
Taxable year, 5.16
Tax-advantaged qualified plans, 6.26
    defined-benefit versus defined-contribution plans, 6.27
    pension versus profit-sharing plans, 6.29
    types of tax-advantaged qualified plans, 6.31
Tax advantages of lifetime gifts, 7.31
Taxation of investments, 4.27
    fully taxable yield, 4.29
    tax-exempt yield, 4.29
Tax avoidance, 5.3
Tax bracket, 5.12
Tax credits, 5.14
Tax doctrines, 5.16
    assignment of income doctrine, 5.18
    constructive receipt doctrine, 5.18
    economic benefit doctrine, 5.17
    fruit and tree doctrine, 5.17
Taxes imposed on transfers of wealth, 7.19
    federal transfer taxes, 7.19
    state death taxes, 7.29
Tax evasion, 5.19
Tax-exempt transactions, 5.24
Tax minimization, 5.3
Tax periods and accounting methods, 5.15
    accrual method, 5.16
    cash-basis method, 5.16
    taxable year, 5.16
Tax preference items, 5.15
Tax-qualified contracts, 2.46
Tax rates and brackets, 5.11
Tax rate schedules for individuals, 5.13
Tax-saving rationale, 4.37
Tax shelters, 5.23
Tax treatment of capital losses, 5.29
Tax treatment of dividends as capital gains, 5.28
Tenancy by the entirety, 7.7
Tenancy in common, 7.6
Termination of benefits under Social Security, 8.9
Termination of group life coverage, 3.27
    conversion, 3.27
    portability of term coverage, 3.27
Term interest, 7.6
Term life insurance, 2.29
Testamentary trust, 7.13
Testator, 7.13
Topic list for CFP certification examinations, A.1
Total disability, 2.39
Traditional IRA, 6.44
    active participant, 6.44
    distributions, 6.46
    monetary limit, 6.45
    special spousal rule, 6.45
Transactions that result in a taxable loss, 5.26
Transfers at death, 7.16, 7.19
    nonprobate estate, 7.17

probate estate, 7.16
Transfers by intestacy, 7.17
Transfers by operation of contract, 7.18
Transfers by operation of law, 7.17
Transfers through will provisions, 7.16
Treasury bills, 4.13
Trends creating opportunities for financial planning advisors, 1.27
True-auction markets, 4.41
Trusts, 7.11
    living (inter vivos) trust, 7.12
    testamentary trust, 7.13
Types of assets, 4.3
    investment assets, 4.3
    personal assets, 4.3
Types of employee benefits, 3.11
    dental insurance, 3.38
    disability income insurance, 3.34
    life insurance, 3.26
    medical expense insurance, 3.12
    miscellaneous fringe benefits, 3.46
    vision insurance, 3.40
    voluntary insurance benefits, 3.41
Types of GSTT transfers, 7.27
    direct skip, 7.27
    taxable distribution, 7.28
    taxable termination, 7.28
Types of medical expense plans, 3.12
    managed care plans, 3.13
    traditional major medical plans, 3.13
Types of Medicare Advantage plans, 8.23
Types of Medicare prescription drug plans, 8.26
Types of property interest, 7.5
    individual ownership of property, 7.5
    joint concurrent ownership of property, 7.6
    other property rights, 7.8
Types of pure risks, 2.5, 2.11
    liability risks, 2.5, 2.11, 2.15
    personal risks, 2.5, 2.11, 2.15
    property risks, 2.5, 2.11, 2.12
Types of tax-advantaged qualified plans, 6.31
    401(k) plans, 6.36
    cash-balance pension plans, 6.33
    defined-benefit pension plans, 6.31
    ESOPs, 6.38
    money-purchase pension plans, 6.34
    profit-sharing plans, 6.34
    stock bonus plans, 6.38
    target-benefit pension plans, 6.34

U

Umbrella liability insurance, 2.58
Uncertainty, 2.3
Understanding the investment, 4.37
Uniform Gifts to Minors Act (UGMA), 7.33
Uniform Transfers to Minors Act (UTMA), 7.33
Unit-benefit formula, 6.31
Universal life insurance, 2.29, 2.34
U.S. Treasury bills (T-bills), 4.13

V

Value stocks, 4.19
Variable life insurance, 2.33
Variable universal life, 2.35
Vision benefit plan, 3.40
Vision insurance, 3.40
Voluntary benefit plans, 3.8, 3.41
Voluntary insurance benefits, 3.8, 3.41
    legal expense insurance, 3.42
    long-term care insurance, 3.44
    property and liability insurance, 3.45
    supplemental medical expense insurance, 3.45

W

Whole life insurance, 2.29, 2.31
Wills, 7.10, 7.16
    requirements for a valid will, 7.10
    what can a valid will accomplish, 7.10